Dewey Decimal Classification and Relative Index

Dewey Decimal Classification and Relative Index

Devised by Melvil Dewey

EDITION 23

Edited by

Joan S. Mitchell, Editor in Chief

Julianne Beall, Assistant Editor

Rebecca Green, Assistant Editor

Giles Martin, Assistant Editor

Michael Panzer, Assistant Editor

VOLUME 3
Schedules 600–999

OCLC

OCLC Online Computer Library Center, Inc.

Dublin, Ohio

2011

Previous editions of the Dewey Decimal Classification:
Copyright 1876, 1885, 1911, 1913, 1915, 1919
by Melvil Dewey
Copyright 1888, 1891, 1894, 1899
by Library Bureau
Copyright 1922, 1927, 1932, 1942, 1952, 1958
by Lake Placid Club Education Foundation
Copyright 1951, 1965, 1967, 1971
by Forest Press, Inc.
© 1979 by Forest Press
A Division of the Lake Placid Education Foundation
© 1989, 1996, 2003
OCLC Online Computer Library Center, Inc.

Library of Congress Cataloging-in-Publication Data
Dewey, Melvil, 1851-1931.
  Dewey decimal classification and relative index / devised by Melvil Dewey. — Ed. 23 / edited by Joan S. Mitchell, Editor in Chief ; Julianne Beall, Assistant Editor ; Rebecca Green, Assistant Editor ; Giles Martin, Assistant Editor ; Michael Panzer, Assistant Editor.
    v. cm.
  Includes bibliographical references and index.
  Contents: v. 1. Manual. Tables — v. 2. Schedules 000-599 — v. 3. Schedules 600-999 — v. 4. Relative index.
    ISBN-13: 978-1-910608-81-4 (set : alk. paper)
    ISBN-10: 1-910608-81-5 (set : alk. paper)
    ISBN-13: 978-1-910608-80-7 (vol. 1 : alk. paper)
    ISBN-10: 1-910608-80-7 (vol. 1 : alk. paper)
    [etc.]
    1. Classification, Dewey decimal. I. Mitchell, Joan S. II. Beall, Julianne, 1946- III. Green, Rebecca, 1952- IV. Martin, Giles. V. Panzer, Michael. VI. Title.
    Z696.D52 2011
    025.4'31—dc22   2011001112

OCLC Online Computer Library Center, Inc.
6565 Kilgour Place
Dublin, OH 43017-3395 USA
www.oclc.org/dewey

The paper used in this publication meets the requirements of ANSI/NISO Z39.48-1992 (Permanence of Paper).

ISBN-13: (set) 978-1-910608-81-4; v. 1 978-1-910608-80-7; v. 2 978-1-910608-76-0; v. 3 978-1-910608-79-1; v. 4 978-1-910608-78-4

ISBN-10: (set) 1-910608-81-5; v. 1 1-910608-80-7; v. 2 1-910608-76-9; v. 3 1-910608-79-3; v. 4 1-910608-78-5

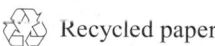 Recycled paper

Schedules

600

600 Technology (Applied sciences)

Class here inventions

See also 303.483 for technology as a cause of cultural change; also 306.46 for sociology of technology; also 338.1–338.4 for economic aspects of industries based on specific technologies; also 338.926 for technology transfer; also 338.927 for appropriate technology

See Manual at 300 vs. 600; also at 363 vs. 302–307, 333.7, 570–590, 600; also at 363.1 vs. 600; also at 583–585 vs. 600

SUMMARY

630	Agriculture and related technologies
.1–.9	Standard subdivisions
631	Specific techniques; apparatus, equipment, materials
632	Plant injuries, diseases, pests
633	Field and plantation crops
634	Orchards, fruits, forestry
635	Garden crops (Horticulture)
636	Animal husbandry
637	Processing dairy and related products
638	Insect culture
639	Hunting, fishing, conservation, related technologies
640	Home and family management
.1–.9	Standard subdivisions; specific aspects of household management; evaluation and purchasing guides
641	Food and drink
642	Meals and table service
643	Housing and household equipment
644	Household utilities
645	Household furnishings
646	Sewing, clothing, management of personal and family life
647	Management of public households (Institutional housekeeping)
648	Housekeeping
649	Child rearing; home care of people with disabilities and illnesses
650	Management and auxiliary services
.01–.09	Standard subdivisions
.1	Personal success in business
651	Office services
652	Processes of written communication
653	Shorthand
657	Accounting
658	General management
659	Advertising and public relations
660	Chemical engineering and related technologies
.01–.09	Standard subdivisions and chemical technologies of specific states of matter
.2–.7	[General topics in chemical engineering, biotechnology, industrial stoichiometry]
661	Technology of industrial chemicals
662	Technology of explosives, fuels, related products
663	Beverage technology
664	Food technology
665	Technology of industrial oils, fats, waxes, gases
666	Ceramic and allied technologies
667	Cleaning, color, coating, related technologies
668	Technology of other organic products
669	Metallurgy
670	Manufacturing
.1–.9	Standard subdivisions and special topics of manufacturing
671	Metalworking processes and primary metal products
672	Iron, steel, other iron alloys
673	Nonferrous metals
674	Lumber processing, wood products, cork
675	Leather and fur processing
676	Pulp and paper technology
677	Textiles
678	Elastomers and elastomer products
679	Other products of specific kinds of materials

680	Manufacture of products for specific uses
681	Precision instruments and other devices
682	Small forge work (Blacksmithing)
683	Hardware and household appliances
684	Furnishings and home workshops
685	Leather and fur goods, and related products
686	Printing and related activities
687	Clothing and accessories
688	Other final products, and packaging technology
690	Construction of buildings
.01–.09	Standard subdivisions
.1–.8	Special topics of construction of buildings
691	Building materials
692	Auxiliary construction practices
693	Construction in specific types of materials and for specific purposes
694	Wood construction
695	Roof covering
696	Utilities
697	Heating, ventilating, air-conditioning engineering
698	Detail finishing

601 Philosophy and theory

602 Miscellany

.18 Standards

Interdisciplinary collections of standards relocated to 389.6

[.72] Patents

Do not use; class in 608

.75 Trademarks and service marks

Class here comprehensive works on trademarks generally used for products rather than services

Class interdisciplinary works on trademarks and service marks in 929.95

.9 **Commercial miscellany**

Class commercial miscellany of products and services used in individual and family living in 640.29; class commercial miscellany of manufactured products in 670.29; class interdisciplinary commercial miscellany in 381.029

603 Dictionaries, encyclopedias, concordances

604 Technical drawing, hazardous materials technology; groups of people

.2 **Technical drawing**

Class here engineering graphics, mechanical drawing

For architectural drawing, see 720.284. For technical drawing in a specific subject, see the subject, e.g., map drawing 526, electronic drafting 621.381

See also 006.6 for computer graphics

.22   Arrangement and organization of drafting rooms, preservation and storage of drawings

.24   Specific drafting procedures and conventions

.242   Production illustration

> Nontechnical graphic representations

.243   Dimensioning; lettering, titling; shades, shadows

.245   Projections

> Including isometric, orthographic, spherical projections; perspectives

.25   Preparation and reading of copies

> Standard subdivisions are added for either or both topics in heading
>
> Including blueprints, photostats
>
> *See also 686.42 for printing blueprints*

.7   Hazardous materials technology

> Methods of extracting, manufacturing, processing, utilizing, handling, transporting, storing solids, liquids, gases of corrosive, explosive, flammable, infectious, radioactive, toxic nature
>
> Class interdisciplinary works on hazardous materials in 363.17. Class technology of a specific hazardous material with the technology, e.g., explosives 662.2; class safety techniques for a specific application of hazardous materials with the application outside 300, plus notation 0289 from Table 1, e.g., safety techniques in working with hazardous paving materials 625.80289 (*not* 363.179)
>
> *See Manual at 604.7 vs. 660.2804*

.8   Groups of people

> Add to base number 604.8 the numbers following —08 in notation 081–089 from Table 1, e.g., women 604.82

605   Serial publications

606   Organizations

[.8]   Management

> Do not use; class in 658

607   Education, research, related topics

> Notation 07 from Table 1 as modified below

.01–.03   Education, research, related topics in areas, regions, places in general; in ancient world

> Add to base number 607.0 notation 1–3 from Table 2, e.g., technical training in ancient Rome 607.0376

[.04–.09]   Education, research, related topics in specific continents, countries, localities in modern world

> Do not use; class in 607.4–607.9

.1   Education

.2   Research

> Class here industrial, products research
>
> Class product planning in management in 658.5038; class management of research for new and improved products in 658.57

[.201–.209]   Geographic treatment of research

> Do not use; class in 607.21–607.29

.21   Research in areas, regions, places in general

> Do not use for research methods; class in 607.2
>
> Add to base number 607.21 the numbers following —1 in notation 11–19 from Table 2, e.g., industrial research in Western Hemisphere 607.21812
>
> Use of this number for historical, descriptive, experimental methods in areas, regions, places in general discontinued; class in 607.2

[.22]   Historical research

> Do not use; class in 607.2

.23   Research in the ancient world

> Do not use for descriptive research; class in 607.2
>
> Add to base number 607.23 the numbers following —3 in notation 31–39 from Table 2, e.g., research in ancient Egypt 607.232
>
> Use of this number for historical, descriptive, experimental methods in the ancient world discontinued; class in 607.2

.24   Research in Europe

> Do not use for experimental research; class in 607.2
>
> Add to base number 607.24 the numbers following —4 in notation 41–49 from Table 2, e.g., industrial research in Norway 607.2481
>
> Use of this number for historical, descriptive, experimental methods in Europe discontinued; class in 607.2

.25   Research in Asia

> Add to base number 607.25 the numbers following —5 in notation 51 59 from Table 2, e.g., industrial research in Japan 607.252
>
> Use of this number for historical, descriptive, experimental methods in Asia discontinued; class in 607.2

.26   Research in Africa

Add to base number 607.26 the numbers following —6 in notation 61–69 from Table 2, e.g., industrial research in South Africa 607.268

Use of this number for historical, descriptive, experimental methods in Africa discontinued; class in 607.2

.27   Research in North America

Do not use for statistical methods; class in 607.2

Add to base number 607.27 the numbers following —7 in notation 71–79 from Table 2, e.g., industrial research in Canada 607.271

Use of this number for historical, descriptive, experimental methods in North America discontinued; class in 607.2

.28   Research in South America

Do not use for presentation of statistical data; class in 607.2

Add to base number 607.28 the numbers following —7 in notation 81–89 from Table 2, e.g., industrial research in Argentina 607.282

Use of this number for historical, descriptive, experimental methods in South America discontinued; class in 607.2

.29   Research in other parts of the world

Add to base number 607.29 the numbers following —9 in notation 91–99 from Table 2, e.g., industrial research in New Zealand 607.2993

Use of this number for historical, descriptive, experimental methods in other parts of the world discontinued; class in 607.2

.3   Other aspects of education, research, related topics

Add to base number 607.3 the numbers following —07 in notation 074–079 from Table 1, e.g., fairs and exhibitions 607.34

Class commercial aspects of fairs and exhibitions in 381.1; class interdisciplinary works on fairs and exhibitions in 907.4

.4–.9   Education, research, related topics in specific continents, countries, localities in modern world

Do not use for museums, collections, exhibits and their activities and services; review and exercise; use of apparatus and equipment in study and teaching; competitions, festivals, awards, financial support; class in 607.3

Add to base number 607 notation 4–9 from Table 2, e.g., education and research in Japan 607.52

608 Patents

> Do not use for history and description of technology with respect to groups of people; class in 604.8
>
> Class here interdisciplinary collections of patents
>
> Class interdisciplinary works on patents in 346.0486
>
> > *For patents in a specific subject, see the subject, plus notation 0272 from Table 1, e.g., patents in chemical engineering 660.0272*
>
> Use of this number for inventions discontinued; class in 600

[.09] **History, geographic treatment, biography**

> Do not use for history and geographic treatment; class in 608.7

[.092] **Biography**

> Do not use; class in 609.2

.7 History and geographic treatment

[.700 1–.700 8] Standard subdivisions

> Do not use; class in 608.01–608.08

[.700 9] History, geographic treatment, biography

> Do not use for history and geographic treatment; class in 608.7

[.700 92] Biography

> Do not use; class in 609.2

.701–.705 Historical periods

> Add to base number 608.70 the numbers following —090 in notation 0901–0905 from Table 1, e.g., 20th century patents 608.704

.71 Areas, regions, places in general; oceans and seas

> Add to base number 608.71 the numbers following —1 in notation 11–18 from Table 2, e.g., patents from developing regions 608.71724

[.72] Biography of inventors, of patentees

> Relocated to 609.2

.73–.79 Specific continents, countries, localities

> Add to base number 608.7 notation 3–9 from Table 2, e.g., patents from Brazil 608.781

609 History, geographic treatment, biography

> Class here technological aspects of industrial archaeology
>
> Class history and geographic treatment of production and economic aspects of industrial archaeology in 338.09; class history of industrial archaeology in 900
>
> *See Manual at 300 vs. 600: Interdisciplinary works*

.2   **Biography**

Class here biography of inventors, of patentees [*both formerly also* 608.72]

610   Medicine and health

Standard subdivisions are added for medicine and health together, for medicine alone

Class here technology of medical services

Class social welfare problems of and services to people with physical illness, interdisciplinary works on social provision of medical services and technology of medical services in 362.1; class home care by nonprofessionals of people with illnesses and disabilities in 649.8

For veterinary medicine, see 636.089

See Manual at 362.1–362.4 vs. 610; also at 571–573 vs. 610; also at 610 vs. 616

SUMMARY

610.1–.9	**[Standard subdivisions; group practice; medical personnel and relationships; nursing; services of allied health personnel]**
611	**Human anatomy, cytology, histology**
.001–.009	**Standard subdivisions**
.01	**Anatomic embryology, cytology, histology**
.1	**Cardiovascular organs**
.2	**Respiratory organs**
.3	**Digestive tract organs**
.4	**Hematopoietic, lymphatic, glandular systems**
.6	**Urogenital system**
.7	**Musculoskeletal system, integument**
.8	**Nervous system**
.9	**Regional and topographical anatomy**
612	**Human physiology**
.001–.009	**Standard subdivisions**
.01–.04	**[Biophysics, biochemistry, control processes, tissue and organ culture, physiology of specific activities]**
.1	**Circulatory system**
.2	**Respiratory system**
.3	**Digestive system**
.4	**Hematopoietic, lymphatic, glandular, urinary systems**
.6	**Reproduction, development, maturation**
.7	**Musculoskeletal system, integument**
.8	**Nervous system**
.9	**Regional physiology**
613	**Personal health and safety**
.04	**Personal health of people by gender, sex, or age group**
.1	**Environmental factors**
.2	**Dietetics**
.4	**Personal cleanliness and related topics**
.5	**Artificial environments**
.6	**Personal safety and special topics of health**
.7	**Physical fitness**
.8	**Substance abuse (Drug abuse)**
.9	**Birth control, reproductive technology, sex hygiene, sexual techniques**

[.23]   Medicine and health as a profession, occupation, hobby

> Do not use; class in 610.69

.28 Auxiliary techniques and procedures; apparatus, equipment, materials

Class here comprehensive works on biomedical engineering

For biological aspects of biomedical engineering, see 570.28

.6 **Organizations, management; group practice; medical personnel and relationships**

Notation 06 from Table 1 as modified below

.65 Group practice

Class economics of group practice in 338.7–338.8; class social aspects in 362.1042

.69 Medical personnel and relationships

Standard subdivisions are added for medical personnel and relationships together, for medical personnel alone

Nature of duties, characteristics of the professions of medical personnel

Class here medical missionaries

Class medical secretaries in 651.3741; class medical records librarians in 651.504261. Class nature of duties, characteristics of profession, relationships of medical personnel of a specific specialty with the specialty, plus notation 023 from table under 616.1–616.9, notation 023 from table under 617, or notation 023 from table under 618.1–618.8, e.g., obstetricians 618.20232, obstetrical nurses 618.20231; class critical appraisal and description of work, individual and collected biographies with the specialty, plus notation 092 from Table 1, e.g., biography of coroners 614.1092, of psychiatrists 616.890092

For nursing personnel, see 610.73069; for allied health personnel, see 610.737069

.695 Physicians

.696 Medical relationships

Including relationships between medical personnel and patients, between medical personnel and the public, within medical professions

.7 **Education, research, nursing, services of allied health personnel**

Notation 07 from Table 1 as modified below

.724 Experimental research

Class here comprehensive works on experimental biomedical research

For experimental biology, see 570.724; for clinical trials, see 615.50724; for experimental medicine, see 616.027

.73 Nursing and services of allied health personnel

Standard subdivisions are added for nursing and services of allied health personnel together, for nursing alone

Class here comprehensive works on the nursing process; comprehensive works on nursing care plans, on nursing interventions so long as the works cover both diagnosis and therapy

For school nursing, see 371.712; for forensic nursing, see 614.1; for patient education by nurses, see 615.5071. For a specific part of the nursing process, a specific part of a nursing care plan, a specific type of nursing intervention, see the part or type in 614–618, e.g., vaccinations provided by nurses 614.47, exercise therapy provided by nurses 615.82, nursing assessment and nursing diagnosis 616.075; for nursing for a specific disease or group of diseases or a specific medical specialty, see the disease or group of diseases or medical specialty in 616–618, plus notation 0231 from table under 616.1–616.9, notation 0231 from table under 617, or notation 0231 from table under 618.1–618.8 if role or work of nursing personnel is emphasized, e.g., a work about cancer nursing that gives much general medical information about cancer 616.994, a work about cancer nursing that focuses on instructions for nurses 616.9940231, a work about geriatric nursing that gives much general information about geriatrics 618.97, a work about geriatric nursing that emphasizes the role and techniques of the geriatric nurse 618.970231

[.730 23] Nursing and work of allied health personnel as a profession, occupation, hobby

Do not use; class in 610.73069

.730 6 Organizations and personnel

Notation 06 from Table 1 as modified below

.730 68 Management

Do not use for management of services of nurses; class in 362.173068

.730 69 Nursing personnel

Nature of duties, characteristics of the profession, relationships

Class here comprehensive works on nursing personnel and allied health personnel

Class comprehensive works on techniques of nursing operations in 610.73

For allied health personnel, see 610.737069

.730 692 Professional nurses

Including associate-degree nurses

Class here nurse practitioners

Class physician assistants in 610.7372069

.730 693 Practical nurses

Including registered nursing assistants

.730 698	Auxiliary nursing personnel
	Class here nurses' aides, nursing assistants other than registered nursing assistants
	Class registered nursing assistants in 610.730693
.730 699	Relationships of nurses
	Including relationships between nurses and patients, between nurses and the public, within nursing profession

---

>   610.732–610.736 Nursing

Class comprehensive works in 610.73

.732	Private duty nursing
.733	Institutional nursing and ward management
	Standard subdivisions are added for either or both topics in heading
	Class nonmedical aspects of ward management in 362.173068
.734	Public health nursing
	Class here Red Cross nursing
.734 3	Community and district nursing
	Standard subdivisions are added for either or both topics in heading
	Including work of health visitors, visiting nurses; home nursing by professionals
	Class home nursing by nonprofessionals in 649.8
.734 6	Occupational health nursing (Industrial nursing)
.734 9	Disaster nursing
.736	Long-term care nursing
.737	Services of allied health personnel
	Class here services of medical assistants, medical technicians

For a specific part of the work of allied health personnel, see the part in 614–618, e.g., exercise therapy provided by medical technicians 615.82; for services of allied health personnel for a specific disease or group of diseases or a specific medical specialty, see the disease or group of diseases or medical specialty in 616–618, plus notation 0233 from table under 616.1–616.9, notation 0233 from table under 617, or notation 0233 from table under 618.1–618.8 if role or work of allied health personnel is emphasized, e.g., a work about services of medical technicians with respect to geriatric patients that gives much general information about geriatrics 618.97, a work that emphasizes the role and techniques of the medical technician with respect to geriatric patients 618.970233

| [.737 023] | Work of allied health personnel as a profession, occupation, hobby |
| | Do not use; class in 610.737069 |

.737 06	Organizations and personnel
	Notation 06 from Table 1 as modified below

.737 069   Allied health personnel

Nature of duties, characteristics of the profession, relationships

Class here medical assistants, medical technicians

Class comprehensive works on techniques of allied health personnel, medical assistants, medical technicians in 610.737

For physician assistants, see 610.7372069

.737 2   Services of physician assistants

[.737 202 3]   Work of physician assistants as a profession, occupation, hobby

Do not use; class in 610.7372069

.737 206   Organizations and personnel

Notation 06 from Table 1 as modified below

.737 206 9   Physician assistants

People educated in the medical model and licensed to perform diagnostic and therapeutic procedures under the supervision of a physician

Nature of duties, characteristics of the profession, relationships

Class nurse practitioners in 610.730692

.92   Biography

See Manual at 610.92 vs. 615.534092

611   Human anatomy, cytology, histology

Standard subdivisions are added for human anatomy, cytology, histology together; for human anatomy alone

For pathological anatomy, see 616.07

See Manual at 599.94 vs. 611; also at 612 vs. 611

SUMMARY

611.001–.009	**Standard subdivisions**
.01	**Anatomic embryology, cytology, histology**
.1	**Cardiovascular organs**
.2	**Respiratory organs**
.3	**Digestive tract organs**
.4	**Hematopoietic, lymphatic, glandular systems**
.6	**Urogenital system**
.7	**Musculoskeletal system, integument**
.8	**Nervous system**
.9	**Regional and topographical anatomy**

.001–.009   Standard subdivisions

.01	Anatomic embryology, cytology, histology
	Class here specific systems, organs, regions
.013	Anatomic embryology
.018	Histology and cytology
	Standard subdivisions are added for histology and cytology together, for histology alone
.018 1	Cytology (Cell biology)
	Connective tissue cells relocated to 611.01826; adipocytes (fat cells) relocated to 611.018276; epithelial cells relocated to 611.01876; cytology and cells of specific systems and organs relocated to 612.1–612.8; cytology and cells of specific regions relocated to 612.9
.018 15	Pathology (Cytopathology)
.018 16	Physiological genetics
	Class here nucleic acids
.018 166	DNA (Deoxyribonucleic acid)
.018 166 3	Molecular structure
	Class here DNA topology, genetic code; chromosome, gene, genome mapping; base, gene, nucleotide sequences
.018 167	Chromosomes
	Class mapping chromosomes in 611.0181663

>   611.018 2–611.018 7   Histology (Tissue biology)

       Class here histogenesis, histophysiology, histopathology, tissue regeneration

       Class comprehensive works in 611.018

.018 2	Connective tissues and connective tissue cells
	Standard subdivisions are added for connective tissues and connective tissue cells together, for connective tissues alone
	Including collagen, elastic tissues, extracellular matrix
	Connective tissues of specific systems and organs relocated to 612.1–612.8; connective tissues of specific regions relocated to 612.9
.018 26	Connective tissue cells [*formerly* 611.0181]
	Including mast cells
.018 27	Adipose tissues and adipocytes
	Standard subdivisions are added for adipose tissues and adipocytes together, for adipose tissues alone
.018 276	Adipocytes (Fat cells) [*formerly* 611.0181]

[.018 3]	Cartilage tissues
	Relocated to 612.7517
[.018 4]	Bone tissues
	Relocated to 612.751045
[.018 5]	Histology of blood and lymph
	Histology of blood relocated to 612.11; histology of lymph relocated to 612.42045
[.018 6]	Muscle tissues
	Relocated to 612.74045
.018 7	Epithelial tissues and cells
	Standard subdivisions are added for epithelial tissues and cells together, for epithelial tissues alone
	Including endothelium; serous and mucous membranes
	Epithelial tissues of specific systems and organs relocated to 612.1–612.8; epithelial tissues of specific regions relocated to 612.9
.018 76	Epithelial cells [*formerly* 611.0181]
[.018 8]	Nerve tissues
	Relocated to 612.81045
[.018 9]	Histology of specific systems, organs, regions
	Histology and tissues of specific systems and organs relocated to 612.1–612.8; histology and tissues of specific regions relocated to 612.9

> ### 611.1–611.9 Gross anatomy

Class comprehensive works in 611

> ### 611.1–611.8 Gross anatomy of specific systems and organs

Class comprehensive works in 611

See Manual at 612.1–612.8

Comprehensive works on gross anatomy and tissue structure of specific systems and organs relocated to 612.1–612.8

.1   Cardiovascular organs

Class hematopoietic system in 611.41

.11   Pericardium

.12   Heart

         Including ventricles, auricles, endocardium, myocardium

         For pericardium, see 611.11

.13   Arteries

         Class here comprehensive works on blood vessels

         For veins, see 611.14; for capillaries, see 611.15. For blood vessels of a specific system or organ, see the system or organ, e.g., cerebral blood vessels 611.81

.14   Veins

.15   Capillaries

.2   **Respiratory organs**

.21   Nose and paranasal sinuses

         Standard subdivisions are added for nose and paranasal sinuses together, for nose alone

.22   Larynx

         Including epiglottis, glottis, laryngeal muscles

.23   Trachea and bronchi

.24   Lungs

.25   Pleura

.26   Diaphragm

.27   Mediastinum

.3   **Digestive tract organs**

.31   Mouth

.313   Tongue

.314   Teeth

.315   Palate

.316   Salivary glands

.317   Lips

.318   Cheeks

.32   Pharynx, tonsils, esophagus

.33   Stomach

         Including pylorus

         Class here comprehensive works on gastrointestinal organs

         For intestine, see 611.34

.34   Intestine

.341	Small intestine
	Including duodenum, jejunum, ileum
.345	Cecum, vermiform appendix
.347	Large intestine
	Including sigmoid colon
	Class here colon

> *For cecum, vermiform appendix, see 611.345; for rectum, see 611.35*

.35	Rectum and anus

> *See also 611.96 for perineum*

.36	Biliary tract and liver

Standard subdivisions are added for biliary tract and liver together, for biliary tract alone

Including gallbladder, bile ducts

.37	Pancreas and islands of Langerhans

Standard subdivisions are added for pancreas and islands of Langerhans together, for pancreas alone

.38	Peritoneum

Including mesentery, omentum

.4   **Hematopoietic, lymphatic, glandular systems**

Class here endocrine system

> *For glandular organs of a specific system, see the system, e.g., salivary glands 611.316*

.41	Bone marrow and spleen

Class here comprehensive works on anatomy of hematopoietic (blood-forming, hemopoietic) system

> *For liver, see 611.36; for lymphatic system, see 611.42*

.42	Lymphatic system

> *For spleen, see 611.41; for lymphatic glands, see 611.46*

.43	Thymus gland
.44	Thyroid and parathyroid glands
.45	Adrenal glands
.46	Lymphatic glands
.47	Carotid body; pituitary and pineal glands
.49	Breasts
.6	**Urogenital system**

.61	Kidneys and ureters

Standard subdivisions are added for kidneys and ureters together, for kidneys alone

Class here comprehensive works on anatomy of urinary organs

For bladder and urethra, see 611.62

.62	Bladder and urethra
.63	Testes, prostate, scrotum

Class here comprehensive works on male genital organs

For penis, see 611.64

.64	Penis
.65	Ovaries and fallopian tubes

Class here comprehensive works on female genital organs

For uterus, see 611.66; for vagina, hymen, vulva, see 611.67

.66	Uterus

Including uterine cervix

.67	Vagina, hymen, vulva
.7	**Musculoskeletal system, integument**

Standard subdivisions are added for musculoskeletal system, integument together; for musculoskeletal system alone

.71	Bones

For ossicles, see 611.85

.711	Bones of spinal column
.712	Bones of chest

Including ribs

For sternum, see 611.713

.713	Sternum
.715	Bones of skull

For bones of face, see 611.715; for mastoid processes, see 611.85

.716	Bones of face
.717	Bones of upper extremities

Including scapulas, clavicles, humeri, radii, ulnas, carpal and metacarpal bones, phalanges and sesamoid bones of hands

Class comprehensive works on bones of extremities in 611.718

.718	Bones of lower extremities

Including hip bones, femurs, patellas, tibias, fibulas, tarsal and metatarsal bones, phalanges and sesamoid bones of feet

Class here comprehensive works on bones of extremities

For bones of upper extremities, see 611.717

.72	Joints and ligaments

Standard subdivisions are added for joints and ligaments together, for joints alone

.73	Muscles

For muscles of a specific system or organ, see the system or organ, e.g., heart muscles 611.12

.731	Muscles of back
.732	Muscles of head
.733	Muscles of neck
.735	Muscles of chest
.736	Muscles of abdomen and pelvis
.737	Muscles of upper extremities

Including muscles of shoulders, arms, hands

Class comprehensive works on muscles of extremities in 611.738

.738	Muscles of lower extremities

Including muscles of hips, buttocks, thighs

Class here leg muscles, comprehensive works on muscles of extremities

For muscles of upper extremities, see 611.737

.74	Connective tissues

Including tendons, fasciae

For ligaments, see 611.72; for bursae, sheaths of tendons, see 611.75

.75	Bursae, sheaths of tendons
.77	Integument

For hair and nails, see 611.78

.78	Hair and nails

Including hair follicles

.8	**Nervous system**

Class here neuroanatomy, sense organs

.81   Brain

> Class here central nervous system
>
> *For spinal cord, see 611.82*

.82   Spinal cord

.83   Nerves and ganglia

> Class nerves of a specific system or organ with the system or organ, e.g., optic nerves 611.84

.84   Eyes

> Class here orbits

.85   Ears

> Including mastoid processes, ossicles

.86   Olfactory organs

.87   Gustatory organs

.88   Tactile organs

.9   Regional and topographical anatomy

> Standard subdivisions are added for either or both topics in heading
>
> Including back
>
> Class specific systems or organs in a region in 611.1–611.8
>
> Comprehensive works on gross anatomy and tissue structure of specific regions relocated to 612.9

.91   Head

> *For face, see 611.92*

.92   Face

> *See also 611.317 for lips; also 611.318 for cheeks*

.93   Neck

.94   Thorax

.95   Abdomen

> Epigastric through lumbar regions

.96   Perineum and pelvic region

.97   Upper extremities

> Class comprehensive works on extremities in 611.98

.98   Lower extremities

> Class here legs, comprehensive works on extremities
>
> *For upper extremities, see 611.97*

612   **Human physiology**

Class here comprehensive works on human anatomy and physiology

Class physiological psychology in 152

> *For human anatomy, cytology, histology, see 611; for pathological physiology, see 616.07*
>
> *See Manual at 612 vs. 611; also at 613 vs. 612, 615.8; also at 616 vs. 612*

SUMMARY

612.001–.009	**Standard subdivisions**
.01–.04	**[Biophysics, biochemistry, control processes, tissue and organ culture, physiology of specific activities]**
.1	**Circulatory system**
.2	**Respiratory system**
.3	**Digestive system**
.4	**Hematopoietic, lymphatic, glandular, urinary systems**
.6	**Reproduction, development, maturation**
.7	**Musculoskeletal system, integument**
.8	**Nervous system**
.9	**Regional physiology**

.001–.009   Standard subdivisions

.01   Biophysics and biochemistry

SUMMARY

612.014	**Biophysics**
.015	**Biochemistry**

.014   Biophysics

.014 2   Physical phenomena in humans

Including human aura when scientifically considered

> *See also 133.892 for the aura as a manifestation of psychic power*

.014 21   Bioenergetics

> *For body heat, see 612.01426; for bioelectricity, see 612.01427; for energy metabolism, see 612.39*

.014 26   Body heat

Including regulation

Class here production, maintenance

.014 27   Bioelectricity

Including electrophysiology

.014 4   Effects of terrestrial agents

Including aerospace physiology

Class space physiology in 612.0145

.014 41   Mechanical forces

.014 412	Gravitational forces
.014 414	Acceleration and deceleration
	Standard subdivisions are added for either or both topics in heading
.014 415	Pressure
	Including submarine physiology
.014 42	Electricity and magnetism
.014 44	Visible light
.014 45	Mechanical vibrations, sound, related vibrations
.014 453	Sound
.014 455	Ultrasonic vibrations
.014 46	Thermal forces
.014 462	Heat and high temperatures
	Standard subdivisions are added for either or both topics in heading
.014 465	Cold and low temperatures
	Standard subdivisions are added for either or both topics in heading
	For cryogenic temperatures, see 612.014467
.014 467	Cryogenic temperatures
.014 48	Radiation (Radiobiology)
	Class radiation sickness and radiation injuries in 616.9897
	For visible light, see 612.01444
.014 480 287	Testing and measurement
	Class here radiometry (radiation dosimetry)
	For a specific application of radiometry, see the application, e.g., use of radiometry in radiotherapy 615.842, use for prevention of diseases due to radiation 616.989705
.014 481	Radio waves and microwaves
	Standard subdivisions are added for either or both topics in heading
.014 482	Infrared radiation
.014 484	Ultraviolet radiation
.014 485	X rays

.014 486	Particle radiation
	Including cosmic rays; beta, gamma, neutron radiation
	For X rays, see 612.014485
.014 5	Extraterrestrial biophysics
	Class here bioastronautics, space physiology
	Class aerospace physiology in 612.0144; class space medicine in 616.980214
.014 53	Effects of mechanical forces
.014 532	Gravitational forces
.014 534	Acceleration and deceleration
	Standard subdivisions are added for either or both topics in heading
.014 535	Pressure
.015	Biochemistry
	Class metabolism in 612.39
	For physiological genetics, see 611.01816
.015 01	Philosophy and theory
	Class theoretical biochemistry in 612.01582
.015 02	Miscellany
.015 028	Auxiliary techniques and procedures; apparatus, equipment, materials
	Class analytical biochemistry in 612.01585
.015 1	Enzymes
	Add to base number 612.0151 the numbers following 572.7 in 572.75–572.79, e.g., saccharolytic enzymes 612.015156, lipolytic enzymes 612.015157
.015 2	Fluids, inorganic constituents, pigments
.015 22	Fluids
	Including fluid balance, water, water-electrolyte balance
	Class here fluid metabolism
.015 24	Inorganic constituents
	Including minerals
	Class inorganic fluids in 612.01522; class inorganic pigments in 612.01528
.015 28	Pigments
	Class biochemistry of skin pigmentation in 612.7927

.015 4	Biosynthesis
.015 7	Organic compounds

> *For nucleic acids, see 611.01816; for enzymes, see 612.0151; for organic fluids, see 612.01522; for organic pigments, see 612.01528; for vitamins, see 612.399; for hormones, see 612.405*

.015 75	Proteins
.015 756	Components of proteins

Class here amino acids, peptides, polypeptides

.015 77	Lipids

Including steroids

Class here fats, fatty acids

.015 78	Carbohydrates

Including sugars

.015 8	Theoretical, physical, analytical biochemistry

Class physical, theoretical, analytical biochemistry of a specific constituent with the constituent, e.g., physical chemistry of carbohydrates 612.01578

.015 82	Theoretical biochemistry
.015 83	Physical biochemistry
.015 85	Analytical biochemistry
.02	Control processes and tissue and organ culture
.022	Control processes

Including biological rhythms, homeostasis

> *For control processes in biophysics, see the process in 612.014, e.g., body heat regulation 612.01426; for control processes in biochemistry, see the process in 612.015, e.g., water-electrolyte balance 612.01522*

.028	Tissue and organ culture
.04	Physiology of specific activities

Class here comprehensive works on the physiology of physical movements in relation to multiple physiological systems

> *For physiology of physical movements in relation to a specific system, see the system, e.g., musculoskeletal system 612.76*

.042	Work

.044	Exercise and sports

> Standard subdivisions are added for either or both topics in heading
>
> Including walking
>
> Class here recreation
>
> *For physiology of exercise on the job, see 612.042*

> **612.1–612.8 Specific functions, systems, organs**

Class here cytology and cells of specific systems and organs [*formerly* 611.0181], connective tissues of specific systems and organs [*formerly* 611.0182], histology and tissues of specific systems and organs [*formerly* 611.0189], comprehensive works on gross anatomy and tissue structure of specific systems and organs [*formerly* 611.1–611.8]

Except for modifications shown under specific entries, add to each subdivision identified by * as follows:

04	Tissues and cells
045	Tissues
	Class here histology (tissue biology); histogenesis, histophysiology, histopathology, tissue regeneration
046	Cells
	Including cytopathology
	Class here cytology (cell biology)

Class comprehensive works in 612

See Manual at 612.1–612.8

.1	***Circulatory system**

> Class here cardiovascular system, circulation
>
> *For lymphatic system, see 612.42. For circulation in a specific system or organ, see the system or organ, e.g., brain 612.824*

.11	Blood

> Class here histology of blood [*formerly* 611.0185], cytology of blood
>
> Class hematopoietic system in 612.41; class blood transfusion in 615.39
>
> *For blood chemistry, see 612.12*

.111	Erythrocytes (Red corpuscles)
.111 1	Biochemistry
	Including hemoglobins
.111 2	Counts and counting
.112	Leukocytes (White corpuscles)
.112 1	Biochemistry
.112 7	Counts and counting

*Add as instructed under 612.1–612.8

.115		Coagulation (Clotting)

Including role of fibrin, fibrinoplastin, plasma, thrombin in clotting

.116		Plasma

Class blood plasma transfusion in 615.39

For role of plasma in clotting, see 612.115

.117		Platelets
.118		Biophysics and biological properties
.118 1		Biophysics

Physical properties and phenomena, effect of physical agents

Including hemorheology (study of blood flow)

For biophysics of a specific component or function, see the compound or function in 612.111–612.117, e.g., biophysics of platelets 612.117

.118 2		Biological properties
.118 25		Blood types and typing (Blood groups and grouping)

Standard subdivisions are added for any or all topics in heading

.12		Blood chemistry

Including cholesterol, lipids, sugar

Class biological properties in 612.1182

For chemistry of a specific component or function, see the component or function in 612.111–612.117, e.g., chemistry of coagulation 612.115

> 612.13–612.18 Circulation

Class comprehensive works in 612.1

.13		*Blood vessels

Class here vascular circulation

For vasomotors, see 612.18

.133		*Arteries

Class here arterial circulation

.134		*Veins

Class here venous circulation

.135		*Capillaries

Class here capillary circulation

.14		Blood pressure

*Add as instructed under 612.1–612.8

.17   *Heart

.171   Biophysics

         Including contraction and dilation of heart cavities, valvular activity

         For blood pressure, see 612.14

.173   Biochemistry

         Including metabolism

.178   *Innervation

.18   *Vasomotors

         Nerves causing dilation (vasodilators) and constriction (vasoconstrictors) of blood vessels

.2   *Respiratory system

         Class here respiration

.21   Biophysics

         Including respiratory sounds

         Class here respiratory mechanics

.22   Biochemistry

         Including oxygen supply, gas exchange, carbon dioxide removal

.23   Nose, paranasal sinuses, larynx, trachea, bronchi

.232   *Nose and paranasal sinuses

         Class here comprehensive works on physiology of the nose

         Subdivisions are added for nose and paranasal sinuses together, for nose alone

         For physiology of the nose as an olfactory organ, see 612.86

.233   *Larynx

         Including epiglottis, glottis

         For physiology of glottis as an organ of speech, see 612.78

.234   *Trachea and bronchi

         Subdivisions are added for either or both topics in heading

.24   *Lungs

.25   Pleura, diaphragm, mediastinum

.26   Tissue respiration

.28   *Innervation of respiratory system

---

*Add as instructed under 612.1–612.8

.3   ***Digestive system**

> Class here digestion, nutrition
>
> *For dietetics and applied nutrition, see 613.2*

.31   *Mouth and esophagus

> Including ingestion and start of digestion
>
> Subdivisions are added for mouth and esophagus together, for mouth alone

.311   *Teeth

> Including mastication

.312   Tongue and tonsils

> Class here comprehensive works on physiology of tongue
>
> *For physiology of tongue as a gustatory organ, see 612.87*

.313   *Salivary glands

> Including saliva

.315   *Esophagus

.32   *Stomach

> Including gastric secretions
>
> Class here comprehensive works on gastrointestinal organs and secretions
>
> *For intestine and intestinal secretions, see 612.33*

.33   *Intestine

> Including intestinal secretions
>
> *For large intestine, see 612.36*

.34   *Pancreas

> Including pancreatic secretions

.35   *Biliary tract and liver

> Including gallbladder, bile and bile ducts
>
> Subdivisions are added for biliary tract and liver together, for biliary tract alone

.352   *Liver

.36   *Large intestine

> Including defecation

*Add as instructed under 612.1–612.8

.38   Absorption

Transfer of digested food from alimentary canal into blood stream

Class absorption in a specific part of the alimentary canal with the part, e.g., intestine 612.33

.39   Metabolism

Including energy metabolism

Class bioenergetics in 612.01421

For biosynthesis, see 612.0154; for metabolism of drugs, see 615.7; for metabolism of toxic substances, see 615.9. For metabolism within a specific function, system, or organ, see the function, system, or organ, e.g., metabolism of plasma 612.116

.391   Hunger and thirst mechanisms

.392   Metabolism of inorganic substances

Class here minerals

.392 3   Water

Class electrolytic, fluid balance; comprehensive works on fluid metabolism in 612.01522

.392 4   Elements

Including iron, phosphorus, sulfur

.392 6   Compounds other than water

Including salts

.396   Carbohydrate metabolism

Class glycemic index as dietetic guide in 613.283

.397   Lipid metabolism

Including fats

.398   Protein metabolism

.399   Vitamins

.4   ***Hematopoietic, lymphatic, glandular, urinary systems**

Class here endocrine system, exocrine glands, secretion

For glands and glandular activity in a specific system or organ, see the system or organ, e.g., salivary glands 612.313, mammary glands and lactation 612.664

.400 1–.400 9   Standard subdivisions

.405   Hormones

*Add as instructed under 612.1–612.8

.41	*Spleen and bone marrow

Class here hematopoiesis, comprehensive works on hematopoietic (blood-forming, hemopoietic) system

For liver, see 612.352; for lymphatic system, see 612.42

.415	*Spleen
.416	*Bone marrow
.42	*Lymphatic system

Class here lymph

For spleen, see 612.415

.420 45	Lymphoid tissue

Number built according to instructions under 612.1–612.8

Class here histology of lymph [*formerly* 611.0185]

.43	*Thymus gland
.44	*Thyroid and parathyroid glands

Subdivisions are added for thyroid and parathyroid glands together, for thyroid gland alone

.448	*Parathyroid glands
.45	*Adrenal glands
.46	*Urinary system

Class here comprehensive works on excretion, excretory system

For defecation, see 612.36

.461	Urine
.463	*Kidneys
.467	Ureters, bladder, urethra
.467 3	*Bladder
.49	Carotid body; pituitary and pineal glands
.492	*Pituitary and pineal glands

Subdivisions are added for pituitary and pineal glands, for pituitary gland alone

.6	***Reproduction, development, maturation**

Class here genital system, comprehensive medical works on sex

Class interdisciplinary works on sex in 306.7

For a specific aspect of sex, see the aspect, e.g., sexual disorders 616.69

---

*Add as instructed under 612.1–612.8

.61	*Male reproductive system
	Including function in sexual activity
	For climacteric, see 612.665
.614	*Testes and scrotum
	Subdivisions are added for testes and scrotum together, for testes alone
.616	*Penis
.618	*Prostate
.62	*Female reproductive system
	Including function in sexual activity
	For pregnancy and childbirth, see 612.63; for menstruation, see 612.662; for climacteric, see 612.665
.625	*Ovaries and fallopian tubes
	Subdivisions are added for ovaries and fallopian tubes together, for ovaries alone
.627	*Uterus
	Including uterine cervix
.628	Vagina, hymen, vulva
.63	Pregnancy and childbirth
	Including placenta
	Class comprehensive works on pregnancy and childbirth in 618.2
	For physiology of embryo and fetus, see 612.64
.64	Physiology of embryo and fetus
	Class here comprehensive works on embryology
	For anatomic embryology, see 611.013
.640 01–.640 09	Standard subdivisions
.640 1	Development of specific systems, organs, regions
	Add to base number 612.6401 the numbers following 611 in 611.1–611.9, e.g., development of the eye 612.640184
.646	Development of embryo
.647	Development of fetus

*Add as instructed under 612.1–612.8

> 612.65–612.67 Postnatal development

Class comprehensive works in 612.6

For postnatal development of a specific system, organ, region, see the system, organ, region, e.g., postnatal development of teeth 612.311

.65   Child development

.652   Development of newborn (neonate)

First month of postnatal development

.654   Development from infancy to beginning of puberty

From second month of postnatal development

.66   Adult development and maturity

For aging, see 612.67

.661   Puberty and development prior to attainment of full maturity

.662   Menstruation

Including menarche

.663   Full maturity

.664   *Mammary glands

Class here lactation

.665   Climacteric

Including menopause

.67   Aging

Class here physical gerontology

See also 616.078 for death

.68   Longevity factors

.7   *Musculoskeletal system, integument

Subdivisions are added for musculoskeletal system, integument together; for musculoskeletal system alone

.74   *Muscles

Class locomotion, exercise, rest in 612.76. Class muscles of a specific system or organ with the system or organ, e.g., cardiac muscles 612.17, eye muscles 612.846

.740 45   Muscle tissues [*formerly* 611.0186]

Number built according to instructions under 612.1–612.8

Including skeletal muscle tissue, smooth muscle tissue

*Add as instructed under 612.1–612.8

.741	Biophysics
	Including contractions, elasticity, irritability, tonus
.743	*Innervation
.744	Biochemistry
	Including fatigue products
.75	Bones, joints, connective tissues
	Class locomotion, exercise, rest in 612.76
.751	*Bones and cartilage
	Subdivisions are added for bones and cartilage together, for bones alone
	Class bone marrow in 612.416
	For mastoid processes, ossicles, see 612.854
.751 045	Bone tissues [*formerly* 611.0184]
	Number built according to instructions under 612.1–612.8
	Including periosteum
.751 7	Cartilage
	Including elastic cartilage, hyaline cartilage; fibrocartilage
	Class here cartilage tissues [*formerly* 611.0183]
.751 76	Cartilage cells (Chondrocytes)
.752	Joints and ligaments
	Standard subdivisions are added for joints and ligaments together, for joints alone
.757	Connective tissues
	Class comprehensive works on histology of connective tissues in 611.0182
	For bone tissues, see 612.751045; for cartilage tissues, see 612.7517; for ligament tissues, see 612.752
.76	Locomotion, exercise, rest
	Including body mechanics
	Class total physiology of physical movements (including muscle contractions, breathing, blood flow, digestion during exercise) in 612.04
.78	Voice and speech
	Standard subdivisions are added for either or both topics in heading
	Class here organs of speech
	Class neurolinguistics in 612.82336

*Add as instructed under 612.1–612.8

.79	*Integument
	Class here integumentary system, skin
.791	Biophysics of skin
	Including absorbency, contractions, irritability, resistivity, tonus
.792	Biochemistry of skin
[.792 1]	Glands of skin
	Relocated to 612.793
.792 7	Pigmentation
.793	Glands of skin [*formerly* 612.7921]
	Including perspiration
	Class here glandular secretions
.798	*Innervation of skin
.799	Hair and nails
	Including hair follicles

.8   Nervous system

Class here neurophysiology, psychophysiology, sensory functions

See Manual at 612.8 vs. 152

SUMMARY

612.804	**Special topics of nervous functions**
.81	**Nerves and nerve fibers**
.82	**Central nervous system**
.83	**Spinal cord**
.84	**Eyes**
.85	**Ears**
.86	**Nose**
.87	**Tongue**
.88	**Other sensory organs**
.89	**Autonomic nervous system**

.804	Special topics of nervous functions
.804 2	Neurochemistry
	Including cerebrospinal fluid
.804 3	Biophysics of nervous system

*Add as instructed under 612.1–612.8

.81   *Nerves and nerve fibers

       Class here peripheral nervous system

       Subdivisions are added for nerves and nerve fibers together, for nerves alone

       Class comprehensive works on nerves, nerve fibers, central nervous system in 612.8

> *For nerves and nerve fibers in central nervous system, see 612.82; for autonomic nervous system, see 612.89. For innervation and neural activity in a specific system or organ, see the system or organ, e.g., heart innervation 612.178*

.810 45   Nerve tissues [*formerly* 611.0188]

       Number built according to instructions under 612.1–612.8

.810 46   Nerve cells

       Number built according to instructions under 612.1–612.8

       Including neuroglia

       Class here neurons

.811   Motor and sensory nerves

.813   Biophysics

       Including electrophysiology

> *For irritability, see 612.816. For biophysics of a specific kind of nerve, see the nerve, e.g., biophysics of cranial nerves 612.819*

.814   Biochemistry

> *For biochemistry of a specific kind of nerve, see the nerve, e.g., biochemistry of motor nerves 612.811*

.816   Irritability

.819   Cranial and spinal nerves

.82   *Central nervous system

       Class here brain

> *For spinal cord, see 612.83*

.821   Sleep phenomena

       Physiology of brain during sleep and dreams

       Class effect of sleep on other psychological activity, interdisciplinary works on sleep in 154.6; class dreams as phenomena that have meaning in themselves or in the life of the dreamer, interdisciplinary works on dreams in 154.63

.822   Biochemistry and biophysics

> *For biochemistry and biophysics of a specific part of brain, see the part, e.g., biophysics of cerebrum 612.825*

*Add as instructed under 612.1–612.8

.823	Emotions, conscious mental processes, intelligence
.823 2	Emotions

Class here feelings

| .823 3 | Conscious mental processes and intelligence |

Standard subdivisions are added for conscious mental processes and intelligence together, for conscious mental processes alone

Class here cognitive neuroscience

Add to base number 612.8233 the numbers following 153 in 153.1–153.9, e.g., neurolinguistics 612.82336, physiology of brain with respect to memory 612.823312, with respect to intelligence 612.82339; however, for kinesthesis, see 612.88

| .824 | Circulation |

For circulation in a specific part of brain, see the part, e.g., circulation in cerebellum 612.827

| .825 | *Cerebrum |

Including cerebral hemispheres, convolutions, corpus striatum, cortex, rhinencephalon

Class here prosencephalon (forebrain)

For cerebral commissures and peduncles, see 612.826; for diencephalon, see 612.8262

.825 2	Localization of motor functions
.825 5	Localization of sensory functions
.826	Diencephalon and brain stem

Including cerebral commissures and peduncles

For medulla oblongata, see 612.828

| .826 2 | *Diencephalon |

Including geniculate bodies, hypothalamus, thalamus

| .826 4 | *Mesencephalon (Midbrain) |

Including corpora quadrigemina

.826 7	*Pons Variolii
.827	*Cerebellum
.828	*Medulla oblongata
.83	*Spinal cord

*Add as instructed under 612.1–612.8

>   612.84–612.88 Sensory functions

    Class here sense organs

    Class comprehensive works in 612.8

.84   *Eyes

    Class here eyeballs; physiological optics; vision

.841   Fibrous tunics, conjunctivas, anterior chambers

    Including corneas, scleras

.842   *Uveas

    Including choroids, ciliary bodies, irises

.843   Optic nerves and retinas

.844   Aqueous humors, crystalline lenses, vitreous bodies

.846   Movements

    Class here ocular neuromuscular mechanism

.847   Eyelids and tear ducts

    Class conjunctivas in 612.841

.85   *Ears

    Class here hearing

.851   *External ears

.854   *Middle ears

    Including eustachian tubes, mastoid processes, ossicles, tympanic membranes

.858   *Internal ears

    Including cochleas, labyrinths, semicircular canals, vestibules

.86   *Nose

    Class here chemical senses, smelling

    Class comprehensive works on physiology of nose in 612.232

    For tasting, see 612.87

.87   *Tongue

    Class here tasting

    Class comprehensive works on physiology of the tongue in 612.312

*Add as instructed under 612.1–612.8

.88   Other sensory organs

> Including kinesthesis, proprioceptive senses; tactile senses; pain sensations and reactions

.89   *Autonomic nervous system

> Including sympathetic and parasympathetic nervous systems

.9   **Regional physiology**

> Including back
>
> Class here cytology and cells of specific regions [*formerly* 611.0181], connective tissues of specific regions [*formerly* 611.0182], epithelial tissues of specific regions [*formerly* 611.0187], histology and tissues of specific regions [*formerly* 611.0189], comprehensive works on gross anatomy and tissue structure of specific regions [*formerly* 611.9]
>
> Add to base number 612.9 the numbers following 611.9 in 611.91–611.98, e.g., physiology of face 612.92
>
> Class physiology, cytology, histology of specific systems and organs in specific regions in 612.1–612.8

613   **Personal health and safety**

> Standard subdivisions are added for personal health and safety together, for personal health alone
>
> Class here measures to promote health and prevent disease taken by individuals and their medical advisers, comprehensive medical works on personal and public measures to promote health and prevent disease
>
> *For public measures to promote health and prevent disease, see 614; for personal measures to prevent poisoning, see 615.905. For personal measures to prevent a specific disease or group of diseases, see the disease or group of diseases in 616–618, plus notation 05 from table under 616.1–616.9, notation 052 from table under 617, or notation 052 from table under 618.1–618.8, e.g., personal measures to prevent cardiovascular diseases 616.105*
>
> *See Manual at 613 vs. 612, 615.8*

SUMMARY

613.04	**Personal health of people by gender, sex, or age group**
.1	**Environmental factors**
.2	**Dietetics**
.4	**Personal cleanliness and related topics**
.5	**Artificial environments**
.6	**Personal safety and special topics of health**
.7	**Physical fitness**
.8	**Substance abuse (Drug abuse)**
.9	**Birth control, reproductive technology, sex hygiene, sexual techniques**

*Add as instructed under 612.1–612.8

.04 Personal health of people by gender, sex, or age group

> Class here comprehensive works on personal health and safety of specific gender, sex, and age groups

> *For personal safety of specific gender, sex, and age groups, see 613.6081–613.6084*

.042 Personal health of specific sex groups

.042 3 Males

.042 32 Males under twelve

> Class here comprehensive works on boys

> *For boys twelve and older, see 613.04233*

.042 33 Males twelve to twenty

.042 34 Adult men

.042 4 Females

.042 42 Females under twelve

> Class here comprehensive works on girls

> *For girls twelve and older, see 613.04243*

.042 43 Females twelve to twenty

.042 44 Adult women

.043 Personal health of specific age groups

> Class personal health of specific age groups of specific sexes in 613.042

.043 2 Infants and children

> Through age eleven

> Class here pediatric preventive measures

.043 3 Young people twelve to twenty

.043 4 Mature adults

> Including young adults, middle-aged people

> *For people in late adulthood, see 613.0438*

.043 8 People in late adulthood

> Class here geriatric preventive measures

[.081–.084] People by gender, sex, or age group

> Do not use; class in 613.04

.1 **Environmental factors**

Class here acclimation, comprehensive works on personal environmental health

For artificial environments, see 613.5; for industrial and occupational health, see 613.62; for travel health, see 613.68; for survival, see 613.69; for environmental toxicology, see 615.902; for environmental diseases, see 616.98

.11 Weather and climate

Standard subdivisions are added for either or both topics in heading

Including humidity, seasonal changes

[.110 911] Weather and climate in frigid zones

Do not use; class in 613.111

[.110 913] Weather and climate in torrid zone (tropics)

Do not use; class in 613.113

.111 Cold weather and climate

Standard subdivisions are added for either or both topics in heading

Including arctic climate

.113 Hot weather and climate

Standard subdivisions are added for either or both topics in heading

Including tropical climate

.12 Physiographic and other regions

Including mountains, seashore

.122 Health resorts

.19 Air and light

.192 Breathing

Class here breathing exercises

Class breathing exercises in respiratory therapy in 615.836; class comprehensive works on exercises in 613.71

.193 Sun bathing

.194 Nudism

.2　　　**Dietetics**

Class here applied nutrition; guides to nutritional aspects of food, of beverages; comprehensive works on personal health aspects of food, of beverages

Class human nutritional requirements considered in relation to physiological processes and the role of nutrients in the body in 612.3; class personal aspects of preventing alcohol abuse in 613.81; class diet therapy in 615.854; class nutritive values of specific beverages in 641.2; class nutritive values of specific foods in 641.33–641.39; class comprehensive works on diet and physical fitness in 613.7; class interdisciplinary works on food safety in 363.192. Class diets to prevent a specific disease with the disease, plus notation 0654 from table under 616.1–616.9, notation 0654 from table under 617, or notation 0654 from table under 618.1–618.8, e.g., diets to prevent hypertension 616.1320654

See also 616.39 for conditions resulting from nutritional deficiencies; also 641.563 for cooking for preventive and therapeutic diets

See Manual at 363.8 vs. 613.2, 641.3

.208 2　　　　Women

Class dietetics for nursing women in 613.269; class dietetics for pregnant women in 618.242

.208 3　　　　Young people

Class home economics and child-rearing aspects of feeding children, interdisciplinary works on feeding children in 649.3

.208 32　　　　Infants

Class breast feeding in 613.269

.208 5　　　　Relatives

.208 52　　　　Mothers

Class dietetics for nursing mothers in 613.269

.23　　　Calories

Class here calorie counters

Class high-calorie diet in 613.24; class low-calorie diet in 613.25

.24　　　Weight-gaining diet

Weight-gaining diet focused on a specific nutritive element relocated to 613.28

.25　　　Weight-losing diet (Reducing diet)

Class here caloric restriction, low-calorie diet

Class diet therapy for obesity in 616.3980654; class comprehensive works on exercise and diet for weight loss in 613.712

Weight-losing diet focused on a specific nutritive element relocated to 613.28

.26   Specific dietary regimens

      Including regimens involving specific foods, e.g., milk-free diet

      Class human breast milk diet in 613.269

        For weight-gaining diet, see 613.24; for weight-losing diet, see 613.25; for regimens involving specific nutritive elements, see 613.28

[.260 1–.260 9]   Standard subdivisions

      Do not use; class in 613.201–613.209

.262   Vegetarian diet

      For macrobiotic diet, see 613.264

.262 2   Vegan diet

.263   High-fiber and low-fiber diets

      Standard subdivisions are added for either or both topics in heading

      Class vegetarian diet in 613.262; class raw food diet in 613.265

.264   Macrobiotic diet

.265   Raw food diet

      Class vegetarian diet in 613.262

.269   Human breast milk diet

      Class here nutritional and general health aspects of breast feeding for both mother and infant, comprehensive medical works on breast feeding

      Class interdisciplinary works on breast feeding in 649.33

        For a specific medical aspect of breast feeding not provided for here, see the aspect, e.g., prolactin and physiology of human lactation 612.664

.28   Specific nutritive elements

      Class here weight-gaining diet focused on a specific nutritive element [*formerly* 613.24], weight-losing diet focused on a specific nutritive element [*formerly* 613.25]

      Class calories in 613.23; class high-fiber and low-fiber diets in 613.263

[.280 1–.280 9]   Standard subdivisions

      Do not use; class in 613.201–613.209

.282   Proteins

.283   Carbohydrates

      Class here glycemic index as dietetic guide

      Class physiology of carbohydrate metabolism in 612.396

.283 3   Low-carbohydrate diet (Carbohydrate-restricted diet)

.283 32   Sugar-free diet

.284   Fats and oils

            Standard subdivisions are added for either or both topics in heading

.284 3   Low-fat diet (Fat-restricted diet)

.284 32   Low-cholesterol diet

.285   Minerals

.285 1   Calcium, iron, copper

            Class here metals

            For metals other than calcium, iron, copper, see 613.2852

.285 16   Calcium

.285 2   Metals other than calcium, iron, copper

.285 22   Sodium

.285 223   Sodium-restricted diet

              Class here low-salt diet, salt-free diet

.286   Vitamins

            Including antioxidants

.287   Water

.4   **Personal cleanliness and related topics**

            Standard subdivisions are added for personal cleanliness and related topics together, for personal cleanliness alone

.41   Bathing

            Including saunas, Turkish baths; showering

.48   Clothing and cosmetics

.482   Clothing

            Only health aspects

            Class clothing selection and dressing with style in 646.3

.488   Cosmetics

            Only health aspects

            Class cosmetics in grooming in 646.72

.5   **Artificial environments**

            In enclosed spaces

            Including homes, offices; indoor air quality; indoor temperatures and air conditioning

            Class toxicology in 615.9

.6 **Personal safety and special topics of health**

  Standard subdivisions are added for personal safety and special topics of health together, for personal safety alone

  Class here accident prevention for individuals, crime prevention for individuals

  Class social services to victims of crimes in 362.88; class public safety programs, interdisciplinary works on safety in 363.1; class works on why individuals become victims of specific crimes in 364.1; class crime prevention for society as a whole in 364.4

   For prevention of identity theft, see 332.024; for household security, see 643.16. For personal safety in a specific field, see the field, plus notation 0289 from Table 1, e.g., personal safety in recreational boating 797.10289

.62 Industrial and occupational health

  Standard subdivisions are added for either or both topics in heading

.66 Self-defense

  Class here prevention of violent crimes for individuals

  Class works on why people become victims of specific violent crimes in 364.15; class martial arts for self-defense, interdisciplinary works on martial arts in 796.8

   See also 362.88 for general works on why people become victims of crimes; also 613.7148 for exercises from martial arts traditions for fitness

.660 82 Women

   Class here self-defense for women

   Class rape prevention in 613.663

.663 Rape prevention for individuals

.68 Travel health

.69 Survival

  After accidents and disasters, in other unfavorable circumstances

  Class here survival housekeeping

  Class survival as a safety aspect of a specific sport with the sport in 796, plus notation 0289 from Table 1, e.g., survival as a safety aspect of mountaineering 796.5220289

   For self-defense, see 613.66

.7 **Physical fitness**

  Class here comprehensive works on diet and physical fitness

   For diet, see 613.2

SUMMARY

613.704	**Special topics of physical fitness**
.71	**Exercise and sports activities**
.72	**Massage**
.78	**Correct posture**
.79	**Relaxation, rest, sleep**

.704   Special topics of physical fitness

\>   613.704 2–613.704 5   Specific age and sex groups

Class physical yoga of specific age and sex groups in 613.7046; class comprehensive works in 613.704

.704 2   Physical fitness of children

.704 3   Physical fitness of young people twelve to twenty

.704 4   Physical fitness of adults

For physical fitness of adult women, see 613.7045

.704 46   Physical fitness of people in late adulthood

Class physical fitness of men in late adulthood in 613.70449

.704 49   Physical fitness of adult men

Class here physical fitness of males

For physical fitness of boys under twelve, see 613.7042; for physical fitness of young men twelve to twenty, see 613.7043

.704 5   Physical fitness of adult women

Class here physical fitness of females

For physical fitness of girls under twelve, see 613.7042; for physical fitness of young women twelve to twenty, see 613.7043

.704 6   Physical yoga

Class here hatha yoga

Class exercises from the martial arts and related traditions in 613.7148

[.708 1–.708 4]   People by gender, sex, or age group

Do not use; class in 613.7042–613.7045

.71 Exercise and sports activities

> Standard subdivisions are added for exercise and sports activities together, for exercise alone
>
> Class here aerobic exercise, comprehensive works on care of physique and form
>
> Class physical yoga in 613.7046; class exercises to aid childbirth in 618.244; class parental supervision of children's exercise and sports activities in 649.57; class exercise and sports activities as recreation in 796; class comprehensive works on physiological processes of exercise and sports in 612.044
>
> *For breathing exercises, see 613.192*

[.710 247 96] The subject for people occupied with athletics and sports

> Do not use; class in 613.711

.710 82 Women

> Class exercise for pregnant women in 618.244

.710 88 Occupational and religious groups

[.710 887 96] People occupied with athletics and sports

> Do not use; class in 613.711

.711 Fitness training for sports

> Including fitness training for specific sports not provided for in 613.713–613.717, e.g., soccer
>
> Class here personal health of athletes
>
> Class a specific kind of fitness training with the kind, e.g., weight lifting 613.713; class fitness training for a specific sport listed in 613.713–613.717 with the sport, e.g., swimming 613.716

.712 Exercise for weight loss

> Class here reducing, reducing exercises, comprehensive works on exercise and diet for weight loss
>
> Class exercise therapy for obesity in 616.398062
>
> *For diet for weight loss, see 613.25*

.713 Weight lifting

> Class here interdisciplinary works on bodybuilding
>
> *For weight lifting as a sport, bodybuilding contests, see 796.41*

.714 Calisthenics and isometric exercises

> Standard subdivisions are added for calisthenics and isometric exercises together, for calisthenics alone
>
> Class here gymnastic exercises
>
> *See also 613.713 for weight lifting; also 613.715 for aerobic dancing; also 613.716 for aquatic exercises*

.714 8   Exercises from the martial arts traditions and related traditions

Standard subdivisions are added for exercises from the martial arts traditions and related traditions together, for exercises from the martial arts traditions alone

Including aikido, karate exercises

Class here tai chi, fitness training for the martial arts

> *See also 796.815 for jujitso and related martial arts as sports*

.714 89   Qi gong

.714 9   Isometric exercises

.715   Aerobic dancing

.716   Aquatic exercises and swimming

.717   Running and walking

> *See also 796.42 for running and walking as sports*

.717 2   Running

Class here jogging

.717 6   Walking

.718   Stretching exercises, and exercises for muscles of specific parts of body

.718 2   Stretching exercises

> *See also 613.72 for massage*

.718 8   Exercises for muscles of specific parts of body

Add to base number 613.7188 the numbers following 611.73 in 611.731–611.738, e.g., abdominal exercises 613.71886

.719   Specific systems of exercises for health

Class physical yoga in 613.7046; class exercises from the martial arts traditions and related traditions in 613.7148

.719 2   Pilates method

.72   Massage

Class here massage for health, fitness, relaxation

Class therapeutic massage, interdisciplinary works on massage in 615.822

.78   Correct posture

.79   Relaxation, rest, sleep

.792   Relaxation

Class breathing for relaxation in 613.192; class massage for relaxation in 613.72

.794   Sleep

.8   **Substance abuse (Drug abuse)**

Only personal preventive aspects

Including abuse of analgesics, depressants, inhalants, sedatives, tranquilizers

Class here appeals to the individual to avoid substance abuse for health reasons

Class comprehensive medical works on addictive drugs in 615.78; class stopping substance abuse, comprehensive medical works on substance abuse as a disease in 616.86; class interdisciplinary works on substance abuse in 362.29

.81   Alcohol

.83   Narcotics, hallucinogens, psychedelics, cannabis

.835   Cannabis

Class here specific kinds of cannabis, e.g., hashish, marijuana

.84   Stimulants and related substances

Standard subdivisions are added for stimulants and related substances together, for stimulants alone

Including amphetamine, ephedrine; cocaine

Class nicotine in 613.85

.85   Tobacco

Class smoking cessation in 616.86506

.9   **Birth control, reproductive technology, sex hygiene, sexual techniques**

Including sexual abstinence as a method of birth control and disease prevention

Class sexual abstinence for birth control in 613.94; class sexual abstinence for disease prevention in 613.95

.907 1   Education

Class sex education of children in the home in 649.65

.94   Birth control and reproductive technology

Standard subdivisions are added for birth control and reproductive technology together, for birth control alone

Only personal health aspects

Including artificial insemination, measures to increase the likelihood of having a child of the desired sex

Class here family planning

Class comprehensive medical works on human reproductive technology in 616.69206; class comprehensive medical works on birth control and family planning in 618.18; class interdisciplinary works on birth control and family planning in 363.96

| .942 | Surgical methods of birth control |

Including tubal sterilization, vasectomy

Class comprehensive works on surgical methods of birth control for males in 617.463; class comprehensive works on surgical methods of birth control for females in 618.1

| .943 | Chemical, natural, mechanical methods of birth control |

| .943 2 | Chemical methods of birth control |

Including contraceptive drug implants, postcoital contraceptives (morning after pills)

| .943 22 | Oral contraceptives |

Class postcoital contraceptives in 613.9432

| .943 4 | Natural family planning |

Class here ovulation detection method, rhythm method

| .943 5 | Mechanical methods of birth control |

Including intrauterine devices, comprehensive works on condoms

For use of condoms for disease prevention, see 613.95

| .95 | Sex hygiene |

Including use of condoms for disease prevention

Class here techniques for disease prevention

See also 613.96 for sexual techniques

| [.950 81–.950 84] | People by gender, sex, or age group |

Do not use; class in 613.951–613.955

| .951 | Sex hygiene of young people |

To age twenty

For sex hygiene of males to age twenty, see 613.953; for sex hygiene of females to age twenty, see 613.955

| .952 | Sex hygiene of adult men |

Class here sex hygiene of males

For sex hygiene of males to age twenty, see 613.953

| .953 | Sex hygiene of males to age twenty |

| .954 | Sex hygiene of adult women |

Class here sex hygiene of females

For sex hygiene of females to age twenty, see 613.955

| .955 | Sex hygiene of females to age twenty |

.96   Sexual techniques

Class here techniques for enhancing sexual enjoyment

See also 613.95 for techniques for disease prevention

614   Forensic medicine; incidence of injuries, wounds, disease; public preventive medicine

Class social provision for public health services other than those concerned with incidence and prevention of disease in 362.1; class environmental problems and services in 363.7; class incidence of poisoning in 615.904

SUMMARY

614.1	**Forensic medicine**
.3	**Incidence of injuries and wounds**
.4	**Incidence of and public measures to prevent disease**
.5	**Incidence of and public measures to prevent specific diseases and kinds of diseases**
.6	**Disposal of the dead**

.1   **Forensic medicine**

Including forensic nursing

Class here forensic pathology, medical jurisprudence

.12   Forensic chemistry

Class forensic toxicology in 614.13

.13   Forensic toxicology

.15   Forensic psychology and psychiatry

Standard subdivisions are added for either or both topics in heading

.17   Forensic anthropology

Class here forensic osteology

.18   Forensic dentistry

.3   **Incidence of injuries and wounds**

Standard subdivisions are added for either or both topics in heading

Including athletic injuries, crash injuries

Add to base number 614.3 the numbers following 617.1 in 617.11–617.19, e.g., gunshot wounds 614.345

Class public safety programs and social provision for prevention of injuries in 363.1

For incidence of injuries and wounds of a specific system, region, organ, see the system, region, organ in 614.59, e.g., eye injuries 614.5997

.4 **Incidence of and public measures to prevent disease**

Class here epidemiology

For incidence of and public measures to prevent specific diseases and kinds of diseases, see 614.5

See also 353.59 for registration and certification of births and deaths

See Manual at 614.4; also at 362.1–362.4 and 614.4–614.5

.409 History, geographic treatment, biography

For geographic treatment of incidence of diseases, see 614.42; for history of epidemics, see 614.49

.42 Incidence

Range, rate, or amount of occurrence

Class here prevalence; health surveys, medical geography

[.420 91] Areas, regions, places in general

Do not use; class in 614.422

[.420 93–.420 99] Specific continents, countries, localities

Do not use; class in 614.423–614.429

.422 Areas, regions, places in general

Add to base number 614.422 the numbers following —1 in notation 11–19 from Table 2, e.g., diseases in the tropics 614.4223

.423–.429 Specific continents, countries, localities

Add to base number 614.42 notation 3–9 from Table 2, e.g., diseases in the United States 614.4273

.43 Disease vectors and disease transmission by water

Standard subdivisions are added for disease vectors and disease transmission by water together, for disease vectors alone

Class here control of disease-carrying pests [*formerly also* 628.96]

Class comprehensive works on water supply in 363.61; class medical microbiology of waterborne pathogens in 616.9041

See also 614.5 for specific diseases transmitted by vectors or by water

.432 Insects

.432 2 Flies

.432 3 Mosquitoes

.432 4 Fleas and lice

Standard subdivisions are added for either or both topics in heading

.433 Arachnids

Including mites, ticks

.434		Birds
.438		Rodents
.44		Public preventive medicine

For specific preventive measures, see 614.45–614.48

> 614.45–614.48 Specific preventive measures

Class comprehensive works in 614.44

.45	Patient isolation

Class quarantine in 614.46

.46	Quarantine

Class patient isolation in 614.45

.47	Immunization

Class here vaccination

.48	Disinfection, fumigation, sterilization

Standard subdivisions are added for any or all topics in heading

.49	History of epidemics

Add to base number 614.49 notation 1–9 from Table 2, e.g., history of epidemics in the United Kingdom 614.4941

.5 **Incidence of and public measures to prevent specific diseases and kinds of diseases**

Class incidence of and public measures to prevent mental and emotional illnesses and disturbances in 362.2; class incidence of injuries and wounds in 614.3

See Manual at 362.1–362.4 and 614.4–614.5

SUMMARY

614.51	**Salmonella infections, bacillary diseases, clostridium infections, diphtheria, cholera, dysenteries, influenza**
.52	**Smallpox, scarlet fever, measles, rubella, chickenpox, rickettsial diseases**
.53	**Protozoan infections**
.54	**Miscellaneous diseases**
.55	**Parasitic diseases and diseases due to fungi (mycoses)**
.56	**Zoonoses**
.57	**Bacterial diseases**
.58	**Virus diseases**
.59	**Diseases of regions, systems, organs; other diseases**

.51	Salmonella infections, bacillary diseases, clostridium infections, diphtheria, cholera, dysenteries, influenza
.511	Salmonella infections
.511 2	Typhoid fever

.511 4	Paratyphoid fever
.512	Clostridium infections, diphtheria

Standard subdivisions are added for clostridium infections and diphtheria together, for clostridium infections alone

Class here bacillaceae infections, bacillary infections

For bacillary dysentery, see 614.516; for anthrax, see 614.561

.512 3	Diphtheria
.512 5	Botulism
.512 8	Tetanus
.514	Cholera
.516	Dysenteries

Including amebic dysentery, bacillary dysentery (shigellosis)

.518	Influenza
.52	Smallpox, scarlet fever, measles, rubella, chickenpox, rickettsial diseases
.521	Smallpox and attenuated forms

Standard subdivisions are added for smallpox and attenuated forms together, for smallpox alone

Including cowpox

.522	Scarlet fever
.523	Measles
.524	Rubella
.525	Chickenpox
.526	Rickettsial diseases

Add to base number 614.526 the numbers following 616.922 in 616.9222–616.9225, e.g., North Queensland tick typhus 614.5263, Q fever 614.5265

.53	Protozoan infections

Add to base number 614.53 the numbers following 616.936 in 616.9362–616.9364, e.g., malaria 614.532

For amebic dysentery, see 614.516

.54	Miscellaneous diseases

Limited to the diseases provided for below

.541	Yellow fever
.542	Tuberculosis
.543	Whooping cough (Pertussis)

.544	Mumps
.545	Puerperal septicemia and pyemia

Standard subdivisions are added for puerperal septicemia and pyemia together, for puerperal septicemia alone

Class comprehensive works on incidence of and public measures to prevent septicemia and pyemia in 614.577

.546	Hansen's disease (Leprosy)
.547	Sexually transmitted diseases

Including chancroid, condylomata acuminata (genital warts), herpes genitalis, lymphogranuloma venereum

For acquired immune deficiency syndrome (AIDS), see 614.599392

.547 2	Syphilis

For neurosyphilis, see 614.5983

.547 8	Gonorrhea
.549	Poliomyelitis

Including postpoliomyelitis syndrome

.55	Parasitic diseases and diseases due to fungi (mycoses)

Add to base number 614.55 the numbers following 616.96 in 616.962–616.969, e.g., schistosomiasis 614.553; however, for trichinosis, see 614.562

For protozoan infections, see 614.53; for parasitic skin diseases, see 614.5957; for fungal skin diseases, see 614.59579

.56	Zoonoses

For incidence of and public measures to prevent a specific zoonotic disease not provided for here, see the disease, e.g., Q fever 614.5265

.561	Anthrax
.562	Trichinosis
.563	Rabies
.564	Glanders
.565	Brucellosis
.566	Psittacosis
.57	Bacterial diseases

Including escherichia coli infections, pseudomonas infections, mycoplasma infections

Class here comprehensive works on gram-negative bacterial infections

For specific bacterial disease or group of bacterial diseases not provided for here, see the diseases, e.g., rickettsial diseases 614.526, brucellosis 614.565

.573   Pasteurella infections, yersinia infections, chlamydia infections, tularemia

         Standard subdivisions are added for pasteurella infections, yersinia infections, chlamydia infections, tularemia together; for pasteurella infections alone

.573 2   Plague

.573 5   Chlamydia infections

.573 9   Tularemia

.574   Borrelia infections

.574 4   Relapsing fevers

.574 6   Lyme disease

.577   Bacterial blood diseases

         Including pyemia, septicemia

         Class puerperal septicemia and pyemia in 614.545

.579   Gram-positive bacterial infections

         Including mycobacterium infections

         For a specific gram-positive bacterial infection or group of gram-positive bacterial infections not provided for here, see the infection or group of infections, e.g., clostridium infections 614.512, anthrax 614.561

.579 7   Staphylococcal infections

         Including toxic shock syndrome

.579 8   Streptococcal infections

         Including necrotizing fasciitis

         For scarlet fever, see 614.522; for erysipelas, see 614.59523

.58   Virus diseases

         For a specific virus disease or group of virus diseases not provided for here, see the disease or group of diseases, e.g., chickenpox 614.525

.581   DNA virus infections

         Including human papillomavirus infections

         For a specific DNA virus infection not provided for here, see the infection, e.g., smallpox 614.521

.581 2   Herpesvirus diseases

         Including infectious mononucleosis

         For a specific herpesvirus disease or group of herpesvirus diseases not provided for here, see the disease or group of diseases, e.g., herpes genitalis 614.547

.588   RNA virus infections

Including Colorado tick fever, hantavirus infections, retroviridae infections, Rift Valley fever

For a specific RNA virus infection or retroviridae infection not provided for here, see the infection, e.g., measles 614.523, HIV infections 614.599392

.588 5   Flavivirus infections

For yellow fever, see 614.541

.588 52   Dengue

Including dengue hemorrhagic fever

.588 56   West Nile fever

.59   Diseases of regions, systems, organs; other diseases

Class here incidence of injuries and wounds of specific regions, systems, organs

Class comprehensive works on incidence of injuries and wounds in 614.3

.591–.598   Diseases of regions, systems, organs

Add to base number 614.59 the numbers following 616 in 616.1–616.8, e.g., epidemic diarrhea 614.593427, erysipelas 614.59523, heart disease 614.5912, nutritional diseases 614.5939, neurosyphilis 614.5983; however, for mental and emotional illnesses, see 362.2; for allergies affecting specific regions, systems, organs, see 614.5993; for tumors (neoplasms) of regions, systems, organs, see 614.5999

.593 9   Nutritional and metabolic diseases

Number built according to instructions under 614.591–614.598

Class here nutrition surveys that emphasize malnutrition

Subdivisions are added for either or both topics in heading

Class comprehensive works on nutrition surveys in 363.82

.599   Other diseases

.599 2   Gynecologic, obstetrical, pediatric, geriatric disorders

Add to base number 614.5992 the numbers following 618 in 618.1–618.9, e.g., pediatric disorders 614.599292; however, for puerperal septicemia and pyemia, see 614.545

.599 3   Diseases of immune system

Class here allergies, failures of immunity

Add to base number 614.5993 the numbers following 616.97 in 616.973–616.979, e.g., acquired immune deficiency syndrome (AIDS) 614.599392

.599 6   Dental diseases

Including fluoridation of water supply

.599 7	Eye diseases
.599 8	Ear diseases
.599 9	Cancers

>   Including benign neoplasms, benign tumors
>
>   Class here carcinoma, malignant neoplasms, malignant tumors, neoplastic diseases; comprehensive works on benign and malignant neoplasms, on benign and malignant tumors
>
>   Class public programs to control cancer-causing agents in 363.179; class public programs to control carcinogens in food in 363.192

.599 94	Specific cancers
[.599 940 1–.599 940 9]	Standard subdivisions

>   Do not use; class in 614.599901–614.599909

.599 941–.599 949	Subdivisions for specific cancers

>   Add to base number 614.59994 the numbers following 616.994 in 616.9941–616.9949, e.g., breast cancer 614.5999449

.6   Disposal of the dead

>   Class social aspects and services in 363.75

615   Pharmacology and therapeutics

> Class comprehensive works on pharmacology in 615.1; class comprehensive works on therapeutics in 615.5

SUMMARY

615.1	**Drugs (Materia medica)**
.2	**Inorganic drugs**
.3	**Organic drugs**
.4	**Prescription filling**
.5	**Therapeutics**
.6	**Methods of administering drugs**
.7	**Pharmacokinetics**
.8	**Specific therapies and kinds of therapies**
.9	**Toxicology**

.1   Drugs (Materia medica)

> Substances used for diagnosis, cure, mitigation, treatment, or prevention of disease
>
> Class here patent medicines, pharmacology, pharmacy
>
> Class drug therapy in 615.58
>
> *For specific drugs and groups of drugs, see 615.2–615.3; for practical pharmacy, see 615.4; for physiological and therapeutic action of drugs, see 615.7*
>
> *See Manual at 615.1 vs. 615.2–615.3; also at 615.1 vs. 615.7*

[.101 513]	Arithmetic
	Do not use; class in 615.1401513
[.101 54]	Chemistry
	Do not use; class in 615.19
.107 24	Experimental research

Class here experimental research on new drugs before they are ready for clinical trials, e.g., testing on cells in vitro or on animals; comprehensive works on drug testing

For experimental research in development and manufacture of drugs, see 615.1900724; for clinical drug trials, see 615.580724

.11	Pharmacopoeias
[.110 93–.110 99]	Specific continents, countries, localities
	Do not use; class in 615.113–615.119
.113–.119	Specific continents, countries, localities

Add to base number 615.11 notation 3–9 from Table 2, e.g., pharmacopoeias of Japan 615.1152

.13	Formularies

Class here dispensatories

[.130 93–.130 99]	Specific continents, countries, localities
	Do not use; class in 615.133–615.139
.133–.139	Specific continents, countries, localities

Add to base number 615.13 notation 3–9 from Table 2, e.g., formularies of United States 615.1373

.14	Prescription writing

Including measures to avoid incompatibilities in prescriptions

Class here dosage determination, posology

.140 151 3	Arithmetic

Class here pharmaceutical arithmetic

.18	Drug preservation techniques

Class here packaging designed to preserve drug quality and potency

.19	Pharmaceutical chemistry

Including specific pharmaceutical dosage forms (forms of medication), e.g., ointments and emulsions; pills, capsules, tablets, troches, powders; solutions and extracts

Class here drug design, drug development, pharmaceutical technology, comprehensive works on drug compounding

For drug compounding closely associated with dispensing, see 615.4

.190 01	Philosophy and theory
.190 02	Miscellany
[.190 028 7]	Testing and measurement
	Do not use; class in 615.1901
.190 03–.190 09	Standard subdivisions
.190 1	Chemical analysis

Class clinical drug trials in 615.580724; class toxicity testing of drugs in 615.7040724

> **615.2–615.3 Specific drugs and groups of drugs**

Class here pharmaceutical chemistry, preservation, general therapeutics

Class a specific drug or group of drugs affecting a specific system in 615.7; class comprehensive works in 615.1

See Manual at 615.1 vs. 615.2–615.3; also at 615.2–615.3 vs. 615.7

.2   Inorganic drugs

Add to base number 615.2 the numbers following 546 in 546.2–546.7, e.g., calomel (mercurous chloride) 615.2663

Class use of radioactive elements, of radioisotopes in 615.842

.3   Organic drugs

.31   Synthetic drugs

Add to base number 615.31 the numbers following 547.0 in 547.01–547.08, e.g., sulfonamides 615.3167

For a specific synthetic drug not provided for here, see the drug, e.g., synthetic vitamins 615.328

.32   Drugs derived from plants and microorganisms

.321   Drugs derived from plants

Class here herbal medicine, herbals, medicinal plants, minimally processed alkaloids, pharmacognosy; comprehensive works on crude drugs and simples (products that serve as drugs with minimal processing, e.g., medicinal teas)

Class enzymes of plant origin in 615.35

For drugs derived from specific plants, see 615.322–615.327

.321 9   Aromatherapy

.322   Drugs derived from bryophytes

Add to base number 615.322 the numbers following 588 in 588.2–588.3, e.g., drugs derived from Musci 615.3222

.323–.327	Drugs derived from specific plants

Add to base number 615.32 the numbers following 58 in 583–587, e.g., belladonna 615.323952

> *For drugs derived from bryophytes, see 615.322; for drugs derived from fungi and algae, see 615.329*

.328	Vitamins

Including synthetic vitamins, vitamins of animal origin

Class here vitamin therapy

.329	Drugs derived from microorganisms, fungi, algae

Class here comprehensive works on antibiotics

Add to base number 615.329 the numbers following 579 in 579.2–579.8, e.g., streptomycin 615.329378

> *For pharmacokinetics of antibiotics, see 615.7922*

.34	Fish-liver oils
.35	Enzymes

Including enzymes of plant origin

.36	Drugs of animal origin

Class here drugs of animal origin prepared by recombinant DNA technology, hormones

> *For a drug of animal origin not provided for here, see the drug, e.g., fish-liver oils 615.34*

.363	Pituitary hormones

Including ACTH (adrenocorticotrophic hormone)

.364	Adrenal hormones

Including aldosterone, cortisone

> *For sex hormones, see 615.366*

.365	Insulin
.366	Sex hormones
.37	Immunologic drugs and immune serums

Standard subdivisions are added for either or both topics in heading

Class here antitoxins, immune gamma globulins, immunoglobulins

.372	Vaccines

Including toxoids

Class here development and manufacture of vaccines

Class use of vaccines in 614.47. Class use of specific vaccines with the disease in 614.5, e.g., use of influenza vaccines 614.518

.39   Human blood products and their substitutes

Standard subdivisions are added for human blood products and their substitutes together, for human blood products alone

Including blood and blood plasma transfusion

For immune gamma globulins, immunoglobulins, immune serums, see 615.37

See also 362.1784 for blood and blood plasma banks

.399   Blood substitutes

Including blood plasma substitutes

.4   Prescription filling

Class here drug compounding closely associated with filling prescriptions

Class comprehensive works on pharmacy in 615.1; class drug compounding by drug manufacturers, comprehensive works on drug compounding in 615.19

See also 615.14 for prescription writing

.401 513   Arithmetic

Class pharmaceutical arithmetic in 615.1401513

.5   Therapeutics

Class here comprehensive works on alternative therapies, on iatrogenic diseases, on patient compliance, on placebo effect

Class works on alternative medicine that include pathology and etiology in addition to therapeutics in 610 (or, if arranged by kind of disease, in 616). Class therapies applied to a specific disease or group of diseases with the disease or group of diseases in 616–618, plus notation 06 from table under 616.1–616.9, notation 06 from table under 617, or notation 06 from table under 618.1–618.8, e.g., therapies for cardiovascular diseases 616.106

For specific therapies and kinds of therapies other than drug therapy, chemotherapy, see 615.8; for emergency care, see 616.025; for intensive care, see 616.028; for palliative and terminal care, see 616.029. For a specific occurrence of iatrogenic diseases, patient compliance, placebo effect, see the occurrence, e.g., drug interactions not anticipated by a doctor 615.7045, surgical infections 617.9195

.501 9   Psychological principles

Do not use for psychological therapies; class in 615.851

.507 1   Education

Class here comprehensive works on patient education

For patient education on a specific topic, see the topic, plus notation 071 from Table 1, e.g., patient education about diabetes mellitus 616.4620071

.507 2   Research

.507 24	Experimental research

Class here comprehensive works on clinical trials

*For clinical trials of diagnostic procedures, see 616.0750724.
For clinical trials of a specific therapy, see the therapy,
plus notation 0724 from Table 1, e.g., clinical drug trials
615.580724; for clinical trials of therapies for a specific
disease or group of diseases, see the disease or group of
diseases in 616–618, plus notation 060724 or other subdivision
of 06 from table under 616.1–616.9, notation 060724 or other
subdivision of 06 from table under 617, or notation 060724
or other subdivision of 06 from table under 618.1–618.8, e.g.,
clinical trials of therapies for cancer 616.994060724, clinical
trials of drugs for cancer 616.9940610724*

.508 3	Young people

Do not use for therapeutics for infants and children up to puberty,
comprehensive works on child and adolescent therapeutics; class in
615.542

.508 35	Young people twelve to twenty

Do not use for therapeutics for young people twelve to twenty who
have not reached puberty; class in 615.542

Class here therapeutics for adolescents

.508 4	People in specific stages of adulthood
[.508 46]	People in late adulthood

Do not use; class in 615.547

.53	General therapeutic systems

Including anthroposophical therapy, botanic and eclectic medicine

Class drug therapy regardless of system in 615.58

*See also 615.321 for botanic remedies, herbal medicine; also 615.88 for
folk remedies, traditional remedies*

See Manual at 615.53

.532	Homeopathy
.533	Osteopathy

As a therapeutic system

Class comprehensive works on osteopathy as a medical science in 610.
Class a specific application of osteopathy with the application, e.g.,
osteopathic discussion of thyroid diseases 616.44

.534	Chiropractic
.534 092	Biography

See Manual at 610.92 vs. 615.534092

.535	Naturopathy
.538	Ayurvedic medicine

.54	Pediatric and geriatric therapeutics
.542	Pediatric therapeutics

Class here comprehensive works on child and adolescent therapeutics

For adolescent therapeutics, see 615.50835. For a specific aspect of pediatric therapeutics, see the aspect, plus notation 083 from Table 1, e.g., exercise therapy for children 615.82083

.547	Geriatric therapeutics

For a specific aspect of geriatric therapeutics, see the aspect, plus notation 0846 from Table 1, e.g., acupuncture as therapy for people in late adulthood 615.8920846

.58	Drug therapy

Class here chemotherapy

Class general therapeutics of a specific drug or group of drugs in 615.2–615.3

For methods of administering drugs, see 615.6

.580 724	Experimental research

Class here clinical drug trials

Class chemical analysis of drugs in 615.1901; class toxicity testing of drugs in 615.7040724. Class clinical trials for drugs for specific diseases or groups of diseases with the disease or group of diseases in 616–618, plus notation 0610724 from table under 616.1–616.9, notation 0610724 from table under 617, or notation 0610724 from table under 618.1–618.8, e.g., clinical trials of drugs for cancer 616.9940610724

.6	**Methods of administering drugs**

Only works that focus narrowly on methods of administering drugs

Including inhalation, oral, topical administration; injections; parenteral infusions

Class here drug administration routes

Class general works on a specific type of therapy with the therapy, e.g., drug therapy 615.58, inhalation therapy 615.836

For methods of administering a specific drug or group of drugs, see 615.2–615.3

.7   **Pharmacokinetics**

Class here biopharmaceutics, pharmacodynamics

Class use of a drug to treat a specific disease or group of diseases with the disease or group of diseases in 616–618, plus notation 061 from table under 616.1–616.9, notation 061 from table under 617, or notation 061 from table under 618.1–618.8, e.g., drug treatment for diseases of liver 616.362061

For toxicology, see 615.9

See Manual at 612.1–612.8; also at 615.1 vs. 615.7; also at 615.2–615.3 vs. 615.7; also at 615.7 vs. 615.9

.704   Special effects and actions of drugs

Class here adverse reactions, toxic reactions

Class toxicity testing of drugs in 615.7040724; class drug allergies in 616.9758

.704 028 7   Testing and measurement

Do not use for toxicity testing of drugs; class in 615.7040724

.704 2   Side effects

.704 5   Interactions

Including drug-herb interactions, drug incompatibilities

.704 52   Drug-nutrient interactions

.71   Drugs affecting cardiovascular and hematopoietic systems

Standard subdivisions are added for drugs affecting cardiovascular and hematopoietic systems together, for drugs affecting cardiovascular system alone

.711   Cardiotonic agents

Class here heart stimulants

.716   Anti-arrhythmia agents

Class here heart depressants, myocardial depressants

.718   Drugs affecting blood and hematopoietic system

.72   Drugs affecting respiratory system

Including bronchodilator agents, cough remedies, expectorants

.73   Drugs affecting digestive system and metabolism

Standard subdivisions are added for drugs affecting digestive system and metabolism together, for drugs affecting digestive system alone

Class drug-nutrient interactions in 615.70452

.732   Cathartics

Class here laxatives

.739	Drugs affecting metabolism

Including antilipemic agents

.74	Drugs affecting lymphatic and glandular systems
.76	Drugs affecting urogenital system
.761	Drugs affecting urinary system

Including diuretics, antidiuretics

.766	Drugs affecting reproductive system

Including abortifacient, contraceptive, fertility drugs

.766 9	Aphrodisiacs
.77	Drugs affecting musculoskeletal system, integument

Standard subdivisions are added for drugs affecting musculoskeletal system, integument together; for drugs affecting musculoskeletal system alone

.771	Drugs affecting bones
.773	Drugs affecting muscles
.778	Drugs affecting integument

For drugs affecting nails and hair, see 615.779

.779	Drugs affecting nails and hair
.78	Drugs affecting nervous system

Class here addictive drugs, psychopharmacology

Class personal aspects of preventing drug addiction in 613.8; class drug therapy for mental disorders in 616.8918; class comprehensive medical works on addictions as diseases in 616.86; class interdisciplinary works on drug addiction in 362.29

See also 178 for the ethics of using addictive drugs

.781	Anesthetics
.782	Central nervous system depressants

Class here hypnotics, sedatives

For anesthetics, see 615.781; for analgesics, see 615.783; for tranquilizers, see 615.7882

.782 1	Barbiturates
.782 2	Narcotics

Including narcotic antagonists

.782 7	Cannabis

Including marijuana

.782 8	Alcohol

.783	Analgesics

Including antipyretics

.784	Anticonvulsants and antispasmodics

Standard subdivisions are added for anticonvulsants and antispasmodics together, for anticonvulsants alone

Including parasympatholytics

.785	Central nervous system stimulants

For aphrodisiacs, see 615.7669

.788	Psychotropic drugs
.788 2	Tranquilizers

Including anti-anxiety, antipsychotic drugs; chlorpromazine, diazepam, meprobamate

.788 3	Hallucinogens

Class here psychedelic drugs

For cannabis, see 615.7827

.79	Miscellaneous classes of drugs

Limited to those provided for below

.792	Anti-infective agents

Including antifungal agents, antiparasitic agents

.792 2	Anti-bacterial agents

Class here antibiotics

Class interdisciplinary works on antibiotics in 615.329

.792 4	Antiviral agents

Including anti-retroviral agents, anti-HIV agents

.794	Anti-inflammatory agents
.796	Anti-allergic agents
.798	Antineoplastic agents
.8	**Specific therapies and kinds of therapies**

Class comprehensive works in 615.5

For drug therapy, see 615.58; for surgery, see 617

See Manual at 615.8; also at 613 vs. 612, 615.8

SUMMARY

615.82	**Physical therapies**
.83	**Phototherapy, thermotherapy, climatotherapy, respiratory therapy; therapeutic use of sound**
.84	**Radiotherapy, electric stimulation therapy, magnetotherapy**
.85	**Miscellaneous therapies**
.88	**Traditional remedies**
.89	**Other therapies**

[.801–.809]   Standard subdivisions

> Do not use; class in 615.501–615.509

.82   Physical therapies

Including Alexander technique

Class here physiotherapy, therapeutic manipulations and exercises

> *For phototherapy, thermotherapy, climatotherapy, respiratory therapy; therapeutic use of sound, see 615.83; for radiotherapy, electric stimulation therapy, magnetotherapy, see 615.84; for hydrotherapy and balneotherapy, see 615.853*

.822   Therapeutic massage

Including Rolfing

Class here interdisciplinary works on massage

Class aromatherapy in 615.3219

> *For massage for health and fitness, see 613.72*

.822 2   Acupressure

Class here shiatsu

Class comprehensive works on acupuncture and acupressure in 615.892

.822 4   Reflexology

.83   Phototherapy, thermotherapy, climatotherapy, respiratory therapy; therapeutic use of sound

Class music therapy in 615.85154

.831   Phototherapy

.831 2   Color therapy

.831 4   Heliotherapy

.831 5   Ultraviolet therapy

Class here actinotherapy

.832   Thermotherapy

.832 3   Diathermy

Class here ultrasonic therapy

.832 9	Cryotherapy
	For cryosurgery, see 617.05
.834	Climatotherapy
.836	Respiratory therapy
	Including breathing exercises, hyperbaric oxygenation, oxygen inhalation therapy
	Class here aerotherapy, inhalation therapy
	Class aromatherapy in 615.3219
.836 2	Artificial respiration
.84	Radiotherapy, electric stimulation therapy, magnetotherapy
.842	Radiotherapy
	Class phototherapy in 615.831
.842 2	X-ray therapy
.842 3	Radium therapy
.842 4	Radioisotope therapy
	Class radium therapy in 615.8423
.845	Electric stimulation therapy and magnetotherapy
	Standard subdivisions are added for electric stimulation therapy and magnetotherapy together, for electric stimulation therapy alone
	Class here electrotherapeutics, therapeutic use of electricity
	Class diathermy in 615.8323; class electroacupuncture in 615.892
.845 4	Magnetotherapy
	Class here therapeutic use of magnetism
.85	Miscellaneous therapies
	Limited to the therapies provided for below
.851	Psychological and activity therapies
	Class mental healing (psychic healing) in 615.8528; class comprehensive works on psychotherapy in 616.8914
.851 2	Hypnotherapy
.851 22	Self-hypnosis
	Class here autogenic training
	Class therapeutic use of biofeedback in 615.8514
.851 4	Biofeedback therapy
	Class here therapeutic use of biofeedback training

.851 5	Activity therapy

Including therapeutic use of gardening

Class here occupational therapy

For bibliotherapy and educational therapies, see 615.8516

.851 53	Recreational therapy

Class here play therapy

Class therapeutic use of horsemanship in 615.851581

.851 54	Music therapy
.851 55	Dance therapy
.851 56	Art therapy
.851 58	Therapeutic use of animals

Class here therapeutic use of pets

Class works that focus on the therapy animal and training it for therapeutic use with the animal in 636, e.g., training therapy dogs 636.7088

.851 581	Therapeutic use of horses

Class here therapeutic use of horsemanship

.851 6	Bibliotherapy and educational therapies
.852	Religious and psychic therapies

Standard subdivisions are added for religious and psychic therapies together, for religious therapies alone

Including healing touch (therapeutic touch), Reiki

Class here faith healing, spiritual therapies

See Manual at 615.852 vs. 203.1, 234.131, 292–299

.852 8	Psychic therapies

Including psychic surgery

Class here healing facilitated by spiritualism; mental healing (psychic healing)

.853	Hydrotherapy and balneotherapy

Standard subdivisions are added for either or both topics in heading

.854	Nutrition therapy

Class here diet therapy

For diet therapy emphasizing a single food, see the food as a type of drug in 615.3, e.g., a diet emphasizing soy 615.32374, a diet emphasizing garlic 615.32433

.854 8	Nutrition support
	Class here artificial feeding
.854 82	Enteral nutrition
	Class here tube feeding
.854 84	Parenteral nutrition
	Class here intravenous feeding
.855	Parenteral therapy

> *For a specific kind of parenteral therapy, see the kind, e.g., parenteral drug therapy 615.58, parenteral feeding 615.85484*

.856	Controversial and spurious therapies

Standard subdivisions are added for either or both topics in heading

Class here quackery

> *For a specific controversial or spurious therapy, see the therapy, e.g., controversial diet therapy 615.854*

.88	Traditional remedies

Only therapeutics

Class here folk remedies, home remedies

Class theoretical works on traditional general therapeutic systems in 615.53; class works on traditional medicine that include pathological or etiological beliefs in 610 (or, if arranged by class of disease, in 616). Class a specific kind of traditional remedy with the kind, e.g., medicinal herbs 615.321, acupuncture 615.892

.880 9	History, geographic treatment, biography
.880 901	To 499 A.D.
	Class here ancient remedies
.880 902	6th–15th centuries, 500–1499
	Class here medieval remedies
.89	Other therapies
.892	Acupuncture

Including moxibustion, electroacupuncture

Class here comprehensive works on acupuncture and acupressure

> *For acupressure, see 615.8222*

.895	Gene therapy

.9   **Toxicology**

Class here poisons and poisoning

Class forensic toxicology in 614.13. Class effects of poisons on a specific system or organ with the system or organ, plus notation 071 from table under 616.1–616.9, notation 071 from table under 617, or notation 061 from table under 618.1–618.8, e.g., effect of poisons on the liver 616.362071

See Manual at 615.7 vs. 615.9

SUMMARY

615.900 1–.900 9	**Standard subdivisions**	
.901–.909	**[Industrial toxicology; incidence, prevention, tests, analysis, detection, treatment of poisoning]**	
.91	**Gaseous poisons**	
.92	**Inorganic poisons**	
.94	**Animal poisons**	
.95	**Organic poisons**	

.900 1   Philosophy and theory

.900 2   Miscellany

[.900 287]   Testing and measurement

Do not use; class in 615.907

.900 3–.900 9   Standard subdivisions

.902   Industrial toxicology

Including toxicology of pollution

Class here environmental toxicology

Class environmental diseases, environmental medicine in 616.98

> *For toxic reactions and interactions of drugs, see 615.704; for toxicology of food additives, see 615.954*

.904   Incidence of poisoning

.905   Prevention of poisoning

Class public safety programs and social provision for prevention of poisoning in 363.1791

.907   Tests, analysis, detection of poisons and poisoning

Class here diagnoses and prognoses of poisoning

Topics listed under 616.075 Diagnoses and prognoses are all included here

.908   Treatment of poisoning

Class here antidotes

.91   Gaseous poisons

> Including asphyxiating gases

> Class here lethal gases

.92   Inorganic poisons

> *For gaseous inorganic poisons, see 615.91; for radiation poisoning, see 616.9897*

.921   Acids

> *For specific acids, see 615.925*

.922   Alkalis

> *For specific alkalis, see 615.925*

.925   Specific inorganic poisons

> Add to base number 615.925 the numbers following 546 in 546.2–546.7, e.g., mercurial poisons 615.925663

.94   Animal poisons

.942   Venoms

> Including bee, scorpion, snake, spider venoms

.945   Poisonous food animals

> Only works that emphasize poisons

> Including poisonous fishes; food animals made poisonous by plants or microorganisms, e.g., shellfish made poisonous by red tides

> Class comprehensive medical works on a specific type of communicable disease that involves poisons with the type of disease in 616.9, e.g., salmonella infections 616.927

.95   Organic poisons

> *For gaseous organic poisons, see 615.91; for animal poisons, see 615.94*

.951   Synthetic and manufactured poisons

> Add to base number 615.951 the numbers following 547.0 in 547.01–547.08, e.g., ethers 615.95135
> Subdivisions are added for either or both topics in heading

.952   Plant and microorganism poisons, poisons derived from plants and microorganisms

> Standard subdivisions are added for all topics in heading together, for plant poisons alone, for poisons derived from plants alone

> Class food animals made poisonous by plants and microorganisms in 615.945

.952 3–.952 8   Specific plant poisons, poisons derived from specific plants

> Add to base number 615.952 the numbers following 58 in 583 588, e.g., opium 615.952335

> *For fungi and algae poisons, poisons derived from fungi and algae, see 615.9529*

.952 9   Microorganism, fungi, algae poisons; poisons derived from microorganisms, fungi, algae

> Only works that emphasize poisons

> Add to base number 615.9529 the numbers following 579 in 579.2–579.8, e.g., bacterial food poisons 615.95293

> Class comprehensive medical works on a specific type of communicable disease that involves poisons with the type of disease in 616.9, e.g., salmonella infections 616.927, botulism 616.9315

.954   Food poisons

> Only works that emphasize poisons

> Including toxicology of food additives

> Class poisonous food animals in 615.945. Class a specific plant poison and poisons derived from specific plants and microorganisms with the poison in 615.952, e.g., bacterial food poisons 615.95293

616   Diseases

Class here clinical medicine, evidence-based medicine, internal medicine

For incidence of and public measures to prevent disease, see 614.4; for therapeutics, see 615.5; for injuries and wounds, surgical treatment of diseases, diseases by body region, diseases of teeth, eyes, ears, see 617; for gynecologic, obstetrical, fetal, pediatric, geriatric diseases, see 618

See Manual at 610 vs. 616; also at 616 vs. 612; also at 616 vs. 616.075; also at 616 vs. 617.4; also at 616 vs. 618.92

SUMMARY

616.001–.009	**Standard subdivisions**
.02–.09	**[General topics of diseases]**
.1	Diseases of cardiovascular system
.2	**Diseases of respiratory system**
.3	**Diseases of digestive system**
.4	**Diseases of endocrine, hematopoietic, lymphatic, glandular systems; diseases of male breast**
.5	**Diseases of integument**
.6	**Diseases of urogenital system**
.7	**Diseases of musculoskeletal system**
.8	**Diseases of nervous system and mental disorders**
.9	**Other diseases**

>   616.001–616.009 Standard subdivisions

Class comprehensive works in 616

See Manual at 610 vs. 616: Standard subdivisions

.001   Philosophy and theory

.001 9   Psychological principles

Do not use for psychosomatic medicine; class in 616.08

.002   Miscellany

[.002 3]   Work with diseases as a profession, occupation, hobby

Do not use; class in 610.69

.002 8   Auxiliary techniques and procedures; apparatus, equipment, materials

[.002 87]   Testing and measurement

Do not use; class in 616.075

.003–.006   Standard subdivisions

.007   Education, research, related topics

[.007 24]   Experimental research

Do not use; class in 616.027

.008   Groups of people

Do not use for incidence of disease in groups of people; class in 614.4208

.008 3   Young people

Do not use for diseases of infants and children up to puberty, comprehensive works on child and adolescent medicine; class in 618.92

.008 35   Young people twelve to twenty

Do not use for diseases of young people twelve to twenty who have not reached puberty; class in 618.92

Class here adolescent medicine

.008 4   People in specific stages of adulthood

[.008 46]   People in late adulthood

Do not use; class in 618.97

.009   History, geographic treatment, biography

Do not use for history and geographic treatment of incidence of disease; class in 614.42. Do not use for history of epidemics; class in 614.49

[.009 11–.009 13]   Frigid, temperate, tropical zones

Do not use; class in 616.9881–616.9883

.009 2 Biography

> Class life with a physical disease in 362.19. Class life with a mental disorder with the disorder in 616.85–616.89, plus notation 0092 from table under 616.1–616.9, e.g., life with manic-depressive illness 616.8950092

SUMMARY

616.02	**Special topics of diseases**
.04	**Special medical conditions**
.07	**Pathology**
.08	**Psychosomatic medicine**
.09	**Case histories**

.02 Special topics of diseases

> Class special topics applied to special medical conditions in 616.04

.024 Domestic medicine

> Diagnosis and treatment of ailments without direction of physician

> Including advice on when to go to a doctor

> *For first aid, see 616.0252. For a specific kind of therapy, see the therapy in 615, e.g., drug therapy 615.58*

.025 Medical emergencies

> Class here emergency care nursing, resuscitation, comprehensive works on emergency medicine

> *For intensive care, see 616.028. For a specific kind of emergency therapy, see the therapy in 615, e.g., oxygen therapy 615.836; for a specific kind of resuscitation, see the kind, e.g., cardiopulmonary resuscitation 616.1025*

.025 2 First aid

.027 Experimental medicine

> Including use of cultured or genetically engineered tissue, use of human fetal tissue

> Class ethics of animal experimentation in 179.4; class ethics of experimentation on human subjects and comprehensive works on ethics of medical experimentation in 174.28; class comprehensive works on clinical trials in 615.50724; class comprehensive works on clinical trials of diagnostic procedures in 616.0750724; class fetal tissue transplantation in 617.954; class breeding, genetic engineering, care, maintenance of laboratory animals in 636.0885

.027 3 Mammals other than humans

> As models for experimental research on human diseases

> Including rabbits, swine

> Class here transgenic mammals as experimental animals

> Class experimental research using mammalian cells in 616.0277

.027 33	Rodents
	Including guinea pigs, hamsters, rats
.027 333	Mice (Mus)
.027 38	Primates
	Including apes, monkeys
.027 7	Cells

Use for experimental research on human diseases

Class here cell lines

| .027 74 | Stem cells |
| .028 | Intensive care |

Class here critical care, intensive care nursing

For a specific kind of intensive care therapy, see the therapy in 615, e.g., oxygen therapy 615.836

| .029 | Palliative and terminal care |

Standard subdivisions are added for either or both topics in heading

Class here terminal care nursing

For a specific kind of palliative and terminal care therapy, see the therapy in 615, e.g., drug therapy 615.58; for palliative treatment of a specific symptom, see the symptom, e.g., pain 616.0472

| .04 | Special medical conditions |
| .042 | Genetic diseases (Hereditary diseases) |

Class here genetic aspects of diseases with complex causation, comprehensive works on medical genetics

For gene therapy, see 615.895; for immunogenetics, see 616.0796; for prenatal procedures to diagnose genetic diseases (e.g., amniocentesis and chorionic villus biopsy), see 618.3204275

| .043 | Congenital diseases |

Including teratology

Class congenital diseases of genetic origin in 616.042

| .044 | Chronic diseases |

For chronic fatigue syndrome, see 616.0478

.047   Symptoms and general pathological processes as problems in their own right

> Including edema, fever, gangrene

> Class here pathology, diagnosis, treatment of symptoms of various etiologies; symptomatology

> Class comprehensive works on palliative care in 616.029; class interpretation of symptoms for diagnosis and prognosis in 616.075; class infections in 616.9; class results of injuries and wounds in 617.2; class surgical complications and sequelae in 617.919. Class symptoms and pathological processes of a specific disease or class of diseases with the disease or class of diseases, e.g., symptoms of heart diseases 616.12

.047 2   Pain

> Class headaches in 616.8491

.047 3   Inflammation

.047 5   Shock and multiple organ failure

> Standard subdivisions are added for either or both topics in heading

> *For shock associated with injury or surgery, see 617.21*

.047 8   Chronic fatigue syndrome

> Class here chronic fatigue syndrome discussed as a specific kind of disease, myalgic encephalomyelitis

> *See also 616.044 for chronic diseases*

>   616.07–616.09   Pathology, psychosomatic medicine, case histories

> Class pathology, psychosomatic medicine, case histories applied to special medical conditions in 616.04; class comprehensive works in 616

.07   Pathology

> *For cytopathology, see 611.01815; for histopathology, see 611.0182–611.0189; for forensic pathology, see 614.1; for medical microbiology, see 616.9041; for symptoms and general pathological processes as problems in their own right, see 616.047*

SUMMARY

616.071	**Etiology**
.075	**Diagnosis and prognosis**
.078	**Death**
.079	**Immunity**

.071   Etiology

Class here pathogenesis, risk factors

Class social factors contributing to spread of a disease in 362.1042; class genetic diseases, genetic aspects of diseases with complex causation in 616.042

For pathogenic microorganisms as causes of communicable diseases, see 616.9041

.075   Diagnosis and prognosis

Standard subdivisions are added for diagnosis and prognosis together, for diagnosis alone

Class here differential diagnosis; disability evaluation; nursing assessment, nursing diagnosis

Class nonprofessional diagnosis in 616.024

See Manual at 616 vs. 616.075

.075 072 4   Experimental research

Class here clinical trials of diagnostic procedures

Class comprehensive works on clinical trials of diagnostic procedures and therapy in 615.50724

.075 1   Medical history taking

.075 4   Physical diagnosis

Including thermography

Class here comprehensive works on diagnostic imaging

For radiological diagnosis, see 616.0757

.075 43   Diagnostic ultrasound

Class here comprehensive works on ultrasonography (sonography, echography)

Class comprehensive works on tomography in 616.0757

For ultrasonic therapy, see 615.8323

.075 44   Diagnosis by sound

Class here auscultation

.075 45   Optical diagnosis

Class here comprehensive works on endoscopy

Class microscopy in 616.0758

For endoscopic surgery, see 617.057

.075 47   Electrodiagnosis

.075 48	Magnetic diagnosis
	Class here magnetic resonance imaging, nuclear magnetic resonance imaging, proton spin tomography
	Class comprehensive works on tomography in 616.0757
.075 6	Chemical diagnosis
	Including diagnostic serology, immunodiagnosis
	Class here clinical chemistry, laboratory diagnosis
	For radioimmunoassay, see 616.0757; for microscopy in diagnosis, see 616.0758
.075 61	Blood analysis
	Including phlebotomy
	See also 616.15075 for diagnosis of diseases of blood
.075 63	Analysis of gastroenteric contents
	See also 616.3075 for diagnosis of diseases of digestive system
.075 66	Urinalysis
	Class radioscopic urinalysis in 616.0757; class urinary manifestations of diseases of urogenital system in 616.63
	See also 616.6075 for diagnosis of diseases of urogenital system
.075 7	Radiological diagnosis
	Including radioimmunoassay, radioscopic urinalysis
	Class here diagnostic radiology; comprehensive works on medical radiology, on tomography
	Class diagnostic radiology limited to use of X-rays in 616.07572; class comprehensive works on diagnostic imaging in 616.0754
	For radiotherapy, see 615.842; for magnetic resonance imaging, see 616.07548
.075 72	Radiography (X-ray examination)
	Including fluoroscopy
	Class diagnostic radiology covering use of X-rays, radioactive materials, other ionizing radiation in 616.0757
.075 722	X-ray computed tomography
	Class here computerized axial tomography (CAT scan, CT)

.075 75	Radioisotope scanning

Variant names: nuclear medicine, radionuclide imaging

Including positron emission tomography (PET), radioimmunoimaging, single-photon emission-computed tomography (SPECT)

See also 616.07548 for nuclear magnetic resonance imaging

.075 8	Microscopy in diagnosis

Class here biopsy

.075 81	Bacteriological examination
.075 82	Cytological examination
.075 83	Histological and histochemical examination
.075 9	Autopsy (Postmortem examination)

Class forensic autopsy in 614.1

.078	Death

Class interdisciplinary works on human death in 306.9

.079	Immunity

Class here disease resistance, immune system, immunochemistry, immunology, leukocytes, lymphocytes

Class immune serums and immunologic drugs in 615.37; class diagnostic immunochemistry, immunodiagnosis in 616.0756; class diseases of hematopoietic system in 616.41; class diseases of immune system in 616.97

>   616.079 1–616.079 6   Immunochemistry

Class comprehensive works in 616.079. Class applications of immunochemistry to a specific type of cell or to reactions associated with a specific type of cell with the cell or reaction in 616.0797–616.0799, e.g., immunochemistry of antigen-antibody reactions 616.07987

.079 1	Interferons
.079 2	Antigens
.079 5	Immune response

Including clonal selection

Class here antigen recognition, comprehensive works on serology

Class immune reactions associated with specific types of cells in 616.0797–616.0799

For diagnostic serology, see 616.0756

.079 6	Immunogenetics

.079 7 T cells (T lymphocytes)

Class here cell-mediated (cellular) immunity, cytotoxic T cells

See also 616.0799 for killer cells

.079 8 B cells (B lymphocytes)

Class here antibodies (immunoglobulins)

For antibody-dependent immune mechanisms, see 616.0799

.079 87 Antigen-antibody reactions

.079 9 Phagocytes and complement

Standard subdivisions are added for phagocytes and complement together, for phagocytes alone

Including granulocytes, killer cells

Class here antibody-dependent immune mechanisms, reticuloendothelial system

See also 616.0797 for cytotoxic T cells

.079 95 Macrophages

.079 97 Complement

Class activation of macrophages by complement in 616.07995

.08 Psychosomatic medicine

Use only for psychosomatic aspects of diseases defined in 616.1–616.7, 616.9

Class somatoform disorders in 616.8524; class diseases caused by stress in 616.98; class comprehensive works on psychological and psychosomatic aspects of disease in 616.0019

.09 Case histories

> **616.1–616.9 Specific diseases**

All notes under 616.02–616.08 are applicable here

Except for modifications shown under specific entries, add to each subdivision identified by * as follows:

001	Philosophy and theory
002	Miscellany
[0023]	The subject as a profession, occupation, hobby
	Do not use; class in 023
0028	Auxiliary techniques and procedures; apparatus, equipment, materials
00284	Apparatus, equipment, materials
	Do not use for self-help devices for people with disabilities; class in 03
[00287]	Testing and measurement
	Do not use; class in 075
003–006	Standard subdivisions
007	Education, research, related topics
[00724]	Experimental research
	Do not use; class in 027
008	Groups of people
	Do not use for incidence of specific diseases or kinds of diseases in groups of people; class in 614.5
0083	Young people
	Do not use for diseases of infants and children up to puberty, comprehensive works on diseases of children and adolescents; class in 618.92
00835	Young people twelve to twenty
	Do not use for diseases of young people twelve to twenty who have not reached puberty; class in 618.92
	Class here diseases of adolescents
0084	People in specific stages of adulthood
[00846]	People in late adulthood
	Do not use; class in 618.97
009	History, geographic treatment, biography
	Do not use for history and geographic treatment of incidence of specific diseases or kinds of diseases; class in 614.5
0092	Biography
	Class life with a physical disease in 362.19. Class life with a mental disease with the disease in 616.85–616.89, plus notation 0092, e.g., life with depression 616.85270092
>01–03	Medical microbiology, special topics, rehabilitation
	Class microbiology, special topics, rehabilitation applied to special classes of diseases in 04; class comprehensive works in 616 without adding from this table

(continued)

> **616.1–616.9 Specific diseases (continued)**

01 Medical microbiology
When the cause of a disease or class of diseases is known to be a single type of microorganism, use 01 without further subdivision for works about the type of microorganism
Class works on a whole disease and its course, cure, and prevention with the disease without adding from this table, e.g., comprehensive works on tuberculosis 616.995
See Manual at 616.1–.9: Add table: 071 vs. 01

014 Medical bacteriology
Including medical microbiology of rickettsiae

015 Medical mycology

016 Medical protozoology

019 Medical virology

02 Special topics

023 Personnel

0231 Nurses
Class here nature of duties, characteristics of profession, relationships; nursing with respect to specific diseases; works that emphasize technology of operations performed by nurses, e.g., works that emphasize techniques used by a cardiovascular nurse 616.10231, by an orthopedic nurse 616.70231
Class works that emphasize a specific technique used by nurses with the technique, e.g., nursing diagnosis 075, nursing diagnosis of cardiovascular diseases 616.1075

0232 Physicians
Class here nature of duties, characteristics of profession, relationships
Do not use for works that emphasize technology of operations performed by physicians; class with the subject without 0232, e.g., works that emphasize techniques used by a physician with respect to cardiovascular diseases 616.1
Class works that emphasize a specific technique used by physicians with the technique, e.g., diagnosis by a physician 075, diagnosis by a physician of cardiovascular diseases 616.1075

(continued)

> **616.1–616.9 Specific diseases (continued)**

0233   Allied health personnel
> Class here nature of duties, characteristics of profession, relationships; works that emphasize technology of operations performed by allied health personnel, e.g., works that emphasize techniques used by allied health personnel with respect to cardiovascular diseases 616.10233
> Class works that emphasize a specific technique used by allied health personnel with the technique, e.g., diagnosis by allied health personnel 075, diagnosis of cardiovascular diseases by allied health personnel 616.1075

02332   Physician assistants

024   Domestic medicine
> Class a specific kind of therapy with the therapy in 06, e.g., drug therapy 061
> *For first aid, see 0252*

025   Medical emergencies
> Class here comprehensive works on emergency therapy for specific diseases or kinds of diseases
> *For intensive care, see 028. For a specific kind of emergency therapy, see the therapy in 06, e.g., emergency drug therapy 061*

0252   First aid

027   Experimental medicine

028   Intensive care
> Class here critical care
> *For a specific kind of intensive care therapy, see the therapy in 06, e.g., drug therapy 061*

029   Palliative and terminal care
> *For a specific kind of palliative or terminal care therapy, see the therapy in 06, e.g., drug therapy 061*

03   Rehabilitation
> Including self-help devices for people with disabilities
> Class rehabilitative therapy in 06; class comprehensive works on rehabilitation in 617.03

04   Special classes of diseases
> Limited to the classes named below

042   Genetic diseases (Hereditary diseases)
> Class here genetic aspects of diseases with complex causation, medical genetics

0421–0423   Microbiology, special topics, rehabilitation
> Add to 042 the numbers following 0 in notation 01–03 from table under 616.1–616.9, e.g., experimental medicine for genetic diseases 04227

0425–0429   Preventive measures, therapy, pathology, psychosomatic medicine, case histories
> Add to 042 the numbers following 0 in notation 05–09 from table under 616.1–616.9, e.g., therapy for genetic diseases 0426, gene therapy 042695

(continued)

> **616.1–616.9 Specific diseases (continued)**

> 043 Congenital diseases
> Class congenital diseases of genetic origin in 042

> 0431–0433 Microbiology, special topics, rehabilitation
> Add to 043 the numbers following 0 in notation 01–03
> from table under 616.1–616.9, e.g., experimental medicine
> for congenital diseases 04327

> 0435–0439 Preventive measures, therapy, pathology, psychosomatic
> medicine, case histories
> Add to 043 the numbers following 0 in notation 05–09
> from table under 616.1–616.9, e.g., therapy for congenital
> diseases 0436

> >05–09 Preventive measures, therapy, pathology, psychosomatic medicine,
> case histories
> Class preventive measures, therapy, pathology, psychosomatic
> medicine, case histories applied to specific classes of diseases in
> 04; class comprehensive works in 616 without adding from this
> table

> 05 Preventive measures
> By individuals and by medical personnel
> Class comprehensive works on public and private measures for
> preventing diseases in 613. Class public measures for preventing
> a specific disease, use of specific vaccines with the disease in
> 614.5, e.g., mosquito control for prevention of malaria 614.532,
> use of influenza vaccines 614.518; class a specific kind of
> therapy used for prevention with the kind of therapy in 061–069,
> e.g., drug therapy 061

> 06 Therapy
> Class here alternative therapy; rehabilitative therapy;
> specific kinds of therapy used in domestic medicine, medical
> emergencies, intensive care, palliative and terminal care
> Class comprehensive works on therapy in 615.5; class
> comprehensive works on therapy for specific diseases or kinds
> of diseases in domestic medicine in 024; class comprehensive
> works on therapy for specific diseases or kinds of diseases in
> medical emergencies in 025; class comprehensive works on
> therapy for specific diseases or kinds of diseases in intensive
> care in 028; class comprehensive works on therapy for specific
> diseases or kinds of diseases in palliative or terminal care in
> 029; class comprehensive works on rehabilitative therapy and
> training for people with a specific disease or kind of disease in
> 03; class comprehensive works on prevention, therapy, etiology
> of a specific disease or kind of disease if all related to a specific
> kind of therapy in 061–069, e.g., diet therapy 0654. Class
> comprehensive works on therapy and pathology of a specific
> disease or kind of disease if not all related to a specific kind of
> therapy with the disease or kind of disease, without adding from
> add table, e.g., cause, course, and cure of heart disease 616.12
> (*not* 616.1206)

(continued)

> **616.1–616.9 Specific diseases (continued)**

060724	Experimental research
	Class here clinical trials
	Class clinical trials of a specific kind of therapy with the kind of therapy, plus notation 0724 from Table 1, e.g., clinical drug trials 0610724
>061–069	Specific therapies
	Class here specific kinds of therapy used for prevention; comprehensive works on prevention, therapy, etiology if these all relate to a specific kind of therapy, e.g., nutritional aspects of a disease and diet therapy 0654
061	Drug therapy
0610724	Experimental research
	Class here clinical drug trials
062–069	Other therapies
	Add to 06 the numbers following 615.8 in 615.82–615.89, e.g., X-ray therapy 06422, psychotherapies 0651
07	Pathology
071	Etiology
	Including effects of poisons on specific systems and organs as cause of disease
	Class social factors contributing to spread of a disease in 362.19; class comprehensive works on medical toxicology in 615.9
	See Manual at 616.1–.9: Add table: 071 vs. 01
075–079	Diagnosis, prognosis, death, immunity
	Add to 07 the numbers following 616.07 in 616.075–616.079, e.g., diagnosis 075, clinical trials of diagnostic procedures 0750724
08	Psychosomatic medicine
09	Case histories

Class comprehensive works in 616. Class a work treating all the complications of a disease with the disease, e.g., all the complications of diabetes mellitus 616.462; class a work that focuses on one specific complication with the complication, e.g., peripheral nerve disorders associated with diabetes mellitus 616.856

See Manual at 612.1–612.8

> **616.1–616.8 Diseases of specific systems and organs**

Class comprehensive works in 616

For diseases of immune system, see 616.97; for tumors and cancers of specific systems and organs, see 616.994; for tuberculosis of specific systems and organs, see 616.995

.1   ***Diseases of cardiovascular system**

Class here cardiopulmonary diseases

Class cardiopulmonary resuscitation (CPR) in 616.1025; class diseases of blood-forming system in 616.41

For pulmonary diseases, see 616.24

SUMMARY

616.11	**Diseases of endocardium and pericardium**
.12	**Diseases of heart**
.13	**Diseases of blood vessels**
.14	**Diseases of veins and capillaries**
.15	**Diseases of blood**

.11   *Diseases of endocardium and pericardium

.12   *Diseases of heart

Including cor pulmonale

Class here cardiology

For diseases of endocardium and pericardium, see 616.11

.122   *Angina pectoris

.123   *Coronary diseases (Ischemic heart diseases)

Class works on heart attacks limited to myocardial infarction in 616.1237; class comprehensive works on cardiac arrest, on heart attacks in 616.123025. Class cardiac arrest and heart attacks not caused by narrowing or blocking of coronary arteries with the cause, e.g., heart attacks caused by congestive heart failure 616.129025

For angina pectoris, see 616.122

.123 028   Intensive care

Number built according to instructions under 616.1–616.9

Class coronary care covering intensive care for any serious heart disease in 616.12028

.123 2   *Coronary arteriosclerosis

.123 7   *Myocardial infarction

.124   *Myocarditis

Class here comprehensive works on diseases of myocardium

For myocardial infarction, see 616.1237

.125   *Valvular diseases

.127   *Rheumatic heart diseases

For rheumatic valvular diseases, see 616.125

*Add as instructed under 616.1–616.9

.128   *Arrhythmia

Class here atrial fibrillation, ventricular fibrillation

Class electric countershock (electric defibrillation) in 616.1280645; class implantation of heart pacers and defibrillators in 617.4120592; class functioning of heart pacers and implanted defibrillators in 617.4120645

.129   *Heart failure

Class here congestive heart failure

Class comprehensive works on cardiac arrest in 616.123025

.13   *Diseases of blood vessels

Including arterial occlusive diseases

Class here angiology; diseases of arteries; diseases of blood vessels in a specific region, e.g., abdominal and pelvic cavities

Class a specific arterial occlusive disease with the disease, e.g., arteriosclerosis 616.136; class diseases of blood vessels in a specific system or organ with the system or organ, e.g., cerebrovascular diseases 616.81

For diseases of veins and capillaries, see 616.14

.131   *Peripheral vascular diseases

> 616.132–616.136 Hypertension, aneurysms, arterial embolisms and thromboses, arteriosclerosis

Class hypertension, aneurysms, embolisms, thromboses, arteriosclerosis of aorta in 616.138; class comprehensive works in 616.13

.132   *Hypertension

Including renal hypertension

For pulmonary hypertension, see 616.24; for portal hypertension, see 616.362

.133   *Aneurysms

.135   *Arterial embolisms and thromboses

Class here comprehensive works on embolisms, on thromboses

For venous embolisms and thromboses, see 616.145; for pulmonary embolisms and thromboses, see 616.249

.136   *Arteriosclerosis

Class here atherosclerosis

.138   *Diseases of aorta

.14   *Diseases of veins and capillaries

Subdivisions are added for diseases of veins and capillaries together, for diseases of veins alone

*Add as instructed under 616.1–616.9

.142   *Phlebitis

    Including thrombophlebitis

.143   *Varicose veins (Varix)

.145   *Venous embolisms and thromboses

    Class thrombophlebitis in 616.142; class comprehensive works on embolisms, on thromboses in 616.135

.148   *Diseases of capillaries

    Including telangiectasis, telangitis

.15   *Diseases of blood

    Class here hematology, comprehensive works on hemic and lymphatic diseases

    For lymphatic diseases, see 616.42; for bacterial blood diseases, see 616.94

    See also 616.07561 for use of blood analysis in diagnosis of diseases in general

.151   *Diseases of erythrocytes

    Class here hemoglobin disorders

    For anemia, see 616.152; for polycythemia, see 616.153

.152   *Anemia

    Including iron-deficiency anemia, thalassemia

.152 7   *Sickle cell anemia

.153   *Polycythemia

.154   *Diseases of leukocytes

    Including agranulocytosis

.157   *Hemorrhagic diseases

    Including von Willebrand disease

    Class here comprehensive works on disorders of blood coagulation, on blood platelet disorders

    For arterial embolisms and thromboses, see 616.135; for venous embolisms and thromboses, see 616.145

.157 2   *Hemophilia

.2   Diseases of respiratory system

    Class here dyspnea

.200 1–.200 3   Standard subdivisions

    As modified under 616.1–616.9

---

*Add as instructed under 616.1–616.9

.200 4	Special topics of diseases of respiratory system

Add to base number 616.2004 the numbers following 0 in notation 01–09 from table under 616.1–616.9, e.g., diagnosis of respiratory diseases 616.200475

.200 5–.200 9	Standard subdivisions

As modified under 616.1–616.9

.201	*Croup

.202	*Respiratory allergies

Class here hay fever

Class asthma in 616.238

.203	*Influenza

.204	*Whooping cough (Pertussis)

.205	*Common cold

.208	*Hyperventilation

.209	*Sleep apnea syndromes

Class here snoring

.21	*Diseases of nose, nasopharynx, paranasal sinuses, larynx

Class here rhinology

Subdivisions are added for diseases of nose, nasopharynx, paranasal sinuses, larynx together; for diseases of nose alone

Class allergic rhinitis in 616.202; class common cold in 616.205; class otolaryngology, comprehensive works on diseases of ears, nose, throat in 617.51

For diseases of larynx, see 616.22

.212	*Diseases of paranasal sinuses

.22	*Diseases of larynx, epiglottis, glottis, vocal cords

Class here laryngology

Subdivisions are added for diseases of larynx, epiglottis, glottis, vocal cords; for diseases of larynx alone

.23	*Diseases of trachea and bronchi

Including bronchiectasis, tracheitis

Subdivisions are added for either or both topics in heading

Class bronchopneumonia in 616.241

.234	*Bronchitis

*Add as instructed under 616.1–616.9

.238   *Asthma

> Class here bronchial asthma
>
> *For cardiac asthma, see 616.12*

.24   *Diseases of lungs

> Including chronic obstructive pulmonary disease, pulmonary hypertension
>
> Class here comprehensive works on diseases of lungs and bronchi
>
> Class cystic fibrosis in 616.372; class pulmonary sarcoidosis in 616.429; class pulmonary tuberculosis in 616.995; class comprehensive works on cardiopulmonary diseases in 616.1
>
> *For diseases of bronchi, see 616.23*

.241   *Pneumonia

> Including Legionnaires' disease
>
> *See also 616.245 for necropneumonia*

.244   *Pneumoconiosis

> Including asbestosis, black lung disease, byssinosis (brown lung disease), pulmonary abscesses, silicosis

.245   *Necropneumonia

.248   *Emphysema

.249   *Pulmonary embolisms and thromboses

> Class comprehensive works on embolisms, on thromboses in 616.135

.25   *Diseases of pleura

> Class pleural pneumonia in 616.241

.27   *Diseases of mediastinum

.3   ***Diseases of digestive system**

> Class allergies of digestive system in 616.975
>
> *See also 616.07563 for use of analysis of gastroenteric contents in diagnosis of diseases in general*

SUMMARY

616.31	**Diseases of mouth and throat**
.32	**Diseases of pharynx and esophagus**
.33	**Diseases of stomach**
.34	**Diseases of intestine**
.35	**Diseases of rectum and anus**
.36	**Diseases of biliary tract and liver**
.37	**Diseases of pancreas**
.38	**Diseases of peritoneum**
.39	**Nutritional and metabolic diseases**

*Add as instructed under 616.1–616.9

.31   *Diseases of mouth and throat

        Subdivisions are added for diseases of mouth and throat together, for diseases of mouth alone

        Class oral region (a broader concept than mouth as a digestive organ) in 617.522; class diseases of teeth and gums in 617.63

        For diseases of larynx, see 616.22; for diseases of pharynx, see 616.32

.312   *Necrotizing ulcerative gingivitis (Trench mouth)

.313   *Mumps

.314   *Diseases of tonsils

.316   *Diseases of salivary glands

        For mumps, see 616.313; for Sjogren's syndrome, see 616.775

.32   *Diseases of pharynx and esophagus

        Subdivisions are added for either or both topics in heading

        Class diseases of tonsils in 616.314

.323   *Deglutition disorders

        Class here dysphagia

.324   *Gastroesophageal reflux

        Class here heartburn

.33   *Diseases of stomach

        Class here gastroenteritis, comprehensive works on gastroenterology (gastrointestinal diseases)

        For diseases of intestine, see 616.34; for typhoid fever, see 616.9272; for cholera, see 616.932; for dysentery, see 616.935; for hiatal hernia, see 617.559

.332   *Functional disorders

        Including disorders of secretion; dyspepsia

        Class gastroesophageal reflux, heartburn in 616.324

.333   *Gastritis

.334   *Stomach ulcers

        Class comprehensive works on ulcers in 616.343

.34   *Diseases of intestine

        Including appendicitis, giardiasis

        For hernias, see 617.559

.342   *Functional disorders

        Including irritable bowel syndrome (irritable colon), obstructions

*Add as instructed under 616.1–616.9

.342 7	*Diarrhea
.342 8	*Constipation
.343	*Peptic ulcers

Class here comprehensive works on stomach and peptic ulcers

For stomach ulcers, see 616.334

.343 3	*Duodenal ulcers
.344	*Enteritis

Including duodenitis, jejunitis

Class here Crohn disease, inflammatory bowel diseases

See also 616.342 for irritable bowel syndrome

.344 5	*Ileitis

Use of this number for Crohn disease discontinued; class in 616.344

.344 7	*Colitis
.344 73	*Ulcerative colitis
.35	*Diseases of rectum and anus

Including fecal incontinence

Class here proctology

Subdivisions are added for diseases of rectum and anus together, for diseases of rectum alone

.352	*Hemorrhoids
.36	*Diseases of biliary tract and liver

Subdivisions are added for diseases of biliary tract and liver together, for diseases of biliary tract alone

.362	*Diseases of liver

Including portal hypertension

For hepatic encephalopathy, Reye syndrome, see 616.83

.362 3	*Hepatitis

Class here viral hepatitis

.362 4	*Cirrhosis
.362 5	*Jaundice
.365	*Diseases of gallbladder and bile duct

Subdivisions are added for diseases of gallbladder and bile duct together, for diseases of gallbladder alone

Class comprehensive works on diseases of biliary tract in 616.36

*Add as instructed under 616.1–616.9

.37	*Diseases of pancreas	

> Class diseases of pancreatic internal secretion in 616.46

.372	*Cystic fibrosis
.38	*Diseases of peritoneum
.39	*Nutritional and metabolic diseases

> Subdivisions are added for either or both topics in heading

> Class inborn (inherited) errors of metabolism in 616.39042. Class nutritional and metabolic diseases of a specific system or organ outside the digestive system with the system or organ, e.g., iron-deficiency anemia 616.152

> *For endocrinology, see 616.4*

> 616.392–616.396 Deficiency diseases

> Class comprehensive works in 616.39

.392	*Beriberi
.393	*Pellagra
.394	*Scurvy
.395	*Rickets
.396	Other deficiency diseases and states

> Including emaciation, kwashiorkor

> Class anorexia nervosa in 616.85262

> *For multiple deficiency states, see 616.399*

.398	*Obesity
.398 08	Psychosomatic medicine

> Number built according to instructions under 616.1–616.9

> *For eating disorders, see 616.8526*

.399	Other nutritional and metabolic diseases

> Including celiac disease, multiple deficiency states, phenylketonuria, porphyria

> Class here malabsorption syndromes

.399 2	*Body fluid disorders

> Including acid-base imbalances

> Class here water-electrolyte imbalances

.399 5	*Diseases of protein metabolism

> Including amyloidosis

*Add as instructed under 616.1–616.9

.399 7	*Diseases of lipid metabolism

Including hypercholesterolemia, hyperlipidemia

.399 8	*Diseases of carbohydrate metabolism

Including lactose intolerance

.399 9	*Gout

.4   *Diseases of endocrine, hematopoietic, lymphatic, glandular systems; diseases of male breast

Class here endocrinology, comprehensive works on diseases of glands

Subdivisions are added for diseases of endocrine, hematopoietic, lymphatic systems, of male breast together; for diseases of endocrine system alone

Class endocrinal obesity in 616.398. Class diseases of glands in a specific system or organ with the system or organ, e.g., diseases of female sex glands 618.1

.41   *Diseases of spleen and bone marrow

Class here diseases of hematopoietic (blood-forming) system

For anemia, see 616.152

.42   *Diseases of lymphatic system

Class filiarial elephantiasis in 616.9652; class Hodgkin disease in 616.99446

For diseases of spleen, see 616.41

.429   *Sarcoidosis

Class here pulmonary sarcoidosis

>   616.43–616.48 Diseases of endocrine system

Class comprehensive works in 616.4

.43   *Diseases of thymus gland

.44   *Diseases of thyroid and parathyroid glands

Subdivisions are added for diseases of thyroid and parathyroid glands together, for diseases of thyroid alone

.442   *Goiter

.443   *Hyperthyroidism

Including Graves' disease

.444   *Hypothyroidism

For myxedema, see 616.858848

*Add as instructed under 616.1–616.9

.445   *Diseases of parathyroid glands

>Including hyperparathyroidism, hypoparathyroidism

.45   *Diseases of adrenal glands

>Including Addison's disease, Cushing syndrome, hyperadrenalism, hypoadrenalism

.46   *Diseases of islands of Langerhans

.462   *Diabetes mellitus

>Class here comprehensive works on diabetes

>Class diabetic nephropathies in 616.61

>*For diabetes insipidus, see 616.47*

.462 2   *Diabetes mellitus, type 1 (Insulin-dependent diabetes)

.462 4   *Diabetes mellitus, type 2 (Non-insulin-dependent diabetes)

.466   *Hypoglycemia

.47   *Diseases of pituitary gland

>Including acromegaly, diabetes insipidus, pituitary dwarfism, pituitary gigantism, hypopituitarism

.48   *Diseases of other glands of endocrine system

>Including hyperpinealism, polyglandular disorders

.49   *Diseases of male breast

>Class comprehensive works on diseases of breast in 618.19

.5   *Diseases of integument

>Class here dermatology, skin diseases

>Class porphyria in 616.399; class mastocytosis in 616.77

>*For allergies of skin, see 616.973; for dermatological manifestations of food and drug allergies, see 616.975*

.51   *Dermatitis, photosensitivity disorders, urticaria

>Including contact dermatitis

>Class here eczema

>Subdivisions are added for dermatitis, photosensitivity disorders, urticaria together; for dermatitis alone

>Class bacterial and viral skin diseases in 616.52

>*For allergic contact dermatitis, see 616.973*

.515   *Photosensitivity disorders

>Including sunburn

*Add as instructed under 616.1–616.9

.517   *Urticaria (Hives)

         Class urticaria pigmentosa in 616.77

.52   Viral and bacterial skin diseases; psoriasis

.522   *Viral skin diseases

         Including herpes labialis (cold sores, fever blisters), shingles (herpes zoster)

         Class herpes genitalis in 616.9518; class comprehensive works on herpesvirus diseases in 616.9112

.523   *Bacterial skin diseases

         Including boils, carbuncles, erysipelas, impetigo, pinta, yaws

.526   *Psoriasis

.53   *Diseases of sebaceous glands

         Including acne, blackheads, seborrhea, wens

.54   *Skin hypertrophies and ulcerations; diseases of scalp, hair, nails

         For pigmentary changes, see 616.55

.544   *Skin hypertrophies

         Including callosities, corns, ichthyosis, keratosis, scleroderma, warts

.545   *Skin ulcerations

         Class here decubitus ulcers (bedsores)

.546   *Diseases of scalp, hair, hair follicles

         Including baldness (alopecia), dandruff, excessive hairiness (hypertrichosis)

.547   *Diseases of nails

.55   *Pigmentary changes

         Including albinism, birthmarks, moles, pigmentary nevi, vitiligo

         Class urticaria pigmentosa in 616.77

         For birthmarks that are capillary hemangiomas, see 616.99315

.56   *Diseases of sweat glands

.57   *Parasitic and fungal skin diseases

         Subdivisions are added for parasitic and fungal skin diseases together, for parasitic skin diseases alone

         Class leishmaniasis in 616.9364

.572   *Lice infestations

         Class here pediculosis

*Add as instructed under 616.1–616.9

.573	*Mite infestations	
	Class here scabies	
.579	*Fungal skin diseases (Dermatomycoses)	
	Including athlete's foot (tinea pedis), ringworm (tinea)	
.58	*Chapping, chilblains, frostbite	
	Subdivisions are added for any or all topics in heading	

.6   ***Diseases of urogenital system**

         Class here diseases of urinary system; urology

>   616.61–616.64   Diseases of urinary system

         Class comprehensive works in 616.6

.61   *Diseases of kidneys and ureters

         Class here diabetic nephropathies, nephrology

         Subdivisions are added for kidneys and ureters together, for kidneys alone

         Class renal hypertension in 616.132; class kidney dialysis in 617.461059

         For kidney stones, see 616.622

.612   *Nephritis

         Class here glomerulonephritis

         For pyelonephritis, see 616.613

.613   *Pyelonephritis and pyelocystitis

         Subdivisions are added for pyelonephritis and pyelocystitis together, for pyelonephritis alone

.614   *Renal failure

         Class here chronic renal failure

         Class hemodialysis, peritoneal dialysis in 617.461059

.62   *Diseases of bladder and urethra

         Including urinary incontinence

         Class here urination disorders

         Subdivisions are added for either or both topics in heading

         For diseases of male urethra, see 616.64; for enuresis, see 616.849

.622   *Urinary calculi

         Class here bladder stones, kidney stones

.623   *Cystitis

---

*Add as instructed under 616.1–616.9

.624   *Urethritis

.63   *Urinary manifestations of diseases of urogenital system

      Including albuminuria, hematuria, proteinuria

      Class interpretation of symptoms for diagnosis and prognosis of diseases of urogenital system in 616.6075. Class urinary manifestations of a specific disease or of disease in a specific organ with the disease or organ, e.g., urinary manifestations of renal failure 616.614

      See also 616.07566 for use of urinalysis to diagnose diseases in general

.635   *Uremia

.64   *Diseases of male urethra

.65   *Diseases of genital system

      Class here diseases of male genital system, diseases of prostate gland

      Class comprehensive works on reproductive toxicology in 616.65071

      For sexual disorders, see 616.69; for diseases of female genital system, see 618.1. For diseases of a specific male genital organ not provided for here, see the organ, e.g., diseases of male urethra 616.64

.66   *Diseases of penis

.67   *Diseases of scrotum

.68   *Diseases of testes and accessory organs

      Subdivisions are added for diseases of testes and accessory organs together, for diseases of testes alone

.69   *Sexual disorders

      Class here male sexual disorders

      For psychiatric sexual disorders, see 616.8583; for female sexual disorders, see 618.17

.692   *Infertility and impotence

      Class here comprehensive works on male and female infertility

      Subdivisions are added for infertility and impotence together, for infertility alone

      For female infertility, artificial insemination, see 618.178

.692 06   Therapy

      Number built according to instructions under 616.1–616.9

      Class here comprehensive medical works on human reproductive technology

      For human reproductive technology applied to female infertility, see 618.17806

*Add as instructed under 616.1–616.9

.692 1	*Male infertility

Class impotence in 616.6922

.692 2	*Impotence

For impotence as a psychological disorder, see 616.85832

.693	*Male climacteric disorders

Class comprehensive works on climacteric disorders in 618.175

.694	*Intersexuality

Class here hermaphroditism, comprehensive medical works on sex differentiation disorders

Class interdisciplinary works on intersexuality in 306.768. Class a specific sex differentiation disorder with the disorder, e.g., congenital adrenal hyperplasia 616.45, congenital adrenal hyperplasia in children 618.9245

See also 616.8583 for gender-identity disorders

.7	***Diseases of musculoskeletal system**

Class here comprehensive works on orthopedics

For orthopedic surgery of musculoskeletal system, see 617.47; for orthopedic regional medicine, orthopedic regional surgery, see 617.5

.71	*Diseases of bones

Class here chronic diseases of skeletal system

Class pituitary gigantism, pituitary dwarfism in 616.47; class Marfan syndrome in 616.773

For diseases of spine, see 616.73; for fractures, see 617.15

.712	*Osteitis

Including osteochondritis, periostitis

Class here osteitis deformans

.715	*Osteomyelitis

.716	*Disorders of metabolic origin

Class here osteoporosis

For rickets, see 616.395

.72	*Diseases of joints

For gout, see 616.3999

.722	*Arthritis

.722 3	*Osteoarthritis

*Add as instructed under 616.1–616.9

.722 7   *Rheumatoid arthritis

For ankylosing spondylitis, see 616.73; for Sjogren's syndrome, see 616.775

.723   *Rheumatism

Class here rheumatology, rheumatic diseases

For a specific rheumatic disease, see the disease, e.g., rheumatoid arthritis 616.7227, rheumatic fever 616.991

.73   *Diseases of spine

Including ankylosing spondylitis

Class backache in 617.564

.74   *Diseases of muscles

Class diseases of muscles in a specific system or organ with the system or organ, e.g., diseases of heart muscle (myocardium) 616.124

.742   *Myalgia

Class here fibromyalgia (muscular rheumatism)

See also 616.0478 for chronic fatigue syndrome

.743   *Myositis

.744   *Neuromuscular diseases

Class myalgic encephalomyelitis in 616.0478; class neuromuscular diseases resulting from disorders of central nervous system in 616.83

.744 2   *Myasthenia gravis

.748   *Muscular dystrophy

.75   *Diseases of tendons and fasciae

See also 616.76 for diseases of sheaths of tendons

.76   *Diseases of bursae and sheaths of tendons

.77   *Diseases of connective tissues

Including Ehlers-Danlos syndrome, mastocytosis

Class here collagen diseases

Class carpal tunnel syndrome in 616.856

For rheumatoid arthritis, see 616.7227; for diseases of tendons and fasciae, see 616.75

.772   *Systemic lupus erythematosus

.773   *Marfan syndrome

.775   *Sjogren's syndrome

*Add as instructed under 616.1–616.9

.8   **Diseases of nervous system and mental disorders**

Class here diseases of brain; neurology; neuropsychiatry

Class diseases of cranial, spinal, peripheral nerves in 616.856; class diseases of autonomic nervous system in 616.8569. Class diseases of nerves needed to make a specific system or organ function properly with the system or organ, e.g., neuromuscular diseases 616.744, diseases of optic nerves 617.732

Diseases of nerves needed to make a region function properly are classed with diseases of nerves, e.g., disease of peripheral nerves needed to make the hand function properly are classed with diseases of peripheral nerves in 616.856

SUMMARY

616.800 1–.800 9	Standard subdivisions
.801–.809	Standard subdivisions and special topics of diseases of nervous system, of diseases of brain
.81	Cerebrovascular diseases
.82	Meningeal diseases
.83	Other organic diseases of central nervous system
.84	Manifestations of nervous system diseases
.85	Miscellaneous diseases of nervous system and mental disorders
.86	Substance abuse (Drug abuse)
.89	Mental disorders

.800 1–.800 9   Standard subdivisions

.801–.803   Standard subdivisions of neurology, of diseases of nervous system, of diseases of brain

As modified under 616.1–616.9

.804   Special topics of diseases of nervous system, of diseases of brain

Add to base number 616.804 the numbers following 0 in notation 01–09 from table under 616.1–616.9, e.g., diagnosis of brain diseases 616.80475
     Subdivisions are added for any or all topics in heading

Class manifestations of neurological diseases as problems in their own right in 616.84

.805–.809   Standard subdivisions of neurology, of diseases of nervous system, of diseases of brain

As modified under 616.1–616.9

.81   *Cerebrovascular diseases

Including vascular dementia

Class here stroke

.82   *Meningeal diseases

Including meningitis

Class meningoencephalitis in 616.832

*Add as instructed under 616.1–616.9

.83   Other organic diseases of central nervous system

Including ataxia telangiectasia, chorea and choreatic disorders other than Huntington disease, Creutzfeldt-Jakob syndrome (both familial form and variant associated with bovine spongiform encephalopathy), Friedreich ataxia, hepatic encephalopathy, neuronal ceroid-lipofuscinosis, neurosyphilis, prion diseases, Reye syndrome, senile dementia, spina bifida, tardive dyskinesia, Tourette syndrome

Class here diseases of basal ganglia, of spinal cord; comprehensive works on dementia, on memory disorders, on movement disorders

Class phenylketonuria in 616.399; class senile dementia of the Alzheimer type in 616.831; class comprehensive works on syphilis in 616.9513

> *For orthopedic aspects of spina bifida, see 616.73; for Huntington disease, see 616.851; for epilepsy, see 616.853. For a specific kind of dementia or dementia-causing disease, see the dementia or disease, e.g., dementia caused by cerebrovascular disease 616.81*

.831   *Alzheimer disease

Class comprehensive works on dementia in 616.83

.832   *Encephalitis

Class here meningoencephalitis

Class postencephalitic Parkinson disease in 616.833

> *See also 616.0478 for myalgic encephalomyelitis*

.833   *Parkinson disease

Including postencephalitic Parkinson disease

.834   *Multiple sclerosis

.835   *Poliomyelitis

Including postpoliomyelitis syndrome

.836   *Cerebral palsy

.839   *Amyotrophic lateral sclerosis

.84   Manifestations of nervous system diseases

Symptoms as problems in their own right

Class here pathology, diagnosis, treatment of symptoms

Class interpretation of symptoms for diagnosis and prognosis of neurological diseases in 616.80475; class manifestations of mental disorders in 616.89. Class diagnostic and prognostic interpretation of symptoms of a specific disease or class of diseases with the disease or class of diseases, e.g., interpretation of symptoms of cerebrovascular diseases 616.81075

.841   Dizziness and vertigo

Standard subdivisions are added for either or both topics in heading

*Add as instructed under 616.1–616.9

.842	Paralysis

         Including neurological aspects of paraplegia

         Class comprehensive works on neurological and surgical aspects of paraplegia in 617.58

.845	Convulsions
.849	Miscellaneous symptoms

         Only those named below

         Including coma, enuresis, pain

         Class comprehensive works on urinary incontinence in 616.62

.849 1	*Headaches

         Class here vascular headaches

.849 12	*Migraine
.849 13	*Cluster headache
.849 14	*Tension headache
.849 8	*Sleep disorders

         Including narcolepsy, somnambulism

         For sleep apnea and snoring, see 616.209

.849 82	*Insomnia
.85	Miscellaneous diseases of nervous system and mental disorders

         Only those named below

SUMMARY

616.851	**Huntington disease**
.852	**Neuroses**
.853	**Epilepsy**
.855	**Speech and language disorders**
.856	**Diseases of cranial, spinal, peripheral nerves; diseases of autonomic nervous system**
.858	**Personality, sexual, gender-identity, impulse-control, factitious, developmental, learning disorders; violent behavior; mental retardation**

.851	*Huntington disease
.852	*Neuroses

         Including adjustment disorders

         Class neurotic aspects of a specific disease with the disease, e.g., neurotic aspects of asthma 616.238

*Add as instructed under 616.1–616.9

.852 1	*Traumatic neuroses

Class here post-traumatic stress disorders

.852 12	*War neuroses (Combat disorders)
.852 2	*Anxiety disorders

For traumatic neuroses, see 616.8521

.852 23	*Panic disorder
.852 25	*Phobic disorders

Including agoraphobia

.852 27	*Obsessive-compulsive disorder

Class comprehensive works on compulsive behavior in 616.8584

.852 3	*Dissociative disorders and amnesia

Subdivisions are added for dissociative disorders and amnesia together, for dissociative disorders alone

.852 32	*Amnesia

Class here amnestic disorders

.852 36	*Multiple personality disorder
.852 4	*Somatoform disorders

Class here conversion disorder, hysteria, somatization disorder

For hypochondria, see 616.8525

See also 616.8581 for histrionic personality disorder

.852 5	*Hypochondria
.852 6	*Eating disorders

Class here appetite disorders, food addiction

.852 62	*Anorexia nervosa
.852 63	*Bulimia
.852 7	*Depressive disorder

Including seasonal affective disorder

Class here comprehensive works on depression, on mood disorders

For manic-depressive illness, see 616.895; for postpartum depression, see 618.76

.852 8	*Neurasthenia

See also 616.0478 for chronic fatigue syndrome

.853	*Epilepsy

*Add as instructed under 616.1–616.9

.855   *Speech and language disorders

> Class here articulation disorders, communication disorders
>
> Subdivisions are added for either or both topics in heading
>
> Class comprehensive works on learning and communication disorders in 616.85889

.855 2   *Neurological language disorders

> Including dysarthria
>
> Class here aphasias
>
> *For written language disorders, see 616.8553*

.855 3   *Written language disorders

> Including agraphia
>
> Class here dyslexia

.855 4   *Stuttering

> Class here stammering

.855 6   *Voice disorders

.856   *Diseases of cranial, spinal, peripheral nerves; diseases of autonomic nervous system

> Including carpal tunnel syndrome, neuralgias, neuritis, polyradiculoneuritis, sciatica; cutaneous sensory disorders, disorders of smell and taste
>
> Subdivisions are added for diseases of cranial, spinal, peripheral nerves and for diseases of autonomic nervous system together; for diseases of cranial, spinal, peripheral nerves alone
>
> Class neurofibromatosis in 616.99383; class comprehensive works on overuse injuries in 617.172
>
> *For shingles, see 616.522; for diseases of optic nerves, see 617.732; for diseases of aural nervous system, see 617.886*

.856 9   *Diseases of autonomic nervous system

> Including parasympathetic nervous system, sympathetic nervous system

.858   Personality, sexual, gender-identity, impulse-control, factitious, developmental, learning disorders; violent behavior; mental retardation

*Add as instructed under 616.1–616.9

SUMMARY

616.858 1	**Personality disorders**
.858 2	**Antisocial personality disorders, family violence and abuse**
.858 3	**Sexual and gender-identity disorders**
.858 4	**Disorders of impulse control; homicidal and suicidal behavior**
.858 5	**Borderline and narcissistic personality disorders**
.858 6	**Factitious disorders**
.858 8	**Mental retardation; developmental and learning disorders**
.858 9	**Attention deficit disorder with hyperactivity**

.858 1   *Personality disorders

Including compulsive, dependent, histrionic, paranoid, passive-aggressive, schizoid, schizotypal personality disorders

Class impulsive personality, comprehensive works on compulsive behavior in 616.8584

> *For a specific type of personality disorder not provided for here, see the disorder, e.g., borderline personality disorder 616.85852*

> *See also 616.85227 for obsessive-compulsive disorder; also 616.8524 for hysteria; also 616.897 for paranoid disorders; also 616.898 for schizophrenia*

.858 2   *Antisocial personality disorders, family violence and abuse

Class here self-destructive behavior, violent behavior

Subdivisions are added for antisocial personality disorders, family violence and abuse together; for antisocial personality disorders alone

Class sexual disorders in 616.8583

> *For a specific type of self-destructive or violent behavior, see the behavior, e.g., suicide 616.858445*

.858 22   *Family violence and abuse

Class here spouse abuse

Subdivisions are added for either or both topics in heading

.858 223   *Child abuse

Including Munchausen syndrome by proxy

Class incest involving children, sexual abuse of children in 616.85836; class abused children in 618.92858223

.858 223 9   *Adult victims of child abuse

Class a specific problem of adult victims of child abuse with the problem, e.g., depression 616.8527

*Add as instructed under 616.1–616.9

.858 3	*Sexual and gender-identity disorders
	Including homosexuality treated as a medical disorder
	Subdivisions are added for sexual and gender-identity disorders together, for sexual disorders alone
	Class interdisciplinary works on gender identity in 305.3; class interdisciplinary works on homosexuality in 306.766; class interdisciplinary works on transgenderism in 306.768
	See also 616.694 for intersexuality
	See Manual at 616.8583
.858 32	*Frigidity and impotence
	Subdivisions are added for either or both topics in heading
	Class comprehensive works on impotence in 616.6922
.858 33	*Sex addiction
	Class here nymphomania, satyromania
.858 35	*Sadism and masochism
	Subdivisions are added for either or both topics in heading
.858 36	*Sexual abuse of children and adolescents
	Class here incest
	Subdivisions are added for either or both topics in heading
	Class sexually abused children in 618.9285836
.858 369	*Adult victims of childhood and adolescent sexual abuse
	Subdivisions are added for either or both topics in heading
	Class a specific problem of adult victims of childhood and adolescent sexual abuse with the problem, e.g., multiple personality disorder 616.85236
.858 4	*Disorders of impulse control; homicidal and suicidal behavior
	Including compulsive shopping
	Class here impulsive personality, comprehensive works on compulsive behavior
	For obsessive-compulsive disorder, see 616.85227; for compulsive eating disorders, see 616.8526; for compulsive personality disorder, see 616.8581; for compulsive sexual disorders, see 616.8583; for substance abuse, see 616.86
.858 41	*Pathological gambling
.858 42	*Kleptomania
.858 43	*Pyromania

*Add as instructed under 616.1–616.9

.858 44	Homicidal and suicidal behavior
.858 445	*Suicidal behavior
.858 5	Borderline and narcissistic personality disorders
.858 52	*Borderline personality disorder
.858 54	*Narcissistic personality disorder
.858 6	*Factitious disorders

Including Munchausen syndrome

Class Munchausen syndrome by proxy in 616.858223

.858 8   *Mental retardation; developmental and learning disorders

Class here mental disorders usually first diagnosed in infancy, childhood, adolescence

Subdivisions are added for mental retardation, developmental and learning disorders together; for mental retardation alone; for developmental disorders alone

For attention deficit disorder with hyperactivity, see 616.8589

.858 82   *Autism

Class here comprehensive works on pervasive development disorders

For pervasive development disorders other than autism, see 616.85883

.858 83   Other pervasive development disorders

Including childhood disintegrative disorder

For Rett syndrome, see 616.85884

.858 832   *Asperger syndrome

.858 84   Mental retardation due to genetic disorders, other congenital abnormalities

Class phenylketonuria in 616.399; class learning disorders due to genetic disorders, other congenital abnormalities, and not associated with mental retardation in 616.85889

.858 841	*Fragile X syndrome
.858 842	*Down syndrome
.858 843	*Hydrocephalus
.858 844	*Microcephaly
.858 845	*Cerebral sphingolipidosis

Class here Tay-Sachs disease

*Add as instructed under 616.1–616.9

.858 848   *Myxedema

Class congenital myxedema in 616.858848043

.858 89   *Learning disorders

Regardless of level of intelligence

Class here learning disorders due to genetic disorders, other congenital abnormalities, and not associated with mental retardation; comprehensive works on learning and communication disorders

Class learning disorders associated with a specific disorder with the disorder, e.g., minimal brain dysfunction 616.8589

For communication disorders, see 616.855

.858 9   *Attention deficit disorder with hyperactivity

Class here hyperkinesia, minimal brain dysfunction

.86   †Substance abuse (Drug abuse)

Including abuse of analgesics, depressants, inhalants, sedatives, tranquilizers

Class here addiction, dependence, habituation, intoxication

Class personal measures to prevent substance abuse in 613.8; class food addiction in 616.8526; class comprehensive medical works on addictive drugs in 615.78; class comprehensive works on compulsive behavior in 616.8584; class interdisciplinary works on substance abuse in 362.29

See Manual at 616.86 vs. 158.1, 204.42, 248.8629, 292–299, 362.29

.861   †Alcohol

Class here alcoholism

.861 9   *Effect of alcoholism on people close to alcoholics

Class here adult children of alcoholics, codependent spouses of alcoholics

Class minor children of alcoholics in 618.928619. Class a specific problem of people close to alcoholics with the problem, e.g., depression 616.8527

>   616.863–616.865 Substances other than alcohol

Including effects on people close to substance abusers

Class minor children of substance abusers in 618.92863–618.92865; class comprehensive works in 616.86. Class a specific problem of people close to substance abusers with the problem, e.g., depression 616.8527

.863   †Narcotics, hallucinogens, psychedelics, cannabis

---

*Add as instructed under 616.1–616.9

†Add as instructed under 616.1–616.9, except do not use 05; class prevention in 613.8 or its subdivisions

.863 2 †Narcotics

Opium and its derivatives and synthetic equivalents

Class here specific narcotics, e.g., heroin, morphine

.863 4 †Hallucinogens and psychedelics

Class here specific hallucinogens and psychedelics, e.g., LSD, mescaline, PCP

Subdivisions are added for either or both topics in heading

Class cannabis in 616.8635

.863 5 †Cannabis

Class here specific kinds of cannabis, e.g., hashish, marijuana

.864 †Stimulants and related substances

Class here specific kinds of stimulants, e.g., amphetamine, ephedrine

Subdivisions are added for stimulants and related substances together, for stimulants alone

Class nicotine in 616.865

.864 7 †Cocaine

Class here specific forms of cocaine, e.g., crack

.865 †Tobacco

.869 *Effect of substance abuse on people close to substance abusers

Class here adult children of substance abusers, codependent spouses of substance abusers

Class minor children of substance abusers in 618.92869. Class effect of abuse of a specific substance on people close to abusers with the abuse of the specific substance, e.g., effect of alcoholism on people close to alcoholics 616.8619, effect of cocaine abuse on people close to cocaine abusers 616.8647; class a specific problem of people close to substance abusers with the problem, e.g., depression 616.8527

*Add as instructed under 616.1–616.9
†Add as instructed under 616.1–616.9, except do not use 05; class prevention in 613.8 or its subdivisions

.89	*Mental disorders

       Including manifestations of mental disorders

       Class here abnormal and clinical psychologies, comparative abnormal behavior of animals, psychiatry, psychoses

       Class a specific organic psychosis not provided for here with the psychosis, e.g., psychosis due to brain tumors 616.99481

       For neuroses, see 616.852; for personality, sexual, gender-identity, impulse-control, factitious, developmental, learning disorders; violent behavior, see 616.858; for puerperal mental disorders, see 618.76

       See Manual at 616.89 vs. 150.195

[.890 6]	Therapy

       Do not use; class in 616.891

.891	Therapy
.891 2	Convulsive therapy

       Variant name: shock therapy

       Including insulin and other drug shock therapies

.891 22	Electroconvulsive therapy
.891 3	Physical therapies

       For electroconvulsive therapy, see 616.89122; for psychosurgery, see 617.481

.891 4	Psychotherapy

       Class psychotherapy applied to a specific disorder with the disorder, plus notation 0651 as instructed under 616.1–616.9, e.g., psychotherapy applied to borderline personality disorder 616.858520651

       For group and family psychotherapy, see 616.8915; for psychological and activity therapies, see 616.8916; for psychoanalysis, see 616.8917

.891 42	Behavior therapy (Behavior modification therapy)
.891 425	Cognitive therapy
.891 43	Gestalt therapy
.891 44	Milieu therapy
.891 45	Transactional analysis
.891 47	Brief psychotherapy

       Class a brief form of a specific kind of psychotherapy with the kind, e.g., brief cognitive therapy 616.891425

*Add as instructed under 616.1–616.9

.891 5   Group and family psychotherapy

                        Class specific psychological and activity therapies in 616.8916

.891 52   Group psychotherapy

.891 523   Psychodrama

                        Including role playing

.891 56   Family psychotherapy

.891 562   Marital psychotherapy

                        Class here couples therapy

.891 6   Psychological and activity therapies

                        Add to base number 616.8916 the numbers following 615.851 in 615.8512–615.8516, e.g., hypnotherapy 616.89162

                        Class psychotherapy in 616.8914; class group and family psychotherapy in 616.8915; class psychoanalysis in 616.8917

.891 7   Psychoanalysis

[.891 701 9]   Psychological principles

                        Do not use for comprehensive works; class in 150.195. Do not use for applications to therapy; class in 616.8917

.891 8   Drug therapy

                        Class drug shock therapy in 616.8912

.895   *Manic-depressive illness (Bipolar disorder)

                        Including depressive reactions, involutional psychoses

                        Class here circular and alternating manic-depressive psychoses

                        Class comprehensive works on depression, on mood disorders in 616.8527

.897   *Paranoid disorders

                        See also 616.8581 for paranoid personality disorder

.898   *Schizophrenia

                        See also 616.8581 for schizoid personality disorder, schizotypal personality disorder

.9   **Other diseases**

                        Class here communicable diseases, infections

---

*Add as instructed under 616.1–616.9

SUMMARY

[.900 1–.900 9]   Standard subdivisions of other diseases

> Do not use; class in 616.001–616.009

.901–.903   Standard subdivisions of communicable diseases

> As modified under 616.1–616.9

.904   Special topics of communicable diseases

> Add to base number 616.904 the numbers following 0 in notation 01–09 from table under 616.1–616.9, e.g., diagnosis of communicable diseases 616.90475

.904 1   Medical microbiology

> Number built according to instructions under 616.904
>
> Class here drug resistance in microorganisms
>
> Class resistance to specific drugs in 615; class comprehensive works on etiology of diseases in 616.071; class comprehensive works on communicable diseases and their course, cure, and prevention in 616.9; class comprehensive works on etiology of communicable diseases in 616.90471. Class medical microbiology of a specific disease or group of diseases with the disease or group of diseases, plus notation 01 from table under 616.1–616.9, e.g., medical microbiology of tuberculosis 616.99501
>
> *See Manual at 579.165 vs. 616.9041*

.904 71   Etiology

> Number built according to instructions under 616.904
>
> Class here comprehensive works on etiology of communicable diseases, e.g., environmental and genetic risk factors plus pathogenic microorganisms
>
> *For pathogenic microorganisms as causes of communicable diseases, see 616.9041*

.905–.908   Standard subdivisions of communicable diseases

> As modified under 616.1–616.9

.909   History, geographic treatment, biography of communicable diseases

[.909 11–.909 13]	Frigid, temperate, tropical zones

Do not use; class in 616.9881 616.9883

> 616.91–616.96 Specific communicable diseases

Class here diseases caused by microorganisms or parasites even if the diseases are not communicable

Class comprehensive works in 616.9

For a specific communicable disease not provided for here, see the disease, e.g., mumps 616.313

.91 *Virus diseases

For a specific virus disease or group of virus diseases not provided for here, see the disease or group of diseases, e.g., viral hepatitis 616.3623

See also 616.0478 for chronic fatigue syndrome

.910 1 Medical virology

Number built according to instructions under 616.1–616.9

Class here medical microbiology of ultramicrobes

.911 *DNA virus infections

Including human papillomavirus infections

For a specific DNA virus infection not provided for here, see the infection, e.g., smallpox 616.912, condylomata acuminata 616.9518

.911 2 *Herpesvirus diseases

For a specific herpesvirus disease or group of herpesvirus diseases not provided for here, see the disease or group of diseases, e.g., shingles 616.522, herpes genitalis 616.9518

.911 22 *Infectious mononucleosis

.912 *Smallpox

For mild forms of smallpox, see 616.913

.913 *Mild forms of smallpox; cowpox

Including alastrim (amaas, Cuban itch, variola minor)

.914 *Chickenpox

.915 *Measles

.916 *Rubella

.918 *RNA virus infections

Including Colorado tick fever, hantavirus infections, Rift Valley fever

For a specific RNA virus infection not provided for here, see the infection, e.g., measles 616.915

*Add as instructed under 616.1–616.9

.918 5	*Flavivirus infections
.918 52	*Dengue
	Including dengue hemorrhagic fever
.918 54	*Yellow fever
.918 56	*West Nile fever
.918 8	*Retroviridae infections

> For a specific retroviridae infection not provided for here, see the infection, e.g., HIV infections 616.9792

.918 801	Medical microbiology of retroviridae

Number built according to instructions under 616.1–616.9

> For retroviridae as oncogenic viruses, see 616.994019

.92	*Bacterial diseases

Including pseudomonas infections, mycoplasma infections

Class here comprehensive works on gram-negative bacterial infections

> For a specific bacterial disease or group of bacterial diseases not provided for here, see the disease or group of diseases, e.g., bacterial skin diseases 616.523, brucellosis 616.957

.922	*Rickettsial diseases
.922 2	*Epidemic louse-borne typhus and endemic flea-borne typhus
.922 3	*Tick-borne rickettsia infections

Including boutonneuse fever

Class here North Queensland tick typhus, Rocky Mountain spotted fever

.922 4	*Tsutsugamushi disease (Scrub typhus)
.922 5	*Q fever
.923	*Pasteurella infections, yersinia infections, chlamydia infections, tularemia

Subdivisions are added for pasteurella infections, yersinia infections, chlamydia infections, tularemia together; for pasteurella infections alone

.923 2	*Plague
.923 5	*Chlamydia infections
.923 9	*Tularemia
.924	*Borrelia infections
.924 4	*Relapsing fevers
.924 6	*Lyme disease

*Add as instructed under 616.1–616.9

.926	*Escherichia coli infections
.927	*Salmonella infections
.927 2	*Typhoid fever
.927 4	*Paratyphoid fever
.929	*Gram-positive bacterial infections

> *For a specific gram-positive bacterial infection or group of gram-positive bacterial infections not provided for here, see the infection or group of infections, e.g., clostridium infections 616.931, anthrax 616.956*

.929 4	*Mycobacterium infections

> *For tuberculosis, see 616.995; for Hansen's disease, see 616.998*

.929 7	*Staphylococcal infections

> Including toxic shock syndrome

.929 8	*Streptococcal infections

> Including necrotizing fasciitis

.929 87	*Scarlet fever
.93	Clostridium infections, diphtheria, cholera, dysenteries, protozoan infections
.931	*Clostridium infections, diphtheria

> Class here bacillaceae infections, bacillary infections

> Subdivisions are added for clostridium infections and diphtheria together, for clostridium infections alone

> *For anthrax, see 616.956*

> *See also 616.9355 for bacillary dysentery*

.931 3	*Diphtheria
.931 5	*Botulism
.931 8	*Tetanus
.932	*Cholera
.935	*Dysenteries
.935 3	*Amebic dysentery
.935 5	*Bacillary dysentery (Shigellosis)
.936	*Protozoan infections

> Class giardiasis in 616.34

> *For amebic dysentery, see 616.9353*

*Add as instructed under 616.1–616.9

.936 2	*Malaria
.936 3	*Trypanosomiasis

> Class here African sleeping sickness (African trypanosomiasis), Chagas disease (South American trypanosomiasis)

.936 4	*Leishmaniasis

> Including cutaneous leishmaniasis (oriental sores), visceral leishmaniasis (kala-azar)

.94	*Bacterial blood diseases
.944	*Septicemia

> Including pyemia

> *For puerperal septicemia, see 618.74*

.95	Sexually transmitted diseases, zoonoses
.951	*Sexually transmitted diseases

> *For acquired immune deficiency syndrome (AIDS), see 616.9792*

.951 3	*Syphilis

> *For neurosyphilis, see 616.83*

.951 5	*Gonorrhea
.951 8	Other sexually transmitted diseases

> Including chancroid, condylomata acuminata (genital warts), herpes genitalis, lymphogranuloma venereum

> Class comprehensive works on chlamydia infections in 616.9235; class comprehensive works on human papillomavirus infections in 616.911; class comprehensive works on herpesvirus diseases in 616.9112

> *See also 616.522 for herpes labialis*

.953	*Rabies
.954	*Glanders
.956	*Anthrax
.957	*Brucellosis
.958	*Psittacosis
.959	*Zoonoses

> *For a specific zoonotic disease, see the disease, e.g., tularemia 616.9239, rabies 616.953*

---

*Add as instructed under 616.1–616.9

.96   *Parasitic diseases and diseases due to fungi (mycoses)

Class here medical parasitology

Subdivisions are added for parasitic diseases and diseases due to fungi together, for parasitic diseases alone

For parasitic skin diseases, see 616.57; for protozoan infections, see 616.936

>   616.962–616.968 Parasitic diseases

Class comprehensive works in 616.96

.962   *Diseases due to endoparasites

Class here comprehensive works on diseases due to worms

For a specific disease due to worms, see 616.963–616.965

>   616.963–616.965 Diseases due to worms

Class here medical helminthology

Class comprehensive works in 616.962

.963   *Diseases due to flukes (Trematode infections)

Including schistosomiasis (bilharziasis)

.964   *Diseases due to tapeworms (Cestode infections)

Including echinococcosis

.965   *Diseases due to roundworms (Nematode infections)

.965 2   *Diseases due to filariae

Including elephantiasis, onchocerciasis

Class here filariasis

.965 4   Diseases due to other nematodes

Including ascariasis, enterobiasis, hookworm infections, trichinosis

.968   *Diseases due to ectoparasites

Class here medical entomology

For a specific entomological disease, see the disease, e.g., lice infestations 616.572

.969   *Diseases due to fungi (Mycoses)

For fungal skin diseases, see 616.579

.969 3   *Candidiasis

---

*Add as instructed under 616.1–616.9

.97   *Diseases of immune system

    Class here comprehensive works on allergies

    Class sarcoidosis in 616.429

    For a specific allergy not provided for here, see the allergy, e.g., hay fever 616.202

.973   *Contact allergies

    Class here allergic contact dermatitis, allergies of skin

    Class comprehensive works on contact dermatitis in 616.51; class dermatological manifestations of food and drug allergies in 616.975

.975   *Food and drug allergies

    Class here allergies of digestive system

    Subdivisions are added for food and drug allergies together, for food allergies alone

.975 8   *Drug allergies

.978   *Autoimmune diseases

    Class here autoimmunity

    For a specific autoimmune disease, see the disease, e.g., systemic lupus erythematosus 616.772

.979   *Immune deficiency diseases

.979 2   *Acquired immune deficiency syndrome (AIDS)

    Class here HIV infections

.98   Noncommunicable diseases and environmental medicine

    Standard subdivisions are added for either or both topics in heading

    Including Persian Gulf syndrome

    Class here communicable diseases as part of environmental medicine, diseases due to stress

    For poisoning, see 615.9. For a specific noncommunicable or environmentally linked disease or type of disease provided for elsewhere, see the disease or type of disease, e.g., mental disorders 616.89, malaria 616.9362, cancer 616.994

.980 01–.980 08   Standard subdivisions

.980 09   History, geographic treatment, biography

[.980 091 1–.980 091 3]   Frigid, temperate, tropical zones

    Do not use; class in 616.9881–616.9883

*Add as instructed under 616.1–616.9

.980 2   Specialized medical fields

Including travel medicine

For industrial and occupational medicine, see 616.9803; for sports medicine, see 617.1027

.980 21   Aerospace medicine

.980 213   Aviation medicine

.980 214   Space medicine

.980 22   Submarine medicine

Class here diving medicine

Class diseases due to compression and decompression in 616.9894

.980 23   Military medicine

For naval medicine, see 616.98024

.980 24   Naval medicine

Class submarine medicine in 616.98022

.980 3   Industrial and occupational medicine

Standard subdivisions are added for either or both topics in heading

See also 613.62 for industrial and occupational health; also 615.902 for industrial toxicology

.988   *Diseases due to climate and weather

Class here medical climatology, medical meteorology

Subdivisions are added for either or both topics in heading

.988 1–.988 3   Diseases of frigid, temperate, tropical zones

Class here communicable diseases of frigid, temperate, tropical zones

Add to base number 616.988 the numbers following —1 in notation 11–13 from Table 2, e.g., diseases due to tropical climate 616.9883

.989   *Diseases due to heat, cold, motion, altitude, compression, decompression, sound, other vibrations, radiation

Including heat exhaustion, hypothermia

Class here comprehensive works on diseases due to physical forces

For diseases due to light, see 616.5; for chapping, chilblains, frostbite, see 616.58

.989 2   *Diseases due to motion

.989 3   *Diseases due to altitude

Class here mountain sickness

*Add as instructed under 616.1–616.9

.989 4   *Diseases due to compression and decompression

                              Subdivisions are added for either or both topics in heading

.989 6   *Diseases due to sound and diseases due to other vibrations

                              Subdivisions are added for diseases due to sound and diseases due to other vibrations together, for diseases due to sound alone

.989 7   *Diseases due to radiation

                              Class here radiation injuries

                              Class comprehensive works on radiation dosimetry in 612.01448

.99   Tumors and miscellaneous communicable diseases

                        Only those named below

[.990 1–.990 9]   Standard subdivisions

                              Do not use; class in 616.99

.991   *Rheumatic fever

.993   †Benign tumors

                        Variant name: benign neoplasms

                        Medical and surgical treatment

                        Including adenomas

.993 1–.993 9   Benign tumors of specific systems and organs

                        Add to base number 616.993 the numbers following 611 in 611.1–611.9, e.g., benign skin tumors 616.99377, neurofibromatosis 616.99383; then add further as instructed under 618.1–618.8, e.g., therapy for neurofibromatosis 616.9938306

.994   †Cancers

                        Variant names: malignant neoplasms, malignant tumors, neoplastic diseases

                        Medical and surgical treatment

                        Class here carcinoma, oncology, tumors

                        For benign tumors, see 616.993

.994 1   †Cancers of cardiovascular organs and blood

.994 11–.994 15   Cancers of cardiovascular organs

                        Add to base number 616.9941 the numbers following 611.1 in 611.11–611.15, e.g., cancer of heart 616.99412; then add further as instructed under 618.1–618.8, e.g., therapy for cancer of heart 616.9941206

*Add as instructed under 616.1–616.9
†Add as instructed under 618.1–618.8

.994 18	†Cancer of blood

Including multiple mycloma

For cancer of leukocytes, see 616.99419

.994 19	†Leukemia

Cancer of leukocytes

.994 2–.994 9	Cancers of other organs and of regions

Add to base number 616.994 the numbers following 611 in 611.2–611.9, e.g., breast cancer 616.99449; then for organs, systems, regions having their own number add further as instructed under 618.1–618.8, e.g., surgery for breast cancer 616.99449059
Subdivisions are added for a specific type of cancer if subdivisions are added for comprehensive works on cancer of the organ or region, e.g., surgery for Hodgkin disease (a cancer of lymphatic glands) 616.99446059

.995	*Tuberculosis

Class here pulmonary tuberculosis

.995 1	Tuberculosis of cardiovascular system

Add to base number 616.9951 the numbers following 611.1 in 611.11–611.15, e.g., tuberculosis of heart 616.99512; then add further as instructed under 616.1–616.9, e.g., therapy for tuberculosis of heart 616.9951206

.995 2	Tuberculosis of respiratory system

.995 21–.995 23	Tuberculosis of nose and nasal accessory sinuses, of larynx, of trachea and bronchi

Add to base number 616.9952 the numbers following 611.2 in 611.21–611.23, e.g., laryngeal tuberculosis 616.99522; then add further as instructed under 616.1–616.9, e.g., therapy for laryngeal tuberculosis 616.9952206

.995 25–.995 27	Tuberculosis of pleura, diaphragm, mediastinum

Add to base number 616.9952 the numbers following 611.2 in 611.25–611.27, e.g., pleural tuberculosis 616.99525; then add further as instructed under 616.1–616.9, e.g., therapy for pleural tuberculosis 616.9952506

.995 3–.995 9	Tuberculosis of other specific systems and organs

Add to base number 616.995 the numbers following 611 in 611.3–611.9, e.g., tuberculosis of teeth and surrounding tissues 616.995314, of bones 616.99571, of eyes 616.99584, of ears 616.99585; then add further as instructed under 616.1–616.9, e.g., therapy for tuberculosis of bones 616.9957106

.998	*Hansen's disease (Leprosy)

*Add as instructed under 616.1–616.9
†Add as instructed under 618.1–618.8

617   **Surgery, regional medicine, dentistry, ophthalmology, otology, audiology**

Standard subdivisions are added for surgery alone; however, do not add for surgery, regional medicine, dentistry, ophthalmology, otology, audiology together; class in 616.001–616.009

Except where contrary instructions are given, all notes under 616.02–616.08 and in table under 616.1–616.9 are applicable here

Except for modifications shown under specific entries, add to each subdivision identified by * as follows:

001–007	Standard subdivisions
	As modified under 616.1–616.9
008	Groups of people
0083	Young people
	Notation 0083 is used for pediatric aspects of specific kinds of wounds and injuries, e.g., burns and scalds in children 617.110083; for surgery of a specific organ, system, disorder, e.g., brain surgery in children 617.4810083; for specific aspects of pediatric dentistry, e.g., caries in children 617.670083
	Class comprehensive works on pediatric dentistry in 617.645; class comprehensive works on surgery for infants and children up to puberty in 617.98; class comprehensive works on pediatrics in 618.92; class regional medicine, ophthalmology, otology, audiology for infants and children up to puberty in 618.92097
00835	Young people twelve to twenty
	Notation 00835 is used for adolescent medicine aspects of all topics in 617, e.g., brain surgery in adolescents 617.48100835, comprehensive works on surgery for adolescents 617.00835
0084	People in specific stages of adulthood
00846	People in late adulthood
	Notation 00846 is used for geriatric aspects of specific kinds of wounds and injuries, e.g., burns and scalds in late adulthood 617.1100846; for surgery of a specific organ, system, disorder, e.g., heart surgery in late adulthood 617.41200846
	Class comprehensive works on geriatric surgery in 617.97; class comprehensive works on geriatrics in 618.97; class regional medicine, dentistry, ophthalmology, otology, audiology for people in late adulthood in 618.9775–618.9778

(continued)

617 Surgery, regional medicine, dentistry, ophthalmology, otology, audiology (continued)

0088	Occupational and religious groups
0088355	Military personnel
	Class military surgery in 617.99
[009]	History, geographic treatment, biography
	Do not use; class in 09
>01–03	Surgical complications, preoperative, intraoperative, postoperative care, special topics, rehabilitation
	Class surgical complications, preoperative, intraoperative, postoperative care, special topics, rehabilitation applied to special classes of diseases in 04; class comprehensive works in 617, without adding from this table
01	Surgical complications; preoperative, intraoperative, postoperative care
	Standard subdivisions are added for any or all topics in heading
	Including surgical shock; complicating preconditions, e.g., heart problems
	Class intensive care in 028
02	Special topics
023	Personnel
0231	Nurses
	Class here specific surgical nursing specialties; nature of duties, characteristics of profession, relationships; works that emphasize technology of operations performed by nurses, e.g., works that emphasize techniques used by a heart surgery nurse 617.4120231
	Class works that emphasize a specific technique used by nurses with the technique, e.g., nursing diagnosis 075, nursing diagnosis with respect to gunshot wounds 617.145075
0232	Physicians
	Class here nature of duties, characteristics of profession, relationships
	Do not use for works that emphasize technology of operations performed by physicians; class with the subject without 0232, e.g., works that emphasize techniques used by a physician with respect to gunshot wounds 617.145
	Class works that emphasize a specific technique used by physicians with the technique, e.g., diagnosis by a physician 075, diagnosis by a physician with respect to gunshot wounds 617.145075
0233	Allied health personnel
	Class here nature of duties, characteristics of profession, relationships; works that emphasize technology of operations performed by allied health personnel, e.g., works that emphasize techniques used by allied health personnel with respect to gunshot wounds 617.1450233
	Class works that emphasize a specific technique used by allied health personnel with the technique, e.g., diagnosis by allied health personnel 075, diagnosis by allied health personnel with respect to gunshot wounds 617.145075
02332	Physician assistants

(continued)

617   **Surgery, regional medicine, dentistry, ophthalmology, otology, audiology (continued)**

024	Domestic medicine
	For first aid, see 0262
026	Emergencies
0262	First aid
027	Experimental medicine
028	Intensive care
03	Rehabilitation
	Including self-help devices for people with disabilities
	Class rehabilitative therapy in 06
04	Special classes of diseases
	Limited to the classes named below
042	Genetic diseases (Hereditary diseases)
0421–0423	Surgical complications, preoperative, intraoperative, postoperative care, special topics, rehabilitation
	Add to 042 the numbers following 0 in notation 01–03 from table under 617, e.g., experimental medicine for genetic diseases 04227
0425–0428	Preventive measures, surgery, therapy, pathology, psychosomatic medicine
	Add to 042 the numbers following 0 in notation 05–08 from table under 617, e.g., diagnosis of genetic diseases 04275
043	Congenital diseases
	Add to 043 the numbers following 042 in notation 0421–0428 from table under 617, e.g., experimental medicine for congenital diseases 04327
	Class congenital diseases of genetic origin in 042
044	Injuries and wounds
	Including results of injuries and wounds
	Class here trauma
	Add to 044 the numbers following 042 in notation 0421–0428 from table under 617, e.g., experimental medicine for injuries 04427
	Subdivisions are added for either or both topics in heading
	See also 01 for surgical shock
>05–08	Preventive measures, surgery, therapy, pathology, psychosomatic medicine
	Class preventive measures, surgery, pathology, psychosomatic medicine applied to special classes of diseases in 04; class comprehensive works on prevention, therapy, etiology of a specific disease or kind of disease if all related to a specific kind of therapy in 061–069, e.g., diet therapy 0654; class comprehensive works in 617, without adding from this table
05	Preventive measures and surgery
052	Preventive measures
	By individuals and by medical personnel
	Class public measures for preventing specific diseases in 614.5; class comprehensive works on prevention in 613. Class a specific kind of therapy used for prevention with the kind of therapy in 061–069, e.g., drug therapy 061

(continued)

617 Surgery, regional medicine, dentistry, ophthalmology, otology, audiology (continued)

059   Surgery
> Limited to operative surgery
> Including surgery utilizing specific instruments or techniques, e.g., catheterization, cryosurgery, microsurgery, radiosurgery
> Class laser microsurgery in 0598; class nonoperative physical procedures in 06
>> *For surgical complications; preoperative, intraoperative, postoperative care, see 01*

0592   Cosmetic and restorative plastic surgery, transplantation of tissue and organs, implantation of artificial organs
> Including implantation and removal of prostheses, other medical devices

0597   Endoscopic surgery

0598   Laser surgery
> Including laser coagulation
> Class here laser microsurgery

06   Therapy
> Class here rehabilitative therapy
> Class comprehensive works on rehabilitative therapy and training for people with a specific disease or kind of disease in 03; class comprehensive works on prevention, therapy, etiology of a specific disease or kind of disease if all related to a specific kind of therapy in 061–069, e.g., diet therapy 0654
>> *For surgery, see 059*
>> *See Manual at 617: Add table: 06*

060724   Experimental research
> Class here clinical trials
> Class clinical trials of a specific kind of therapy with the kind of therapy, plus notation 0724 from Table 1, e.g., clinical drug trials 0610724

>061–069   Specific therapies
> Class here specific kinds of therapy used for prevention; comprehensive works on prevention, therapy, etiology if these all relate to a specific kind of therapy, e.g., nutritional aspects of a disease and diet therapy 0654

061   Drug therapy

0610724   Experimental research
> Class here clinical drug trials

062–069   Other therapies
> Add to 06 the numbers following 615.8 in 615.82–615.89, e.g., X-ray therapy 06422, rehabilitative activity therapies 06515

07   Pathology

071   Etiology
> Including effects of poisons on specific systems and organs as cause of disease
> Class social factors contributing to spread of a disease in 362.19; class comprehensive works on medical toxicology in 615.9

075–079   Diagnosis, prognosis, death, immunity
> Add to 07 the numbers following 616.07 in 616.075–616.079, e.g., physical diagnosis 0754

(continued)

617   Surgery, regional medicine, dentistry, ophthalmology, otology, audiology (continued)

08   Psychosomatic medicine
09   History, geographic treatment, biography
0901–0905   Historical periods
                Add to 09 the numbers following —090 in notation
                0901–0905 from Table 1, e.g., the subject in late 20th century
                09045
091–099   Geographic treatment and biography
                Add to 09 notation 1–9 from Table 2, e.g., the subject in India
                0954

Class comprehensive works on minor surgery in 617.024; class comprehensive works on emergency surgery in 617.026; class comprehensive works on surgery by instrument and technique in 617.05; class comprehensive works on surgical pathology in 617.07; class comprehensive works on operative surgery and special fields of surgery in 617.9

For surgical treatment of tumors, see 616.993–616.994

See Manual at 618.92097 vs. 617; also at 618.977 vs. 617

SUMMARY

617.001–.008   **Standard subdivisions of surgery**
.02–.09   **General topics of surgery; history, geographic treatment, biography of
                surgery**
.1   **Injuries and wounds**
.2   **Results of injuries and wounds**
.4   **Surgery by systems**
.5   **Regional medicine**
.6   **Dentistry**
.7   **Ophthalmology**
.8   **Otology and audiology**
.9   **Operative surgery and special fields of surgery**

>   617.001–617.008 Standard subdivisions of surgery

            Class comprehensive works in 617

.001   Philosophy and theory of surgery

.002   Miscellany of surgery

[.002 3]   Surgery as a profession, occupation, hobby

                    Do not use; class in 617.023

[.002 8]   Auxiliary techniques and procedures; apparatus, equipment, materials

                    Do not use; class in 617.9

[.002 87]   Testing and measurement

                    Do not use; class in 617.075

.003–.007   Standard subdivisions of surgery

.008   Surgery for groups of people

.008 3   Young people

Do not use for surgery for infants and children up to puberty; class in 617.98

.008 35   Young people twelve to twenty

Do not use for comprehensive works on surgery for young people twelve to twenty who have not reached puberty; class in 617.98

Class here adolescent surgery

.008 4   People in specific stages of adulthood

[.008 46]   People in late adulthood

Do not use; class in 617.97

.008 8   Occupational and religious groups

[.008 835 5]   Military personnel

Do not use; class in 617.99

[.009]   History, geographic treatment, biography of surgery

Do not use; class in 617.09

\>   617.02–617.09   General topics of surgery; history, geographic treatment, biography of surgery

Class comprehensive works in 617

.02   Special topics of surgery

.023   Personnel

.023 1   Surgical nurses

Class here general surgical nursing, general works that emphasize technology of operations performed by surgical nurses; nature of duties, characteristics of profession, relationships

Class works that emphasize a specific technique used by surgical nurses with the technique, e.g., physical diagnosis by surgical nurses 617.0754

.023 2   Surgeons

Class here nature of duties, characteristics of profession, relationships

Do not use for general works on technology of operations that surgeons perform; class in 617

Class works that emphasize a specific technique used by surgeons with the technique, e.g., physical diagnosis by surgeons 617.0754

.023 3   Surgical allied health personnel

> Class here nature of duties, characteristics of profession, relationships of surgical technicians and assistants; general works that emphasize technology of operations performed by surgical technicians and assistants

> Class works that emphasize a specific technique used by surgical technicians and assistants with the technique, e.g., techniques of sterilization for surgery by surgical assistants 617.9101

.023 32   Surgical physician assistants

> Class here nature of duties, characteristics of profession, relationships; general works that emphasize technology of operations performed by surgical physician assistants

> Class works that emphasize a specific technique used by surgical physician assistants with the technique, e.g., physical diagnosis by surgical physician assistants 617.0754

.024   Minor surgery

> Class here outpatient surgery

.026   Emergency surgery

.03   Rehabilitation

> Class here comprehensive works on rehabilitation

> Class rehabilitative therapy in 617.06. Class rehabilitation from a specific disease or injury with the disease or injury in 616–618, plus notation 03 from table under 616.1–616.9, notation 03 from table under 617, or notation 03 from table under 618.1–618.8, e.g., rehabilitation for patients with heart disease 616.1203

.033   Self-help devices for people with disabilities

> Including wheelchairs

> *For orthopedic self-help devices for people with disabilities, see 617.9*

.05   Surgery utilizing specific instruments and techniques or specific groups of instruments and techniques

> Including catheterization, cryosurgery, microsurgery; geriatric surgery, pediatric surgery, or military surgery utilizing a specific instrument or technique not provided in 617.91–617.96

> Class radiosurgery in 617.481059

.057   Endoscopic surgery

> Class comprehensive works on endoscopy in 616.07545

.058   Laser surgery

> Including laser coagulation

> Class here laser microsurgery

.06   Nonsurgical therapy

                Class here rehabilitative therapy

                Add to base number 617.06 the numbers following 615.8 in 615.82–615.89, e.g., X-ray therapy 617.06422, rehabilitative activity therapies in 617.06515

                Class comprehensive works on rehabilitative therapy and training in 617.03

.07   Pathology

                Add to base number 617.07 the numbers following 616.07 in 616.071–616.079, e.g., physical diagnosis 617.0754

.075   Diagnosis and prognosis

                Number built according to instructions under 617.07

                Class comprehensive works on a diagnostic technique used in general medicine, including techniques that involve minor surgery, with the technique in 616.075, e.g., biopsy 616.0758

.09   History, geographic treatment, biography of surgery

.090 1–.090 5   Historical periods

                Add to base number 617.090 the numbers following —090 in notation 0901–0905 from Table 1, e.g., history of surgery in late 20th century 617.09045

.091–.099   Geographic treatment and biography

                Add to base number 617.09 notation 1–9 from Table 2, e.g., collected biographies of surgeons 617.0922

.1   **Injuries and wounds**

                Standard subdivisions are added for either or both topics in heading

                Class here traumatology

                Class frostbite in 616.58; class heat stress disorders in 616.989; class motion sickness in 616.9892; class results of injuries and wounds in 617.2

                For injuries and wounds of a specific system, region, or organ, see the system, region, or organ in 617.4–617.5, plus notation 044 from table under 617, e.g., thoracic injuries 617.54044

.100 1–.100 9   Standard subdivisions

.102   Special topics of injuries and wounds

.102 6   Emergencies

.102 62   First aid

                For first aid for a specific type of injury or wound, see the type, plus notation 0262 from table under 617, e.g., first aid for athletic injuries 617.1027, first aid for gunshot wounds 617.1450262

.102 7   Athletic and dance injuries

> Standard subdivisions are added for athletic and dance injuries together, for athletic injuries alone

> Class here sports medicine

> Class a specific branch of sports medicine with the branch, e.g., promotion of health of athletes 613.711

.102 75   Dance injuries

.102 76–.102 79   Injuries associated with specific kinds of sports

> Add to base number 617.1027 the numbers following 79 in 796–799, e.g., skiing injuries 617.1027693

.102 8   Crash injuries

> Injuries resulting from transportation accidents

.103   Rehabilitation

> Including self-help devices for people with disabilities

> Class rehabilitative therapy in 617.106

.106   Nonsurgical therapy

> Class here rehabilitative therapy

> Add to base number 617.106 the numbers following 615.8 in 615.82–615.89, e.g., therapeutic massage 617.10622, rehabilitative activity therapies 617.106515

> Class comprehensive works on rehabilitative therapy and training in 617.103

.107   Pathology

> Add to base number 617.107 the numbers following 616.07 in 616.071–616.079, e.g., physical diagnosis 617.10754

.11   *Burns and scalds

> Subdivisions are added for either or both topics in heading

> Class burns and scalds resulting from injuries from electricity in 617.12

.12   *Injuries from electricity

.13   *Abrasions, contusions, lacerations

> Subdivisions are added for any or all topics in heading

.14   *Penetrating wounds

.143   *Incisions and punctures

> Class here needlestick injuries, stab wounds

> Subdivisions are added for either or both topics in heading

*Add as instructed under 617

.145   *Gunshot wounds

.15   Fractures

> Add to base number 617.15 the numbers following 611.71 in 611.711–611.718, e.g., fracture of femur 617.158

.16   *Dislocations

.17   *Sprains and strains

> Subdivisions are added for either or both topics in heading

.172   *Cumulative trauma disorders

> Variant names: overuse injuries, repetitive strain injuries

> *For a specific cumulative trauma disorder, see the disorder, e.g., carpal tunnel syndrome 616.856*

.18   *Asphyxia

> Including drowning, near drowning

.19   *Blast injuries

> *For a specific kind of blast injuries, see the kind of injury, e.g., fractures 617.15*

.2   Results of injuries and wounds

> Standard subdivisions are added for either or both topics in heading

> *For results of injuries and wounds of a specific system, region, or organ, see the system, region, or organ in 617.4–617.5, plus notation 044 from table under 617, e.g., results of thoracic injuries 617.54044*

> *See also 617.103 for rehabilitation; also 617.106 for rehabilitative therapy*

.21   Traumatic and surgical shock

> Standard subdivisions are added for either or both topics in heading

> Class comprehensive medical works on shock in 616.0475

.22   Fever, infections, inflammation

> *See also 617.9195 for fever, infections, inflammation as surgical complications*

> **617.4–617.5   Surgery by systems and regions**

> Class here injuries and wounds of specific systems, regions, organs; surgery of specific organs

> Class comprehensive works in 617

*Add as instructed under 617

.4   **Surgery by systems**

> *For respiratory system, see 617.54*

> *See Manual at 612.1–612.8; also at 616 vs. 617.4*

SUMMARY

617.41	**Cardiovascular system**
.43	**Digestive system**
.44	**Blood-forming, lymphatic, glandular systems**
.46	**Urogenital system**
.47	**Musculoskeletal system, integument**
.48	**Nervous system**

.41   †Cardiovascular system

.412   †Heart

> Class implantation of heart pacers in 617.4120592; class functioning of heart pacers in 617.4120645

.413   †Arteries

> Class here comprehensive works on surgery of blood vessels (vascular surgery)

> Class surgery of blood vessels in a specific system or organ with the system or organ, e.g., cerebrovascular surgery 617.481

> *For veins, see 617.414; for capillaries, see 617.415*

.414   †Veins

.415   †Capillaries

.43   †Digestive system

> Including surgical treatment of morbid obesity

> *For surgery of specific organs of digestive system, see 617.5*

> *See also 617.952 for lipectomy*

.44   †Blood-forming, lymphatic, glandular systems

> Class here endocrine system

> *For surgery of a specific gland, see the gland, e.g., thyroid gland 617.539*

.441   †Bone marrow

.46   †Urogenital system

> *For gynecologic and obstetrical surgery, see 618*

---

†Add as instructed under 617, except use 059 by itself only for surgery utilizing specific instruments or techniques and do not use 06 by itself

.461	†Kidneys, adrenal glands, ureters

Class here comprehensive works on surgery of urinary organs

Subdivisions are added for kidneys, adrenal glands, ureters together; for kidneys alone

Class hemodialysis, peritoneal dialysis in 617.461059

For bladder and urethra, see 617.462

.462	†Bladder and urethra

.463	†Male genital organs

Including circumcision; surgical methods of birth control in males, vasectomy

.47	†Musculoskeletal system, integument

Class here orthopedic surgery

Subdivisions are added for musculoskeletal system, integument together; for musculoskeletal system alone

Class orthopedic regional surgery in 617.5

For amputations, see 617.58059

.471	†Bones

Class chronic diseases of skeletal system in 616.71; class spine surgery involving both spinal column and spinal cord in 617.56059

For skull, see 617.514; for jaws, see 617.522

See also 617.441 for bone marrow

.471 044	Injuries and wounds

Number built according to instructions under 617

For fractures, see 617.15

.472	†Joints

For jaws, see 617.522; for joints of extremities, see 617.58

.472 044	Injuries and wounds

Number built according to instructions under 617

For dislocations, see 617.16

.473	†Muscles

.473 044	Injuries and wounds

Number built according to instructions under 617

For sprains and strains, see 617.17

---

†Add as instructed under 617, except use 059 by itself only for surgery utilizing specific instruments or techniques and do not use 06 by itself

.474	†Tendons
.475	†Bursae
.477	†Integument

Including surgery of nails

Class here surgery of skin

.477 044	Injuries and wounds

Number built according to instructions under 617

For abrasions, see 617.13

.477 9	†Hair

Including removal

.48	†Nervous system

Class here neurosurgery

For ophthalmologic surgery, see 617.71; for otologic surgery, see 617.8059

.481	†Brain

Including psychosurgery

.481 03	Rehabilitation

Number built according to instructions under 617

Class rehabilitation of brain-injured patients in 617.4810443

.482	†Spinal cord

Including surgical treatment of spina bifida

Class surgery involving both spinal column and spinal cord in 617.56059

.483	†Nerves

Class surgery of nerves of a specific system or organ with the system or organ, e.g., neuromuscular surgery 617.473

.5 Regional medicine

Class here regional surgery; orthopedic regional medicine, orthopedic regional surgery

Class nonsurgical medicine of specific systems or organs in specific regions in 616; except as provided for below, class surgery of a specific system in a specific region in 617.4

See also 617.15 for fractures

See Manual at 617.5

---

†Add as instructed under 617, except use 059 by itself only for surgery utilizing specific instruments or techniques and do not use 06 by itself

SUMMARY

617.508	**Groups of people**
.51	**Head**
.52	**Face**
.53	**Neck**
.54	**Thorax (Chest) and respiratory system**
.55	**Abdominal and pelvic cavities**
.56	**Back**
.57	**Upper extremities**
.58	**Lower extremities**

.508 3   Young people

> Do not use for nonsurgical regional medicine of infants and children up to puberty, comprehensive works on child and adolescent medicine; class in 618.920975

.508 35   Young people twelve to twenty

> Do not use for nonsurgical regional medicine of young people twelve to twenty who have not reached puberty; class in 618.920975

> Class here comprehensive works on nonsurgical regional medicine of adolescents

.508 4   People in specific stages of adulthood

.508 46   People in late adulthood

> Do not use for nonsurgical regional medicine; class in 618.9775

.51   *Head

> Class here otolaryngology, otorhinolaryngology, comprehensive works on diseases of ears, nose, throat

> *For face, see 617.52; for throat, see 617.531; for eyes, see 617.7; for ears, see 617.8*

.514   †Skull

> Limited to surgery

> Class here skull base

.52   *Face

> Class eyes in 617.7

.522   *Oral region

> Including lips, tongue, jaws, parotid gland

> Class nonsurgical works on mouth as a digestive organ in 616.31

> *For teeth, see 617.6*

---

*Add as instructed under 617

†Add as instructed under 617, except use 059 by itself only for surgery utilizing specific instruments or techniques and do not use 06 by itself

.522 059		Surgery

> Number built according to instructions under 617
>
> Class comprehensive works on kinds of oral surgery commonly performed by dentists in 617.605. Class a specific kind of oral surgery performed by dentists with the kind in 617.6, e.g., periodontal surgery 617.632059, tooth extraction 617.66

.522 5	*Palate
.523	*Nose

> Class here comprehensive works on nose and throat
>
> Class comprehensive works on diseases of ears, nose, throat in 617.51
>
> *For throat, see 617.531*

.53	*Neck
.531	*Throat

> *For pharynx, see 617.532; for larynx and trachea, see 617.533*

.532	†Pharynx

> Limited to surgery
>
> Including tonsils

.533	†Larynx and trachea

> Limited to surgery
>
> Including epiglottis, vocal cords

.539	†Thyroid and parathyroid glands

> Limited to surgery

.54	*Thorax (Chest) and respiratory system

> Regional medicine and surgery of thorax; surgery of respiratory system
>
> Subdivisions are added for thorax and respiratory system together, for thorax alone
>
> *For surgery of heart, see 617.412; for surgery of nose, see 617.523; for surgery of larynx and trachea, see 617.533*

.542	†Lungs

> Limited to surgery

.543	†Pleura

> Limited to surgery

---

*Add as instructed under 617

†Add as instructed under 617, except use 059 by itself only for surgery utilizing specific instruments or techniques and do not use 06 by itself

.544	†Bronchi
	Limited to surgery
.545	†Mediastinum
	Limited to surgery
.546	†Thymus gland
	Limited to surgery
.547	†Diaphragm
	Limited to surgery
.548	†Esophagus
	Limited to surgery
.549	†Male breast
	Limited to surgery
	Class comprehensive works on surgery of breast in 618.19059
.55	*Abdominal and pelvic cavities
	For urogenital system, see 617.46
.551	†Spleen
	Limited to surgery
.553	†Stomach
	Limited to surgery
	Including pylorus
.554	†Intestine
	Limited to surgery
.554 1	†Small intestine
	Limited to surgery
	Including duodenum, jejunum, ileum
.554 5	†Cecum, vermiform appendix
	Limited to surgery
	Subdivisions are added for either or both topics in heading

---

*Add as instructed under 617
†Add as instructed under 617, except use 059 by itself only for surgery utilizing specific instruments or techniques and do not use 06 by itself

.554 7	†Large intestine
	Limited to surgery
	Including sigmoid colon
	Class here colon

For cecum and vermiform appendix, see 617.5545; for rectum, see 617.555

.555	†Rectum, anus, perineum
	Limited to surgery
	Subdivisions are added for rectum, anus, perineum together; for rectum alone

.556	†Biliary tract and liver
	Limited to surgery
	Subdivisions are added for biliary tract and liver together, for biliary tract alone

.556 2	†Liver
	Limited to surgery

.556 5	†Gallbladder
	Limited to surgery

.556 7	†Bile ducts
	Limited to surgery

.557	†Pancreas and islands of Langerhans
	Limited to surgery
	Subdivisions are added for pancreas and islands of Langerhans together, for pancreas alone

.558	†Peritoneum
	Limited to surgery
	Including mesentery, omentum

.559	*Hernias in abdominal region
	Including hiatal hernia
	Class here inguinal hernia

.56	*Back
	Class shoulders in 617.572; class hips in 617.581

.564	*Backache

*Add as instructed under 617
†Add as instructed under 617, except use 059 by itself only for surgery utilizing specific instruments or techniques and do not use 06 by itself

.57   *Upper extremities

        Class here surgery of joints of upper extremities

        Class comprehensive works on extremities in 617.58; class comprehensive works on amputations, on surgery of joints of extremities in 617.58059

.572   *Shoulders

.574   *Arms, elbows, wrists

        Subdivisions are added for arms, elbows, wrists together; for arms alone

        Class carpal tunnel syndrome in 616.856

.575   *Hands

        Class carpal tunnel syndrome in 616.856

.58   *Lower extremities

        Class here legs; comprehensive works on extremities, on paraplegia

        Class works about "legs" when used to mean segment of lower limb between knee and ankle in 617.584

        For neurological aspects of paraplegia, see 616.842; for upper extremities, see 617.57

        See also 616.72 for nonsurgical medical aspects of joints

.580 59   Surgery

           Number built according to instructions under 617

           Class here comprehensive works on amputations, on surgery of joints of extremities

           For amputations of upper extremities, surgery of joints of upper extremities, see 617.57059. For surgery of a specific joint, see the joint, e.g., surgery of knees 617.582059

.581   *Hips

.582   *Knees and thighs

        Subdivisions are added for knees and thighs together, for knees alone

.584   *Legs between knee and ankle, ankles

.585   *Feet

        Class here podiatry

.6   ***Dentistry**

.600 83   Young people

           Do not use for dentistry for infants and children up to puberty; class in 617.645

---

*Add as instructed under 617

.600 835   Young people twelve to twenty

> Do not use for dentistry for young people twelve to twenty who have not reached puberty; class in 617.645

> Class here adolescent dentistry

.601   Oral hygiene and preventive dentistry

> Do not use for surgical complications, preoperative, intraoperative, postoperative care; class in 617.605

> Standard subdivisions are added for either or both topics in heading

> Class here dental hygiene

.605   Surgery

> Number built according to instructions under 617

> Do not use for preventive measures; class in 617.601

> Including surgical complications; preoperative, intraoperative, postoperative care

> > *For a specific kind of dental surgery, see the kind, e.g., extractions 617.66, dental implantation 617.693*

[.605 9]   Surgery

> Do not use; class in 617.605

.63   *Dental diseases

> Class here diseases of teeth

> > *For tumors of teeth and surrounding tissues, see 616.994314; for tuberculosis of teeth and surrounding tissues, see 616.995314*

.632   *Diseases of gums and tooth sockets

> Including gingivitis, periapical abscesses, periodontitis

> Class here periodontics

> Subdivisions are added for either or both topics in heading

.634   *Diseases of tooth tissues

> Including diseases of cementum, dentin, enamel

> > *For caries, see 617.67*

.634 2   *Diseases of dental pulp

> Class here endodontics

.64   Orthodontics and pediatric dentistry

.643   *Orthodontics

---

*Add as instructed under 617

.645	*Pediatric dentistry

Class here comprehensive works on pediatric and adolescent dentistry

For adolescent dentistry, see 617.600835. For a specific aspect of pediatric dentistry, see the aspect, plus notation 0083 from table under 617, e.g., periodontics for children 617.6320083

.66	*Extraction

Class here exodontics

.67	*Caries (Cavities)
.672	Preparation and treatment

Standard subdivisions are added for either or both topics in heading

.675	Fillings and inlays

Standard subdivisions are added for either or both topics in heading

Including metallic and ceramic fillings and inlays

.69	Prosthodontics

Class here dental restoration

For fillings and inlays, see 617.675

.690 284	Apparatus and equipment

Do not use for materials; class in 617.695

.692	Dentures, bridges, crowns

Standard subdivisions are added for dentures, bridges, crowns; for dentures alone

For implant-supported dentures, see 617.693

.692 2	Crowns
.693	Dental implantation

Class here dental implants, implant-supported dentures

.695	Materials

Class here dental materials used for dental restoration

For materials used as fillings and inlays, see 617.675

.7	***Ophthalmology**

Class here eye diseases

For tumors of eyes, see 616.99484; for tuberculosis of eyes, see 616.99584

[.704 4]	Injuries and wounds

Do not use; class in 617.713

*Add as instructed under 617

[.705 9]	Surgery

> Do not use; class in 617.71

[.707]	Pathology

> Do not use; class in 617.71

.71	Pathology and surgery of eyes

> Class surgical complications; preoperative, intraoperative, postoperative care in 617.701. Class pathology and surgery of a specific disease or part of eyes with the disease or part, e.g., diagnosis of glaucoma 617.741075

.712	*Blindness and partial blindness

> Subdivisions are added for either or both topics in heading

> > *See also 617.75 for disorders of refraction and accommodation, color vision defects*

.713	*Injuries and wounds

> Class here trauma

> Subdivisions are added for either or both topics in heading

.715	Diagnosis and prognosis

> Add to base number 617.715 the numbers following 616.075 in 616.0751–616.0759, e.g., physical diagnosis 617.7154
> > Subdivisions are added for diagnosis and prognosis together, for diagnosis alone

.719	*Diseases of corneas and scleras

> Subdivisions are added for corneas and scleras together, for corneas alone

> > *See also 362.1783 for eye banks*

.72	*Diseases of uveas

> Including diseases of choroids, ciliary bodies, irises

.73	*Diseases of optic nerves, of retinas
.732	*Diseases of optic nerves

> Class diseases of ocular neuromuscular mechanism in 617.762

.735	*Diseases of retinas
.74	*Diseases of eyeballs

> > *For diseases of corneas and scleras, see 617.719; for diseases of uveas, see 617.72; for diseases of retinas, see 617.735*

.741	*Glaucoma
.742	*Diseases of crystalline lenses

> Class here cataracts

*Add as instructed under 617

.742 059 2	Cosmetic and restorative plastic surgery, transplantation of tissue and organs, implantation of artificial organs

Number built according to instructions under 617

Do not use for implantation of intraocular lenses; class in 617.7524

.746	*Diseases of vitreous bodies
.75	Disorders of refraction and accommodation, color vision defects

Class here optometry

See also 617.712 for blindness and partial blindness

.750 3	Rehabilitation

Number built according to instructions under 617

Do not use for eyeglasses, contact lenses; class in 617.752

.752	Eyeglasses, contact lenses, intraocular lenses

Class here opticianry

.752 2	Eyeglasses
.752 3	Contact lenses
.752 4	Intraocular lenses

Including implantation of intraocular lenses

.755	Disorders of refraction and accommodation

Including astigmatism, hyperopia, myopia, presbyopia

For correction of disorders of refraction or accommodation by eyeglasses, contact lenses, intraocular lenses, see 617.752; for aniseikonia, see 617.758. For surgical correction of disorders of refraction or accommodation, see the specific part of the eye upon which surgery is done, e.g., surgery on corneas to correct myopia 617.719059

.758	Aniseikonia
.759	Color vision defects
.76	Diseases of ocular neuromuscular mechanism and lacrimal apparatus
.762	*Diseases of ocular neuromuscular mechanism

Including diplopia, strabismus

Class here ocular motility disorders, orthoptics

.764	*Diseases of lacrimal apparatus

For Sjogren's syndrome, see 616.775

.77	Diseases of eyelids and conjunctivas

*Add as instructed under 617

.771	*Diseases of eyelids
.772	*Trachoma
.773	*Conjunctivitis

> For trachoma, see 617.772

.78	*Diseases of orbits
.79	Artificial eyes

> Class intraocular lenses in 617.7524; class orbital implants in 617.780592

.8   *Otology and audiology

> Class here deafness, partial hearing loss

> Subdivisions are added for either or both topics in heading

> *For tumors of ears, see 616.99485; for tuberculosis of ears, see 616.99585*

.803	Rehabilitation

> Number built according to instructions under 617

> Do not use for hearing aids; class in 617.89

.81	*Diseases of external ears

> *For diseases of auricles, see 617.82; for diseases of auditory canals, see 617.83*

.82	*Diseases of auricles
.83	*Diseases of auditory canals
.84	*Diseases of middle ears

> *For diseases of tympanic membranes, see 617.85; for diseases of eustachian tubes, see 617.86; for diseases of mastoid processes, see 617.87*

.842	*Diseases of ossicles
.85	*Diseases of tympanic membranes
.86	*Diseases of eustachian tubes
.87	*Diseases of mastoid processes
.88	*Diseases of internal ears and of aural nervous system
.882	*Diseases of internal ears

> Including Meniere's disease; semicircular canals, vestibules

> Class here diseases of labyrinths

> Class vertigo as a symptom of neurological disease in 616.841; class motion sickness in 616.9892

.882 2	*Diseases of cochleas

*Add as instructed under 617

.886   *Diseases of aural nervous system

                   Including sensorineural hearing loss

.89   Correction of impaired hearing

                   Including hearing aids

                   *For surgical methods of correction that are limited to a specific part
                   of the hearing apparatus, see the part in 617.81–617.88, plus notation
                   059 from table under 617, e.g., cochlear implants 617.88220592; for
                   nonsurgical methods of correction that are limited to a specific part
                   of the hearing apparatus, see the part in 617.81–617.88, plus notation
                   06 from table under 617, e.g., drug therapy for diseases of middle ears
                   617.84061*

.9   Operative surgery and special fields of surgery

                   Class here orthopedic equipment; auxiliary techniques and procedures;
                   apparatus, equipment, materials; comprehensive works on surgical equipment,
                   on prostheses

                   Class comprehensive works on orthopedic and nonorthopedic self-help devices
                   for people with disabilities in 617.033

                   *For a specific piece of equipment or prosthesis, see the use of the equipment
                   or prosthesis, e.g., dentures 617.692*

SUMMARY

617.91	**Operative surgery**
.93	**Surgical dressings**
.95	**Cosmetic and restorative plastic surgery, transplantation of tissue and organs, implantation of artificial organs**
.96	**Anesthesiology**
.97	**Geriatric surgery**
.98	**Pediatric surgery**
.99	**Military surgery**

> 617.91–617.96 Surgical techniques, procedures, apparatus, equipment,
materials

                   Class comprehensive works in 617.9. Except for anesthesiology, class
                   techniques, procedures, apparatus, equipment, materials of surgery of a specific
                   system, organ, or region with the surgical therapy of the system, organ, or
                   region, e.g., preoperative care in neck surgery 617.53059

.91   Operative surgery

                   For anesthesiology, see 617.96

.910 01   Philosophy and theory

.910 02   Miscellany

[.910 028]   Auxiliary techniques and procedures; apparatus, equipment,
                       materials

                       Do not use; class in 617.9178

*Add as instructed under 617

.910 03–.910 09	Standard subdivisions
.910 1	Asepsis and antisepsis

> Standard subdivisions are added for either or both topics in heading

> Class here sterilization

.917	Operating rooms
.917 8	Surgical instruments, apparatus, equipment, materials

> *For surgical dressings, see 617.93*

.919	Surgical complications; preoperative, intraoperative, postoperative care

> Including complicating preconditions, e.g., heart problems

> *For surgical complications associated with anesthesia, see 617.96041*

.919 2	Preoperative care
.919 5	Postoperative care and complications

> Standard subdivisions are added for either or both topics in heading

> Including surgical infections

> *For surgical shock, see 617.21*

.93	Surgical dressings
.95	Cosmetic and restorative plastic surgery, transplantation of tissue and organs, implantation of artificial organs
.952	Cosmetic and restorative plastic surgery

> Standard subdivisions are added for either or both topics in heading

> Class transplantation of tissue for cosmetic and restorative purposes in 617.954; class implantation of artificial tissue for cosmetic and restorative purposes in 617.956

> *For cosmetic and restorative plastic surgery of a specific system, region, or organ, see the system, region, or organ in 617.4–617.5, plus notation 0592 from table under 617, e.g., plastic surgery of face 617.520592; for cosmetic and restorative plastic surgery in gynecologic and obstetrical surgery, see the tissue or organ in 618, plus notation 0592 from table under 618.1–618.8, e.g., mammaplasty 618.190592*

.954   **Transplantation of tissue and organs**

Including transplantation of fetal tissue

Class blood and blood plasma transfusion in 615.39; class transplantation of fetal tissue in experimental medicine in 616.027

For transplantation of tissue of a specific system, region, or organ; or transplantation of a specific organ, see the system, region, or organ in 617.4–617.5, plus notation 0592 from table under 617, e.g., skin transplantation 617.4770592, heart transplantation 617.4120592; for transplantation of tissue of a specific system, region, or organ; or transplantation of a specific organ in gynecological or obstetrical surgery, see the system, region, or organ in 618, plus notation 0592 from table under 618.1–618.8, e.g., transplantation of ovarian tissue 618.110592

See also 362.1783 for tissue and organ banks; also 618.1780599 for gamete, zygote, embryo transfer for purpose of human reproduction

.956   **Implantation of artificial tissue and organs**

Including implantation and removal of prostheses, other medical devices

For implantation of artificial tissue of a specific system, region, or organ; or implantation of an artificial substitute, artificial part, or assistive device for a specific organ, see the system, region, or organ in 617.4–617.5, plus notation 0592 from table under 617, e.g., implantation of bone substitutes 617.4710592, implantation of heart-assist devices 617.4120592; for implantation of artificial tissue, artificial organs, or medical devices in gynecologic and obstetrical surgery, see the tissue or organ in 618, plus notation 0592 from table under 618.1–618.8, e.g., breast implants 618.190592

.96   **Anesthesiology**

Class acupuncture anesthesia in 615.892

.960 4   Special topics of anesthesiology

.960 41   Complications

.960 42   Emergencies

Class resuscitation in 616.025

>   617.962–617.966   Types of anesthesia

Class anesthesiology regardless of type for specific kinds of surgery in 617.967; class comprehensive works in 617.96

.962   **General anesthesia**

Including inhalation, intravenous, rectal anesthesias

.964   **Regional anesthesia**

Including epidural, spinal anesthesias

Class here conduction anesthesia

For local anesthesia, see 617.966

.966   Local anesthesia

.967   Anesthesiology for specific kinds of surgery

General, regional, local anesthesia

Add to base number 617.967 the numbers following 617 in 617.1–617.9, e.g., dental anesthesia 617.9676

For anesthesiology for gynecology and obstetrics, see 617.968

.968   Anesthesiology for gynecology and obstetrics

.968 1   Gynecology

.968 2   Obstetrics

>   617.97–617.99 Special fields of surgery

Class comprehensive works in 617.9

For surgery of tumors and cancers, see 616.993–616.994; for gynecologic surgery, see 618.1059. For surgery of a specific organ, system, region, or disorder, see the organ, system, region, or disorder in 617, e.g., brain surgery in children 617.4810083, abdominal surgery in children 617.55059083

.97   *Geriatric surgery

[.970 59]   Operative surgery

Do not use for comprehensive works; class in 617.97; do not use for comprehensive works on geriatric surgery utilizing a specific instrument or technique not provided in 617.91–617.96; class in 617.05, e.g., cryosurgery on people in late adulthood 617.05, laser surgery on people in late adulthood 617.0580846; do not use for a specific surgical technique provided in 617.91–617.96; class in 617.91–617.96, e.g., anesthesiology of people in late adulthood 617.960846

[.970 592]   Cosmetic and restorative plastic surgery, transplantation of tissue and organs, implantation of artificial organs

Do not use; class in 617.950846

.98   *Pediatric surgery

Class here comprehensive works on pediatric and adolescent surgery

For adolescent surgery, see 617.00835

[.980 59]   Operative surgery

Do not use for comprehensive works; class in 617.98; do not use for comprehensive works on pediatric surgery utilizing a specific instrument or technique not provided in 617.91–617.96; class in 617.05, e.g., cryosurgery on children 617.05, laser surgery on children 617.058083; do not use for a specific surgical technique provided in 617.91–617.96; class in 617.91–617.96, e.g., anesthesiology of children 617.96083

*Add as instructed under 617

| [.980 592] | Cosmetic and restorative plastic surgery, transplantation of tissue and organs, implantation of artificial organs |

Do not use; class in 617.95083

.99   *Military surgery

| [.990 59] | Operative surgery |

Do not use for comprehensive works; class in 617.99; do not use for comprehensive works on military surgery utilizing a specific instrument or technique not provided in 617.91–617.96; class in 617.05, e.g., cryosurgery on military personnel 617.05, laser surgery on military personnel 617.058088355; do not use for a specific surgical technique provided in 617.91–617.96; class in 617.91–617.96, e.g., military anesthesiology 617.96088355

| [.990 592] | Cosmetic and restorative plastic surgery, transplantation of tissue and organs, implantation of artificial organs |

Do not use; class in 617.95088355

618   Gynecology, obstetrics, pediatrics, geriatrics

Standard subdivisions are added for gynecology, obstetrics, pediatrics, geriatrics together; for gynecology and obstetrics together

SUMMARY

618.01–.09	Standard subdivisions and special topics of gynecology, obstetrics, pediatrics, geriatrics
.1	Gynecology
.2	Obstetrics
.3	Diseases and complications of pregnancy
.4	Childbirth
.5	Labor complications
.6	Normal puerperium
.7	Puerperal diseases
.8	Obstetrical surgery
.9	Pediatrics and geriatrics

.01   Philosophy and theory

.02   Miscellany

| [.028 7] | Testing and measurement |

Do not use; class in 618.0475

.03   Dictionaries, encyclopedias, concordances

.04   Special topics of gynecology, obstetrics, pediatrics, geriatrics

Add to base number 618.04 the numbers following 0 in notation 01–09 from table under 618.1–618.8, e.g., drug therapy 618.0461; however, for gynecology, obstetrics, pediatrics, geriatrics as a profession, occupation, hobby, see 618.023

.05–.07   Standard subdivisions

.08   Groups of people

*Add as instructed under 617

.083   Young people

> Do not use for infants and children up to puberty; class in 618.92098

.083 5   Young people twelve to twenty

> Do not use for young people twelve to twenty who have not reached puberty; class in 618.92098

> Class here adolescent gynecology and obstetrics

.084   People in specific stages of adulthood

.084 6   People in late adulthood

> Do not use for patients; class in 618.978

.09   History, geographic treatment, biography

> Class life with a disease in 362.198

>   **618.1–618.8 Gynecology and obstetrics**

Medical and surgical

Except where contrary instructions are given, all notes under 616.02–616.08 and in table under 616.1–616.9 are applicable here

Except for modifications shown under specific entries, add to each subdivision identified by * as follows:

```
001–007   Standard subdivisions
              As modified under 616.1–616.9
008       Groups of people
0083          Young people
                  Do not use for infants and children up to puberty; class in
                  618.92098
00835         Young people twelve to twenty
                  Do not use for young people twelve to twenty who have
                  not reached puberty; class in 618.92098
                  Class here adolescent gynecology and obstetrics
0084          People in specific stages of adulthood
00846         People in late adulthood
                  Do not use for patients; class in 618.978
009       History, geographic treatment, biography
0092          Biography
                  Class life with a disease in 362.198
```

(continued)

> **618.1–618.8 Gynecology and obstetrics (continued)**

01–03	Microbiology, special topics, rehabilitation
	Add to 0 the numbers following 0 in notation 01–03 from table under 616.1–616.9, e.g., experimental medicine 027
	Class microbiology, special topics, rehabilitation applied to special classes of diseases in 04
04	Special classes of diseases
	Limited to the classes named below
042	Genetic diseases (Hereditary diseases)
0421–0423	Microbiology, special topics, rehabilitation
	Add to 042 the numbers following 0 in notation 01–03 from table under 616.1–616.9, e.g., experimental medicine for genetic diseases 04227
0425–0429	Preventive measures, surgery, therapy, pathology, psychosomatic medicine, case histories
	Add to 042 the numbers following 0 in notation 05–09 from table under 618.1–618.8, e.g., therapy for genetic diseases 0426
043	Congenital diseases
	Add to 043 the numbers following 042 in notation 0421 0429 from table under 618.1–618.8, e.g., experimental medicine for congenital diseases 04327
	Class congenital diseases of genetic origin in 042
>05–09	Preventive measures, surgery, therapy, pathology, psychosomatic medicine, case histories
	Class preventive measures, surgery, therapy, pathology, psychosomatic medicine applied to special classes of diseases in 04; class comprehensive works on prevention, therapy, etiology of a specific disease or kind of disease if all related to a specific kind of therapy in 061–069, e.g., diet therapy 0654; class comprehensive works in 618.1–618.8, without adding from this table
05	Preventive measures and surgery
052	Preventive measures
	By individuals and by medical personnel
	Class public measures preventing specific diseases in 614.5992; class comprehensive works on prevention in 613. Class a specific kind of therapy used for prevention with the kind of therapy in 061–069, e.g., drug therapy 061
059	Surgery
	Limited to operative surgery
	Including preoperative, intraoperative, postoperative care; surgery utilizing specific instruments or techniques, e.g., catheterization, cryosurgery, microsurgery, radiosurgery; surgical complications
	Class laser microsurgery in 0598; class nonoperative physical procedures in 06
0592	Cosmetic and restorative plastic surgery, transplantation of tissue and organs, implantation of artificial organs
	Including implantation and removal of prostheses, other medical devices

(continued)

>   **618.1–618.8 Gynecology and obstetrics (continued)**

0597	Endoscopic surgery
0598	Laser surgery

            Including laser coagulation

            Class here laser microsurgery

06   Therapy

       Class here rehabilitative therapy

       Class comprehensive works on rehabilitative therapy and education for living with handicaps and disabilities in 03; class comprehensive works on prevention, therapy, etiology of a specific disease or kind of disease if all related to a specific kind of therapy in 061–069, e.g., diet therapy 0654

       For surgery, see 059

060724   Experimental research

            Class here clinical trials

            Class clinical trials of a specific kind of therapy with the kind of therapy, plus notation 0724 from Table 1, e.g., clinical drug trials 0610724

>061–069   Specific therapies

       Class here specific kinds of therapy used for prevention; comprehensive works on prevention, therapy, etiology if these all relate to a specific kind of therapy, e.g., nutritional aspects of a disease and diet therapy 0654

061   Drug therapy

0610724   Experimental research

            Class here clinical drug trials

062–069   Other therapies

       Add to 06 the numbers following 615.8 in 615.82–615.89, e.g., X-ray therapy 06422

07   Pathology

071   Etiology

       Including effects of poisons on specific systems and organs as cause of disease

       Class social factors contributing to spread of a disease in 362.19; class comprehensive works on medical toxicology in 615.9

075–079   Diagnosis, prognosis, death, immunity

       Add to 07 the numbers following 616.07 in 616.075–616.079, e.g., physical diagnosis 0754

08   Psychosomatic medicine

09   Case histories

     Class comprehensive works in 618

.1   ***Gynecology**

     Including endocrine gynecology, endometriosis

     Class tumors of genital system in 616.99465

     For puerperal diseases, see 618.7

     See also 616.9297 for toxic shock syndrome

⁺Add as instructed under 618.1–618.8

.100 83   Young people

                          Do not use for gynecology for infants and children up to puberty;
                          class in 618.92098

.100 835   Young people twelve to twenty

                          Do not use for gynecology for young people twelve to twenty
                          who have not reached puberty; class in 618.92098

                          Class here adolescent gynecology

.11   *Diseases of ovaries

.12   *Diseases of fallopian tubes

.14   *Diseases of uterus

                   Class here diseases of uterine cervix

                   See also 618.1 for endometriosis

[.140 59]   Surgery

                          Do not use; class in 618.145

.142   *Infections

                   Including cervicitis, endometritis

                   For leukorrhea, see 618.15

                   See also 618.1 for endometriosis

.144   *Malformations

                   Including prolapse of uterus

.145   Surgery

.145 3   Hysterectomies

.145 8   Dilatation and curettage

                       See also 618.88 for surgical abortion

.15   *Diseases of vagina

                   Including leukorrhea

.16   *Diseases of vulva

.17   *Functional and systemic disorders

                   Class here female sexual disorders

                   Class comprehensive medical works on sexual disorders in 616.69

.172   *Menstruation disturbances

                   Including amenorrhea, dysmenorrhea, menorrhagia, oligomenorrhea,
                   premenstrual syndrome (PMS)

*Add as instructed under 618.1–618.8

.175   *Menopause disorders

              Class here disorders of perimenopause, of postmenopause;
              comprehensive works on climacteric disorders

              For male climacteric disorders, see 616.693

.178   *Infertility

              Including artificial insemination

              Class comprehensive works on male and female infertility in 616.692

.178 059   Surgery

                  Number built according to instructions under 618.1–618.8

.178 059 9   Gamete, zygote, embryo transfer; fertilization in vitro

                  Standard subdivisions are added for any or all topics in
                  heading

.178 06   Therapy

                  Number built according to instructions under 618.1–618.8

                  Class here human reproductive technology applied to female
                  infertility

                  Class comprehensive works on human reproductive technology in
                  616.69206

                  For surgery, see 618.178059

.18   Birth control

              Class here contraception, family planning

              Class personal health aspects of birth control in 613.94; class
              interdisciplinary works on birth control in 363.96. Class surgical methods
              of birth control in females with the kind of surgery in 618.1, e.g., tubal
              sterilization 618.12059

              *For nonsurgical methods of birth control in males, see 616.65; for
              surgical methods of birth control in males, see 617.463*

.182   Chemical methods of birth control

              Including contraceptive drug implants, spermatocidal agents

              Class pharmacokinetics of chemical contraceptives in 615.766

.182 2   Oral contraceptives

                  Class postcoital contraceptives in 618.1825

.182 5   Postcoital contraceptives

                  Class here morning after pills

.184   Natural family planning

              Class here ovulation detection method, rhythm method

*Add as instructed under 618.1–618.8

.185 Mechanical methods of birth control

Including female condoms, vaginal diaphragms

.185 2 Intrauterine devices

.19 *Diseases of breast

Class here comprehensive works on diseases of male and female breast

For diseases of male breast, see 616.49; for tumors of breast, see 616.99449; for diseases of lactation, see 618.71

.190 59 Surgery

Number built according to instructions under 618.1–618.8

Class here comprehensive works on surgery of male and female breast

For surgery of male breast, see 617.549

.2 ***Obstetrics**

Class here midwifery, comprehensive works on pregnancy and childbirth

For physiology of pregnancy and childbirth, see 612.63; for diseases, disorders, management of pregnancy, childbirth, puerperium, see 618.3–618.8

.200 835 Young people twelve to twenty

Class here adolescent obstetrics

[.205 2] Preventive measures

Do not use; class in 618.24

[.205 9] Surgery

Do not use; class in 618.8

.207 5 Diagnosis

Number built according to instructions under 618.1–618.8

Class here comprehensive works on diagnosis of diseases and complications of pregnancy, diagnosis of labor complications, diagnosis of puerperal diseases

To be classed here a work should be broader than diagnosis of diseases and complications of pregnancy; it should include also diagnosis of labor complications (618.5) or diagnosis of puerperal diseases (618.7075)

For diagnosis of diseases and complications of pregnancy, see 618.3075; for diagnosis of labor complications, see 618.5; for diagnosis of puerperal diseases, see 618.7075

.24 Prenatal care and preparation for childbirth

Standard subdivisions are added for either or both topics in heading

*Add as instructed under 618.1–618.8

.242	Dietetics and nutrition for pregnant women

Standard subdivisions are added for either or both topics in heading

See also 641.56319 for cooking for pregnant women

.244	Exercise for pregnant women
.25	*Multiple pregnancy and childbirth

Subdivisions are added for either or both topics in heading

.29	Nonsurgical methods of abortion

Class here use of abortifacient agents

Class surgical abortion, comprehensive works on induced abortion in 618.88

>   **618.3–618.8 Diseases, disorders, management of pregnancy, childbirth, puerperium**

Class comprehensive works in 618.2

See also 618.25 for multiple pregnancy and childbirth

.3	*Diseases and complications of pregnancy
.31	*Ectopic pregnancy

Including abdominal, tubal pregnancies

.32	*Fetal disorders

Class here perinatal medicine (perinatology)

Class neonatal medicine in 618.9201; class comprehensive works on congenital diseases in 616.043

For childbirth, see 618.4

.320 75	Diagnosis

Number built according to instructions under 618.1–618.8

Class procedures to diagnose genetic diseases, e.g., amniocentesis and chorionic villi sampling, in 618.3204275

.326	Diseases of specific systems and organs
.326 1	*Diseases of cardiovascular system
.326 8	*Diseases of nervous system

---

*Add as instructed under 618.1–618.8

.326 86   *Substance-related disorders

                   Effects on fetus of use of substances by mother

                   Including effect of tobacco use

                   Class here drug dependence; comprehensive works on fetal disorders and pregnancy complications associated with substance use and abuse

                      For pregnancy complications associated with substance use and abuse, see 618.3686

.326 861   *Alcohol-related disorders

                   Class here fetal alcohol syndrome

.34   *Diseases of placenta and amniotic fluid

               Subdivisions are added for diseases of placenta and amniotic fluid together, for diseases of placenta alone

.36   Pregnancy complications due to co-occurrence of pregnancy and disease in the mother

               Pre-existing diseases and diseases induced by pregnancy

               Including communicable diseases

.361   *Diseases of cardiovascular system

.361 3   *Diseases of blood vessels

.361 32   *Hypertension

                   Including eclampsia

                   Class here pregnancy toxemias

                      For puerperal eclampsia, see 618.7

.364   *Diseases of endocrine, hematopoietic, lymphatic systems

               Class here diseases of glands

               Subdivisions are added for diseases of endocrine, hematopoietic, lymphatic systems together; for diseases of endocrine system alone

.364 6   *Diabetes

               Class here diabetes mellitus, gestational diabetes

.368   *Diseases of nervous system and mental disorders

---

*Add as instructed under 618.1–618.8

.368 6		*Substance abuse (Drug abuse)

Including alcohol, tobacco

Class here substance use that would not be considered a problem except during pregnancy

Class comprehensive works on fetal disorders and pregnancy complications associated with maternal substance use and abuse in 618.32686

.39 Miscarriage, stillbirth, premature labor

.392 *Miscarriage and stillbirth

Subdivisions are added for either or both topics in heading

Class here perinatal death, spontaneous abortion

See also 155.937085 for psychology of bereavement

.397 *Premature labor

Class here premature birth

.4 Childbirth

Class here labor

Class a specific aspect not provided for here with the aspect, e.g., Cesarean section 618.86

.42 Presentation

.45 Natural childbirth

.5 Labor complications

Class here dystocia

.54 Uterine hemorrhage

.6 Normal puerperium

Class here postnatal care

.7 *Puerperal diseases

Including postpartum hemorrhage, Sheehan's syndrome

[.707 8] Death

Do not use; class in 618.79

.71 *Diseases of lactation

.74 *Puerperal infections

Including infectious puerperal peritonitis, puerperal metritis, puerperal pyemia

Class here childbed fever, puerperal septicemia

*Add as instructed under 618.1–618.8

.76   *Puerperal mental disorders

        Class here postpartum depression

        Class comprehensive works on depression in 616.8527

.79   Maternal death

.8   Obstetrical surgery

        Class embryo transfer in 618.1780599

.82   Version and extraction

.85   Minor surgery

        Including episiotomy

.86   Cesarean section

.88   Surgical abortion

        Including embryotomy

        Class here comprehensive medical works on abortion

        Class interdisciplinary works on abortion in 362.19888

          For nonsurgical methods of abortion, see 618.29

          See also 615.766 for abortifacient drugs

.9   Pediatrics and geriatrics

.92   Pediatrics

        Medicine for infants and children up to puberty

        Class here comprehensive works on child and adolescent medicine

          For medicine for young people who have reached puberty (adolescent medicine), see 616.00835; for pediatric aspects of injuries and wounds, see 617.10083; for pediatric aspects of results of injuries and wounds, see 617.2083; for pediatric dentistry, see 617.645; for pediatric surgery, see 617.98

          See Manual at 616 vs. 618.92

.920 001–.920 007   Standard subdivisions

        As modified under 616.1–616.9

.920 008   Groups of people

.920 009   History, geographic treatment, biography

.920 009 2   Biography

        Class life with a physical disease in 362.19892. Class life with a mental disorder with the disorder in 618.9285–618.9289, e.g., life with depression 618.9285270092

---

*Add as instructed under 618.1–618.8

.920 01–.920 09	General topics of pediatrics

Add to base number 618.920 notation 01–09 from table under 616.1–616.9, e.g., congenital diseases 618.920043; however, for pediatric preventive measures, see 613.0432; for pediatric therapeutics, see 615.542

Class chronic diseases; symptoms and general pathological processes as problems in their own right in 618.9204

.920 1	Newborn infants (Neonates)

In first month after birth

Class here neonatal medicine (neonatology)

Class perinatal medicine in 618.32; class comprehensive works on congenital diseases in 616.043

.920 11	Premature infants

Class here low birth weight infants

.920 2	Infants

Through age two

Class a specific medical condition or disease not provided for here with the condition or disease, e.g., pain in infants 618.9204720832, diarrhea in infants 618.92342700832

For infants in first month after birth, see 618.9201

.920 26	†Sudden infant death

Variant names: cot death, crib death, sudden infant death syndrome (SIDS)

.920 4	Chronic diseases; symptoms and general pathological processes as problems in their own right

Add to base number 618.9204 the numbers following 616.04 in 616.044–616.047, e.g., pain in childen 618.920472

.920 9	Special branches of medicine

Class pediatric sports medicine in 617.1027083; class pediatric dentistry in 617.645; class pediatric surgery in 617.98

.920 97	Regional medicine, ophthalmology, otology, audiology

See Manual at 618.92097 vs. 617

.920 975	Regional medicine

Add to base number 618.920975 the numbers following 617.5 in 617.51–617.58, e.g., disorders of face 618.92097522; however, for pediatric regional surgery, see 617.5083

†Add as instructed under 616.1–616 9

.920 977–.920 978	Ophthalmology, otology, audiology

Add to base number 618.92097 the numbers following 617 in 617.7–617.8, e.g., trachoma in children 618.92097772; however, for pediatric surgery of eyes, see 617.71; for pediatric surgery of ears, see 617.8059083

.920 98	†Gynecology

For pediatric gynecologic surgery, see 618.1059083

.920 981	Specific diseases

Add to base number 618.920981 the numbers following 618.1 in 618.11–618.19, e.g., diseases of uterus 618.9209814; however, for surgery for pediatric gynecologic diseases, see 618.11–618.19

.921–.929	Specific diseases

Add to base number 618.92 the numbers following 616 in 616.1–616.9, e.g., heart diseases in children 618.9212

Class sudden infant death in 618.92026

For pediatric dental diseases, see 617.645; for pediatric regional medicine diseases, pediatric diseases of eyes and ears, pediatric gynecologic diseases, see 618.9209

.97	†Geriatrics

For geriatric aspects of injuries and wounds, see 617.100846; for geriatric aspects of results of injuries and wounds, see 617.20846; for geriatric surgery, see 617.97

[.970 42]	Genetic diseases (Hereditary diseases)

Do not use; class in 618.976042

[.970 43]	Congenital diseases

Do not use; class in 618.976043

[.970 52]	Preventive measures

Do not use; class in 613.0438

[.970 6]	Therapy

Do not use; class in 615.547

.976	Special medical conditions, specific diseases
[.976 01–.976 03]	Standard subdivisions

Do not use; class in 618.97001–618.97003

.976 04	Special medical conditions

Add to base number 618.97604 the numbers following 616.04 in 616.042–616.047, e.g., pain in geriatric patients 618.9760472

---

†Add as instructed under 616.1–616.9

[.976 05–.976 09]   Standard subdivisions

Do not use; class in 618.97005–618.97009

.976 1–.976 9   Specific diseases

Add to base number 618.976 the numbers following 616 in 616.1–616.9, e.g., geriatric mental disorders 618.97689

.977   Miscellaneous branches of medicine other than surgery

Only those branches named below

See Manual at 618.977 vs. 617

[.977 01–.977 02]   Standard subdivisions

Do not use; class in 618.977

.977 03   Rehabilitation

Do not use for dictionaries, encyclopedias, concordances; class in 618.977

Class rehabilitation from a specific disease with the disease in 618.976–618.978, plus notation 03 from table under 616.1–616.9, notation 03 from table under 617, or notation 03 from table under 618.1–618.8, e.g., rehabilitation for geriatric patients with heart disease 618.9761203

[.977 04–.977 09]   Standard subdivisions

Do not use; class in 618.977

.977 5–.977 8   Regional medicine, dentistry, ophthalmology, otology, audiology

Add to base number 618.977 the numbers following 617 in 617.5–617.8, e.g., geriatric dentistry 618.9776; however, for geriatric regional surgery, see 617.50846; for geriatric dental surgery, see 617.6050846; for geriatric surgery of eyes, see 617.71; for geriatric surgery of ears, see 617.80590846

.978   †Gynecology

For geriatric gynecologic surgery, see 618.10590846

.978 1   Specific diseases

Add to base number 618.9781 the numbers following 618.1 in 618.11–618.19, e.g., diseases of uterus 618.97814; however, for surgery for geriatric gynecologic diseases, see 618.11–618.19

[619]   [Unassigned]

Most recently used in Edition 21

---

†Add as instructed under 616.1–616.9

620   Engineering and allied operations

Standard subdivisions are added for engineering and allied operations together, for engineering alone

Class here manufacturing of products of various branches of engineering

Class comprehensive works on manufacturing in 670

For chemical engineering, see 660

SUMMARY

620.001–.009	**Standard subdivisions and engineering design and quality**
.1	**Engineering mechanics and materials**
.2	**Sound and related vibrations**
.3	**Mechanical vibration**
.4	**Engineering for specific kinds of geographic environments, fine particle and remote control technology, surface engineering**
.5	**Nanotechnology**
.8	**Human factors and safety engineering**
621	**Applied physics**
.04	**Special topics of applied physics**
.1	**Steam engineering**
.2	**Hydraulic-power technology**
.3	**Electrical, magnetic, optical, communications, computer engineering; electronics, lighting**
.4	**Prime movers and heat engineering**
.5	**Pneumatic, vacuum, low-temperature technologies**
.6	**Blowers, fans, pumps**
.8	**Machine engineering**
.9	**Tools**
622	**Mining and related operations**
.1	**Prospecting**
.2	**Excavation techniques**
.3	**Mining for specific materials**
.4	**Mine environment**
.5	**Mine drainage**
.6	**Mine transport systems**
.7	**Ore dressing**
.8	**Mine health and safety**
623	**Military and nautical engineering**
.04	**Special topics of military engineering**
.1	**Fortifications**
.2	**Mine laying and clearance, demolition**
.3	**Engineering of defense**
.4	**Ordnance**
.5	**Ballistics and gunnery**
.6	**Military transportation technology**
.7	**Communications, vehicles, sanitation, related topics**
.8	**Nautical engineering and seamanship**
624	**Civil engineering**
.029	**Commercial miscellany**
.1	**Structural engineering and underground construction**
.2	**Bridges**

625		**Engineering of railroads and roads**
	.1	**Railroads**
	.2	**Railroad rolling stock**
	.3	**Inclined, mountain, ship railroads**
	.4	**Local rail transit systems**
	.5	**Cable and aerial railways**
	.6	**Light rail transit systems**
	.7	**Roads**
	.8	**Artificial road surfaces**
627		**Hydraulic engineering**
	.04	**Special topics of hydraulic engineering**
	.1	**Inland waterways**
	.2	**Harbors, ports, roadsteads**
	.3	**Port facilities**
	.4	**Flood control**
	.5	**Reclamation, irrigation, related topics**
	.7	**Underwater operations**
	.8	**Dams and reservoirs**
	.9	**Other hydraulic structures**
628		**Sanitary engineering**
	.1	**Water supply**
	.2	**Sewers**
	.3	**Sewage treatment and disposal**
	.4	**Waste technology, public toilets, street cleaning**
	.5	**Pollution control technology and industrial sanitation engineering**
	.7	**Sanitary engineering for rural and sparsely populated areas**
	.9	**Other branches of sanitary and municipal engineering**
629		**Other branches of engineering**
	.04	**Transportation engineering**
	.1	**Aerospace engineering**
	.2	**Motor land vehicles, cycles**
	.3	**Air-cushion vehicles (Ground-effect machines, Hovercraft)**
	.4	**Astronautics**
	.8	**Automatic control engineering**

.001   Philosophy and theory

.001 1   Systems

Class design of engineering systems in 620.0042; class manufacturing systems in 670.11; class interdisciplinary works covering systems of agriculture, home economics, or management in addition to engineering in 601.1; class interdisciplinary works on systems in 003

.001 13   Computer modeling and simulation

Class computer-aided design in 620.00420285

.001 17   Kinds of systems

.001 171   Large-scale systems

Class here systems engineering

.001 5   Scientific principles

[.001 53]   Physical principles in engineering

Do not use; class in 621

[.001 531]		Mechanical principles in engineering
		Do not use; class in 620.1
[.001 534]		Principles of sound and related vibrations in engineering
		Do not use; class in 620.2
.002	Miscellany	
[.002 87]		Testing and measurement
		Do not use; class in 620.0044
[.002 88]		Maintenance and repair
		Do not use; class in 620.0046
[.002 89]		Safety measures
		Do not use; class in 620.86
.003	Dictionaries, encyclopedias, concordances	
.004	Design, testing, measurement, quality, maintenance, repair	
.004 2		Engineering design
.004 202 85		Computer applications

Class here computer-aided design (CAD)

Class comprehensive works on computer-aided design and computer-aided manufacturing (CAD/CAM) in 670.285

.004 4		Testing and measurement

Including inspection, simulation

Class interdisciplinary works on measurement in 530.8

.004 5		Quality

Including interchangeability, maintainability, precision

Class testing and measurement for quality in 620.0044; class maintenance in 620.0046

.004 52		Reliability
.004 54		Durability
.004 6		Maintenance and repair

Class here interdisciplinary works on maintenance and repair

For maintenance and repair in a specific subject, see the subject, plus notation 0288 from Table 1, e.g., clock and watch repair 681.110288

.005–.008	Standard subdivisions	
.009	History, geographic treatment, biography	

.009 1	Areas, regions, places in general

Class engineering to overcome problems of specific kinds of geographic environments in 620.41

.009 2	Biography

Class biography of engineers known primarily as entrepreneurs in 338.76

.009 9	Other parts of the world
[.009 99]	Treatment by extraterrestrial worlds

Do not use; class in 620.419

.1 Engineering mechanics and materials

Standard subdivisions are added for engineering mechanics and materials together, for engineering mechanics alone

Class here applied mechanics

SUMMARY

620.100 1–.100 9	**Standard subdivisions**
.103–.107	**Engineering mechanics (Applied mechanics)**
.11	**Engineering materials**
.12	**Wood**
.13	**Masonry materials**
.14	**Ceramic and allied materials**
.16	**Metals**
.17	**Ferrous metals**
.18	**Nonferrous metals**
.19	**Other engineering materials**

.100 1–.100 9	Standard subdivisions

>   620.103–620.107 Engineering mechanics (Applied mechanics)

Class comprehensive works in 620.1

For fine particle technology, see 620.43

See also 531 for mechanics as a subject in physics

.103	Applied statics

For applied solid statics, see 620.1053; for applied fluid statics, see 620.1063; for applied gas statics, see 620.1073

.104	Applied dynamics

For applied solid dynamics, see 620.1054; for applied fluid dynamics, see 620.1064; for applied gas dynamics, see 620.1074

.105	Applied solid mechanics

Class structural theory in 624.17

For mechanical vibration, see 620.3

See also 621.811 for physical principles of machinery

.105 3	Statics	
.105 4	Dynamics	
.106	Applied fluid mechanics	

Class here applied hydromechanics, comprehensive works on fluid-power technology

For applied gas mechanics, see 620.107; for steam engineering, see 621.1; for hydraulic-power technology, see 621.2; for hydraulic engineering, see 627

.106 3   Statics

.106 4   Dynamics

Including cavitation, pressure surge, water hammer

Class here flow

See also 621.4022 for convective transport, heat convection

.107   Applied gas mechanics

Class here applied aeromechanics

For steam engineering, see 621.1; for pneumatic and vacuum technology, see 621.5; for aeromechanics of flight, see 629.1323; for air-conditioning engineering, see 697.93

.107 3   Statics

.107 4   Dynamics

.11   Engineering materials

Class comprehensive works on materials, manufacture of materials in 670

For specific kinds of materials, see 620.12–620.19

.110 287   Testing and measurement

Do not use for nondestructive testing; class in 620.1127

.112   Properties of materials and nondestructive testing

Standard subdivisions are added for properties of materials and nondestructive testing together, for properties of materials alone

Class here failure, resistance, strength of materials

Class properties and nondestructive testing of porous, organic, composite materials in 620.116–620.118

> 620.112 1–620.112 6 Resistance to specific forces

Class comprehensive works in 620.112

.112 1   Resistance to thermal forces

Class resistance to thermal radiation in 620.11228

See also 620.11296 for thermal properties

.112 15	Changes in temperature
.112 16	Low temperatures
	Including cryogenic temperatures
.112 17	High temperatures
.112 2	Resistance to decay, decomposition, deterioration
	Standard subdivisions are added for any or all topics in heading
	Physicochemical actions not basically thermal or mechanical
	Including action of pests
.112 23	Biodegradation, corrosion, weathering
	Including rot, rust
.112 28	Resistance to radiation
.112 3	Resistance to mechanical deformation (Mechanics of materials)
	For resistance to specific mechanical stresses, see 620.1124; for resistance to fracture, see 620.1126
.112 302 87	Testing and measurement
	Including strain gauges
.112 32	Temporary deformation (Elasticity)
	Including elastic limit
.112 33	Permanent deformation (Plasticity)
	Including creep, plastic flow
	For properties affecting permanent deformation, see 620.1125
.112 4	Resistance to specific mechanical stresses
	Class resistance to change of form, regardless of stress, in 620.1125; class resistance to fracture, regardless of stress, in 620.1126
.112 41	Tension
.112 42	Compression
.112 43	Torsion
.112 44	Flexure
.112 45	Shearing
.112 48	Vibrations
.112 5	Properties affecting permanent deformation
	Including impact strength, rigidity, shock resistance; ductility, malleability

.112 6	Resistance to fracture (Fracture mechanics)

Including brittleness, hardness

Class here crack resistance, resistance to penetration and breaking; fatigue; fatigue, fracture, rupture strength

.112 7	Nondestructive testing
.112 72	Radiographic testing

Class here X-ray testing

.112 73	Tracer testing
.112 74	Ultrasonic testing
.112 78	Magnetic testing
.112 9	Other properties
.112 92	Mechanical properties

Including adhesiveness, roughness, texture; friction and wear resistance

Class comprehensive works on friction in 621.89

See also 620.44 for surface technology

.112 94	Acoustical properties
.112 95	Optical properties

Including luminescence, photoelasticity, refractivity

.112 96	Thermal properties

Including heat conductivity

See also 620.1121 for resistance to thermal forces

.112 97	Electrical, electronic, magnetic properties
.112 972	Semiconductivity
.112 973	Superconductivity
.112 99	Microphysical properties

Including crystallographic and molecular properties; microstructure

For electronic properties, see 620.11297

> 620.115–620.118 Nanostructured, porous, organic, composite materials

Class comprehensive works in 620.11

For a specific kind of nanostructured, porous, organic, composite material, see 620.12–620.19

.115   *Nanostructured materials

> Class nanoporous materials in 620.116; class nanostructured organic materials in 620.117; class nanostructured composite materials in 620.118

.116   *Porous materials

> Including nanoporous materials

> Class porous organic materials in 620.117; class porous composite materials in 620.118

.117   *Organic materials

> Class organic composite materials in 620.118

.118   *Composite materials

> *For a specific composite material, see the predominant component in 620.12–620.19, e.g., reinforced concrete 620.137*

>   620.12–620.19 Specific kinds of materials

> Add to each subdivision identified by * as follows:
> 0287   Testing and measurement
>   Do not use for nondestructive testing; class in 7
> 1–9   Specific properties and nondestructive testing
>   Add the numbers following 620.112 in 620.1121–620.1129, e.g., nondestructive testing 7

> Class comprehensive works in 620.11. Class manufacturing and chemical properties of a specific kind of material with the material, e.g., wood 674

> *For porous, organic, composite materials, see 620.116–620.118*

.12   *Wood

> Including laminated wood

.13   Masonry materials

> *For brick, terra-cotta, tile, see 620.142*

.130 287   Testing and measurement

> Do not use for nondestructive testing; class in 620.130427

.130 4   Special topics of masonry materials

.130 42   *Specific properties and nondestructive testing

.132   *Natural stones

.135   *Cement

> Class here masonry adhesives

---

*Add as instructed under 620.12–620.19

.136	*Concrete

For reinforced and prestressed concrete, see 620.137; for concrete blocks, see 620.139

.137	*Reinforced and prestressed concrete

Subdivisions are added for either or both topics in heading

.139	Artificial stones

Including cinder and concrete blocks

.139 028 7	Testing and measurement

Do not use for nondestructive testing; class in 620.1390427

.139 04	Special topics of artificial stones
.139 042	*Specific properties and nondestructive testing

.14	Ceramic and allied materials

Standard subdivisions are added for ceramic and allied materials together, for ceramic materials alone

Class masonry materials in 620.13

.140 287	Testing and measurement

Do not use for nondestructive testing; class in 620.140427

.140 4	Special topics of ceramic and allied materials
.140 42	*Specific properties and nondestructive testing
.142	Brick, terra-cotta, tile
.143	*Refractory materials

Including fireclays

Class refractory metals in 620.16

For asbestos, see 620.195

.144	*Glass

Including fiber glass

.146	Enamel and porcelain
.16	*Metals

Class here alloys

For ferrous metals, see 620.17; for nonferrous metals, see 620.18

.17	*Ferrous metals

Class here iron, steel

*Add as instructed under 620.12–620.19

.18	Nonferrous metals

Class here nonferrous alloys

.180 287	Testing and measurement

Do not use for nondestructive testing; class in 620.180427

.180 4	Special topics of nonferrous metals
.180 42	*Specific properties and nondestructive testing
.182	*Copper

Class here brass, Muntz metal; bronze, gunmetal; copper-aluminum alloys; copper-beryllium alloys

.183	*Lead
.184	Zinc and cadmium
.184 2	*Zinc

For brass, Muntz metal, see 620.182

.184 6	*Cadmium
.185	*Tin

For bronze, gunmetal, see 620.182

.186	*Aluminum

For copper-aluminum alloys, see 620.182

.187	*Magnesium
.188	*Nickel
.189	Other metals
.189 1	*Mercury
.189 2	Precious, rare-earth, actinide-series metals

Add to base number 620.1892 the numbers following 669.2 in 669.22–669.29, e.g., uranium 620.1892931

.189 3	Metals used in ferroalloys

For nickel, see 620.188

.189 302 87	Testing and measurement

Do not use for nondestructive testing; class in 620.18930427

.189 304	Special topics of metals used in ferroalloys
.189 304 2	*Specific properties and nondestructive testing
.189 32	Titanium, manganese, vanadium
.189 322	*Titanium

*Add as instructed under 620.12–620.19

.189 33	*Cobalt	
.189 34	Chromium, molybdenum, tungsten	
.189 35	Zirconium and tantalum	
.189 352	*Zirconium	
.189 4	*Beryllium	

> For copper-beryllium alloys, see 620.182

.189 5	Antimony, arsenic, bismuth
.189 6	Alkali and alkaline-earth metals
.189 602 87	Testing and measurement

> Do not use for nondestructive testing; class in 620.18960427

.189 604	Special topics of alkali and alkaline-earth metals
.189 604 2	*Specific properties and nondestructive testing
.19	Other engineering materials
.191	Soils and related materials

Standard subdivisions are added for soils and related materials together, for soils alone

Including aggregates, clay, gravel, sand

Class foundation soils in 624.151; class interdisciplinary works on soils in 631.4

.191 028 7	Testing and measurement

> Do not use for nondestructive testing; class in 620.1910427

.191 04	Special topics of soils and related materials
.191 042	*Specific properties and nondestructive testing
.192	Polymers

> For elastomers, see 620.194

.192 028 7	Testing and measurement

> Do not use for nondestructive testing; class in 620.1920427

.192 04	Special topics of polymers
.192 042	*Specific properties and nondestructive testing
.192 3	*Plastics

Class here plastic laminating materials

.192 4	*Gums and resins

Subdivisions are added for either or both topics in heading

*Add as instructed under 620.12–620.19

.193	Nonmetallic elements
	Including carbon, silicon
.193 028 7	Testing and measurement
	Do not use for nondestructive testing; class in 620.1930427
.193 04	Special topics of nonmetallic elements
.193 042	*Specific properties and nondestructive testing
.194	*Elastomers
	Class here rubber
.195	Insulating materials
	Including asbestos, corkboard, kapok, rock wool; dielectric materials
.195 028 7	Testing and measurement
	Do not use for nondestructive testing; class in 620.1950427
.195 04	Special topics of insulating materials
.195 042	*Specific properties and nondestructive testing
.196	Bituminous materials
	Including asphalt, tar
.196 028 7	Testing and measurement
	Do not use for nondestructive testing; class in 620.1960427
.196 04	Special topics of bituminous materials
.196 042	*Specific properties and nondestructive testing
.197	Organic fibrous materials
	Including paper, paperboard, rope, textiles
.197 028 7	Testing and measurement
	Do not use for nondestructive testing; class in 620.1970427
.197 04	Special topics of organic fibrous materials
.197 042	*Specific properties and nondestructive testing
.198	Other natural and synthetic minerals
	Including corundum, feldspar, gems, graphite, oil, quartz, water
.199	Adhesives and sealants
	Class here comprehensive works on laminating materials
	For masonry adhesives, see 620.135; for plastic laminating materials, see 620.1923

*Add as instructed under 620.12–620.19

.199 028 7	Testing and measurement
	Do not use for nondestructive testing; class in 620.1990427
.199 04	Special topics of adhesives and sealants
.199 042	*Specific properties and nondestructive testing

.2   **Sound and related vibrations**

> Standard subdivisions are added for sound and related vibrations together, for sound alone

> Class here applied acoustics (acoustical engineering)

> *See also 534 for physics of sound*

>   620.21–620.25   Applied acoustics (Acoustical engineering)

> Class electroacoustical communications in 621.3828; class engineering works on architectural acoustics in 690.2; class comprehensive works in 620.2; class interdisciplinary works on architectural acoustics in 729.29

.21   General topics of applied acoustics

> Including reflection and refraction of sound

.23   Noise and countermeasures

> Standard subdivisions are added for either or both topics in heading

.25   Acoustics in specific physical environments

> Including underwater acoustics

.28   Applied subsonics and ultrasonics

> *For ultrasonic testing of materials, see 620.11274*

.3   **Mechanical vibration**

> Class effects of vibrations on materials in 620.11248

> *For sound and related vibrations, see 620.2*

.31   Generation and transmission

.37   Effects and countermeasures

> Standard subdivisions are added for either or both topics in heading

.4   **Engineering for specific kinds of geographic environments, fine particle and remote control technology, surface engineering**

.41   Engineering for specific kinds of geographic environments

> Class a specific technology with the technology, plus notation 091 from Table 1 when the environment is not inherent in the subject, e.g., ergonomics for deserts 620.8209154, nautical engineering 623.8

*Add as instructed under 620.12–620.19

.411–.417   Specific kinds of terrestrial environments

> Add to base number 620.41 the numbers following —1 in notation 11–17 from Table 2, e.g., ocean engineering 620.4162; however, for engineering of estuaries, see 627.124

> Class hydraulic engineering in 627

.419   Extraterrestrial environments

.43   Fine particle technology

> Including dust, liquid particle technology

> Class here powder technology

.44   Surface engineering

.46   Remote control and telecontrol

> Standard subdivisions are added for either or both topics in heading

.5   Nanotechnology

> Technology that manipulates matter on the atomic or molecular scale

> Class a specific application of nanotechnology with the technology, e.g., nanostructured materials 620.115, nanotechnology used in manufacturing thin-film circuits 621.3815

.8   Human factors and safety engineering

> Class here work environment engineering

> Class a specific application of human factors engineering with the application, e.g., engineering of the home kitchen work environment 643.3

> *See also 628 for environmental protection engineering*

.82   Human factors engineering

> Variant names: biotechnology, design anthropometry, ergonomics

.86   Safety engineering

> Class interdisciplinary works on safety in 363.1

> *For safety engineering of a specific technology, see the technology, plus notation 0289 from Table 1, e.g., safety in machine engineering 621.80289*

621   Applied physics

> Class here mechanical engineering

> Class a specific application of applied physics with the application, e.g., military engineering 623

> *For engineering mechanics, see 620.1; for applied acoustics, see 620.2*

SUMMARY

.04   Special topics of applied physics

.042   Energy engineering

> Class here engineering of alternative and renewable energy sources

> Class interdisciplinary works on energy in 333.79

.044   Plasma engineering

> Class interdisciplinary works on plasma in 530.44

\>   **621.1–621.2 Fluid-power technologies**

> Class comprehensive works in 620.106

.1   **Steam engineering**

\>   621.15–621.16 Specific kinds of steam engines

> Class comprehensive works in 621.1

> *For marine steam engines, see 623.8722; for steam locomotives, see 625.261; for steam tractors and rollers, see 629.2292*

.15   Portable engines

> Class comprehensive works on specific structural types of steam engines in 621.16

.16   Stationary engines

> Class here comprehensive works on specific structural types of steam engines

> *For portable engines of specific structural types, see 621.15*

.164   Reciprocating engines

.165   Turbines

.18   Generating and transmitting steam

> Standard subdivisions are added for generating and transmitting steam together, for generating steam alone

> Class generating steam in specific kinds of steam engines in 621.15–621.16; class generating steam in central stations in 621.19

>   621.182–621.183   Generating steam

        Class comprehensive works in 621.18

.182   Fuels

.183   Boilers and boiler furnaces

          Standard subdivisions are added for either or both topics in heading

          Including chimneys, mechanical stokers

.185   Transmitting steam

          Including insulation, pressure regulators, safety valves, steam pipes

.19   Central stations

.194   Boiler operations (Boiler-house practices)

.197   Accessories

          Including condensers, cooling towers, superheaters

.199   Cogeneration of electric power and heat

          Class interdisciplinary works on cogeneration of electricity and heat in 333.793

.2   **Hydraulic-power technology**

        Class hydraulic control in 629.8042

.204   Special topics of hydraulic-power technology

.204 2   Specific liquids

[.204 201–.204 209]   Standard subdivisions

          Do not use; class in 621.201–621.209

.204 22   Water

.204 24   Hydraulic fluids

          Other than water

.21   Water mills

        Class here comprehensive works on waterwheels

        For waterwheels used as water-lifting devices, see 621.69

.24   Turbines

.25   Pumps and accumulators

.252   Pumps

        Class comprehensive works on pumps in 621.69

.254   Accumulators

.26   Hydraulic transmission

> Class specific liquids in hydraulic transmission in 621.2042

> *For rams, see 621.27*

.27   Rams

.3   Electrical, magnetic, optical, communications, computer engineering; electronics, lighting

> Standard subdivisions are added for electromagnetic engineering, for combined electrical and electronic engineering, for electrical engineering alone

> *See also 537 for physics of electricity and electromagnetism*

SUMMARY

621.302 8	**Auxiliary techniques and procedures; apparatus, equipment, materials**
.31	**Generation, modification, storage, transmission of electric power**
.32	**Lighting**
.33	**Electric power transmission for railroads**
.34	**Magnetic engineering**
.35	**Superconductivity**
.36	**Optical engineering**
.37	**Testing and measurement of electrical quantities**
.38	**Electronics, communications engineering**
.39	**Computer engineering**

.302 84   Apparatus, equipment, materials

> Do not use for electrical equipment; class in 621.31042

.302 87   Testing and measurement

> Do not use for electrical testing and measurement; class in 621.37

.31   Generation, modification, storage, transmission of electric power

> Class here alternating current

SUMMARY

621.310 4	**Special topics of generation, modification, storage, transmission of electric power**
.312	**Generation, modification, storage**
.313	**Generating machinery and converters**
.314	**Transformers**
.315	**Capacitors (Condensers)**
.316	**Details and parts of generators**
.317	**Control devices**
.319	**Transmission**

.310 4   Special topics of generation, modification, storage, transmission of electric power

.310 42	Electrical machinery and equipment

Standard subdivisions are added for either or both topics in heading

Including eddy currents, shaft currents

Class a specific application with the application, e.g., refrigerators 621.57

For electric motors, see 621.46

.312	Generation, modification, storage

For equipment for generation, modification, control, see 621.313–621.317

.312 1	Generation

Class here central and auxiliary power plants, mechanical generation

For direct energy conversion, see 621.3124

.312 13	Specific kinds of mechanical generation
[.312 130 1–.312 130 9]	Standard subdivisions

Do not use; class in 621.312101–621.312109

.312 132	Steam-powered generation

Class here comprehensive works on generation from fossil fuels

For generation by internal-combustion engines, see 621.312133; for nuclear steam-powered generation of electricity, see 621.483

.312 133	Generation by internal-combustion engines
.312 134	Hydroelectric generation

Including tidal generation

Class engineering of dams for hydroelectric power in 627.8

.312 136	Wind-powered generation
.312 4	Direct energy conversion
.312 42	Electrochemical energy conversion

Class here batteries

Class comprehensive works on electrochemical engineering in 660.297

For solar batteries, see 621.31244

.312 423	Primary batteries
.312 424	Secondary batteries (Storage batteries)
.312 429	Fuel cells

.312 43	Thermoelectric generation

Including radioisotope thermoelectric generation; thermionic converters

Class generation of electricity from solar radiation in 621.31244

.312 44	Generation of electricity from solar radiation

Class here photovoltaic generation, use of solar batteries and cells

.312 45	Magnetohydrodynamic generation

.312 6	Modification and storage

Including operation of transformer, converter substations

For storage of electrical energy by chemical methods, see 621.312424

> **621.313–621.317 Machinery and equipment for generation, modification, control**

Class comprehensive works in 621.31042

.313	Generating machinery and converters

Standard subdivisions are added for either or both topics in heading

Class here comprehensive works on generators and motors

For details and parts of generators, see 621.316; for electric motors, see 621.46

.313 2	Direct-current machinery

Including converters to alternating current, dynamos

.313 3	Alternating-current machinery

Class here synchronous machinery

For synchronous generators, see 621.3134; for synchronous converters to direct current, see 621.3135; for asynchronous machinery, see 621.3136

.313 4	Synchronous generators

.313 5	Synchronous converters to direct current

For rectifiers, see 621.3137

.313 6	Asynchronous machinery

For rectifiers, see 621.3137

.313 7	Rectifiers
.314	Transformers
.315	Capacitors (Condensers)

.316	Details and parts of generators

Including armatures, brushes, commutators, contactors, electromagnets

For a specific part not provided for here, see the part, e.g., transformers 621.314

.317	Control devices

Including circuit breakers, fuses, grounding devices, lightning arresters, relays, rheostats

Class here power electronics, switching equipment

Class switches at service end of line in 621.31924

.319	Transmission

Including power failure

Class here electrification

Class interdisciplinary works on electrification, on power failure in 333.7932

For electric power transmission for railroads, see 621.33

[.319 011]	Systems

Do not use; class in 621.3191

.319 1	Systems

Class circuitry and lines in 621.3192

.319 12	Direct-current systems

.319 13	Alternating-current systems

Including high-tension systems

.319 15	Composite current systems

Direct and alternating currents combined

.319 2	Networks (Circuitry and lines)

.319 21	Physical phenomena in circuits

Including heat losses in lines, transients

.319 22	Overhead lines

.319 23	Underground lines

.319 24	Apparatus at service end of line

Including extension cords, outlets, sockets, switches

Class here interior wiring

For exterior wiring, see 621.31925

.319 25	Exterior wiring

.319 3	Equipment and components

Class equipment for generation, modification, control in 621.313–621.317; class use of equipment and components in lines and circuitry in 621.3192

.319 33	Wires
.319 34	Cables
.319 37	Insulators

Class here insulation

.32	Lighting

Class here electric lighting

.321	Principles of lighting

Class principles of specific kinds of lighting with the kind, e.g., principles of residential lighting 621.3228

.321 1	Layouts, calculations, photometry
.321 4	Floodlighting

Class here directed lighting

Class exterior floodlighting in 621.3229

.322	Lighting in specific situations

Class here interior lighting

Class specific forms of lighting in 621.323–621.327

For public lighting, see 628.95; for lighting of airports, see 629.1365

.322 01–.322 09	Standard subdivisions for interior lighting

Do not use for comprehensive works on lighting in specific situations; class in 621.3201–621.3209

.322 5–.322 8	Interior lighting for specific kinds of buildings

Add to base number 621.322 the numbers following 72 in 725–728, e.g., lighting for office buildings 621.322523

.322 9	Exterior lighting

Including advertising and display lighting, garden and patio lighting

---

> 621.323–621.327 Specific forms of lighting

Class comprehensive works in 621.32

.323	Nonelectrical lighting

Including candles, oil-burning devices, torches

For gas lighting, see 621.324

.324	Gas lighting

> 621.325–621.327 Electric lighting

Class comprehensive works in 621.32

.325   Arc lighting

Electric-discharge lighting in which light is produced by consumable electrodes or by vapors emanating from consumable electrodes

.326   Incandescent lighting

.327   Vapor lighting (Luminous-tube lighting)

.327 3   Fluorescent lighting

.327 4   Mercury-vapor lighting

.327 5   Neon lighting

.327 6   Sodium-vapor lighting

.33   Electric power transmission for railroads

.34   Magnetic engineering

Class here artificial magnets, electromagnets

Class electromagnets as parts of generators in 621.316; class electromagnets as parts of electric motors in 621.46; class comprehensive works on electromagnetic technology in 621.3

See also 538 for physics of magnetism; also 538.4 for natural magnets

.35   Superconductivity

Class here superconductors

Class superconductor circuits in 621.3815

.36   Optical engineering

Class here applied optics; works on infrared and ultraviolet technology together

Class manufacture of optical instruments in 681.4; class interdisciplinary works on photography in 770

For lighting, see 621.32

See also 535 for optics and light as subjects in physics; also 620.11295 for optical properties of engineering materials

.361   Spectroscopy

> 621.362–621.364 Infrared and ultraviolet technology

Class infrared and ultraviolet spectroscopy in 621.361; class infrared and ultraviolet photography in 621.3672; class comprehensive works in 621.36

.362   Infrared technology

.364   Ultraviolet technology

.365	Photonics
.366	Lasers

> *For laser communications, see 621.3827*

.366 1	Solid-state lasers
.366 2	Fluid-state lasers

> *For gaseous-state lasers, see 621.3663*

.366 3	Gaseous-state lasers
.366 4	Chemical and dye lasers
.367	Technological photography and photo-optics

Standard subdivisions are added for either or both topics in heading

Including spectrography, stroboscopic photography

Class here image processing, optical data processing

> *For photoelectric and photoelectronic devices, see 621.381542; for optical communications, see 621.3827*

> *See Manual at 006.37 vs. 006.42, 621.367, 621.391, 621.399*

.367 2	Infrared and ultraviolet photography
.367 3	Radiography (Gamma-ray and X-ray photography)
.367 5	Holography
.367 8	Remote sensing technology

> *For photogrammetry, see 526.982*

.369	Other branches of applied optics
.369 2	Fiber optics

> *See also 621.381045 for optoelectronics*

.369 3	Integrated optics
.369 4	Nonlinear optics
.37	Testing and measurement of electrical quantities

Instruments and their use

> *For testing and measurement of a specific apparatus, part, or function, see the apparatus, part, or function, plus notation 0287 from Table 1, e.g., testing overhead lines 621.319220287*

.372	Units and standards of measurement

Including calibration of electrical instruments

.373	Recording meters

Class meters recording specific electrical quantities in 621.374

.374	Instruments for measuring specific electrical quantities

[.374 01–.374 09]   Standard subdivisions

>Do not use; class in 621.3701–621.3709

.374 2   Instruments for measuring capacitance, inductance, resistance

>Including bridges, ohmmeters, resistance boxes, shunts; comprehensive works on electrical bridges (bridge circuits)

>*For frequency bridges, see 621.3747*

.374 3   Instruments for measuring potential

>Including electrometers, potentiometers, voltage detectors, voltmeters

.374 4   Instruments for measuring current

>Including ammeters, ampere-hour meters, coulometers, galvanometers, milliammeters, voltameters

.374 5   Instruments for measuring energy

>Including electric meters, watt-hour meters

.374 6   Instruments for measuring power

>Including electrodynamometers, volt-ammeters, wattmeters

.374 7   Instruments for measuring frequency

>Including frequency bridges, oscillographs

>Class electric phasemeters in 621.3749

.374 9   Instruments for measuring phase

>Including power-factor meters, synchroscopes

.38   Electronics, communications engineering

>Unless other instructions are given, class a subject with aspects in two or more subdivisions of 621.38 in the number coming last, e.g., antennas for amateur radio 621.38416 (*not* 621.384135)

SUMMARY

621.381	**Electronics**
.382	**Communications engineering**
.383	**Telegraphy**
.384	**Radio and radar**
.385	**Telephony**
.386	**Telephone terminal equipment**
.387	**Telephone transmission and nonterminal equipment**
.388	**Television**
.389	**Security, sound recording, related systems**

.381   Electronics

>Class here microelectronics, molecular electronics

>Class signal processing in 621.3822; class electronic interference and noise in 621.38224. Class a specific application of electronics with the application, e.g., laser technology 621.366

>*See also 537.5 for physics of electronics*

SUMMARY

621.381 04	Special topics of electronics
.381 3	Microwave electronics
.381 5	Components and circuits

.381 04   Special topics of electronics

.381 044   Power and energy in electronic systems

.381 045   Optoelectronics

> *See also 621.3678 for remote sensing technology; also 621.3692 for fiber optics*

.381 046   Packaging

.381 3   Microwave electronics

.381 31   Wave propagation and transmission

         Including interference

.381 32   Circuits

> Add to base number 621.38132 the numbers following 621.38153 in 621.381532–621.381537, e.g., amplifiers 621.381325

.381 33   Components and devices

> Standard subdivisions are added for either or both topics in heading

> Class use of components in specific circuits in 621.38132

.381 331   Wave guides

.381 332   Cavity resonators

.381 333   Klystrons

.381 334   Magnetrons

.381 335   Traveling-wave tubes

.381 336   Masers

.381 5   Components and circuits

> Standard subdivisions are added for either or both topics in heading

> Class here analog, digital, integrated, microelectronic, semiconductor, superconductor, thin-film circuits; circuits and components common to electronics and communications engineering

> Class components and circuits of a specific branch of communications engineering in 621.383–621.389; class very large scale integration in 621.395

> *For microwave components and circuits, see 621.3813*

[.381 502 87]   Testing and measurement

> Do not use; class in 621.381548

>   621.381 51–621.381 52   Components

Class use of components in specific circuits in 621.38153; class devices not intrinsic to circuits in 621.38154; class analog-to-digital and digital-to-analog converters in 621.38159; class comprehensive works in 621.3815

.381 51	Electronic tubes
.381 512	Vacuum tubes
.381 513	Gas tubes
.381 52	Semiconductors

Class here crystal devices, miniaturization, optoelectronic devices, thin-film technology

.381 522	Diodes

Including junction, light-emitting, tunnel (Esaki), Zener diodes; varactors

.381 528	Transistors and thyristors

Standard subdivisions are added for transistors and thyristors together, for transistors alone

Including phototransistors

Class here bipolar transistors

.381 528 2	Junction transistors
.381 528 4	Field-effect transistors
.381 528 7	Thyristors
.381 53	Printed circuits and circuits for specific functions
.381 531	Printed circuits

Including microlithography

Class printed circuits for specific functions in 621.381532–621.381537

>   621.381 532–621.381 537   Circuits for specific functions

Class comprehensive works in 621.3815

.381 532	Converters, filters, interference eliminators
.381 532 2	Converters (Rectifiers and inverters)
.381 532 4	Filters
.381 533	Oscillators

Class use of oscillators in pulse circuits in 621.381534

.381 534	Pulse circuits
	Including counting circuits, pulse generators and processes
	Class modulation and demodulation (detection) of pulses in 621.3815365
.381 535	Amplifiers and feedback circuits
	Standard subdivisions are added for amplifiers and feedback circuits together, for amplifiers alone
	Class operational amplifiers in 621.395
.381 536	Modulators and demodulators (detectors)
	Class here modulation, demodulation (detection)
.381 536 2	Amplitude
	Including attenuators
.381 536 3	Frequency
	See also 621.3815486 for frequency synthesizers
.381 536 4	Phase
	Including phase-locked loops
.381 536 5	Pulse
.381 537	Switching, control, trigger circuits, relays
.381 537 2	Switching theory
	Class switching theory in logic circuit design in 621.395
.381 54	Supplementary components
	Devices not intrinsic to circuits
	Class here electronic instrumentation (applications of electronics)
	Class instrumentation in a specific field with the field, e.g., electronic control 629.89
.381 542	Photoelectric and photoelectronic components
	Including electric eyes; photoconductive, photoemissive, photovoltaic cells; photomultipliers; phototubes
	See also 621.367 for image processing; also 621.381045 for optoelectronics
.381 542 2	Video display components
	Including liquid crystal displays

.381 548	Testing and measuring components

Including bridges (bridge circuits); signal, square-wave, sweep generators; thermistors

Class here testing and measuring electronic circuits and components, instruments for testing and measuring electronic signals

Class testing and measuring a specific circuit or component with the circuit or component, plus notation 0287 from Table 1, e.g., testing amplifiers 621.3815350287

.381 548 3	Oscilloscopes

Including oscillographs

.381 548 6	Frequency synthesizers
.381 59	Analog-to-digital and digital-to-analog converters

Standard subdivisions are added for either or both topics in heading

Class analog-to-digital and digital-to-analog converters in data communications engineering in 621.39814

.382	Communications engineering

Class here analog, digital, electronic communications; telecommunications; comprehensive works on digital data and telecommunications engineering

Unless other instructions are given, class a subject with aspects in two or more subdivisions of 621.382 in the number coming last, e.g., signal processing in acoustical communications 621.3828 (*not* 621.3822)

Class comprehensive works on wireless communication in 621.384. Class a component or circuit common to electronics and communications engineering with the component or circuit in 621.3815, e.g., amplifiers 621.381535, switching circuits 621.381537

For specific communications systems, see 621.383–621.389; for data communications engineering, see 621.3981

See Manual at 004.6 vs. 621.382, 621.3981

[.382 028 546 2]	Interfacing and communications protocols (standards)

Do not use; class in 621.38212

[.382 028 546 5]	Communications network architecture

Do not use; class in 621.38215

[.382 028 546 6]	Data transmission modes and data switching methods

Do not use; class in 621.38216

.382 1	Communications networks

For communications networks based on a specific technology, see the technology, e.g., telephone networks 621.385

.382 12	Communications protocols (Communications standards)
[.382 120 218]	Standards
	Do not use; class in 621.38212
.382 15	Communications network architecture
	Class here systems analysis, design, topology (configuration) of communications networks
.382 16	Data transmission modes and data switching methods
	Including circuit and packet switching, multiplexing, asynchronous and synchronous transfer modes
.382 2	Signal processing
	Class here information theory
	Class interdisciplinary works on information theory in 003.54
.382 23	Signal analysis and theory
	Standard subdivisions are added for either or both topics in heading
.382 24	Interference and noise
	Standard subdivisions are added for either or both topics in heading
	Class here electronic interference and noise
.382 3	Miscellaneous topics
	Limited to studios, transmission facilities, and the topics provided for below
.382 32	Power supply in communications systems
.382 34	Recording devices
	Including discs, tapes
	For a recording device of a specific communication system, see the device in 621.383–621.389, e.g., video recorders 621.38833, sound recorders 621.38932
.382 35	Facsimile transmission
	By wire or radio wave
	Class here telefacsimile
.382 38	Space communications
	See also 621.3825 for satellite communication
.382 4	Antennas and propagation
.382 5	Relay communication
	Class here satellite communication
.382 54	Antennas and propagation

.382 7   Optical communications

       Transmission of sound, visual images, other information by light

       Including optical disc technology

       Class here laser communications

       Class optoacoustic communications in 621.3828

.382 75   Optical-fiber communication

       Class here guided-light communication

.382 8   Acoustical communications

       Audio systems covering broadcasting and transmission as well as recording and reproduction of sound

       Including acousto-optical communications

       Class here electroacoustical communications

       Class audio systems limited to recording and reproduction of sound in 621.3893

.382 84   Specific devices

       Including microphones, speakers

       Class antennas in 621.3824

>   621.383–621.389   Specific communications systems

       Class comprehensive works in 621.382

.383   Telegraphy

       For radiotelegraphy, see 621.3842

.384   Radio and radar

       Including digital audio broadcasting

       Standard subdivisions are added for radio and radar together, for radio alone

       Class here broadcasting stations; comprehensive engineering works on radio and television, on wireless communication

       Class interdisciplinary works on radio and television in 384.5; class interdisciplinary works on broadcasting stations in 384.5453

       For satellite communication, see 621.3825; for television, see 621.388

.384 028 8   Maintenance and repair

       Class maintenance and repair of radio receiving sets in 621.384187

>   621.384 1–621.384 5   Radio

       Class comprehensive works in 621.384

.384 1	Specific topics in general radio
[.384 101–.384 109]	Standard subdivision
	Do not use; class in 621.38401–621.38409
.384 11	Wave propagation and transmission
	Including interference
	See also 384.54524 for allocation of frequencies
.384 12	Circuits
	Including amplifiers, filters, interference eliminators, modulation circuits, oscillators, rectifiers
	Class a specific application of circuits with the application, e.g., receiving set circuits 621.38418
.384 13	Components and devices
	Standard subdivisions are added for either or both topics in heading
.384 131	Transmitters
.384 132	Tubes
	Class use of tubes in specific circuits in 621.38412
.384 133	Miscellaneous supplementary devices
	Limited to condensers (capacitors), grounding devices, inductors, microphones, resistors, testing equipment
.384 134	Semiconductor devices
	Class use of semiconductor devices in specific circuits in 621.38412
.384 135	Antennas
.384 15	Systems by wave type, satellite and relay systems
	Standard subdivisions are added for systems by wave type, satellite and relay systems together; for systems by wave type alone

---

> 621.384 151–621.384 153 Systems by wave type

Class relay and satellite systems of a specific wave type in 621.384156; class comprehensive works in 621.38415

.384 151	Shortwave systems
	Including ultrahigh frequency (UHF), very-high-frequency (VHF) systems
	For frequency-modulation systems, see 621.384152
.384 152	Frequency-modulation (FM) systems

.384 153	Long-wave systems
	Including amplitude modulation (AM), single-sideband, very-low-frequency (VLF) systems
.384 156	Relay and satellite systems
.384 16	Amateur radio (Ham radio)
	Limited to long distance communication
	Class here comprehensive works on amateur and citizens band radio
	For citizens band radio, see 621.38454
.384 18	Radio receiving sets
[.384 180 288]	Maintenance and repair
	Do not use; class in 621.384187
.384 187	Maintenance and repair
.384 19	Special developments
.384 191	Direction and position finding
	Standard subdivisions are added for either or both topics in heading
	Including loran, radio beacons, radio compasses
	Class here GPS receivers
	Identification and locating relocated to 621.384192; real-time locating systems (RTLS) relocated to 621.384192; radio frequency identification (RFID) systems relocated to 621.384192
.384 192	Identification and locating [*formerly* 621.384191]
	Standard subdivisions are added for either or both topics in heading
	Including radio frequency identification (RFID) systems [*formerly* 621.384191]
	Class here real-time locating systems (RTLS) [*formerly* 621.384191]; automatic identification and data capture (AIDC)
.384 196	Radio control
	Variant names: remote control, telecontrol
.384 197	Space communication
.384 2	Radiotelegraphy

.384 5	Radiotelephony
	Including portable radios, walkie-talkies
	Class here mobile radio stations, comprehensive works on radio transmission in telephony
	For radio relays, see 621.38782
.384 54	Citizens band radio
	Limited to local communication (ca. 10 miles or 15 kilometers)
	Class comprehensive works on amateur and citizens band radio in 621.38416
.384 56	Cellular telephone systems
	Variant names: cellular radio, portable telephone systems
.384 8	Radar
.384 83	Specific instruments and devices
	Including antennas
.384 85	Systems
	Including continuous, monopulse, pulse-modulated systems
.385	Telephony
	Class here telephone systems based on wires, cables, lasers, optical fibers; Internet telephony
	Class cellular telephone systems in 621.38456; class data communications engineering in 621.3981; class interdisciplinary works on telephony in 384.6
	For radiotelephony, see 621.3845; for telephone terminal equipment, see 621.386; for telephone transmission and nonterminal equipment, see 621.387
.385 1	Network analysis
.385 7	Automatic and semiautomatic switching systems
	Including direct distance dialing
.386	Telephone terminal equipment
	Dialing, transmitting, receiving equipment
.386 7	Telephone answering and message recording devices
.386 9	Pay telephones
.387	Telephone transmission and nonterminal equipment
	Including switching systems
.387 8	Transmission
	Class comprehensive works on radio transmission in telephony in 621.3845

.387 82	Long-distance systems
	Including radio relays
.387 83	Local systems
.387 84	Transmission lines and cables
.388	Television

Class here interactive television (TV programming with interactive content and/or enhancements, e.g., interactive program guides, personalized multi-camera angles, real-time voting, video-on-demand)

.388 001	Philosophy and theory
.388 002	Miscellany
.388 002 88	Maintenance and repair

Class here maintenance and repair of broadcast and transmission equipment, of comprehensive works on television repair

For maintenance and repair of receiving sets, see 621.38887

.388 003–.388 009	Standard subdivisions
.388 02	Black-and-white television
.388 04	Color television
.388 06	High-definition television (HDTV)
.388 07	Digital television
.388 1	Wave propagation and transmission
	Including interference
.388 3	Components and devices

Standard subdivisions are added for either or both topics in heading

.388 31	Transmitters
.388 32	Semiconductors, transistors, tubes
.388 33	Video recorders and video recordings

Standard subdivisions are added for video recorders and video recordings together, for video recorders alone

[.388 330 288]	Maintenance and repair

Do not use; class in 621.388337

.388 332	Video recordings
	Including cassettes, discs
[.388 332 028 8]	Maintenance and repair

Do not use; class in 621.388337

.388 337	Maintenance and repair of video recorders and video recordings
.388 34	Cameras and components
.388 35	Antennas
.388 5	Communication systems
.388 53	Satellite television
.388 57	Cable television
.388 6	Stations
.388 8	Television sets
[.388 802 88]	Maintenance and repair

Do not use; class in 621.38887

.388 87	Maintenance and repair
.389	Security, sound recording, related systems
.389 2	Public address, security, related systems

Including paging systems, sirens

.389 28   Security electronics

Including surveillance systems, e.g., electronic eavesdropping devices

Class here alarm systems

For fire alarms, see 628.9225

.389 3   Sound recording and reproducing systems

Audio systems limited to recording and reproduction of sound

Class here digital audio engineering

Class telephone message recording in 621.3867; class comprehensive works on acoustical communications, on audio systems covering transmission as well as recording and reproduction in 621.3828

.389 32   Recorders and recordings

Including compact discs

.389 324   Tape recorders and recordings

Including cassettes

.389 33   Reproducers

Including compact disc players, jukeboxes, phonographs

Class combination recorders-reproducers in 621.38932

.389 332   High-fidelity systems (Hi-fi)

For stereophonic systems, see 621.389334

.389 334	Stereophonic systems
	Including quadraphonic systems
.389 5	Sonar
.389 7	Audiovisual engineering
.39	Computer engineering

Class here electronic digital computers, central processing units, computer reliability, general computer performance evaluation

Unless other instructions are given, class a subject with aspects in two or more subdivisions of 621.39 in the number coming last, e.g., circuitry of computer internal storage 621.3973 (*not* 621.395)

Class selection and use of computer hardware, works treating both hardware and either programming or programs in 004. Class a specific application of computers with the application, e.g., use of computers to regulate processes automatically 629.895

See Manual at 004–006 vs. 621.39

[.390 287]	Testing and measurement
	Do not use; class in 621.392
.391	General works on specific types of computers

Including optical computers

Class here specific types of processors, e.g., multiprocessors

Class programmable calculators in 681.14

See Manual at 006.37 vs. 006.42, 621.367, 621.391, 621.399

>	621.391 1–621.391 6 Digital computers

Class comprehensive works in 621.39

See Manual at 004.11–004.16

.391 1	Supercomputers
.391 2	Mainframe computers
	For supercomputers, see 621.3911
.391 4	Midrange computers

Class here minicomputers, server class computers

Class comprehensive works on midrange and personal computers in 621.3916

.391 6	Personal computers
	Former heading: Microcomputers
	Class here specific types of personal computers; comprehensive works on midrange and personal computers
	For midrange computers, see 621.3914
.391 67	Handheld computing devices
	Class here specific types of handheld computing devices
.391 9	Analog and hybrid computers
	Standard subdivisions are added for either or both topics in heading
.392	Systems analysis and design, computer architecture
	Including hardware description languages
	See Manual at 004.21 vs. 004.22, 621.392
.395	Circuitry
	Class here logic circuits, logic design of circuits, very large scale integration (VLSI)
.397	Storage
.397 3	Internal storage (Main memory)
	Class here random-access memory (RAM), read-only memory (ROM)
	Class CD-ROM (compact disc read-only memory) in 621.3976
.397 32	Semiconductor memory
	Class here bipolar, metal-oxide-semiconductor (MOS), thin-film memory
.397 6	External storage (Auxiliary storage)
	Including punched cards
.397 63	Magnetic storage
	Including floppy disks, floppy disk drives; magnetic tapes, e.g., cartridges, cassettes, reel-to-reel tapes; tape drives
	Class here hard disks, hard disk drives; magnetic bubble memory
.397 67	Optical storage
	Including CD-ROM (compact disc read-only memory), DVD, WORM (write once read many) discs and drives
	Class storage of pictorial data in optical storage devices in 621.367
.397 68	Semiconductor storage
	Class here solid-state storage; flash drives, memory cards
.398	Interfacing and communications devices, peripherals

.398 1   Interfacing and communications devices

               Class here data communications engineering

               Class Internet telephony in 621.385

                 See Manual at 004.6 vs. 621.382, 621.3981

.398 14   Analog-to-digital and digital-to-analog converters

               Standard subdivisions are added for either or both topics in heading

               Including modems

.398 4   Peripherals

               Class peripheral storage in 621.3976

                 For peripherals combining input and output functions, see 621.3985; for input peripherals, see 621.3986; for output peripherals, see 621.3987

.398 5   Peripherals combining input and output functions

               Class here computer terminals

               Class tape and disk devices in 621.3976

.398 6   Input peripherals

               Including keyboards

.398 7   Output peripherals

               Including monitors (video display screens), printers

                 See also 621.3996 for computer graphics

.399   Devices for special computer methods

               Including computer sound synthesis

                 See Manual at 006.37 vs. 006.42, 621.367, 621.391, 621.399

.399 3   Computer vision

.399 4   Computer pattern recognition

.399 6   Computer graphics

.4   **Prime movers and heat engineering**

               Standard subdivisions are added for prime movers and heat engineering together, for prime movers alone

               Class here engines, power plants, propulsion systems

                 For steam engineering, see 621.1; for hydraulic-power technology, see 621.2

SUMMARY

621.400 1–.400 9	**Standard subdivisions**
.402–.406	**[Heat engineering and turbines]**
.42	**Stirling engines and air motors**
.43	**Internal-combustion engines**
.44	**Geothermal engineering**
.45	**Wind engines**
.46	**Electric and related motors**
.47	**Solar-energy engineering**
.48	**Nuclear engineering**

.400 1–.400 9   Standard subdivisions

.402   Heat engineering

> *For low-temperature technology, see 621.56. For a kind of heat engineering, see the kind, e.g., geothermal engineering 621.44, heating buildings 697*
>
> *See also 536 for physics of heat*

.402 1   Thermodynamics

.402 2   Heat transfer

> Including heat exchange

.402 23   Conduction

.402 25   Convection

.402 27   Radiation

.402 3   Fuels and combustion

> Class pollution by-products of combustion in 628.532

.402 4   Insulation

.402 5   Equipment

> Including furnaces, heat engines, heat exchangers, heat pumps
>
> Class solar furnaces in 621.477

.402 8   Specific heat systems

> Not provided for elsewhere
>
> Including distribution and storage systems; electric heating
>
> Class a specific aspect of a specific heat system with the aspect, e.g., heat transfer in electric heating 621.4022

.406   Turbines

> Class here turbomachines

.42   Stirling engines and air motors

> *For wind engines, see 621.45*

.43   Internal-combustion engines

Class generation of electricity by internal-combustion engines in 621.312133

For internal-combustion engines for a specific type of transportation, see the type, e.g., internal-combustion engines of ships 623.8723

>   621.433–621.436   Specific internal-combustion engines

Class parts and accessories of specific engines in 621.437; class comprehensive works in 621.43

.433   Gas turbines and free-piston engines

Standard subdivisions are added for gas turbines and free-piston engines, for gas turbines alone

For turbojet engines, see 621.4352

.433 5   Free-piston engines

.434   Spark-ignition engines

Nondiesel piston engines

Including rotary spark-ignition engines

Class here reciprocating spark-ignition engines

.435   Jet and rocket engines

.435 2   Jet engines

Including turbojet engines

.435 6   Rocket engines

Class here interdisciplinary works on rocketry

For a specific aspect of rocketry, see the aspect, e.g., rocket weapons 623.4519, booster rockets 629.475

.436   Diesel and semidiesel engines

Standard subdivisions are added for either or both topics in heading

Class here compression-ignition engines

[.436 028 8]   Maintenance and repair

Do not use; class in 621.4368

.436 1   General topics of diesel and semidiesel engines

Including combustion

.436 2   Design and construction

.436 8   Operation, maintenance, repair

.437   Parts and accessories of internal-combustion engines

Including carburetors, connecting rods, cylinders, governors, ignition devices, pistons, valves

.44 Geothermal engineering

.45 Wind engines

Class wind-powered generation of electricity in 621.312136

.453 Windmills

.46 Electric and related motors

Standard subdivisions are added for electric and related motors together, electric motors alone

.47 Solar-energy engineering

Class engineering of secondary sources of solar energy with the secondary source, e.g., generation of electricity from solar radiation 621.31244, wind energy 621.45

.471 General topics of solar-energy engineering

.471 2 Heat storage

.472 Solar collectors

.473 Solar engines

.477 Solar furnaces

.48 Nuclear engineering

Fission and fusion technology

See also 539.7 for nuclear physics

.483 Nuclear reactors, power plants, by-products

Standard subdivisions are added for nuclear reactors, power plants, by-products together; for nuclear reactors alone; for nuclear power plants alone

Class here fission reactors, nuclear steam-powered generation of electricity; comprehensive works on fission and fusion reactor, power plants, by-products

For fusion reactors, power plants, by-products, see 621.484

.483 015 3 Physical principles

Do not use for reactor physics; class in 621.4831

.483 028 6 Green technology (Environmental technology)

Do not use for waste technology; class in 621.4838

[.483 028 9] Safety measures

Do not use; class in 621.4835

.483 1	Reactor physics

Including critical size

Class here physics of reactor cores

Class physics of a specific component, material, or process with the component, material, or process, plus notation 0153 from Table 1, e.g., nuclear reactions in fuel elements 621.483350153976

.483 2	Design, construction, shielding, siting
.483 23	Shielding
.483 3	Materials
.483 32	Structural materials
.483 35	Fuel element materials

Fuels and cladding

.483 36	Coolants
.483 37	Moderators
.483 4	Specific types of reactors

Classified by neutron energy, moderator, fuel and fuel conversion, coolant

Including breeder reactors

Class a specific aspect of a specific type with the aspect, e.g., shielding of fast reactors 621.48323

.483 5	Operation, control, safety measures
.483 7	Radioactive isotopes

Class here comprehensive technological works on radioisotopes

> *For a specific application of radioisotopes, see the application, e.g., radioactive isotope therapy 615.8424, radioisotope thermoelectric generation 621.31243*

.483 8	Waste technology
.484	Fusion reactors, fusion power plants, by-products

Standard subdivisions are added for fusion reactors, fusion power plants, by-products together; for fusion reactors alone; for fusion power plants alone

Variant name for fusion reactors: thermonuclear reactors

Including tokamaks

Class comprehensive works on fission and fusion reactor, power plants, by-products in 621.483

.485	Nuclear propulsion
.5	**Pneumatic, vacuum, low-temperature technologies**

.51   Pneumatic technology

Class here air compression technology, air compressors

For a specific kind of pneumatic technology, see the kind, e.g., compressed-air transmission 621.53, pneumatic control 629.8045

.53   Compressed-air transmission

.54   Pneumatic conveying and cleaning

Including carriers, cleaners, sandblasters

.55   Vacuum technology

Including vacuum pumps

See also 533.5 for vacuum physics

.56   Low-temperature technology

Class here refrigeration

For freezers and refrigerators, see 621.57; for ice manufacture, see 621.58; for cryogenic technology, see 621.59

See also 536.56 for physics of low temperatures

.563   Heat pumps

.564   Refrigerants

.57   Freezers and refrigerators

.58   Ice manufacture

.59   Cryogenic technology

Including liquefaction and solidification of gases having low boiling points

.6   **Blowers, fans, pumps**

.61   Blowers and fans

Standard subdivisions are added for either or both topics in heading

For rotary blowers and fans, see 621.62; for centrifugal blowers and fans, see 621.63

.62   Rotary blowers and fans

Standard subdivisions are added for either or both topics in heading

.63   Centrifugal blowers and fans

Standard subdivisions are added for either or both topics in heading

---

>   621.64–621.69   Pumps

Class hydraulic pumps in 621.252; class comprehensive works in 621.69

.64   Hand pumps

.65   Reciprocating pumps

.66   Rotary pumps

.67   Centrifugal pumps

.69   Pneumatic pumps

> Class here water-lifting devices, comprehensive works on pumps
>
> *For a specific kind of pump, see the kind, e.g., hydraulic pumps 621.252*

.691   Jet pumps

.699   Density and direct-fluid-pressure displacement pumps

.8   Machine engineering

> Class a specific kind of machinery not provided for here with the kind, e.g.,
> hydraulic machinery 621.2; class a specific use of machinery with the use, e.g.,
> gears in clocks 681.112

SUMMARY

621.802 87	**Testing and measuring**
.81	**General topics of machine engineering**
.82	**Machine parts**
.83	**Gears and cams**
.84	**Valves and pistons**
.85	**Power transmission systems**
.86	**Materials-handling equipment**
.87	**Cranes and elevators**
.88	**Fasteners**
.89	**Tribology**

[.801 53]   Physical principles

> Do not use; class in 621.811

.802 87   Testing and measuring

> Class here strength tests of mechanisms

[.802 88]   Maintenance and repair

> Do not use; class in 621.816

.81   General topics of machine engineering

.811   Physical principles

> Including vibration

.812   Power and speed control devices

.815   Machine design

.816   Maintenance and repair

> Including balancing

.82   Machine parts

> Including rotors
>
> *For gears, ratchets, cams, see 621.83; for valves, pistons, see 621.84*

.821	Journals
.822	Bearings

Including ball, roller, sliding bearings

Class journals in 621.821

.823	Shafts

Including axles

Class bearings in 621.822

For journals, see 621.821

.824	Springs
.825	Clutches, couplings, universal joints
.827	Connecting rods, cranks, eccentrics
.83	Gears and cams

Including pawls, ratchets

.833	Gears

Class here gearing

.833 1	Spur gears
.833 2	Bevel and skew bevel gears
.833 3	Spiral and worm gears
.838	Cams
.84	Valves and pistons

Standard subdivisions are added for valves and pistons, for valves alone

Variant names for valves: cocks, faucets, taps

.85	Power transmission systems

Class power transmission systems for materials-handling equipment in 621.86. Class a specific machine part of a transmission system with the part, e.g., shafts 621.823

.852	Power transmission by belt
.853	Power transmission by rope
.854	Power transmission by wire
.859	Power transmission by chain
.86	Materials-handling equipment

For cranes, elevators, see 621.87

.862	Hoisting equipment

For chain hoists, fork lifts, tackles, see 621.863; for capstans, winches, windlasses, see 621.864

.863	Chain hoists, fork lifts, tackles
.864	Capstans, winches, windlasses
.865	Excavating machinery

Class here earthmoving machinery, power shovels

.867	Conveying equipment

For telpherage, see 621.868

.867 2	Pipes

Including pipe laying

Class here pipelines

Class coal pipelines in 662.624; class petroleum pipelines in 665.544; class industrial gases pipelines in 665.744. Class manufacturing pipes of a specific material with the material, e.g., metal pipes 671.832

.867 5	Belt conveyors
.867 6	Escalators
.868	Telpherage

Including chair lifts, ski tows

Class here comprehensive works on people movers

For escalators, see 621.8676; for elevators, see 621.877

.87	Cranes and elevators
.873	Cranes

Including cherry pickers, derricks

.877	Elevators

Including jacks

.88	Fasteners

See also 621.97 for fastening equipment

.882	Bolts, nuts, screws
.883	Cotters
.884	Nails and rivets
.885	Sealing devices
.89	Tribology

Including lubrication, lubricants, wear

Class here friction

For bearings, see 621.822

.9 **Tools**

> Class here fabricating equipment
>
> Class a specific use with the use, e.g., lathes in woodworking 684.08

.900 1–.900 9   Standard subdivisions

.902   Machine tools

.902 3   Numerical control

.904   Pneumatic tools

.908   Hand tools

.91   Planing and milling tools

> *See also 671.35 for machining metal*

.912   Planers, shapers, slotters

.914   Crushing tools

.92   Abrading and grinding tools

> Standard subdivisions are added for either or both topics in heading

.922   Lapping tools

> Including buffing, polishing tools

.923   Emery wheels and grindstones

.924   Filing tools

.93   Cutting, disassembling, sawing tools

> Including axes, crowbars, scissors, shears, slicers, trimmers

.932   Knives

.934   Saws

.94   Turning tools

> Class turning tools used for perforating in 621.95

.942   Lathes

.944   Gear-cutting, pipe-threading, screw-cutting tools

> *For tapping tools, see 621.955*

.95   Perforating and tapping tools

> Standard subdivisions are added for perforating and tapping tools together, for perforating tools alone
>
> *For punching tools, see 621.96*

.952   Drilling tools

> Class here boring tools

.954   Broaching and reaming tools

.955   Tapping tools

See also 621.84 for taps (valves)

.96   Punching tools

Class die punches in 621.984

.97   Fastening and joining equipment

Standard subdivisions are added for either or both topics in heading

Class fasteners in 621.88

.972   Screwdrivers and wrenches

Variant name for wrenches: spanners

.973   Hand hammers

.974   Power hammers

.977   Soldering and welding equipment

.978   Riveting equipment

.98   Pressing, impressing, molding equipment

Standard subdivisions are added for pressing, impressing, molding equipment together; for pressing equipment alone

.982   Bending tools

.984   Impressing and molding equipment

Including dies, molds, stamps

.99   Other tools and equipment

.992   Guiding, holding, safety equipment

Including chucks, clamps, guards, jigs, vises

622   Mining and related operations

Standard subdivisions are added for mining and related operations together, for mining alone

SUMMARY

[.028 9]   Safety measures

Do not use; class in 622.8

.1   **Prospecting**

Class here exploratory operations

\>   622.12–622.17   General topics of prospecting

Class general topics of prospecting applied to specific materials in 622.18; class general topics of prospecting applied to treasure in 622.19; class comprehensive works in 622.1

.12   Surface exploration

Including biogeochemical, geobotanical, geological prospecting

.13   Geochemical prospecting

Including mineral surveys (qualitative and quantitative measurement of mineral content)

Class biogeochemical prospecting in 622.12

.14   Mine surveys

Determination of size, depth, shape of mines

.15   Geophysical prospecting

.152   Gravitational prospecting

.153   Magnetic prospecting

.154   Electrical prospecting

.159   Other methods of prospecting

Including gas-detection, geothermal, radioactivity prospecting

.159 2   Seismic prospecting

Variant names: acoustical, vibration prospecting

.17   Underwater prospecting

.18   Prospecting for specific materials

Add to base number 622.18 the numbers following 553 in 553.2–553.9, e.g., prospecting for petroleum 622.1828; however, for prospecting for water, see 628.11

Standard subdivisions are added for specific materials even if only one type of prospecting is used, e.g., seismic exploration for petroleum in Texas 622.182809764

.19   Prospecting for treasure

Underground and underwater

Class here treasure hunting

Class archaeological methods and equipment in 930.1028

.2   **Excavation techniques**

Class here underground (subsurface) mining

Class extraction techniques for specific materials in 622.3

See also 622.4–622.8 for nonextractive mining technologies

>   622.22–622.28   Underground mining

Class comprehensive works in 622.2

.22   In-situ processing

Class here leach mining wells, solution mining

See Manual at 622.22, 622.7 vs. 662.6, 669

.23   Underground blasting and drilling

.24   Underground boring

.25   Shaft sinking

Class here shafts

.26   Tunneling

Class here tunnels

.28   Supporting structures

Class here control of roof and wall failure (rock failure)

.29   Surface and underwater mining

.292   Surface mining

Class here open-pit and strip mining

Class reclamation after surface mining in 631.64

For quarrying, see 622.35

.292 7   Alluvial mining

Including hydraulic and placer mining

.295   Underwater mining

Class here offshore mining, mineral extraction from ocean floor

.3   ***Mining for specific materials**

Class here extraction techniques of specific materials

Class prospecting for specific materials in 622.18. Class a nonextractive mining technology relating to specific materials with the technology in 622.4–622.8, e.g., ore dressing 622.7

For surface mining of specific materials, see 622.292

---

*Do not use notation 0289 from Table 1 for safety measures; class in 622.8

.33	*Carbonaceous materials

.331–.337   Coal, graphite, solid and semisolid bitumens

Add to base number 622.33 the numbers following 553.2 in 553.21–553.27, e.g., coal 622.334; however, for safety measures, see 622.8

.338   *Oil, oil shales, tar sands, natural gas

Use 622.338 for extraction of petroleum covering oil and gas, use 622.3382 for petroleum limited to oil

Class comprehensive technical works on petroleum in 665.5; class interdisciplinary works on petroleum in 553.28

.338 1   *Drilling techniques

Including use of drilling muds (drilling fluids)

.338 19   *Offshore drilling

Class here comprehensive works on offshore petroleum extraction

For a specific aspect of offshore petroleum extraction, see the aspect, e.g., offshore enhanced oil recovery 622.3382

.338 2   *Oil

Including well blowouts

Class here reservoir engineering; enhanced, secondary, tertiary recovery; well flooding

Class techniques of drilling for oil in 622.3381

.338 27   *Specific enhanced oil recovery methods

Including enhanced recovery by use of bacteria

.338 3   *Oil shale and tar sands

Variant names for oil shale: bituminous, black shale; for tar sands: bituminous, oil sands

Class extraction of oils from oil shale and tar sands in 665.4

.338 5   *Natural gas

Class techniques of drilling for natural gas in 622.3381

.339   *Fossil resins and gums

Standard subdivisions are added for fossil resins and gums together, for fossil resins alone

.34   *Metals

Class here the ore of the metal

.341   *Iron

---

*Do not use notation 0289 from Table 1 for safety measures; class in 622.8

>   622.342–622.349   Nonferrous metals

                 Class comprehensive works in 622.34

.342   *Precious metals

.342 2   *Gold

.342 3   *Silver

.342 4   *Platinum

.343–.349   Other nonferrous metals

                 Add to base number 622.34 the numbers following 553.4 in 553.43–553.49, e.g., uranium ores 622.34932; however, for safety measures, see 622.8

.35–.39   Other materials

                 Add to base number 622.3 the numbers following 553 in 553.5–553.9, e.g., gem diamonds 622.382; however, for safety measures, see 622.8; for water, see 628.114

.35   Structural and sculptural stone

                 Number built according to instructions under 622.35–622.39

                 Class here quarrying

                    For quarrying of other economic materials, see 622.36

>   **622.4–622.8   Nonextractive mining technologies**

                 Class here nonextractive mining technologies relating to specific materials

                 Class comprehensive works in 622

.4   **Mine environment**

                    For mine drainage, see 622.5; for mine health and safety, see 622.8

.42   Ventilation and air conditioning

                    For temperature control, see 622.43

.43   Temperature control

.47   Illumination

.473   Portable lamps

.474   Electric lighting systems

.48   Electricity

                 Class electricity applied to a specific operation with the operation, e.g., temperature control 622.43

.49   Sanitation

*Do not use notation 0289 from Table 1 for safety measures; class in 622.8

.5	**Mine drainage**
.6	**Mine transport systems**
	Haulage and hoisting
.65	Hand and animal haulage
.66	Mechanical haulage
	Including mine railroads
	Class vertical haulage in 622.68
.67	Direct-driven and gear-driven hoists
.68	Elevators
	Including skips
.69	Surface transportation
	Including loading, unloading, transshipment
.7	**Ore dressing**
	Class here dressing of specific mineral ores
	See Manual at 622.22, 622.7 vs. 662.6, 669
.73	Crushing and grinding
.74	Sizing
	Including screening

> 622.75–622.77 Ore concentration

Variant names: beneficiation, ore separation

Class comprehensive works in 622.7

.75	Mechanical separation
.751	Gravity concentration
.752	Flotation
.77	Electrostatic and magnetic separation
.79	Milling plants
	Class specific milling-plant operations in 622.73–622.77

.8   **Mine health and safety**

Standard subdivisions are added for either or both topics in heading

Class control of roof and wall failure (rock failure) in 622.28; class interdisciplinary works on mine safety in 363.119622

> *For comprehensive works on safety measures for excavation techniques, see 622.20289; for sanitation, see 622.49. For safety measures for a specific excavation technique, see the technique in 622.22–622.29, plus notation 0289 from Table 1, e.g., safety measures in tunneling 622.260289*

.82   Control of gas and explosions

Class here comprehensive works on fire control, on respiratory safety

> *For dust control, see 622.83*

.83   Dust control

.89   Rescue operations

623   Military and nautical engineering

Standard subdivisions are added for military and nautical engineering together, for military engineering alone

See Manual at 355–359 vs. 623

SUMMARY

623.04		**Special topics of military engineering**
.1		**Fortifications**
.2		**Mine laying and clearance, demolition**
.3		**Engineering of defense**
.4		**Ordnance**
.5		**Ballistics and gunnery**
.6		**Military transportation technology**
.7		**Communications, vehicles, sanitation, related topics**
.8		**Nautical engineering and seamanship**

.04   Special topics of military engineering

.042   Optical engineering

Class here infrared and ultraviolet technology

.043   Electronic engineering

.044   Nuclear engineering

.045   Mechanical engineering

.047   Construction engineering

>   **623.1–623.7 Military engineering**

Class special topics of military engineering in 623.04; class naval engineering in 623.8; class comprehensive works in 623

.1 **Fortifications**

> Class here forts and fortresses
>
> Class architectural aspects in 725.18

.109 History and biography

> > Do not use for geographic treatment; class in 623.19

.15 Temporary fortifications

.19 Geographic treatment

> > Add to base number 623.19 notation 1–9 from Table 2, e.g., forts in France 623.1944

.2 **Mine laying and clearance, demolition**

.26 Mine laying and clearing

> > Standard subdivisions are added for either or both topics in heading
> >
> > *See also 623.45115 for manufacture of mines*

.27 Demolition

.3 **Engineering of defense**

> Class warning systems in 623.737
>
> *See also 623.4 for ordnance*

.31 Defense against invasion

> > Including countermining, flooding, mechanical barriers, moats, traps
> >
> > Class architectural aspects of moats in 725.98
> >
> > *For fortifications, see 623.1; for mine laying, demolition, see 623.2*

.38 Protective construction

> > Including air raid shelters

.4 **Ordnance**

> Class combat ships in 623.82
>
> *For combat vehicles, see 623.74*

SUMMARY

623.41	**Artillery**
.42	**Specific pieces of artillery**
.43	**Gun mounts**
.44	**Small arms and other weapons**
.45	**Ammunition and other destructive agents**
.46	**Accessories**

.41 Artillery

> > *For specific pieces of artillery, see 623.42; for artillery projectiles, see 623.4513*

.412	Field artillery
.417	Coast artillery
.418	Naval artillery
.419	Space artillery
.42	Specific pieces of artillery

> Including cannons, howitzers, mortars, crew-served rocket launchers

| .43 | Gun mounts |
| .44 | Small arms and other weapons |

> Standard subdivisions are added for small arms and other weapons together, for small arms alone

> Class here side arms

> Class artistic aspects of arms and armor in 739.7. Class vehicle-mounted small arms with the vehicle, e.g., armored cars 623.7475

> *See also 623.455 for small arms ammunition*

| .441 | Weaponry of prefirearm origin |

> Including armor, bayonets, bows and arrows, catapults, knives, maces, shields, spears, swords, tomahawks

| .442 | Portable firearms |

> *For handguns, see 623.443*

| .442 4 | Automatic firearms |

> Including automatic rifles, machine and submachine guns

> Class automatic pistols and revolvers in 623.443

.442 5	Carbines, muskets, rifles
.442 6	Portable rocket launchers (Bazookas)
.443	Handguns
.443 2	Pistols
.443 6	Revolvers
.445	Chemical weapons

> Including flame throwers; rifle attachments for launching smoke and gas canisters

> Class artillery for launching chemical projectiles in 623.41; class chemical delivery devices in 623.4516

> *For chemical agents, see 623.4592*

| .446 | Destructive radiation weapons |

> Including laser weapons, thermal weapons

.447   Destructive vibration weapons

> Including ultrasonic weapons

.45   Ammunition and other destructive agents

> Standard subdivisions are added for ammunition and other destructive agents together, for ammunition alone

.451   Charge-containing devices

> Class here bombs, missiles, projectiles
>
> Class interdisciplinary works on bombs in 355.8251; class interdisciplinary works on missiles in 358.17182
>
> *For tactical rockets, see 623.4543*
>
> *See also 623.455 for small arms ammunition*

.451 1   Grenades, mines, nuclear weapons

> Class grenades and mines with special types of charges in 623.4516–623.4518

.451 14   Grenades

> Class here hand and rifle grenades

.451 15   Mines

> Class mine laying and clearance in 623.26

.451 19   Nuclear weapons

> Including artillery projectiles, bombs
>
> *For nuclear missiles, see 623.4519*

.451 3   Artillery projectiles

> Class artillery projectiles with special types of charges in 623.4516–623.4518; class nuclear artillery projectiles in 623.45119

.451 4   Antipersonnel devices

> Including booby traps
>
> Class here shrapnel devices
>
> *For a specific antipersonnel device other than booby traps and shrapnel devices, see the device, e.g., antipersonnel hand grenades 623.45114*

>   623.451 6–623.451 8   Devices with special types of charges
>
> Class comprehensive works in 623.451
>
> *For nuclear weapons, see 623.45119*

.451 6	Chemical and biological devices

Projectiles and related devices containing incendiary materials, microbes, poison gas, smoke

Standard subdivisions are added for chemical and biological devices together, for chemical devices alone

Class here weapons of mass destruction

Class chemical agents in 623.4592; class biological agents in 623.4594

For nuclear weapons, see 623.45119

.451 7	High-explosive devices

Including blockbusters, high-explosive-antitank (HEAT) projectiles, torpedoes

For bangalore torpedoes, see 623.4545

.451 8	Armor-piercing devices
.451 9	Guided missiles

Nuclear and nonnuclear missiles

Class here storage and launching equipment, launch vehicles; strategic missiles, comprehensive works on rocket weapons

Class comprehensive works on rocketry in 621.4356

For tactical rockets, see 623.4543

.451 91	Air-to-air guided missiles
.451 92	Air-to-surface guided missiles
.451 93	Air-to-underwater guided missiles
.451 94	Surface-to-air guided missiles

Class here antimissile missiles, interceptor missiles

.451 95	Ballistic missiles

Class here Surface-to-surface guided missiles

.451 952	Short-range ballistic missiles
.451 953	Intermediate-range ballistic missiles
.451 954	Long-range ballistic missiles

Class here intercontinental ballistic missiles

.451 96	Surface-to-underwater guided missiles
.451 97	Underwater guided missiles

Including underwater-to-air, underwater-to-surface, underwater-to-underwater missiles

.451 98	Space guided missiles

.452   Explosives

.452 6   Burning and deflagrating explosives

      Including cordite, guncotton, gunpowder, smokeless powder

      Class here propellant explosives

.452 7   High explosives

      Including dynamite, nitroglycerin, TNT

.454   Detonators, tactical rockets, demolition charges

.454 2   Detonators

      Including fuses, percussion caps, primers

.454 3   Tactical rockets

      Unguided nuclear and nonnuclear rockets

      Class comprehensive works on rocket weapons, on rocket-propelled guided missiles in 623.4519

.454 5   Demolition charges

      Including bangalore torpedoes, destructors, shaped charges

      Class shaped charges in bombs, missiles, projectiles in 623.451

.455   Small arms ammunition

      Including bazooka rockets, bullets, cartridges

.459   Nonexplosive agents

      Class here detection of nonexplosive agents

.459 2   Chemical agents

      Including tear gas

      Class here poisons and gases

.459 4   Biological agents

.46   Accessories

      Including range finders, sighting apparatus

.5   **Ballistics and gunnery**

.51   Ballistics

.513   Interior ballistics

      Motion of projectiles within the bore

.514   Exterior ballistics

      Motion of projectiles after leaving gun tube

.516   Terminal ballistics

      Effect of projectiles on targets

.55	Gunnery

> *For recoil, see 623.57*

.551	Land gunnery
.553	Naval gunnery
.555	Aircraft gunnery
.556	Spacecraft gunnery
.557	Target selection and detection

> Class range and sighting apparatus in 623.46; class application to specific types of gunnery in 623.551–623.556

.558	Firing and fire control

> Standard subdivisions are added for either or both topics in heading

> Class application to specific types of gunnery in 623.551–623.556

> *For target selection and detection, see 623.557*

.57	Recoil
.6	**Military transportation technology**

> *For vehicles, see 623.74*

.61	Land transportation

> *For roads, see 623.62; for railroads, see 623.63; for bridges, see 623.67; for tunnels, see 623.68*

.62	Roads
.63	Railroads
.631	The way

> Earthwork and track

.633	Rolling stock
.64	Naval facilities

> Including artificial harbors, docks

> Class here naval bases

> Class architectural aspects of naval facilities in 725.34

.66	Air facilities

> Class here air bases, airports, comprehensive works on military aerospace engineering

> Add to base number 623.66 the numbers following 629.136 in 629.1361–629.1368, e.g., airstrips 623.6612

> Class architectural aspects of air facilities in 725.39

> *For military astronautics, see 623.69; for aircraft, see 623.746*

.67   Bridges

.68   Tunnels

.69   Space facilities

> Class here comprehensive works on military astronautics
>
> *For spacecraft, see 623.749*

.7   Communications, vehicles, sanitation, related topics

SUMMARY

623.71	**Intelligence and reconnaissance topography**
.72	**Photography and photogrammetry**
.73	**Communications technology**
.74	**Vehicles**
.75	**Sanitation and safety engineering**
.76	**Electrical engineering**
.77	**Camouflage and concealment**

.71   Intelligence and reconnaissance topography

> Standard subdivisions are added for intelligence and reconnaissance topography together, for intelligence alone
>
> Including sketching and map making
>
> *For photography and photogrammetry, see 623.72*

.72   Photography and photogrammetry

.73   Communications technology

> Class comprehensive works on military electronics in 623.043

.731   Visual signals

.731 2   Flag signals, heliographs, semaphores

.731 3   Pyrotechnical devices

.731 4   Electrooptical devices

.732   Telegraphy

> *For radiotelegraphy, see 623.7342*

.733   Telephony

> *For radiotelephony, see 623.7345*

.734   Radio and radar

> Standard subdivisions are added for radio and radar together, for radio alone

.734 1   Shortwave radio

.734 2   Radiotelegraphy

> Class shortwave radiotelegraphy in 623.7341

.734 5	Radiotelephony

Class shortwave radiotelephony in 623.7341

.734 8	Radar
.735	Television
.737	Warning systems

Class here air raid warning systems

.74	Vehicles

Support vehicles, combat vehicles and their ordnance

For ammunition and other destructive agents, see 623.45; for railroad rolling stock, see 623.633; for nautical craft, see 623.82

See Manual at 629.046 vs. 388

.741	Lighter-than-air aircraft

For specific types of lighter-than-air aircraft, see 623.742 623.744

> 623.742–623.744 Specific types of lighter-than-air aircraft

Class comprehensive works in 623.741

.742	Free balloons

Class here comprehensive works on military balloons

For barrage balloons, see 623.744

.743	Airships (Dirigibles)
.743 5	Rigid airships
.743 6	Semirigid airships
.743 7	Nonrigid airships
.744	Barrage balloons
.746	Heavier-than-air aircraft

Class here comprehensive works on aircraft

For lighter-than-air aircraft, see 623.741

.746 04	Special topics of aircraft

> 623.746 042–623.746 047 General types of heavier-than-air aircraft

Class here piloting general types of heavier-than-air aircraft

Class comprehensive works in 623.746; class comprehensive works on piloting in 623.746048

.746 042	Propeller-driven airplanes
.746 044	Jet planes

.746 045	Rocket planes
.746 047	Vertical-lift aircraft (VTOL aircraft)
	Including helicopters
.746 048	Piloting

Class piloting of a specific type of heavier-than-air aircraft with the aircraft, e.g., piloting jet planes 623.746044, piloting fighters 623.7464

.746 049	Components

Including engines, escape equipment, instrumentation (avionics)

Class components of a specific type of aircraft with the aircraft, e.g., components of jet planes 623.746044, of fighters 623.7464

For aircraft ordnance, see 623.7461

.746 1	Aircraft ordnance

For charge-containing devices, see 623.451

>   **623.746 2–623.746 7 Heavier-than-air aircraft for specific uses**

Class here piloting heavier-than-air aircraft for specific uses

Class aircraft ordnance regardless of type of aircraft in 623.7461; class pilotless aircraft regardless of type in 623.7469; class comprehensive works in 623.746; class comprehensive works on piloting in 623.746048

.746 2	Trainers
.746 3	Bombers and fighter-bombers

     Standard subdivisions are added for either or both topics in heading

     Including attack airplanes, close support aircraft

     Class here close support aircraft

.746 4	Fighters
.746 5	Transport aircraft
	Cargo and personnel
.746 6	Rescue aircraft
.746 7	Reconnaissance aircraft
.746 9	Pilotless aircraft (Guided aircraft)
	Variant name: drones
	Reconnaissance and combat
.747	Motor land vehicles

.747 2	Motor land vehicles for transporting personnel

Class armored personnel carriers in 623.7475

.747 22	Jeeps and similar vehicles

Standard subdivisions are added for jeeps and similar vehicles together, for jeeps alone

.747 23	Buses
.747 24	Ambulances
.747 4	Motor land vehicles for transporting supplies
.747 5	Motor land vehicles for combat

Including armored personnel carriers

.747 52	Tanks
.748	Air-cushion vehicles
.748 2	Overland air-cushion vehicles
.748 4	Overwater air-cushion vehicles
.748 5	Amphibious air-cushion vehicles
.749	Spacecraft
.75	Sanitation and safety engineering

Class here health engineering

.751	Water supply
.753	Sewage treatment and disposal
.754	Garbage and refuse treatment and disposal
.76	Electrical engineering
.77	Camouflage and concealment
.8	**Nautical engineering and seamanship**

Nautical engineering: engineering of ships and boats and their component parts

Standard subdivisions are added for nautical engineering and seamanship together, for nautical engineering alone

Class here naval engineering, comprehensive works on military water transportation

Class harbors, ports, roadsteads in 627.2

For naval facilities, see 623.64

SUMMARY

623.802 84	**Apparatus, equipment, materials**
.81	**Naval architecture**
.82	**Nautical craft**
.83	**Shipyards**
.84	**Hulls of nautical craft**
.85	**Engineering systems of nautical craft**
.86	**Equipment and outfit of nautical craft**
.87	**Power plants of nautical craft**
.88	**Seamanship**
.89	**Navigation**

.802 84   Apparatus, equipment, materials

> Do not use for equipment and outfit of nautical craft; class in 623.86

.81   Naval architecture

> Variant names: marine architecture, naval design

.812   Design of craft

.812 04   Design of general types of craft

> Add to base number 623.81204 the numbers following 623.820 in 623.8202–623.8205, e.g., design of submersible craft 623.812045

.812 1–.812 9   Design of specific kinds of craft

> Add to base number 623.812 the numbers following 623.82 in 623.821–623.829, e.g., design of sailboats 623.81223

.817   Structural analysis and design

> Add to base number 623.817 the numbers following 624.17 in 624.171–624.177, e.g., structural analysis 623.8171, wreckage studies 623.8176

> Class structural analysis and design of general and specific kinds of craft in 623.812; class structural analysis and design of specific metals in 623.818

.818   Design in specific materials

> Add to base number 623.818 the numbers following 624.18 in 624.182–624.189, e.g., design in steel 623.81821

> Class design of general and specific kinds of craft in a specific material in 623.812

.82   Nautical craft

> Class shipyards in 623.83; class overwater hovercraft in 629.324

> *For naval architecture, see 623.81; for parts and details of nautical craft, see 623.84–623.87*

> *See Manual at 629.046 vs. 388*

SUMMARY

623.820 01–.820 09	Standard subdivisions
.820 1–.820 7	[Models and miniatures, general types of craft, craft of specific materials]
.821	Ancient and medieval craft
.822	Modern wind-driven ships
.823	Small and medium power-driven ships
.824	Power-driven merchant and factory ships
.825	Power-driven warships
.826	Support warships and other government ships
.827	Nonmilitary submersible craft
.828	Other power-driven ships
.829	Hand-propelled and towed craft

.820 01   Philosophy and theory

.820 02   Miscellany

[.820 022 8]   Models and miniatures

Do not use; class in 623.8201

.820 03–.820 09   Standard subdivisions

.820 1   Models and miniatures

Class ships in bottles in 745.5928

.820 104   Models and miniatures of general types of craft

Add to base number 623.820104 the numbers following 623.820 in 623.8202–623.8205, e.g., models of sailing craft 623.8201043

.820 11–.820 19   Models and miniatures of specific types of craft

Add to base number 623.8201 the numbers following 623.82 in 623.821–623.829, e.g., models of battleships 623.820152

> 623.820 2–623.820 5 General types of craft

Class general types of craft in specific materials in 623.8207; class specific types of craft in 623.821–623.829; class comprehensive works in 623.82

.820 2   *Small craft

Class small sailing craft in 623.8203; class small submersible craft in 623.8205; class small power-driven craft in 623.823

.820 23   *Pleasure craft

Including yachts

.820 26   *Working craft

.820 3   *Sailing ships

*Do not use notation 0228 from Table 1 for models and miniatures; class in 623.8201

.820 4	*Power-driven ships

Including hydrofoils, steamships

Class power-driven submersible craft in 623.8205; class small power-driven craft in 623.823

.820 5	*Submersible craft

.820 7	*Craft of specific materials

Class works limited to hulls of specific materials in 623.84

.821	*Ancient and medieval craft

Including biremes, caravels, galleys, triremes

> ### 623.822–623.829 Modern craft

Class comprehensive works in 623.82

.822	*Modern wind-driven ships

Including rotor ships

Class comprehensive works on ancient, medieval, and modern wind-driven ships in 623.8203

.822 3	*Pleasure craft

Including sailing yachts

.822 4	*Merchant ships

Including clipper ships

.822 5	*Warships

.822 6	*Work ships

Including research ships

For merchant ships, see 623.8224

> ### 623.823–623.828 Power-driven craft

Class comprehensive works in 623.8204

.823	*Small and medium power-driven ships

For small and medium power-driven craft not provided for here, see 623.824–623.828

.823 1	*Motorboats

Class here speedboats

.823 13	*Outboard motorboats

---

*Do not use notation 0228 from Table 1 for models and miniatures; class in 623.8201

.823 14	*Inboard motorboats
	Including hydroplanes, motor yachts
.823 15	*Inboard-outboard motorboats
.823 2	*Tugboats and towboats
.823 4	*Ferryboats
.824	*Power-driven merchant and factory ships

Standard subdivisions are added for power-driven merchant and factory ships together, for power-driven merchant ships alone

Class trawlers in 623.828

.824 3	*Passenger ships

Class ferryboats in 623.8234

.824 32	*Ocean liners
.824 36	*Inland-waterway ships
	Including river steamers
.824 5	*Cargo ships
	Including bulk carriers, freighters, tankers
.824 8	*Factory ships
	Including ship canneries, whaleboats
.825	*Power-driven warships

For support warships, see 623.826

.825 1	Naval ordnance

Class here armor, weapons

For naval artillery, see 623.418; for charge-containing devices, see 623.451

> 　　　　　　623.825 2–623.825 8　Specific types of combat warships

Class naval ordnance in 623.8251; class comprehensive works in 623.825

.825 2	*Battleships
.825 3	*Cruisers
.825 4	*Destroyers and destroyer escorts

Standard subdivisions are added for destroyers and destroyer escorts together, for destroyers alone

.825 5	*Aircraft carriers
.825 6	*Landing craft

*Do not use notation 0228 from Table 1 for models and miniatures; class in 623.8201

.825 7	*Submarines
	Class comprehensive works on submersible craft in 623.8205
.825 72	*Diesel-engine and electric-motor powered submarines
.825 74	*Nuclear-powered submarines
.825 8	*Light combat craft
	Including torpedo boats
.826	*Support warships and other government ships
.826 2	*Minelayers and minesweepers
.826 3	*Coast guard ships, police boats, revenue cutters
.826 4	*Hospital ships and military transports
.826 5	*Military supply ships
.827	*Nonmilitary submersible craft
	Including bathyscaphes, bathyspheres
	Class comprehensive works on submersible craft in 623.8205
.828	*Other power-driven ships
	Including dredgers, drilling ships, icebreakers
	Lightships relocated to 623.8943
.828 2	*Fishing boats
	Including trawlers
	For whaling ships, see 623.8248
.829	*Hand-propelled and towed craft
	Including barges, canoes, coracles, lifeboats, rafts, rowboats, scows, towed canalboats
.83	Shipyards
	Including dry docks, floating dry docks

> **623.84–623.87 Parts and details of nautical craft**

Class here design

Class comprehensive works in 623.82

.84	Hulls of nautical craft
	Class hydrodynamics of hulls in 623.812
.842	Lofting
.843	Metalwork

*Do not use notation 0228 from Table 1 for models and miniatures; class in 623.8201

.843 2	Riveting and welding
.843 3	Ship fitting
.844	Carpentry
.845	Construction with ceramics, masonry, allied materials

> Add to base number 623.845 the numbers following 624.183 in 624.1832–624.1838, e.g., concrete hulls 623.8454

.848	Resistant construction

> Including corrosion-resistant, fire-resistant construction

.85	Engineering systems of nautical craft

> *For power plants, see 623.87*

.850 01–.850 09	Standard subdivisions
.850 1	Mechanical systems
.850 3	Electrical systems
.850 4	Electronic systems
.852	Electric lighting
.853	Temperature controls and air conditioning

> Standard subdivisions are added for temperature controls and air conditioning together, for temperature controls alone

.853 5	Cooling

> Including refrigeration

.853 7	Heating and air conditioning
.854	Water supply and sanitation
.854 2	Potable water
.854 3	Seawater

> Used for fire fighting and sanitation

.854 6	Sanitation

> Class seawater for sanitation in 623.8543

.856	Communication systems

> Add to base number 623.856 the numbers following 623.73 in 623.731–623.737, e.g., flag systems 623.85612

.86	Equipment and outfit of nautical craft

> Including flares, other portable lights

> Class use of equipment and outfit in 623.88

.862	Gear and rigging

> Including anchors, cordage, masts, rope, rudders, sails, spars

.863	Nautical instruments
.865	Safety equipment

Including fire fighting, lifesaving equipment

Class comprehensive works on marine safety technology in 623.888

.866	Furniture
.867	Cargo-handling equipment

Class cargo handling in 623.8881

For onshore cargo-handling equipment, see 627.34

.87	Power plants of nautical craft

Class here marine engineering

.872	Specific kinds of engines
[.872 01–.872 09]	Standard subdivisions

Do not use; class in 623.8701–623.8709

.872 2	Steam engines
.872 3	Internal-combustion engines

Class here inboard motors

Add to base number 623.8723 the numbers following 621.43 in 621.433–621.437, e.g., outboard motors 623.87234, diesel engines 623.87236

.872 6	Electric engines
.872 7	Solar engines
.872 8	Nuclear engines
.873	Engine auxiliaries

Including boilers, pipes, propellers, pumps, shafts

.874	Fuels
.88	Seamanship

For navigation, see 623.89

[.880 289]	Safety measures

Do not use; class in 623.888

.881	Ship handling

Class safety and related topics in handling craft in 623.888

For handling specific types of craft, see 623.882

.881 2–.881 5	Handling general types of craft

Add to base number 623.881 the numbers following 623.820 in 623.8202–623.8205, e.g., handling small craft 623.8812

.882   Handling various specific types of craft

Class safety and related topics in handling specific types of craft in 623.888

[.882 01–.882 09]   Standard subdivisions

Do not use; class in 623.88101–623.88109

.882 1–.882 9   Specific types of craft

Add to base number 623.882 the numbers following 623.82 in 623.821–623.829, e.g., handling power-driven merchant ships 623.8824

.888   Specific topics of seamanship

Class here marine safety technology

For safety equipment, see 623.865

[.888 01–.888 09]   Standard subdivisions

Do not use; class in 623.8801–623.8809

.888 1   Loading and unloading of nautical craft

Standard subdivisions are added for either or both topics in heading

Class here cargo handling

.888 2   Knotting and splicing ropes and cables

Class here interdisciplinary works on knotting and splicing

For a specific application of knotting and splicing, see the application, e.g., knotting in camping 796.545

.888 4   Prevention of collision and grounding

Including rules of the road

.888 5   Wreckage studies

Class wreckage studies in marine architecture in 623.8176

.888 6   Fire fighting technology

See also 623.865 for manufacture of fire fighting equipment

.888 7   Rescue operations

.89   Navigation

Selection and determination of course

Class navigation procedures to prevent collision and grounding in 623.8884

.892   Geonavigation

For electronic aids to geonavigation, see 623.893

.892 021   Tabulated and related materials

Do not use for tide and current tables; class in 623.8949

.892 2	Piloting and pilot guides

Positioning craft by visual observation of objects of known position

Standard subdivisions are added for either or both topics in heading

Class here nautical charts

For piloting in and pilot guides to specific marine harbors and shores, see 623.8929

[.892 209 163–.892 209 167]	Treatment by specific oceans and seas

Do not use; class in 623.89223–623.89227

.892 209 168	Treatment by specific oceanographic forms

Do not use for inland seas; class in 623.89229

.892 209 169	Treatment by fresh and brackish waters

Do not use for specific inland waters; class in 623.89229

.892 23–.892 27	Piloting in and pilot guides to specific oceans and intercontinental seas

Add to base number 623.8922 the numbers following —16 in notation 163–167 from Table 2, e.g., pilot guides to North Sea 623.8922336; however, for piloting in and pilot guides to specific marine harbors and shores, see 623.8929

.892 29	Piloting in and pilot guides to specific inland waters

Add to base number 623.89229 notation 4–9 from Table 2, e.g., pilot guides to Great Lakes 623.8922977; however, for piloting in and pilot guides to specific marine harbors and shores, see 623.8929

.892 3	Dead reckoning
.892 9	Piloting in and pilot guides to specific marine harbors and shores

Standard subdivisions are added for either or both topics in heading

Class here approach and harbor piloting and pilot guides

[.892 909 1]	Areas, regions, places in general

Do not use; class in 623.89291

[.892 909 3–.892 909 9]	Specific continents, countries, localities

Do not use; class in 623.89293–623.89299

.892 91	Piloting in and pilot guides to specific areas, regions, places in general

Add to base number 623.89291 the numbers following —1 in notation 11–19 from Table 2, e.g., pilot guides of developing countries 623.89291724; however, for approach and harbor piloting and pilot guides dealing comprehensively with specific oceans and intercontinental seas, see 623.89223–623.89227

Subdivisions are added for either or both topics in heading

.892 93–.892 99   Piloting in and pilot guides to specific continents, countries, localities

Add to base number 623.8929 notation 3–9 from Table 2, e.g., pilot guides of India 623.892954
Subdivisions are added for either or both topics in heading

.893   Geonavigation aids

Class here navigation aids [*formerly also* 627.92], electronic aids to geonavigation

For nonelectronic aids to geonavigation, see 623.894

>   623.893 2–623.893 3   Direction-finding and position-finding devices

Class comprehensive works in 623.893

.893 2   Radio aids

Including compasses, loran, radio

.893 3   Microwave aids

Including racon, radar, shoran

Class here GPS receivers

.893 8   Sounding devices

Including echo-ranging and sound-ranging devices, e.g., sonar

.894   Nonelectronic aids to geonavigation

.894 2   Lighthouses [*formerly also* 627.922]

Class interdisciplinary works on lighthouses in 387.155

.894 3   Lightships [*formerly also* 623.828]

.894 4   Light beacons, buoys, daymarks [*all formerly also* 627.924]

.894 5   Light lists

.894 9   Tide and current tables

Standard subdivisions are added for either or both topics in heading

624   Civil engineering

Including engineering of landscape architecture

Class here construction engineering

For military construction engineering, see 623.047. For a specific branch of civil engineering not provided for here, see the branch, e.g., construction of buildings 690

See Manual at 624 vs. 624.1; also at 624 vs. 690

SUMMARY

.029   Commercial miscellany

> Class interdisciplinary works on quantity surveying in 692.5

.1   **Structural engineering and underground construction**

> Standard subdivisions are added for structural engineering and underground construction together, for structural engineering alone

> Class a specific application of structural engineering with the application, e.g., structural engineering of dams 627.8

> *See Manual at 624 vs. 624.1*

SUMMARY

.101   Philosophy and theory

> Class structural theory, theory of structure in 624.17

.15   Foundation engineering and engineering geology

> Standard subdivisions are added for foundation engineering and engineering geology together, for foundation engineering alone

.151   Engineering geology

> Class here properties of foundation soils

.151 09   History, geographic treatment, biography

> Class soil surveys in 624.1517

.151 3   Rock and soil mechanics

.151 32   Rock mechanics

.151 36   Soil mechanics

> Including drainage properties, permeability; permafrost

.151 362   Soil consolidation

.151 363   Soil stabilization

> Class here soil compaction

.151 4   Soil content analysis

.151 7   Soil surveys

                    Class interdisciplinary works on soil surveys in 631.47

[.151 709 1]   Areas, regions, places in general

                    Do not use; class in 624.15171

[.151 709 3–.151 709 9]   Specific continents, countries, localities

                    Do not use; class in 624.15173–624.15179

.151 71   Areas, regions, places in general

                    Add to base number 624.15171 the numbers following —1 in notation 11–19 from Table 2, e.g., soil survey of tropical regions 624.151713

.151 73–.151 79   Specific continents, countries, localities

                    Add to base number 624.1517 notation 3–9 from Table 2, e.g., soil survey of Japan 624.151752

>   624.152–624.158 Foundation engineering

                    Class engineering geology of foundations in 624.151; class comprehensive works in 624.15

.152   Excavation

                    Including grading, shoring

                    Class here earthwork

                    Class embankments in 624.162

.152 6   Blasting

.153   Foundation materials

                    Add to base number 624.153 the numbers following 620.1 in 620.12–620.19, e.g., iron 624.1537

                    Class foundation materials for specific types of foundations in 624.154–624.158

>   624.154–624.158 Specific types of foundations

                    Class comprehensive works in 624.15

.154   Pile foundations

.156   Floating foundations

                    Including cantilever and platform foundations

.157   Underwater foundations

                  Including caissons, cofferdams

                  Class underwater pier foundations in 624.158; class comprehensive works on underwater constuction in 627.702

.158	Pier foundations
.16	Supporting structures other than foundations

Class temporary supporting structures during excavation in 624.152

.162	Embankments
.164	Retaining walls
.17	Structural analysis and design

Standard subdivisions are added for structural analysis and design together, for structural analysis alone

Class here mechanics of structures, structural elements, structural theory, interdisciplinary works on structural analysis and design

Unless other instructions are given, class a subject with aspects in two or more subdivisions of 624.17 in the number coming last, e.g., wind loads on shells 624.17762 (*not* 624.175)

For a specific application of structural analysis and design, see the application, e.g., structural analysis of aircraft 629.1341

.170 1–.170 9	Standard subdivisions [*formerly also* 624.17101–624.17109]
.171	Specific elements of structural analysis

Including structural control, failures, stability

For loads, see 624.172; for stresses and strains, see 624.176

Use of this number for comprehensive works on structural analysis discontinued; class in 624.17

[.171 01–.171 09]	Standard subdivisions

Relocated to 624.1701–624.1709

.171 2	Graphic statics
.171 3	Statically indeterminate structures

Including static determinacy and indeterminacy

.171 4	Deflections
.171 5	Moment distribution method
.172	Loads

For wind loads, see 624.175

.175	Wind loads
.176	Stresses and strains (Deformation)

Standard subdivisions are added for either or both topics in heading

Including blast-resistant construction

Class here wreckage studies

.176 2	Earthquake engineering

.177	Structural design and specific structural elements
[.177 01–.177 09]	Standard subdivisions
	Do not use; class in 624.1701–624.1709
.177 1	Structural design
	For design with specific materials, see 624.18
.177 13	Structural optimization

>   624.177 2–624.177 9 Specific structural elements

Class here specific structural elements in metal, design and construction of specific elements

Class specific structural elements in materials other than metal in 624.18; class comprehensive works in 624.17

.177 2	Beams, girders, cylinders, columns, slabs
.177 23	Beams and girders
	Standard subdivisions are added for either or both topics in heading
.177 25	Columns
.177 3	Trusses and frames
	Standard subdivisions are added for either or both topics in heading
.177 4	Cables, wires, bars, rods
.177 5	Arches and domes
.177 6	Shells and plates
.177 62	Shells
.177 65	Plates
.177 9	Sandwich and honeycomb constructions
	Standard subdivisions are added for either or both topics in heading
	Class specific sandwich and honeycomb constructions in 624.1772–624.1776
.18	Materials
	Class here design and construction
.182	Metals
	Class specific structural elements in metal in 624.1772–624.1779
.182 1	Iron and steel (Ferrous metals)
	Standard subdivisions are added for either or both topics in heading

.182 2–.182 9	Nonferrous metals

Add to base number 624.182 the numbers following 620.18 in 620.182–620.189, e.g., construction in aluminum 624.1826

.183	Masonry, ceramic, allied materials
.183 2	Stone

Including artificial stone, e.g., concrete blocks

.183 3	Cement
.183 4	Concrete

Class concrete and cinder blocks in 624.1832

See also 721.0445 for visual concrete

.183 41	Reinforced concrete (Ferroconcrete)

Class a specific concrete structural element of reinforced concrete in 624.18342–624.18349

.183 412	Prestressed concrete
.183 414	Precast concrete
.183 42–.183 49	Specific concrete structural elements

Add to base number 624.1834 the numbers following 624.177 in 624.1772–624.1779, e.g., concrete shells 624.183462

.183 6	Brick and tile
.183 8	Glass
.184	Wood and laminated wood

Standard subdivisions are added for wood and laminated wood together, for wood alone

.189	Other materials

Add to base number 624.189 the numbers following 620.19 in 620.191–620.199, e.g., design in plastics 624.18923

.19	Underground construction

Class here ventilation

Class subsurface mining in 622.2

For construction of underground waste disposal facilities, see 628.44566

.192	Mountain tunnels
.193	Tunnels

Class architectural aspects in 725.98

For military tunnel engineering, see 623.68; for mountain tunnels, see 624.192; for underwater tunnels, see 624.194

.194	Underwater tunnels

.2	**Bridges**

        Class here compound bridges, long-span bridges

        Unless other instructions are given, class a subject with aspects in two or more subdivisions of 624.2 in the number coming last, e.g., movable truss bridges 624.24 (*not* 624.217)

        Class architecture of bridges in 725.98

        For military bridge engineering, see 623.67

.209 3–.209 9   Specific continents, countries, localities

        Class specific bridges of a specific kind in 624.21–624.24

>   624.21–624.24 Specific kinds of bridges

        Class comprehensive works in 624.2

.21   Girder and related kinds of bridges

        Standard subdivisions are added for girder and related kinds of bridges together, for girder bridges alone

        Including beam bridges, tubular bridges

        Class here continuous bridges

.215   Box-girder bridges

.217   Iron and steel truss bridges

        Standard subdivisions are added for either or both topics in heading

.218   Timber truss bridges

        Class here covered bridges

.219   Cantilever bridges

.22   Arch bridges

.225   Masonry arch bridges

.23   Suspension and cable-stayed bridges

        Standard subdivisions are added for suspension and cable-stayed bridges together, for suspension bridges alone

.238   Cable-stayed bridges

.24   Movable bridges

.25   Structural analysis and design

        Standard subdivisions are added for either or both topics in heading

        Class structural analysis and design of specific kinds of bridges in 624.21–624.24

.252   Loads, stresses, strains

.257   Specific structural elements

For floors and foundations, see 624.28

[.257 01–.257 09]   Standard subdivisions

Do not use; class in 624.201–624.209

.28   Floors and foundations

.283   Floors

Class here structural analysis and design of floors

.284   Foundations

Class here structural analysis and design of foundations

625   Engineering of railroads and roads

Class tunnel engineering in 624.193; class bridge engineering in 624.2; class land transportation engineering in 629.048

SUMMARY

625.1	**Railroads**	
.2	**Railroad rolling stock**	
.3	**Inclined, mountain, ship railroads**	
.4	**Local rail transit systems**	
.5	**Cable and aerial railways**	
.6	**Light rail transit systems**	
.7	**Roads**	
.8	**Artificial road surfaces**	

.1   **Railroads**

Including comprehensive works on special-purpose railroads

Class here comprehensive works on broad-gage, narrow-gage, standard-gage railroads

Class electrification of railroads in 621.33; class interdisciplinary works on railroads in 385

For military railroad engineering, see 623.63; for railroad rolling stock, see 625.2; for special-purpose railroads, see 625.3–625.6

.100 1   Philosophy and theory

.100 2   Miscellany

[.100 228]   Models and miniatures

Do not use; class in 625.19

.100 288   Maintenance and repair

Including snow removal operations

.100 3–.100 9   Standard subdivisions

[.103]   Monorail systems

Relocated to 625.44

.11 Surveying and design

Including final location surveys; determination of grades, switchbacks, right-of-way

---

> 625.12–625.16 Permanent way

Class comprehensive works in 625.1

For permanent way of special-purpose railroads, see 625.3–625.6

.12 Earthwork

.122 Engineering geology

Including rock and soil mechanics

Class here properties of soils that support structures (foundation soils)

.123 Roadbed preparation

Including excavation

.13 Protective structures

Including retaining walls, snow fences, snowsheds

.14 Track

For rails and rail fastenings, see 625.15; for track accessories, see 625.16

.141 Ballast

.143 Ties (Sleepers)

Including tie plates

.144 Track laying

For laying of tracks over ice, see 625.147

[.146] Monorail tracks

Relocated to 625.44

.147 Tracks over ice

.15 Rails

Including rail fastenings

.16 Track accessories

.163 Turnouts and crossings

Including frogs, switches, sidings

.165 Control devices

Including signals, signs

.18 Railroad yards

.19   Model and miniature railroads and trains

Standard subdivisions are added for either or both topics in heading

Add to base number 625.19 the numbers following 625.2 in 625.21–625.26, e.g., models of steam locomotives 625.1961

Class play with model railroads and trains in 790.133

> *For models and miniatures of a specific kind of special-purpose railroad, see the kind in 625.3–625.6, e.g., models of subways 625.420228, models of monorail rolling stock 625.44*

.2   **Railroad rolling stock**

Class here comprehensive works on specific types of cars, on rolling stock for roads with two running rails

> *For rolling stock for special-purpose railroads, see 625.3–625.6*

> *See Manual at 629.046 vs. 388*

[.202 28]   Models and miniatures

Do not use; class in 625.19

.21   *Running gear

Including axles, bearings, springs, wheels

Class here running gear for specific types of cars

\>   625.22–625.24   Specific types of cars

Class running gear for specific types of cars in 625.21; class accessory equipment for specific types of cars in 625.25; class comprehensive works in 625.2

.22   *Work cars (Nonrevenue rolling stock)

Including cabooses, handcars, railroad snowplows

.23   *Passenger-train cars

Including coaches; baggage, dining, sleeping cars

.24   *Freight cars

Including boxcars, gondola cars, refrigerator cars, tank cars

.25   *Accessory equipment

Including brakes, buffers, couplings

Class here accessory equipment for specific types of cars

.26   *Locomotives

Class running gear in 625.21; class accessory equipment in 625.25

.261   *Steam locomotives

*Do not use notation 0228 from Table 1; class in 625.19

.262	*Gas-turbine locomotives
.263	*Electric locomotives

> For diesel-electric locomotives, see 625.2662

.265	*Air-compression-powered locomotives
.266	*Diesel and semidiesel locomotives

> Standard subdivisions are added for either or both topics in heading

.266 2	*Diesel-electric locomotives
.266 4	*Diesel-hydraulic locomotives
.27	Mechanical operation
[.28]	Monorail rolling stock

> Relocated to 625.44

> **625.3–625.6 Special-purpose railroads**

> Class here roadbeds, tracks and accessories, rolling stock

> Class comprehensive works in 625.1

> *For mine railroads, see 622.66*

.3	**Inclined, mountain, ship railroads**
.32	Funicular railroads
.33	Rack railroads
.39	Ship railroads
.4	**Local rail transit systems**

> Including guided-way systems

> Class here local surface rail systems using conventional (heavy) rail technology [*formerly* 625.6], commuter rail systems, rapid transit rail systems, urban and suburban rail systems; comprehensive works on local rail transit systems with multiple transit modes

> *For light rail transit systems, see 625.6*

.42	Underground systems (Subways)
.44	Elevated systems

> Including monorail systems [*formerly also* 625.103], monorail tracks [*formerly also* 625.146], monorail rolling stock [*formerly also* 625.28]

.5	**Cable and aerial railways**

> *For funicular railroads, see 625.32*

---

*Do not use notation 0228 from Table 1; class in 625.19

.6   **Light rail transit systems**

> Including trolleybus systems
>
> Class here interurban railroads (streetcar lines running between urban areas or from urban to rural areas); streetcar systems, tramways, trolley-car systems
>
> Local surface rail systems using conventional (heavy) rail technology relocated to 625.4

.65   Roadbeds, tracks, accessories

.66   Rolling stock

> Including horse-drawn streetcars, trolleybuses
>
> Class here streetcars, trams, trolley cars

.7   **Roads**

> Class here highways, streets
>
> Class grade crossings (road crossings of railroads) in 625.163; class interdisciplinary works on roads and highways in 388.1; class interdisciplinary works on urban roads and streets in 388.411
>
> *For military road engineering, see 623.62; for artificial road surfaces, see 625.8; for forestry roads, see 634.93*

[.702 88]   Maintenance and repair

> Do not use; class in 625.76

.72   Surveying and design

.723   Surveying

> Class soil surveys in 625.732

.725   Design

> Including determination of bankings, grades

.73   Earthwork

.732   Engineering geology

> Including rock and soil mechanics
>
> Class here properties of soils that support structures (foundation soils)

.733   Foundation preparation

> Including excavation

.734   Drainage

> Including conduits, dikes, ditches, gutters, pipes

.734 2   Culverts

.735   Subsurface highway materials

.74   Dirt roads

> Stabilized and unstabilized
>
> Including soil stabilization processes
>
> *For surfacing dirt roads, see 625.75*

.75   Surfacing dirt roads

.76   Maintenance and repair

> Class maintenance and repair of a specific kind of road or associated feature with the road or feature, plus notation 0288 from Table 1, e.g., maintenance of dirt roads 625.740288, of roadside areas 625.770288

.761   Damages and their repairs

> Standard subdivisions arc added for either or both topics in heading
>
> Including resurfacing, shoulder maintenance

.763   Snow and ice control measures

> Including use of snowplows, snow fences

.77   Roadside areas

> Including parking turnouts, picnic areas, rest areas; planting and cultivation of roadside vegetation

.79   Ice crossings, traffic control equipment, protective roadside barriers

> *For public lighting for roads, see 628.95*

.792   Ice crossings

> Class here ice and snow-compacted roads

.794   Traffic control equipment

> Including markings, signals, signs

.795   Protective roadside barriers

> Including dividers, fences
>
> Class snow fences in 625.763; class curbs in 625.888

.8   **Artificial road surfaces**

> Class here comprehensive works on paving
>
> *For a paving surface not provided for here, see the surface, e.g., airport runways 629.13634*

[.802 88]   Maintenance and repair

> Do not use; class in 625.76

>   625.81–625.86   Pavements in specific materials

> Class sidewalks in specific materials in 625.881–625.886; class comprehensive works in 625.8

.81   Flagstones

.82   Brick and stone

       Including gravel and crushed stone pavements

        For flagstones, see 625.81

.83   Wood

.84   Concretes

        For asphalt concrete, see 625.85

.85   Bituminous materials

       Including tar

       Class here asphalt, asphalt concrete

        For macadam, see 625.86

.86   Macadam and telford surfaces

.88   Sidewalks and auxiliary pavements

       Standard subdivisions are added for sidewalks and auxiliary pavements together, for sidewalks alone

.881–.886   Sidewalks in specific materials

       Add to base number 625.88 the numbers following 625.8 in 625.81–625.86, e.g., brick sidewalks 625.882

.888   Curbs

.889   Auxiliary pavements

       Including driveways, parking aprons

        For curbs, see 625.888

[626]   [Unassigned]

       Most recently used in Edition 14

627   Hydraulic engineering

       The branch of engineering dealing with utilization and control of natural waters of the earth

       Class here hydraulic structures, water resource engineering

       Class comprehensive works on ocean engineering in 620.4162

        For water supply engineering, see 628.1

SUMMARY

627.04		**Special topics of hydraulic engineering**
	.1	**Inland waterways**
	.2	**Harbors, ports, roadsteads**
	.3	**Port facilities**
	.4	**Flood control**
	.5	**Reclamation, irrigation, related topics**
	.7	**Underwater operations**
	.8	**Dams and reservoirs**
	.9	**Other hydraulic structures**

[.015 325]   Hydrodynamics

Do not use; class in 627.042

.04   Special topics of hydraulic engineering

.042   Hydrodynamics of waterways and water bodies

Standard subdivisions are added for either or both topics in heading

.046   Recreational waters

.1   Inland waterways

For underwater operations, see 627.7

.12   Rivers and streams

Standard subdivisions are added for either or both topics in heading

Class interdisciplinary works on rivers and streams in 551.483

For canalized rivers, see 627.13

[.120 153 25]   Hydrodynamics

Do not use; class in 627.125

.122   Sediment and silt

Standard subdivisions are added for either or both topics in heading

.123   Water diversion

Including construction of barrages

.124   Estuaries and river mouths

Standard subdivisions are added for either or both topics in heading

.125   Applied hydrodynamics

.13   Canals

Class here canalized rivers, comprehensive engineering works on canals

Class tunnels carrying canals in 624.193; class bridges carrying canals in 624.2; class interdisciplinary works on canals in 386.4

For irrigation canals, see 627.52

.131   Surveying and design

.133   Bank protection and reinforcement

> Standard subdivisions are added for either or both topics in heading

.135   Auxiliary devices

.135 2   Gates, locks, sluices

.135 3   Inclines, lifts, ramps

> 627.137–627.138 Specific types of navigation canals

> Class engineering and construction details of specific types of canals in 627.131–627.135; class comprehensive works in 627.13

.137   Ship canals

.138   Barge canals

.14   Lakes

.2   **Harbors, ports, roadsteads**

> Standard subdivisions are added for harbors, ports, roadsteads together; for harbors alone; for ports alone

> Class interdisciplinary works on harbors, ports, roadsteads in 387.1

> *For port facilities, see 627.3; for underwater operations, see 627.7*

.22   Roadsteads, anchorages, mooring grounds

> Standard subdivisions are added for any or all topics in heading

> Including supertanker berthing areas

> Class freestanding mooring and berthing structures in 627.32

.23   Channels

> Class here fairways

.24   Protective structures

> Including breakwaters, jetties, seawalls

> Class comprehensive works on seawalls in 627.58

.3   **Port facilities**

> Class architectural aspects in 725.34

> *For navigation aids, see 623.893*

> 627.31–627.34 Specific types of structures and equipment

> Class specific types of structures in marinas in 627.38; class comprehensive works in 627.3

.31   Docks

> Class here piers, quays, wharves

.32	Freestanding mooring and berthing structures
.34	Cargo-handling equipment

Class comprehensive works on cargo-handling equipment in 623.867

.38	Marinas

.4 **Flood control**

Including flood wreckage studies

Class here use of dams and reservoirs for flood control

Class construction of dams and reservoirs for flood control in 627.8. Class flood control for and wreckage studies of a specific type of structure with the structure, e.g., flood wreckage studies of bridges 624.2

.42   Flood barriers

Including seawalls

Class here embankments, levees; comprehensive works on dikes

Class comprehensive works on seawalls in 627.58

For dikes and seawalls in reclamation from sea, see 627.549

.44	Water impoundment
.45	Water diversion

.5 **Reclamation, irrigation, related topics**

Class here comprehensive technological works on erosion and its control

Class interdisciplinary works on land reclamation in 333.73153; class interdisciplinary works on erosion in 551.302

For erosion of agricultural soils and its control, see 631.45; for reclamation of agricultural soils, see 631.6; for revegetation and surface mine reclamation, see 631.64

.52   Irrigation

Class here construction and use of irrigation canals

Class construction of dams and reservoirs for irrigation in 627.8

For on-farm irrigation, see 631.587

.54   Drainage and reclamation from sea

Standard subdivisions are added for drainage and reclamation from sea together, for drainage alone

.549   Reclamation from sea

Including dikes

Class here polders

.56   Artificial recharge of groundwater

Class comprehensive works on engineering of groundwater in 628.114

.58 Shore protection

> Including stabilization of coastal dunes by engineering means, comprehensive works on seawalls
>
> Class here beach erosion and its control, shore reclamation, comprehensive works on coastal engineering
>
> Class dune stabilization by revegetation, comprehensive works on dune stabilization in 631.64
>
> *For harbor seawalls, see 627.24; for seawalls as flood barriers, see 627.42. For a specific aspect of coastal engineering, see the aspect, e.g., reclamation from sea 627.549*

.7 **Underwater operations**

.700 1–.700 9 Standard subdivisions

> 627.702–627.704 General topics of underwater operations

> Class comprehensive works in 627.7

.702 Underwater construction

.703 Salvage operations

.704 Research operations

.72 Diving

> Class here interdisciplinary works on diving
>
> *For diving sports, see 797.2*

.73 Dredging

.74 Blasting

.75 Drilling

.8 **Dams and reservoirs**

> Standard subdivisions are added for dams and reservoirs together, for dams alone
>
> Class here construction of dams and reservoirs for specific purposes
>
> Class a specific use of dams and reservoirs with the use, e.g., water storage and conservation 628.132

.81 Earthwork, planning, surveying

> Class earthwork, planning, surveying for specific kinds of dams in 627.82–627.84; class earthwork, planning, surveying for reservoirs in 627.86; class earthwork, planning, surveying for ancillary structures in 627.88

> 627.82–627.84 Specific kinds of dams

Class ancillary structures of specific kinds of dams in 627.88; class comprehensive works in 627.8

.82   Masonry dams

.83   Earth-fill and rock-fill dams

Standard subdivisions are added for either or both topics in heading

.84   Movable dams

.86   Reservoirs

Including silting control

Class ancillary structures of reservoirs in 627.88

.88   Ancillary structures

.882   Gates, penstocks, sluices

.883   Spillways and weirs

.9   Other hydraulic structures

[.92]   Navigation aids

Relocated to 623.893

[.922]   Lighthouses

Relocated to 623.8942

[.924]   Light beacons, buoys, daymarks

Relocated to 623.8944

.98   Offshore structures

Class here artificial islands, drilling platforms

Class a specific use of offshore structures with the use, e.g., use of drilling platforms in petroleum extraction 622.33819

For freestanding mooring and berthing structures, see 627.32

628 Sanitary engineering

Class here environmental engineering (environmental health engineering, environmental protection engineering), green technology (environmental technology), municipal engineering, public sanitation technology, sustainable engineering

Class interdisciplinary works on environmental protection in 363.7

> *For military sanitary engineering, see 623.75; for plumbing, see 696.1. For a specific aspect of municipal engineering not provided for here, see the aspect, e.g., road and street engineering 625.7, laying gas pipelines 665.744; for a specific aspect of environmental engineering, green technology, sustainable engineering not provided for here, see the aspect, plus notation 0286 from Table 1, e.g., green technology in electronic circuits 621.38150286*

> *See Manual at 300 vs. 600; also at 363 vs. 302–307, 333.7, 570–590, 600*

SUMMARY

[.091 734]   Treatment in rural regions

Do not use; class in 628.7

.1 Water supply

Class here comprehensive works on engineering of water supply, sewers, sewage treatment and disposal

Class interdisciplinary works on water supply in 363.61

> *For sewers, see 628.2; for sewage treatment and disposal, see 628.3; for water supply for rural and sparsely populated areas, see 628.72*

SUMMARY

.102 87   Measurement

Do not use for testing; class in 628.161

.11   Sources

      Class here protection and engineering evaluation of sources

      Class economic and social evaluation of adequacy, development requirements, conservation of sources in 333.91; class hydraulic engineering in 627; class interdisciplinary works on sources, on evaluation of sources in 553.7

      See also 628.132 for reservoirs

.112   Lakes, rivers, springs

      Class artesian wells in 628.114

.114   Groundwater

      Including artesian wells, prevention of seawater intrusion, prospecting for water

      Class here wells

.116   Seawater

      Class desalinization in 628.167

.13   Storage and conservation

      Standard subdivisions are added for either or both topics in heading

      Including storage tanks, water towers

      Class construction of dams for water storage and conservation in 627.8

.132   Reservoirs

      Including evaporation control

      Class engineering of reservoirs for water supply, comprehensive works on protection of reservoirs in 627.86

.14   Collection and distribution systems

      For construction of dams and reservoirs, see 627.8; for storage and conservation, see 628.13; for water mains and service pipes, see 628.15

.142   Collection systems

.144   Distribution systems

.15   Water mains and service pipes

      Class here aqueducts

.16   Testing, analysis, treatment, pollution countermeasures

      See Manual at 363.61

.161   Testing and analysis

      Class here testing and measurement of pollution

.162   Treatment

Class here treatment of sewage effluent for reuse; comprehensive engineering works on treatment of water supply and sewage

For mechanical treatment, see 628.164; for chemical treatment, see 628.166; for desalinization, see 628.167; for sewage treatment, see 628.3

.162 2   Coagulation (Flocculation), screening, sedimentation (settling)

.164   Mechanical treatment

Including filtration, membrane (osmotic) processes

Class membrane processes for desalinization in 628.1674

For screening, sedimentation, see 628.1622

.165   Aeration

Including deaeration

See also 628.1662 for ozone treatment

.166   Chemical treatment

For coagulation, see 628.1622; for aeration, see 628.165

.166 2   Disinfection

Including chlorination, copper sulfate treatment, ozone treatment, ultraviolet radiation

.166 3   Fluoridation

Class interdisciplinary works on fluoridation in 614.5996

.166 6   Demineralization

Including softening

For desalinization, see 628.167

.167   Desalinization

.167 2   Distillation

.167 23   Distillation using nuclear energy

.167 25   Solar desalinization

.167 3   Electrolysis

.167 4   Membrane processes

.167 44   Reverse osmosis

.168   Pollution countermeasures

Class prevention of natural pollution of water sources in 628.11; class interdisciplinary works on water pollution countermeasures in 363.7394

For countermeasures that consist of routine water treatment, see 628.162; for countermeasures that consist of sewage treatment, see 628.3

[.168 028 7]	Testing and measurement
	Do not use; class in 628.161
.168 2	Countermeasures for domestic wastes and sewage
.168 25	Wastes in sanitary landfills
.168 3	Countermeasures for industrial wastes

For countermeasures for radioactive wastes, see 628.1685. For countermeasures in a specific technology other than sanitary engineering, see the technology, plus notation 0286 from Table 1, e.g., pollution control in metallurgy plants 669.0286

.168 31	Thermal pollution
.168 32	Acid mine drainage
.168 33	Oil spills
.168 36	Wastes from chemical and related industries

Standard subdivisions are added for wastes from chemical and related industries together, for wastes from chemical industries alone

.168 37	Manufacturing wastes

Class thermal pollution from manufacturing processes in 628.16831

For wastes from chemical and related technologies, see 628.16836

.168 4	Countermeasures for agricultural wastes
.168 41	Soil improvement wastes

Including fertilizers, irrigation return flow

.168 42	Pesticides
.168 46	Animal wastes

Class here feedlot runoff

.168 5	Countermeasures for radioactive wastes
.2	**Sewers**

Class road drainage in 625.734

.21	Sewer systems for handling precipitation

Including overflows

Class here urban runoff

.212	Storm sewers
.214	Combined sewers
.23	Deodorization and ventilation of sewers

Including ventilators

.24   Design and construction

.25   Appurtenances of sewers

        Including catch basins, house connections, manholes

.29   Pumping stations

.3   Sewage treatment and disposal

        Standard subdivisions are added for sewage treatment and disposal together, for sewage treatment alone

        For unsewered sewage disposal, see 628.742. For treatment and disposal of sewage in a specific technology, see the technology, plus notation 0286 from Table 1, e.g., treatment of sewage from beverage plants by beverage makers 663.0286

        See Manual at 363.61

>   628.32–628.35   Treatment

        Class comprehensive works in 628.3

.32   Disinfection

.34   Primary treatment

        Including primary sedimentation, screening

        Class comprehensive works on a specific process used in both primary and secondary treatment in 628.351–628.354

.35   Secondary and tertiary treatment

        Standard subdivisions are added for secondary and tertiary treatment together, for secondary treatment alone

        Class here aeration, biological treatment

>   628.351–628.354   Secondary treatment

        Class comprehensive works in 628.35

.351   Oxidation ponds

        Variant names: sewage lagoons, stabilization ponds

        Including oxidation ditches

.352   Filtration

.353   Secondary sedimentation

.354   Activated sludge process

.357   Tertiary treatment

Including nitrogen removal

Class comprehensive works on a specific process used in both secondary and tertiary treatment in 628.351–628.354

For demineralization, see 628.358

.358   Demineralization

.36   Disposal

For disposal into water, see 628.39

.362   Sewage effluent disposal

For disposal by artificial recharge of groundwater, see 627.56; for treatment for reuse as water supply, see 628.162

.362 3   Sewage irrigation

.364   Sewage sludge disposal

Including sanitary landfills

For underground disposal of sludge other than in sanitary landfills, see 628.366; for incineration of sludge, see 628.37; for utilization of sludge, see 628.38

.366   Underground disposal of sludge

Other than in sanitary landfills

Including construction of facilities, storage

.37   Incineration of sludge

.38   Utilization of sludge

Class here biosolids

For a specific use of sludge, see the use, e.g., use as fertilizer 631.869

.39   Disposal of sewage, sewage effluent, sewage sludge into water

.4   Waste technology, public toilets, street cleaning

Standard subdivisions are added for waste technology, public toilets, street cleaning together; for waste technology alone

Class here industrial waste treatment and disposal

Class pollution from wastes in 628.5; class interdisciplinary works on wastes in 363.728

For gaseous wastes, see 628.53; for waste technology for rural and sparsely populated areas, see 628.74. For control and utilization of wastes in a specific technology, see the technology, plus notation 0286 from Table 1, e.g., waste technology in fuel processing 662.60286

.42	Hazardous and toxic wastes

Standard subdivisions are added for either or both topics in heading

Waste technology only

Class social services for hazardous and toxic wastes in 363.7287

For hazardous and toxic liquid wastes, see 628.43; for hazardous and toxic solid wastes, see 628.44; for hazardous and toxic gaseous wastes, see 628.53

.43	Liquid wastes

For liquid wastes released into bodies of water, see 628.168; for sewage treatment and disposal, see 628.3

.44	Solid wastes (Refuse)
.442	Collection
.445	Treatment and disposal

Standard subdivisions are added for either or both topics in heading

---

> 628.445 6–628.445 9 Disposal

Class comprehensive works in 628.445

.445 6	Disposal on land and underground
.445 62	Open dumps
.445 64	Sanitary landfills
.445 66	Underground disposal

Other than in sanitary landfills

Including construction of facilities, storage

.445 7	Incineration
.445 8	Conversion into useful products

Class here recycling technology

For a specific conversion technology, see the technology, e.g., converting garbage into fertilizer 668.6375

.445 9	Disposal into water
.45	Public toilets
.46	Street cleaning

.5   **Pollution control technology and industrial sanitation engineering**

Standard subdivisions are added for pollution control technology and industrial sanitation engineering together, for pollution control technology alone

Class here industrial pollution technology

Class interdisciplinary works on pollution in 363.73

For noise control, see 620.23; for water pollution control, see 628.168. For pollution control technology in a specific technology, see the technology, plus notation 0286 from Table 1, e.g., engineering to control pollution in fuel processing plants 662.60286

.51   Industrial sanitation engineering

Class here plant sanitation

.52   Specific kinds of pollutants

Class here movement through environment

Class specific kinds of pollutants in water in 628.168; class specific kinds of pollutants in air in 628.53; class specific kinds of pollutants in soil in 628.55

.529   Pesticides

.53   Air pollution

Class here gaseous wastes, dispersal of pollutants from source

Class air quality surveys in 363.73922

.532   Products of combustion

Class here smog

.535   Radioactive substances

Including radon

.536   Microorganisms

.55   Soil pollution

.7   **Sanitary engineering for rural and sparsely populated areas**

Standard subdivisions are added for either or both topics in heading

Class pollution in rural and sparsely populated areas in 628.5091734; class pest control in rural and sparsely populated areas in 628.96091734

.72   Water supply

.74   Waste technology

.742   Unsewered sewage disposal

Including septic tanks

.744   Solid waste technology

Class agricultural solid waste technology in 628.746

.746   Agricultural waste technology

> Class water pollution from agricultural wastes in 628.1684

> > *For utilization of agricultural wastes in a specific technology, see the technology, e.g., utilization for biogas 665.776*

.746 6   Animal wastes

> Class here animal manures

.9   Other branches of sanitary and municipal engineering

.92   Fire safety and fire fighting technology

> Including general disaster and rescue technology

> Class interdisciplinary works on fire hazards and their control in 363.37

> > *For a specific disaster and rescue technology, see the technology, e.g., first aid 616.0252*

.922   Fire safety technology

> Including fire escapes, rescue operations

> Class here fire prevention

.922 2   Flammability studies and testing

> Standard subdivisions are added for either or both topics in heading

> Class development of fire resistance in products in 628.9223

.922 3   Fireproofing and fire retardation

> Including fire doors, fire retardants

> > *For fireproofing a specific product, see the product, e.g., textiles 677.689, buildings 693.82*

.922 5   Fire detection and alarms

.925   Fire fighting technology

> Class here use of equipment and supplies, comprehensive works on their manufacture

> > *For shipboard fire fighting technology, see 623.8886; for fire fighting technology in airports, see 629.1368; for forest fire technology, see 634.9618. For manufacture of a specific kind of equipment and supplies, see the kind, e.g., nautical fire fighting equipment 623.865, fire resistant clothing 687.16, fire stations 690.519*

.925 2   Extinction with water

> Including hydraulic systems, sprinkler systems

.925 4   Extinction with chemicals

.925 9   Fire fighting vehicles

> Class here fire engines

> > *For construction of fire engines, see 629.225*

.95 Public lighting

Class lighting of airports in 629.1365

.96 Pest control

Class here household pests, comprehensive works on pest control technology

Class interdisciplinary works on pest control in 363.78

For control of plant pests, see 628.97; for control of agricultural pests, see 632.6

Control of disease-carrying pests relocated to 614.43

.964 Mollusks

Class here slugs, snails

.965 Terrestrial invertebrates

.965 7 Insects

Including ants, cockroaches, house flies, mosquitoes, termites

.968 Birds

.969 Mammals

.969 3 Rodents

Class here rat control

.97 Control of plant pests

629 Other branches of engineering

SUMMARY

.04 Transportation engineering

Unless other instructions are given, class a subject with aspects in two or more subdivisions of 629.04 in the number coming last, e.g., land vehicles 629.049 (*not* 629.046)

Class military transportation technology in 623.6; class operation of transportation equipment for recreational purposes in 796–797; class interdisciplinary works on transportation in 388. Class technical problems peculiar to transportation of a specific commodity with the commodity, e.g., slurry transportation of coal 662.624

.040 289 Safety measures

Including comfort equipment, e.g., air conditioning; control devices, e.g., markings, signals, signs

.045   Navigation

> *For celestial navigation, see 527*

.046   Transportation equipment

> Including remote-control vehicles
>
> Class here vehicles
>
> *See Manual at 629.046 vs. 388*

.046 022 8   Models and miniatures

> Class interdisciplinary works on remote-control models in 796.15
>
> *See Manual at 796.15 vs. 629.0460228*

.047   Stationary transportation facilities

> Class here trafficways
>
> *For transportation buildings, see 690.53*

\>   629.048–629.049   Engineering of transportation in specific mediums

> Class comprehensive works in 629.04
>
> *For aerospace engineering, see 629.1*

.048   Water transportation engineering

> *For nautical engineering and seamanship, see 623.8; for inland waterways, see 627.1; for harbors, ports, roadsteads, see 627.2; for overwater air-cushion vehicles, see 629.324*

.049   Land transportation engineering

> *For pipes and pipelines, see 621.8672; for railroads, roads, highways, see 625; for motor land vehicles, cycles, see 629.2; for overland air-cushion vehicles, see 629.322; for nonmotor land vehicles, see 688.6*

.1   **Aerospace engineering**

> Class military aerospace engineering in 623.66
>
> *For astronautics, see 629.4*

SUMMARY

629.11	**Mechanics and operation of aerospace flight**
.12	**Aerospace vehicles and stationary facilities**
.13	**Aeronautics**
.14	**Portable flight vehicles**

.11   Mechanics and operation of aerospace flight

> Class mechanics and operation of a specific type of aerospace flight with the type, e.g., astromechanics 629.411

.12   Aerospace vehicles and stationary facilities

       Aerospace vehicles: vehicles that function equally well in the atmosphere and space

       Class a specific facility with the facility, e.g., air-cushion vehicles 629.3

       For vehicles that function primarily in the atmosphere, see 629.133; for vehicles that function primarily in space, see 629.47

.13   Aeronautics

       See Manual at 629.046 vs. 388

SUMMARY

629.130 01–.130 09	**Standard subdivisions**
.130 1–.130 9	**Standard subdivisions of flight**
.132	**Mechanics of flight; flying and related topics**
.133	**Aircraft types**
.134	**Aircraft components and general techniques**
.135	**Aircraft instrumentation (Avionics)**
.136	**Airports**

.130 01–.130 09   Standard subdivisions

.130 1   Philosophy and theory of flight

[.130 153 36]   Aeromechanics of flight

       Do not use; class in 629.1323

[.130 155 15]   Aviation meteorology

       Do not use; class in 629.1324

.130 2–.130 8   Standard subdivisions of flight

.130 9   History, geographic treatment, biography of flight

       Do not use for flight guides; class in 629.13254

       Record of flying activities in all types of aircraft

.130 92   Biography of flight

       Class here fliers, pilots

.132   Mechanics of flight; flying and related topics

[.132 01–.132 09]   Standard subdivisions

       Do not use; class in 629.1301–629.1309

.132 2   Aerostatics

.132 3   Aerodynamics

       Including aircraft noise

       Class here comprehensive works on aeromechanics

       For aerostatics, see 629.1322; for weather aerodynamics, see 629.1324

.132 300 1–.132 300 9	Standard subdivisions
.132 303	Subsonic aerodynamics
.132 304	Transonic aerodynamics

Including sonic booms

.132 305	Supersonic aerodynamics
.132 306	Hypersonic aerodynamics
.132 31	Gliding and soaring

Standard subdivisions are added for either or both topics in heading

.132 32	Airflow

Including turbulence

For boundary layers, see 629.13237

.132 322	Incompressible airflow
.132 323	Compressible airflow
.132 327	Air pockets (Air holes)
.132 33	Lift and thrust
.132 34	Drag (Air resistance)
.132 35	Pressure distribution and aerodynamic load

Standard subdivisions are added for either or both topics in heading

.132 36	Stability and control
.132 362	Aeroelasticity, flutter, vibration
.132 364	Moments of inertia

Including pitch, roll, yaw; restoring torques and damping

.132 37	Boundary layers
.132 38	Propulsion principles
.132 4	Aviation meteorology

Weather conditions and aerodynamics

Class piloting in bad weather in 629.1325214

.132 5	Flying and related topics

Standard subdivisions are added for flying and related topics together, for flying alone

Class flying model airplanes in 796.154; class flying kites in 796.158; class air sports in 797.5

For aviation meteorology, see 629.1324; for automatic control, see 629.1326

See Manual at 796.15 vs. 629.0460228

[.132 509]	History, geographic treatment, biography of flight

Do not use; class in 629.1309

.132 51	Navigation
.132 52	Piloting

Class here comprehensive works on piloting and navigation, on piloting airplanes

For navigation, see 629.13251

[.132 520 92]	Biography

Do not use; class in 629.13092

.132 521	General topics of piloting

Unless other instructions are given, class a subject with aspects in two or more subdivisions of 629.132521 in the number coming first, e.g., landing during bad weather 629.1325213 (*not* 629.1325214)

Class general topics of specific types of aircraft in 629.132522–629.132528

.132 521 2	Takeoff
.132 521 3	Landing
.132 521 4	Piloting under adverse conditions

Including bad weather, disablement of craft, nighttime

Class here instrument flying

.132 521 6	Piloting commercial craft
.132 521 7	Piloting private craft
.132 522	Piloting lighter-than-air aircraft
.132 523–.132 528	Piloting specific types of heavier-than-air aircraft

Add to base number 629.13252 the numbers following 629.1333 in 629.13333–629.13338, e.g., piloting helicopters 629.1325252; however, for comprehensive works on piloting airplanes, see 629.13252; for piloting commercial craft, see 629.1325216; for piloting private craft, see 629.1325217

Class hang gliding in 629.14

.132 54   Flight guides (Pilot guides)

Class here charts, logbooks, maps

[.132 540 91–.132 540 99]   Geographic treatment

Do not use; class in 629.132541–629.132549

.132 541–.132 549   Specific geographic areas

Add to base number 629.13254 notation 1–9 from Table 2, e.g., pilot guides to Spain 629.1325446

.132 55   Wreckage studies

.132 6   Automatic control

Manned and guided aircraft

See also 629.1352 for automatic pilots

.133   Aircraft types

Class components of specific aircraft types in 629.134

[.133 022 8]   Models and miniatures

Do not use; class in 629.1331

[.133 028 7]   Testing and measurement

Do not use; class in 629.1345

[.133 028 8]   Maintenance and repair

Do not use; class in 629.1346

.133 028 9   Safety measures

Class safety equipment in 629.13443

.133 1   Models and miniatures

Add to base number 629.1331 the numbers following 629.133 in 629.1332–629.1333, e.g., models of helicopters 629.1331352

Class comprehensive works on models and miniatures of military aircraft in 623.7460228; class flying model aircraft, interdisciplinary works on building and flying model aircraft in 796.154. Class models and miniatures of a specific type of military aircraft with the type in 623.741–623.746, plus notation 0228 from Table 1, e.g., models of fighters 623.74640228; class models and miniatures of a specific aircraft component with the component in 629.134–629.135, plus notation 0228 from Table 1, e.g., models of turboprop engines 629.13435320228

See Manual at 796.15 vs. 629.0460228

.133 2   *Lighter-than-air aircraft

*Do not use notation 0228 from Table 1; class in 629.1331

.133 22	*Free and captive balloons
	Including hot air balloons
	Class dirigible balloons in 629.13324
.133 24	*Airships (Dirigibles)
	For specific types of airships, see 629.13325–629.13327

> 629.133 25–629.133 27 Specific types of airships

Class comprehensive works in 629.13324

.133 25	*Rigid airships
.133 26	*Semirigid airships
.133 27	*Nonrigid airships (Blimps)
.133 3	*Heavier-than-air aircraft
.133 32	*Kites
	Class flying kites in 796.158
.133 33	*Gliders
	Class hang gliders in 629.14
.133 34	Airplanes
	For rocket planes, see 629.13338
[.133 340 228]	Models and miniatures
	Do not use; class in 629.133134
[.133 340 287]	Testing and measurement
	Do not use; class in 629.1345
[.133 340 288]	Maintenance and repair
	Do not use; class in 629.1346
.133 340 4	Special topics of airplanes
.133 340 42	General topics of airplanes
.133 340 422	*Private airplanes
	Class private short takeoff and landing airplanes in 629.133340426
.133 340 423	*Commercial airplanes
	Class commercial short takeoff and landing airplanes in 629.133340426
.133 340 426	*Short takeoff and landing airplanes (STOL airplanes)

*Do not use notation 0228 from Table 1; class in 629.1331

.133 343	*Propeller-driven airplanes
	Piston and turboprop
	Including ultralight airplanes
	Class propeller-driven seaplanes in 629.133347; class propeller-driven amphibious planes in 629.133348
.133 347	*Seaplanes
.133 348	*Amphibious planes
.133 349	*Jet airplanes
	Class jet seaplanes in 629.133347; class jet amphibious planes in 629.133348
.133 35	*Vertical-lift craft (VTOL craft)
	Including autogiros, convertiplanes, flying jeeps
.133 352	*Helicopters
.133 36	*Orthopters (Ornithopters)
.133 38	*Rocket planes
.134	Aircraft components and general techniques
	For aircraft instrumentation, see 629.135
[.134 028 7]	Testing and measurement
	Do not use; class in 629.1345
[.134 028 8]	Maintenance and repair
	Do not use; class in 629.1346
.134 1	Analysis and design
	Class analysis and design of parts in 629.1343; class analysis and design of interiors and special equipment in 629.1344
.134 2	Manufacturing and assembling
	Class manufacturing and assembling of parts in 629.1343; class manufacturing and assembling of interiors and special equipment in 629.1344
.134 3	Parts
	Class here components
	For interiors and special equipment, see 629.1344
.134 31	Airframes
	Class a specific component part with the component, e.g., fuselages 629.13434

*Do not use notation 0228 from Table 1; class in 629.1331

.134 32	Airfoils

Including wing accessories

Class here wings

For control surfaces, see 629.13433; for propellers, vertical lift rotors, see 629.13436

.134 33	Control surfaces

Including ailerons, flaps, rudders

.134 34	Fuselages

.134 35	Engines and fuels

Standard subdivisions are added for engines and fuels together, for engines alone

Including pollution control

.134 351	Fuels

Class here propellants

Class fuels and propellants for specific engines in 629.134352–629.134355

.134 352	Reciprocating and compound engines

Piston and compound piston-turbine engines

Class comprehensive works on reciprocating, compound, gas-turbine, jet engines in 629.13435

.134 353	Gas-turbine and jet engines

Standard subdivisions are added for either or both topics in heading

.134 353 2	Turboprop engines
.134 353 3	Turbojet engines
.134 353 4	Turboramjet engines
.134 353 5	Ramjet engines
.134 353 6	Pulse-jet engines
.134 353 7	Fan-jet engines
.134 354	Rocket engines
.134 355	Nuclear power plants
.134 36	Propellers and vertical lift rotors
.134 37	Rigging and bracing equipment

Standard subdivisions are added for either or both topics in heading

.134 38	Other equipment

.134 381   Landing gear

See also 678.32 for manufacture of tires

.134 386   Escape equipment

Including capsule cockpits, parachutes, pilot ejection seats

.134 4   Interiors and special equipment

.134 42   Comfort equipment

Including air conditioning, heating, pressurization, soundproofing, ventilating equipment

.134 43   Safety equipment

Including fire prevention equipment, life rafts, safety belts

.134 45   Interiors

Including cabins

.134 5   Tests and measurements

Standard subdivisions are added for either or both topics in heading

Aircraft and airplanes in general

Class wreckage studies in 629.13255

For test and measurements of a specific type of aircraft other than airplanes in general or a specific part, see the type of aircraft or part, plus notation 0287 from Table 1, e.g., tests and measurements of seaplanes 629.1333470287, of interiors 629.134450287

.134 52   Ground tests and inspection

Standard subdivisions are added for either or both topics in heading

Including wind and shock tunnels

.134 53   Flight tests

.134 6   Maintenance and repair

Standard subdivisions are added for either or both topics in heading

Aircraft and airplanes in general

For maintenance and repair of specific types of aircraft other than airplanes in general or of a specific part, see the type of aircraft or part, e.g., maintenance and repair of seaplanes 629.1333470288, of interiors 629.134450288

.135   Aircraft instrumentation (Avionics)

.135 1   Navigation instrumentation

Including landing and navigation lights

.135 2	Flight instrumentation

Including accelerometers, altimeters, Machmeters; automatic pilots; air-speed, vertical-speed, turn and bank indicators; directional gyros, gyrohorizons

.135 3	Power-plant monitoring instrumentation
.135 4	Electrical systems

Class electrical systems of a specific kind of instrumentation in 629.1351–629.1353

.135 5	Electronic systems

Class electronic systems of a specific kind of instrumentation in 629.1351–629.1353

.136	Airports

Class here commercial land airports

.136 1	Types other than commercial land airports

Including floating airports (seadromes)

Class details of airports in 629.1363–629.1368

.136 12	Airstrips
.136 16	Heliports

>   629.136 3–629.136 8   Details of airports

Class comprehensive works in 629.136

.136 3	Runways
.136 34	Pavements
.136 35	Drainage systems
.136 37	Snow removal and compaction
.136 5	Lighting systems
.136 6	Air traffic control systems

See Manual at 629.1366 vs. 387.740426

.136 8	Fire fighting equipment
.14	Portable flight vehicles

Units intended to be carried by a single person

Including hang gliders and gliding

Class hang gliding as a sport in 797.55

.2   **Motor land vehicles, cycles**

Standard subdivisions are added for motor land vehicles, cycles together; for motor land vehicles alone

Class here automotive engineering

Class military motor land vehicles in 623.747

See Manual at 629.046 vs. 388

SUMMARY

629.201–.209	**Standard subdivisions and special topics of motor land vehicles**	
.22	**Types of vehicles**	
.23	**Design, materials, construction**	
.24	**Chassis**	
.25	**Engines**	
.26	**Bodies**	
.27	**Other equipment**	
.28	**Tests, driving, maintenance, repair**	
.29	**Specialized land vehicles**	

[.202 28]   Models and miniatures

Do not use; class in 629.221

.202 84   Apparatus and equipment

Do not use for materials; class in 629.232

[.202 87]   Testing and measurement

Do not use; class in 629.282

[.202 88]   Maintenance and repair

Do not use; class in 629.287

.202 89   Safety measures

Class safety engineering of motor land vehicles in 629.2042

.204   Special topics of motor land vehicles

.204 2   Safety engineering of motor land vehicles

Class here comprehensive works on motor land vehicle and highway safety engineering

For highway safety engineering, see 625.70289

.22   Types of vehicles

Class design, materials, construction of a specific type of vehicle in 629.23; class parts of a specific type of vehicle in 629.24–629.27; class driving a specific type of vehicle in 629.283; class nonsurface motor land vehicles, vehicles for extraterrestrial surfaces in 629.29

[.220 228]   Models and miniatures

Do not use; class in 629.221

[.220 287]	Testing and measurement	

Do not use; class in 629.282

[.220 288]	Maintenance and repair

Do not use; class in 629.287

.220 289	Safety measures

Class safety accessories in 629.276

.220 4	Special topics of types of vehicles

Including three-wheel vehicles

.220 42	*Off-road vehicles

Including all-terrain vehicles, snowmobiles

For dune buggies, see 629.222

.220 43	*Natural gas vehicles
.221	Models and miniatures

Including models and miniatures of off-road vehicles

Add to base number 629.221 the numbers following 629.22 in 629.222–629.229, e.g., models of racing cars 629.2218

Class comprehensive works on models and miniatures of military motor land vehicles in 623.7470228; class operating remote-control models in 796.156. Class models and miniatures of a specific type of military motor land vehicles with the type in 623.7472–623.7475, plus notation 0228 from Table 1, e.g., models of tanks 623.747520228

See Manual at 796.15 vs. 629.0460228

> 629.222–629.228 Gasoline-powered, oil-powered, man-powered vehicles

Class comprehensive works in 629.22

.222	*Passenger automobiles

Including dune buggies, minivans, station wagons

Class passenger automobiles rebuilt or modified for high speed in 629.2286

See also 629.2234 for vans

.222 1	*Sports cars

Class racing cars in 629.228

For specific named sports cars, see 629.2222

*Do not use notation 0228 from Table 1 for models and miniatures; class in 629.221. Do not use notation 0287 from Table 1 for testing and measurement; class in 629.282. Do not use notation 0288 from Table 1 for maintenance and repair; class in 629.287

.222 2	Specific named passenger automobiles
	Arrange alphabetically by name or make of car
[.222 201–.222 209]	Standard subdivisions
	Do not use; class in 629.22201–629.22209
.222 3	*Passenger automobiles for public transportation
.222 32	*Taxicabs and limousines
.222 33	*Buses

> *For guided-way ststems, see 625.4; for trolleybuses, see 625.66*

.222 34	*Ambulances
.223	*Light trucks
.223 2	*Pickup trucks
.223 4	*Vans

> *See also 629.222 for minivans*

.224	*Trucks (Lorries)

Class here tractor trailers (articulated lorries, semi-trailers)

> *For light trucks, see 629.223*

.225	*Work vehicles

Including bulldozers, fire engines

> *For automotive materials-handling equipment, see 621.86; for trucks, see 629.224*

.225 2	*Tractors

> *For steam tractors, see 629.2292*

.226	*Campers, motor homes, trailers (caravans)

Standard subdivisions are added for any or all topics in heading

Class here comprehensive works on recreational vehicles (RVs)

Class construction of towed mobile homes in 690.879

> *For a specific kind of recreational vehicle not provided for here, see the vehicle, e.g., dune buggies 629.222*

> *See also 629.224 for tractor trailers*

> *See Manual at 643.29, 690.879, 728.79 vs. 629.226*

.227	*Cycles
.227 1	*Monocycles

*Do not use notation 0228 from Table 1 for models and miniatures; class in 629.221. Do not use notation 0287 from Table 1 for testing and measurement; class in 629.282. Do not use notation 0288 from Table 1 for maintenance and repair; class in 629.287

.227 2	*Bicycles

> *For mopeds and motor bicycles, see 629.2275; for tandem bicycles, see 629.2276*

.227 3	*Tricycles
.227 5	*Motorcycles

Including minibikes, mopeds, motor bicycles

Class here motorscooters

.227 6	*Tandem bicycles
.228	*Racing cars

Conventional and converted

Including karts

.228 6	*Hot rods
.229	*Other types of vehicles
.229 2	*Steam-powered vehicles

Including steam tractors and steamrollers

Class comprehensive works on tractors in 629.2252

.229 3	*Electric-powered vehicles

> *For trolleybuses, see 625.66*

.229 4	*Air-compression-powered vehicles
.229 5	*Solar energy-powered vehicles
.229 6	*Nuclear-powered vehicles
.23	Design, materials, construction

Class materials for, design and construction of parts in 629.24–629.27

.231	Analysis and design

Standard subdivisions are added for either or both topics in heading

Including ergonomic and safety design

Class safety accessories in 629.276

.232	Materials
.234	Manufacturing techniques

Including factory inspection

---

*Do not use notation 0228 from Table 1 for models and miniatures; class in 629.221. Do not use notation 0287 from Table 1 for testing and measurement; class in 629.282. Do not use notation 0288 from Table 1 for maintenance and repair; class in 629.287

> 629.24–629.27 Parts

Class comprehensive works in 629.2

.24 Chassis

.242 Supporting frames

.243 Suspension systems

Class here springs and shock absorbers

.244 Transmission devices

.244 6 Automatic transmission devices

.245 Rear axles, differentials, drive shafts

.246 Brakes

Including brake fluids

.247 Front axles and steering gear

.248 Wheels

.248 2 Tires

See also 678.32 for manufacture of tires

.25 Engines

Class here pollution control

Most works covering automobile engines as a whole focus on spark-ignition engines and are classed in 629.2504

.250 01–.250 09 Standard subdivisions

> 629.250 1–629.250 9 Specific types of engines

Class comprehensive works in 629.25

.250 1 Steam engines

.250 2 Electric engines

.250 3–.250 6 Internal-combustion engines

Add to base number 629.250 the numbers following 621.43 in 621.433–621.436, e.g., spark-ignition engines 629.2504

.250 7 Air-compression engines

.250 8 Solar engines

.250 9 Nuclear engines

>   **629.252–629.258 Parts and auxiliary systems of internal-combustion engines**

> Class here comprehensive works on specific kinds of parts and auxiliary systems of automotive engines

> Class comprehensive works in 629.25

> *For a specific part and auxiliary system of noninternal-combustion engines, see 629.25*

.252   **Motor parts of internal-combustion engines**

> Including mufflers (silencers)

.252 8   Emission control devices

.253   **Fuel systems and fuels of internal-combustion engines**

> Standard subdivisions are added for fuel systems and fuels together, for fuel systems alone

> Class here electronic fuel injection systems

.253 3   Carburetors

.253 8   Fuels

.254   **Ignition, electrical, electronic systems of internal-combustion engines**

> Standard subdivisions are added for ignition, electrical, electronic systems together; for ignition systems alone; for electrical systems alone

> Class a specific use of electrical and electronic systems with the use, e.g., electronic fuel injection 629.253, electric starters 629.257

.254 2   Batteries

.254 8   Auxiliary electrical systems

> *For lighting equipment, see 629.271*

.254 9   Electronic systems

.255   **Lubricating systems of internal-combustion engines**

> Class here lubricants

.256   **Cooling systems of internal-combustion engines**

> Including antifreeze solutions

.257   **Starting devices of internal-combustion engines**

.258   **Throttles and spark control devices of internal-combustion engines**

.26   **Bodies**

> Including convertible tops, doors, fenders, running boards, seats

.260 288	Maintenance and repair
	Class here bodywork
	Class comprehensive works on customizing and detailing in 629.287
.262	Decorations
.266	Windows and windshields
	Standard subdivisions are added for either or both topics in heading
.27	Other equipment
.271	Lighting equipment
.272	Electronic systems
	Class here computer systems
	For electronic fuel injection systems, see 629.253; for electronic systems of internal-combustion engines, see 629.2549
.273	Panel instrumentation
.275	Hardware
	Including handles, hinges, locks
.276	Safety accessories
	Including air bags, bumpers, mirrors, seat belts, windshield wipers and washers
	Class comprehensive works on safety design in 629.231
.277	Comfort, convenience, entertainment equipment
	Including audio systems, glove compartments, telephones, televisions, two-way radios
.277 2	Heaters, ventilators, air-conditioners
.28	Tests, driving, maintenance, repair
.282	Tests and related topics
	Class testing and measurement of a specific part with the part, plus notation 0287 from Table 1, e.g., testing brakes 629.2460287
	For factory inspection, see 629.234
.282 4	Road tests (Performance tests)
.282 5	Periodic inspection and roadability tests
.282 6	Wreckage studies
	Determination of mechanical failure through examination of remains

.283	Driving (Operation)

Class here driving private passenger automobiles

> *For driving vehicles other than internal-combustion passenger vehicles, see 629.284*

.283 04	Special topics of driving

Including factors in safe driving

.283 042	Driving off-road vehicles

Including all-terrain vehicles, snowmobiles

.283 3	Driving public transportation vehicles
.283 32	Taxicabs and limousines
.283 33	Buses
.283 34	Ambulances
.284	Driving vehicles other than internal-combustion passenger vehicles

Add to base number 629.284 the numbers following 629.22 in 629.223–629.229, e.g., driving trucks 629.2844

.286	Services provided by garages and service stations

> *For maintenance and repair, see 629.287*

> *See also 690.538 for construction of garage and service stations*

.287	Maintenance and repair

Standard subdivisions are added for either or both topics in heading

Class here customizing, detailing

Class works on car tune-ups limited to maintenance and repair of the engine in 629.250288. Class maintenance and repair of a specific part with the part, plus notation 0288 from Table 1, e.g., maintenance of bodies 629.260288

.287 04	Special topics of maintenance and repair of types of vehicles

Including three-wheel vehicles

.287 042	Maintenance and repair of off-road vehicles

Including all-terrain vehicles, snowmobiles

> *For dune buggies, see 629.2872*

.287 043	Maintenance and repair of natural gas vehicles
.287 1–.287 9	Maintenance and repair of specific kinds of vehicles and of models and miniatures

Add to base number 629.287 the numbers following 629.22 in 629.222–629.229, e.g., repair of motorcycles 629.28775

Arrange alphabetically by trade name under each type of vehicle (Option: Arrange all vehicles regardless of type alphabetically by trade name)

.29   Specialized land vehicles

> *For overland air-cushion vehicles, see 629.322*

.292   Nonsurface motor land vehicles

> Including subterranean, ocean floor vehicles

.295   Vehicles for extraterrestrial surfaces

> Including moon cars

.3   **Air-cushion vehicles (Ground-effect machines, Hovercraft)**

> Class military air-cushion vehicles in 623.748

.31   General topics of air-cushion vehicles

> Class general topics applied to specific types of vehicles in 629.32

.313   Lift systems

.314   Propulsion systems

.317   Structural analysis and design

.32   Types of vehicles

.322   Overland air-cushion vehicles

> Class amphibious air-cushion vehicles in 629.325

.324   Overwater air-cushion vehicles

> Class amphibious air-cushion vehicles in 629.325

.325   Amphibious air-cushion vehicles

.4   **Astronautics**

> Class military astronautics in 623.69; class interdisciplinary works on space policy in 333.94

> *See also 500.5 for space sciences*

> *See Manual at 629.046 vs. 388*

SUMMARY

629.409 2	**Astronautical engineers**	
.41	**Space flight**	
.43	**Unmanned space flight**	
.44	**Auxiliary spacecraft**	
.45	**Manned space flight**	
.46	**Engineering of unmanned spacecraft**	
.47	**Astronautical engineering**	

[.401 521]   Astromechanics

> Do not use; class in 629.411

.409 2   Astronautical engineers

> Class astronauts in 629.450092

.41   Space flight

> Class preparation for flight to a specific celestial body with the flight, e.g., preparation for manned lunar flight 629.454
>
> > *For unmanned space flight, see 629.43; for manned space flight, see 629.45*

.411   Astromechanics

.411 1   Gravitation

.411 3   Orbits

.415   Planetary atmospheres

> Including reentry problems

.415 1   Aerodynamics

.415 2   Atmospheric thermodynamics

.416   Space phenomena and environments affecting flight

> Standard subdivisions are added for either or both topics in heading
>
> Including meteoroids, radiation

.418   Weightlessness

.43   Unmanned space flight

> *See Manual at 629.43, 629.45 vs. 559.9, 919.904*

.432   Launching

.433   Guidance and homing

> Class here mission control
>
> > *For communication and tracking, see 629.437*

.434   Flight of artificial satellites

> Class satellite flight for a specific purpose with the purpose, e.g., weather satellites 551.6354

.435   Astronautical exploratory and data-gathering flights

.435 2   Ionospheric and near-space flights

> > Standard subdivisions are added for either or both topics in heading

.435 3   Lunar flights

.435 4   Planetary flights

> Add to base number 629.4354 the numbers following 523.4 in 523.41–523.49, e.g., Venusian probes 629.43542

.437   Communications and tracking

.44   Auxiliary spacecraft

.441   Space shuttles

.442	Space stations

Class here space colonies, laboratories

.45	Manned space flight

Class auxiliary spacecraft in 629.44

See Manual at 629.43, 629.45 vs. 559.9, 919.904

.450 01–.450 09	Standard subdivisions
.450 7	Selection and training of astronauts

Standard subdivisions are added for either or both topics in heading

.452	Launching and takeoff

Standard subdivisions are added for either or both topics in heading

.453	Guidance, homing, navigation

Class here mission control

For communication and tracking, see 629.437

.454	Circumterrestrial and lunar flights
.455	Planetary flights

Class here flights to planetary satellites

Add to base number 629.455 the numbers following 523.4 in 523.41–523.49, e.g., flights to Mars 629.4553; then add further as follows:
[001–009]   Standard subdivisions
                Relocated to 01–09
   01–09   Standard subdivisions [*formerly* 001–009]

.457	Communications and tracking
.458	Piloting and related activities
.458 2	Piloting
.458 3	Rendezvous with other spacecraft
.458 4	Extravehicular activities

Including space walks

.458 5	Rescue operations
.458 8	Atmospheric entry and landing
.46	Engineering of unmanned spacecraft

Class here artificial satellites

Add to base number 629.46 the numbers following 629.47 in 629.471–629.478, e.g., environmental control 629.467

.47	**Astronautical engineering**

Class here comprehensive works on spacecraft

For auxiliary spacecraft, see 629.44; for engineering of unmanned spacecraft, see 629.46

.471	Structural analysis and design of spacecraft

Standard subdivisions are added for either or both topics in heading

.472	Spacecraft materials and components
.473	Spacecraft construction
.474	Spacecraft engineering systems

For propulsion systems, see 629.475; for life-support systems, see 629.477

.474 2	Flight operations systems

Including guidance, homing, landing, navigation, piloting systems

.474 3	Communication and tracking systems
.474 4	Auxiliary power systems
.474 43	Nuclear power systems
.474 45	Electric and magnetohydrodynamic power systems
.475	Propulsion systems

Including fuels, auxiliary equipment and instrumentation

Class here booster rockets, engines

Class fuels, auxiliary equipment and instrumentation of a specific type of propulsion in 629.4752–629.4755; class comprehensive works on rocketry in 621.4356

.475 2	Chemical propulsion
.475 22	Liquid propellant
.475 24	Solid propellant
.475 3	Nuclear propulsion
.475 4	Photon propulsion
.475 5	Electric and magnetohydrodynamic propulsion

Including plasma and ion propulsion

.477	Environmental control and life-support systems

Standard subdivisions are added for either or both topics in heading

.477 2	Space suits
.477 3	Food and water supply

.477 4	Sanitation and sterilization
	Including control of wastes
.477 5	Control of temperature, humidity, air supply and pressure
.478	Terrestrial facilities
	Including launch complexes, space ports; spacecraft maintenance, ground testing, repair facilities

.8 Automatic control engineering

Class here automatons that are not computer controlled

Class a specific application with the application, e.g., numerical control of machine tools 621.9023

.801	Philosophy and theory
	For control theory, see 629.8312
.804	Special topics of automatic control engineering
.804 2	Hydraulic control
	Class here fluidics
.804 3	Electric control
	Class computer control in 629.89
.804 5	Pneumatic control
.82	Open-loop systems

Mechanisms in which outputs have no effect on input signals

Including vending machines

Class computer control of open-loop systems in 629.89

.83 Closed-loop systems (Feedback systems)

Mechanisms which maintain prescribed relationships between the controlled outputs and the inputs

Class computer control of closed-loop systems in 629.89

830 1	Philosophy and theory
	For control theory, see 629.8312
.831	General principles

Class general principles of specific mechanisms and systems in 629.832–629.836

.831 2	Control theory

Mathematical design, analysis, synthesis

Including optimal control

Class here comprehensive works on control theory

Class interdisciplinary works on control theory in 003.5

> *For control theory for open-loop systems, see 629.82; for computer control theory, see 629.89*

.831 3	Circuitry
.831 4	Feedback characteristics
.831 5	. System components

Including error correctors, error detectors

.831 7	Construction and assembly

> 629.832–629.836 Specific systems

Including components, circuitry

Class here mechanisms

Class comprehensive works in 629.83

.832	Linear systems
.832 3	Servomechanisms
.833	Multiple-loop systems
.836	Nonlinear systems

Including adaptive control systems

.89	Computer control

Class here electronic control, comprehensive works on computer control

For computer factory operations in manufacturing, see 670.427

.892	Robots

Unless it is redundant, add to base number 629.892 the numbers following 00 in 004–006, e.g., use of digital personal computers 629.892416, but use of digital computers as a whole 629.892 (*not* 629.8924)

For specific kinds of robots, see 629.893

.893	Specific kinds of robots
.893 2	Mobile robots
.893 3	Manipulators

Class here robot hands

.895   Computerized process control

Use of computers to keep conditions of continuous processes as close as possible to desired values or within a desired range by controlling continuous variables such as temperature or pressure

Unless it is redundant, add to base number 629.895 the numbers following 00 in 004–006, e.g., use of digital personal computers 629.895416, but use of digital computers as a whole 629.895 (*not* 629.8954)

630   Agriculture and related technologies

Standard subdivisions are added for agriculture and related technologies together, for agriculture alone

Class here farming, farms, plant crops; interdisciplinary works on plants of agricultural importance

Class agricultural sociology in 306.349; class agricultural economics in 338.1

For a specific nonagricultural aspect of domestic plants, see the aspect, e.g., biology of domestic plants 580

See also 307.72 for rural sociology; also 333.76 for agricultural land economics; also 909.09734 for general works on rural conditions and civilization; also 930–990, plus notation 009734 from table under 930–990, for rural conditions and civilization in specific areas

See Manual at 571–575 vs. 630; also at 630 vs. 579–590, 641.3

SUMMARY

633	**Field and plantation crops**
.1	Cereals
.2	Forage crops
.3	Legumes, forage crops other than grasses and legumes
.5	Fiber crops
.6	Sugar, syrup, starch crops
.7	Alkaloidal crops
.8	Other crops grown for industrial processing
634	**Orchards, fruits, forestry**
.04	Cultivation, harvesting, related topics of orchards, of fruits, of trees
.1	Pomaceous fruits
.2	Stone fruits
.3	Citrus and moraceous fruits
.4	Other fruits
.5	Nuts
.6	Tropical and subtropical fruits
.7	Berries and herbaceous tropical and subtropical fruits
.8	Grapes
.9	Forestry
635	**Garden crops (Horticulture)**
.04	Cultivation, harvesting, related topics
.1	Edible roots
.2	Edible tubers and bulbs
.3	Edible leaves, flowers, stems
.4	Cooking greens and rhubarb
.5	Salad greens
.6	Edible garden fruits and seeds
.7	Aromatic and sweet herbs
.8	Mushrooms and truffles
.9	Flowers and ornamental plants
636	**Animal husbandry**
.001–.009	Standard subdivisions
.01–.08	[General topics in animal husbandry]
.1	Horses
.2	Cattle and related animals
.3	Sheep and goats
.4	Swine
.5	Chickens and other kinds of domestic birds
.6	Birds other than poultry
.7	Dogs
.8	Cats
.9	Other mammals
637	**Processing dairy and related products**
.1	Milk processing
.2	Butter processing
.3	Cheese processing
.4	Manufacture of frozen desserts
.5	Egg processing
638	**Insect culture**
.1	Bee keeping (Apiculture)
.2	Silkworms
.5	Other insects

639	Hunting, fishing, conservation, related technologies
.091 6	Treatment in air and water
.1	Hunting
.2	Commercial fishing, whaling, sealing
.3	Culture of cold-blooded vertebrates
.4	Mollusk fisheries and culture
.5	Crustacean fisheries
.6	Crustacean culture
.7	Harvest and culture of invertebrates other than mollusks and crustaceans
.8	Aquaculture
.9	Conservation of biological resources

[.15] Scientific principles

Do not use; class in 630.21–630.29

.2 Miscellany and scientific principles

Notation 02 from Table 1 as modified below

.201 Tabulated, illustrative, related materials; humorous treatment; audiovisual treatment

.201 1–.201 2 Tabulated, illustrative, related materials

Add to base number 630.201 the numbers following   02 in notation 021–022 from Table 1, e.g., agricultural pictures 630.20122

.201 7 Humorous treatment

.201 8 Audiovisual treatment

.202 Synopses and outlines

.203–.209 Other miscellany

Add to base number 630.20 the numbers following —02 in notation 023–029 from Table 1, e.g., directories 630.205; however, for apparatus, equipment, materials, see 631

.21–.29 Scientific principles

Do not use for miscellany; class in 630.201–630.209

Add to base number 630.2 the numbers following 5 in 510–590, e.g., agricultural meteorology 630.2515; however, for agricultural genetics, see 631.5233

.7 Education, research, related topics

.71 Education

Notation 071 from Table 1 as modified below

.715 Adult education and on-the-job training

Class here extension departments and services

For extension work for young people, see 630.717

.717 Extension work for young people

631   Specific techniques; apparatus, equipment, materials

Topics common to plant and animal husbandry or limited to plant culture

Class comprehensive works on apparatus, equipment, materials used in a specific auxiliary technique or procedure in 630.208, e.g., computers 630.2085

> *For plant injuries, diseases, pests, see 632; for specific techniques, apparatus, equipment, materials for specific plant crops, see 633–635; for specific techniques, apparatus, equipment, materials for animal husbandry, see 636.08*

SUMMARY

631.2	**Agricultural structures**
.3	**Tools, machinery, apparatus, equipment**
.4	**Soil science**
.5	**Cultivation and harvesting**
.6	**Clearing, drainage, revegetation**
.7	**Water conservation**
.8	**Fertilizers, soil conditioners, growth regulators**

[.01–.09]   Standard subdivisions

Do not use; class in 630.1–630.9

.2   Agricultural structures

Class construction of farm buildings and structures other than farmhouses in 690.537

.21   Farmhouses

Class construction of farmhouses in 690.86

.22   General-purpose buildings

Class here barns

> *For housing for domestic animals, see 636.0831*

.25   Machine and equipment sheds

.27   Fences, hedges, walls

Construction and use

.28   Roads, bridges, dams

Class construction of bridges in 624.2; class construction of farm roads in 625.74; class construction of dams in 627.8

.3   Tools, machinery, apparatus, equipment

Class manufacture of tools, machinery, apparatus, equipment in 681.763. Class manufacture of a specific article with the article, e.g., tractors 629.2252

> *See also 631.2 for agricultural structures*

.304   Workshops

.34   Equipment for care and shelter of plants

> *For equipment for a specific purpose, see the purpose, e.g., greenhouses 631.583*

.37   Power and power machinery

> *For a specific use of power and power machinery, see the use, e.g., use of combines 633.1045*

.371   Kinds of power

> Including human, animal, mechanical, electric power

.372   Tractors

.373   Transport equipment

> Including trucks, wagons

.4   Soil science

> Class here interdisciplinary works on soils

> *For a specific aspect of soils, see the aspect, e.g., soil formation 551.305, engineering use of soils 624.151*

[.401 2]   Classification of soils

> Do not use; class in 631.44

[.401 5]   Scientific principles

> Do not use; class in 631.4

[.409]   History, geographic treatment, biography

> Do not use; class in 631.49

.41   Soil chemistry

> *For soil fertility, acidity, alkalinity, see 631.42*

.416   Inorganic chemistry

> Including salinity

> Class use of soil conditioners in 631.82

.417   Organic chemistry

> Including humus

> Class here soil biochemistry

.42   Soil fertility, acidity, alkalinity

.422   Soil fertility

> *For use of fertilizers, see 631.8*

.43   Soil physics

.432   Moisture and hydromechanics

> Standard subdivisions are added for either or both topics in heading

.433	Soil mechanics

> Including effect of gas content, micropedology
>
> Class here soil texture
>
> Class interdisciplinary works on soil mechanics in 624.15136
>
> *For hydromechanics, see 631.432*

.436	Soil temperature
.44	Soil classification
.45	Soil erosion

> Class here control of soil erosion, soil conservation, comprehensive agricultural works on soil and water conservation
>
> Class comprehensive technological works on soil erosion in 627.5; class interdisciplinary works on soil conservation in 333.7316; class interdisciplinary works on soil erosion in 551.302
>
> *For revegetation, see 631.64; for water conservation, see 631.7*

.451	Conservation tillage

> Including mulch tillage
>
> *For tillage for water conservation, see 631.586*

.452	Crop rotation and cover crops

> Class comprehensive works on crop rotation in 631.582

.455	Contouring and terracing
.456	Strip cropping
.46	Soil biology

> *For soil biochemistry, see 631.417*

.47	Soil and land-use surveys

> Standard subdivisions are added for either or both topics in heading
>
> Soil surveys are detailed studies covering small areas (the size of a county or smaller)
>
> Class geographic studies of soils (less detailed than soil surveys and usually covering larger areas) in 631.49

.470 01–.470 08	Standard subdivisions
[.470 09]	History, geographic treatment, biography

> Do not use for history without subdivision; class in 631.47

[.470 090 1–.470 090 5]	Historical periods

> Do not use; class in 631.4701–631.4705

[.470 091–.470 099]	Geographic treatment

> Do not use; class in 631.471–631.479

.470 1–.470 5   Historical periods

> Add to base number 631.470 the numbers following —090 in notation 0901–0905 from Table 1, e.g., 20th century soil surveys 631.4704
> > Subdivisions are added for either soil or land-use surveys or both together

.471–.479   Geographic treatment

> Class here soil types in specific areas

> Add to base number 631.47 notation 1–9 from Table 2, e.g., soil survey of Gonzales County, Texas 631.47764257
> > Subdivisions are added for either soil or land-use surveys or both together

.49   History, geographic treatment, biography of soil science

> Class here geographic studies of soils (less detailed than soil surveys and usually covering areas larger than jurisdictions like counties)

> *For soil and land-use surveys, see 631.47*

.490 1–.490 5   Historical periods

> Add to base number 631.490 the numbers following —090 in notation 0901–0905 from Table 1, e.g., 20th century soil studies 631.4904

.491–.499   Geographic treatment, biography

> Add to base number 631.49 notation 1–9 from Table 2, e.g., soil science in China 631.4951

.5   **Cultivation and harvesting**

> Standard subdivisions are added for cultivation and harvesting together, for cultivation alone

.51   Soil working (Tillage)

> Before and after planting

> Class here cultivation limited to tillage

> Class soil working in special methods of cultivation in 631.58

> *For conservation tillage, see 631.451*

.52   Production of seeds, bulbs, tubers, new varieties

> Standard subdivisions are added for production of seeds, bulbs, tubers, new varieties together; for production of seeds, bulbs, tubers alone

> Including domestication, plant selection, seedlings

> Class here nursery practice, plant breeding

.521   Seeds

.523		Development of new varieties

Including plant introduction

Class here germ plasm, hybrids

Class interdisciplinary works on germ plasm in 333.9534

.523 3		Agricultural genetics

Class here genetic engineering

.526		Bulbs and tubers

Standard subdivisions are added for either or both topics in heading

.53		Plant propagation

Class here comprehensive works on plant propagation and nursery practice

For nursery practice, see 631.52; for grafting, pruning, training, see 631.54

.531	Propagation from seeds (Sowing)
.532	Propagation from bulbs and tubers

Standard subdivisions are added for either or both topics in heading

.533	Propagation from suckers, runners, buds

Class propagation from tubers in 631.532; class propagation from cuttings in 631.535

.534	Propagation by layering
.535	Propagation from cuttings and slips
.536	Transplanting

Class here planting seedlings

.54	Grafting, pruning, training

Most works on grafting and pruning will be classed in 634.044 and cognate numbers in 634.1–634.8 or in 635.9

.541	Grafting
.542	Pruning
.546	Training
.55	Harvesting

Including mowing, reaping

Class operations subsequent to harvesting in 631.56

.558	Yields

See Manual at 338.1 vs. 631.558

.56	Operations subsequent to harvesting

Including cleaning, husking, packing

.567   Grading

.568   Storage

.57   Varieties and kinds of organisms used in agriculture

> Class here description of cultivated varieties that contain little or no information on how to grow them
>
> Class biology of varieties of agricultural plants in 580
>
> *For development of new varieties, see 631.523*

.58   Special methods of cultivation

> Including double cropping, multiple cropping, permaculture
>
> Class special methods of cultivation as topics in land economics in 333.76; class special methods of cultivation as topics in agricultural economics in 338.162

.581   Reduced cultivation methods

> Class here minimum tillage, surface tillage

.581 2   Fallowing

.581 4   No-tillage

.581 8   Shifting cultivation (Slash-and-burn agriculture)

.582   Crop rotation

> *For crop rotation to control erosion, see 631.452*

.583   Controlled-environment agriculture

> Including forcing, retarding, hotbeds, use of artificial light
>
> Class here greenhouse agriculture
>
> Most works on use of artificial light in agriculture will be classed in 635.0483 and 635.9826
>
> *For greenhouse gardening, see 635.0483*

.584   Organic farming

> *For organic gardening, see 635.0484. For a specific aspect of organic farming, see the aspect, e.g., compost 631.875*

.585   Soilless culture (Hydroponics)

> Most works on soilless culture will be classed in 635.0485 and cognate numbers in 635.1–635.9

.586   Dry farming

> Class here tillage for water conservation

.587   Irrigation

> Use only for works describing what is done on the farm, e.g., installation and use of center-pivot sprinkler systems

> Class digging wells in 628.114; class interdisciplinary works on technological aspects of irrigation, works on obtaining irrigation water from off-farm sources in 627.52; class interdisciplinary works on irrigation in 333.913

> *For sewage irrigation, see 628.3623*

.6   **Clearing, drainage, revegetation**

> Class here reclamation

> Class interdisciplinary works on technological aspects of reclamation in 627.5

.61   Clearing

.62   Drainage

> Class off-farm drainage projects, interdisciplinary works on technological aspects of drainage in 627.54

.64   Revegetation

> Including inland dune stabilization, surface mine reclamation

> Class reforestation in 634.956

.7   **Water conservation**

> *For tillage for water conservation, see 631.586*

.8   **Fertilizers, soil conditioners, growth regulators**

> Standard subdivisions are added for fertilizers, soil conditioners, growth regulators together; for fertilizers alone

> Class here interdisciplinary works on agricultural chemicals

> Class comprehensive works on soil fertility in 631.422

> *For pesticides, see 632.95; for manufacture of agricultural chemicals, see 668.6*

.81   Nutritive principles, complete fertilizers, methods of application

> *For nutritive principles and methods of application of specific fertilizers, see 631.83–631.87*

.811   Nutritive principles

.813   Complete fertilizers

.816   Methods of application

.82   Soil conditioners

> Including conditioners for control of salinity

.821   Acid-soil conditioners

> Including lime

.825	Alkaline-soil conditioners
.826	Conditioners for soil texture

Including peat

> 631.83–631.87 Specific kinds of fertilizers

Class comprehensive works in 631.8

.83	Potassium fertilizers
.84	Nitrogen fertilizers
.841	Ammonium, cyanamide, urea fertilizers

For ammonium nitrate, see 631.842

.842	Nitrate fertilizers

Including ammonium nitrate

.843	Slaughterhouse residues

For bone meal, see 631.85

.847	Biological methods of soil nitrification

Use of nitrifying bacteria, nitrifying crops

.85	Phosphorus fertilizers

Including bone meal

.86	Organic fertilizers

Class here animal wastes

For slaughterhouse residues, see 631.843; for vegetable manures and converted household garbage, see 631.87

.861	Farm manure
.866	Guano
.869	Biosolids (Sewage sludge)
.87	Vegetable manures and converted household garbage

Standard subdivisions are added for vegetable manures and converted household garbage together, for vegetable manure alone

.874	Green manures
.875	Compost

Including converted household garbage

.89	Growth regulators

632　Plant injuries, diseases, pests

Standard subdivisions are added for plant injuries, diseases, pests together; for plant injuries alone

Class here pathology of agricultural plants; comprehensive works on plant and animal injuries, diseases, pests

Class works on both physiology and pathology of agricultural plants in 571.2; class use of agricultural plants in studies of basic pathological processes in 571.92

> *For injuries, diseases, pests of specific plant crops, see 633–635; for veterinary medicine, see 636.089*

.1　Damages caused by environmental factors

Class here damages caused by climatic change, by weather

.11　Frost injury

Including other low-temperature injuries

.12　Drought and heat damage

.14　Hail damage

.15　Lightning damage

.16　Wind and rain damage

.17　Flood damage

.18　Fire damage

.19　Pollution damages

Class here air pollution damages, diseases caused by pollution

---

>　632.2–632.8　Specific diseases and pests

Class here control of specific diseases

Class comprehensive works on diseases and pests together in 632; class comprehensive works on diseases in 632.3; class comprehensive works on pests in 632.6; class comprehensive works on disease and pest control in 632.9

> *For pesticides regardless of disease or pest, see 632.95*

> *See Manual at 632.95 vs. 632.2–632.8*

.2　Galls

Class here gall-producing organisms

.3　Diseases

Including protozoan diseases, radiation injury

Class here disease control

> *For diseases caused by pollution, see 632.19; for galls, see 632.2; for fungus diseases, see 632.4; for viral diseases, see 632.8; for pesticides used in disease control, see 632.95*

.32   Bacterial diseases

> Including rickettsial diseases

.4   **Fungus diseases**

> Add to base number 632.4 the numbers following 579.5 in 579.52–579.59, e.g., rusts 632.492, smuts 632.493

.5   **Weeds**

> Including poisonous plants
>
> Class here plant pests, weed control
>
> *For herbicides, see 632.954*

.52   Parasitic weeds

> Class parasitic microorganisms in 632.3

.6   **Animal pests**

> Class here pests, control of specific animal pests
>
> Add to base number 632.6 the numbers following 59 in 592–599, e.g., nematodes 632.6257, common rats 632.69352; however, for gall-producing animal pests, see 632.2; for protozoan diseases, see 632.3; for insect pests, see 632.7
>
> Class comprehensive works on agricultural pest control, on specific topics of pest control other than pesticides in 632.9; class interdisciplinary works on pest control technology in 628.96; class interdisciplinary works on pests, works on pest control services in 363.78
>
> *For weeds, see 632.5; for pesticides, see 632.95; for predator control in animal husbandry, see 636.0839*

.7   **Insect pests**

> Add to base number 632.7 the numbers following 595.7 in 595.72–595.79, e.g., locusts 632.726, beetles 632.76

.8   **Virus diseases**

.9   **General topics of pest and disease control**

> Standard subdivisions are added for pest and disease control together, for pest control alone
>
> Including genetic engineering for pest resistance
>
> Class here control of animal pests, integrated pest management
>
> *For disease control, see 632.3; for weed control, see 632.5; for control of specific animal pests, see 632.6*

.902 84   Apparatus and equipment

> Do not use for materials; class in 632.95

.93   Plant quarantine

.94   Crop-dusting, fumigation, spraying

.940 284	Apparatus and equipment
	Do not use for materials; class in 632.95
.95	Pesticides

Including algicides

Class here interdisciplinary works on pesticides [*formerly also* 668.65], pesticides used to control animal pests

Class chemicals used in biological control in 632.960284

For manufacture of pesticides, see 668.65

See Manual at 632.95 vs. 632.2–632.8

.950 4	Special topics of pesticides

Including fumigants

.950 42	Undesired effects and their control

Including pesticide resistance

Class interdisciplinary works on environmental effects of pesticides in 363.7384

.951	**Pesticides used to control specific kinds of animal pests**

Including rodenticides, vermicides

Class comprehensive works on pesticides used to control animal pests in 632.95

[.951 01–.951 09]	Standard subdivisions

Do not use; class in 632.9501–632.9509

.951 7	Insecticides

Including DDT

Class here pesticides used to control arthropods

.952	Fungicides
.953	Bactericides
.954	Herbicides
.96	Biological control

> **633–635 Specific plant crops**

Add to each subdivision identified by * as follows:
1–6   Cultivation and harvesting
      Add the numbers following 631.5 in 631.51–631.56, e.g., harvesting 5
      For special cultivation methods, see 8
7   Varieties and kinds
      Class specific techniques of cultivation and harvesting specific varieties in 1–6; class fertilizers, soil conditioners, growth regulators for specific varieties in 89; class injuries, pests, diseases of specific varieties in 9
8   Special cultivation methods; fertilizers, soil conditioners, growth regulators
81–87   Special cultivation methods
      Add to 8 the numbers following 631.58 in 631.581–631.587, e.g., organic farming 84
89   Fertilizers, soil conditioners, growth regulators
      Add to 89 the numbers following 631.8 in 631.81–631.89, e.g., compost 8975
9   Injuries, diseases, pests
      Add to 9 the numbers following 632 in 632.1–632.9, e.g., insect pests 97

Class comprehensive works in 630

See Manual at 633–635

633   Field and plantation crops

Large-scale production of crops intended for agricultural purposes or industrial processing other than preservation

Standard subdivisions are added for either or both topics in heading

Class truck farming in 635

For a specific field or plantation crop not provided for here, see the crop, e.g., bananas 634.772

SUMMARY

633.1	**Cereals**
.2	**Forage crops**
.3	**Legumes, forage crops other than grasses and legumes**
.5	**Fiber crops**
.6	**Sugar, syrup, starch crops**
.7	**Alkaloidal crops**
.8	**Other crops grown for industrial processing**

[.028]   Auxiliary techniques and procedures; apparatus, equipment, materials

      Do not use for auxiliary techniques and procedures; class in 630.208

[.028 4]   Apparatus, equipment, materials

      Do not use; class in 631

.1	**Cereals**

Including grain amaranths

For cereal crops grown for forage, see 633.25

.104	*Cultivation, harvesting, related topics
.11	*Wheat
.12	*Buckwheat
.13	*Oats
.14	*Rye
.15	*Corn

Variant names: Indian corn, maize

Class sweet corn in 635.672

For popcorn, see 635.677

.16	*Barley
.17	Millets, grain sorghums, upland and wild rice
.171	*Millets (Panicum and related genera)
.174	*Grain sorghums

Class sweet sorghums in 633.62

.178	*Wild rice
.179	*Upland rice
.18	*Rice

Class here paddy rice

For upland rice, see 633.179

See also 633.178 for wild rice

.2	**Forage crops**

Class here forage grasses, Pooideae grasses

For forage crops other than grasses, see 633.3

| .200 1–.200 9 | Standard subdivisions |
| .202 | Pastures and their grasses |

Class here range management

Class pasture use of forests in 634.99; class comprehensive works on ranches and farms devoted to livestock in 636.01

For specific pasture grasses, see 633.21–633.28

| .208 | *Cultivation, harvesting, related topics of forage crops |

*Add as instructed under 633–635

.21   *Bluegrasses (Poa)

.22   *Orchard grass

         Variant name: cocksfoot

.23   *Bent grasses (Agrostis)

.24   *Timothy

.25   Cereal grasses

         Add to base number 633.25 the numbers following 633.1 in 633.11–633.18, e.g., rye grasses 633.254

.26   Sedges

.27   Panicoideae grasses

         For corn, see 633.255; for millets, see 633.2571; for sorghums, see 633.2574

.28   Other Pooideae grasses

         Including fescues (Festuca)

.3   Legumes, forage crops other than grasses and legumes

         Standard subdivisions are added for legumes and forage crops other than grasses and legumes together, for legumes alone

         Class here forage legumes, grain legumes

         Class interdisciplinary works on legumes as food in 641.3565

         For leguminous fruits, see 634.46; for garden legumes, see 635.65

.304   *Cultivation, harvesting, related topics

.31   *Alfalfa

         Variant name: lucerne

.32   *Trifolium clovers

         Class here trefoils

         Class sweet clovers in 633.366

.33   *Cowpeas

         Variant name: black-eyed peas

.34   *Soybeans

         Variant names: sojas, soyas

.35   *Vetches

.36   Lespedeza, sweet clovers, lupines, peanuts, field peas

.364   *Lespedeza

         Variant name: bush clover

*Add as instructed under 633–635

.366	*Sweet clovers (Melilotus)

.367   *Lupines

.368   *Peanuts

         Variant name: groundnuts

.369   *Field peas

         Variant names: Austrian winter peas, Pisum arvense

.37   Other legumes

         Including chick-peas, fava beans (broad beans), lentils, lima beans, Pisum sativum

.372   *Common beans (Phaseolus vulgaris)

         Former heading: Kidney beans

.39   Forage crops other than grasses and legumes

.5   **Fiber crops**

         Class here soft-fiber crops

         Class fiber plants grown for paper pulp in 633.89

>   633.51–633.56   Soft fibers

         Class comprehensive works in 633.5

.51   *Cotton

.52   *Flax

.53   *Hemp (Cannabis sativa)

         See also 633.79 for marijuana

.54   *Jute

.55   *Ramie

.56   Other soft fibers

         Including kenaf

.57   Hard fibers

         For hard fibers not provided for below, see 633.58

.571   *Manila hemp

         Variant name: abaca

.576   *Pineapple fibers

.577   *Sisal (Agave fibers)

*Add as instructed under 633–635

.58   Other hard fibers

> Including bamboo, rattan, other basketwork and wickerwork plants

.6   Sugar, syrup, starch crops

> Standard subdivisions are added for sugar, syrup, starch crops together; for sugar crops alone; for syrup crops alone

.61   *Sugarcane

.62   *Sorgo

> Variant name: sweet sorghums

.63   *Sugar beets

.64   *Sugar maples

.68   Starch crops

> Including arrowroot, sago, taro

> Class a crop raised for starch and another product with the other product, e.g., potatoes 635.21

.682   *Cassava (Manioc)

.7   Alkaloidal crops

.71   *Tobacco

.72   *Tea

.73   *Coffee

.74   *Cacao

.75   *Poppies (Papaver somniferum)

.76   *Kola nuts (Cola nuts)

.77   *Maté

> Variant name: Paraguay tea

.78   *Chicory

.79   *Marijuana

> Class here hashish

> *See also 633.53 for hemp*

.8   Other crops grown for industrial processing

.81   Perfume-producing plants

*Add as instructed under 633–635

.82   Flavoring-producing plants

    Including hops, mints, sassafras, vanilla, wintergreen

     For spices, see 633.83; for alliaceous plants, see 635.26; for aromatic and sweet herbs, see 635.7

.83   Spices

    Including allspice, cinnamon, clove, ginger, nutmeg

    Class here sweet spices

     For hot spices, see 633.84

.84   Hot spices

    Including black pepper, chili, horseradish, mustard, paprika

.85   Plants producing nonvolatile oils

    Class here oilseed plants

     For a specific plant producing a nonvolatile oil not provided for here, see the plant, e.g., corn 633.15; coconuts 634.61; olives 634.63

.851   *Oil palms

.853   *Rapeseed

.86   Dye-producing plants

.87   Tannin-producing plants

    Including canaigre

.88   Medicine-producing plants

    Add to base number 633.88 the numbers following 58 in 583–588, e.g., ginsengs 633.88384; however, for a crop producing medicine as a secondary product, see the primary product, e.g., poppy 633.75

.89   Crops grown for other industrial purposes

.895   Rubber-producing and resin-producing plants

.895 2   *Rubber tree (Hevea brasiliensis)

.895 9   *Turpentine-producing plants

.898   Insecticide-producing plants

*Add as instructed under 633–635

634   Orchards, fruits, forestry

Fruits: reproductive bodies of seed plants having an edible more or less sweet pulp associated with the seed

Standard subdivisions are added for orchards, fruits, forestry together; for orchards alone; for fruits alone

Class here comprehensive works on tree crops

For trees grown for plantation crops, see 633; for pepos, see 635.61; for ornamental trees, see 635.977

SUMMARY

634.04	**Cultivation, harvesting, related topics of orchards, of fruits, of trees**
.1	**Pomaceous fruits**
.2	**Stone fruits**
.3	**Citrus and moraceous fruits**
.4	**Other fruits**
.5	**Nuts**
.6	**Tropical and subtropical fruits**
.7	**Berries and herbaceous tropical and subtropical fruits**
.8	**Grapes**
.9	**Forestry**

.04   *Cultivation, harvesting, related topics of orchards, of fruits, of trees

---

> ### 634.1–634.6 Orchards and their fruits

Class comprehensive works in 634

.1   Pomaceous fruits

.11   *Apples

.13   *Pears

See also 634.653 for alligator pears

.14   *Quinces

.15   *Medlars (Mespilus germanica)

See also 634.16 for Japanese medlars

.16   *Loquats

Variant name: Japanese medlars

.2   Stone fruits

Variant name: Drupaceous fruits

.21   *Apricots

.22   *Plums

.23   *Cherries

*Add as instructed under 633–635

.25	*Peaches
.257	Varieties and kinds
	Number built according to instructions under 633–635
	Including nectarines
.3	**Citrus and moraceous fruits**
.304	*Citrus fruits
	For specific citrus fruits, see 634.31–634.34
.31	*Oranges
.32	*Grapefruit
.33	Citron group
.331	*Citrons
.334	*Lemons
.337	*Limes
.34	*Kumquats
.36	*Moraceous fruits
	For figs, see 634.37; for mulberries, see 634.38; for breadfruit, see 634.39
.37	*Figs
.38	*Mulberries
.39	*Breadfruit
.4	**Other fruits**
	Class tropical and subtropical fruits not provided for here in 634.6
.41	Annonaceous fruits
	Including papaws
.42	Myrtaceous and passifloraceous fruits
.421	*Guavas
.425	*Passion fruit
.43	Sapotaceous fruits
.44	Anacardiaceous fruits
	Including mangoes
	Class cashews in 634.573
.45	*Persimmons

*Add as instructed under 633–635

.46 Leguminous fruits

  Including carob

  Class comprehensive works on legumes in 633.3

.5   **Nuts**

.51   *Walnuts

.52   *Pecans

.53   *Chestnuts

.54   *Filberts

.55   *Almonds

.57   Cashews, pistachios, Brazil nuts

.573   *Cashews

.574   *Pistachios

.575   *Brazil nuts

.6   **Tropical and subtropical fruits**

  Not provided for elsewhere

  For herbaceous tropical and subtropical fruits, see 634.77

.61   *Coconuts

.62   *Dates

.63   *Olives

.64   *Pomegranates

.65   Papayas, avocados, mangosteens

.651   *Papayas

.653   *Avocados

  Variant name: alligator pears

.655   *Mangosteens

.7   **Berries and herbaceous tropical and subtropical fruits**

  Standard subdivisions are added for berries and herbaceous tropical and subtropical fruits together, for berries alone

  Class here comprehensive works on small fruits

  For a specific small fruit not provided for here, see the fruit, e.g., mulberries 634.38, grapes 634.8

.71   Cane fruits (Rubus)

.711   *Raspberries

*Add as instructed under 633–635

.713	*Blackberries
.714	*Loganberries
.717	*Dewberries
.718	*Boysenberries
.72	Ribes
.721	*Currants
.725	*Gooseberries
.73	Huckleberries and blueberries
.732	*Huckleberries (Gaylussacia)
.737	*Blueberries (Vaccinium)
.74	Other bush fruits

Including barberries, juneberries

.75	*Strawberries
.76	*Cranberries
.77	Herbaceous tropical and subtropical fruits

Class comprehensive works on tropical and subtropical fruits in 634.6

.772	*Bananas
.773	*Plantains
.774	*Pineapples
.775	Cactus fruits

.8 **Grapes**

Class here viticulture

.82　Injuries, diseases, pests

Add to base number 634.82 the numbers following 632 in 632.1–632.9, e.g., fungus diseases 634.824

.83　Varieties and kinds

Class a specific aspect of varieties and kinds with the aspect, e.g., fungus diseases of muscadines 634.824

.88　Cultivation and harvesting

Add to base number 634.88 the numbers following 631.5 in 631.51–631.58, e.g., pruning 634.8842; however, for varieties, see 634.83

.9 **Forestry**

*Add as instructed under 633–635

SUMMARY

634.92	**Forest management**
.93	**Access and safety features**
.95	**Silviculture**
.96	**Injuries, diseases, pests**
.97	**Kinds of trees**
.98	**Forest exploitation and products**
.99	**Agroforestry**

[.906 85]   Management of production

> Do not use; class in 634.92

>   634.92–634.96   General topics of forestry

Class general topics applied to a specific kind of tree in 634.97; class comprehensive works in 634.9

For exploitation and products, see 634.98

.92   Forest management

Class here production management in forestry

Class comprehensive works on management in forestry in 634.9068. Class production management of a specific aspect of forestry with the aspect, e.g., production management of logging 634.980685

.928   Production planning and mensuration

.928 3   Production planning

.928 5   Mensuration

Including estimation

.93   Access and safety features

Including lookout towers, roads

.95   Silviculture

.953   Forest thinning

.955   Brush disposal

Including prescribed burning

.956   Forestation

Class here afforestation, reforestation, plant breeding

Class interdisciplinary works on afforestation in 333.75152; class interdisciplinary works on reforestation in 333.75153

.956 2   Producing seeds and seedlings

See also 634.9565 for propagation with seeds and seedlings

.956 4   Nursery practice

For producing seeds and seedlings, see 634.9562

.956 5	Propagation at permanent site
	Including seeding at permanent site
.96	Injuries, diseases, pests
	Add to base number 634.96 the numbers following 632 in 632.1–632.9, e.g., forest fire technology 634.9618
.97	Kinds of trees
	Class here general topics of forestry applied to specific kinds of trees

Add to each subdivision identified by † as follows:
- 2–6   General topics
  - Add the numbers following 634.9 in 634.92–634.96, e.g., reforestation 56
  - *For exploitation and products, see 8*
- 7   Varieties and kinds
  - Class a specific general topic with respect to a specific variety or kind with the topic, e.g., reforestation of a variety 56
- 8   Exploitation and products
  - Standard subdivisions are added for either or both topics in heading
  - Class here logging, logs, lumbering
  - *For minor products, see 634.985–634.987; for sawmill operations, see 674.2*
- 83   Pulpwood

.972	Dicotyledons
	Class here hardwoods
	For other dicotyledons, see 634.973
.972 1	†Oaks
.972 2	†Maples
.972 3	†Poplars
	Class aspens, cottonwoods in 634.97365
	See also 634.97322 for yellow poplar (tulip tree)
.972 4	†Chestnuts
.972 5	†Beeches
.972 6	†Birches
.972 7	†Lindens
.972 77	Varieties and kinds
	Number built according to instructions under 634.97
	Including basswood (American linden), lime (European linden)
.972 8	†Elms

†Add as instructed under 634.97

.973   Other dicotyledons

         Add to base number 634.973 the numbers following 583 in 583.2–583.9, e.g., eucalyptus 634.973766

.974   Monocotyledons

         Class here palm forestry

            See also 633.58 for rattan palms; also 633.851 for oil palms; also 634.61 for coconut palm; also 635.97745 for ornamental palms

.975   Gymnosperms

>   634.975 1–634.975 8   Coniferous trees

       Class comprehensive works in 634.975

       For coniferous trees not provided for here, see 634.9759

.975 1   †Pines

         Class dammar, huon pines in 634.97593

.975 2   †Spruces

.975 3   †Hemlocks

.975 4   †Firs

.975 5   †Cypresses

.975 6   †Cedars

.975 7   †Larches

.975 8   †Sequoias

.975 9   Other gymnosperms

         Add to base number 634.9759 the numbers following 585 in 585.2–585.9, e.g., kauris (dammar pines) 634.97593

.98   Forest exploitation and products

       Standard subdivisions are added for either or both topics in heading

       Class here logging, logs, comprehensive works on lumbering

       Class exploitation and products of specific kinds of trees in 634.97; class lumber in 674. Class trees cultivated for a specific product other than lumber or pulp with the product, e.g., turpentine trees 633.8959, pecan trees 634.52

       For sawmill operations, see 674.2

.983   Pulpwood

       Class nonwoody plants grown for paper pulp in 633.89

†Add as instructed under 634.97

> 634.985–634.987 Exploitation of minor forest products

    Use only for products that have not been cultivated

    Class here minor products of specific kinds of trees

    Class comprehensive works in 634.987

.985   Bark

.986   Sap

.987   Minor forest products

        Including fruits, seeds, nuts

          For bark, see 634.985; for sap, see 634.986

.99   Agroforestry

       Forestry in combination with other farming

       Including farm forestry, woodlots; pasture use of forestry

       Class a specific forestry aspect of agroforestry with the aspect, e.g., logging 634.98

635   Garden crops (Horticulture)

    Class here vegetables (crops grown primarily for human consumption without intermediate processing other than cooking and preservation); home gardening, truck farming

    Class orchards in 634

SUMMARY

635.04		**Cultivation, harvesting, related topics**
	.1	**Edible roots**
	.2	**Edible tubers and bulbs**
	.3	**Edible leaves, flowers, stems**
	.4	**Cooking greens and rhubarb**
	.5	**Salad greens**
	.6	**Edible garden fruits and seeds**
	.7	**Aromatic and sweet herbs**
	.8	**Mushrooms and truffles**
	.9	**Flowers and ornamental plants**

.04   *Cultivation, harvesting, related topics

> **635.1–635.8 Edible garden crops**

    Class comprehensive works in 635

.1   **Edible roots**

      For cassava, see 633.682

*Add as instructed under 633–635

.11   *Beets

.12   Turnips, rutabagas, celeriac

.125   *Turnips

> Class rutabagas in 635.126

.126   *Rutabagas

> Variant names: Russian turnips, swedes, Swedish turnips

.128   *Celeriac

.13   *Carrots

.14   *Parsnips

.15   *Radishes

.16   *Salsify

.2   Edible tubers and bulbs

> Standard subdivisions are added for edible tubers and bulbs together, for edible tubers alone

> *For taro, see 633.68*

.21   *Potatoes

.22   *Sweet potatoes

.23   *Yams (Dioscorea)

.24   *Jerusalem artichokes

.25   *Onions

.26   Alliaceous plants

> Including chives, garlic, leeks, shallots

> *For onions, see 635.25*

.3   Edible leaves, flowers, stems

> *For cooking greens and rhubarb, see 635.4; for salad greens, see 635.5*

.31   *Asparagus

.32   *Artichokes

> *See also 635.24 for Jerusalem artichokes*

.34   *Cabbage

> Class here comprehensive works on cultivation of Brassica oleracea

> *For cauliflower and broccoli, see 635.35; for Brussels sprouts, see 635.36*

*Add as instructed under 633–635

.347   Varieties and kinds

                   Number built according to instructions under 633–635

                   Including kale (collards)

.35   *Cauliflower and broccoli

                   Subdivisions are added for either or both topics in heading

.36   *Brussels sprouts

.4   Cooking greens and rhubarb

                   Standard subdivisions are added for cooking greens and rhubarb together, for cooking greens alone

.41   *Spinach

.42   *Chard

.48   *Rhubarb

.5   Salad greens

.51   *Dandelions

.52   *Lettuce

.53   *Celery

                   See also 635.128 for celeriac

.54   *Chicory

.55   *Endive

.56   Sorrel and cresses

.6   Edible garden fruits and seeds

.61   Pepos

                   Class here melons

                   For squashes and pumpkins, see 635.62; for cucumbers, see 635.63

.611   *Muskmelons

.615   *Watermelons

.62   *Squashes and pumpkins

                   Subdivisions are added for either or both topics in heading

.63   *Cucumbers

.64   Other garden fruits

.642   *Tomatoes

.643   *Sweet peppers

                   Variant names: bell, green peppers

*Add as instructed under 633 635

.646	*Eggplants
.648	*Okra
.65	Garden legumes

Class comprehensive works on legumes in 633.3

.651	*Broad beans
.652	*Common beans (Phaseolus vulgaris)

Former heading: Kidney beans

.653	*Lima beans
.655	*Soybeans

Variant names: sojas, soyas

.656	*Peas

Variant names: English peas, garden peas, Pisum sativum

.657	*Chick-peas
.658	*Lentils
.659	Other garden legumes
.659 2	*Black-eyed peas

Variant name: cowpeas

.659 6	*Peanuts

Variant name: groundnuts

.67	Corn

Variant names: Indian corn, maize

.672	*Sweet corn
.677	*Popcorn

.7 **Aromatic and sweet herbs**

Standard subdivisions are added for either or both topics in heading

Class here herb gardens

.8 **Mushrooms and truffles**

Standard subdivisions are added for mushrooms and truffles together, for mushrooms alone

*Add as instructed under 633–635

.9   **Flowers and ornamental plants**

Standard subdivisions are added for either or both topics in heading

Class here floriculture

Class landscape architecture of flower gardens in 712

For planting and cultivation of roadside vegetation, see 625.77

See Manual at 635.9 vs. 582.1

SUMMARY

635.91	**Specific techniques; apparatus, equipment, materials**
.92	**Injuries, diseases, pests**
.93	**Groupings by life duration; taxonomic groupings**
.94	**Plants propagated from bulbs and tubers**
.95	**Groupings by environmental factors**
.96	**Groupings by special areas and purposes**
.97	**Other groupings of ornamental plants**
.98	**Special methods of cultivation in floriculture**

[.902 84]   Apparatus, equipment, materials

Do not use; class in 635.91

.91   Specific techniques; apparatus, equipment, materials

Add to base number 635.91 the numbers following 631 in 631.2–631.8, e.g., propagating ornamental plants 635.9153; however, for propagation from bulbs and tubers, see 635.94; for special methods of cultivation, see 635.98

Class specific techniques, apparatus, equipment, materials of specific groupings of ornamental plants in 635.93–635.97

.92   Injuries, diseases, pests

Add to base number 635.92 the numbers following 632 in 632.1–632.9, e.g., fungus diseases 635.924

For injuries, diseases, pests of specific groupings of plants, see 635.93–635.97

>   635.93–635.97   Groupings of plants

Unless other instructions are given, class a subject with aspects in two or more subdivisions of 635.93–635.97 in the number coming first in the schedule, e.g., succulent house plants 635.9525 (*not* 635.965)

Class comprehensive works in 635.9

.93   Groupings by life duration; taxonomic groupings

.931   Groupings by life duration

Class specific taxonomic kinds regardless of life duration in 635.933–635.938

For perennials, see 635.932

.931 2	*Annuals
.931 4	*Biennials
.932	*Perennials
.933–.938	Taxonomic groupings

Add to base number 635.93 the numbers following 58 in 583–588, e.g., cacti 635.93356, roses 635.933734, orchids 635.9344; however, for everlastings, see 635.973; for comprehensive works on dicotyledons, see 635.9; for taxonomic groupings of trees, see 635.9773–635.9775

.94	Plants propagated from bulbs and tubers

Standard subdivisions are added for either or both topics in heading

Class here propagating ornamental plants from bulbs, from tubers

.95	Groupings by environmental factors
.951	Native habitats

Add to base number 635.951 notation 4–9 from Table 2, e.g., ornamentals native to Scotland 635.951411

.952	Groupings by climatic factors

Including arctic plants

Class comprehensive works on temperate-zone plants in 635.9

.952 3	*Tropical plants
.952 5	*Desert plants

Including drought-resistant plants

Class here succulent plants

Class works on succulent plants emphasizing cactus in 635.93356

.952 8	*Alpine plants

Including alpine gardens, high-altitude plants

Class"alpine gardens" in the sense synonymous with rock gardens (that is, as rock gardens with nonalpine as well as alpine plants) in 635.9672

.953	Groupings by seasonal and diurnal factors

Including winter-flowering plants, morning-blooming and night-blooming plants

.954	Groupings by natural light factors

Including plants favoring sunlight

See also 635.9826 for artificial-light gardening

.954 3	*Shade-tolerant plants

*Add as instructed under 633–635

.955	Groupings by soil factors
	Including plants favoring difficult, problem, sandy soils
	Class plants suitable for rock gardens in 635.9672
.96	Groupings by special areas and purposes
	Class comprehensive works on plants for all purposes in 635.9
	For foliage plants, see 635.975; for butterfly gardening, see 638.5789
.962	*Flower beds
.963	*Borders and edgings
	Subdivisions are added for either or both topics in heading
.964	Ground cover
	Class here grass
.964 2	*Turf
	Class lawns in 635.9647
.964 7	*Lawns
.965	*House plants
	Class here indoor gardening in the home
	Class window-box gardening in 635.9678; class comprehensive works on container gardening in 635.986
	For bonsai, see 635.9772
.966	*Flowers for cutting
	Class flower arrangement in 745.92
.967	Special kinds of gardens
.967 1	Roof, balcony, patio gardens
	Class comprehensive works on container gardening in 635.986
.967 2	*Rock gardens
	See also 635.9528 for alpine gardening
.967 4	*Water gardens
.967 6	*Wild-flower gardens
	Class wild flowers of a specific native habitat in 635.951
.967 8	*Window-box gardens
.968	Plants grown for fragrance and color
.97	Other groupings of ornamental plants
.973	*Everlastings

*Add as instructed under 633–635

.974   *Vines

    Class here climbing plants

.975   *Foliage plants

.976   *Shrubs and hedges

    Subdivisions are added for either or both topics in heading

    Class hedges used as fences in 631.27

.977   Trees

    Class here urban forestry; potted, shade, street trees

    Including tree planting

    Class comprehensive works on container gardening in 635.986

.977 1   General kinds of ornamental trees

    Class general kinds of trees of a specific taxa in 635.9773–635.9775; class comprehensive works in 635.977

    For bonsai, see 635.9772

.977 13   *Flowering trees

.977 15   *Evergreen trees

    Class Christmas trees, evergreen trees in the sense of conifers in 635.9775

.977 2   *Bonsai

    Class here dwarf potted trees, miniature trees, penjing

    Class specific taxonomic kinds of bonsai in 635.9773–635.9775

.977 3–.977 5   Taxonomic groupings

    Add to base number 635.977 the numbers following 58 in 583–585, e.g., elms 635.977345; however, for comprehensive works on dicotyledonous trees, see 635.977

.98   Special methods of cultivation in floriculture

    Class special methods of cultivation of specific groupings of plants in 635.93–635.97, class comprehensive works on special methods of cultivating vegetables and ornamental plants in 635.048

.982   Controlled-environment gardening

    For bell-jar gardening, see 635.985

.982 3   *Greenhouse gardening

.982 4   *Terrariums

.982 6   *Artificial-light gardening

.985   *Bell-jar gardening

*Add as instructed under 633–635

.986   *Container gardening

          Class here pot gardening

.987   Organic gardening

          Class a specific aspect of organic gardening in floriculture with the
          aspect in 635.91–635.98, e.g., compost 635.91875

636   **Animal husbandry**

Class here interdisciplinary works on species of domestic mammals

*For culture of nondomesticated animals, see 639. For a specific nonagricultural
aspect of domestic mammals, see the aspect, e.g., biology 599*

See Manual at 800, T3C—362 vs. 398.245, 590, 636

SUMMARY

636.001–.009	**Standard subdivisions**	
.01–.08	**[General topics in animal husbandry]**	
.1	**Horses**	
.2	**Cattle and related animals**	
.3	**Sheep and goats**	
.4	**Swine**	
.5	**Chickens and other kinds of domestic birds**	
.6	**Birds other than poultry**	
.7	**Dogs**	
.8	**Cats**	
.9	**Other mammals**	

.001   Philosophy and theory

[.001 576 5]   Genetics

          Do not use; class in 636.0821

.002   Miscellany

[.002 77]   Ownership marks

          Do not use; class in 636.0812

.003–.006   Standard subdivisions

.007   Education, research, related topics

.007 9   Competitions, festivals, awards, financial support

          Do not use for animal shows and related awards; class in 636.0811

.008–.009   Standard subdivisions

.01   Ranches and farms

          Class feeding livestock in 636.084

          See also 636.0845 for range management

*Add as instructed under 633–635

.07   **Young of animals**

       Class production and maintenance, rearing for specific purposes, veterinary medicine of young animals in 636.08

.08   **Specific topics in animal husbandry**

       Unless other instructions are given, class a subject with aspects in two or more subdivisions of this schedule in the number coming last, e.g., care and maintenance of pets 636.0887 (*not* 636.083)

       For ranches and farms, see 636.01; for young of animals, see 636.07

SUMMARY

636.081	**Selection, showing, ownership marks**
.082	**Breeding**
.083	**Care, maintenance, training**
.084	**Feeding**
.085	**Feeds and applied nutrition**
.086	**Field-crop feeds**
.088	**Animals for specific purposes**
.089	**Veterinary medicine**

[.080 1–.080 9]   Standard subdivisions

       Do not use; class in 636.001–636.009

.081   **Selection, showing, ownership marks**

       For selection in breeding, see 636.082

.081 1   Showing

       Class here judging; show animals

.081 2   Ownership marks

       Class here branding

.082   **Breeding**

       Including breeding stock

.082 1   Genetics

       Including germ plasm

       Class here genetic engineering

       Class interdisciplinary works on livestock genetic resources in 333.954

.082 2   Breeding records

       Class here herdbooks, pedigrees, studbooks

.082 4   Breeding and reproduction methods

.082 45   Artificial insemination

.083	Care, maintenance, training

Including transportation

Class here stable management

For feeding, see 636.084

.083 1	Housing

Including barns, cages, stockyards

Class waste management in 636.0838; class construction of housing for domestic animals in 690.892

See also 636.0843 for feedlot management

.083 2	Animal welfare

Class here animal rescue, animal shelters, condition of livestock

Class veterinary care of animals in 636.089

See also 179.3 for ethical aspects of animal care

.083 21	Animal hospitals

Variant name: veterinary hospitals

.083 3	Individual tending

Including dipping, shearing

Class here grooming

.083 5	Training

Class training for a specific purpose in 636.088

.083 7	Harnesses and accessories

Most works on harnesses and accessories will be classed under horses in 636.10837

.083 8	Animal waste management
.083 9	Predator control

For predator control in wildlife conservation, see 639.966

.084	Feeding

For feeds and applied nutrition, see 636.085

.084 3	Feedlot management

For feedlot waste management, see 636.0838

.084 5	Grazing

Class here browsing, herding, range management

For development of pasturage, see 633.202; for pasture use of forests, see 634.99

.085	Feeds and applied nutrition

.085 2   Applied nutrition

                             Class here composition and food value

                             For composition and food value of a specific feed, see the feed, e.g., food value of silage 636.0862

.085 21   Nitrogen

.085 22   Proteins

.085 27   Minerals

                             Class here trace elements

.085 28   Vitamins

.085 5   Feeds

                             Class growing forage crops in 633.2; class grazing in 636.0845

                             For field-crop feeds, see 636.086

.085 56   Feed from wastes

                             Class here feed from agricultural wastes

.085 57   Feed additives and formula feeds

.086   **Field-crop feeds**

                             Including dry fodder, green fodder

.086 2   Silage

.088   **Animals for specific purposes**

                           See Manual at 636.1–636.8 vs. 636.088

.088 2   Beasts of burden

                             Class here draft animals, pack animals

                             Class comprehensive works on work animals in 636.0886

.088 3   Animals raised for food

                           For animals raised for eggs and milk, see 636.08842

.088 4   Animals raised for special products

                         For animals raised for food, see 636.0883

.088 42   Animals raised for eggs and milk

                             Class milk processing in 637.1; class egg processing in 637.5

                             See Manual at 636.1–636.8 vs. 636.088

.088 44   Animals raised for hide

                           Class fur farming in 636.97

                           For hair, see 636.08845

.088 45	Animals raised for hair and feathers
	Including bristles, wool
.088 5	Laboratory animals
.088 6	Work animals
	Including animals used to guard and herd

> *For beasts of burden, see 636.0882; for sport and stunt animals, see 636.0888*

.088 7	Pets

Class here obedience training

Class reminiscences about and true accounts of pets in 808.883. Class reminiscences about and true accounts of pets in a specific literature with the literature in 800, plus notation 803 from Table 3B under the appropriate language, e.g., reminiscences in English about pets 828.03; class literary treatment of pets other than reminiscences with the appropriate literary form in 800, e.g., a late 20th century English novel about pets 823.914

> *See Manual at 800, T3C—362 vs. 398.245, 590, 636*

.088 8	Sport and stunt animals

Including circus, fighting, hunting, game, racing animals

Class show animals in 636.0811; class comprehensive works on work animals in 636.0886

.088 9	Zoo animals
.089	Veterinary medicine

Class here veterinary sciences

Add to base number 636.089 the numbers following 61 in 610–618, e.g., veterinary viral diseases 636.089691

Class animal welfare in 636.0832; class animal hospitals in 636.08321

> ### 636.1–636.8 Specific kinds of domestic animals

Except for modifications shown under specific entries, add to each subdivision identified by * as follows:

01	Philosophy and theory	
[015765]		Genetics
		Do not use; class in 2
02–06	Standard subdivisions	
07	Education, research, related topics	
079	Competitions, awards, financial support	
		Do not use for animal shows and related awards; class in 1
08–09	Standard subdivisions	
1	Showing	
	Class here judging	
2	Breeding	
22	Breeding records	
	Class here origin of the breed or breeds; herdbooks, pedigrees, studbooks	
3	Care, feeding, training, veterinary medicine	
35	Training	
39	Veterinary medicine	

Class comprehensive works in 636

See Manual at 636.1–636.8 vs. 636.088

.1   Horses

Class here equines

.100 1–.100 9   Standard subdivisions

Notation from Table 1 as modified under 636.001–636.009

.101–.108   Specific topics in husbandry of horses

Add to base number 636.10 the numbers following 636.0 in 636.01–636.08, e.g., housing horses 636.10831; however, for racehorses, see 636.12; for riding horses, see 636.13; for draft horses, see 636.15

Class training of riders and drivers, comprehensive works on training horses and their riders and drivers in 798

.109   Miniature horses

Regardless of breed

> ### 636.11–636.17 Specific breeds and kinds of horses

Class miniature horses regardless of breed in 636.109; class comprehensive works in 636.1

.11   Oriental horses

.112   *Arabian horse

---

*Add as instructed under 636.1–636.8

.12   *Racehorses

> *For a specific breed of racehorse, see the breed, e.g., Thoroughbred horse 636.132*

.13   Saddle horses (Riding horses)

> Including American saddlebred, Tennessee walking horses; American paint, Appaloosa, Morab, mustang, pinto
>
> *For wild mustang, see 599.6655; for Oriental horses, see 636.11; for comprehensive works on racehorses, see 636.12*

.132   *Thoroughbred horse

.133   *Quarter horse

.138   *Lippizaner horse

.14   *Carriage horses

> Including Cleveland bay and Hackney horses
>
> Class here coach horses, comprehensive works on harness horses (carriage horses and light harness horses)
>
> Class comprehensive works on harness and draft horses in 636.15
>
> *For light harness horses, see 636.17*

.15   *Draft horses

> Including Belgian draft, Clydesdale, Shire horses
>
> Class here comprehensive works on harness and draft horses
>
> *For harness horses, see 636.14*

.16   *Ponies

> Including Chincoteague, Iceland, Shetland, Welsh ponies

.17   *Light harness horses

.175   *Standardbred horse

> Class here trotters

.177   *Morgan horse

.18   Other equines

> Including zebras

.182   *Donkeys (Burros)

.183   *Mules

*Add as instructed under 636.1–636.8

.2   **Cattle and related animals**

Class here bovidae, bovines, ruminants

Subdivisions are added for cattle and related animals together, for cattle alone

For sheep and goats, see 636.3; for Tragulidae, see 636.963

.200 1–.200 9   Standard subdivisions

Notation from Table 1 as modified under 636.001–636.009

.201–.208   Specific topics on husbandry of cattle and related animals together, of cattle alone

Add to base number 636.20 the numbers following 636.0 in 636.01–636.08, e.g., heifers 636.207; however, for cattle for specific purposes, see 636.21

.21   Cattle for specific purposes

Class here production, maintenance, training

Add to base number 636.21 the numbers following 636.088 in 636.0882–636.0889, e.g., raising cattle for beef 636.213, for milk 636.2142

Class veterinary science in 636.2089; class specific breeds of cattle for specific purposes in 636.22–636.28; class milking and milk processing in 637.1

\>   636.22–636.28   Specific breeds of cattle

Class comprehensive works in 636.2

.22   British breeds of cattle

.222   English beef breeds

Including Hereford and Shorthorn cattle

.223   Scottish, Welsh, Irish beef breeds

Including Aberdeen Angus, Galloway, Highland cattle

.224   Channel Island dairy breeds

Including Guernsey and Jersey cattle

.225   Scottish and Irish dairy breeds

Including Ayrshire and Dexter cattle

.226   Dual-purpose breeds

Including Devon, English Longhorn, Polled Shorthorn cattle

.23   German, Dutch, Danish, Swiss breeds of cattle

.232   Beef breeds

.234   Dairy breeds

Including Brown Swiss and Holstein-Friesian cattle

.236	Dual-purpose breeds
.24	French and Belgian breeds of cattle
.242	Beef breeds
.244	Dairy breeds
.246	Dual-purpose breeds
.27	Other European breeds of cattle
.28	Non-European breeds of cattle
.29	Other larger ruminants and Camelidae

Including Giraffidae

.291	Zebus (Brahmans)
.292	Bison

Variant names: American buffalo, buffalo

See also 636.293 for water buffalo

.293	Other Bovoidea

Including water buffalo

.294	Cervidae (Deer)

Use of this number for Giraffidae discontinued; class in 636.29

.294 4	Cervus
.294 42	*Cervus elephas

Variant names: American elk, red deer, wapiti

.294 5	*Dama (Fallow deer)
.294 8	*Rangifer

Variant names: caribou, reindeer

.295	*Camels

Subdivisions are added for specific breeds

.296	Camelidae

Including vicuña

For camels, see 636.295

.296 6	*Llamas (Guanaco, Alpacas)

Subdivisions are added for specific breeds

.3   Sheep and goats

Subdivisions are added for sheep and goats together, for sheep alone

---

* Add as instructed under 636.1–636.8

.300 1–.300 9   Standard subdivisions

>   Notation from Table 1 as modified under 636.001–636.009

.301–.308   Specific topics in husbandry of sheep and goats together, of sheep alone

> Add to base number 636.30 the numbers following 636.0 in 636.01–636.08, e.g., sheep ranches 636.301; however, for sheep for specific purposes, see 636.31

.31   Sheep for specific purposes

> Class here production, maintenance, training

> Add to base number 636.31 the numbers following 636.088 in 636.0882–636.0889, e.g., raising sheep for mutton 636.313, for wool 636.3145

> Class veterinary science in 636.3089; class specific breeds of sheep for specific purposes in 636.32–636.38

\>   636.32–636.38 Specific breeds of sheep

> Class comprehensive works in 636.3

.32   British breeds of sheep

.33   German, Dutch, Swiss breeds of sheep

.34   French and Belgian breeds of sheep

.35   Italian breeds of sheep

.36   Merino breeds

> Class here Spanish breeds of sheep

.366   Spanish Merino breeds

.367   Other European Merino breeds

.368   Non-European Merino breeds

.37   Other European breeds of sheep

.38   Non-European breeds of sheep

> *For non-European Merino breeds, see 636.368*

.381   American breeds

.385   Asian breeds

.386   African breeds

.39   Goats

.390 01–.390 09   Standard subdivisions

> Notation from Table 1 as modified under 636.001–636.009

.390 1–.390 8	Specific topics in husbandry of goats

Add to base number 636.390 the numbers following 636.0 in 636.01–636.08, e.g., goat farms 636.301; however, for goats for specific purposes, see 636.391

.391	Goats for specific purposes

Class here production, maintenance, training

Add to base number 636.391 the numbers following 636.088 in 636.0882–636.0889, e.g., raising goats for hair 636.39145

Class veterinary science in 636.39089; class specific breeds of goats for specific purposes in 636.392–636.398

.392–.398	Specific breeds of goats

Add to base number 636.39 the numbers following 636.3 in 636.32–636.38, e.g., Angora goat 636.3985

.4　　　　Swine

.400 1–.400 9	Standard subdivisions

Notation from Table 1 as modified under 636.001–636.009

.401–.408	Specific topics in husbandry of swine

Add to base number 636.40 the numbers following 636.0 in 636.01–636.08, e.g., swine for specific purposes other than food 636.4088

Class swine for food in 636.4

> 　　　　　　636.42–636.48　Specific breeds of swine

Class comprehensive works in 636.4

.42–.47	European breeds of swine

Add to base number 636.4 the numbers following 636.3 in 636.32–636.37, e.g., British breeds 636.42

.48	Non-European breeds of swine
.482	Poland China swine
.483	Duroc-Jersey swine
.484	American breeds

Including Cheshire, Chester White, Hampshire, Victoria swine

For Poland China swine, see 636.482; for Duroc-Jersey swine, see 636.483

.485	Asian breeds
.486	African breeds
.489	Pacific Ocean island breeds

.5 **Chickens and other kinds of domestic birds**

Class here poultry, comprehensive works on raising birds, interdisciplinary works on species of domestic birds

Subdivisions are added for chickens and other kinds of domestic birds together, for chickens alone

For birds other than poultry, see 636.6. For a specific nonagricultural aspect of domestic birds, see the aspect, e.g., biology of domestic birds 598

.500 1–.500 9   Standard subdivisions

Notation from Table 1 as modified under 636.001–636.009

.501–.508   Specific topics of husbandry of chickens and other kinds of domestic birds together, of chickens alone

Add to base number 636.50 the numbers following 636.0 in 636.01–636.08, e.g., chicken breeding 636.5082; however, for poultry for specific purposes, see 636.51

.51   Poultry for specific purposes

Class here production, maintenance, training

Add to base number 636.51 the numbers following 636.088 in 636.0882–636.0889, e.g., raising chickens for meat 636.513, for eggs 636.5142

Class veterinary science in 636.5089; class specific breeds of chickens for specific purposes in 636.52–636.58; class poultry other than chickens for specific purposes in 636.59

>   636.52–636.58 Specific breeds of chickens

Class comprehensive works in 636.5

.52–.57   European breeds of chickens

Add to base number 636.5 the numbers following 636.3 in 636.32–636.37, e.g., Leghorn 636.55

For diminutive varieties of European breeds of chickens, see 636.587

.58   Non-European and diminutive breeds of chickens

.581   American breeds

For Plymouth Rock chicken, see 636.582; for Wyandotte chicken, see 636.583; for Rhode Island Red chicken, see 636.584; for diminutive varieties of American breeds, see 636.587

.582   Plymouth Rock chicken

.583   Wyandotte chicken

.584   Rhode Island Red chicken

.585   Asian breeds

For diminutive varieties of Asian breeds, see 636.587

.587	Diminutive varieties
.587 1	*Bantams
.587 2	Cornish fowl
.59	Other poultry
.592	Turkeys

.592 001–.592 009   Standard subdivisions

                 Notation from Table 1 as modified under 636.001–636.009

.592 01–.592 08   Specific topics in husbandry of turkeys

                 Add to base number 636.5920 the numbers following 636.0 in 636.01–636.08, e.g., raising turkeys for meat 636.5920883

.593	Guinea fowl
.594	Pheasants
.595	Peafowl
.596	*Pigeons

            Subdivisions are added for specific breeds

.597	*Ducks

            Subdivisions are added for specific breeds

.598	Geese

.6   Birds other than poultry

            Class comprehensive works on birds in 636.5

.61   Birds raised for feathers

            Class a specific kind of bird raised for feathers with the kind, e.g., ostriches 636.694

.63   Game birds

.68   Ornamental birds, songbirds, hawks

            Standard subdivisions are added for ornamental birds, songbirds, hawks together; for ornamental birds alone; for songbirds alone

            Including mynas, toucans

            Class here aviary birds, cage birds

            For peafowl, see 636.595

.681   Swans

.686   Finches, parrots, hawks

.686 2   *Finches

---

*Add as instructed under 636.1–636.8

.686 25	*Canaries

Subdivisions are added for specific varieties

.686 4	*Budgerigars

Variant names: lovebirds; grass, shell parakeets

Subdivisions are added for specific varieties

Class comprehensive works on parakeets in 636.6865

See also 636.6865 for lovebirds (Agapornis)

.686 5	*Parrots

Including cockatoos, conures, lories, lovebirds (Agapornis), macaws, comprehensive works on parakeets

For budgerigars (lovebirds), see 636.6864

.686 56	*Cockatiels

Subdivisions are added for specific varieties

.686 9	*Hawks

Class here falcons

Subdivisions are added for specific varieties

.69	Ratites
.694	*Ostriches

.7   Dogs

.700 1–.700 9	Standard subdivisions

Notation from Table 1 as modified under 636.001–636.009

.701–.708	Specific topics in husbandry of dogs

Add to base number 636.70 the numbers following 636.0 in 636.01–636.08, e.g., breeding 636.7082; however, for sled dogs, watchdogs, see 636.73; for hunting dogs, see 636.75

See also 636.73 for working dogs as a recognized group of dog breeds; also 636.752 for sporting dogs as a recognized group of dog breeds

See Manual at 636.70886, 636.70888 vs. 636.73, 636.752

.71	Breeds of dogs

For specific breeds, see 636.72–636.76

*Add as instructed under 636.1–636.8

>   636.72–636.75   Specific breeds and groups of dogs

Class comprehensive works in 636.71

For toy dogs of any breed, see 636.76

See Manual at 636.72–636.75

.72   Nonsporting dogs

Including bichon frise, Boston terrier, bulldog, Chinese Shar-Pei, chow chow, Dalmatian, Finnish spitz, French bulldog, Keeshond, Lhasa apso, Schipperke, Tibetan spaniel, Tibetan terrier

Class here utility breeds (United Kingdom)

Class comprehensive works on terriers in 636.755

.728   *Poodles

Class here miniature poodle

Subdivisions are added for specific breeds

.73   Working and herding dogs

Standard subdivisions are added for working and herding dogs together, for working dogs alone

Including sled dogs, watchdogs (guard dogs)

Including akita, Alaskan Malamute, Bernese mountain dog, boxer, bullmastiff, Eskimo dogs, Great Dane, Great Pyrenee, Komondor, Kuvasz, mastiffs, Newfoundland, Portuguese water dog, Rottweiler, Saint Bernard, Samoyed, Schnauzers (standard and giant), Siberian husky

Class Finnish spitz in 636.72; class Norwegian elkhound in 636.753; class miniature Schnauzer in 636.755

See also 636.70886 for dogs as working animals

See Manual at 636.70886, 636.70888 vs. 636.73, 636.752

.736   *Doberman pinscher

Class miniature pinscher in 636.76

.737   Herding dogs

Including Australian cattle dog, Belgian Malinois, Belgian Tervuren, Bouvier des Flandres, Briard, puli, Welsh corgis; sheep dogs other than collies and German shepherd dog

.737 4   *Collies

Subdivisions are added for specific breeds

.737 6   *German shepherd dog (German police dog)

*Add as instructed under 636.1–636.8

.75 Sporting dogs, hounds, terriers

Class here hunting dogs, sporting dogs (United Kingdom)

.752 Sporting dogs

Including Brittany, Vizsla, Weimaraner, wirehaired pointing griffon

Class here bird dogs, gundogs (United Kingdom)

See also 636.70888 for dogs as sport animals

See Manual at 636.70886, 636.70888 vs. 636.73, 636.752

.752 4 *Spaniels

Subdivisions are added for specific breed

See also 636.72 for Tibetian spaniel; also 636.76 for Japanese spaniel (chin)

.752 5 *Pointers

Subdivisions are added for specific breeds

.752 6 *Setters

Subdivisions are added for specific breeds

.752 7 *Retrievers

Subdivisions are added for specific breeds

.753 Hounds

Including Norwegian elkhound

See Manual at 636.72–636.75: Hounds

.753 2 Gazehounds (Sighthounds)

Including Ibizan hound, Saluki, Scottish deerhound, whippet

For Afghan hound, see 636.7533; for greyhound, see 636.7534; for Borzoi, Irish wolfhound, see 636.7535

.753 3 *Afghan hound

.753 4 *Greyhound

Class Italian greyhound in 636.76; class greyhound racing in 798.8

.753 5 *Wolfhounds

Including Borzoi, Irish wolfhound

.753 6 Scent hounds (Tracking hounds)

Including Basenji, basset hound, black and tan coonhound, bloodhound, foxhounds, harrier, otterhound, petit basset griffon vendéen, pharaoh hound, Rhodesian ridgeback

For beagle, see 636.7537; for dachshund, see 636.7538

*Add as instructed under 636.1–636.8

.753 7	*Beagle

.753 8	*Dachshund

Class miniature dachshund in 636.76

.755	Terriers

Including miniature Schnauzer

For Boston and Tibetan terriers, see 636.72; for toy terriers, see 636.76

.755 9	*Bull terriers

Class here pit bull terriers

Subdivisions are added for specific breeds

.76	Toy dogs

Including affenpinscher, Brussels griffon, Chihuahua, Chinese crested, English toy spaniel, Italian greyhound, Japanese chin, Maltese, Mexican hairless (Xoloitzcuintli), miniature dachshund, miniature pinscher, Papillon, Pekingese, Pomeranian, pug, shih tzu, silky terrier, toy Manchester terrier, toy poodle, Yorkshire terrier

Class miniature poodle in 636.728; class miniature Schnauzer in 636.755

.8	**Cats**

.800 1–.800 9	Standard subdivisions

Notation from Table 1 as modified under 636.001–636.009

.801–.808	Specific topics in husbandry of cats

Add to base number 636.80 the numbers following 636.0 in 636.01–636.08, e.g., breeding cats 636.8082, cats for specific purposes other than pets 636.8088

Class cats as pets in 636.8

>   636.82–636.83   Specific breeds and kinds of domestic cats

Class comprehensive works in 636.8

See Manual at 636.82–636.83

.82	Shorthair cats

Including Chartreaux, Russian blue cats

Class here foreign (Oriental) shorthair cats

.822	Common shorthair cats

Breeds of British Isles, Canada, United States

Including Bengal, Manx, rex cats

*Add as instructed under 636.1 636.8

.824   *Burmese cat

> Subdivisions are added for specific varieties

.825   *Siamese cat

> Subdivisions are added for specific varieties

.826   *Abyssinian cat

> Subdivisions are added for specific varieties

.83   Longhair cats

> Including Himalayan, Maine coon, Turkish Angora, Turkish Van cats

.832   *Persian cat

> Subdivisions are added for specific varieties

.89   Nondomestic cats

> Including cheetah, ocelot

.9   Other mammals

> Class here other mammals as pets

> Add to base number 636.9 the numbers following 599 in 599.2–599.8, e.g., hamsters 636.9356, fur-bearing animals 636.97; however, for Equidae, see 636.1; for ruminants other than Tragulidae, see 636.2; for Camelidae, see 636.296; for Felidae, see 636.8

637   Processing dairy and related products

> Class comprehensive works on dairy farming in 636.2142

.1   Milk processing

> 637.12–637.14   Cow's milk

> Class comprehensive works in 637.1

.12   Milking and inspection of cow's milk

.124   Milking

.127   Inspection and testing

> Standard subdivisions are added for either or both topics in heading

.127 6   Butterfat tests

.127 7   Bacterial counts

.14   Processing specific forms of cow's milk

> 637.141–637.146   Whole milk

> Class comprehensive works in 637.1

*Add as instructed under 636.1–636.8

.141	Fresh whole milk

Including comprehensive works on pasteurization, homogenization, vitamin D treatment

For pasteurization, homogenization, vitamin D treatment of products other than fresh whole milk, see the product, e.g., cream 637.148

.141 028 7	Measurement

Do not use for testing; class in 637.127

.142	Concentrated liquid forms of whole milk
.142 2	Evaporated milk
.142 4	Sweetened condensed milk
.143	Dried whole milk
.146	Cultured whole milk

For yogurt from whole milk, see 637.1476

.147	Skim milk
.147 3	Dried skim milk
.147 6	Cultured skim milk

Class here yogurt

.148	Cream
.17	Milk other than cow's milk
.2	**Butter processing**
.24	By-products

Class here buttermilk

.3	**Cheese processing**

Including by-products

.35	Varieties
.352	Cream cheese
.353	Ripened soft cheeses

Including Brie

.354	Hard cheeses

Including cheddar and Swiss cheeses

.356	Fresh cheeses

Including cottage cheese

For cream cheese, see 637.352

.358	Cheese foods

.4   **Manufacture of frozen desserts**

> Class here ice cream

.5   **Egg processing**

> Class raising hens for eggs in 636.5142; class raising poultry other than chickens for eggs in 636.59

.54   Dried eggs

> Including dried egg whites and yolks

638   Insect culture

.1   **Bee keeping (Apiculture)**

.12   Varieties of bees

> Class a specific aspect of a specific variety of bee with the aspect, e.g., pasturage 638.13

.13   Pasturage for bees

.14   Hive management

.144   Supplementary feeding of bees

.145   Queen rearing

.146   Swarming control

.15   Injuries, diseases, pests

.151–.158   Specific injuries, diseases, pests

> Add to base number 638.15 the numbers following 632 in 632.1–632.8, e.g., diseases 638.154

> *For adverse effects of pesticides, see 638.159*

.159   Adverse effects of pesticides

.16   Honey processing

> Class here comprehensive works on bee products

> *For wax, see 638.17*

.17   Wax

.2   **Silkworms**

.5   **Other insects**

.57   Specific insects

> Add to base number 638.57 the numbers following 595.7 in 595.72–595.79, e.g., butterfly gardening 638.5789

639 Hunting, fishing, conservation, related technologies

Class here culture of nondomesticated animals

For sports hunting and fishing, see 799

SUMMARY

.091 6   Treatment in air and water

Class aquaculture in 639.8

.1 Hunting

Class here trapping, subsistence hunting

Class comprehensive works on commercial and sports hunting in 799.2

.11 Hunting mammals

Add to base number 639.11 the numbers following 599 in 599.2–599.8, e.g., bison (buffalo) hunting 639.11643, hunting fur-bearing animals 639.117; however, for whaling, see 639.28; for sealing, see 639.29

Most works on trapping mammals are on fur trapping, and will be classed in 639.117

See also 333.9549 for resource economics of game mammals in general; also 333.959 for resource economics of specific mammals; also 636.97 for fur farming; also 799.2 for sports hunting

.12 Hunting birds

Most works on hunting game birds will be classed in 333.958 (resource economics) or 799.24 (sports hunting)

.128 Specific kinds of birds

Add to base number 639.128 the numbers following 598 in 598.3–598.9, e.g., waterfowl 639.12841

.13 Hunting amphibians

See also 639.378 for amphibian farming

.14 Reptile hunting

Add to base number 639.14 the numbers following 597.9 in 597.92–597.98, e.g., hunting alligators 639.148

See also 639.39 for reptile farming

.2   **Commercial fishing, whaling, sealing**

> Standard subdivisions are added for commercial fishing, whaling, sealing together; for commercial fishing alone
>
> Class here works on fisheries encompassing culture as well as capture, on fisheries encompassing invertebrates as well as fishes
>
> Class comprehensive works on aquaculture in 639.8
>
> *For culture of fishes, see 639.3; for fisheries for invertebrates, see 639.4*

> **639.21–639.22 Fishing in specific types of water**
>
> Class fishing for specific kinds of fishes regardless of kind of water in 639.27; class comprehensive works in 639.2

.21   Fishing in fresh water

.22   Fishing in salt waters

> Including fishing in brackish waters
>
> Class here deep-sea fishing

.27   Fishing for specific kinds of fishes

> Add to base number 639.27 the numbers following 597 in 597.2–597.7, e.g., salmon fishing 639.2756

.28   Whaling

.29   Sealing

.3   **Culture of cold-blooded vertebrates**

> Class here cold-blooded vertebrates as pets; culture of fishes

---

> **639.31–639.34 Fish culture**
>
> Class comprehensive works in 639.3
>
> *For culture of specific kinds of fishes, see 639.372–639.377*

.31   Fish culture in fresh water

> Class here fishponds, freshwater fish farming
>
> *For fish culture in freshwater aquariums, see 639.34*

.311   Fish hatcheries

.312   Fish culture in lakes

.313   Fish culture in streams

> Class here fish culture in rivers

.32   Fish culture in salt waters

               Including fish culture in brackish waters

                    For fish culture in marine aquariums, see 639.342

.34   Fish culture in aquariums

               Class here freshwater aquariums, home aquariums

               Class interdisciplinary works on aquariums in 597.073

.342   Marine aquariums

.344   Institutional aquariums

               Class interdisciplinary works on educational and scientific aquariums in
               597.073

                    For marine aquariums, see 639.342

.37   Culture of amphibians and specific kinds of fishes

[.370 1–.370 9]   Standard subdivisions

               Do not use; class in 639.301–639.309

.372–.377   Culture of specific kinds of fishes

               Add to base number 639.37 the numbers following 597 in 597.2–597.7,
               e.g., carp, koi 639.37483; goldfish 639.37484

.378   Amphibian culture

               Add to base number 639.378 the numbers following 597.8 in
               597.82–597.89, e.g., frog culture 639.3789

.39   Reptile culture

               Add to base number 639.39 the numbers following 597.9 in 597.92–597.98,
               e.g., turtle culture 639.392

.4   Mollusk fisheries and culture

               Standard subdivisions are added for either or both topics in heading

               Class here Bivalvia; comprehensive works on harvest and culture of
               invertebrates, on shellfish fisheries and culture

                    *For crustacean fisheries, see 639.5; for crustacean culture, see 639.6; for
                    harvest and culture of invertebrates other than mollusks and crustaceans,
                    see 639.7*

               ───────────────

>   639.41–639.46 Bivalvia

               Class comprehensive works in 639.4

.41   Oysters

               Class here edible oysters

.412   Pearl oysters

.42   Mussels

.44   Clams

.46   Scallops

.48   Mollusks other than Bivalvia

> Add to base number 639.48 the numbers following 594 in 594.2–594.5, e.g., land snails 639.4838

.5   Crustacean fisheries

Class here comprehensive works on crustacean fisheries and culture

Add to base number 639.5 the numbers following 595.38 in 595.384–595.388, e.g., shrimps 639.58

For crustacean culture, see 639.6

.6   Crustacean culture

Add to base number 639.6 the numbers following 595.38 in 595.384–595.388, c.g., crayfish culture 639.64

.7   Harvest and culture of invertebrates other than mollusks and crustaceans

Standard subdivisions are added for either or both topics in heading

For insect culture, see 638

.75   Worms

Class here bait worm culture, earthworms (night crawlers), fishworms, worm farming

.8   Aquaculture

Class here mariculture

Class aquaculture of a specific kind of animal with the kind, e.g., aquaculture of fishes 639.3

.89   Aquaculture of plants

Class hydroponics in 631.585

.9   Conservation of biological resources

Class here conservation of animals, game animals, mammals, vertebrates, wildlife; game protection

Class interdisciplinary works on conservation of biological resources in 333.9516; class interdisciplinary works on conservation of animals, vertebrates, mammals in 333.95416

See also 636.0888 for raising warm-blooded game animals

> 639.92–639.96 Specific topics in conservation

Class specific topics in conservation of specific kinds of animals in 639.97; class specific topics in conservation of plants in 639.99; class comprehensive works in 639.9

.92   Habitat improvement

.93   Population control

.95   Maintenance of reserves and refuges

> Standard subdivisions are added for either or both topics in heading

.96   Control of injuries, diseases, pests

.964   Diseases

.966   Pests

> Class here predator control
>
> Class comprehensive works on pest control in agriculture in 632.6; class comprehensive works on predator control in agriculture in 636.0839

.969   Adverse effects of pesticides

.97   Specific kinds of animals

> Other than vertebrates taken as a whole, mammals taken as a whole
>
> *See Manual at 333.955–333.959 vs. 639.97*

[.970 1–.970 9]   Standard subdivisions

> Do not use; class in 639.901–639.909

.971–.978   Specific kinds of animals other than mammals

> Add to base number 639.97 the numbers following 59 in 591–598, e.g., protecting marine animals 639.97177, attracting birds 639.978
>
> *See also 598.07234 for bird watching; also 638.5789 for butterfly gardening; also 639.3 for raising game fishes; also 690.8927 for building bird houses*

.979   Specific kinds of mammals

> Class comprehensive works on mammals in 639.9

[.979 01–.979 09]   Standard subdivisions

> Do not use; class in 639.901–639.909

.979 1–.979 8   Subdivisions for specific kinds of mammals

> Add to base number 639.979 the numbers following 599 in 599.1–599.8, e.g., habitat improvement for deer 639.97965

.99   Plant conservation

640   Home and family management

Standard subdivisions are added for home and family management together, for home management alone

Class here home economics, household management

Use 640 for housekeeping covering activities related to running the home, e.g., preparing meals and doing routine repairs as well as cleaning. Use 648 for housekeeping limited to cleaning

Class personal health in 613; class management of public households in 647

SUMMARY

640.1–.9	**Standard subdivisions; specific aspects of home management; evaluation and purchasing guides**
641	**Food and drink**
642	**Meals and table service**
643	**Housing and household equipment**
644	**Household utilities**
645	**Household furnishings**
646	**Sewing, clothing, management of personal and family life**
647	**Management of public households (Institutional housekeeping)**
648	**Housekeeping**
649	**Child rearing; home care of people with disabilities and illnesses**

[.288]   Maintenance and repair

> Do not use; class in 643.7

.29   Commercial miscellany

> Do not use for evaluation and purchasing manuals; class in 640.73

.4   Specific aspects of home management

> Class comprehensive works on home management in 640

.41   Helpful hints and miscellaneous recipes

.43   Time management

> Class interdisciplinary works on time management in 650.11

.46   Management of household employees

> Duties, hours, selection, training

> Class management of institutional household employees in 647.2

.6   Organizations

[.68]   Management

> Do not use for comprehensive works; class in 640. Do not use for specific aspects; class in 640.4

.7   Education, research, related topics; evaluation and purchasing guides

> Notation 07 from Table 1 as modified below

.73 Evaluation and purchasing guides

Class here consumer education for home and personal needs

Class comprehensive works on managing household money in 332.024; class interdisciplinary evaluation and purchasing guides and works on consumer education in 381.33. Class evaluation and purchasing guides for a specific product or service with the product or service, plus notation 029 from Table 1, e.g., manual on evaluating automobiles 629.222029

641 Food and drink

Class applied nutrition in 613.2

For meals and table service, see 642

SUMMARY

641.01	**Philosophy and theory, gastronomy**
.2	**Beverages (Drinks)**
.3	**Food**
.4	**Food preservation and storage**
.5	**Cooking**
.6	**Cooking specific materials**
.7	**Specific cooking processes and techniques**
.8	**Cooking specific kinds of dishes and preparing beverages**

.01 Philosophy and theory, gastronomy

Notation 01 from Table 1 as modified below

.013 Gastronomy

Class here pleasures of food and drink, comprehensive works on the slow food movement

For a specific aspect of the slow food movement, see the aspect, e.g., purchasing food at farmers markets 381.4, growing heirloom tomatoes 635.642, slow food cooking in restaurants 641.572

.2 Beverages (Drinks)

Class here interdisciplinary works on beverages

Class comprehensive works on nutritive values of beverages in 613.2. Class nutritive values of a specific beverage with the beverage, e.g., nutritive value of wine 641.22

For a specific aspect of beverages, see the aspect, e.g., manufacture (commercial preparation) 663

.21 Alcoholic beverages

Class home preparation of alcoholic beverages, bartending in 641.874

For wine, see 641.22; for brewed and malted beverages, see 641.23; for distilled liquor, see 641.25

.22   Wine

Class here grape wine, comprehensive works on white and red wine, comprehensive works on specific white and red wines (specific brands, estate wines)

Class home preparation of wine in 641.872

See also 641.23 for mead, rice wine

.222   Kinds of grape wine

Including ice wine

[.222 01–.222 09]   Standard subdivisions

Do not use; class in 641.2201–641.2209

.222 2   White wine

Class here specific white wines (specific brands, estate wines, varietals)

Class comprehensive works on white and red wine in 641.22; class white ice wine in 641.222

For sparkling white wine, see 641.2224; for fortified white wine, see 641.2226

.222 3   Red wine

Class here specific red wines (specific brands, estate wines, varietals)

Class red ice wine in 641.222

For sparkling red wine, see 641.2224; for fortified red wine, see 641.2226

.222 32   Rosé wine

Class here specific rosé wines (specific brands, estate wines, varietals)

.222 4   Sparkling wine

Class here specific sparkling wines (specific brands, estate wines, varietals)

Class comprehensive works on white wine in 641.2222; class comprehensive works on red wine in 641.2223

.222 6   Fortified wine

Class here specific fortified wines (specific brands, estate wines, varietals)

Class comprehensive works on white wine in 641.2222; class comprehensive works on red wine in 641.2223

.229   Nongrape wine

Including fermented cider

.23   Brewed and malted beverages

Including mead (honey wine), pulque, rice wine

Class here beer, ale

Class malt whiskey in 641.252; class home brewing in 641.873

.25   Distilled liquor

Including mescal, potato whiskey, tequila, vodka

.252   Whiskey

Class potato whiskey in 641.25

.253   Brandy

.255   Compound liquors

Including absinthe, gin

Class here cordials, liqueurs

.259   Rum

.26   Nonalcoholic beverages

Including carbonated, malted, mineralized beverages

For specific nonalcoholic beverages made from a single principal ingredient, see 641.3, e.g., orange juice 641.3431; for nonalcoholic beverages made from multiple ingredients, see 641.875

.3   Food

Class here interdisciplinary works on food

For interdisciplinary works on specific dishes, see 641.8. For a specific aspect of food, see the aspect, e.g., manufacture (commercial preparation) 664

See Manual at 363.8 vs. 613.2, 641.3; also at 630 vs. 579–590, 641.3

.300 1   Philosophy and theory

.300 2   Miscellany

.300 29   Commercial miscellany

Do not use for evaluation and purchasing manuals; class in 641.31

.300 3–.300 9   Standard subdivisions

.302   Health foods

Including substitutes for food regarded as unhealthy, e.g., dairy substitutes

Class here natural foods, organically grown foods

Class dietetics in 613.2

See also 641.563 for health cooking

.303   Food from plants

      Class here vegetarian foods

        For specific food from plant crops, see 641.33–641.35

        See also 641.5636 for vegetarian cooking

.306   Food from animals

        For specific food from animals, see 641.36–641.39

.308   Food additives

.31   Evaluation and purchasing manuals

      Class comprehensive works on applied nutrition in 613.2; class evaluation and purchasing manuals of specific food in 641.33–641.39

.33–.35   Specific food from plant crops

      Class here nutritive values

      Add to base number 641.3 the numbers following 63 in 633–635, e.g., field legumes 641.3565

      Class comprehensive works on food from plants in 641.303

>   641.36–641.39   Specific food from animals

      Class here nutritive values

      Class comprehensive works on food from animals in 641.306

.36   Meat

      Add to base number 641.36 the numbers following 636 in 636.1–636.8, e.g., ham 641.364

        For game and seafood, see 641.39

.37   Dairy and related products

      Add to base number 641.37 the numbers following 637 in 637.1–637.5, e.g., skim milk 641.37147

.38   Honey

.39   Game and seafood

      Add to base number 641.39 the numbers following 641.69 in 641.691–641.696, e.g., oysters 641.394

.4   **Food preservation and storage**

      Standard subdivisions are added for food preservation and storage together, for food preservation alone

      Class interdisciplinary works on food preservation in 664.028

> 641.41–641.46 Preservation techniques for fruit and vegetables, for food as a whole

Class comprehensive works in 641.4

For preservation techniques for meat and allied food, see 641.49

.41 Preliminary treatment

.42 Canning

.44 Drying and dehydrating

Including freeze-drying

.45 Low-temperature techniques

.452 Cold storage

.453 Deep freezing

For freeze-drying, see 641.44

.46 Pickling, brining, smoking

Class here chemical preservation

.462 Pickling

Class here pickles

.48 Storage

.49 Meat

Class storage of meat in 641.48

.492 Red meat

Add to base number 641.492 the numbers following 641.4 in 641.41–641.46, e.g., canning red meat 641.4922

.493 Poultry

Add to base number 641.493 the numbers following 641.4 in 641.41–641.46, e.g., freezing poultry 641.49353

.494 Seafood

Add to base number 641.494 the numbers following 641.4 in 641.41–641.46, e.g., brining seafood 641.4946

.495 Other animal flesh

.5   **Cooking**

Preparation of food with and without use of heat

Unless other instructions are given, observe the following table of preference, e.g., outdoor cooking for children 641.5622 (*not* 641.578):

Cooking for special situations, reasons, ages	641.56
Quantity, institutional, travel, outdoor cooking	641.57
Money-saving and timesaving cooking	641.55
Cooking with specific fuels, appliances, utensils	641.58
Cooking specific meals	641.52–641.54
Beginner and gourmet cooking	641.51
Cooking characteristic of specific geographic environments, ethnic cooking	641.59

Class menus and meal planning in 642

For cooking specific materials, see 641.6; for specific cooking processes and techniques, see 641.7; for cooking specific kinds of dishes, preparing beverages, see 641.8

SUMMARY

641.501–.509	**Standard subdivisions**
.51	**Beginner and gourmet cooking**
.52	**First meal of the day**
.53	**Light meals**
.54	**Main meal of the day**
.55	**Money-saving and timesaving cooking**
.56	**Cooking for special situations, reasons, ages**
.57	**Quantity, institutional, travel, outdoor cooking**
.58	**Cooking with specific fuels, appliances, utensils**
.59	**Cooking characteristic of specific geographic environments, ethnic cooking**

.502   Miscellany

.502 8   Auxiliary techniques and procedures

[.502 84]   Apparatus, equipment, materials

Do not use; class in 643.3

.508   Cooking with respect to groups of people

.508 3   Cooking with respect to young people

Do not use for cooking by children; class in 641.5123. Do not use for cooking for young people; class in 641.5622

.508 4   Cooking with respect to people in specific ages of adulthood

Do not use for cooking for people in specific ages of adulthood; class in 641.562

.508 7   Cooking with respect to people with disabilities, gifted people

Do not use for cooking for people with illnesses; class in 641.5631

.508 8   Cooking with respect to occupational groups

[.508 82]	Cooking with respect to religious groups

Do not use; class in 641.567

[.508 9]	Cooking with respect to ethnic and national groups

Do not use for Jewish cooking; class in 641.5676. Do not use for cooking with respect to other ethnic and national groups; class in 641.592

.509	History, geographic treatment, biography

Do not use for cooking characteristic of specific geographic environments; class in 641.59

Class here collections of recipes from specific restaurants

.51	Beginner and gourmet cooking
.512	Beginner cooking

Class here easy dishes

.512 3	Children's cooking

Class cooking of food for consumption by children in 641.5622

.514	Gourmet cooking

Gourmet cooking characteristic of specific geographic environments, ethnic cooking relocated to 641.59

> 641.52–641.54 Cooking specific meals

Class comprehensive works in 641.5

.52	First meal of the day

Class here brunches [*formerly* 641.532], breakfasts

.53	Light meals

Class here snacks; dinners, lunches, suppers, teas as light meals

Class breakfasts and brunches in 641.52; class dinners, lunches, suppers, teas as main meals in 641.54

[.532]	Brunches

Relocated to 641.52

[.534–.539]	Box and bag lunches, afternoon teas, suppers, snacks

Numbers discontinued; class in 641.53

.54	Main meal of the day

Class here dinners, lunches, suppers, teas as main meals

Class breakfasts and brunches in 641.52; class dinners, lunches, suppers, teas as light meals in 641.53

.55	Money-saving and timesaving cooking

| .552 | Money-saving cooking |

Including leftovers

| .555 | Timesaving cooking |

Class here make-ahead meals

| .56 | Cooking for special situations, reasons, ages |

SUMMARY

641.561	Cooking for one or two people
.562	Cooking for people of specific ages
.563	Cooking for health, appearance, personal reasons
.564	Seasonal cooking
.566	Cooking for Christian church limitations and observances
.567	Cooking for religious limitations and observances
.568	Cooking for special occasions

| .561 | Cooking for one or two people |

| .561 1 | Cooking for one |

| .561 2 | Cooking for two |

| .562 | Cooking for people of specific ages |

| .562 2 | Young people |

Class here cooking for children

Class cooking by children in 641.5123

| .562 22 | Cooking for infants |

Class here baby food

Class comprehensive works on baby food in 641.300832

| .562 7 | People in late adulthood |

| .563 | Cooking for health, appearance, personal reasons |

Standard subdivisions are added for cooking for health, appearance, personal reasons together; for cooking for health alone

Class here cooking to prevent illness

| .563 1 | Cooking for people with medical conditions |

Class cooking for specific dietary regimens for specific medical conditions in 641.5632–641.5638

| .563 11 | People with heart disease |

| .563 14 | People with diabetes |

| .563 18 | People with food allergies |

| .563 19 | Pregnant women |

| .563 2 | Cooking with specified vitamin and mineral content |

.563 23	Low-salt cooking
	Class here low-sodium cooking, salt-free cooking
.563 5	Low-calorie cooking

Class here cooking for overweight people

Class cooking with respect to low carbohydrate, fat, protein content in 641.5638

| .563 6 | Vegetarian cooking |

Class comprehensive works on vegetarian foods in 641.303

See also 641.65 for cooking vegetables

| .563 7 | Health-food cooking |

Class comprehensive works on health cooking in 641.563

.563 8	Cooking with respect to carbohydrate, fat, protein content
.563 83	Low-carbohydrate cooking
.563 837	Sugar-free cooking
.563 84	Low-fat cooking

Class here fat-free cooking

| .563 847 | Low-cholesterol cooking |
| .564 | Seasonal cooking |

Class cooking for special occasions in 641.568

| .566 | Cooking for Christian church limitations and observances |

Including Lent

Class here cooking for specific Christian groups

For cooking for Christmas, see 641.5686

| .567 | Cooking for religious limitations and observances |

Class here cooking for days of feast and fast, cooking with respect to religious groups

Add to base number 641.567 the numbers following 29 in 292–299, e.g., Jewish cooking 641.5676

For cooking for Christian church limitations and observances, see 641.566

| .568 | Cooking for special occasions |

Class here cooking for holidays, for parties

Class cooking that emphasizes religious aspects of holidays in 641.567; class comprehensive works on food service and cooking for parties in 642.4

| .568 6 | Christmas cooking |

.57	Quantity, institutional, travel, outdoor cooking

> Including cooking for armed services
>
> Class here short-order cooking
>
> Class naval cooking in 641.5753

.571	School cooking
.572	Hotel and restaurant cooking

> Standard subdivisions are added for either or both topics in heading

.575	Travel cooking

> Including airline, bus, camper (caravan), dining car cooking

.575 3	Marine cooking (Shipboard cooking)

> Class here naval cooking

.577	Canteen cooking

> Temporary or mobile facilities for serving food

.578	Outdoor cooking

> Class here cookouts
>
> Class cooking in campers (caravans) in 641.575

.578 2	Camp cooking
.578 4	Cooking at an outdoor grill

> Class here cooking at outdoor barbecues
>
> Class comprehensive works on techniques of barbecuing in 641.76

.579	Cooking for health care facilities

> Class here cooking for hospitals

.58	Cooking with specific fuels, appliances, utensils

> Including convection-oven cooking, wood-stove cooking
>
> Class outdoor cooking in 641.578. Class a specific use of a specific appliance or utensil with the use, e.g., frying with frying pans 641.77

.584	Gas
.585	Alcohol-based fuels

> Class here cooking with chafing dishes

.586	Electricity

> Cooking with electric ranges and appliances
>
> Class convection-oven cooking in 641.58; class microwave cooking in 641.5882; class electric slow cooking in 641.5884

.587	Steam and pressure cooking

> Standard subdivisions are added for either or both topics in heading

.588	Slow and fireless cooking
.588 2	Microwave cooking
.588 4	Electric slow cooking
.589	Specific utensils

Including clay pots, Dutch ovens, foils, specially coated utensils

Class cooking with specific utensils using specific fuels in 641.584–641.588

.589 2	Food processors
.589 3	Blenders
.59	Cooking characteristic of specific geographic environments, ethnic cooking

Class here gourmet cooking characteristic of specific geographic environments, ethnic cooking [*formerly* 641.514]; international cooking

Class history and geographic treatment of general cooking, collections of recipes from specific restaurants, in 641.509

.591	Cooking characteristic of areas, regions, places in general

Add to base number 641.591 the numbers following —1 in notation 11–19 from Table 2, e.g., arctic and cold-weather cooking 641.5911, tropical and hot-weather cooking 641.5913

.592	Ethnic cooking
.592 05–.592 09	Specific ethnic and national groups with ethnic origins from more than one continent, of European descent

Add to base number 641.592 notation 05–09 from Table 5, e.g., cooking of ethnic groups of European descent 641.59209

.592 1–.592 9	Specific ethnic and national groups

Add to base number 641.592 notation 1–9 from Table 5, e.g., African American cooking 641.59296073; however, for Jewish cooking, see 641.5676; for cooking of ethnic groups dominant in their areas, see 641.593–641.599

.593–.599	Cooking characteristic of specific continents, countries, localities

Add to base number 641.59 notation 3–9 from Table 2, e.g., Southern cooking (United States) 641.5975

Class ethnic cooking of nondominant groups in 641.592

.6	**Cooking specific materials**

Class specific kinds of dishes featuring specific materials in 641.8

For leftovers, see 641.552

.61   Cooking preserved foods

> Add to base number 641.61 the numbers following 641.4 in 641.42–641.46, e.g., cooking using frozen foods 641.6153
>
> Class home preservation in 641.4; class cooking using specific preserved foods in 641.63–641.69

.62   Cooking with beverages and their derivatives

> Including vinegar
>
> Class home preparation of beverages in 641.87. Class cooking with a specific nonalcoholic beverage with the product from which it is derived, e.g., cooking with chocolate 641.6374, with apple juice 641.6411

.622   Wine

.623   Beer and ale

> Standard subdivisions are added for either or both topics in heading

.625   Distilled liquor

> 641.63–641.69 Specific foods

> Class comprehensive works in 641.6

.63–.67   Cooking food derived from plant crops and domesticated animals

> Add to base number 641.6 the numbers following 63 in 633–637, e.g., legumes 641.6565 (*not* 641.633), garden legumes 641.6565, meat 641.66, chicken meat 641.665; however, for ices, sherbet, sorbet, see 641.863
>
> Class vegetarian cooking in 641.5636; class comprehensive works on cooking with beverages in 641.62
>
> *For cooking with honey, see 641.68*

.68   Cooking with honey

.69   Cooking game and seafood

> Class here cooking nondomesticated animals

.691   Game

> Mammals and birds

.692   Fish

> Class here seafood
>
> *For mollusks, see 641.694; for crustaceans, see 641.695*

.694   Mollusks

> Including clams, mussels, octopuses, oysters, snails, squid
>
> Class here shellfish
>
> *For crustaceans, see 641.695*

.695	Crustaceans

> Including crabs, lobsters, shrimp

.696	Amphibians, insects, reptiles

.7   Specific cooking processes and techniques

> Class specific processes applied to specific materials in 641.6; class specific processes applied to specific kinds of dishes, preparing beverages in 641.8

[.701–.709]	Standard subdivisions

> Do not use; class in 641.501–641.509

.71	Baking and roasting

> Standard subdivisions are added for baking and roasting together, for baking alone

.73	Braising [*formerly* 641.77], boiling, simmering, steaming, stewing
.76	Barbecuing, broiling, grilling

> Standard subdivisions are added for barbecuing, broiling, grilling together; for barbecuing alone

> Including skewer cooking

> *For barbecuing, broiling, grilling at outdoor grills, see 641.5784*

.77	Frying and sautéing

> Standard subdivisions are added for either or both topics in heading

> Braising relocated to 641.73

.774	Stir frying

> Class here wok cooking

.79	Preparation of cold dishes

> Class here chilled dishes

.8   Cooking specific kinds of dishes and preparing beverages

> Class here interdisciplinary works on specific dishes

> *For manufacture (commercial preparation) of complete dishes, see 664.65*

SUMMARY

641.81	**Side dishes, sauces, garnishes**
.82	**Main dishes**
.83	**Salads**
.84	**Sandwiches and related dishes**
.85	**Preserves and candy**
.86	**Desserts**
.87	**Preparing beverages**

[.801–.809]	Standard subdivisions

> Do not use; class in 641.501–641.509

.81 **Side dishes, sauces, garnishes**

> Standard subdivisions are added for side dishes, sauces, garnishes together; for side dishes alone

> Side dishes other than salads, sandwiches, desserts

> Including fondues, stuffing

> Class here specific side dishes treated as entrées

.812 **Appetizers**

>> Including dips, pâtés, relishes

>> Class here finger foods, hors d'oeuvres, savories, starters, tapas

.813 **Soups**

.814 **Sauces and salad dressings**

> Standard subdivisions are added for sauces and salad dressings together, for sauces alone

.815 **Bread and bread-like foods**

> Standard subdivisions are added for bread and bread-like foods together, for bread alone

> Including crackers, unleavened breads

> Class here yeast breads, comprehensive works on baked goods

> Class main dishes based on bread and bread-like foods in 641.82; class sandwiches and related dishes in 641.84

> *For pastries, see 641.865*

.815 3 **Crepes, pancakes, waffles**

>> Standard subdivisions are added for any or all topics in heading

.815 7 **Quick breads**

>> Class here biscuits, muffins, scones

>> *See also 641.8654 for biscuits (cookies)*

.819 **Garnishes**

.82 **Main dishes**

> Including quiches, soufflés, sushi

> Class here entrées, one-dish cooking

> Class a side dish, salad, sandwich or stuffed food regarded as a main dish with the topic elsewhere in 641.8, e.g., soup 641.813, hamburger on a roll 641.84

.821 **Casserole dishes**

.822 **Noodle and pasta dishes**

> Standard subdivisions are added for either or both topics in heading

.823	Stews
.823 6	Chili
.824	Meat and cheese pies
	Including meat loaf
.824 8	Pizza
.83	Salads
.84	Sandwiches and related dishes

> Standard subdivisions are added for either or both topics in heading

> Class here sandwiches and related dishes of any type, e.g., open-faced sandwiches, grilled sandwiches, wraps

.85	Preserves and candy
.852	Jams, jellies, marmalades, preserves

> Standard subdivisions are added for any or all topics in heading

> *See also 641.8642 for jellies (gelatin desserts)*

.853	Candy

> Variant name: sweets

.86	Desserts

> Class here comprehensive works on candies and desserts

> *For preserves and candy, see 641.85*

.862	Frozen desserts

> Including frozen yogurt, ice milk

> Class here ice cream

> *For ices, sherbet, sorbet, see 641.863*

.863	Ices, sherbet, sorbet

> Standard subdivisions are added for any or all topics in heading

.864	Gelatin dessserts; puddings
.864 2	Gelatin desserts

> Variant name: jellies

> *See also 641.852 for jellies (preserves)*

.864 4	Puddings
.865	Pastries

> Class comprehensive works on baked goods in 641.815

.865 2	Pies and tarts

> Standard subdivisions are added for either or both topics in heading

.865 3		Cakes

        See also 641.8659 for coffee cakes

.865 39   Cake decoration

         Class here cake icing, sugar art

.865 4   Cookies

         Variant name: biscuits

        See also 641.815 for crackers; also 641.8157 for biscuits (quick breads)

.865 9   Danish, French, related pastries

         Including coffee cakes, cream puffs, eclairs

.87   Preparing beverages

         Class interdisciplinary works on beverages in 641.2

        See also 641.62 for cooking with beverages

.872   Wine

.873   Alcoholic brewed beverages

         Class here beer, ale

.874   Alcoholic beverages

         Class here bartending, comprehensive works on cocktails (mixed drinks)

        For wine, see 641.872; for alcoholic brewed beverages, see 641.873; for bottled and canned cocktails, see 663.1

.875   Nonalcoholic beverages

         Including carbonated drinks, fruit drinks, juices, malted drinks

        For nonalcoholic brewed beverages, see 641.877

.877   Nonalcoholic brewed beverages

         Including cocoa, coffee, teas; their concentrates and substitutes

         Class cooking with cocoa, coffee, tea in 641.637

642   Meals and table service

     Class here menus, menu cookbooks, specific meals

     Class banquets, catered meals in 642.4; class comprehensive works on cookbooks in 641.5

> ### 642.1–642.5 Meals in specific situations

> Class here comprehensive works on meals and table service in specific situations

> Class comprehensive works in 642

> *For table service in specific situations, see 642.6*

.1   **Meals for home, family, individuals**

Standard subdivisions are added for meals for home, family, individuals together; meals for home alone, for family alone

Class family and individual meals for camp, picnic, travel in 642.3

.3   **Meals for camp, picnic, travel**

.4   **Meals for social and public occasions**

Including banquets, catered meals

Class here entertaining and catering for social and public occasions

Class party cooking in 641.568; class picnics in 642.3; class catering that includes restaurant operations in 647.95; class interdisciplinary works on entertaining in 793.2

.5   **Meals in public and institutional eating places**

Standard subdivisions are added for either or both topics in heading

Class here meals in cafeterias and restaurants

Class meals for social and public occasions in 642.4; class operation of public eating places in 647.95

.56   Health care facilities

Class here hospitals

.57   Schools

Regardless of level

.6   **Table service**

Including carving, place setting, seating guests

Class here table service at specific meals, waiting on tables

Class comprehensive works on meals and table service in specific situations in 642.1–642.5

For table furnishings, see 642.7; for table decorations, see 642.8

.7   **Table furnishings**

Including dinnerware, glassware, silverware, table linens

For table decorations other than folded napkins, see 642.8

.79   Napkin folding

.8 **Table decorations**

For folded napkins, see 642.79

643 Housing and household equipment

Works for owner-occupants or renters covering activities of members of household

SUMMARY

[.028 4]   Apparatus, equipment, materials

Do not use; class in 643

[.028 8]   Maintenance and repair

Do not use; class in 643.7

.1 **Housing**

For special-purpose housing and special kinds of housing, see 643.2

See also 690.8 for construction of houses; also 728 for comprehensive works on design and construction of houses

See Manual at 363.5 vs. 643.1

[.102 88]   Maintenance and repair

Do not use; class in 643.7

.102 9   Commercial miscellany

Do not use for evaluation and purchasing guides; class in 643.12

.12   Selecting, buying, selling homes

Standard subdivisions are added for any or all topics in heading

Including site selection, supervision of construction

Class here evaluation and purchasing guides; home buying, home inspection

Class moving in 648.9

See also 333.338 for economics of home acquisition; also 346.043 for law of real property

.16   Household security

Class here burglarproofing

Class burglary in 364.1622

.2   **Special-purpose housing and special kinds of housing**

Including houseboats, modular and prefabricated houses

Class comprehensive works on single-family houses in 643.1. Class a specific aspect of special-purpose housing or a special kind of housing with the aspect, e.g., renovating vacation homes 643.7

.25   Vacation homes

.27   Apartments

Including condominium and cooperative apartments

Class management of condominiums and cooperative apartment houses in 647.92

.29   Mobile homes

See also 388.346 for motorized homes

See Manual at 643.29, 690.879, 728.79 vs. 629.226

\>   **643.3–643.5 Specific areas of the home**

Class household utilities in 644; class household furnishings in 645; class comprehensive works in 643.1

See also 684.08 for home workshops

.3   ***Kitchens**

Including cooking apparatus, equipment, materials

Class cooking with specific appliances and utensils not limited to a specific kind of cooking in 641.58. Class a specific appliance or utensil used for a specific kind of cooking with the kind of cooking, e.g., frying with frying pans 641.77

.4   ***Eating and drinking areas**

Standard subdivisions are added for either or both topics in heading

Class here dining areas

.5   ***Other areas of the home**

Including attics, basements, storage areas

.52   *Bathrooms

Class plumbing, plumbing fixtures in 644.6

.53   *Bedrooms

Bedclothes relocated to 645.4

.54   *Living rooms, drawing rooms, parlors

Standard subdivisions are added for any or all topics in heading

---

*Do not use notation 0284 from Table 1; class in base number

.55   *Recreation areas

         Indoor and outdoor

         Including family and recreation rooms, patios, porches

.556   *Swimming pools

.58   *Study and work areas

         Including dens

         See also 658.0412 for management of home-based enterprises

.6   Appliances and laborsaving installations

         Standard subdivisions are added for either or both topics in heading

         Class appliances and installations for specific areas in 643.3–643.5; class appliances and installations for specific household utilities in 644; class appliances and installations for specific kinds of household furnishings in 645. Class appliances and installations for a specific purpose with the purpose, e.g., sewing machines 646.2044

         See also 683.8 for manufacture of household appliances

.602 88   Maintenance and repair

         Class here maintenance and repair by members of household, maintenance and repair of electrical appliances

.7   Renovation, improvement, remodeling

         Standard subdivisions are added for any or all topics in heading

         Class here do-it-yourself work, home repairs; comprehensive works on maintenance and repair in home economics, on maintenance and repair by members of household

         Class renovation, improvement, remodeling of specific areas of the home in 643.3–643.5; class renovation, improvement, remodeling of specific household utilities in 644; class renovation, improvement, remodeling of specific kinds of household furnishings in 645

         For maintenance and repair of a specific item in the home, see the item, plus notation 0288 from Table 1, e.g., repair of appliances 643.60288, repair of furniture 645.40288

         See Manual at 690 vs. 643.7

[.702 88]   Maintenance and repair

         Do not use; class in 643.7

644   Household utilities

         Works for owner-occupants or renters covering activities by members of household

         Class here home energy conservation

         See Manual at 647 vs. 647.068, 658.2, T1—0682

*Do not use notation 0284 from Table 1; class in base number

.1 **Heating**

.3 **Lighting**

> Class lighting fixtures as furnishings in 645.5

.5 **Ventilation and air conditioning**

.6 **Plumbing**

> Class here water fixtures

645 Household furnishings

Works for owner-occupants or renters covering activities by members of household

Class here household furnishings of residential buildings, comprehensive works on household furnishings and interior decoration

Class manufacture of household furnishings in 684

For home construction of fabric furnishings, see 646.21; for interior decoration, see 747

.04 Special topics of household furnishings

.046 Fabrics

> Description, selection, purchase, care, use
>
> Class home construction of household articles made of fabric in 646.21

> **645.1–645.5 Specific kinds of interior furnishings**
>
> Class comprehensive works in 645

.1 **Floor covering**

.12 Rugs

> Class here carpets

.2 **Wall and ceiling coverings**

> Standard subdivisions are added for wall and ceiling coverings together, for wall coverings alone
>
> Including hangings, paint, paneling, wallpaper

.3 **Window furnishings**

> Including awnings, blinds, shades

.32 Draperies

> Class here curtains

.4   **Furniture and accessories**

Standard subdivisions are added for furniture and accessories together, for furniture alone

Including bedclothes [*formerly also* 643.53], upholstery, slipcovers

Class home construction of furniture in 684.1; class artistic aspects of furniture and accessories in 749

For outdoor furniture and accessories, see 645.8

.5   **Lighting fixtures**

.6   **Furnishings for specific rooms**

Class interior furnishings of specific kinds regardless of room in 645.1–645.5

See also 644 for utilities for specific rooms

.8   **Outdoor furnishings**

Including furnishings for balconies, gardens, patios, roofs

Class here outdoor furniture and accessories

646   Sewing, clothing, management of personal and family life

SUMMARY

.1   **Sewing materials and equipment**

Standard subdivisions are added for sewing materials and equipment together, for sewing materials alone

Including leathers and furs

See also 646.30284 for materials and equipment used for clothing

.11   Fabrics

Class here comprehensive works on fabrics in the home

For fabrics for a specific use, see the use, e.g., use in furnishings 645.046

.19   Sewing equipment, fasteners

Standard subdivisions are added for either or both topics in heading

Including needles, pins, scissors, shears, thimbles, thread

Class here notions

For sewing machines, see 646.2044

.2   **Sewing and related operations**

Standard subdivisions are added for sewing and related operations together, for sewing alone

Class here mending, sewing for the home

Class clothing construction in 646.4; class mending clothes in 646.6

For a specific technique in textile arts, see the technique in 746, e.g., weaving 746.14

[.202 84]   Apparatus, equipment, materials

Do not use; class in 646.1. Do not use for sewing machines; class in 646.2044

[.202 88]   Maintenance and repair

Do not use; class in 646.2

.204   Basic sewing operations

Class here darning

.204 2   Hand sewing

.204 4   Machine sewing

Including serging

.21   Construction of home furnishings

Including making bedclothes, curtains, hangings, slipcovers, table linens, towels

Class basic sewing operations in 646.204; class artistic and decorative aspects of construction of interior furnishings in 746.9

.25   Reweaving

.3   **Clothing and accessories**

Standard subdivisions are added for clothing and accessories together, for clothing alone

Description, selection, purchase of clothing and accessories for utility, quality, economy, appearance, style

Class here casual wear (sportswear)

Class interdisciplinary works on clothing and accessories in 391

For clothing and accessories construction, see 646.4; for care of clothing and accessories, see 646.6

See Manual at 391 vs. 646.3, 746.92

[.302 88]   Maintenance and repair

Do not use; class in 646.6

[.308 1]   Clothing for men and women

Do not use; class in 646.32–646.34

.308 3	Clothing for young people

> Do not use for children under twelve; class in 646.36

.308 4	Clothing for people in specific stages of adulthood

> Do not use for clothing for men in specific stages of adulthood; class in 646.32. Do not use for clothing for women in specific stages of adulthood; class in 646.34

.308 7	Clothing for gifted people

> Do not use for clothing for people with disabilities and illnesses; class in 646.31

.31–.36	Clothing for people with disabilities and illnesses; men, women, children

> Add to base number 646.3 the numbers following 646.40 in 646.401–646.406, e.g., women's clothing 646.34

> Class clothing for young people twelve to twenty in 646.30835

.4   Clothing and accessories construction

> Standard subdivisions are added for clothing and accessories construction together, for clothing construction alone

> Class here dressmaking, tailoring; construction of casual wear (sportswear)

> *For construction of headwear, see 646.5; for commercial manufacture of clothing, see 687. For clothing construction by a specific technique in textile arts, see the technique in 746, e.g., knitting sweaters 746.4320432*

> *See also 646.47 for construction of activewear (clothing for athletic and outdoor sports)*

SUMMARY

646.400 1–.400 9	**Standard subdivisions**
.401–.409	**[Clothing for people with disabilities and illnesses, men, women, children; patterns; fitting and alterations]**
.42	**Construction of undergarments and hosiery**
.43	**Construction of specific kinds of garments**
.45	**Construction of outerwear**
.47	**Construction of garments for special purposes**
.48	**Accessories construction**

.400 1–.400 7	Standard subdivisions
.400 8	Clothing with respect to groups of people
[.400 811]	Clothing for men

> Do not use; class in 646.402

[.400 82]	Clothing for women

> Do not use; class in 646.404

.400 83	Clothing for young people

> Do not use for children under twelve; class in 646.406

.400 84	Clothing for people in specific stages of adulthood

Do not use for clothing for men in specific stages of adulthood; class in 646.402. Do not use for clothing for women in specific stages of adulthood; class in 646.404

.400 87	Clothing for gifted people

Do not use for clothing for people with disabilities and illnesses; class in 646.401

.400 9	History, geographic treatment, biography
.401	Clothing for people with disabilities and illnesses

>   646.402–646.406 Clothing for men, women, children

Class construction of clothing for people with disabilities and illnesses regardless of age or sex in 646.401; class patterns regardless of groups of people in 646.407; class fitting and alterations regardless of groups of people in 646.408; class comprehensive works in 646.4

.402	Men's clothing
.404	Women's clothing
.406	Children's clothing

From birth through age eleven

Class clothing for young people twelve to twenty in 646.400835

.407	Patterns
.407 2	Pattern design and patternmaking

Standard subdivisions are added for either or both topics in heading

.408	Fitting and alterations

Standard subdivisions are added for either or both topics in heading

>   646.42–646.48   Specific kinds of clothing

       Add to each subdivision identified by * as follows:

001–007	Standard subdivisions
008	Clothing with respect to groups of people
[00811]	Clothing for men
	Do not use; class in 02
[0082]	Clothing for women
	Do not use; class in 04
0083	Clothing for young people
	Do not use for children under twelve; class in 06
0084	Clothing for people in specific stages of adulthood
	Do not use for clothing for men in specific stages of adulthood; class in 02. Do not use for clothing for women in specific stages of adulthood; class in 04
0087	Clothing for gifted people
	Do not use for clothing for people with disabilities and illnesses; class in 01
009	History, geographic treatment, biography
01–06	Clothing for people with disabilities and illnesses, men, women, children
	Add to 0 the numbers following 646.40 in 646.401–646.406, e.g., clothing for people with physical disabilities 01

      Class comprehensive works in 646.4

.42   *Construction of undergarments and hosiery

       Subdivisions are added for construction of undergarments and hosiery together, for construction of undergarments alone

        See also 646.433 for vests (waistcoats); also 646.436 for pants (trousers)

.43   *Construction of specific kinds of garments

       Not provided for elsewhere

.432   *Dresses

.433   *Suits

        Class here jackets, sport coats, vests (waistcoats)

        Class skirts in 646.437; class outerwear, comprehensive works on coats and jackets in 646.45

         See also 646.42 for vests (undergarments)

        Pants (trousers) relocated to 646.436

.435   *Shirts, blouses, tops

        Subdivisions are added for any or all topics in heading

.436   *Pants (Trousers) [*formerly* 646.433]

.437   *Skirts

*Add as instructed under 646.42–646.48

.45   *Construction of outerwear

Including capes, cloaks, stoles, sweaters

Class here overcoats, topcoats, raincoats; comprehensive works on coats and jackets

Class garments for special purposes in 646.47

For suit jackets, sport coats, see 646.433

[.452–.457]   Overcoats, raincoats, sweaters, cloaks, jackets, stoles

Numbers discontinued; class in 646.45

.47   *Construction of garments for special purposes

Including activewear (clothing for athletic and outdoor sports), maternity garments

Class accessories for special purposes in 646.48

See also 646.4 for casual wear (sportswear)

.475   *Sleepwear and loungewear

Former heading: Nightclothes

Subdivisions are added for either or both topics in heading

.476   *Evening and formal dress, wedding clothes

Subdivisions are added for evening and formal dress, wedding clothes together; for evening and formal dress together; for evening dress alone; for formal dress alone

.478   *Costumes

Including party, period costumes

Class here theatrical costumes

.48   Accessories construction

Including aprons, belts, gloves and mittens, handbags, handkerchiefs, neckwear, scarves

Class hosiery in 646.42; class headwear in 646.5; class footwear in 685.3; class handcrafted costume jewelry in 745.5942

.5   **Construction of headwear**

Class here bonnets, caps, hats

For construction of headwear by a specific technique in textile arts, see the technique in 746, e.g., crocheting hats 746.4340432

.500 1–.500 7   Standard subdivisions

.500 8   Construction of headwear with respect to groups of people

*Add as instructed under 646.42–646.48

[.500 811]	Men
	Do not use; class in 646.502
[.500 82]	Women
	Do not use; class in 646.504
[.500 83]	Young people
	Do not use; class in 646.506

.500 84   People in specific stages of adulthood

> Do not use for headwear for men in specific stages of adulthood; class in 646.502. Do not use for headwear for women in specific stages of adulthood; class in 646.504

.500 9   History, geographic treatment, biography

.502   Men's headwear

.504   Women's headwear

> Class here millinery

.506   Young people's headwear

> Class here children's headwear

.6   Care of clothing and accessories

Standard subdivisions are added for care of clothing and accessories together, for care of clothing alone

Including mending, reweaving; packing, storage

For laundering and related operations, see 648.1

.7   Management of personal and family life

Class here grooming; life skills, success in personal and family life

Class clothing selection and dressing with style in 646.3; class training children in grooming in 649.63; class interdisciplinary works on success in 650.1

For parapsychological and occult means for achievement of well-being, happiness, success, see 131; for psychological means for achievement of personal well-being, happiness, success, see 158; for etiquette, see 395; for care of physique and form, see 613.71; for success in business and other public situations, see 650.1

See also 362.82 for social services to families

SUMMARY

.700 1–.700 7	Standard subdivisions of management of personal and family life
.700 8	Management of personal and family life with respect to groups of people
[.700 846]	Management of personal and family life with respect to people in late adulthood
	Do not use; class in 646.79
.700 9	History, geographic treatment, biography of management of personal and family life
.701–.703	Standard subdivisions of grooming
.704	Grooming for women, men, young people
.704 2	Grooming for women
.704 4	Grooming for men
.704 6	Grooming for young people
	Class here grooming for children
.705–.707	Standard subdivisions of grooming
.708	Grooming for groups of people
[.708 1–.708 3]	Grooming for men, women, young people
	Do not use; class in 646.704
.708 4	Grooming for people in specific stages of adulthood
	Do not use for grooming for women in specific stages of adulthood; class in 646.7042. Do not use for grooming for men in specific stages of adulthood; class in 646.7044
.709	History, geographic treatment, biography of grooming
.72	Care of hair, face, skin, nails
	Class here cosmetology, cosmetics, makeup
	Class cosmetology, cosmetics, makeup limited to face in 646.726
.724	Care of hair
	Including care of beard, shaving; dyeing, hairweaving, permanent waving, relaxing
	Class here barbering, haircutting, hairdressing, hairstyling
.724 7	Braiding
.724 8	Wigs
	Including cleaning, dyeing, selection, styling
.726	Care of face and skin
	Standard subdivisions are added for either or both topics in heading
	Including care of eyes, lips
	Class manicuring and pedicuring in 646.727

.727 Care of nails

Class here manicuring, pedicuring

.76 Social skills

Class social skills in family living in 646.78

For dating and choice of mate, see 646.77

.77 Dating and choice of mate

Standard subdivisions are added for either or both topics in heading

.78 Family life

Class here guides to harmonious intrafamily relationships

For child rearing, see 649.1

.782 Spousal relationship

Class here husband-wife relationship, married people

.79 Guides for people in late adulthood

Class here guides to retirement

Class family life in 646.78

See also 362.6 for social services to people in late adulthood

647 Management of public households (Institutional housekeeping)

See Manual at 647 vs. 647.068, 658.2, T1—0682

SUMMARY

647.068	**Management**
.2	**Employees**
.6	**Employee hours and duties**
.9	**Specific kinds of public households and institutions**

.068 Management

See Manual at 647 vs. 647.068, 658.2, T1—0682

[.068 3] Personnel management (Human resource management)

Do not use; class in 647.2

.2 Employees

Class here personnel management

Class comprehensive home economics works on household employees in 640.46. Class employees and personnel management in a specific field of institutional housekeeping with the field, e.g., waiters 642.6, personnel management of waiters 642.60683

For hours and duties, see 647.6

.6 Employee hours and duties

.9   **Specific kinds of public households and institutions**

> Class a specific aspect of public households and institutions with the aspect, e.g., grounds keeping 635.9, laundering 648.1
>
> *See Manual at 647 vs. 647.068, 658.2, T1—0682*

[.901–.909]   Standard subdivisions

> Do not use; class in 647.01–647.09

.92   Multiple dwellings for long-term residents

> Including apartment hotels, condominiums, cooperatives, public housing, tenements; trailer and mobile home parks
>
> Class here apartment houses
>
> Class recreation vehicle (RV), trailer camps in 647.942
>
> *For boarding and rooming houses for temporary residents, see 647.94*

.94   Lodging for temporary residents

> Class here household management in hospitality industry, bed and breakfast establishments, hostels, hotels, inns, motels, resorts
>
> Class interdisciplinary works on hospitality industry in 338.4791; class interdisciplinary works on tourism in 910; class interdisciplinary and descriptive works on lodging for temporary residents, hotels, inns, motels in 910.46; class interdisciplinary and descriptive works on resorts in 910.462; class interdisciplinary and descriptive works on bed and breakfast establishments in 910.464; class interdisciplinary and descriptive works on hostels in 910.466; class interdisciplinary and descriptive works on campsites in 910.468
>
> *For eating and drinking places, see 647.95*
>
> *See Manual at 913–919: Add table: 04: Guidebooks*

.940 25   Directories of persons and organizations

> Limited to directories of personnel and organizations concerned with household management of lodging for temporary residents
>
> Do not use for directories of lodging for temporary residents; class in 910.46

.942   Campsites

> Class here recreation vehicle (RV) camps, trailer camps
>
> Class trailer and mobile home parks in 647.92

.95   Eating and drinking places

> Standard subdivisions are added for either or both topics in heading
>
> Class here catering establishments
>
> Class interdisciplinary works on facilities for travelers in 910.46
>
> *See Manual at 913–919: Add table: 04: Guidebooks*

[.950 253–.950 259]　　　　　Directories of specific continents, countries, localities

　　　　　　　　　　　　Do not use; class in 647.953–647.959

[.950 93–.950 99]　　　Specific continents, countries, localities

　　　　　　　　　　　　Do not use; class in 647.953–647.959

.953–.959　　　Specific continents, countries, localities

　　　Class here directories

　　　Add to base number 647.95 notation 3–9 from Table 2, e.g., restaurants of Hawaii 647.95969

.96　　　Miscellaneous institutional households

　　　Not provided for elsewhere

　　　Add to base number 647.96 the numbers following 725 in 725.1–725.9, e.g., office buildings 647.9623

.98　　　Religious institutions

　　　Add to base number 647.98 the numbers following 726 in 726.1–726.9, e.g., monasteries 647.987

.99　　　Educational and research institutions

　　　Add to base number 647.99 the numbers following 727 in 727.1–727.9, e.g., libraries 647.998

648　　Housekeeping

Class here household sanitation

Use 640 for housekeeping covering activities related to running the home, e.g., preparing meals and doing routine repairs as well as cleaning. Use 648 for housekeeping limited to cleaning

See Manual at 647 vs. 647.068, 658.2, T1—0682

.1　　Laundering and related operations

Standard subdivisions are added for laundering and related operations together, for laundering alone

Including bleaching, drying, dyeing, ironing, spot removal

Class dry cleaning in 667.12; class commercial laundering, interdisciplinary works on laundering in 667.13

.5　　Housecleaning

Class here cleaning floors, furnishings

.7　　Pest control

.8　　Storage

.9　　Moving

649   Child rearing; home care of people with disabilities and illnesses

SUMMARY

649.1	Child rearing	
.3	Feeding children	
.4	Child health care	
.5	Children's activities and recreation	
.6	Child training	
.7	Moral and character training of children	
.8	Home care of people with disabilities and illnesses	

.1   Child rearing

Class here supervision

Unless other instructions are given, class a subject with aspects in two or more subdivisions of 649.1 in the number coming last, e.g., gifted boys 649.155 (*not* 649.132)

Class specific elements of home care of children regardless of age, sex, or other characteristics in 649.3–649.7

For child training, see 649.6

.102 4	Works for specific types of users

Including child rearing for people in specific occupations

Do not add as instructed in Table 1

.102 42	Works for expectant parents
.102 43	Works for single parents
.102 45	Works for older children in family
.102 48	Works for babysitters
.108	Child care with respect to groups of people

Do not use for care of specific groups of children; class in 649.12–649.15

.12	Children of specific age groups

Add to base number 649.12 the numbers following —083 in notation 0832–0835 from Table 1, e.g., preschool children 649.123

.13	Children of specific sexes

Class children of specific sexes belonging to specific age groups in 649.12

.132	Boys
.133	Girls
.14	Children of specific status, type, relationships

Add to base number 649.14 the numbers following 155.44 in 155.442–155.446, e.g., the only child 649.142

.15 Exceptional children; children by social and economic levels, with social disadvantages, by ethnic and national origin

Standard subdivisions are added for all topics in heading together, for exceptional children alone

.151–.155 Exceptional children

Add to base number 649.15 the numbers following 371.9 in 371.91–371.95, e.g., home care of gifted children 649.155

.156 Children by social and economic levels, with social disadvantages

.156 7 Children with social disadvantages

Class here children with cultural disadvantages

.157 Children by ethnic and national origin

.157 001–.157 009 Standard subdivisions

.157 05–.157 09 Ethnic and national groups with ethnic origins from more than one continent, of European descent

Add to base number 649.157 notation 05–09 from Table 5, e.g., American native children of mixed ancestry with ethnic origins from more than one continent 649.1570597

.157 1–.157 9 Specific ethnic and national groups

Add to base number 649.157 notation 1–9 from Table 5, e.g., Japanese children 649.157956, Japanese-American children 649.157956073

> ### 649.3–649.7 Specific elements of home care of children

Class comprehensive works in 649.1

.3 Feeding children

.33 Breast feeding

Class here interdisciplinary works on breast feeding

For nutritional aspects of breast feeding, see 613.269

.4 Child health care

Class feeding in 649.3; class home care of children with disabilities and illnesses in 649.8

.48 Substance abuse

.5 Children's activities and recreation

.51 Creative activities

Including modeling, music, painting, paper work

.55   Play with toys

> Including games
>
> Class sports games in 649.57

.57   Exercise, gymnastics, sports

> Standard subdivisions are added for any or all topics in heading

.58   Reading and related activities

> Standard subdivisions are added for reading and related activities together, for reading alone
>
> Including storytelling, reading aloud to children, listening
>
> *For home teaching of reading, see 649.68*

.6   **Child training**

> Class religious training in 204.4; class Christian religious training in 248.845
>
> *For moral and character training, see 649.7*

.62   Toilet training

.63   Training in grooming and self-reliance

> Including bathing, dressing, feeding self

.64   Behavior modification, discipline, obedience

> Standard subdivisions are added for any or all topics in heading
>
> Class a specific application with the application, e.g., behavior modification in dressing habits 649.63

.65   Sex education

.68   Home preschool education

> Development of learning ability, of readiness for school by parents in the home
>
> Including home teaching of reading
>
> Class primary level home schools and schooling in 372.104242; class techniques of study at primary level for parents in 372.130281; class home schools and schooling in reading at primary level in 372.4

.7   **Moral and character training of children**

> Standard subdivisions are added for either or both topics in heading
>
> Class religious training of children in the home in 204.4; class Christian religious training of children in the home in 248.845

.8   **Home care of people with disabilities and illnesses**

> Class social services to people with disabilities and illnesses in 362.1–362.4; class nursing aspects in 610.73
>
> *For home care of children with disabilities, see 649.151*

650 Management and auxiliary services

Class here business

See Manual at 330 vs. 650, 658

SUMMARY

.01–.09   Standard subdivisions

.1   **Personal success in business**

Including creative ability

Class here interdisciplinary works on success

For success in personal and family life, see 646.7; for success as an executive, see 658.409. For a specific aspect of success, see the aspect, e.g., techniques of study for success as a student 371.30281

.11   Time management

Class here personal efficiency, interdisciplinary works on time management

For time management in personal life, see 640.43; for executive time management, see 658.4093

.12   Financial success

.13   Personal improvement and success in business relationships

Standard subdivisions are added for either or both topics in heading

.14   Success in obtaining jobs and promotions

Standard subdivisions are added for either or both topics in heading

.142   Résumés, cover letters, job applications

Standard subdivisions are added for résumés, cover letters, job applications together; for résumés alone

Including writing cover letters for job hunting

Class here résumé writing

.144   Employment interviewing

Class here employment interviewing from the job seeker's viewpoint, comprehensive works on employment interviewing

For employment interviewing from the employer's viewpoint, see 658.31124

>   **651–657 Auxiliary services**

Class comprehensive works in 650

For advertising and public relations, see 659

651   **Office services**

Including problems of security and confidentiality

Class a specific aspect of security and confidentiality in office services with the aspect, e.g., security and confidentiality in records management 651.5

For processes of written communication, see 652; for accounting, see 657

SUMMARY

[.028 4]   Apparatus, equipment, materials

> Do not use for apparatus and equipment; class in 651.2. Do not use for materials; class in 651.29

[.028 5]   Computer applications

> Do not use; class in 651.8

.2 Equipment and supplies

> Standard subdivisions are added for equipment and supplies together, for equipment alone

> Class procurement of office equipment and supplies in 658.72

> *For a specific type of equipment, see the use of the equipment, e.g., computers 651.8, photocopying machines 652.4*

.23 Furniture

.26 Processing equipment

> Class here electronic office machines

.29 Forms and supplies

> Standard subdivisions are added for forms and supplies together, for forms alone

> Including materials

.3 Office management

.37 Clerical services

> *For written communication, see 652*

> *See also 657 for accounting*

.374 Secretarial and related services

> Class here office practice

.374 1 Secretarial services

> Work of secretaries, stenographers, typists

.374 3 Related services

> Including work of filers, messengers, receptionists

> Class work of stenographers, typists in 651.3741

.5   **Records management**

Class clerical services associated with records management in 651.37

For creation and transmission of records, see 651.7

.504   Special topics of records management

.504 2   Records management in specific types of enterprises

[.504 201–.504 209]   Standard subdivisions

Do not use; class in 651.501–651.509

.504 26   Records management in technical enterprises

.504 261   Medical records management

.51   Retention, maintenance, final disposition of records

Standard subdivisions are added for any or all topics in heading

Class filing systems and storage in 651.53

.53   Filing systems

Including comprehensive works on storage of records

Class here filing procedures

For specific aspects of storage, see 651.54–651.59

.530 285   Computer applications

Do not use for digitization of files; class in 651.59

\>   651.54–651.59   Specific aspects of storage

Class here space, equipment, control, protection, preservation

Class comprehensive works in 651.53

.54   Storage of original documents

Including storage in filing cabinets, visible and rotary files

For storage of inactive files, see 651.56

.56   Storage of inactive files

Original documents in permanent (dead) storage

.58   Microreproduction of files

Active and inactive

.59   Digitization of files

Active and inactive

.7 **Communication**

Class here creation and transmission of records

Class communication as a technique of management in 658.45; class interdisciplinary works on communication in 302.2

See Manual at 658.45 vs. 651.7, 808.06665

.73 Oral communication

Including use of telephone, telephone answering machines, voice mail

.74 Written communication

Including dictating and use of dictating equipment

For specific types of written communication, see 651.75–651.78; for processes of written communication, see 652

See also 653.14 for recording in shorthand and transcribing shorthand notes

> 651.75–651.78 Specific types of written communication

Class comprehensive works in 651.74

.75 Correspondence

Including layout of letters

.752 Form letters

.755 Memorandums

.759 Mail handling

.77 Minutes

.78 Reports

.79 Internal communication

Including electronic mail

Class interdisciplinary works on electronic mail in 004.692

For oral internal communication, see 651.73; for written internal communication, see 651.74

.792 Intranets

Class interdisciplinary works on intranets in 004.682

.8   **Computer applications**

Use in carrying out office functions

Unless it is redundant, add to base number 651.8 the numbers following 00 in 004–006, e.g., use of digital personal computers 651.8416, but use of digital computers as a whole 651.8 (*not* 651.84)

Class interdisciplinary works on data processing in 004

For computer applications in a specific office activity, see the activity, e.g., digitization of files 651.59

.9   **Office services in specific kinds of enterprises**

Class specific elements of office services in specific kinds of enterprises in 651.2–651.8

[.900 01–.900 09]   Standard subdivisions

Do not use; class in 651.01–651.09

.900 1–.999 9   Subdivisions for office services in specific kinds of enterprises

Add to base number 651.9 notation 001–999, e.g., office services in libraries 651.902

652   Processes of written communication

For word processing, see 005.52; for shorthand, see 653

.1   **Penmanship**

See also 745.61 for calligraphy

.3   **Keyboarding**

Class here typing

.300 1–.300 6   Standard subdivisions

.300 7   Education, research, related topics

.300 76   Review and exercise

Do not use for speed and accuracy tests and drills; class in 652.307

.300 8–.300 9   Standard subdivisions

.302   Specific levels of skill

Class speed and accuracy tests and drills in 652.307

[.302 01–.302 09]   Standard subdivisions

Do not use; class in 652.3001–652.3009

.302 4   Basic level

Class here beginning level

.302 5   Intermediate level

.302 6   Advanced level

.307   Speed and accuracy

> Standard subdivisions are added for either or both topics in heading

> Class here tests, drills

[.307 076]   Review and exercise

> Do not use; class in 651.307

.32   Keyboarding for specific purposes

> Other than general commercial and professional keyboarding

> Including keyboarding for personal use

[.320 1–.320 9]   Standard subdivisions

> Do not use; class in 652.3001–652.3009

.326   Keyboarding for specific kinds of enterprises

> Including legal, medical keyboarding

[.326 01–.326 09]   Standard subdivisions

> Do not use; class in 652.3001–652.3009

.4   Copying

> Class here photocopying

> Class interdisciplinary works on photocopying in 686.4

.8   Cryptography

> Class here interdisciplinary works on cryptography

> *For cryptographic techniques used for a specific purpose, see the purpose, e.g., cryptographic techniques used for security in computer systems 005.82*

653   Shorthand

.076   Review and exercise

> Do not use for speed and accuracy tests and drills; class in 653.15

.1   Basic shorthand practice

> Class basic practice in a specific system with the system, e.g., Gregg shorthand transcription 653.4270424

.14   Taking dictation, and transcription

> Standard subdivisions are added for either or both topics in heading

> *See also 651.74 for dictating and use of dictating equipment*

.15   Speed and accuracy

> Standard subdivisions are added for either or both topics in heading

> Class here tests, drills

> Class speed and accuracy in transcription in 653.14

[.150 76]	Review and exercise
	Do not use; class in 653.15
.18	Specific uses
	Including court reporting; medical, personal uses
[.180 1–.180 9]	Standard subdivisions
	Do not use; class in 653.101–653.109

>   **653.2–653.4 Systems**

Class comprehensive works in 653

.2   **Abbreviated longhand systems**

Systems using conventional letters

.3   **Machine systems**

Add to base number 653.3 the numbers following 653.1 in 653.14–653.18, e.g., specific uses 653.38

.4   **Handwritten systems**

For abbreviated longhand systems, see 653.2

.41	Multilingual systems
.42	English-language systems
.424	Pitman systems
.424 04	Special topics of Pitman systems
.424 042	Basic shorthand practice

Add to base number 653.424042 the numbers following 653.1 in 653.14–653.18, e.g., speed and accuracy 653.4240425

.424 07	Education, research, related topics
.424 076	Review and exercise

Do not use for speed and accuracy tests and drills; class in 653.4240425

.427	Gregg systems
.427 04	Special topics of Gregg systems
.427 042	Basic shorthand practice

Add to base number 653.427042 the numbers following 653.1 in 653.14–653.18, e.g., transcription 653.4270424

.427 07	Education, research, related topics
.427 076	Review and exercise

Do not use for speed and accuracy tests and drills; class in 653.4270425

.428 Script systems

Including Dewey system (1936)

.43–.49 Systems used in other languages

Add to base number 653.4 notation 3–9 from Table 6, e.g., French-language systems 653.441

[654] [Unassigned]

Most recently used in Edition 14

[655] [Unassigned]

Most recently used in Edition 17

[656] [Unassigned]

Most recently used in Edition 14

657 Accounting

Class here financial accounting

Class use of accounting information by management in 658.1511

SUMMARY

657.04	**Levels of accounting**
.1	**Constructive accounting**
.2	**Bookkeeping (Recordkeeping)**
.3	**Financial reports (Financial statements)**
.4	**Specific fields of accounting**
.6	**Specific kinds of accounting**
.7	**Accounting for specific phases of business activity**
.8	**Accounting for enterprises engaged in specific kinds of activities**
.9	**Accounting for enterprises of specific sizes or specific kinds of legal or ownership form**

.04 Levels of accounting

.042 Elementary level

.044 Intermediate level

Including college-level accounting

.046 Advanced level

>   **657.1–657.9 Elements of accounting**

Unless other instructions are given, observe the following table of preference, e.g., accounting for cost of inventory in a corporation engaged in manufacturing 657.867072 (*not* 657.42, 657.72, 657.95):

Accounting for enterprises engaged in specific kinds of activities	657.8
Financial reports (Financial statements)	657.3
Accounting for specific phases of business activity	657.7
Constructive accounting	657.1
Bookkeeping (Recordkeeping)	657.2
Specific fields of accounting	657.4
Accounting for enterprises of specific sizes or specific kinds of legal or ownership form	657.9
Specific kinds of accounting	657.6

Class comprehensive works in 657

.1   **Constructive accounting**

Development of accounting systems to fit the needs of individual organizations

.2   **Bookkeeping (Recordkeeping)**

Including secretarial bookkeeping and accounting

Class elementary accounting in 657.042

.3   **Financial reports (Financial statements)**

Class here consolidated financial statements

Class use of financial reports by management to improve business performance in 658.1512

.32   Preparing financial statements

.4   **Specific fields of accounting**

Including human resources accounting

For constructive accounting, see 657.1; for bookkeeping, see 657.2; for payroll accounting, see 657.742

See also 658.1511 for managerial accounting; also 658.4013 for management audits

[.401–.409]   Standard subdivisions

Do not use; class in 657.01–657.09

.42   Cost accounting

Class here activity-based costing

.45   Auditing

See also 658.4013 for management audits

.450 285   Computer applications

                  Class auditing of computer-processed accounts in 657.453

.452   Audit reports

          Class here audit reporting

.453   Auditing of computer-processed accounts

.458   Internal auditing

.46   Tax accounting

          Including accounting for social security taxes

.47   Fiduciary accounting

          Accounting for receiverships, estates, trusts

.48   Inflation accounting

.6   **Specific kinds of accounting**

[.601–.609]   Standard subdivisions

          Do not use; class in 657.01–657.09

.61   Public accounting

.63   Private accounting

.7   **Accounting for specific phases of business activity**

          Including accounting for income, for profit

[.701–.709]   Standard subdivisions

          Do not use; class in 657.01–657.09

.72   Current assets

          Including accounts receivable, cash, inventory

.73   Fixed assets

          Including depreciation, valuation and revaluation of land, buildings, equipment; insurance

.74   Current liabilities

          Including accounts payable, notes payable

          For tax accounting, see 657.46

.742   Payroll accounting

.75   Fixed liabilities

          Including bonds payable, leases, mortgages, pension plans, purchase contracts

.76   Capital accounting

> Accounting for ownership equity
>
> Including accounting for stock and dividends

.8   **Accounting for enterprises engaged in specific kinds of activities**

> Except for modifications shown under specific entries, add to each subdivision identified by * as follows:
> 001–009   Standard subdivisions
> 01–07   Specific aspects of accounting
>   Add to 0 the numbers following 657 in 657.1–657.7, e.g., auditing 045

[.801–.809]   Standard subdivisions

> Do not use; class in 657.01–657.09

.83   Services and professional activities

> Standard subdivisions are added for services and professional activities together, for services alone
>
> Class here service industries

.832   Social services

> Including libraries, prisons, religious institutions

.832 2   *Health care facilities

> Class here hospitals

.832 7   *Educational institutions

.833   Finance and real estate

.833 3   *Finance

> *For insurance, see 657.836*

.833 5   *Real estate

.834   Professions

.835   *Government

> Including military accounting
>
> Class accounting for government corporations (*except* municipalities) in 657.95. Class accounting for a specific government service other than military with the service in a subdivision of 657.83, e.g., educational institutions 657.8327

.835 045   Government auditing

> Number built according to instructions under 657.8
>
> Class here manuals of government audit procedure

.836   *Insurance

*Add as instructed under 657.8

.837	*Hotels and restaurants
	Class here hospitality industry
.837 4	*Hotels
.837 5	*Restaurants
.838	*Public utilities
.839	*Commerce
	Class here wholesale trade, retail trade
.84	Communications and entertainment media
	Including motion-picture producers and theaters, publishing houses, television and radio networks and stations, theaters
.86	Other activities
	See also 657.83 for services and professional activities
.861	*Labor unions
.862	*Mining
.863	*Agriculture
.867	*Manufacturing
.869	*Construction

.9 Accounting for enterprises of specific sizes or specific kinds of legal or ownership form

[.901–.903]	Standard subdivisions
	Do not use; class in 657.01–657.03
.904	Enterprises of specific sizes
.904 2	Small business
[.905–.909]	Standard subdivisions
	Do not use; class in 657.05–657.09
.91	Individual proprietorships
.92	Partnerships
	For international partnerships, see 657.96
.95	Corporations
	For multinational corporations, see 657.96
.96	Combinations
	Class here mergers, multinational organizations
.97	Cooperatives

*Add as instructed under 657.8

.98   Nonprofit organizations

658   General management

Management comprises the conduct of all types of enterprises (for profit and not for profit) except government agencies that do not themselves provide direct services

Class here general business management, general industrial management; management of public agencies that themselves provide direct services (in contrast to public agencies that regulate, support, or control services provided by other organizations)

Class analysis and description of behavior in complex organizations, sociology of management in 302.35; class specific principles of management in 658.401–658.403; class comprehensive works on management and economics in 330

> *For public administration, see 351. For management of enterprises engaged in a specific field of activity, see the field, plus notation 068 from Table 1, e.g., management of commercial banks 332.12068, management of automobile manufacturing 629.222068*

> *See also 306.36 for industrial sociology*

> *See Manual at T1—068 vs. 353–354; also at 330 vs. 650, 658*

SUMMARY

658.001–.009	**Standard subdivisions**	
.02–.05	**[Management of enterprises of specific sizes, scope, forms; computer applications]**	
.1	**Organization and financial management**	
.2	**Plant management**	
.3	**Personnel management (Human resource management)**	
.4	**Executive management**	
.5	**Management of production**	
.7	**Management of materials**	
.8	**Management of marketing**	

.001   Philosophy and theory

[.001 1]   Systems

> Do not use for systems theory and analysis; class in 658.4032. Do not use for operations research; class in 658.4034. Do not use for models and simulation; class in 658.40352

.002   Miscellany

[.002 85]   Computer applications

> Do not use; class in 658.05

.003–.009   Standard subdivisions

.02   Management of enterprises of specific sizes and scope

> Class management of enterprises of specific forms regardless of size or scope in 658.04

[.020 1–.020 9]	Standard subdivisions	

            Do not use; class in 658.001–658.009

.022   Small enterprises *[handwritten: ← starting a business]*

.022 08   Groups of people

            Class here minority enterprises

.023   Big enterprises

.04   Management of enterprises of specific forms

            For initiation of specific forms of ownership organization, management of new enterprises of specific forms, see 658.114

            See Manual at 658.04 vs. 658.114, 658.402

[.040 1–.040 9]   Standard subdivisions

            Do not use; class in 658.001–658.009

>   658.041–658.046 For-profit organizations

            Class international for-profit organizations in 658.049; class comprehensive works in 658

.041   Individual proprietorships

            Including part-time enterprises

            Class here one-person enterprises, self-employment enterprises

            Class executive management by entrepreneurs in 658.421

            For one-person corporations, see 658.045

.041 2   Home-based businesses

.042   Partnerships

            General and limited

            Class partnership associations in 658.044

.044   Unincorporated business enterprises

            Including joint stock companies, joint ventures, partnership associations

            For individual proprietorships, see 658.041; for partnerships, see 658.042

.045   Corporations

            Including close, family, one-person corporations

            Class government corporations as part of the public administrative process in 352.266; class general works on management that do not emphasize the organizational form corporation even though the works may be predominently about managing corporations in 658; class combinations in 658.046

.046   Combinations

> Including conglomerates, holding companies, interlocking directorates, subsidiaries, trusts

> Class mergers in 658.16

.047   Cooperatives

.048   Nonprofit organizations

> Class international nonprofit organizations in 658.049

> *See also 658.047 for cooperative organizations*

.049   International enterprises

> Class organization of international enterprises and activities in 658.18

.05   Computer applications

> Unless it is redundant, add to base number 658.05 the numbers following 00 in 004–006, e.g., use of digital personal computers 658.05416, but use of digital computers as a whole 658.05 (*not* 658.054); however, for data security, see 658.478

> *See also 651.8 for computer applications in clerical operations; also 658.4032 for systems analysis in decision making*

.1   Organization and financial management

> Standard subdivisions are added for organization and finance together, for organization alone

> *For internal organization, see 658.402*

SUMMARY

658.11	**Initiation of business enterprises**
.12	**Management for legal compliance**
.15	**Financial management**
.16	**Reorganization and dissolution of enterprises**
.18	**Organization of international enterprises**

.11   Initiation of business enterprises

> Including location

> Class here management of new business enterprises

> Class capitalization in 658.152; class reorganization and dissolution of business enterprises in 658.16

.114   Initiation of business enterprises by form of ownership organization

> Add to base number 658.114 the numbers following 658.04 in 658.041–658.049, e.g., initiation of corporations 658.1145

> Class comprehensive works on management of specific forms of ownership organization in 658.04

> *See Manual at 658.04 vs. 658.114, 658.402*

.12   Management for legal compliance

Former heading: Legal administration

Including use of legal counsel

> *For management for legal compliance with respect to a specific subject, see the subject in 658, e.g., management for legal compliance with respect to collective bargaining 658.3154*
>
> *See also 346.06 for law of organizations*

.15   Financial management

Including insolvency, bankruptcy; valuation of businesses

Class here financial decision making, financial planning

Class reorganization and dissolution of business enterprises because of business failure in 658.16. Class a specific aspect of valuation of businesses with the aspect, e.g., valuation of capital 658.1522

> *See Manual at 332 vs. 338, 658.15*

.151   Financial control

> *For budgeting, see 658.154; for management of income and expense, see 658.155*

.151 1   Managerial accounting

Design and use of accounting procedures to provide internal reports needed for day-to-day management

Class accounting in 657; class internal auditing in 657.458; class budgeting in 658.154

> *See also 658.4013 for management audits*

.151 2   Use of reports

Including balance sheets, income and expense statements, profit and loss statements

Class here financial reports made to directors, stockholders, top management

.152   Management of financial operations

Class here management of investment, comprehensive works on capital and its management

> *For capital, see 332.041; for budgeting (including capital budgets), see 658.154; for management of income and expense, see 658.155; for compensation management, see 658.32; for management of credit extended by seller to buyer, see 658.88*

>   658.152 2–658.152 4 Capital and its management

Class comprehensive works in 658.152

.152 2	Procurement of capital

Class here costs and valuation of capital

For procurement of specific kinds of capital, see 658.1524

.152 24	External sources

Including conversion of closely held corporations to corporations whose stocks are publicly traded; endowments, grants; issue and sale of stocks and bonds; loans

Class here fund raising

Class debt management in 658.1526

For fund raising for enterprises engaged in a specific field of activity, see the field, plus notation 0681 from Table 1, e.g., private charitable and philanthropic fund raising for social welfare 361.70681

.152 26	Internal sources

Including reserves, savings

.152 4	Procurement and management of specific kinds of capital
[.152 401–.152 409]	Standard subdivisions

Do not use; class in 658.152201–658.152209

.152 42	Fixed capital

Class here long-term capital

Including land, buildings, associated industrial equipment; long-term loans receivable; leasing

See also 658.72 for procurement of other kinds of equipment

.152 44	Working capital

Including accounts receivable, cash, inventory, 30–90 day loans receivable

Class here short-term capital

.152 6	Debt management

Including accounts payable, bonds outstanding, notes payable

.153	Taxes, insurance, charitable donations

Including ways that management can deal with taxes, what insurance is needed for the organization

Class interdisciplinary works on and economic aspects of business taxes in 336.207; class interdisciplinary works on charitable donations in 361.765; class interdisciplinary works on insurance in 368

See also 343.068 for law of business taxes

.154	Budgeting

Including capital budgets, zero-base budgeting

.155   Management of income and expense

Including distribution of profits, dividend policy

Class here management of profit and loss, risk management

Class interdisciplinary works on risk management in 368; class increasing profits in 658.1554

For use of income and expense statements, see 658.1512; for taxes, insurance, charitable donations, see 658.153; for health and safety programs, see 658.382; for business security, see 658.47; for pricing, see 658.816

.155 2   Cost analysis and control

Standard subdivisions are added for cost analysis and control together, for cost control alone

Class managerial accounting in 658.1511

For cost accounting, see 657.42; for analysis and control of specific kinds of costs, see 658.1553; for cost-benefit analysis, cost-volume-profit analysis, see 658.1554

.155 3   Kinds of costs

Including fixed and overhead costs; variable costs; labor, material costs

For costs of capital, see 658.1522

.155 4   Income (Revenue)

Including break-even analysis, cost-benefit analysis, cost-volume-profit analysis

Class here increasing profits

.159   Financial management in enterprises of specific sizes, scope, forms

Including financial management in nonprofit organizations

For a specific aspect of financial management in enterprises of specific sizes, scope, forms, see the aspect in 658.151–658.155, e.g., budgeting management in small business 658.154

[.159 01–.159 09]   Standard subdivisions

Do not use; class in 658.1501–658.1509

.159 2   Small business

.159 208   Groups of people

Class here minority enterprises

.159 9   International enterprises

.16 Reorganization and dissolution of enterprises

> Standard subdivisions are added for reorganization and dissolution of enterprises together, for reorganization of enterprises alone

> Class here comprehensive works on reorganization, comprehensive works on reorganization resulting from business failure

> Class financial management of insolvency, of bankruptcy in 658.15

> *For internal reorganization, see 658.402*

.162 Mergers

> Class here acquisitions, consolidations, take-overs

.164 Sales

> Class here corporate divestiture

.166 Dissolution

> Class here dissolution resulting from business failure

> Class reorganization resulting from business failure in 658.16

.18 Organization of international enterprises

> Including foreign licensing

> Class here organization of international business activities

> Class initiation of international enterprises and activities in 658.1149

.2 Plant management

> Class procurement of land and buildings in 658.15242

> *See Manual at 647 vs. 647.068, 658.2, T1—0682*

.200 1–.200 9 Standard subdivisions

.202 Maintenance management

> Including total productive maintenance

.21 Location

> Class location of businesses in 658.11

.23 Layout

.24 Lighting

.25 Heating, ventilating, air conditioning

.26 Utilities

> Including electricity, gas, power and power distribution, water

> Class here comprehensive business works on energy management

> *For lighting, see 658.24; for heating, ventilating, air conditioning, see 658.25. For a specific aspect of energy management, see the aspect, e.g., energy management to promote efficiency in production 658.515*

.27 Equipment

Class procurement of industrial equipment associated with plants in 658.15242; class procurement of other kinds of equipment in 658.72

For office equipment, see 651.2; for utilities, see 658.26; for equipment for safety and comfort, see 658.28

.28 Equipment for safety and comfort

Including equipment for noise control, for sanitation

.3 Personnel management (Human resource management)

Class interdisciplinary works on industrial relations, on labor in 331

For management of executive personnel, see 658.407

SUMMARY

658.300 1–.300 9	**Standard subdivisions**
.301–.306	**[General topics of personnel management]**
.31	**Elements of personnel management**
.32	**Compensation management**
.38	**Employee health, safety, welfare**

.300 1–.300 7   Standard subdivisions

.300 8   Groups of people

Class here affirmative action, discrimination in employment, equal employment opportunity, workplace diversity

.300 9   History, geographic treatment, biography

.301   Personnel planning and policy

Standard subdivisions are added for either or both topics in heading

.302   Supervision

By immediate supervisors

Class employee development in 658.3124; class personnel management of supervisors in 658.4071245

.303   Personnel management in enterprises of specific sizes

[.303 01–.303 09]   Standard subdivisions

Do not use; class in 658.3001–658.3009

.304   Management of personnel occupying specific types of positions and management of problem employees

.304 4   Management of personnel occupying specific types of positions

Including blue collar and professional employees; sales personnel

For management of office personnel, see 651.30683; for management of supervisors, executive personnel, see 658.407

[.304 401–.304 409]   Standard subdivisions

Do not use; class in 658.3001–658.3009

.304 5	Management of problem employees

Class management of problem employees occupying specific types of positions in 658.3044. Class management of a specific type of problem employee provided for elsewhere with the type, e.g., alcoholic employees 658.300874

.306	Job analysis

Including specifications of qualifications required of personnel in each position

Class here job description, job evaluation, position classification

.31	Elements of personnel management

SUMMARY

658.311	**Recruitment and selection of personnel**
.312	**Conditions of employment, performance rating, utilization of personnel**
.313	**Separation from service**
.314	**Motivation, morale, discipline**
.315	**Employer-employee relationships**

.311	Recruitment and selection of personnel
.311 1	Recruitment
.311 2	Selection

Including drug testing, handwriting analysis, security clearance, background investigation, use of lie detector

Class here comprehensive works on selection and placement

For placement, see 658.3128

See also 658.383 for payment of moving expenses

.311 24	Interviewing

Class employment interviewing from the job seeker's viewpoint, comprehensive works on employment interviewing in 650.144

.311 25	Testing

Class here aptitude testing

.312	Conditions of employment, performance rating, utilization of personnel

Standard subdivisions are added for conditions of employment, performance rating, utilization of personnel together; for conditions of employment alone

---

> 658.312 1–658.312 4 Conditions of employment

Class comprehensive works in 658.312

For compensation management, see 658.32; for personnel health, safety, welfare, see 658.38

.312 1	Hours

Former heading: Days and hours of work

Including workday, overtime; flexible hours, shift work, part-time work; compressed workweek; night, holy day, Sunday, holiday work

Class here workweek

For leave and rest periods, see 658.3122

Lunch periods and breaks relocated to 658.3122

.312 2	Leave and rest periods (breaks)

Standard subdivisions are added for leave and rest periods together, for leave alone

Including lunch periods and breaks [*both formerly* 658.3121]; educational, parental, sabbatical, sick leave

Class here annual leave, holidays, paid vacations

Class absenteeism in 658.314

.312 3	Telecommuting

.312 4	Education and training

Standard subdivisions are added for either or both topics in heading

Including mentoring

Class here employee development

.312 404	Development and administration of training programs

Standard subdivisions are added for either or both topics in heading

Including evaluation of training programs, selection and training of training personnel, teaching methods

.312 42	Orientation

Class here induction

.312 43	In-house work training

Training needed to enable an employee to do his or her job

Including retraining, adjustment to automation

.312 44	Other kinds of training

Including attitude training, literacy training, rehabilitation training, safety training, training in human relations

.312 45	Training of personnel occupying specific types of positions
	Including blue collar and professional employees; sales personnel
	Class induction and orientation of personnel occupying specific types of positions in 658.31242; class in-house work training of personnel occupying specific types of positions in 658.31243; class other kinds of training regardless of type of position occupied by employee in 658.31244
	For training of supervisors, see 658.4071245
[.312 450 1–.312 450 9]	Standard subdivisions
	Do not use; class in 658.312401–658.312409
.312 5	Performance rating (Evaluation)
	Class here performance standards
.312 8	Utilization of personnel
	Including allocation of staff to specific responsibilities, staffing patterns; placement, transfer of employees from one position to another
	Class training in 658.3124; class performance rating in 658.3125; class motivation in 658.314; class work teams in 658.4022
.313	Separation from service
	Including dismissal for cause
.313 2	Retirement
.313 4	Reduction in force
	Class here downsizing
.314	Motivation, morale, discipline
	Standard subdivisions are added for any or all topics in heading
	Including absenteeism, misconduct, retention, turnover
	Class here promotion of creativity, productivity
	Class performance rating in 658.3125
.314 2	Incentives
	For incentive payments, see 658.3225
.314 22	Job satisfaction
	Class job enrichment in 658.31423
.314 23	Job enrichment
.314 24	Promotion
	See also 650.14 for how to obtain a promotion (employee's viewpoint)

.314 4	Penalties

> Including demotion, fines, reprimands
>
> *For dismissal for cause, see 658.313*

.314 5	Interpersonal relations

> Including informal, day-to-day relations between superiors and subordinates; conflict management, prevention of sexual harassment
>
> Class comprehensive works on employer-employee relationships from a management perspective in 658.315

.315	Employer-employee relationships

> Class here labor relations
>
> *For informal relations, see 658.3145*

.315 2	Employee participation in management

> Including open-book management, worker self-management
>
> Class industrial democracy in 331.0112; class worker control of industry in 338.6

.315 3	Labor unions and other employee organizations

> Standard subdivisions are added for labor unions and other employee organizations together, for labor unions alone
>
> *For collective bargaining, see 658.3154; for role of employee organizations in grievance procedures, see 658.3155*

.315 4	Collective bargaining

> Including arbitration, mediation, negotiation of contracts, strikes

.315 5	Grievance procedures
.32	Compensation management

> Class here wage administration, salary administration
>
> Class management of labor costs in 658.1553

.321	Payroll administration

> Class clerical techniques involved in maintaining payroll records in 651.37; class payroll accounting procedures in 657.74

.322	Compensation plans
.322 2	Wage and salary scales

> Standard subdivisions are added for either or both topics in heading
>
> Hourly or other periodic scales
>
> Including locality pay (weighting), longevity pay, overtime pay, severance pay

.322 5	Incentive compensation

Including merit awards, merit pay; bonuses, piecework rates, profit sharing

Class comprehensive works on incentives in 658.3142

.322 59	Employee stock ownership plans

Class here employee stock options

.325	Employee benefits

For personnel health, safety, welfare programs and services, see 658.38

.325 3	Pensions
.325 4	Insurance and workers' compensation
.38	Employee health, safety, welfare

Class comprehensive management works on employee benefits in 658.325

.382	Health and safety programs

Including mental health programs

Class safety of plant and equipment in 658.200289; class safety training in 658.31244; class provision of health and accident insurance in 658.3254; class comprehensive works on safety management in 658.408; class interdisciplinary works on industrial safety in 363.11

.382 2	Programs for substance abuse

Including alcohol abuse and drug abuse programs; drug testing

Class drug testing in employee selection in 658.3112

.383	Economic services

Including discounts, housing, moving expenses, transportation

.385	Counseling services

Including retirement counseling services, vocational guidance services

Class mental health programs and services in 658.382

.4	**Executive management**

Limited to those activities named below

Class here role, function, powers, position of top and middle management

Class supervision in 658.302; class comprehensive works on management for legal compliance in 658.12. Class a specific executive managerial activity not provided for here with the activity in management, e.g., personnel management 658.3; class application of a specific activity named below in another branch of management with the branch, e.g., production planning 658.503

SUMMARY

.400 1–.400 9   Standard subdivisions

> 658.401–658.409 Specific executive management activities

Unless other instructions are given, observe the following table of preference, e.g., planning for change 658.406 (*not* 658.4012):

Personal aspects of executive management	658.409
Management of executive personnel	658.407
Internal organization	658.402
Managing change	658.406
Negotiation, conflict management, crisis management, contracting out	658.405
Planning, policy making, control, quality management	658.401
Decision making and information management	658.403
Social responsibility of executive management	658.408
Project management	658.404

Class comprehensive works in 658.4

For communication, see 658.45; for use of consultants, see 658.46; for business intelligence and security, see 658.47

SUMMARY

.401   Planning, policy making, control, quality management

.401 2   Planning and policy making

Standard subdivisions are added for either or both topics in heading

Class here management by objectives, strategic management

Class decision making in 658.403; class forecasting in 658.40355

.401 3	Control and quality management

> Standard subdivisions are added for either or both topics in heading

> Class here management audits (assessments of management effectiveness), total quality management

> Class management audits applied to a specific function with the function, e.g., management audits applied to production management 658.5; class total quality management applied to a specific function with the function, e.g., total quality management in marketing 658.8

> > *See also 657.45 for financial audits; also 658.562 for quality control of products*

.402	Internal organization

> Including line and staff, functional, departmental organization; decentralization, distribution and delegation of authority and responsibility; internal reorganization

> Class sociology of economic institutions in 306.3; class comprehensive management works on organization in 658.1; class comprehensive management works on reorganization in 658.16

> > *For allocation of personnel to specific responsibilities, see 658.3128*

> > *See also 302.3 for social interaction within groups*

> > *See Manual at 658.04 vs. 658.114, 658.402*

.402 2	Work teams

> Class here work groups

.403	Decision making and information management

> Class here problem solving

.403 001–.403 009	Standard subdivisions
.403 01	Philosophy and theory of decision making
[.403 011]	Systems in decision making

> Do not use; class in 658.4032

.403 015	Scientific principles
[.403 015 1]	Mathematical techniques of decision making

> Do not use; class in 658.4033

.403 02–.403 09	Standard subdivisions of decision making
.403 2	Systems theory and analysis

> Standard subdivisions are added for either or both topics in heading

> Including critical path method (CPM), network analysis, program evaluation review technique (PERT)

> > *For decision theory, see 658.40301; for operations research, see 658.4034; for simulation, see 658.40352; for decision analysis, see 658.40354; for forecasting, see 658.40355*

.403 3	Mathematical techniques of decision making
	Including mathematical programming
	Class here econometrics as an aid in decision making
	For simulation, see 658.40352
.403 4	Operations research
	Including probability theory, queuing theory
	Class mathematical methods in 658.4033; class simulation in 658.40352; class games in 658.40353
.403 5	Other techniques of decision making
.403 52	Simulation
	Class here models
.403 53	Games
.403 54	Decision analysis
.403 55	Forecasting
.403 6	Group decision making
	Class specific techniques of group decision making in 658.4032–658.4035
	See also 658.4052 for negotiation
.403 8	Information management
	Class here gathering of information by management for use in managerial decision making; information resources, knowledge management
	Class communication in 658.45
.403 801 1	Systems
	Class here information systems
.404	Project management
.405	Negotiation, conflict management, crisis management, contracting out
.405 2	Negotiation
	See also 658.4036 for group decision making
.405 3	Conflict management
.405 6	Crisis management

.405 8	Contracting out

Contracting for services

Class here subcontracting

Class contracting out a particular managerial service with the service in 658, e.g., personnel management 658.3; class contracting out a particular nonmanagerial service with the service, plus notation 0684 from Table 1, e.g., contracting out hospital care 362.110684

See also 658.723 for contracting for materials

.406	Managing change

Class here expansion, modernization

Class comprehensive works on reorganization of enterprises in 658.16

For internal reorganization, see 658.402. For managing change in a specific branch of management, see the branch, e.g., changes in production 658.5

.406 2	Externally induced change

Including technological innovations

.406 3	Innovation by management

Including corporate turnarounds

Class here reengineering

.407	Management of executive personnel

Add to base number 658.407 the numbers following 658.3 in 658.31–658.38, e.g., training of supervisors 658.4071245

.408	Social responsibility of executive management

Class here comprehensive works on safety management

Class managing welfare services for employees in 658.38; class managing welfare services for people other than employees in 361.7; class interdisciplinary works on safety in 363.1

For a specific aspect of safety management, see the aspect, e.g., product safety 658.56

See Manual at 363.1

.408 3	Protection of environment

Class interdisciplinary works on protection of environment in 363.7

.409	Personal aspects of executive management

Class here success as an executive

Class general success in business in 650.1

.409 2	Executive leadership

.409 3	Time management

Class here personal efficiency (management by executives of their own time and work)

.409 4	Personal characteristics of executives

Including creative ability

.409 5	The management environment

Including interpersonal relations, job stress, social pressures

.42	Top management

Class initiation of business enterprises in 658.11; class comprehensive works on top and middle management in 658.4

For a specific activity of top management, see the activity, e.g., decision making by top management 658.403

.421	Entrepreneurial management

Class management of small business in 658.022

.422	Boards of directors

Class here boards of trustees

.43	Middle management
.45	Communication

As a technique of management

Class mechanics of communication in 651.7

See Manual at 658.45 vs. 651.7, 808.06665

.452	Oral communication

Class here business presentations

See also 808.51 for techniques of public speaking

.453	Written communication
.455	Informational programs

Including bulletin boards, house organs

Class here communication of information by management in order to guide people and control activities

See also 658.4038 for gathering of information by management for use in managerial decision making

.456	Meetings

Class interdisciplinary works on meetings in 060; class general rules of order in 060.42

.46   Use of consultants

Class here techniques of management consulting

For use of consultants in a specific branch of management, see the branch, e.g., use of consultants in market research 658.83

.47   Business security and intelligence

Standard subdivisions are added for business security and intelligence together, for business security alone

Class insurance in 658.153

.472   Business intelligence, and security of information and ideas

Standard subdivisions are added for any or all topics in heading

Class here industrial espionage, countering industrial espionage, trade secrets

For security of information stored in computers, see 658.478

.473   Physical security

Including protection from fraud, theft, violence

Class here crime prevention

For protection against fires and other disasters, see 658.477; for physical security of computers, see 658.478

.477   Protection against fires and other disasters

.478   Computer security

Class here data security

Class comprehensive works on security of information in 658.472; class interdisciplinary works on computer security in 005.8

.5   Management of production

Class here production management in manufacturing enterprises, production management in service industries, comprehensive works on logistics

Class marketing in 658.8; class comprehensive works on energy management in 658.26

For materials handling, see 658.781; for physical distribution, see 658.788; for factory operations engineering, see 670.42. For production management in enterprises engaged in a specific kind of activity other than manufacturing, see the activity, plus notation 0685 from Table 1, e.g., management of agricultural production 630.685

.500 1–.500 9   Standard subdivisions

.503   General production planning

.503 6   Decision making and use of information

Standard subdivisions are added for either or both topics in heading

.503 8	Product planning

Including diversification

Class marketing in 658.8

For new product development, see 658.575

.51	Organization of production

For sequencing, see 658.53; for work studies, see 658.54

.514	Use of technology

Including automation, man-machine ratios, modernization, technological innovations

See also 658.577 for development of technology

.515	Promotion of efficiency

For use of technology, see 658.514

.53	Sequencing

Including dispatching, routing

Class here scheduling, workflow

.533	Kinds of sequences

Including assembly-line, team methods

.54	Work studies

Including work load

.542	Time and motion studies
.542 1	Time studies
.542 3	Motion studies
.544	Fatigue and monotony studies

Standard subdivisions are added for either or both topics in heading

.56	Product control, packaging; waste control and utilization

Including product liability, recall, safety

Class product planning in 658.5038; class product design in 658.5752; class comprehensive works on safety management in 658.408

.562	Quality control

Class comprehensive works on quality control in 658.4013

For inspection, see 658.568

.564   Packaging

Including labeling

Class here interdisciplinary works on packaging

> *For storage containers, see 658.785; for packing for shipment, see 658.7884; for use of packaging in sales promotion, see 658.823; for packaging technology, see 688.8*

.567   Waste control and utilization

Standard subdivisions are added for either or both topics in heading

.568   Inspection

Class comprehensive works on quality control in production management in 658.562

.57   Research and development (R and D)

Standard subdivisions are added for research and development together, for research alone

.571   Fundamental research

.575   New product development

> *For decisions to develop new products, see 658.5038; for market research on new products, see 658.83*

.575 2   Product design

.577   Equipment and process research

Standard subdivisions are added for either or both topics in heading

.7   Management of materials

Class here management of supplies

Class comprehensive works on energy management in 658.26; class comprehensive works on logistics in 658.5

> *For management of office supplies, see 651.29*

.72   Procurement

Acquisition of equipment, materials, parts, subassemblies, supplies, tools

Class here procurement of office equipment and supplies, comprehensive works on procurement

Class management of costs of materials in 658.1553

> *For procurement of land, buildings, associated industrial equipment, see 658.15242*

.722   Vendor selection

.723   Contracts

Class here negotiation of contracts

Class contracting out, subcontracting for services in 658.4058

.728   Receiving

.78   Internal control of materials and physical distribution

.781   Materials handling

.785   Storage

                  Including storage containers

                  Class here warehouse management

                  Class location of warehouses in 658.21

.787   Inventory control

                  Class here stock control

                  Class financial control of inventories in 658.15244

                  For receiving, see 658.728; for storage, see 658.785

.788   Physical distribution

                  Class here shipment

                  Class internal movement of materials in 658.781

.788 2   Transportation management

                  Selection of carrier and routing

.788 4   Packing for shipment

                  Class interdisciplinary works on packaging in 658.564

.788 5   Loading and unloading

                  Standard subdivisions are added for either or both topics in heading

.8   Management of marketing

           Class here management of distribution; management of marketing goods, marketing services; management of merchandising

           Class product design in 658.5752; class comprehensive works on logistics in 658.5

                  For physical distribution, see 658.788; for advertising and public relations, see 659

SUMMARY

658.800 1–.800 9	**Standard subdivisions**
.802–.804	**[General topics of marketing management; marketing to specific kinds of buyers]**
.81	**Sales management**
.82	**Sales promotion**
.83	**Market research**
.84	**Export marketing**
.85	**Personal selling**
.86	**Wholesale marketing**
.87	**Marketing channels**
.88	**Credit management**

.800 1	Philosophy and theory
[.800 11]	Systems
	Do not use; class in 658.802
.800 19	Psychological principles
	For consumer psychology, see 658.8342
.800 2–.800 6	Standard subdivisions
.800 7	Education, research, related topics
.800 72	Research
	For market research, see 658.83
.800 8–.800 9	Standard subdivisions
.802	General topics of marketing management
	Including communication in marketing, green marketing, market segmentation
	Class application of general topics to marketing to specific kinds of buyers in 658.804
.804	Marketing to specific kinds of buyers
	Including governments and their agencies, hospitals; key accounts
	Class here industrial marketing
	Class consumer research in 658.834
	For marketing to foreign buyers, see 658.84
.804 01–.804 09	Standard subdivisions of industrial marketing
	Do not use for marketing to specific kinds of buyers; class in 658.8001–658.8009
.81	Sales management
	Class management of sales personnel in 658.3044
	For sales promotion, see 658.82
.810 01	Philosophy and theory
.810 011 2	Forecasting and forecasts
	Do not use for sales forecasting; class in 658.818
.810 02–.810 09	Standard subdivisions
.810 1	Sales planning
	For market research, see 658.83
.810 2	Organization of sales force
	Including organization by area, by product, by type of customer, by key accounts

.810 6	Sales meetings

Class comprehensive management works on business meetings in 658.456

.812	Customer relations

Including claims, complaints, returns, servicing of products

.816	Pricing
.818	Sales forecasting
.82	Sales promotion

Including use of coupons, discounts, gifts, prizes, samples, trading stamps

For servicing of products, see 658.812; for use of credit to promote sales, see 658.88

.823	Use of packaging

Class interdisciplinary works on packaging in 658.564

.827	Use of brands and trademarks

Standard subdivisions are added for either or both topics in heading

Including business names; producer and distributor brands

.83	Market research

Class here market analysis, market study; interviewing, use of consultants and research agencies, techniques of consulting in market research

Unless other instructions are given, class a subject with aspects in two or more subdivisions of 658.83 in the number coming first, e.g., research in Germany on consumer preferences 658.83430943 (*not* 658.83943)

Class results of market research in 381–382

For sales forecasting, see 658.818

[.830 9]	History, geographic treatment, biography

Do not use; class in 658.839

.834	Consumer research
.834 019	Psychological principles

Do not use for consumer psychology; class in 658.8342

.834 2	Consumer behavior

Including motivation research

Class here consumer psychology

For consumer attitudes, preferences, reactions, see 658.8343

.834 3	Consumer attitudes, preferences, reactions

Standard subdivisions are added for any or all topics in heading

Including brand preferences, consumer satisfaction

.839   History, geographic treatment, biography

.839 01–.839 05   Historical periods

> Add to base number 658.8390 the numbers following —090 in notation 0901–0905 from Table 1, e.g., market research 2000–2009 658.8390511

.839 1–.839 9   Geographic treatment and biography

> Add to base number 658.839 notation 1–9 from Table 2, e.g., market research in Germany 658.83943

.84   Export marketing

.85   Personal selling

> Techniques for the individual, regardless of channel
>
> Class here personal salesmanship

.86   Wholesale marketing

> Class personal selling through wholesale channels in 658.85; class wholesale marketing through specific channels in 658.87. Class management of enterprises doing wholesale marketing of a specific type of product with the product in 381.4, plus notation 068 from Table 1, e.g., management of wholesale food marketing 381.4564130068, financial management of wholesale food marketing 381.45641300681

.87   Marketing channels

> Including consumer cooperatives, managing producers' cooperatives; convenience stores, shopping centers; fairs, markets; garage, yard sales
>
> Class here marketing through specific wholesale channels, marketing through retail channels; comprehensive works on marketing channels
>
> Class personal selling through specific channels, e.g., personal selling by telephone, in 658.85; class comprehensive works on wholesale marketing in 658.86; class direct-mail advertising in 659.133. Class management of enterprises selling a specific type of product with the product in 381.4, plus notation 068 from Table 1, e.g., management of bookstores 381.45002068, financial management of bookstores 381.450020681; class a specific aspect of managing chain stores, outlet stores, franchise businesses if there is no emphasis on a specific kind of product with the kind of store or business in 658.8702–658.8708, plus notation 0681–0687 from Table 1, e.g., financial management of chain stores 658.87020681; class a specific aspect of managing enterprises in a specific channel if there is no emphasis on a specific kind of product with the channel in 658.871–658.879, plus notation 0681–0687 from Table 1, e.g., financial management of department stores 658.8710681
>
> *For export marketing, see 658.84*

.870 01–.870 09   Standard subdivisions

.870 2   Chain stores

> Including voluntary retail chains
>
> Class chain department stores in 658.871

.870 5   Outlet stores

> Class here discount stores that are outlet stores, factory outlets, manufacturers' outlets, wholesale outlets

.870 8   Franchise businesses

.871   Department stores

> Class department stores that are discount stores or superstores in 658.879

.872   Telemarketing and direct marketing

> Standard subdivisions are added for either or both topics in heading

> Class here catalog, mail-order, online, telephone-order marketing; direct-mail marketing, direct selling, multilevel marketing, pyramid marketing; television selling

> *See also 659.143 for television advertising; also 659.144 for online advertising*

.877   Auctions

[.877 028 5]   Computer applications

> Do not use; class in 658.8777

.877 7   Online auctions

.879   Discount stores

> Including customer, warehouse, wholesale clubs

> Class here supermarkets that are not predominantly food stores; hypermarkets, superstores

> Class discount stores that are outlet stores in 658.8705

> *For management of food retailing in supermarkets, see 381.4564130068*

.88   Credit management

> Limited to credit extended by seller to buyer

> Including collections, credit investigations

> Class comprehensive works on management of financial operations in 658.152. Class credit management by banks and other financial institutions with the institution or type of credit in 332, plus notation 0685 from Table 1, e.g., management of loans issued by commercial banks 332.17530685

.882   Mercantile credit management

.883   Consumer credit management

> Class here retail credit management

(.9)   Management of enterprises engaged in specific fields of activity

> (Optional number; prefer specific subject, plus notation 068 from Table 1)

(.91)	Enterprises other than those engaged in extraction, manufacturing, construction

(Optional number; prefer specific subject, plus notation 068 from Table 1)

Add to base number 658.91 notation 001–999, e.g., management of banks 658.913321; however, for management of election campaigns, see 324.7

(.92–.99)	Enterprises engaged in extraction, manufacturing, construction

(Optional number; prefer specific subject, plus notation 068 from Table 1)

Add to base number 658.9 the numbers following 6 in 620–690, e.g., management of mines 658.922

659   Advertising and public relations

Class here publicity

.1   Advertising

See also 658.81 for sales management; also 658.85 for personal selling

.104   Special topics of advertising

.104 2   Social aspects of advertising

Class social aspects of use of specific images and themes in advertising in 659.10452–659.10459, e.g., social aspects of images of women in advertising 659.1045522

.104 5   Use of images and themes in advertising

Standard subdivisions are added for either or both topics in heading

Class here iconography of advertising

Add to base number 659.1045 the numbers following —3 in notation 32–39 from Table 3C, e.g., use of images of women in advertising 659.1045522, use of sports themes in advertising 659.1045579

.11   General topics of advertising

Class application of general topics to advertising in specific media in 659.13; class application of general topics to specific kinds of advertising in 659.131; class application of general topics to advertising specific kinds of organizations, products, services in 659.19

.111   Planning and control

Standard subdivisions are added for either or both topics in heading

.112   Organization

Managerial organization only

See also 338.7616591 for economics and history of advertising organizations

.112 2   Advertising departments

.112 5   Advertising agencies

.113   Advertising campaigns

.13 Kinds of advertising and advertising in specific media

Class advertising of specific kinds of organizations, products, services in a specific kind of medium in 659.19

For advertising in electronic media, see 659.14; for display advertising, see 659.15; for contests and lotteries, see 659.17

.131 Kinds of advertising

Including classified advertising, specialty advertising

Class advertising of specific kinds of organizations, products, services by a specific kind of advertising in 659.19. Class a specific kind of advertising in a specific medium with the medium, e.g., classified advertising in print media 659.132, online classified advertising 659.144

.131 2 National advertising

.131 4 Retail advertising

.131 5 Industrial advertising

Class here business-to-business advertising

See also 659.19 for advertising specific kinds of organizations, products, services

.132 Advertising in print media

Including directory advertising

For direct advertising, see 659.133

.133 Direct advertising

Printed advertising delivered or handed directly to consumer

Including circulars, letters, mail-order catalogs; direct-mail advertising

Class direct-mail marketing in 658.872; class online advertising in 659.144

.134 Advertising by location of media

For point-of-sale advertising, see 659.157

.134 2 Outdoor advertising

Including billboards, roadside signs

Class outdoor transportation advertising in 659.1344

For advertising by electric signs, see 659.136

.134 4 Transportation advertising

Including airplane banners, car cards, traveling displays on exteriors of vehicles, station posters

.136 Advertising by electric signs

.14 Advertising in electronic media

> Including advertising in motion pictures

> Class advertising of specific kinds of organizations, products, services, issues in a specific electronic medium in 659.19

.142 Radio

.143 Television

> *See also 658.872 for television selling*

.144 Advertising in digital media

> Class here online advertising

> *See also 658.872 for online marketing*

.15 Display advertising

.152 Exhibitions and shows

> Standard subdivisions are added for either or both topics in heading

> Including fashion modeling

> Class interdisciplinary works on fashion modeling in 746.92

.157 Point-of-sale advertising

> Including counter, showcase, window displays

.17 Advertising by contests and lotteries

> Standard subdivisions are added for either or both topics in heading

> *See also 659.19790134 for advertising of contests; also 659.1979538 for advertising of lotteries*

.19 Advertising specific kinds of organizations, products, services

> Class here advertising to influence behavior or public opinion with respect to specific subjects; advertising specific kinds of organizations, products, services in a specific kind of medium; advertising specific kinds of organizations, products, services by a specific kind of advertising

[.190 001–.190 009] Standard subdivisions

> Do not use; class in 659.101–659.109

.190 01–.199 99 Subdivisions for specific kinds of organizations, products, services

> Add to base number 659.19 notation 001–999, e.g., library advertising 659.1902, traffic safety advertising 659.19363125, advertising pharmaceutical drugs 659.196151; however, for advertising for political election campaigns, see 324.73

.2 Public relations

.28 Public relations in enterprises of specific forms

> Class public relations in enterprises producing specific kinds of products and services, or pursuing specific objectives, regardless of form of enterprise in 659.29

[.280 1–.280 9]   Standard subdivisions

> Do not use; class in 659.201–659.209

.281–.289   Subdivisions for enterprises of specific forms

> Add to base number 659.28 the numbers following 658.04 in 658.041–658.049, e.g., corporations 659.285

.29   Public relations in organizations producing specific kinds of products and services, or pursuing specific objectives

[.290 001–.290 009]   Standard subdivisions

> Do not use; class in 659.201–659.209

.290 01–.299 99   Subdivisions for organizations producing specific kinds of products and services, or pursuing specific objectives

> Add to base number 659.29 notation 001–999, e.g., public relations for computer industry 659.29004, public relations for lobbying in general 659.293244, public relations for public welfare lobbying 659.293616; however, for public relations in libraries, see 021.7; for public relations for religion, see 200; for public relations for conduct of political election campaigns, see 324.7; for public relations for government, see 352.748; for public relations for armed forces, see 355.342

660   Chemical engineering and related technologies

Standard subdivisions are added for chemical engineering and related technologies together, for chemical engineering alone

Class military applications in 623

For pharmaceutical chemistry, see 615.19; for pulp and paper technology, see 676; for elastomers and elastomer products, see 678

SUMMARY

660.01–.09	**Standard subdivisions and chemical technologies of specific states of matter**
.2–.7	**[General topics in chemical engineering, biotechnology, industrial stoichiometry]**
661	**Technology of industrial chemicals**
662	**Technology of explosives, fuels, related products**
663	**Beverage technology**
664	**Food technology**
665	**Technology of industrial oils, fats, waxes, gases**
666	**Ceramic and allied technologies**
667	**Cleaning, color, coating, related technologies**
668	**Technology of other organic products**
669	**Metallurgy**

.01   Philosophy and theory

.011 5   Theory of communication and control

> Do not use for process control; class in 660.2815

.02   Miscellany

[.028 4]	Apparatus, equipment, materials

Do not use for materials; class in 660.282. Do not use for apparatus and equipment; class in 660.283

[.028 9]	Safety measures

Do not use; class in 660.2804

.03	Dictionaries, encyclopedias, concordances
.04	Chemical technologies of specific states of matter

Add to base number 660.04 the numbers following 530.4 in 530.41–530.44, e.g., plasma technology 660.044

Class industrial gases in 665.7

.05–.09	Standard subdivisions

.2 General topics in chemical engineering

For biochemical engineering, see 660.63; for industrial stoichiometry, see 660.7

.28	Specific types of chemical plant and specific activities in chemical plants
.280 01–.280 09	Standard subdivisions
.280 4	Safety measures

See also 363.179 for interdisciplinary works on hazardous chemicals

See Manual at 604.7 vs. 660.2804

.280 7	Specific types of chemical plant
.280 71	Bench-scale plants
.280 72	Pilot plants
.280 73	Full-scale plants

> 660.281–660.283 Process and materials

Class specific applications in unit operations in 660.2842; class specific applications in unit processes in 660.2844; class comprehensive works in 660.28

.281	Process design, assembly, control
.281 2	Process design

.281 5	Process control

Class here computerized process control

Unless it is redundant, add to base number 660.2815 the numbers following 00 in 004–006, e.g., use of digital personal computers 660.2815416, but use of digital computers 660.2815 (*not* 660.28154)

Class interdisciplinary works on computerized process control in 629.895

.282	Materials
.283	Process equipment

Including piping

Class computer equipment in process control in 660.2815; class interdisciplinary works on piping in 621.8672; class interdisciplinary works on pressure vessels in 681.76041

.283 04	Control of corrosion

Class interdisciplinary works on corrosion in 620.11223

.283 2	Chemical reactors
.284	Unit operations and unit processes
.284 2	Unit operations

Unit operations: operations basically physical

Class here separation processes; transport phenomena engineering

.284 22	Crushing, grinding, screening
.284 23	Mass transfer

Including absorption, gas chromatography

For precipitation, filtration, solvent extraction, see 660.28424; for fractional distillation, see 660.28425

.284 235	Adsorption
.284 24	Precipitation, filtration, solvent extraction
.284 245	Filtration
.284 248	Solvent extraction
.284 25	Fractional distillation
.284 26	Evaporative and drying processes

For dehumidification of air and gas, see 660.28429

.284 27	Heat transfer

Class a specific heat transfer process with the process, e.g., melting 660.284296

.284 29	Other unit operations

Including dehumidification of air and gas

.284 292		Momentum transfer and fluidization
		Including mixing
.284 293		Humidification
.284 296		Melting
.284 298		Crystallization
.284 4		Unit processes
		Operations basically chemical
		For polymerization, see 668.92
.284 43		Oxidation-reduction reaction (Redox reaction)
		Including hydrogenation
		Class here oxidation, reduction
.284 49		Fermentation
.29		Applied physical chemistry

Add to base number 660.29 the numbers following 541.3 in 541.33–541.39, e.g., catalytic reactions 660.2995; however, for absorption, see 660.28423; for adsorption, see 660.284235; for synthesis (e.g., addition, condensation, hydrolysis, oxidation, reduction) and name reactions, see 660.2844; for polymerization, see 668.92

.6   **Biotechnology**

Application of living organisms or their biological systems or processes to the manufacture of useful products

See also 620.82 for human factors engineering

.62   Industrial microbiology

Class a specific aspect of industrial microbiology with the aspect, e.g., fermentation 660.28449, use of microorganisms in biochemical engineering 660.63

.63   Biochemical engineering

.634   Enzyme technology

.65   Genetic engineering

.7   **Industrial stoichiometry**

661   Technology of industrial chemicals

Production of chemicals used as raw materials or reagents in manufacture of other products

For industrial gases, see 665.7

SUMMARY

.001–.009   Standard subdivisions

> **661.03–661.08 Inorganic compounds**

Class acids, bases, salts in 661.2–661.6; class comprehensive works in 661

.03   Metallic compounds

Class here alkali and alkaline-earth compounds

Add to base number 661.03 the numbers following 546.3 in 546.38–546.39, e.g., sodium compounds 661.0382

For metallic compounds other than those of alkali and alkaline-earth metals, see 661.04–661.07

.04–.07   Other inorganic compounds

Add to base number 661.0 the numbers following 546 in 546.4–546.7, e.g., sulfur compounds 661.0723

For hydrogen compounds, see 661.08

.08   Hydrogen compounds

Including heavy water (deuterium oxide), hydrides

.1   Nonmetallic elements

For carbon, see 662.9; for gaseous elements, see 665.8

> **661.2 661.6 Acids, bases, salts**

Class organic acids, bases, salts in 661.8; class comprehensive works in 661

.2   Acids

.22   Sulfuric acid

.23   Hydrochloric acid

.24   Nitric acid

.25   Phosphoric acid

.3   Bases

Class here alkalis

.32	Sodas
.322	Caustic soda (Sodium hydroxide)
.323	Sodium bicarbonate
.324	Sodium carbonate
.33	Potassium alkalis
.332	Caustic potash (Potassium hydroxide)
.333	Potassium bicarbonate
.334	Potassium carbonate

Class here comprehensive works on potash

For a specific potash compound other than potassium carbonate, see the compound, e.g., caustic potash 661.332

.34	Ammonia and ammonium hydroxide

Standard subdivisions are added for ammonia and ammonium hydroxide together, for ammonia alone

.35	Other alkalis

Including hydroxides and carbonates of cesium, francium, lithium, rubidium, alkaline-earth metals

.4	**Salts**

For ammonium salts, see 661.5; for sulfur and nitrogen salts, see 661.6

.42	Halogen salts

Including chlorides, chlorites, chlorates, corresponding salts of other halogens

.43	Phosphorus and silicon salts

Including phosphides, phosphites, phosphates, corresponding salts of silicon

.5	**Ammonium salts**
.6	**Sulfur and nitrogen salts**

For ammonium salts, see 661.5

.63	Sulfur salts

Including sulfides, sulfites, sulfates

For plaster of paris, see 666.92

.65	Nitrogen salts

Including nitrides, nitrites, nitrates

.8	**Organic chemicals**
.800 1–.800 9	Standard subdivisions

>   661.802–661.804   Derived chemicals

       Class derived special-purpose chemicals in 661.806–661.808; class comprehensive works in 661.8

.802   Cellulose derivatives

.803   Coal tar chemicals

.804   Petrochemicals

       Industrial chemicals produced from petroleum or natural gas

       Class comprehensive works on petrochemicals in 665.538

       For a specific petrochemical, see the chemical, e.g., alcohols 661.82, carbon black 662.93

.805   Synthetic chemicals

>   661.806–661.808   Special-purpose chemicals

       Class comprehensive works in 661.8

.806   Essential oils

       Class essential oils used for manufacture of perfumes in 668.54

.807   Solvents, diluents, extenders

.808   Photographic chemicals and photosensitive surfaces

       Including sensitometry

       Class here comprehensive works on chemical engineering of organic and inorganic photographic chemicals

       For inorganic photographic chemicals, see 661.1–661.6

.81   Hydrocarbons

.814   Aliphatic hydrocarbons

.815   Alicyclic hydrocarbons

.816   Aromatic hydrocarbons

> 661.82–661.89 Compounds based on specific elements other than carbon

Add to each subdivision identified by * the numbers following 661.81 in 661.814–661.816, e.g., aliphatic esters 661.834

Unless other instructions are given, observe the following table of preference, e.g., phosphoric acids 661.87 (*not* 661.86):

Sulfur compounds	661.896
Phosphorus compounds	661.87
Silicon compounds	661.88
Organometallic compounds	661.895
Nitrogen compounds	661.894
Oxy and hydroxy compounds	661.82–661.86
Halogenated compounds	661.891

Class comprehensive works in 661.8

> 661.82–661.86 Oxy and hydroxy compounds

Class comprehensive works in 661.8

.82 *Alcohols and phenols

For glycerin, see 668.2

.83 *Esters

.84 *Ethers

.85 *Aldehydes and ketones

Subdivisions are added for either or both topics in heading

.86 *Acids

.87 *Phosphorus compounds

.88 *Silicon compounds

.89 Other organic compounds

.891 *Halogenated compounds

.894 *Nitrogen compounds

.895 *Organometallic compounds

.896 *Sulfur compounds

662 Technology of explosives, fuels, related products

.1 Fireworks (Pyrotechnics)

*Add as instructed under 661.82–661.89

.2 **Explosives**

Class nuclear explosives in 621.48

For fireworks, see 662.1

.26 Propellants

Including black powder (gunpowder), cordite, flashless and coated powders, nitrocellulose (guncotton), smokeless powder

Class here low (deflagrating) explosives

For rocket propellants, see 662.666

.27 High explosives

Including dynamite, PETN (pentaerythritol tetranitrate); primary explosives, e.g., mercury fulminate

.4 **Detonators**

Including boosters, firing mechanisms, fuses, percussion caps, primers

Class explosives used in detonators in 662.27

.5 **Matches**

.6 **Fuels**

Class industrial oils, fats, waxes, gases as fuels in 665

For a specific fuel not provided for here, see the fuel, e.g., nuclear fuels 621.48335, biomasss as fuel 662.88, petroleum 665.5

See also 621.4023 for combustion of fuels

See Manual at 622.22, 622.7 vs. 662.6, 669

.602 86 Green technology (Environmental technology)

Class wastes as fuels, comprehensive works on chemical technology of energy from waste materials in 662.87

.62 Coal

For coke, see 662.72

[.620 287] Testing and measurement

Do not use; class in 662.622

.622 Properties, tests, analysis

.622 09 History and biography

Do not use for properties, tests, analysis of coal from specific places; class in 662.6229

.622 1–.622 5 Properties, tests, analysis of specific types of coal

Add to base number 662.622 the numbers following 553.2 in 553.21–553.25, e.g., analysis of bituminous coal 662.6224

.622 9   Properties, tests, analysis of coal from specific places

> Add to base number 662.6229 notation 1–9 from Table 2, e.g., properties of Virginia coal 662.6229755

> Class specific types of coal regardless of place in 662.6221–662.6225

.623   Treatment of coal

> Including desulfurization, sizing, washing; conversion to slurry, slurry dewatering

.624   Storage, transportation, distribution of coal

.625   Uses of coal

> Including as a fuel, as a raw material

> Class a specific use with the use, e.g., metallurgical use 669.81

.65   Wood and wood derivatives

> Standard subdivisions are added for wood and wood derivatives together, for wood alone

> Including sawdust, wood briquettes

> *For charcoal, see 662.74*

.66   Synthetic fuels

> Class synthetic fuel gases in 665.77

.662   Synthetic petroleum

.662 2   Production of synthetic petroleum through hydrogenation and liquefaction of coal

> Including Bergius process

> Class production from coal gas in 662.6623

.662 3   Production of synthetic petroleum through hydrogenation of carbonaceous gases

> Including Fischer-Tropsch processes

.666   Rocket fuels (Rocket propellants)

> Liquid and solid

.669   Other liquid fuels

> Including benzene from waste products

.669 2   Alcohol as fuel

> Including ethanol, gasohol, methanol

.7   **Coke and charcoal**

.72   Coke

.74   Charcoal

.8   **Other fuels**

.82 Colloidal and mud fuels

.86 Boron fuels

.87 Wastes as fuels

Class here comprehensive works on the chemical technology of energy from waste materials

Class waste biomass as fuel in 662.88; class interdisciplinary works on energy from waste materials in 333.7938

For a specific form of energy from waste materials, see the form, e.g., benzene made from waste products 662.669

.88 Biomass as fuel

Including bagasse

Class here plant biomass as fuel, comprehensive works on the chemical technology of biomass as fuel

Class interdisciplinary works on biomass as fuel in 333.9539

For wood and wood derivatives as fuels, see 662.65; for biodiesel fuel, see 665.37

See also 665.776 for gases manufactured from biological wastes

.9 Nonfuel carbons

.92 Graphite and graphite products

Standard subdivisions are added for graphite and graphite products together, for graphite alone

.93 Adsorbent carbons

Including activated carbons, adsorbent charcoals, animal black, bone char, carbon black, decolorizing carbons, lampblack

663 Beverage technology

Commercial preparation, preservation, packaging

Class household preparation of beverages in 641.87; class interdisciplinary works on beverages in 641.2

.1 Alcoholic beverages

For wine, see 663.2; for brewed and malted beverages, see 663.3; for distilled liquor, see 663.5

.102 84 Apparatus and equipment

Do not use for materials; class in 663.11

.11 Materials

.12 Preliminary preparations

.13 Fermentation

.14 Packing

.15	Refrigeration and pasteurization
.16	Distillation
.17	Aging
.19	Bottling

.2   Wine

Class here grape wine, comprehensive works on white and red wine, comprehensive works on specific white and red wines (specific brands, estate wines)

See also 663.4 for mead; also 663.49 for rice wine

.200 1	Philosophy and theory
.200 2	Miscellany
.200 284	Apparatus and equipment

Do not use for materials; class in 663.201

.200 3–.200 9	Standard subdivisions
.201–.209	Materials, processes, operations

Add to base number 663.20 the numbers following 663.1 in 663.11–663.19, e.g., fermentation 663.203

.22	Kinds of grape wine

Including ice wine

[.220 1–.220 9]	Standard subdivisions

Do not use; class in 663.2001–663.2009

.222	White wine

Class here specific white wines (specific brands, estate wines, varietals)

Class comprehensive works on white and red wine in 663.2; class white ice wine in 663.22

For sparkling white wine, see 663.224; for fortified white wine, see 663.226

.223	Red wine

Class here specific red wines (specific brands, estate wines, varietals)

Class red ice wine in 663.22

For sparkling red wine, see 663.224; for fortified red wine, see 663.226

.223 2	Rosé wine

Class here specific rosé wines (specific brands, estate wines, varietals)

.224 Sparkling wine

Class here specific sparkling wines (specific brands, estate wines, varietals)

Class comprehensive works on white wine in 663.222; class comprehensive works on red wine in 663.223

.226 Fortified wine

Class here specific fortified wines (specific brands, estate wines, varietals)

Class comprehensive works on white wine in 663.222; class comprehensive works on red wine in 663.223

.29 Nongrape wine

Including fermented cider

.3 Brewed and malted beverages

Standard subdivisions are added for either or both topics in heading

For specific kinds of brewed and malted beverages, see 663.4

.302 84 Apparatus and equipment

Do not use for materials; class in 663.31

.31–.39 Materials, processes, operations

Add to base number 663.3 the numbers following 663.1 in 663.11–663.19, e.g., fermentation 663.33

.4 Specific kinds of brewed and malted beverages

Including mead (honey wine)

Class malt whiskey in 663.52

.42 Beer and ale

Standard subdivisions are added for either or both topics in heading

.49 Rice wine; pulque

Standard subdivisions are added for rice wine and pulque together, for rice wine alone

Class here specific kinds of rice wine

.5 Distilled liquor

Including mescal, potato whiskey, tequila, vodka

.500 1 Philosophy and theory

.500 2 Miscellany

.500 284 Apparatus and equipment

Do not use for materials; class in 663.501

.500 3–.500 9 Standard subdivisions

.501–.509	Materials, processes, operations

Add to base number 663.50 the numbers following 663.1 in 663.11–663.19, e.g., distillation 663.506

.52 Whiskey

Including bourbon

Class potato whiskey in 663.5

.53 Brandy

.55 Compound liquors

Distilled spirits flavored with various seeds, roots, leaves, flowers, fruits

Including cordials (liqueurs), gin

.59 Rum

.6 Nonalcoholic beverages

Including fruit drinks

For nonalcoholic brewed beverages, see 663.9; for milk, see 637.1

.61 Bottled drinking water

Including carbonated water

Class here potable mineral water

.62 Carbonated and mineralized beverages

Standard subdivisions are added for carbonated and mineralized beverages together, for carbonated beverages alone

Class carbonated and mineralized water in 663.61

.63 Fruit and vegetable juices

Standard subdivisions are added for fruit and vegetable juices together, for fruit juices alone

Class here drinks in which the principal ingredient is juice

Class fermented cider in 663.2; class fruit drinks in 663.6; class carbonated juices in 663.62

.64 Milk substitutes

Including coconut milk, nondairy coffee whiteners, soybean milk

.9 **Nonalcoholic brewed beverages**

Add to each subdivision identified by * as follows:
0284   Apparatus and equipment
                 Do not use for materials; class in 1
    1   Materials
    2   Preliminary preparations
    3   Fermentation and oxidation
    4   Firing, roasting, curing
    5   Blending
    7   Specific varieties
    8   Concentrates
    9   Packaging

.92   *Cocoa and chocolate

Subdivisions are added for either or both topics in heading

.93   *Coffee

.94   *Tea

.96   Herb teas

Including catnip, maté, sassafras

.97   Coffee substitutes

Including acorns, cereal preparations, chicory

664   Food technology

Commercial preparation, preservation, packaging

Class here comprehensive works on commercial food and beverage technology

Class household preservation, storage, cooking in 641.4–641.8; class interdisciplinary works on food in 641.3

For commercial processing of dairy and related products, see 637; for commercial beverage technology, see 663

SUMMARY

664.001–.009	Standard subdivisions
.01–.09	[Materials, processes, operations, by-products]
.1	Sugars, syrups, their derived products
.2	Starches and jellying agents
.3	Fats and oils
.4	Food salts
.5	Flavoring aids
.6	Special-purpose food and aids
.7	Grains, other seeds, their derived products
.8	Fruits and vegetables
.9	Meats and allied foods

.001   Philosophy and theory

*Add as instructed under 663.9

.001 15	Theory of communication and control
	Do not use for process control; class in 664.02
.001 5	Scientific principles
.001 579	Microorganisms, fungi, algae
	Class here food microbiology
.002	Miscellany
.002 84	Apparatus and equipment
	Do not use for materials; class in 664.01
[.002 87]	Testing and measurement
	Do not use; class in 664.07
.003–.009	Standard subdivisions
.01	Materials
	For additives, see 664.06
.02	Processes
	Class here process design, control, equipment
.022	Extraction
.023	Refining
.024	Manufacturing processes
	Not provided for elsewhere
	Including fermentation, food biotechnology, food processing with microorganisms
.028	Preservation techniques
	Class here interdisciplinary works on food preservation
	For home preservation of foods, see 641.4
.028 1	Preliminary treatment
	Including peeling
.028 2	Canning
.028 4	Drying and dehydrating
	Standard subdivisions are added for either or both topics in heading
.028 42	Drying and dehydrating by slow, thermal processes
.028 43	Drying and dehydrating through pulverizing and flaking
.028 45	Drying and dehydrating by freeze-drying
.028 5	Low-temperature preservation techniques
	For freeze-drying, see 664.02845

.028 52	Cold storage
.028 53	Deep freezing
.028 6	Chemical preservation

        Including brining, pickling, smoking

           For chemical preservation by use of additives, see 664.0287

.028 7	Chemical preservation by use of additives
.028 8	Irradiation
.06	Additives

        Production, properties, use

        Class flavoring aids in 664.5

           For chemical preservation by use of additives, see 664.0287

| .062 | Food colors |
| .07 | Tests, analyses, quality controls |

        For color, contaminants, flavor, odor, texture

        Including grading

        Class tests, analyses, quality controls of additives in 664.06

.072	Sensory evaluation of food
.08	By-products
.09	Packaging
.1	**Sugars, syrups, their derived products**

        Standard subdivisions are added for sugars, syrups, their derived products together; for sugars and syrups together; for sugars alone

        Class here sweeteners

           For artificial sweeteners, see 664.5

| .102 84 | Apparatus and equipment |

        Do not use for materials; class in 664.111

| [.102 87] | Testing and measurement |

        Do not use; class in 664.117

>   664.11–664.13 Sugars and syrups

        Class comprehensive works in 664.1

| .11 | Materials, techniques, processes, operations, by-products of sugars and syrups |

        Class materials, techniques, processes, operations, by-products of specific sugars and syrups in 664.12–664.13

.111	Materials
.112	Preliminary preparations
.113	Extraction and purification
.114	Concentration

Production of syrup

| .115 | Crystallization |

Production of sugar

| .116 | Additives |
| .117 | Tests, analyses, quality controls |

For color, contaminants, flavor, texture

Class tests, analyses, quality controls of additives in 664.116

| .118 | By-products |

Including molasses

Class utilization in 664.19

| .119 | Packaging |

> 664.12–664.13 Specific sugars and syrups

Class comprehensive works in 664.1

.12 Cane and beet sugar and syrup

Standard subdivisions are added for cane and beet sugar and syrup together, for cane and beet sugar alone

.122 Cane sugar and syrup

Standard subdivisions are added for cane sugar and syrup together, for cane sugar alone

.122 028 4 Apparatus and equipment

Do not use for materials; class in 664.1221

[.122 028 7] Testing and measurement

Do not use; class in 664.1227

.122 1–.122 9 Materials, processes, operations, by-products

Add to base number 664.122 the numbers following 664.11 in 664.111–664.119, e.g., cane molasses 664.1228

.123 Beet sugar and syrup

Standard subdivisions are added for beet sugar and syrup together, for beet sugar alone

.13 Other sugars and syrups

For honey, see 638.16

.132   Maple sugar and syrup

> Standard subdivisions are added for maple sugar and syrup together, for maple syrup alone

.133   Corn and sorghum sugars and syrups

.139   Jerusalem artichoke sugar and syrup

.15   Sugar products

.152   Jams, jellies, marmalades, preserves

> Standard subdivisions are added for any or all topics in heading

> *See also 664.26 for jellies (gelatin desserts)*

.153   Candy (Sweets)

> *See also 664.6 for chewing gum*

.19   By-product utilization

> Class a specific use with the use, e.g., molasses for rum 663.59

.2   Starches and jellying agents

> Standard subdivisions are added for starches and jellying agents together, for starches alone

---

>   664.22–664.23   Starches

> Class comprehensive works in 664.2

.22   Cornstarch and potato starch

.23   Cassava and arrowroot starches

.25   Jellying agents

> Class here pectin

> *For gelatin, see 664.26*

.26   Gelatin

.3   Fats and oils

> Class interdisciplinary works on animal fats and oils in 665.2; class interdisciplinary works on vegetable fats and oils in 665.3

> *For butter, see 637.2; for peanut butter, see 664.726*

.32   Margarine

.34   Lard

.36   Salad and cooking oils

.362   Olive oil

.363   Cottonseed oil

.368   Soy oil

.37   Salad dressings

> Including mayonnaise

.4   **Food salts**

> Including monosodium glutamate, table salt, tenderizers, sodium-free and other dietetic salts
>
> Class comprehensive works on commercial technology of food flavoring aids in 664.5

.5   **Flavoring aids**

> Including artificial sweeteners, chocolate, sugar substitutes
>
> Class here condiments
>
> Class flavoring aids in a specific kind of food with the kind of food, e.g., chocolate candies 664.153
>
> *For food salts, see 664.4. For a specific flavoring aid not provided for here, see the aid, e.g., sugar 664.1*

.52–.54   Essences and spices

> Add to base number 664.5 the numbers following 633.8 in 633.82–633.84, e.g., vanilla extract 664.52

.55   Vinegar

.58   Complex condiments

> Including catsup, chutney, miso, sauces
>
> Class salad dressings in 664.37

.6   **Special-purpose food and aids**

> Including chewing gum, snack food
>
> Class special-purpose flavoring aids in 664.5

>   664.62–664.66 Special-purpose food

> Class comprehensive works in 664.6. Class a specific food with the food, e.g., vegetables 664.8

.62   Baby food

.63   Low-calorie food

.64   Meatless high-protein food

> Including synthetic meat

.65   Complete dishes

> Including complete meals, packaged ingredients for complete recipes
>
> Class packaged ingredients for recipes based on a specific kind of food with the kind, e.g., mixes and prepared doughs for bakery goods 664.753

.66   Food for animals

            Class here pet food

            For animal feed made from grains and other seeds, see 664.76

.68   Leavening agents and baking aids

            Including baking powder, baking soda, cream of tartar, yeast

.7   **Grains, other seeds, their derived products**

            Class sugars and syrups from grain and other seeds in 664.13; class starches and jellying agents from grain and other seeds in 664.2; class fats and oils from grains and other seeds in 664.3

.72   Milling and milling products

            Standard subdivisions are added for milling and milling products together, for milling alone

            For animal feeds, see 664.76

.720 01   Philosophy and theory

.720 02   Miscellany

[.720 028 7]   Testing and measurement

                Do not use; class in 664.7204

.720 03–.720 09   Standard subdivisions

.720 1   Preliminary treatment

.720 3   Grinding and deflaking

.720 4   Sifting, grading, quality controls

.720 7   Products

            Including flour, meal, refined grain

            See also 664.7208 for by-products

.720 8   By-products

            Including bran, siftings

.720 9   Packaging

.722   Wheat

.722 7   Products

            See also 664.7228 for by-products

.722 72   Flour

.722 73   Meal

.722 8   By-products

            Including bran, siftings

.724	Corn

Variant names: Indian corn, maize

.725	Rice
.726	Nuts, legumes, other non-cereal seeds and their flours, meals, by-products

Including cottonseeds, sunflower seeds

Class comprehensive works on commercial processing of nuts in 664.8045; class comprehensive works on commercial processing of legumes in 664.80565

For salad and cooking oils, see 664.36

.75	Secondary products
.752	Bakery goods

Including crackers

Class mixes and prepared doughs for bakery goods in 664.753

.752 3	Breads

Including biscuits, quick breads

.752 5	Pastries

Including cakes, cookies (biscuits), pies

.753	Mixes and prepared doughs

Including biscuit, cake, pancake mixes

.755	Noodles and pastas

Standard subdivisions are added for either or both topics in heading

.756	Ready-to-eat cereals
.76	Animal feeds

Class comprehensive works on commercial processing of foods for animals in 664.66

.762	Cereal grains

Individual grains and mixtures

Class formula feeds in 664.768

.763	Other seeds

Individual seeds and mixtures

Class formula feeds in 664.768

.764	Cereal grain and seed mixtures
.768	Formula feeds

Cakes, flakes, granules, pellets, powders basically of cereal grains and other seeds and fortified with vitamins and minerals

.8   **Fruits and vegetables**

Class a specific product derived from fruits and vegetables with the product, e.g., jams 664.152, fats and oils 664.3

.800 1   Philosophy and theory

.800 2   Miscellany

[.800 287]   Testing and measurement

Do not use; class in 664.807

.800 3–.800 9   Standard subdivisions

.804   Specific fruits and groups of fruits

Add to base number 664.804 the numbers following 634 in 634.1–634.8, e.g., citrus fruits 664.804304, nuts 664.8045

.805   Specific vegetables and groups of vegetables

Add to base number 664.805 the numbers following 635 in 635.1–635.8, e.g., salad greens 664.8055

.806–.809   Additives, tests, analyses, quality controls, by-products, packaging

Add to base number 664.80 the numbers following 664.0 in 664.06–664.09, e.g., packaging vegetables 664.809

Class additives, tests, analyses, quality controls, by-products, packaging applied to specific fruits and groups of fruits in 664.804; class additives, tests, analyses, quality controls, by-products, packaging applied to specific vegetables and groups of vegetables in 664.805

See also 664.81–664.88 for preservation techniques

.81–.88   Preservation techniques

Add to base number 664.8 the numbers following 664.028 in 664.0281–664.0288, e.g., deep freezing fruits 664.853

Class preservation techniques applied to specific fruits and groups of fruits in 664.804; class preservation techniques applied to specific vegetables and groups of vegetables in 664.805

.9   **Meats and allied foods**

Standard subdivisions are added for meats and allied foods together, for meats alone

.900 1   Philosophy and theory

.900 2   Miscellany

[.900 287]   Testing and measurement

Do not use; class in 664.907

.900 3–.900 9   Standard subdivisions

.902   Preservation techniques, slaughtering, meat cutting

.902 8		Preservation techniques

Add to base number 664.9028 the numbers following 664.028 in 664.0281–664.0288, e.g., canning 664.90282

.902 9   Slaughtering and meat cutting

Standard subdivisions are added for either or both topics in heading

.906–.909   Additives, tests, analyses, quality controls, by-products, packaging

Add to base number 664.90 the numbers following 664.0 in 664.06–664.09, e.g., packaging meats and allied foods 664.909

Class additives, tests, analyses, quality controls, by-products, packaging applied to specific meats or allied foods with the meat or food, e.g., packaging red meats 664.9299

See also 664.9028 for preservation techniques

.92   Red meat

[.920 287]   Testing and measurement

Do not use; class in 664.9297

.921–.928   Preservation techniques

Add to base number 664.92 the numbers following 664.028 in 664.0281–664.0288, e.g., canning red meat 664.922
Subdivisions are added for specific red meats, e.g., canning beef 664.922

.929   Additives, tests, analyses, quality controls, by-products, packaging

Add to base number 664.929 the numbers following 664.0 in 664.06–664.09, e.g., packaging red meat 664.9299
Subdivisions are added for specific red meats, e.g., packaging beef 664.9299

See also 664.921–664.928 for preservation techniques

.93   Poultry

[.930 287]   Testing and measurement

Do not use; class in 664.9397

.931–.938   Preservation techniques

Add to base number 664.93 the numbers following 664.028 in 664.0281–664.0288, e.g., deep freezing 664.9353
Subdivisions are added for specific kinds of poultry, e.g., deep freezing turkeys 664.9353

.939   Additives, tests, analyses, quality controls, by-products, packaging

Add to base number 664.939 the numbers following 664.0 in 664.06–664.09, e.g., poultry by-products 664.9398
Subdivisions are added for specific kinds of poultry, e.g., turkey by-products 664.9398

See also 664.931–664.938 for preservation techniques

.94   Fishes and shellfish

Standard subdivisions are added for fish and shellfish together, for fishes alone

Class here seafood

[.940 287]   Testing and measurement

Do not use; class in 664.9497

.941–.948   Preservation techniques

Add to base number 664.94 the numbers following 664.028 in 664.0281–664.0288, e.g., canning seafood 664.942
Subdivisions are not added for specific kinds of fishes and shellfish, e.g., canning oysters 664.94 (*not* 664.942)

.949   Additives, tests, analyses, quality controls, by-products, packaging

Add to base number 664.949 the numbers following 664.0 in 664.06–664.09, e.g., quality controls for seafood 664.9497
Subdivisions are not added for specific kinds of fishes and shellfish, e.g., quality controls for catfish 664.94 (*not* 664.9497)

See also 664.941–664.948 for preservation techniques

.95   Other meats and allied foods

Including frogs, turtles, snails, insects

665   Technology of industrial oils, fats, waxes, gases

SUMMARY

665.028	**Techniques, procedures, apparatus, equipment, materials**
.1	**Waxes**
.2	**Animal fats and oils**
.3	**Vegetable fats and oils**
.4	**Mineral oils and waxes**
.5	**Petroleum**
.7	**Natural gas and manufactured gases**
.8	**Other industrial gases**

.028   Auxiliary techniques and procedures; apparatus, equipment, materials

Notation 028 from Table 1 as modified below

Class here basic techniques and procedures

.028 2   Extraction

Including pressurizing, rendering, steam distilling

.028 3   Refining

Including bleaching, blending, coloring, fractionating, purifying

.028 7   Maintenance and repair

Do not use for testing and measurement; class in 665.0288

.028 8   Tests, analyses, quality controls

> Do not use for maintenance and repair; class in 665.0287

.1   **Waxes**

> Class polishing waxes in 667.72
>
> *For mineral waxes, see 665.4*

.12   Vegetable waxes

> Including bayberry, candleberry, carnauba, laurel, myrtle waxes

.13   Animal waxes

> Including lanolin (wool wax), spermaceti
>
> *For beeswax, see 638.17*

.19   Blended waxes

.2   **Animal fats and oils**

> Standard subdivisions are added for either or both topics in heading
>
> Including fish, neat's-foot, whale oils; tallow; biodiesel fuel from animal fats and oils
>
> Class here interdisciplinary works on animal fats and oils
>
> Class comprehensive works on biodiesel fuel in 665.37
>
> *For animal fats and oils used in food or food preparation, see 664.3*
>
> *See also 665.13 for spermaceti*

.3   **Vegetable fats and oils**

> Class here interdisciplinary works on vegetable fats and oils
>
> Class interdisciplinary works on specific vegetable oils used primarily as food with the vegetable oil in 641.3, e.g., olive oil 641.3463
>
> *For the food technology of vegetable fats and oils used in food and food preparation, see 664.3*

.33   Wood oil

> Class here comprehensive works on naval stores
>
> *For a specific kind of naval store, see the kind, e.g., pitch 665.5388*

.332   Crude turpentine

> Class turpentine oils in 661.806

.333   Tung oil (Chinese wood oil)

.35   Seed oils

> Class biodiesel fuel in 665.37
>
> *For tung oil, see 665.333*

.352   Linseed oil (Flaxseed oil)

.353   Castor oil

.354   Cocoa butter (Cacao butter)

.355   Coconut oil

.37   Biodiesel fuel

> Class here comprehensive works on biodiesel fuel
>
> *For biodiesel fuel from animal fats and oils, see 665.2*

.4   Mineral oils and waxes

> Including natural asphalt, shale oil, tar sand
>
> *For petroleum, see 665.5*

.5   Petroleum

> Class here comprehensive works on technology of petroleum and natural gas
>
> Class synthetic petroleum in 662.662
>
> *For technology of extraction of petroleum and natural gas, see 622.338; for comprehensive works on technology of natural gas, see 665.7*

.53   Refinery treatment and products

> Standard subdivisions are added for refinery treatment and products together, for refinery treatment alone
>
> Class preliminary refining of oil sands and oil shale to obtain distillable fluids in 665.4

.530 286   Green technology (Environmental technology)

> Do not use for pollution control technology, waste technology; class in 665.5389

.532   Fractional distillation

.533   Cracking processes

> Including thermal and catalytic cracking, hydrogenation of residual petroleum distillates

.534   Purification and blending of distillates

.538   Refinery products and by-products

> Including waste products
>
> Class here petrochemicals
>
> *For petrochemicals as a type of industrial chemical, see 661.804*

.538 2   Highly volatile products

.538 24   Naphthas

.538 25   Aviation fuel

> Including high-octane-rating gasoline, jet and turbojet fuel
>
> Class interdisciplinary works on gasoline in 665.53827

.538 27   Gasoline

> *For high-octane-rating gasoline, see 665.53825*

.538 3   Kerosene

> *For jet and turbojet fuel, see 665.53825*

.538 4   Heavy fuel oil

> Including absorber oil, diesel fuel, gas oil, heating oil

> *See also 665.37 for biodiesel fuel*

.538 5   Lubricating oil and grease

> Including paraffin wax and petrolatum

.538 8   Residues (Bottoms)

> Including asphalt, bunker and road oils, petroleum coke, pitch

> Class unusable residues (wastes) in 665.538; class asphalt concrete in 666.893

.538 9   Waste control

> Class here pollution control

.54   Storage, transportation, distribution

.542   Storage

.543   Transportation

> Including transportation by tankers

> *For pipeline transportation, see 665.544*

.544   Pipeline transportation

.55   Uses

> Class a specific use with the use, e.g., automobile engine lubricants 629.255

.7   Natural gas and manufactured gases

> Standard subdivisions are added for natural gas and manufactured gases together, for natural gas alone

> Class here comprehensive works on technology of industrial gases

> *For technology of extracting natural gas, see 622.3385; for technology of industrial gases not provided for here, see 665.8*

.702 86   Green technology (Environmental technology)

> Class production of manufactured gases from biological wastes in 665.776

.73   Processing natural gas

> Including extraction of helium

.74 Storage, transportation, distribution of natural gas and manufactured gases

>Standard subdivisions are added for natural gas, manufactured gases, or both

.742 Storage

>Standard subdivisions are added for natural gas, manufactured gases, or both

.743 Transportation

>Standard subdivisions are added for natural gas, manufactured gases, or both

>*For pipeline transportation, see 665.744*

.744 Pipeline transportation

>Standard subdivisions are added for natural gas, manufactured gases, or both

.75 Uses of natural gas and manufactured gases

>Standard subdivisions are added for either or both topics in heading

>Class a specific use with the use, e.g., heating buildings 697.043

.77 Production of manufactured gases

>Class here comprehensive works on technology of manufactured gases

>*For storage, transportation, distribution, see 665.74; for uses, see 665.75*

.772 Production of manufactured gases from coal and coke

>Including blast-furnace, carbureted-blue, city, coke-oven, producer, water gases

>Class here coal gasification

.773 Production of manufactured gases from petroleum and natural gas

>Including oil, refinery, reformed natural, reformed refinery, liquefied petroleum gases, e.g., butane, butene, pentane, propane, and their mixtures

.776 Production of manufactured gases from biological wastes

>Class here biogas

.779 Production of manufactured gases by mixing fuel gases from several sources

.8 Other industrial gases

>*For ammonia, see 661.34*

.81 Hydrogen

.82 Gases derived from liquefaction and fractionation of air

.822   Noble gases

> Variant names: inert, rare gases
>
> Including argon, helium, krypton, neon, radon, xenon
>
> Class extraction of helium from natural gases in 665.73

.823   Oxygen

.824   Nitrogen

.83   Halogen gases

.84   Sulfur dioxide

.85   Acetylene

.89   Carbon dioxide, ozone, hydrogen sulfide

666   Ceramic and allied technologies

Standard subdivisions are added for ceramic and allied technologies together, for ceramic technologies alone

SUMMARY

666.04		**Special topics of ceramic and allied technologies**
.1		**Glass**
.2		**Enamels**
.3		**Pottery**
.4		**Pottery materials, equipment, processes**
.5		**Porcelain**
.6		**Earthenware and stoneware**
.7		**Refractories and structural clay products**
.8		**Synthetic and artificial minerals and building materials**
.9		**Masonry adhesives**

.04   Special topics of ceramic and allied technologies

.042   Ceramic-to-metal bonding

.1   Glass

[.102 8]   Auxiliary techniques and procedures

> Do not use; class in 666.13

[.102 84]   Apparatus, equipment, materials

> Do not use; class in 666.12

.102 86   Green technology (Environmental technology)

> Do not use for pollution control technology, waste technology; class in 666.14

.104   Special topics of glass

.104 2   Physicochemical phenomena occurring during glassmaking processes

> Including phase and structural transformations

> 666.12–666.14 General topics of glass

> Class general topics of specific types of glass in 666.15; class general topics of products in 666.19; class comprehensive works in 666.1

.12 Techniques, procedures, apparatus, equipment, materials

For auxiliary techniques and procedures, see 666.13

.121 Materials

> 666.122–666.129 Specific operations in glassmaking

> Class tests, analyses, quality controls in 666.137; class comprehensive works in 666.12

.122 Blowing

.123 Pressing

.124 Drawing

.125 Molding and casting

Standard subdivisions are added for either or both topics in heading

.126 Multiform processes

Cold-molding glass powder under pressure, and firing at high temperatures

.129 Annealing and tempering

.13 Auxiliary techniques and procedures

Add to base number 666.13 the numbers following —028 in notation 0285–0289 from Table 1, e.g., quality control in glassmaking 666.137; however, for waste technology, see 666.14

.14 Waste technology

Including recycling

Class here pollution control

Class recycling a specific type of glass or glass product with the type of glass or product, e.g., recycling bottles 666.192

.15 Specific types of glass

See also 669.94 for metallic glass

.152 Window glass

Sheet glass that differs from plate glass primarily in being annealed more quickly and in not being ground and polished

.153 Plate glass

Class laminated plate glass in 666.154

.154 Laminated glass

.155	Heat-resistant glass
.156	Optical glass
.157	Fiber glass and foam glass

> Class fiberglasss-reinforced plastic in 668.4942

.19	Products
.192	Bottles and jars

> Standard subdivisions are added for either or both topics in heading

.2   Enamels

.3   Pottery

> Class here comprehensive works on clay technology
>
> Class pottery limited to earthenware or stoneware in 666.6
>
> *For techniques and procedures, see 666.44; for specific types of pottery, see 666.5–666.6; for structural clay products, see 666.73*

[.301–.309]   Standard subdivisions

> Do not use; class in 666.31–666.39

.31–.39   Standard subdivisions

> Add to base number 666.3 the numbers following —0 in notation 01–09 from Table 1, e.g., auxiliary techniques and procedures 666.328; however, for apparatus, equipment, materials, see 666.4

.4   Pottery materials, equipment, processes

> Add to base number 666.4 the numbers following 738.1 in 738.12–738.15, e.g., kilns 666.436

.44   Techniques and procedures

> Number built according to instructions under 666.4
>
> *For auxiliary techniques and procedures, see 666.328*
>
> auxiliary techniques and procedures relocated to 666.328

> **666.5–666.6 Specific types of pottery**
>
> Class comprehensive works in 666.3

.5   Porcelain

.58   Specific products

> Including figurines, tableware, vases

.6   Earthenware and stoneware

> Standard subdivisions are added for either or both topics in heading

.68	Specific products

Including containers, figurines, industrial products, tableware

.7   Refractories and structural clay products

.72	Refractory materials

Including alumina, asbestos, chrome, fireclays, mica, talc, zirconia

.73	Structural clay products
.732	Roofing tiles
.733	Tile drains and piping
.737	Bricks

For hollow and perforated bricks, see 666.738

.738	Hollow and perforated bricks

.8   Synthetic and artificial minerals and building materials

.86	Synthetic and artificial minerals

Standard subdivisions are added for either or both topics in heading

Including cryolite, feldspar, graphite, mica

For synthetic and artificial gems, see 666.88

.88	Synthetic and artificial gems

Standard subdivisions are added for either or both topics in heading

Including diamonds, garnets, rubies, sapphires

.89	Synthetic building materials

Including drywall

For structural clay products, see 666.73

.893	Concrete

Including asphalt concrete, ready-mix concrete

Class concrete blocks in 666.894

.894	Hollow concrete and cinder blocks

Class here interdisciplinary works on concrete blocks

For solid concrete blocks, see 666.895

.895	Solid concrete blocks

.9   Masonry adhesives

Class concrete in 666.893

.92	Gypsum plasters

Including Keene's cement, plaster of paris

.93   Lime mortars

.94   Portland cement

> Class here comprehensive works on cement

> *For Keene's cement, see 666.92; for other cements, see 666.95*

.95   Other cements

> Including high-alumina cement, magnesia

667   Cleaning, color, coating, related technologies

> Standard subdivisions are added for cleaning, color, coating, related technologies together; for color technology alone

.1   Cleaning and bleaching

> Of textiles, leathers, furs, feathers

> Class household bleaching, cleaning, laundry in 648

.12   Dry cleaning

> Including manufacture of dry-cleaning materials

.13   Laundering and finishing operations

> *For soaps, see 668.12; for detergents, see 668.14*

.14   Bleaching

> Including manufacture of bleaching materials

.2   Dyes and pigments

> Standard subdivisions are added for dyes and pigments together, for dyes alone

> Including stains

>   667.25–667.26   Dyes

> Class comprehensive works in 667.2

.25   Synthetic dyes

.252   Nitro and nitroso dyes

.253   Azo-oxy and azo-tetrazo dyes

.254   Diphenylmethane and triphenylmethane dyes

.256   Hydroxyketone dyes

> Including alizarines, quinoidals

.257   Indigoid dyes

> *See also 667.26 for indigo*

.26   Natural dyes

> Including indigo

.29	Pigments

.3 Dyeing and printing

Standard subdivisions are added for dyeing and printing together, for dyeing alone

Class here dyeing and printing of textiles, of textile fibers

Class dyeing and printing of a specific material not provided for here with the material, e.g., dyeing leather 675.25

For dyes, see 667.25–667.26

See also 686.2 for printing of books and related products

.31–.35	Dyeing specific textiles

Add to base number 667.3 the numbers following 677 in 677.1–677.5, e.g., dyeing nylon 667.3473

.38	Textile printing

.4 Inks

For printing ink, see 667.5

.5 Printing ink

.6 Paints and painting

Standard subdivisions are added for either or both topics in heading

Including paint removers, sign painting

.62	Oil-soluble paint
.622	Oils, driers, plasticizers
.623	Pigments and extenders

For carbon black, see 662.93

.624	Diluents (Thinners)
.63	Water-soluble paint

Including latex paint, whitewash

.69	Special-purpose paints

Including fire-resistant, luminous, rust-resistant paints

.7 Polishes, lacquers, varnishes

Class here methods of applying polishes, lacquers, varnishes

.72	Polishes and polishing

Standard subdivisions are added for either or both topics in heading

.75   Lacquers and lacquering

     Standard subdivisions are added for either or both topics in heading

     Including japans, japanning [*both formerly* 667.8]

.79   Varnishes and varnishing

     Standard subdivisions are added for either or both topics in heading

     Including shellac, spar varnish

     Class here spirit varnishes

        For lacquers and lacquering, see 667.75

[.8]   **Japans and japanning**

     Relocated to 667.75

.9   **Coatings and coating**

     Standard subdivisions are added for either or both topics in heading

     Comprehensive works on methods and materials for producing protective and decorative coatings

        For a coating made of a specific material, see the material, e.g., enamel coatings 666.2, thermoset plastic coatings 668.422; for methods of applying a specific kind of coating, see the kind of coating, e.g., painting 667.6; for coatings applied to a specific thing and methods of applying the coatings, see the thing to which the coating is applied, e.g., coatings for metal 671.73, metal coatings for polymers 668.9, painting a building 698.1, varnishing a violin 787.21923

668   Technology of other organic products

SUMMARY

668.1	**Surface-active agents (Surfactants)**
.2	**Glycerin**
.3	**Adhesives and related products**
.4	**Plastics**
.5	**Perfumes and cosmetics**
.6	**Agricultural chemicals**
.9	**Polymers and polymerization**

.1   **Surface-active agents (Surfactants)**

.12   Soaps

.124   Soluble soaps

     Including liquid concentrates, powders

.125   Insoluble soaps (Metallic soaps)

     Including oleates and stearates of aluminum

.127   Scouring compounds

.14   Detergents and wetting agents

> Nonsoap materials that manifest surface activity
>
> Standard subdivisions are added for detergents and wetting agents together, for detergents alone
>
> Including fatty-alcohol sulfates, sulfated oils and hydrocarbons

.2   **Glycerin**

.3   **Adhesives and related products**

> Standard subdivisions are added for adhesives and related products together, for adhesives alone
>
> *For masonry adhesives, see 666.9*

> 668.31–668.37   Specific kinds of adhesives

> Class products made from specific kinds of adhesives in 668.38; class comprehensive works in 668.3

.31   Synthetic glue

.32   Animal glue

> Including casein glue

.33   Vegetable glue

> Including mucilage
>
> *See also 668.37 for gum*

.34   Crude gelatin

.37   Gum and resin

> Standard subdivisions are added for either or both topics in heading

.372   Natural gum and resin

> Standard subdivisions are added for either or both topics in heading
>
> *See also 668.33 for mucilage*

.374   Synthetic gum and resin

> Standard subdivisions are added for either or both topics in heading
>
> Including epoxy resin

.38   Products made from adhesives

> Including tape
>
> Class here sealants

.4   **Plastics**

[.402 8]   Auxiliary techniques and procedures; apparatus, equipment, materials

> Do not use; class in 668.41

.404   Special topics of plastics

.404 2   Physicochemical phenomena of plastics manufacture

.41   Techniques, procedures, apparatus, equipment, materials

> Class application to specific kinds of plastics in 668.42–668.45; class application to forms and products in 668.49

.411   Materials

> Including fillers, plasticizers

\>   668.412–668.419 Specific operations

Class comprehensive works in 668.41

.412   Molding and casting

> Standard subdivisions are added for either or both topics in heading

.413   Extrusion

.414   Laminating

.415   Welding

.416   Reinforcing

.419   Auxiliary techniques and procedures

.419 2   Waste technology

> Class here pollution control

.419 5–.419 9   Miscellaneous auxiliary techniques and procedures

> Add to base number 668.419 the numbers following —028 in notation 0285–0289 from Table 1, e.g., quality control in plastics manufacture 668.4197; however, for waste technology, see 668.4192

\>   668.42–668.45 Specific kinds of plastics

Class forms and products of specific kinds of plastics in 668.49; class comprehensive works in 668.4

.42   Polymerization plastics

.422   Thermosetting plastics

.422 2   Phenolics

.422 3   Ureas

.422 4   Melamines

.422 5   Polyesters

> Including polyurethanes
>
> Class interdisciplinary works on polyurethanes in 668.4239

.422 6   Epoxies

.422 7		Silicones
.423		Thermoplastic plastics

Including acetals, acetates, butyrates, polycarbonates, polyethers

.423 2		Acrylics (Polyacrylics)
.423 3		Styrenes (Polystyrenes)
.423 4		Polyolefins

Including polyethylenes, polyisobutylenes, polypropylenes

.423 5		Polyamides (Nylons)
.423 6		Vinyls (Polyvinyls)
.423 7		Vinylidene chlorides
.423 8		Polyfluoro hydrocarbons
.423 9		Polyurethanes

Class here interdisciplinary works on polyurethanes

For thermosetting polyurethanes, see 668.4225; for polyurethane rubber, see 678.72

.43   Protein plastics

Including plastics derived from casein

.44   Cellulosics

Including celluloid

.45   Plastics from natural resins

Including lignin-derived plastics

For protein plastics, see 668.43

.49   Forms and products

Class plastic fibers and fabrics in 677.4

> 668.492–668.495 Specific forms

Class comprehensive works in 668.49

.492   Laminated plastic

.493   Plastic foams

Including structural foam

.494   Reinforced plastic

.494 2   Glass-reinforced plastic

Class here fiberglass-reinforced plastic

.495   Plastic films

.497   Containers

.5   **Perfumes and cosmetics**

.54   Perfumes

.542   Natural perfumes

                 Including floral oils and waters; potpourris

.544   Synthetic perfumes

.55   Cosmetics

.6   **Agricultural chemicals**

.62   Fertilizers

                 Add to base number 668.62 the numbers following 631.8 in 631.83–631.85, e.g., superphosphates 668.625

                 For organic fertilizers, see 668.63

.63   Organic fertilizers

                 Add to base number 668.63 the numbers following 631.8 in 631.86–631.87, e.g., manufacture of fertilizers from animal wastes 668.636, converting household garbage 668.6375

.64   Soil conditioners

                 Manufactured and organic

.65   Pesticides

                 Interdisciplinary works on pesticides relocated to 632.95

.651   Insecticides, rodenticides, vermicides

.652   Fungicides and algicides

.653   Bactericides

.654   Herbicides (Weed killers)

.9   **Polymers and polymerization**

                 Standard subdivisions are added for polymers and polymerization together, for polymers alone

                 Class here synthetic polymers

                 Class a specific application with the application, e.g., manufacture of nylon hosiery 687.3; class a specific polymer with the polymer, e.g., plastics 668.4

.92   Polymerization

669 Metallurgy

Class here alloys, extractive metallurgy, process metallurgy, interdisciplinary works on metals

For a specific aspect of metals, see the aspect, e.g., chemistry 546.3, metalworking and primary metal products 671

See Manual at 669; also at 622.22, 622.7 vs. 662.6, 669

SUMMARY

669.01–.09	**Standard subdivisions and special topics of metallurgy**
.1	**Ferrous metals**
.2	**Precious and group 3 metals**
.3	**Copper**
.4	**Lead**
.5	**Zinc and cadmium**
.6	**Tin**
.7	**Other nonferrous metals**
.8	**Metallurgical furnace technology**
.9	**Physical and chemical metallurgy**

.028   Auxiliary techniques and procedures; apparatus, equipment

Notation 028 from Table 1 as modified below

.028 2   Pyrometallurgy

Extraction by furnace methods, e.g., smelting

Class electrical zone melting in 669.0284

.028 3   Hydrometallurgy

Extraction by leaching methods

.028 4   Electrometallurgy

Do not use for apparatus and equipment; class in 669.028. Do not use for materials; class in 669.042

Including electrical zone melting, vacuum metallurgy

Class here electrorefining, electrowinning

.04   Special topics of metallurgy

.042   Materials

Class here prepared ores and scrap metals

Class furnace materials in 669.8

> **669.1–669.7 Metallurgy of specific metals and their alloys**

Class comprehensive works in 669

For physical and chemical metallurgy of specific metals and their alloys, see 669.96

.1   **Ferrous metals**

.14	Reduction and refining of ferrous ores

Class comprehensive works on production of iron and steel in 669.1

[.140 1–.140 9]	Standard subdivisions

Do not use; class in 669.101–669.109

.141	Production of iron

For production of ingot iron, see 669.1423

.141 3	Blast-furnace practice

Class here casting as a part of the refining process, production of pig iron and crude cast iron

Class iron casting as a metalworking process in 672.25; class cast iron products in 672.8

.141 4	Puddling furnace practice

Class here production of wrought iron

.142	Production of steel

Class here stainless steel

.142 2	Open-hearth furnace practice (Siemens process)
.142 3	Bessemer converter practice

Including production of duplex-process steel, ingot iron

.142 4	Electric furnace practice

Including arc furnace practice

.142 9	Production of crucible steel

> ### 669.2–669.7 Nonferrous metals

Class comprehensive works in 669

.2	**Precious and group 3 metals**

Standard subdivisions are added for precious and group 3B metals together, for precious metals alone

---

> 669.22–669.24 Precious metals

Class comprehensive works in 669.2

.22	Gold
.23	Silver
.24	Platinum
.29	Group 3 metals
.290 01–.290 09	Standard subdivisions

.290 1	Scandium
.290 3	Yttrium
.291–.294	Rare earth elements (Lanthanide series) and actinide series

> Add to base number 669.29 the numbers following 546.4 in
> 546.41–546.44, e.g., rare earth elements 669.291, actinide series metals
> 669.292, uranium 669.2931

.3 Copper

> Class here brass, Muntz metal; bronze, gunmetal; copper-aluminum alloys;
> copper-beryllium alloys

.4 Lead

.5 Zinc and cadmium

.52	Zinc

> *For brass, Muntz metal, see 669.3*

.56	Cadmium

.6 Tin

> *For bronze, gunmetal, see 669.3*

.7 Other nonferrous metals

> Including iridium, osmium, palladium, rhodium, ruthenium; rhenium

> *See also 669.24 for platinum*

.71	Mercury
.72	Light, alkali, alkaline-earth metals

> Standard subdivisions are added for light, alkali, alkaline-earth metals
> together; for light metals alone

> *For titanium, see 669.7322; for zirconium, see 669.735*

.722	Aluminum

> *For copper-aluminum alloys, see 669.3*

.723	Magnesium
.724	Beryllium

> *For copper-beryllium alloys, see 669.3*

.725	Alkali and alkaline-earth metals

> Including barium, calcium, cesium, francium, lithium, potassium,
> radium, rubidium, sodium, strontium

> *For magnesium, see 669.723; for beryllium, see 669.724*

.73	Metals used in ferroalloys
.732	Titanium, vanadium, manganese

.732 2	Titanium
.733	Nickel and cobalt
.733 2	Nickel
.734	Chromium, molybdenum, tungsten
.735	Zirconium and tantalum
.75	Antimony, arsenic, bismuth
.79	Miscellaneous rare metals and metalloids

> Limited to gallium, hafnium, indium, niobium, polonium, thallium; germanium, selenium, tellurium

.8   **Metallurgical furnace technology**

> Class metallurgical furnace technology used for a specific metal with the metal, e.g., nickel 669.7332

.802 8	Auxiliary techniques and procedures; apparatus, equipment, materials

> Do not use for refractory material; class in 669.82

.81	Fuel
.82	Refractory material

> Class comprehensive works on technology of refractory materials in 666.72

.83	Firing and heat control
.84	Fluxes and slag
.85	Physical processes

> Including heat exchange

.9   **Physical and chemical metallurgy**

> Standard subdivisions are added for either or both topics in heading

> Physical and chemical phenomena occurring during metallurgical processes; physical and chemical analyses of metals; formation of alloys

> Class metalworking and manufacture of primary metal products in 671–673

.92	Chemical analysis

> Including assaying

> Class chemical analysis of specific metals and their alloys in 669.96

.94	Physicochemical metallurgical phenomena

> Including alloy binary systems, intermetallic compounds, metallic glass, solid solutions, solidification; phase diagrams

> Class physicochemical metallurgical phenomena of specific metals and their alloys in 669.96

.95	Metallography

.950 28	Specific kinds of techniques and procedures; apparatus, equipment, materials
.950 282	Microscopical metallography
	Optical and electron metallography
.950 283	X-ray metallography
.951–.957	Metallography of specific metals and their alloys

> Add to base number 669.95 the numbers following 669 in 669.1–669.7, e.g., aluminum 669.95722

.96	Physical and chemical metallurgy of specific metals and their alloys

> Add to base number 669.96 the numbers following 669 in 669.1–669.7, e.g., titanium 669.967322

> *For metallography of specific metals and their alloys, see 669.951–669.957*

670 Manufacturing

Including planning and design for manufactured products

Class here manufactured products

Class military applications in 623; class planning and design for specific kinds of products in 671–679; class the arts in 700. Class comprehensive works on products made by a specific process with the process, e.g., seasoned wood 674.38; however, if a specific provision is made for the product, class with the product, e.g., coated papers 676.283 (*not* 676.235)

> *For manufacture of products based on specific branches of engineering, see 620; for manufacture of products based on chemical technologies, see 660; for manufacture of final products for specific uses not provided for elsewhere, see 680*

> *See Manual at T1—025 vs. T1—029*

SUMMARY

670.1–.9	Standard subdivisions and special topics of manufacturing
671	Metalworking processes and primary metal products
672	Iron, steel, other iron alloys
673	Nonferrous metals
674	Lumber processing, wood products, cork
675	Leather and fur processing
676	Pulp and paper technology
677	Textiles
678	Elastomers and elastomer products
679	Other products of specific kinds of materials

.285   Computer applications

Class here computer-aided design / computer-aided manufacture (CAD/CAM), computer integrated manufacturing systems (CIM), comprehensive works on computer use in the management of manufacturing and computer-aided design or computer-aided manufacture

Class computer-aided design (CAD) in 620.00420285; class computer use in the management of manufacturing in 658.05

For computer-aided manufacture (CAM), flexible manufacturing systems limited to factory operations, see 670.427

.4   Special topics of manufacturing

.42   Factory operations engineering

Class here shop and assembly-line technology

For tools and fabricating equipment, see 621.9; for packaging technology, see 688.8

[.420 685]   Management of factory operations

Do not use; class in 658.5

.423   Machine-shop practice

.425   Inspection technology

.427   Mechanization and automation of factory operations

Standard subdivisions are added for either or both topics in heading

Class here assembling machines, computer control of factory operations; computer-aided manufacture (CAM), flexible manufacturing systems if limited to factory operations

Class computer-aided design (CAD) in 620.00420285; class computer-aided design / computer-aided manufacture (CAD/CAM), computer integrated manufacturing systems (CIM), computer-aided manufacture (CAM), flexible manufacturing systems if applied to design and production of manufactured products in 670.285; class automated machine-shop practice in 670.423; class automated inspection technology in 670.425; class comprehensive works on computer control in 629.89

.427 2   Robots

Unless it is redundant, add to base number 670.4272 the numbers following 00 in 004–006, e.g., use of digital personal computers 670.4272416, but use of digital computers 670.4272 (*not* 670.42724)

.427 5   Computerized process control

Unless it is redundant, add to base number 670.4275 the numbers following 00 in 004–006, e.g., use of digital personal computers 670.4275416, but use of digital computers 670.4275 (*not* 670.42754)

Class comprehensive works on computerized process control in 629.895

[.685]   Management of production

Do not use; class in 658.5

> ## 671–679 Manufacture of products from specific materials

Class here manufacture of primary products

Class comprehensive works in 670

For manufacture of ceramic products, see 666; for manufacture of plastic products, see 668.49

See Manual at 671–679 vs. 680

671 Metalworking processes and primary metal products

Standard subdivisions are added for metalworking processes and primary metal products together, for metalworking processes alone

Class metallurgy and interdisciplinary works on metals in 669

For metalworking processes and primary metal products with iron, steel, other iron alloys as the main metal, see 672; for metalworking processes and primary metal products with nonferrous metals as the main metal, see 673

> ### 671.2–671.7 Specific metalworking processes

Class specific processes applied to specific primary products in 671.8; class comprehensive works in 671

.2   **Founding (Casting)**

See also 671.3 for hot-working operations

.202 84   Materials

Do not use for apparatus and equipment; class in 671.22

.22   Foundry equipment

.23   Patternmaking and moldmaking

.24   Melting

.25   Specific methods of casting

.252   Sand casting

.253   Permanent-mold casting

Including die casting

.254   Centrifugal casting

.255   Investment casting

Variant names: cire perdue, lost-wax, precision casting

Including lost-foam casting

.256   Continuous casting

.3	**Mechanical working and related processes**

Standard subdivisions are added for mechanical working and related processes together, for mechanical working alone

Class here hot-working operations, cold-working operations, high-energy forming

For small forge work, see 682

.32	Rolling
.33	Forging, pressing, stamping
.332	Forging
.334	Stamping
.34	Extruding and drawing
.35	Machining

Including grinding

Class here cutting as a machining process, milling

Class comprehensive works on cutting metal in 671.53

.36	Heat treatment and hardening

Including age-hardening, annealing, quenching, shot peening, tempering

.37	Powder metallurgical processes (Powder metallurgy)
.373	Sintering
.4	**Electroforming of metals**
.5	**Joining and cutting of metals**

Standard subdivisions are added for joining and cutting together, for joining alone

Class ceramic-to-metal bonding in 666.042

.52	Welding

Including laser welding, underwater welding

Class underwater welding of a specific type with the type, e.g., underwater arc welding 671.5212

[.520 287]	Testing and measurement

Do not use; class in 671.520423

.520 4	Special topics of welding
.520 42	Welds (Welded joints)
.520 422	Weldability, weld stability, weld defects
.520 423	Inspection and testing
.521	Electric welding

.521 2	Arc welding
.521 3	Resistance welding
	Including flash, projection, seam, spot welding
.521 4	Electron beam welding
.521 5	Induction welding
.522	Gas welding
.529	Pressure and thermit welding
	Including diffusion welding, forge welding, ultrasonic welding

.53 **Cutting**

Class cutting as a machining process in 671.35

.56 **Soldering and brazing**

Standard subdivisions are added for either or both topics in heading

.58 **Bonding**

.59 **Riveting**

.7 Finishing and surface treatment of metals; metal coating of nonmetals

Including cleaning, deburring

.72 **Polishing and buffing**

Standard subdivisions are added for polishing and buffing together, for polishing alone

.73 **Coating**

Including cladding; coating of various metals with a specific metal and metal coating of nonmetals

Class enameling in 666.2; class coating various metals with a specific metal and metal coating of nonmetals using a specific type or method of coating in 671.732–671.736; class comprehensive works on coating in 667.9. Class metal coating of a specific material with the material, e.g., metal coating of plastics 668.4, metal coating of ferrous metals 672.73

.732 **Electroplating**

Add to base number 671.732 the numbers following 669 in 669.1–669.7, e.g., nickel plating 671.7327332

.733 **Hot-metal dipping**

.734 **Metal spraying**

Class here metallizing

For vacuum metallizing, see 671.735

.735 **Vapor plating (Vacuum deposition)**

Including vacuum metalizing, vapor-phase deposition

.736 **Diffusion coating**

.8 **Primary products**

Class here comprehensive works on technology of metal products

For a specific metal product not provided for here, see the product, e.g., metal furniture 684.105

.82 Rolled products

.821 Patternmaking

.823 Strips and sheets

.83 Forged, pressed, stamped products

.832 Pipes

.84 Extruded and drawn products

Including cables

.842 Wires

.87 Powder metal products

672 Iron, steel, other iron alloys

Metalworking processes and primary products

Add to base number 672 the numbers following 671 in 671.2–671.8, e.g., heat treatment 672.36, galvanizing 672.732
Subdivisions are added for any or all topics in heading

For small forge work, see 682

673 Nonferrous metals

Metalworking processes and primary products

Class here alloys of nonferrous metals

Add to each subdivision identified by * the numbers following 671 in 671.2–671.8, e.g., welding aluminum 673.72252

Class metalworking processes and primary products in which nonferrous metals are not the main metal of the final product with the process or the main metal, e.g., nickel plating of various metals 671.7327332, zinc coating of steel 672.73252

.2 **Precious metals**

.22 *Gold

.23 *Silver

.24 *Platinum

.3 ***Copper**

Class here brass, Muntz metal; bronze, gunmetal; copper-aluminum alloys; copper-beryllium alloys

.4 ***Lead**

*Add as instructed under 673

.5   **Zinc and cadmium**

.52   *Zinc

> *For brass, Muntz metal, see 673.3*

.56   *Cadmium

.6   ***Tin**

> *For bronze, gunmetal, see 673.3*

.7   **Other nonferrous metals**

.72   Light, alkali, alkaline-earth metals

> Standard subdivisions are added for light, alkali, alkaline-earth metals together; for light metals alone

> *For titanium, see 673.7322; for zirconium, see 673.735*

.722   *Aluminum

> *For copper-aluminum alloys, see 673.3*

.723   *Magnesium

.724   *Beryllium

> *For copper-beryllium alloys, see 673.3*

.73   Metals used in ferroalloys

.732   Titanium, vanadium, manganese

.732 2   *Titanium

.733   Nickel and cobalt

.733 2   *Nickel

.734   Chromium, molybdenum, tungsten

.735   Zirconium and tantalum

674   Lumber processing, wood products, cork

.001–.009   Standard subdivisions

.01   Philosophy and theory of lumber technology

.02   Miscellany of lumber technology

.021 2   Tables and formulas

> Do not use for specifications; class in 674.5

.028 6   Green technology (Environmental technology)

> Do not use for pollution control technology, waste technology; class in 674.84

*Add as instructed under 673

.028 7   Testing and measurement

> Do not use for grading lumber; class in 674.5

.03–.09   Standard subdivisions of lumber technology

> **674.1–674.5 Lumber technology**

Class physical properties of lumber in 620.12; class comprehensive works in 674

.1   **Structure, chemical properties, types of lumber**

.12   Structure

> Gross and microscopic

.13   Chemical properties

> Including chemical properties of wood extracts

.14   Specific types of lumber

> Class structure of specific types of lumber in 674.12; class chemical properties of specific types of lumber in 674.13

.142   Hardwoods

> Including basswood, beech, chestnut, elm, maple, oak, poplar

.144   Softwoods

> Including cedar, cypress, fir, hemlock, larch, pine, redwood, spruce

.2   **Sawmill operations**

> Class wood waste and residues in 674.84

.28   Rough lumber

> Class here dimension stock (cut stock)

.3   **Storage, seasoning, preservation of lumber**

.32   Storage in lumberyards

.38   Seasoning and preservation

> Standard subdivisions are added for seasoning and preservation together, for seasoning alone

> Class here drying

.382   Use of air

.384   Use of kilns

.386   Use of chemicals

> Class here preservation

.4   **Production of finished lumber**

.42   Production of surfaced lumber

.43	Production of pattern lumber

Including shiplap, sidings, tongue-and-groove products

.5 **Grading lumber**

Including inspection and specifications

.8 **Wood products**

Class here comprehensive works on wood-using technologies

For a specific product or wood-using technology not provided for here, see the product or technology, e.g., wood as a fuel 662.65, finished lumber 674.4, pulp and paper technology 676, wooden furniture 684.104, carpentry 694

.82 Containers and pallets

Including barrels, boxes, casks, crates

.83 Composite woods; veneers

Standard subdivisions are added for veneers and composite woods together, for composite woods alone

.833 Veneers

> 674.834–674.836 Composite woods

Class comprehensive works in 674.83

.834 Plywood

See also 674.835 for specialty plywoods

.835 Laminated wood (Sandwich panels, Specialty plywoods)

.836 Particle board

.84 Wood waste and residues

Standard subdivisions are added for either or both topics in heading

Including excelsior, sawdust, wood flour and shavings

Class here pollution control technology, waste technology

Class utilization of wood waste and residues in making a specific product with the product, e.g., particle board 674.836

.88 Other products

Including picture frames, signs, spools, toothpicks, wood-cased pencils, woodenware

.9 **Cork**

675 Leather and fur processing

Standard subdivisions are added for leather and fur processing together, for leather processing alone

For leather and fur goods, see 685

.2 Processing of natural leather

[.202 87] Testing and measurement

Do not use; class in 675.29

.22 Preliminary operations

Including fleshing, unhairing (liming), bating hides and skins

.23 Tanning

.24 Dressing

.25 Finishing

Including dyeing, embossing, glazing, production of patent leather

.29 Properties, tests, quality controls

.3 Fur processing

Including manufacture of imitation furs

.4 Manufacture of imitation leathers

676 Pulp and paper technology

Standard subdivisions are added for pulp and paper technology together, for paper technology alone

Class here comprehensive works on paper and paper products, on the total process of making paper out of logs or other sources of pulp

Class the process of making pulp, through bleaching, in 676.1; class conversion of pulp into paper or paper products, starting with beating and refining the pulp, in 676.2

SUMMARY

676.04		**Special topics of pulp and paper technology**
	.1	**Pulp**
	.2	**Conversion of pulp into paper, and specific types of paper and paper products**
	.3	**Paper and paperboard containers**
	.4	**Purified pulp**
	.5	**Pulp by-products**
	.7	**Paper from man-made and noncellulosic fibers**

.028 6 Green technology (Environmental technology)

Do not use for pollution control technology, waste technology; class in 676.042

.04 Special topics of pulp and paper technology

.042 Waste technology

> Class here pollution control
>
> Class paper recycling in 676.142

.1 Pulp

> Class here the process of making pulp, through bleaching
>
> Class conversion of pulp into paper, starting with beating and refining the pulp, in 676.2; class pulp by-products in 676.5

[.102 87] Testing and measurement

> Do not use; class in 676.17

> 676.12–676.14 Specific pulps

> Class comprehensive works in 676.1
>
> *For purified pulp, see 676.4*

.12 Wood pulp

[.120 287] Testing and measurement

> Do not use; class in 676.121

.121 Properties, tests, quality controls

> 676.122–676.127 Specific processes

> Class comprehensive works in 676.12

.122 Mechanical process (Ground wood process)

.124 Soda process

.125 Sulfite process

.126 Sulfate process (Kraft process)

.127 Semichemical process

.13 Rag pulp

.14 Other pulps

> Including bagasse, bamboo, cornstalks, hemp, jute, straw

.142 Wastepaper

> Class here paper recycling

.17 Properties, tests, quality controls

> Class properties, tests, quality controls of specific pulps in 676.12–676.14

.18 Molded products and pulpboards

.182 Molded products

.183	Pulpboards

Including chip boards, fiberboards, wallboards

See also 666.89 for drywall

> **676.2–676.5 Pulp products**

Class comprehensive works in 676

For molded products and pulpboards, see 676.18

.2	**Conversion of pulp into paper, and specific types of paper and paper products**

Class paper recycling in 676.142

[.202 87]	Testing and measurement

Do not use; class in 676.27

> 676.22–676.27 General topics of conversion of pulp into paper

Class general topics of specific types of paper and paper products in 676.28; class comprehensive works in 676.2

.22	Production by hand
.23	Specific processes of machine production
.232	Basic processes
.234	Finishing

Including calendering, coloring, creping, sizing

For coating, see 676.235

.235	Coating
.27	Properties, tests, quality controls
.28	Specific types of paper and paper products

For photographic paper, see 661.808

.280 27	Patents and identification marks

Including watermarks

.282	Graphic arts paper
.282 3	Stationery

Including onionskin paper

.282 4	Book paper

Class coated book paper in 676.283

.282 5	Drawing and art paper

Standard subdivisions are added for either or both topics in heading

.282 6   Currency paper

              Papers for printing money, bonds, securities

.283   Coated paper

            For specific kinds of coated paper, see the kind, e.g., coated wallpaper 676.2848

.284   Specialty paper

.284 2   Tissue paper

            Including cleansing tissues, toilet paper

            Class onionskin paper in 676.2823

.284 4   Blotting and saturating paper

            Standard subdivisions are added for either or both topics in heading

.284 5   Vulcanized and parchment papers

            See also 685 for parchment prepared from the skin of an animal

.284 8   Wallpaper

.286   Unsized paper

            Including newsprint

.287   Wrapping and bag papers

            Including bogus wrapping, butcher, kraft wrapping, Manila paper

.288   Paperboard

            Including bristol board, cardboard, food board, pasteboard

.289   Roofing and building papers

.3   **Paper and paperboard containers**

.32   Boxes and cartons

            Standard subdivisions are added for either or both topics in heading

            Including corrugated and solid paperboard boxes, folding boxes

            For food board containers, see 676.34

.33   Bags

.34   Food board containers

            Including food cartons, paper plates and cups

.4   **Purified pulp**

            Production of alpha cellulose from wood pulp and cotton linters

.5   **Pulp by-products**

            Including fatty acids, lignin, resins, tall oil, turpentine

            Class comprehensive works on naval stores in 665.33

.7   **Paper from man-made and noncellulosic fibers**

677   **Textiles**

Production of fibers, fabrics, cordage

Class here comprehensive works on manufacture of textiles and clothing

For manufacture of clothing, see 687

SUMMARY

677.001–.009	**Standard subdivisions**
.02	**General topics of textiles**
.1	**Textiles of bast fibers**
.2	**Textiles of seed-hair fibers**
.3	**Textiles of animal fibers**
.4	**Textiles of man-made fibers**
.5	**Other textiles of specific fibers**
.6	**Special-process fabrics regardless of composition**
.7	**Cordage, trimmings and allied products**
.8	**Surgical gauze and cotton**

.001   Philosophy and theory

.002   Miscellany

.002 8   Auxiliary techniques and procedures

[.002 84]   Apparatus, equipment, materials

Do not use; class in 677.028

.002 86   Green technology (Environmental technology)

Class waste and reused wool and hair in 677.36; class waste and reused silk in 677.394

[.002 87]   Testing and measurement

Do not use; class in 677.0287

.003–.009   Standard subdivisions

.02   General topics of textiles

.022   Designs (Working patterns)

.028   Techniques, procedures, apparatus, equipment, materials, products

For auxiliary techniques and procedures, see 677.0028

.028 2   Operations

.028 21   Preliminary operations

Including carding, combing

.028 22   Spinning, twisting, reeling

Standard subdivisions are added for spinning, twisting, reeling together; for spinning alone

.028 24   Weaving, knitting, felting

.028 242	Weaving
.028 245	Knitting
.028 25	Basic finishing

                          Physical and chemical processes

                          Including beetling, calendering, creping, mercerizing, pressing, shearing, singeing, tentering

                          For dyeing and printing, see 667.3

.028 3	Materials
.028 32	Fibers
.028 35	Textile chemicals
.028 5	Power equipment
.028 52	Spinning machines
.028 54	Looms and loom equipment

                          Standard subdivisions are added for looms and loom equipment together, for looms alone

.028 55	Basic finishing machines
.028 6	Products

                          For tests and quality controls of products, see 677.0287; for cordage, trimmings and allied products, see 677.7; for surgical gauze and cotton, see 677.8

.028 62	Yarns and threads

                          Standard subdivisions are added for either or both topics in heading

.028 64	Fabrics

                          For special-process fabrics, see 677.6

.028 7	Testing and measurement

                          Including tests and quality controls of products

---

> ### 677.1–677.5 Textiles of specific composition

        Class here specific kinds of textile fibers

        Class special-process fabrics regardless of composition in 677.6; class comprehensive works in 677

.1	**Textiles of bast fibers**
.11	Flax
[.110 284]	Apparatus, equipment, materials

                          Do not use; class in 677.112–677.117

.112–.117	Techniques, procedures, apparatus, equipment, materials, products

Add to base number 677.11 the numbers following 677.028 in 677.0282–677.0287, e.g., linen fabrics 677.1164

For auxiliary techniques and procedures, see 677.11028

.12	Hemp
.13	Jute
.15	Ramie
.18	Coir

.2 Textiles of seed-hair fibers

.21	Cotton
[.210 284]	Apparatus, equipment, materials

Do not use; class in 677.212–677.217

.212–.217	Techniques, procedures, apparatus, equipment, materials, products

Add to base number 677.21 the numbers following 677.028 in 677.0282–677.0287, e.g., cotton ginning, carding, combing 677.2121

For auxiliary techniques and procedures, see 677.21028

.23	Kapok

.3 Textiles of animal fibers

.31	Sheep wool

Class here comprehensive works on technology of wool textiles

For llama, alpaca, vicuña, guanaco wool textiles, see 677.32

[.310 284]	Apparatus, equipment, materials

Do not use; class in 677.312–677.317

.312–.317	Techniques, procedures, apparatus, equipment, materials, products

Add to base number 677.31 the numbers following 677.028 in 677.0282–677.0287, e.g., sheep wool fibers 677.3132

For auxiliary techniques and procedures, see 677.31028

.32	Llama, alpaca, vicuña, guanaco wools
.33	Goat hair
.34	Camel's hair
.35	Rabbit hair
.36	Waste and reused wool and hair

Standard subdivisions are added for any or all topics in heading

.39	Silk
.391	Cultivated silk

[.391 028 4]	Apparatus, equipment, materials
	Do not use; class in 677.3912–677.3917
.391 2–.391 7	Techniques, procedures, apparatus, equipment, materials, products

Add to base number 677.391 the numbers following 677.028 in 677.0282–677.0287, e.g., beetling cultivated silk 677.39125

For auxiliary techniques and procedures, see 677.391028

| .392 | Wild silk (Tussah silk) |
| .394 | Waste and reused silk |

Standard subdivisions are added for either or both topics in heading

.4 Textiles of man-made fibers

| .46 | Cellulosics (Rayon and acetates) |

For textiles of paper fibers, see 677.5

| .460 01–.460 09 | Standard subdivisions |
| .460 1–.460 9 | Standard subdivisions of rayon |

> 677.461–677.463 Rayon

Class comprehensive works in 677.46

.461	Nitrocellulose
.462	Cuprammonium rayon
.463	Viscose rayon
.464	Cellulose acetate
.47	Noncellulosics

For fiber glass, see 677.52

.472	Azlon
.473	Polyamides (Nylons)
.474	Other polymerization textiles
.474 2	Acrylics

Class here polyacrylics

| .474 3 | Polyesters |
| .474 4 | Vinyls |

Including nytrils, sarans, vinyons

Class here polyvinyls

| .474 5 | Olefins |

Including polyethylene, polypropylene

.474 8	Polyfluoro hydrocarbons

.5 Other textiles of specific fibers

.51 Textiles of asbestos fibers

.52 Textiles of fiber glass

.53 Textiles of metal fibers

.54 Textiles of unaltered vegetable fibers

> Including bamboo, cane, raffia, rattan, rush

.55 Textiles of elastic fibers

.6 Special-process fabrics regardless of composition

> Class here nonwoven fabrics

.61 Fancy-weave fabrics

> *For tapestries, carpets, rugs, see 677.64; for openwork fabrics, see 677.65*

.615 Fabrics in dobby weave

> Including bird's-eye, figured madras, huckaback, sharkskin

.616 Fabrics in Jacquard weave

> Including brocade, brocatelle, damask, lamé, upholstery fabrics

.617 Fabrics in pile weave

> Including chenille, corduroy, frieze, plush, terry cloth, velour, velvet, velveteen

.62 Woven felt

> Class comprehensive works on felt in 677.63

.624 Flannel and swanskin yard goods

.626 Blankets, lap robes, coverlets

.63 Felt

> *For woven felt, see 677.62*

.632 Yard goods and carpets

.64 Tapestries, carpets, rugs

.642 Tapestry yard goods

.643 Rugs

> Class here carpets

> *For nonwoven felt carpets, see 677.632*

.65 Openwork fabrics

> *For chain-stitch and knotted fabrics, see 677.66*

.652   Fabrics in leno weave

        Including grenadines, marquisettes

.653   Laces

        Including bobbin, machine, needlepoint laces

.654   Tulles

.66   Chain-stitch and knotted fabrics

.661   Knitted fabrics

.662   Crocheted fabrics

.663   Tatted fabrics

.664   Netted fabrics

.68   Fabrics with functional finishes

        Including drip-dry, durable press fabrics

        Class specific types of special-process fabrics regardless of finish in 677.61–677.66

.681   Crease-resistant and wrinkle-resistant fabrics

        Standard subdivisions are added for either or both topics in heading

.682   Waterproof and water-repellent fabrics

        Standard subdivisions are added for either or both topics in heading

.688   Shrinkage-controlled fabrics

.689   Flameproof and flame-resistant fabrics

        Standard subdivisions are added for either or both topics in heading

.69   Bonded and laminated fabrics

        Standard subdivisions are added for either or both topics in heading

.7   Cordage, trimmings and allied products

.71   Ropes, twines, strings

        Class here cordage

        For passementerie, see 677.76

.76   Passementerie

        Including decorative bias bindings, braids, cords, gimps, lacings, ribbons, tapes, tinsel; upholstery trimmings

.77   Machine embroidery

        Including clip spot, lappet, Schiffli, swivel (dotted swiss) embroidery

        Class laces in 677.653

.8   **Surgical gauze and cotton**

Including bandages, sanitary napkins

678   Elastomers and elastomer products

Standard subdivisions are added for elastomers and elastomer products together, for elastomers alone

.2   **Rubber**

For rubber products, see 678.3; for properties of rubber, see 678.4; for natural rubber, see 678.62; for synthetic rubber, see 678.72

.202 84   Apparatus and equipment

Do not use for materials; class in 678.21

.202 86   Green technology (Environmental technology)

Do not use for pollution control technology, waste technology; class in 678.29

.21   Materials

For reclaimed rubber, see 678.29

.22   Mastication

.23   Compounding

Including use of accelerators, antioxidants, pigments, solvents

.24   Vulcanization

.27   Molding, extruding, calendering

.29   Reclaimed rubber and waste control

Including devulcanizing

Class here pollution control technology, waste technology

.3   **Rubber products**

Class elastic fiber textiles in 677.55

For natural rubber products, see 678.63; for synthetic rubber products, see 678.723

.32   Tires

.33   Overshoes

.34   Articles molded and vulcanized in presses

Including doorstops, hollow ware, hot-water bottles, tiles

.35   Extruded articles

Including inner tubes, rubber bands, weather stripping, windshield wipers

.36   Articles made by dipping, spreading, electrodeposition

Including conveyor and driving belts, hose, sheeting

.72   Synthetic rubber and derivatives

> Standard subdivisions are added for synthetic rubber and derivatives together, for synthetic rubber alone
>
> Including acrylonitrile rubber (GR-A), butadiene-styrene rubber (GR-S), chloroprene rubber (GR-M), isobutylene rubber (GR-I), polybutadiene rubber, polyurethane rubber
>
> Class comprehensive works on polyurethanes in 668.4239

.720 28   Auxiliary techniques and procedures; apparatus, equipment, materials

> Do not use for auxiliary techniques and procedures, apparatus, equipment, materials for synthetic rubber; class in 678.722

.722   Techniques, procedures, apparatus, equipment, materials for synthetic rubber

.723   Synthetic rubber products

.724   Properties of synthetic rubber

.728   Chemical derivatives of synthetic rubber

.73   High-styrene resins (Elastoplastics)

679   Other products of specific kinds of materials

.4   **Products of keratinous and dentinal materials**

.43   Ivory products

.47   Feather products

.6   **Products of fibers and bristles**

> Including brooms, brushes, mops

.7   **Products of tobacco**

> *See also 688.4 for tobacco substitutes*

.72   Cigars

.73   Cigarettes

680   Manufacture of products for specific uses

> Not provided for elsewhere
>
> Class here interdisciplinary works on handicrafts
>
> Class repairs of household equipment by members of household in 643.7. Class manufacture of a product based on a specific branch of engineering with the branch of engineering in 620, e.g., military engineering 623, manufacture of motor vehicles 629.2; except for products provided for in 681 688, class manufacture of products of a specific material with the material in 671–679, e.g., manufacture of steel pipes 672.832, but manufacture of steel toys 688.72
>
> *For artistic handicraft work, see 745.5*
>
> *See Manual at 671–679 vs. 680; also at 680 vs. 745.5*

SUMMARY

681   **Precision instruments and other devices**
682   **Small forge work (Blacksmithing)**
683   **Hardware and household appliances**
684   **Furnishings and home workshops**
685   **Leather and fur goods, and related products**
686   **Printing and related activities**
687   **Clothing and accessories**
688   **Other final products, and packaging technology**

681   Precision instruments and other devices

Standard subdivisions are added for precision instruments and other devices together, for precision instruments alone

SUMMARY

681.1   **Instruments for measuring time, counting and calculating machines and instruments**
.2   **Testing, measuring, sensing instruments**
.4   **Optical instruments**
.6   **Printing, writing, duplicating machines and equipment**
.7   **Other scientific and technological instruments, machinery, equipment**
.8   **Musical instruments**

.1   Instruments for measuring time, counting and calculating machines and instruments

For testing, measuring, sensing instruments, see 681.2

.11   Instruments for measuring time

.111   Ancient and primitive instruments

Including hourglasses, water clocks

.111 2   Sundials

.112   Constituent parts (Clockwork)

Including gears, escapements, bearings, regulating devices

.113   Clocks

Class here interdisciplinary works on clocks

For constituent parts, see 681.112; for pneumatic clocks, see 681.115; for electric clocks, see 681.116; for chronographs, chronoscopes, chronometers, see 681.118; for clocks considered as works of art, see 739.3

.114   Watches

Class here interdisciplinary works on watches

For constituent parts, see 681.112; for chronographs, chronoscopes, chronometers, see 681.118; for watches considered as works of art, see 739.3

.115   Pneumatic clocks

.116   Electric clocks

.118   Chronographs, chronoscopes, chronometers

> Including metronomes, stopwatches, tachometers, time clocks, time and date recorders

.14   Counting and calculating machines and instruments

> Including cash registers, slide rules, sorting machines, voting machines

> *For computers, see 621.39*

.145   Calculators

.2   Testing, measuring, sensing instruments

> Standard subdivisions are added for any or all topics in heading

> Including calorimeters

> Class here testing, measuring, sensing instruments of general application in science or technology; testing, measuring, sensing instruments for nontechnological application; instruments for measuring physical quantities; electrical and electronic instruments for measuring nonelectrical and nonelectronic quantities

> Class testing, measuring, sensing instruments for a specific branch of science (other than instruments for measuring physical quantities) in 681.75. Class testing, measuring, sensing instruments for a specific technological application with the manufacturing number, e.g., aircraft instrumentation 629.135, medical diagnostic equipment 681.761

> > *For instruments for measuring electrical quantities, see 621.37; for instruments for testing and measuring electronic signals, see 621.381548; for instruments for measuring time, see 681.11*

.25   Optical testing, measuring, sensing instruments

> Including polarimeters

> Class here fiber optic sensors

> Class optical testing, measuring, sensing instruments applied to a specific property with the property, e.g., fiber optic sensors to measure flow 681.28

> > *For spectroscopes, see 681.414; for photometers, see 681.415*

.28   Flowmeters

.4   Optical instruments

.41   Specific instruments

> Including contact lenses

> > *For component parts of specific instruments, see 681.42–681.43*

.411   Eyeglasses

.412   Telescopes and binoculars

.412 3   Telescopes

.412 5	Binoculars
	Including opera glasses
	Class here field glasses
.413	Microscopes
.414	Spectroscopes
.414 2–.414 6	Optical, infrared, ultraviolet spectroscopes
	Add to base number 681.414 the numbers following 535.84 in 535.842–535.846, e.g., infrared spectroscopes 681.4142
.414 8	Other spectroscopes
	Including magnetic resonance, microwave, radio-frequency, X-ray and gamma-ray spectroscopes
.415	Photometers
.418	Photographic equipment
	Including cameras, projectors, accessories
	Class film and other chemical photographic supplies in 661.808
	For photometers, see 681.415; for photocopying equipment, see 681.65

>   **681.42–681.43 Component parts**

Class comprehensive works in 681.4

.42	Lenses, prisms, mirrors
.423	Lenses
.428	Mirrors
.43	Frames and other housings
.6	**Printing, writing, duplicating machines and equipment**

Including computer output microform (COM) devices, pens, mechanical pencils, rubber stamps

Class here comprehensive works on manufacturing of office equipment

Class facsimile recorders in 621.38235; class wood-cased pencils in 674.88; class interdisciplinary works on office equipment in 651.2

For manufacturing a specific kind of office equipment, see the kind, e.g., calculators 681.145

.61	Stenographic and composing machines, typewriters
.62	Printers and printing presses
	Class here computer output printers
.65	Photocopying equipment

.7   **Other scientific and technological instruments, machinery, equipment**

Not provided for elsewhere

.75   Scientific instruments and equipment

Standard subdivisions are added for either or both topics in heading

Class here testing, measuring, sensing equipment for specific branches of science

Class comprehensive works on scientific testing, measuring, sensing instruments in 681.2

.753   Physical instruments and equipment

Standard subdivisions are added for either or both topics in heading

Including instruments with multiple applications based on physical principles, e.g., gyroscopes

Class instruments for measuring physical quantities in 681.2

.754   Chemical instruments and equipment

Standard subdivisions are added for either or both topics in heading

.755   Geological instruments and equipment

Standard subdivisions are added for either or both topics in heading

.757   Biological instruments and equipment

Standard subdivisions are added for either or both topics in heading

.76   Technological equipment

Including construction, pollution control, mining, surveying equipment

Class here instruments, machinery; testing, measuring, sensing instruments in specific branches of technology not provided for elsewhere

Class comprehensive works on technological testing, measuring, sensing instruments in 681.2

.760 4   Special topics of technological equipment

.760 41   Pressure vessels

Class a specific use of pressure vessels with the use, e.g., nuclear pressure vessels 621.483

.761   Medical and health equipment

Standard subdivisions are added for medical and health equipment together, for medical equipment alone

Including condoms, crutches, diagnostic equipment, exercise equipment, prosthetic devices

Class interdisciplinary works on medical and health equipment in 610.284; class interdisciplinary works on exercise equipment in 613.710284

.763   Agricultural and related equipment

> Standard subdivisions are added for agricultural and related equipment together, for agricultural equipment alone

> Including subsistance hunting, fishing, shooting equipment

> Class comprehensive works on commercial and sports hunting, fishing, shooting equipment in 688.79

.763 1   Equipment for plant culture

.763 6   Equipment for animal culture

.766   Equipment for chemical and related technologies

.766 4   Equipment for food and beverage technology

.766 5   Equipment for petroleum and industrial gas technologies

.766 6   Equipment for ceramic technology

.766 8   Equipment for plastic and elastomer technologies

.766 9   Equipment for metallurgy

.767   Equipment for nonchemical manufactures

.767 1   Equipment for metal manufactures

.767 6   Equipment for wood and paper technologies

.767 7   Equipment for textile and clothing technologies

.8   **Musical instruments**

> Add to base number 681.8 the numbers following 78 in 786–788, e.g., manufacture of pianos 681.862

> Class hand construction of specific instruments or groups of instruments in 786–788; class comprehensive works on hand construction in 784.1923

682   Small forge work (Blacksmithing)

.1   **Horseshoeing**

.4   **Ironwork and hand-forged tools**

> Standard subdivisions are added for ironwork and hand-forged tools together, for ironwork alone

683   Hardware and household appliances

> Standard subdivisions are added for hardware and household appliances together, for hardware alone

> Class here comprehensive works on manufacture of hardware and building supplies

> *For a specific hardware or building supply product not provided for here, see the product, e.g., tools 621.9, paints 667.6*

.3   **Locksmithing**

.31	Bolts and latches

Standard subdivisions are added for either or both topics in heading

.32	Locks and keys

Standard subdivisions are added for either or both topics in heading

.34	Safes and strongboxes

Standard subdivisions are added for either or both topics in heading

.4   **Small firearms**

Class here interdisciplinary works on small firearms, on gunsmithing

For military small firearms, see 623.442

.400 1	Philosophy and theory
.400 2	Miscellany
[.400 288]	Maintenance and repair

Do not use; class in 683.403

.400 3–.400 9	Standard subdivisions

>   683.401–683.406 General topics of small firearms

Class comprehensive works in 683.4

.401	Design
.403	Maintenance and repair

Standard subdivisions are added for either or both topics in heading

.406	Ammunition
.42	Rifles and shotguns
.422	Rifles
.426	Shotguns
.43	Handguns
.432	Pistols

Class here single-shot pistols

.432 5	Automatic pistols
.436	Revolvers

.8   **Household utensils and appliances**

Including tableware

For nonmetallic household utensils and appliances, see the material from which they are made, e.g., porcelain tableware 666.58, woodenware 674.88

.802 88	Maintenance and repair

> *For maintenance and repair by members of household, see 643.60288*

.82	Kitchen utensils

Including cutlery, pots, pans, pails

.83	Electrical appliances

Class comprehensive works on electrical equipment in 621.31042

> *For electrical equipment requiring special installation, see 683.88*

.88	Heavy equipment

Electrical, gas, other equipment requiring special installation

Including dishwashers, dryers, garbage-disposal units, ranges, stoves, washing machines, water heaters

> *For refrigerators and freezers, see 621.57; for heating, ventilating, air-conditioning equipment, see 697*

684   Furnishings and home workshops

Standard subdivisions are added for furnishings and home workshops together, for furnishings alone

Class here home furnishings

> *For lighting fixtures, see 621.32*

.001–.009	Standard subdivisions
.08	Woodworking

Class here comprehensive works on home (amateur) workshops

> *For metalworking in home workshops, see 684.09; for furniture making in home workshops, see 684.1*

.082	Woodworking with hand tools

Including woodworking with specific hand tools, e.g., planes

.083	Woodworking with power tools

Add to base number 684.083 the numbers following 621.9 in 621.91–621.95, e.g., routers 684.08321, power saws 684.08334

.084	Surface finishing
.09	Metalworking

.1   Furniture

Class here home construction of furniture

.100 1–.100 9	Standard subdivisions

>   684.104–684.106   General topics of furniture

       Class comprehensive works in 684.1

.104   Wooden furniture

       Class here cabinetmaking

[.104 028 8]   Maintenance and repair

       Do not use; class in 684.1044

.104 2   Basic construction

.104 3   Surface finishing

.104 4   Maintenance and repair

       Standard subdivisions are added for either or both topics in heading

.104 42   Body restoration

.104 43   Surface refinishing

.105   Metal furniture

.106   Furniture in other materials

       Including composite materials, plastics, rattan, tiles

>   684.12–684.16   Specific kinds of furniture

       Class outdoor furniture in 684.18; class comprehensive works in 684.1

.12   Upholstered furniture

       Including couches, sofas, upholstered chairs

.13   Chairs and tables

.132   Chairs

       For upholstered chairs, see 684.12

.135   Tables

       For desks, see 684.14

.14   Desks

.15   Beds

       Including frames, springs, mattresses

.16   Cabinets and built-in furniture

       Standard subdivisions are added for cabinets and built-in furniture together, for cabinets alone

       Including chests, china cabinets, dressers, file cabinets

       Class here furniture used for storage

       See also 684.104 for cabinetmaking

.162   Shelving

Class here bookcases

For built-in wooden shelves, see 694.6

.18   Outdoor furniture

Including garden, patio, porch furniture

Class camping furniture in 685.53

.3   **Fabric furnishings**

Including bedclothes, curtains, draperies, hangings, slipcovers

Class home construction of fabric furnishings in 646.21

For carpets and rugs, see 677.643

685   **Leather and fur goods, and related products**

Standard subdivisions are added for leather and fur goods and related products together, for leather goods alone

Including parchment prepared from the skin of an animal

See also 676.2845 for parchment paper made from pulp

.1   **Saddlery and harness making**

.2   **Leather and fur clothing and accessories**

Class leather and fur footwear in 685.3; class leather and fur gloves and mittens in 685.4

.22   Leather clothing and accessories

Including aprons, belts, jackets, skirts, trousers

.24   Fur clothing and accessories

Standard subdivisions are added for fur clothing and accessories together, for fur clothing alone

Including coats, hats, jackets, muffs, neckpieces, stoles

.3   **Footwear and related products**

For overshoes, see 678.33; for hosiery, see 687.3

.31   Boots and shoes

Standard subdivisions are added for either or both topics in heading

Class shoes for specific activities in 685.36; class shoes for people with disabilities in 685.38

For wooden shoes and clogs, see 685.32

.310 01   Philosophy and theory

.310 02   Miscellany

[.310 028 8]	Maintenance and repair

Do not use; class in 685.3104

.310 03–.310 09	Standard subdivisions
.310 2	Design
.310 3	Construction
.310 4	Maintenance and repair

Standard subdivisions are added for either or both topics in heading

.32	Wooden shoes and clogs
.36	Footwear for specific activities

Footwear used as equipment in a specific sport relocated to the sport in 688.7

[.361]	Ice skates

Relocated to 688.7691

[.362]	Roller skates and skateboards

Roller skates relocated to 688.7621; Skateboards relocated to 688.7622

[.363]	Snowshoes

Relocated to 688.7692

[.364]	Skis

Relocated to 688.7693

[.367]	Stilts

Relocated to 688.7

.38	Footwear and related products for people with disabilities

Standard subdivisions are added for footwear and related products together, for footwear alone

Including orthopedic shoes

.4	**Gloves and mittens**

Standard subdivisions are added for either or both topics in heading

Regardless of material

.41	Conventional gloves
.43	Gloves and mittens for specific activities

Including protective gloves for industry

Gloves and mittens used as equipment in a specific sport relocated to the sport in 688.7

.47	Conventional mittens
.5	**Luggage, handbags, camping equipment**

.51	Luggage and handbags

Including briefcases, attaché cases

.53	Camping equipment

Including sleeping bags, tents

686   Printing and related activities

Class here design and manufacture of publications, book arts

Class interdisciplinary works on the book in 002

For book illustration, see 741.64

See also 681.6 for manufacture of printing equipment

SUMMARY

686.1	Invention of printing
.2	Printing
.3	Bookbinding
.4	Photocopying

.1   Invention of printing

.2   Printing

Class here printing in the Latin alphabet

Class works on desktop publishing that emphasize typography in 686.22; class comprehensive works on printing and publishing in 070.5; class interdisciplinary works on print media in 302.232

See also 070.593 for self-publishing

.209	History, geographic treatment, biography

Class invention of printing in 686.1

.21	Printing in non-Latin alphabets and characters

Standard subdivisions are added for either or both topics in heading

Class here typefounding, typecasting, typefaces for non-Latin alphabets and characters

For other specific aspects of printing in non-Latin alphabets and characters, see the aspect, e.g., letterpress printing 686.2312

.218	Greek alphabet
.219	Other non-Latin alphabets and characters

Add to base number 686.219 the numbers following —9 in notation 91–99 from Table 6, e.g., Cyrillic alphabet 686.21918

.22	Typography
.221	Typefounding and typecasting

Standard subdivisions are added for either or both topics in heading

.224	Typefaces

Design, style, specimens of letters, ornaments, other characters and devices

Class here typefaces for the Latin alphabet

Class typefaces for non-Latin alphabets and characters in 686.21; class typefaces for braille and other raised characters in 686.282

.224 7	Specific typefaces and kinds of typefaces for the Latin alphabet

Including Gothic, italic, roman type; Bodoni, Garamond, Times Roman type

.225	Composition (Typesetting)
[.225 028 5]	Computer applications

Do not use; class in 686.22544

.225 2	Page design

Including paste-up

Class here layout

.225 3	Hand composition
.225 4	Machine composition
.225 42	Composition by use of human-operated equipment

Including linotype composition

.225 44	Composition by use of automatic equipment

Including phototypesetting (photocomposition)

Class here computerized typesetting

Unless it is redundant, add to base number 686.22544 the numbers following 00 in 004–006, e.g., personal computer programs for typesetting 686.22544536, the use of digital personal computers 686.22544416, but the use of digital computers 686.22544 (*not* 686.225444)

[.225 5]	Proofreading

Number discontinued; class in 686.225

.225 6	Imposition and lockup
.23	Presswork (Impression)

Class interdisciplinary works on use of computer printers as low-volume output devices in 004.77. Class a specific use with the use, e.g., use in typesetting 686.22544477

For printing special graphic materials, see 686.28

See also 621.38235 for facsimile transmission; also 681.6 for manufacture of printing equipment

.230 4	Special topics of presswork

.230 42	Color printing
.231	Mechanical techniques

For photomechanical techniques, see 686.232

.231 2	Printing from type

Class here comprehensive works on letterpress techniques

For printing from plates, see 686.2314

.231 4	Printing from plates

Printing from stereotypes, electrotypes, autotypes, engraved plates, paper mats

See also 686.2315 for printing from planographic plates

.231 5	Planographic (Flat-surface)

Class here lithography and offset (offset lithography)

For photolithography, photo-offset, collotype, see 686.2325

.231 6	Stencil techniques

Including silk-screen printing

.232	Photomechanical techniques
.232 5	Photolithography, photo-offset, collotype (gelatin process)

See also 621.381531 for photolithography in manufacture of printed circuits (microlithography)

.232 7	Photoengraving (Photointaglio)

Including line and halftone cuts, photogravure

.233	Nonimpact techniques

Including electrographic, electrophotographic, laser processes

See also 686.44 for electrophotographic processes in photocopying

.28	Printing special graphic materials
.282	Braille and other raised characters

Standard subdivisions are added for braille and other raised characters together, for braille alone

Class comprehensive works on braille and other raised-character alphabets in 411

.283	Maps
.284	Music
.288	Materials of direct monetary value

Including postage stamps, securities

.3   **Bookbinding**

Processes and materials

.300 1–.300 9   Standard subdivisions

.302   Hand and fine binding

Standard subdivisions are added for either or both topics in heading

.303   Specific kinds of commercial binding

.303 2   Library binding

.303 4   Edition binding

.34   Types of covers

.342   Leather

.343   Cloth and imitation leather

.344   Paper

.35   Methods of fastening

Including hand sewing, oversewing, side-sewing, wire-stitching; perfect binding and other kinds of gluing

.36   Ornamentation

Including gilding, lettering, marbling, tooling

.4   **Photocopying**

Class here photoduplication, interdisciplinary works on photocopying

Class facsimile transmission in 621.38235

For a specific aspect of photocopying, see the aspect, e.g., library photocopying services 025.12

See also 681.65 for manufacture of photocopying equipment

.42   Blueprinting

.43   Microphotography

Production of microforms

Class here production of microfiche and microfilms

.44   Electrostatic and electrophotographic processes

.442   Xerography

.45   Production of photostats

687   Clothing and accessories

Standard subdivisions are added for clothing and accessories together, for clothing alone

Class here dressmaking, casual wear (sportswear)

Unless other instructions are given, class a subject with aspects in two or more subdivisions of 687 in the number coming last, e.g., military headwear 687.4 (*not* 687.15)

Class interdisciplinary works on clothing in 391; class interdisciplinary works on clothing construction in 646.4

> *For leather and fur clothing, see 685.2*

SUMMARY

.04   General topics of clothing

.042   Patternmaking and grading

> Standard subdivisions are added for patternmaking and grading together, for patternmaking alone

.043   Cutting

.044   Tailoring

.1   Specific kinds of garments

> *For footwear, see 685.3; for gloves and mittens, see 685.4; for undergarments, see 687.2; for hosiery, see 687.3; for headwear, see 687.4*

.11   Miscellaneous kinds of garments

Limited to those provided for below

.112   Dresses

Use of this number for dressmaking discontinued; class in 687

.113   Suits

Class here jackets, sport coats, vests (waistcoats)

Class skirts in 687.117

Pants (trousers) relocated to 687.116

.115   Shirts, blouses, tops

Standard subdivisions are added for any or all topics in heading

.116   Pants (Trousers) [*formerly* 687.113]

> *See also 687.2 for pants (undergarments)*

.117	Skirts
.14	Outerwear

Class here overcoats, topcoats, raincoats; comprehensive works on coats and jackets

For suit jackets, sport coats, see 687.113

[.140 811]	Outerwear for men

Do not use; class in 687.141

[.140 82]	Outerwear for women

Do not use; class in 687.142

.140 83	Outerwear for young adults

Do not use for outerwear for children; class in 687.143

For outerwear for young adult men aged twenty-one and over, see 687.141; for outerwear for young adult women twenty-one and over, see 687.142

.140 84	Outerwear for people in specific stages of adulthood

Class outerwear for adult men regardless of age in 687.141; class outerwear for adult women regardless of age in 687.142

.141	Outerwear for men

Class outerwear for young adult men in 687.1408351

.142	Outerwear for women

Class outerwear for young adult women in 687.1408352

.143	Outerwear for children
[.144–.147]	Sweaters, wraps, specific types of outer coats

Numbers discontinued; class in 687.14

.15	Uniforms and symbolic garments

Including civil and military uniforms, ceremonial and academic robes, ecclesiastical vestments

.16	Garments for special purposes

Including activewear (clothing for athletic and outdoor sports), costumes, evening and formal dress, maternity garments, wedding clothes

For uniforms and symbolic garments, see 687.15

See also 687 for casual wear (sportswear)

.162	Protective clothing

Including fire-resistant clothing

.165　　　　　Sleepwear and loungewear

　　　　　　　　Former heading: Nightclothes

　　　　　　　　Standard subdivisions are added for either or both topics in heading

.19　　　　　Accessories

　　　　　　　　Including aprons, belts, cuffs, handkerchiefs, muffs, neckwear, scarves

　　　　　　　　Headscarves relocated to 687.4

　　　　　　　　Class interdisciplinary works on accessories in 391.44; class interdisciplinary works on making costume jewelry in 688.2; class interdisciplinary works on making jewelry in 739.27

　　　　　　　　For gloves and mittens, see 685.4; for handbags, see 685.51; for headwear, see 687.4

.2　　　Undergarments

　　　　　　　　See also 687.3 for hosiery

[.208 11]　　　　Undergarments for men

　　　　　　　　　Do not use; class in 687.21

[.208 2]　　　　Undergarments for women

　　　　　　　　　Do not use; class in 687.22

[.208 3]　　　　Undergarments for young people

　　　　　　　　　Do not use; class in 687.23

.208 4　　　　Undergarments for people in specific stages of adulthood

　　　　　　　　　Class undergarments for adult men regardless of age in 687.21; class undergarments for adult women regardless of age in 687.22

.208 7　　　　Undergarments for people with disabilities and illnesses

　　　　　　　　　Class supporting undergarments worn for medical or health reasons in 687.25

.21　　　　　Men's undergarments

.22　　　　　Women's undergarments

　　　　　　　　Class here comprehensive works on lingerie

　　　　　　　　For women's sleepwear and loungewear, see 687.165082

.23　　　　　Children's undergarments

　　　　　　　　Class young men's undergarments in 687.21; class young women's undergarments in 687.22

.25　　　　　Supporting undergarments worn for medical or health reasons

.3　　　Hosiery

.4   **Headwear**

> Including headscarves [*formerly* 687.19], helmets, protective headwear
>
> Class here bonnets, caps, hats
>
>> For helmets as armor, see 623.441
>
> Headwear used as equipment in a specific sport relocated to 688.7

[.408 11]   Men's headwear

> Do not use; class in 687.41

[.408 2]   Women's headwear

> Do not use; class in 687.42

[.408 3]   Young people's headwear

> Do not use; class in 687.43

.408 4   Headwear for people in specific stages of adulthood

> Class headwear for adult men regardless of age in 687.41; class headwear for adult women regardless of age in 687.42

.41   Men's headwear

.42   Women's headwear

.43   Children's headwear

> Class headwear for young men in 687.41; class headwear for young women in 687.42

.8   **Items auxiliary to clothing construction (Notions)**

> Including buttons
>
> Class here comprehensive works on manufacture of sewing equipment and supplies
>
> Class interdisciplinary works on sewing equipment and supplies in 646.1
>
>> For manufacture of sewing machinery and equipment, see 681.7677. For manufacture of a specific kind of sewing supply, see the kind, e.g., thread 677.02862

688   Other final products, and packaging technology

.1   **Models and miniatures**

> Standard subdivisions are added for either or both topics in heading
>
> Class here interdisciplinary works on models and miniatures
>
> Class interdisciplinary works on handcrafted models and miniatures in 745.5928
>
>> For models and miniatures of a specific object, see the object, plus notation 0228 from Table 1, e.g., scale models of space stations 629.4420228
>
> See Manual at 745.5928

.2 Costume jewelry

Class here interdisciplinary works on making costume jewelry

Class handcrafted costume jewelry in 745.5942; class interdisciplinary works on costume jewelry in 391.7; class interdisciplinary works on making jewelry in 739.27

.4 Supplies for tobacco users

Including ash trays, cigarette holders and cases, hookahs, lighters, tobacco pouches, tobacco substitutes

Class here supplies for smoking tobacco, for chewing tobacco

.42 Pipes

.5 Accessories for personal grooming

Including combs, electric shavers, nail-care tools, razors, razor blades, tweezers

For cosmetics, see 668.55; for brushes, see 679.6

.6 Nonmotor land vehicles

Including carriages, carts, wagons, wheelbarrows

For cycles, see 629.227

See also 688.7622 for skateboards

See Manual at 629.046 vs. 388

.7 Recreational equipment

Including stilts [*formerly* 685.367]

Class here footwear used as equipment in a specific sport [*formerly* 685.36], gloves and mittens used as equipment in a specific sport [*formerly* 685.43], headwear used as equipment in a specific sport [*formerly* 687.4]

See also 681.761 for exercise equipment

.72 Toys

Class here interdisciplinary works on mass-produced and handcrafted toys

For handcrafted toys, see 745.592

.722 Dolls, puppets, marionettes

.722 1 Dolls

.722 4 Puppets and marionettes

.723 Dollhouses and furniture

Standard subdivisions are added for either or both topics in heading

.724 Soft toys

Class stuffed dolls in 688.7221

.724 3 Teddy bears

.725   **Educational toys**

Including construction toys, science sets

.726   **Novelties, ornaments, puzzles, tricks**

Not provided for elsewhere

.728   **Action toys**

Mechanical, electrical, electronic, others

Class scale-model action toys in 688.1

>   **688.74–688.79 Equipment for sports and games**

Not provided for elsewhere

Class comprehensive works in 688.7

.74   **Equipment for indoor games of skill**

Add to base number 688.74 the numbers following 794 in 794.1–794.8, e.g., chessmen 688.741

.75   **Equipment for games of chance**

Add to base number 688.75 the numbers following 795 in 795.1–795.4, e.g., playing cards 688.754

.76   **Equipment for outdoor sports and games**

Add to base number 688.76 the numbers following 796 in 796.1–796.9, e.g., roller skates 688.7621 [*formerly* 685.362], skateboards 688.7622 [*formerly* 685.362], tennis rackets 688.76342, ice skates 688.7691 [*formerly* 685.361], baseball helmets 688.76357 [*formerly* 687.4], snowshoes 688.7692 [*formerly* 685.363], skis 688.7693 [*formerly* 685.364]; however, for camping equipment, see 685.53; for baseball caps, see 687.4

For equipment for equestrian sports and animal racing, see 688.78; for equipment for fishing, hunting, shooting, see 688.79

.78   **Equipment for equestrian sports and animal racing**

Including hurdles

For saddles and harnesses, see 685.1

.79   **Equipment for fishing, hunting, shooting**

Add to base number 688.79 the numbers following 799 in 799.1–799.3, e.g., artificial flies 688.79124

For small firearms, see 683.4

See also 681.763 for subsistence hunting, fishing, shooting equipment

.8 **Packaging technology**

Materials, equipment, techniques

Class interdisciplinary works on packaging in 658.564. Class manufacture and use of containers made of a specific material with the material, e.g., paper containers 676.3; class artistic aspects of containers with the aspect in 700, e.g., earthenware vases 738.38; class containers for a specific product with the product, e.g., beer cans 663.42

[689] **[Unassigned]**

Most recently used in Edition 14

690 Construction of buildings

Planning, analysis, engineering design, construction, destruction of habitable structures and their utilities

Class interdisciplinary works on design and construction of buildings in 720

See Manual at 624 vs. 690; also at 690 vs. 643.7

SUMMARY

690.01–.09	**Standard subdivisions**
.1–.8	**Special topics of construction of buildings**
691	**Building materials**
692	**Auxiliary construction practices**
693	**Construction in specific types of materials and for specific purposes**
694	**Wood construction**
695	**Roof covering**
696	**Utilities**
697	**Heating, ventilating, air-conditioning engineering**
698	**Detail finishing**

.01 Philosophy and theory

.02 Miscellany

.021 2 Formulas

Do not use for specifications; class in 692.3

[.022 3] Maps, plans, diagrams

Do not use; class in 692.1

.028 Auxiliary techniques and procedures; apparatus, equipment

.028 4 Apparatus and equipment

Do not use for materials; class in 691

.028 6   Green technology (Environmental technology)

— sustainable building (handwritten)

Do not use for comprehensive works on environmental engineering of buildings; class in 696

Including pollution control technology; comprehensive works on waste technology

> *For water drainage, see 696.13; for chimneys and flues, see 697.8; for air quality components of air conditioning systems, see 697.9324*

> *See also 696 for comprehensive works on energy engineering of buildings*

[.028 8]   Maintenance and repair

Do not use; class in 690.24

[.028 9]   Safety measures

Do not use; class in 690.22

.029   Commercial miscellany

Do not use for estimates of labor, time, materials; class in 692.5

.03–.09   Standard subdivisions

>   **690.1–690.8 Special topics of construction of buildings**

Unless other instructions are given, observe the following table of preference, e.g., maintenance and repair of residential buildings 690.80288 (*not* 690.24):

Specific parts of buildings	690.4
Specific types of buildings	690.5–690.8
Structural elements	690.1
General activities of buildings	690.2
Buildings by shape, buildings with atriums	690.38
Portable and temporary buildings	690.34
Special topics of buildings (without subdivision)	690.3

.1   **Structural elements**

Add to base number 690.1 the numbers following 721 in 721.1–721.8, e.g., auxiliary roof structures 690.15; however, for fireplaces, see 697.1; for chimneys, see 697.8

Class construction of structural elements in wood in 694

.2   **General activities of buildings**

Including architectural acoustics

Class interdisciplinary works on architectural acoustics in 729.29

.21   Structural analysis

Including statics, dynamics, stability, strength of buildings

.22	Provision for safety

Engineering for safe buildings, safety during construction

.24	Maintenance and repair

Including remodeling

For home repairs by members of household, see 643.7

See Manual at 690 vs. 643.7

.26	Wrecking and razing

.3   **Special topics of buildings**

.34	Portable and temporary buildings
.342	Portable buildings
.344	Temporary buildings
.38	Buildings by shape, buildings with atriums

Including circular, single-story buildings

.383	Tall buildings

.4   **Specific parts of buildings**

Class plumbing in specific parts of buildings in 696.18

.42	Bathrooms and lavatories

Standard subdivisions are added for either or both topics in heading

Class interdisciplinary works on bathrooms and lavatories in 643.52

.43	Laundries

Class interdisciplinary works on laundries in 667.13

.44	Kitchens

Class interdisciplinary works on kitchens in 643.3

.5–.8   **Specific types of buildings**

Add to base number 690 the numbers following 72 in 725–728, e.g., airport terminal buildings 690.539; however, for construction of buildings for defense against military action, see 623.1; for naval facilities, see 623.64; for military air facilities, see 623.66; for port facilities, see 627.3

.879	Mobile homes

Number built according to instructions under 690.5–690.8

See Manual at 643.29, 690.879, 728.79 vs. 629.226

691   **Building materials**

Class here construction properties, selection

Class construction in a specific type of material in 693

.1 **Timber**

.12   Prevention of decay

            Including impregnation, painting, spraying with fungicides

.14   Prevention of termite damage

.15   Treatment for fire resistance

.2 **Natural stones**

            Including granite, limestone, marble, sandstone, serpentine, slate, soapstone

.3 **Concrete and artificial stones**

            Including concrete blocks, cinder blocks

.4 **Ceramic and clay materials**

            Including brick, terra-cotta, tile, sun-dried blocks

.5 **Masonry adhesives**

.6 **Glass**

.7 **Iron and steel (Ferrous metals)**

            Standard subdivisions are added for either or both topics in heading

.8 **Metals**

            Add to base number 691.8 the numbers following 669 in 669.2–669.7, e.g., aluminum 691.8722

            For iron and steel, see 691.7

.9 **Other building materials**

.92   Plastics and their laminates

            Standard subdivisions are added for either or both topics in heading

.95   Insulating materials

            Including asbestos, corkboard, diatomaceous earth, kapok, rock wool

.96   Bituminous materials

            Including asphalts, tar

.97   Prefabricated materials

.99   Adhesives and sealants

            For masonry adhesives, see 691.5; for plastics and their laminates, see 691.92

692   Auxiliary construction practices

            Class application of a specific auxiliary practice to a specific subject with the subject, e.g., construction specifications for air conditioning 697.93

.1 **Plans and drawings**

    Interpretation and use of rough sketches, working drawings, blueprints

    For detail drawings, see 692.2

.2 **Detail drawings**

    Interpretation and use of large-scale drawings of trims, moldings, other details

.3 **Construction specifications**

.5 **Estimates of labor, time, materials**

    Class here interdisciplinary works on quantity surveying

    Class estimates for a specific subject in building with the subject, plus notation 029 from Table 1, e.g., estimates for air conditioning 697.93029

.8 **Contracting**

    Provision of construction materials and services in accordance with specifications

693 Construction in specific types of materials and for specific purposes

    Class comprehensive works on construction in all types of materials in 690

    For selection, preservation, construction properties of building materials, see 691; for wood construction, see 694; for roofing materials, see 695

[.01–.09]   Standard subdivisions

    Do not use; class in 690.01–690.09

> **693.1–693.7 Construction in specific materials**

    Class construction in specific materials for specific purposes in 693.8; class comprehensive works in 690

    For construction in other materials, see 693.9

.1 **Masonry**

    Including construction in natural stone

    For masonry using materials other than natural stone, see 693.2–693.5

> **693.2–693.5 Masonry using materials other than natural stone**

    Class comprehensive works in 693.1

.2 **Stabilized earth materials**

.21   Bricks

    For hollow bricks, see 693.4

.22	Sun-dried blocks

Including adobe, cob, pisé, tabby, tapia

.3 Tiles and terra-cotta

For hollow tiles, see 693.4

.4 Artificial stones and hollow bricks

Including cinder blocks, concrete blocks, hollow tiles

.5 Concrete

For concrete blocks, see 693.4

.52 Concrete without reinforcement

.521 Poured concrete

.522 Precast concrete

.54 Concrete with reinforcement (Ferroconcrete)

.541 Poured concrete

.542 Prestressed concrete

.544 Precast concrete

.6 Lathing, plastering, stuccowork

Including drywall construction

.7 Metals

.71 Iron and steel (Ferrous metals)

Standard subdivisions are added for either or both topics in heading

.72–.77 Nonferrous metals

Add to base number 693.7 the numbers following 669 in 669.2–669.7, e.g., tin 693.76

.8 Construction for specific purposes

.82 Fireproof construction

.83 Insulated construction

.832 Thermal insulation

.834 Acoustical insulation (Soundproofing)

.84 Pest-resistant construction

.842 Termite-resistant construction

.844 Rodent-resistant construction

.85 Shock-resistant construction

.852 Earthquake-resistant construction

.854   Blast-resistant construction

.89   Waterproof, moistureproof, lightning-resistant construction

.892   Waterproof construction

Class moistureproof construction in 693.893

.893   Moistureproof construction

.898   Lightning-resistant construction

.9   Construction in other materials

.91   Ice and snow

.92   Sandwich panels

Class sandwich panels in a specific substance with the substance, e.g., wood 694

.96   Glass

.97   Prefabricated materials

Class materials prefabricated in a specific substance with the substance, e.g., precast concrete 693.522

.98   Nonrigid materials

Including pneumatic construction

.99   Miscellaneous materials

Add to base number 693.99 the numbers following 620.19 in 620.191–620.199, e.g., plastics 693.9923; however, for nonrigid materials, see 693.98

694   Wood construction

Class here carpentry

.1   Planning, analysis, engineering design

> **694.2–694.6 Carpentry**

Class comprehensive works in 694

.2   Rough carpentry (Framing)

Construction of ceilings, floors, foundations, frames, openings, partition frames, posts, roofs, sidings, walls

.6   Finish carpentry (Joinery)

On-site construction of doors, doorways; blinds, shutters, windows; balconies, porches, verandas; balustrades, rails, ramps, stairs; trims, e.g., inlays, moldings, paneling; built-in cases and shelves

Class off-site manufacture of finishing items in 680

695 Roof covering

Class wooden roofs in 694.2; class comprehensive works on roofs as structural elements in 690.15

696 Utilities

Class here comprehensive works on energy and environmental engineering of buildings

Class interior electric wiring in 621.31924; class comprehensive works on waste technology in buildings in 690.0286; class interdisciplinary works on energy for use in buildings in 333.7962

For heating, ventilating, air-conditioning engineering, see 697. For a specific aspect of energy engineering, see the aspect, e.g., thermal insulation 693.832; for a specific aspect of environmental engineering not provided for here, see the aspect, plus notation 0286 from Table 1, e.g., environmental engineering of building materials 691.0286, environmental engineering in hot water heating 697.30286

.1 Plumbing

Design and installation of water fixtures and pipes

.12 Water supply

Including intake pipes, water receiving fixtures, water-softening equipment

For water supply in specific parts of buildings, see 696.18; for hot-water supply, see 696.6

.13 Water drainage

For water drainage in specific parts of buildings, see 696.18

.18 Plumbing in specific parts of buildings

Class here water supply in specific parts of buildings, drainage in specific parts of buildings

[.180 1–.180 9] Standard subdivisions

Do not use; class in 696.101–696.109

.182 Bathrooms and lavatories

Standard subdivisions are added for either or both topics in heading

.183 Laundries

.184 Kitchens

Including installation of dishwashers and garbage-disposal units

.2 Pipe fitting

Including gas pipes (gas fitting)

For water pipes, see 696.1; for steam fitting, see 696.3

.3 Steam pipes (Steam fitting)

.6   **Hot-water supply**

Including pipes, water heaters, water-softening equipment

697   Heating, ventilating, air-conditioning engineering

Standard subdivisions are added for heating, ventilating, air-conditioning engineering together; for heating alone

SUMMARY

697.001–.009	**Standard subdivisions**
.02–.07	**[Local and central heating, heating with specific sources of energy, heating equipment]**
.1	**Heating with open fires (Radiative heating)**
.2	**Heating with space heaters (Convective heating)**
.3	**Hot-air heating**
.4	**Hot-water heating**
.5	**Steam heating**
.7	**Other heating methods**
.8	**Chimneys and flues**
.9	**Ventilation and air conditioning; heating, ventilation, air-conditioning in specific kinds of buildings**

[.000 1–.000 9]   Standard subdivisions

Relocated to 697.001–697.009

.001–.009   Standard subdivisions [*formerly also* 697.0001–697.0009]

.001   Philosophy and theory

.002   Miscellany

.002 8   Auxiliary techniques and procedures; apparatus, equipment, materials

.002 84   Apparatus, equipment, materials

Do not use for heating apparatus and equipment; class in 697.07

.003–.009   Standard subdivisions

.02   Local heating

Class local heating by source of heat in 697.1–697.2

.03   Central heating

Class here comprehensive works on district heating

> For district heating by hot water, see 697.4; for district heating by steam, see 697.54. For a specific type of central heating, see the type in 697.3–697.7, e.g., solar heating 697.78

.04   Heating with specific sources of energy

Class here fuels

Class a specific fuel used in local heating in 697.02; class a specific fuel used in central heating in 697.03

> For solar heating, see 697.78; for nuclear heating, see 697.79

.042   Coal and coke heating

.043   Gas heating

.044   Oil heating

.045   Electric heating

.07   Heating equipment

Including boilers, furnaces, radiators, thermostats

Class here heating apparatus

>   **697.1–697.8 Heating**

Class heating in specific kinds of buildings in 697.95–697.98; class comprehensive works in 697

>   **697.1–697.2 Local heating**

Class chimneys and flues for local heating in 697.8; class comprehensive works in 697.02

.1   **Heating with open fires (Radiative heating)**

Including braziers, fireplaces

Class fireplace-like stoves that have visible fires but which are convective heaters in 697.2

.2   **Heating with space heaters (Convective heating)**

Class comprehensive works on local heating in 697.02

.22   Stationary stoves

Class cooking stoves in 683.88

.24   Portable heaters

>   **697.3–697.7 Central heating**

Class chimneys and flues for central heating in 697.8; class comprehensive works in 697.03

.3   **Hot-air heating**

Class radiant panel hot-air heating in 697.72

.4   **Hot-water heating**

Class hot-water supply in 696.6; class radiant panel hot-water heating in 697.72; class comprehensive works on district heating in 697.03

.5   **Steam heating**

Class steam fitting in 696.3; class radiant panel steam heating in 697.72

.500 1   Philosophy and theory

.500 2	Miscellany
.500 28	Auxiliary techniques and procedures; materials
.500 284	Materials

> Do not use for apparatus and equipment; class in 697.507

.500 3–.500 9	Standard subdivisions
.507	Equipment

> Including boilers, furnaces, radiators

> Class here apparatus

.54	District heating

> Heating a group of buildings from a central station

> Class comprehensive works on steam and hot-water district heating in 697.03

> *See also 697.4 for hot-water district heating*

.7	**Other heating methods**
.72	Radiant panel heating
.78	Solar heating

> Class building of solar houses in 690.83704724

.79	Nuclear heating
.8	**Chimneys and flues**
.9	**Ventilation and air conditioning; heating, ventilation, air-conditioning in specific kinds of buildings**
.92	Ventilation

> Class ventilation in specific kinds of buildings in 697.95–697.98

.93	Air conditioning

> Class heating in 697.1–697.8

.931	General topics of air conditioning

> Class general topics applied to specific components in 697.932; class general topics applied to specific systems in 697.933; class general topics applied to specific types of buildings in 697.95–697.98

.931 2	Design principles
.931 5	Psychrometrics

> Determination and control of enclosed atmospheric environments for optimum comfort

.931 6	Industrial and commercial applications

> Determination and control of enclosed atmospheric environment for effective operations

.932	Components

Class here manufacturing

.932 2	Cooling and heating components

Including cooling and heating coils, thermostats

.932 3	Humidifying and dehumidifying components

Including humidistats

.932 4	Air quality components

Devices for removing particulates, e.g., dust, pollen

Class here filters

.932 5	Air circulation components

Including blowers

.933	Systems

Class system components in 697.932; class systems in specific types of buildings in 697.95–697.98

.933 2	Winter systems
.933 3	Summer systems
.933 4	Year-round systems
[.935–.938]	Air conditioning in specific types of buildings

Relocated to 697.95–697.98

.95–.98	Air-conditioning in specific types of buildings [*formerly* 697.935–697.938]; heating, ventilation in specific types of buildings

Add to base number 697.9 the numbers following 72 in 725–728, e.g., heating, ventilation, air-conditioning of industrial buildings 697.954 Subdivisions are added for any or all topics in heading

Class components of air-conditioning systems for specific types of buildings in 697.932

698 Detail finishing

Including cladding, siding, suspended ceilings

Class roof covering in 695

For lathing, plastering, stuccowork, see 693.6; for wooden moldings, paneling, inlays, see 694.6

.1	**Painting**
.102	Miscellany
.102 8	Auxiliary techniques and procedures; apparatus, equipment, materials
.102 83	Paint mixing

[.102 88]	Maintenance and repair

Do not use; class in 698.1028

.12   Exteriors

.14   Interiors

Class painting woodwork in 698.35

.142   Walls

.146   Floors

.147   Ceilings

.2   Calcimining and whitewashing

Standard subdivisions are added for either or both topics in heading

.3   Finishing woodwork

.32   Staining

Including graining and marbling

.33   Polishing with wax and oil

.34   Lacquering and varnishing

.35   Painting

.5   Glazing and leading windows

.6   Paperhanging

.9   Floor coverings

Including carpets, rugs; linoleum, tiles

Class comprehensive works on floors in 690.16

[699]   [Unassigned]

Most recently used in Edition 14

700 The arts

Description, critical appraisal, techniques, procedures, apparatus, equipment, materials of the fine, decorative, literary, performing, recreational arts

Class here conceptual art, fine and decorative arts, government policy on the arts, plastic arts (visual arts), visual arts

Use 700 and standard subdivisions 700.1–700.9 for artists' books, performance art covering the arts in general; use 702.81 and 709 for artists' books, performance art limited to fine and decorative arts

Class plastic arts when limited to the three-dimensional arts in 730

For book arts, see 686; for literature, see 800

SUMMARY

780	Music
.000 1–.099 9	Relation of music to other subjects
.1–.9	Standard subdivisions; analytical guides, program notes; texts; treatises on music scores and recordings; performances
781	General principles and musical forms
782	Vocal music
783	Music for single voices
784	Instruments and instrumental ensembles and their music
785	Ensembles with only one instrument per part
786	Keyboard, mechanical, electrophonic, percussion instruments
787	Stringed instruments (Chordophones)
788	Wind instruments (Aerophones)
790	Recreational and performing arts
.01–.09	Standard subdivisions of recreation; recreation centers
.1–.2	[General kinds of recreational activities and the performing arts in general]
791	Public performances
792	Stage presentations
793	Indoor games and amusements
794	Indoor games of skill
795	Games of chance
796	Athletic and outdoor sports and games
797	Aquatic and air sports
798	Equestrian sports and animal racing
799	Fishing, hunting, shooting

> ### 700.1–700.9 Standard subdivisions of the arts

Use this standard subdivision span for material that includes two or more of the fine and decorative arts and one or more of the other arts, e.g., a work about a painter who is also a sculptor and a poet 700.92. If only one fine or decorative art and one of the other arts is involved, class in the number coming first in the schedule, e.g., a United States painter and poet 759.13

Class comprehensive works in 700

.1 **Philosophy and theory of the arts**

Notation 01 from Table 1 as modified below

Class here effects of other topics on the arts

.103 Effects of social conditions and factors on the arts

.104 Effects of humanities on the arts

.105 Effects of science and technology on the arts

.108 Effects of other concepts on the arts

Including humor, mythology, nature, parapsychology

.2 **Miscellany**

.285 Computer applications

Class here computers used as a technique to support traditional techniques in the arts

Class computer art in 776

See Manual at 776 vs. 006.5–006.7

.3 **Dictionaries, encyclopedias, concordances**

.4 **Special topics in the arts**

.41 Arts displaying specific qualities of style, mood, viewpoint

Add to base number 700.41 the numbers following —1 in notation 11–18 from Table 3C, e.g., horror in the arts 700.4164

Class arts dealing with specific themes and subjects regardless of quality displayed in 700.42–700.49

.42–.49 Arts dealing with specific themes and subjects

Add to base number 700.4 the numbers following —3 in notation 32–39 from Table 3C, e.g., historical themes in the arts 700.458

.5–.8 **Standard subdivisions of the arts**

.9 **History, geographic treatment, biography of the arts**

.92 Biography

Class here the works themselves and critical appraisal and description of works of an artist or artists

See Manual at 700.92

> **701–708 Standard subdivisions of fine and decorative arts**

Other than history, geographic treatment, biography

Class standard subdivisions of specific schools, styles, periods of development in 709.012–709.05; class comprehensive works in 700

701 **Philosophy and theory of fine and decorative arts**

Notation 01 from Table 1 as modified below

Including appreciative aspects, inherent features

Class here effects of other topics on the arts

.03–.08 Special topics of philosophy and theory of fine and decorative arts

Add to base number 701.0 the numbers following 700.10 in 700.103–700.108, e.g., effects of social conditions and factors on fine and decorative arts 701.03

.1 **Appreciative aspects**

Do not use for systems; class in 701

Including use of audiovisual aids

See also 709 for history of the fine arts

.15 Psychological principles

Fine arts as products of creative imagination

.17 Aesthetics

Class interdisciplinary works in 111.85

.18 Criticism and appreciation

Class here theory, technique, history

Class works of critical appraisal in 709

.8 Inherent features

Including composition, decorative values, form, light, movement, space, style, symmetry, time, vision

.82 Perspective

See also 742 for drawing aspects of perspective

.85 Color

See also 752 for painting aspects of color

.9 Methodology

Do not use for psychological principles; class in 701.15

702 Miscellany of fine and decorative arts

.8 Auxiliary techniques and procedures; apparatus, equipment, materials

Notation 028 from Table 1 as modified below

Including testing and measurement, use of artists' models

Class here basic techniques and procedures

.81 Mixed-media and composites

Including artists' books; performance art

Class finished works of mixed-media and composite art in 709; class two-dimensional mixed-media art or composites in 760

.812 Collage

Class decoupage in 745.546

.813 Montage

.814 Assemblage

.85 Computer applications

Class here computers used as a technique to support traditional techniques in fine and decorative arts

Class computer art in 776

See Manual at 776 vs. 006.5–006.7

.87 Techniques of reproduction, execution, identification

Do not use for testing and measurement; class in 702.8

.872	Reproductions and copies
.874	Forgeries and alterations
.88	Maintenance and repair

Including expertizing

Class identification of reproductions, copies, forgeries, alterations in 702.87

.9 **Commercial miscellany**

Class auction and sales catalogs in which an exhibition is involved in 707.4

703 Dictionaries, encyclopedias, concordances of fine and decorative arts

704 Special topics in fine and decorative arts

\> 704.03–704.08 Groups of people

Unless other instructions are given, class a subject with aspects in two or more subdivisions of 704.03–704.08 in the number coming last, e.g., women with disabilities 704.87 (*not* 704.042)

Class description, critical appraisal, works, biography of artists as individuals in 709.2; class comprehensive works in 704

.03 Ethnic and national groups

Class people by gender or sex of a specific ethnic or national group in 704.04; class groups of miscellaneous specific groups of people of a specific ethnic or national group in 704.08; class ethnic and national groups in places where they predominate in 709.1–709.9

.030 5–.030 9 Specific ethnic and national groups with ethnic origins from more than one continent, of European descent

Add to base number 704.03 notation 05–09 from Table 5, e.g., art of ethnic groups of European descent 704.0309

.031–.039 Specific ethnic and national groups

Add to base number 704.03 notation 1–9 from Table 5, e.g., art of North American native peoples 704.0397

.04 People by gender or sex

Class groups of miscellaneous specific groups of people of a specific gender or sex in 704.08

For transgendered people, see 704.0867

.041 Men

Works specifically emphasizing male sex

.042 Women

.08   Miscellaneous specific groups of people

Add to base number 704.08 the numbers following —08 in notation 083–088 from Table 1, e.g., people with disabilities 704.087; however, for art dealers, see 381.457092; for nonliterate peoples, see 709.011

See Manual at 709.2 vs. 381.457092

.9   Iconography

See Manual at 704.9 and 753–758

.94   Specific subjects

A work with two or more subjects is classed with the subject that is the center of interest, e.g., cityscapes with incidental human figures 704.944 (*not* 704.942), church interiors displaying Stations of the Cross 704.9484 (*not* 704.944)

SUMMARY

704.942	**Human figures**
.943	**Nature and still life**
.944	**Architectural subjects and cityscapes**
.946	**Symbolism and allegory**
.947	**Mythology and legend**
.948	**Religion**
.949	**Other specific subjects**

[.940 1–.940 9]   Standard subdivision

Do not use; class in 704.901–704.909

.942   Human figures

Class here portraits

Unless other instructions are given, observe the following table of preference, e.g., groups of children 704.9425 (*not* 704.9426):

Erotica	704.9428
Nudes	704.9421
Specific groups of people	704.9423–704.9425
Groups of human figures	704.9426

Class symbolism of human figures in 704.946. Class human figures engaged in a specific occupation with the occupation, e.g., farmers 704.943092, doctors 704.94961092, circus clowns 704.94979133

For human figures associated with mythology and legend, see 704.947; for human figures associated with religion, see 704.948

.942 092   Biography

Artists and critics

Class works about the person portrayed in 704.942

.942 1   Nudes

Class here nudes of men [*formerly* 704.9423], nudes of women [*formerly* 704.9424], nudes of children [*formerly* 704.9425], groups of nudes [*formerly* 704.9426]

[.942 2]	Draped figures
	Number discontinued; class in 704.942

> 704.942 3–704.942 5 Specific groups of people

Class comprehensive works in 704.942

.942 3	Men
	Nudes of men relocated to 704.9421
.942 4	Women
	Nudes of women relocated to 704.9421
.942 5	Children
	Nudes of children relocated to 704.9421
.942 6	Groups of human figures
	Groups of nudes relocated to 704.9421; hunters relocated to 704.94979929
.942 8	Erotica
	Including pornography

.943 Nature and still life

Standard subdivisions are added for nature and still life together, for nature alone

Class here agriculture

Class symbolism of nature and still life in 704.946; class comprehensive works on science in 704.9495

For nature and still life associated with mythology and legend, see 704.947; for nature and still life associated with religion, see 704.948

.943 2	Animals
	Class here pets
	Add to base number 704.9432 the numbers following 59 in 592–599, e.g., eagles 704.94328942
	Class symbolism of animals in 704.946
.943 4	Plants
	Class symbolism of plants in 704.946
.943 43	Flowers
.943 5	Still life
.943 6	Landscapes
	Add to base number 704.9436 notation 1–9 from Table 2, e.g., landscapes of Utah 704.9436792

.943 7	Marine scenes and seascapes
	Standard subdivisions are added for either or both topics in heading
.944	Architectural subjects and cityscapes
	Standard subdivisions are added for either or both topics in heading
	Add to base number 704.944 notation 1–9 from Table 2, e.g., cityscapes of England 704.94442
.946	Symbolism and allegory
	Standard subdivisions are added for either or both topics in heading
	For religious symbolism, see 704.948
.947	Mythology and legend
	Class religious mythology in 704.948
.948	Religion
	Class here religious mythology, religious symbolism
	Class significance and purpose of art in religion in 203.7; class significance and purpose of art in Christianity in 246; class significance and purpose of art in non-Christian religions in 292–299
(.948 1)	(Permanently unassigned)
	(Optional number used to provide local emphasis and a shorter number for a specific religion other than Christianity; prefer the number for the specific religion in 704.9489)
.948 2	Christianity
	Class here icons, santos, votive offerings
	For specific Christian subjects, see 704.9484–704.9487

>   704.948 4–704.948 7 Specific Christian subjects

Class comprehensive works in 704.9482

.948 4	Biblical characters and events
	For Trinity and Holy Family and its members, see 704.9485; for apostles, saints, angels, see 704.9486; for devils, see 704.9487
.948 5	Trinity and Holy Family and its members
.948 52	Trinity
.948 53	Jesus Christ
.948 55	Madonna and Child
	Class here Mary without Child

.948 56	Holy Family

Presented as a group

Class Jesus Christ in 704.94853; class Mary with or without Child in 704.94855; class Saint Joseph in 704.94863

.948 6	Apostles, saints, angels
.948 62	Apostles
.948 63	Saints

For Apostles, see 704.94862

.948 64	Angels
.948 7	Devils
.948 9	Other religions

Add to base number 704.9489 the numbers following 29 in 292–299, e.g., Buddhism in art 704.948943; however, for Old Testament characters and events, see 704.9484

(Option: To give local emphasis and a shorter number to iconography of a specific religion, class in 704.9481, which is permanently unassigned)

.949	Other specific subjects

Add to base number 704.949 notation 001–999, e.g., hunters 704.94979929 [*formerly* 704.9426], technological subjects 704.9496; however, for agriculture, see 704.943

705 Serial publications of fine and decorative arts

706 Organizations and management of fine and decorative arts

707 Education, research, related topics of fine and decorative arts

.4 Temporary and traveling collections and exhibits

Do not use for museums and permanent collections and exhibits; class in 708

Class here permanent collections on tour, temporary exhibits of a private collection, auction and sales catalogs in which an exhibition is involved

For temporary in-house exhibits selected from a museum's or gallery's permanent collection, see 708

708 Galleries, museums, private collections of fine and decorative arts

Do not use for groups of people; class in 704.03–704.08

General art collections

Class here annual reports dealing with acquisitions, activities, programs, projects

For temporary and traveling collections and exhibits, see 707.4

.001–.008	Standard subdivisions
.009	History and biography

Do not use for geographic treatment; class in 708.1–708.9

> ### 708.1–708.9 Geographic treatment

Class here guidebooks and catalogs of specific galleries, museums, private collections

Class comprehensive works in 708

(Option: To give local emphasis and a shorter number to galleries, museums, private collections of a specific country, use one of the following:

(Option A: Place them first by use of a letter or other symbol, e.g., galleries, museums, private collections in Japan 708.J [preceding 708.1]

(Option B: Class them in 708.1; in that case class galleries, museums, private collections in North America in 708.97)

.1 North America

For galleries, museums, private collections in Middle America, see 708.972

(Option: To give local emphasis and a shorter number to galleries, museums, private collections of a specific country other than United States and Canada, class them in this number; in that case class galleries, museums, private collections in North America in 708.97)

.11 Canada

Add to base number 708.11 the numbers following —71 in notation 711–719 from Table 2, e.g., galleries, museums, private collections in British Columbia 708.111

.13–.19 United States

Add to base number 708.1 the numbers following —7 in notation 73–79 from Table 2, e.g., galleries, museums, private collections in Pennsylvania 708.148

For galleries, museums, private collections in Hawaii, see 708.9969

> **708.2–708.8 Europe**

Class comprehensive works in 708.94

For galleries, museums, private collections not provided for here, see 708.949, e.g., galleries, museums, private collections in Belgium 708.9493

.2   British Isles

Class here England

.21–.28   England

Add to base number 708.2 the numbers following —42 in notation 421–428 from Table 2, e.g., galleries, museums, private collections in Manchester 708.2733

.29   Scotland, Ireland, Wales

Add to base number 708.29 the numbers following —4 in notation 41–42 from Table 2, e.g., galleries, museums, private collections in Wales 708.2929

.3–.8   Miscellaneous parts of Europe

Add to base number 708 the numbers following —4 in notation 43–48 from Table 2, e.g., galleries, museums, private collections in France 708.4

.9   Other geographic areas

Add to base number 708.9 notation 1–9 from Table 2, e.g., comprehensive works on galleries, museums, private collections in Islamic areas 708.91767, in European countries 708.94, in Belgium 708.9493, in Middle America 708.972, in Hawaii 708.9969

Class parts of Europe in notation 41–48 from Table 2 in 708.2–708.8

709   History, geographic treatment, biography

Development, description, critical appraisal, works

Class here finished works of experimental and mixed-media art that do not fit easily into a recognized medium

Class two-dimensional experimental and mixed-media art in 760

See also 364.16287 for looting, plundering, theft of art as a crime; also 364.164 for destruction of art as a crime

SUMMARY

709.01	Arts of nonliterate peoples, and earliest times to 499
.02	6th–15th centuries, 500–1499
.03	Modern period, 1500–
.04	20th century, 1900–1999
.05	21st century, 2000–2099
.1	Areas, regions, places in general
.2	Biography
.3–.9	Specific continents, countries, localities

.01	Arts of nonliterate peoples, and earliest times to 499

Notation 0901 from Table 1 as modified below

.011	Nonliterate peoples

Regardless of time or place, but limited to nonliterate peoples of the past and nonliterate peoples clearly not a part of contemporary society

.011 2	Paleolithic art
.011 3	Rock art

>   709.012–709.015   Periods of development to 499 A.D.

Class here schools and styles not limited by country or locality, comprehensive works on European art limited by period, school, or style

Add to each subdivision identified by † notation 01–08 from Table 1, e.g., exhibits of prehistoric art 709.012074

Class comprehensive works in 709

For European art limited to a specific location, see the location in 709.4, e.g., art of Germany 709.43

See Manual at 704.9 and 753–758; also at 709.012–709.015, 709.02–709.05 vs. 709.3–709.9

.012	†To 4000 B.C.
.013	†3999–1000 B.C.
.014	†999–1 B.C.
.015	†1st–5th centuries, 1–499 A.D.

>   709.02–709.05   Periods of development, 500–

Notation 0902–0905 from Table 1 as modified below

Class here schools and styles not limited by country or locality, comprehensive works on European art limited by period, school, or style

Add to each subdivision identified by * notation 01–08 from Table 1, e.g., exhibits of cubism 709.04032074

Class comprehensive works in 709

For European art limited to a specific location, see the location in 709.4, e.g., art of Germany 709.43

See Manual at 704.9 and 753–758; also at 709.012–709.015, 709.02–709.05 vs. 709.3–709.9

.02	*6th–15th centuries, 500–1499

Class here medieval art

*Add as instructed under 709.02–709.05
†Add as instructed under 709.012–709.015

.021	*6th–12th centuries, 500–1199
.021 2	*Early Christian art
	For early Christian art before 500, see 709.015
.021 4	*Byzantine art
	For Byzantine art before 500, see 709.015
.021 6	*Romanesque art
.022	*13th century, 1200–1299
	Class here Gothic art
	For Gothic art of an earlier or later period, see the specific period, e.g., 500–1199 709.021
.023	*14th century, 1300–1399
.024	*15th century, 1400–1499
	Class here Renaissance art
	For Renaissance art of an earlier or later period, see the specific period, e.g., 16th century 709.031
.03	*Modern period, 1500–
	For 20th century, 1900–1999, see 709.04; for 21st century, 2000–2099, see 709.05
.031	*16th century, 1500–1599
.032	*17th century, 1600–1699
	Class here baroque art
	For baroque art of 18th century, see 709.033
.033	*18th century, 1700–1799
.033 2	*Rococo art
.034	*19th century, 1800–1899
.034 1	*Classical revival (Neoclassicism)
	For classical revival of 18th century, see 709.033
.034 2	*Romanticism
	For romanticism of 18th century, see 709.033
.034 3	*Naturalism and realism
	For naturalism and realism of an earlier or later period, see the specific period, e.g., 18th century 709.033
.034 4	*Impressionism
	Including luminism, pleinairism

*Add as instructed under 709.02–709.05

.034 5	*Neo-impressionism
	Including divisionism, pointillism
.034 6	*Postimpressionism
.034 7	*Symbolism and synthetism
.034 8	*Kitsch (Trash)
	For kitsch of a later period, see the period, e.g., 20th century 709.04013
.034 9	*Art nouveau
	For art nouveau of a later period, see the period, e.g., 20th century 709.04014
.04	20th century, 1900–1999
	Class here modern art
	For 19th century, 1800–1899, see 709.034; for 21st century, 2000–2099, see 709.05; for computer art (Digital art), see 776
.040 01–.040 08	Standard subdivisions
[.040 09]	History
	Do not use; class in 709.04
.040 1	*Art deco, kitsch, art nouveau
.040 12	*Art deco
.040 13	*Kitsch (Trash)
	Class comprehensive works on kitsch in 709.0348
.040 14	*Art nouveau
	Class comprehensive works on art nouveau in 709.0349
.040 2	*Functionalism
.040 3	*Cubism and futurism
	Including geometric design
.040 32	*Cubism
.040 33	*Futurism
.040 4	*Expressionism and fauvism
.040 42	*Expressionism
	Class abstract expressionism in 709.04052
.040 43	*Fauvism
.040 5	*Abstractionism, nonobjectivity, constructivism

*Add as instructed under 709.02–709.05

.040 52	*Abstractionism
	Including abstract expressionism, geometric abstractionism, neoplasticism
.040 56	*Nonobjectivity
	Class here concrete art
.040 57	*Constructivism
.040 58	*Minimalism
.040 6	*Dadaism and surrealism
.040 62	*Dadaism
.040 63	*Surrealism
.040 7	*Composite media and sensations
	Class techniques of composite media in 702.81
	For specific composite media, see 709.0408
.040 71	*Pop art
.040 72	*Optical art (Op art)
	See also 776 for computer art
[.040 73]	Kinetic art
	Number discontinued; class in 709.0407
.040 74	*Happenings, environments, events
.040 75	*Conceptual art
	For happenings, environments, events, see 709.04074
.040 752	*Body art
.040 755	*Performance art
.040 76	*Land art (Earthworks)
[.040 77]	Structuralism
	Number discontinued; class in 709.0407
[.040 78]	Multiple art
	Number discontinued; class in 709.0407
[.040 79]	Space art
	Number discontinued; class in 709.0407
.040 8	Specific composite media
	Class techniques of composite media in 702.81
.040 82	*Artists' books

*Add as instructed under 709.02–709.05

.040 84	*Mail art (Correspondence art)
.040 9	*Outsider art (Art brut)
.041–.049	Periods

Add to base number 709.04 the numbers following —0904 in notation 09041–09049 from Table 1, e.g., arts of 1960–1969 709.046

Class a specific school or style in a specific period in 709.0401–709.0407

.05	21st century, 2000–2099
.050 01–.050 08	Standard subdivisions [*formerly* 709.0501–709.0508]
[.050 09]	History

Do not use; class in 709.05

| [.050 1–.050 8] | Standard subdivisions |

Relocated to 709.05001–709.05008

| .051 | *2000–2019 |

Class a specific school or style in a specific period in 709.05

| .051 1 | *2000–2009 |
| .051 2 | *2010–2019 |

.1   Areas, regions, places in general

Class groups of people in 704.03–704.08; class art of nonliterate peoples regardless of place in 709.011

.2   Biography

Class here description, critical appraisal, works of artists not limited to or chiefly identified with a specific form, e.g., painting, or group of forms, e.g., graphic arts

See Manual at 709.2 vs. 381.457092

.22   Collected biography

Class works of more than one artist in the same geographic area not limited by continent, country, locality in 709.1; class works of more than one artist in the same continent, country, locality in 709.3–709.9

.3–.9   Specific continents, countries, localities

Class here art of specific periods, e.g., art of 1800–1899 in Germany 709.4309034

Class groups of people in 704.03–704.08; class art of nonliterate peoples regardless of place in 709.011. Class comprehensive works on European art of specific periods with the period in 709.01–709.05 (*not* 709.4), e.g., art of 1800–1899 in Europe 709.034 (*not* 709.409034)

See Manual at 709.012–709.015, 709.02–709.05 vs. 709.3–709.9

*Add as instructed under 709.02–709.05

710 Area planning and landscape architecture

Former heading: Civic and landscape art

Class comprehensive works on area planning, landscape architecture, and architecture in 720

SUMMARY

711	**Area planning (Civic art)**
712	**Landscape architecture (Landscape design)**
713	**Landscape architecture of trafficways**
714	**Water features in landscape architecture**
715	**Woody plants in landscape architecture**
716	**Herbaceous plants in landscape architecture**
717	**Structures in landscape architecture**
718	**Landscape design of cemeteries**
719	**Natural landscapes**

711 Area planning (Civic art)

Design of physical environment for public welfare, convenience, pleasure

Class here plans

Unless other instructions are given, observe the following table of preference, e.g., planning of pedestrian malls in business districts 711.5522 (*not* 711.74):

Specific kinds of areas	711.5
Specific elements	711.6–711.8
Specific levels	711.2–711.4
Procedural and social aspects	711.1

Class comprehensive works on area planning and architecture in 720; class interdisciplinary works on area planning in 307.12

SUMMARY

711.1	**Procedural and social aspects**
.2	**International and national planning**
.3	**Interstate, state, provincial, county planning**
.4	**Local community planning (City planning)**
.5	**Specific kinds of areas**
.6	**Structural elements**
.7	**Transportation facilities**
.8	**Nontransportation utilities**

.1 Procedural and social aspects

.12 Professional practice and technical procedures

Including collection of data, preparation and presentation of plans and models

.13 Social factors affecting planning

.14 Economic factors affecting planning

>   **711.2–711.4   Specific levels**

         Class comprehensive works in 711

.2   **International and national planning**

.3   **Interstate, state, provincial, county planning**

         For urban counties, see 711.4; for metropolitan areas, see 711.43

.4   **Local community planning (City planning)**

         Class here urban renewal (conservation, rehabilitation, redevelopment)

         Class interdisciplinary works on city planning in 307.1216; class interdisciplinary works on urban renewal in 307.3416

         For urban renewal of specific kinds of areas, see 711.5

.409 3–.409 9   Specific continents, countries, localities

         Class here specific types of plans for specific cities

>   711.41–711.45   Specific types of plans

         Unless other instructions are given, class a subject with aspects in two or more subdivisions of 711.4 in the number coming last, e.g., plans for small cities in cold climates 711.43 (*not* 711.42)

         Class comprehensive works in 711.4

.41   *Plans based on street patterns

         Including gridiron, radial, studied irregularity plans

.42   *Plans based on environment

         Including plans based on topography and climate

.43   *Plans based on size

         Including plans for villages, small and large cities, metropolitan areas

.45   *Plans based on function

         Including new towns; plans for cities serving primarily as governmental, industrial, residential centers

.5   **Specific kinds of areas**

         Class here planning for urban renewal (conservation, rehabilitation, redevelopment) of specific kinds of areas

         Class interdisciplinary works on urban renewal in 307.3416

---

*Do not use notation 093–099 from Table 1 for specific cities; class in 711.4093–711.4099

.55   **Functional areas**

       Class here plazas, squares

       For religious centers, see 711.56; for cultural and educational areas, see 711.57; for residential areas, see 711.58; for parking areas, see 711.73

.551   Civic, administrative, governmental areas

       Standard subdivisions are added for any or all topics in heading

.552   Commercial and industrial areas

       Class planning of transportation facilities in 711.7

.552 2   Commercial areas

       Class here business districts, shopping centers

.552 4   Industrial areas

       Class here industrial parks

.554   Agricultural areas

.555   Medical centers

.556   Prison and reformatory areas

.557   Hotel and restaurant areas

       Including trailer camps for temporary residents

.558   Recreational areas

       Including parks, playgrounds, theatrical and performing arts centers

.56   Religious centers

.57   Cultural and educational areas

       Including areas for libraries, museums, colleges and universities

       Class theatrical and performing arts centers in 711.558

.58   Residential areas

       Urban, suburban, rural areas

       Including apartment-house districts, trailer parks for long-term residents

       For hotel areas, trailer camps for temporary residents, see 711.557; for housing renewal, see 711.59

.59   Housing renewal

       Class interdisciplinary works on housing renewal in 307.34

>   **711.6–711.8 Specific elements**

       Class comprehensive works in 711.6

.6   **Structural elements**

> Adaptation to site and use
>
> Class here comprehensive works on specific elements
>
> *For utilities, see 711.7*

.7   **Transportation facilities**

> Class here comprehensive works on utilities
>
> *For nontransportation utilities, see 711.8*

.72   Bicycle transportation facilities

.73   Motor vehicle transportation facilities

> Including motorcycle transportation facilities, parking areas

.74   Pedestrian transportation facilities

> Including pedestrian malls

.75   Railroad transportation facilities

> Including rapid transit facilities

.76   Marine transportation facilities

.78   Air transportation facilities

.8   **Nontransportation utilities**

> Including water, gas, electricity transmission and supply; communication lines; sanitation and flood control facilities

712   Landscape architecture (Landscape design)

> Class engineering aspects of landscape architecture in 624; class comprehensive works on landscape architecture and architecture in 720
>
> *For specific elements in landscape architecture, see 714–717*

.01   Philosophy and theory

> Class aesthetics, composition, style in 712.2

>   **712.2–712.3 General considerations**

> Class general considerations of design of specific kinds of land tracts in 712.5–712.7; class comprehensive works in 712

.2   **Principles**

> Including aesthetics, composition, effect, style

.3   **Professional practice and technical procedures**

> Including collection of data, preparation and presentation of plans and models, supervision of operations

> ### 712.5–712.7   Specific kinds of land tracts

Class comprehensive works in 712

> *For trafficways, see 713; for cemeteries, see 718; for natural landscapes, see 719*

.5   **Public parks and grounds**

Class here amusement parks, commons, fairgrounds, zoological and botanical gardens; comprehensive works on parks

> *For private parks, see 712.6; for parks of public reserved lands, see 719.3*

.6   **Private parks and grounds**

Class here estates, home gardens, penthouse gardens, yards

.7   **Semiprivate and institutional grounds**

Class here grounds of churches, country clubs, hospitals, hotels, industrial plants, schools

713   Landscape architecture of trafficways

> *See also 625.77 for planting and cultivation of roadside vegetation*

> ### 714–717   Specific elements in landscape architecture

Class comprehensive works in 712

714   Water features in landscape architecture

Including cascades, fountains

Class here natural and artificial pools

Class comprehensive works on fountains in 731.724

715   Woody plants in landscape architecture

Cultivated for flowers or for other attributes

Class here comprehensive works on plants in landscape architecture

Class comprehensive works on plants cultivated for their flowers in landscape architecture in 716

> *For herbaceeous plants in landscape architecture, see 716*

> *See also 635.97 for planting and cultivation of woody plants*

.1   **Topiary work**

> ### 715.2–715.4   Specific kinds of plants

Class topiary work on specific kinds of plants in 715.1; class comprehensive works in 715

.2	**Trees**
.3	**Shrubs**
.4	**Vines**

716 Herbaceous plants in landscape architecture

Cultivated for flowers or for other attributes

Including ground cover

Class here comprehensive works on plants cultivated for their flowers in landscape architecture

For woody plants cultivated for their flowers, see 715

See also 635.9 for planting and cultivation of herbaceous plants

717 Structures in landscape architecture

Relationship of buildings, terraces, fences, gates, steps, ornamental accessories to other elements of landscape architecture

Including pedestrian facilities, street furniture

718 Landscape design of cemeteries

.8 **National cemeteries**

719 Natural landscapes

Class natural water features in 714

.3 **Reserved lands**

.32 Public parks and natural monuments

Standard subdivisions are added for either or both topics in heading

.33 Forest and water-supply reserves

.36 Wildlife reserves

720 Architecture

Class here architectural structure; comprehensive works on architecture, area planning, and landscape architecture; on architecture and area planning; on architecture and landscape architecture; on architecture and structural engineering; interdisciplinary works on design and construction of buildings

For structural engineering, see 624.1; for engineering design and construction of buildings, see 690; for area planning and landscape architecture, see 710

SUMMARY

.1 **Philosophy and theory [*formerly also* 721.01]**

> Notation 01 from Table 1 as modified below

.103–.108 **Special topics of philosophy and theory**

> Add to base number 720.10 the numbers following 700.10 in 700.103–700.108, e.g., effects of social conditions and factors on architecture 720.103

.2 **Miscellany [*formerly also* 721.02]**

.22 Illustrations, models, miniatures

> Class architectural drawing in 720.284

.222 Pictures and related illustrations

> Class here architectural drawings

> Add to base number 720.222 notation 1–9 from Table 2, e.g., architectural drawings from England 720.22242

> Class drawings in the vertical plane, e.g., elevations, in 729.1; class drawings in the horizontal plane, e.g., floor plans in 729.2. Class architectural drawings for one structure or a specific type of structure with the structure in 725–728, plus notation 0222 from table under 721–729, e.g., architectural drawings of palaces 728.820222

.28 Auxiliary techniques and procedures; apparatus, equipment

> Including site planning

> Green technology (environmental technology) relocated to 720.47; waste technology relocated to 720.475, architectural materials relocated to 721.04

.284 Architectural drawing

> Do not use for apparatus and equipment; class in 720.28. Do not use for materials; class in 721.04

> Class drawings, illustrations, models in 720.22

.286 Remodeling

> Do not use for green technology; class in 720.47

.288   Maintenance and repair

> Class here conservation, preservation, restoration

> Class interdisciplinary works on conservation, preservation, restoration in 363.69

> *See Manual at 930–990: Historic preservation*

.3   **Dictionaries, encyclopedias, concordances [*formerly also* 721.03]**

.4   **Special topics of architecture**

> Unless other instructions are given, observe the following table of preference, e.g., temporary circular buildings 720.48 (*not* 720.444):

Architecture and the environment	720.47
Buildings by shape, buildings with atriums	720.48
Multiple-purpose buildings	720.49
Portable and temporary buildings	720.44

.44   Portable and temporary buildings

.442   Portable buildings

.444   Temporary buildings

.47   Architecture and the environment [*formerly also* 721.0467]

> Including pollution control technology

> Class here green technology (environmental technology) [*formerly* 720.28], sustainable architecture

.472   Energy resources

> Class here energy conservation

.472 4   Use of solar energy

> *For solar heating, see 697.78; for daylighting, see 729.28*

.473   Earth-sheltered buildings

> Class here underground architecture

.475   Waste technology [*formerly* 720.28]

.48   Buildings by shape, buildings with atriums [*both formerly also* 721.042]

> Including circular, single-story buildings

.483   Tall buildings

> Class here skyscrapers

.49   Multiple-purpose buildings [*formerly also* 721.0469]

> Class a multiple-purpose building with one primary purpose with the single-purpose buildings of that type, e.g., an apartment building with a floor of commercial space 728.314

.5–.8   **Standard subdivisions [*formerly also* 721.05–721.08]**

.9   **History, geographic treatment, biography [*formerly also* 721.09]**

> Class here architectural aspects of historic buildings, schools and styles limited to a specific country or locality
>
> Class architectural drawings in 720.222; class comprehensive works on specific schools and styles not limited to a specific country or locality in 722–724
>
> *See Manual at 913–919: Historic sites and buildings; also at 930–990: Historic preservation*

[.901–.905]   Historical periods

> Do not use; class in 722–724

[.93]   Ancient world

> Do not use; class in 722

.95   Asia

> Class here Buddhist, Oriental architecture
>
> Class Buddhist architecture of a national style with the style, e.g., Japanese Buddhist architecture 720.952

.954   India and neighboring south Asian countries

> Class here Hindu, Jain architecture

>   **721–729   Specific aspects of architecture**

> Add to each subdivision identified by * as follows:
> 01   Philosophy and theory
>   Notation 01 from Table 1 as modified below
> 0103–0108   Special topics
>   Add to 010 the numbers following 700.10 in 700.103–700.108, e.g., effects of social conditions and factors on architecture 0103
> 02   Miscellany
> 0222   Pictures and related illustrations
>   Class here architectural drawings
>   Add to 0222 notation 1–9 from Table 2, e.g., architectural drawings from England 022242
> 028   Auxiliary techniques and procedures; apparatus, equipment, materials
>   Notation 028 from Table 1 as modified below
> 0286   Remodeling
>   Do not use for green technology; class in 047
> 03   Dictionaries, encyclopedias, concordances
> 04   Special topics
>   Add to 04 the numbers following 720.4 in 720.44–720.49, e.g., energy conservation 0472
> 05–08   Standard subdivisions
> 09   History, geographic treatment, biography.
>   Class architectural drawings in 0222
>   *See Manual at 913–919: Historic sites and buildings; also at 930–990: Historic preservation*
> Class comprehensive works in 720

721   Architectural materials and structural elements

Use of this number for architectural structure discontinued; class in 720

[.01]   Philosophy and theory

Relocated to 720.1

[.02]   Miscellany

Relocated to 720.2

[.03]   Dictionaries, encyclopedias, concordances

Relocated to 720.3

.04   Architectural materials [*formerly also* 720.28]

For engineering design and construction in specific materials, see 693

.040 1–.040 9   Standard subdivisions [*formerly* 721.04401–721.04409]

[.042]   Buildings by shape, buildings with atriums

Relocated to 720.48

.044   Specific materials

[.044 01–.044 09]   Standard subdivisions

Relocated to 721.0401–721.0409

.044 1–.044 6   Masonry

Add to base number 721.044 the numbers following 693 in 693.1–693.6, e.g., architectural construction in reinforced concrete 721.04454

.044 7   Metals

Add to base number 721.0447 the numbers following 669 in 669.1–669.7, e.g., architectural construction in aluminum 721.0447722

.044 8   Wood

.044 9   Other materials

Add to base number 721.0449 the numbers following 693.9 in 693.91–693.99, e.g., architectural construction in glass 721.04496

[.046]   Architecture and the environment, multiple-purpose buildings

Provision discontinued because without meaning in context

[.046 7]   Architecture and the environment

Relocated to 720.47

[.046 9]   Multiple-purpose buildings

Relocated to 720.49

[.05–.08]   Standard subdivisions

Relocated to 720.5–720.8

[.09] History, geographic treatment, biography

Relocated to 720.9

> **721.1–721.8 Structural elements**

Class here decoration; interdisciplinary works on design and construction

Class decoration of structural elements in specific mediums in 729.4–729.8; class comprehensive works in 721

For engineering design and construction, see 690.1

.1 **Foundations**

.2 **Walls**

Including footings, entablatures; colonnades, partitions; bearing and retaining walls

See also 725.96 for free-standing walls

.3 **Columnar constructions**

Including abutments, colonnettes, columns, pedestals, piers, pilasters, posts

For colonnades, entablatures, see 721.2

.36 Architectural orders

.4 **Curved constructions and details**

.41 Arcades and arches

For groined arches, see 721.44

See also 725.96 for free-standing arches

.43 Vaults

For specific types of vaults, see 721.44–721.45

> 721.44–721.45 Specific types of vaults

Class comprehensive works in 721.43

.44 Groined vaults

Including groined arches

.45 Other types of vaults

Including expanding, fan, rib, tunnel vaults

.46 Domes

Class cupolated roofs in 721.5

.48 Niches

.5 **Roofs and roof structures**

> Standard subdivisions are added for roofs and roof structures together, for roofs alone
>
> Including dormers, gables; cornices, pediments; cupolas, pinnacles, spires, towers; chimneys, skylights

.6 **Floors**

.7 **Ceilings**

.8 **Other elements**

> Including balustrades, fastenings, fireplaces

.82 Openings

> Class here blinds

.822 Doors and doorways

> Standard subdivisions are added for either or both topics in heading

.823 Windows

> Class windows as parts of roof structures in 721.5

.83 Means of vertical access

> Including ramps

.832 Stairs

> Including escalators

.833 Elevators

.84 Semi-enclosed and uncovered spaces

> Former heading: Extensions
>
> Including balconies, courtyards, decks, patios, porches, verandas
>
> *For arcades, see 721.41; for decks and patios of residential buildings, see 728.93*

> **722–724 Architectural schools and styles**

> Class architects of specific schools and styles not limited to a specific type of structure in 720.92; class details of construction of specific schools and styles in 721; class specific types of structures regardless of school or style in 725–728; class design and decoration of structures of specific schools and styles in 729; class comprehensive works, schools and styles from ca. 300 limited to a specific country or locality in 720.9

722 **Architecture from earliest times to ca. 300**

.1	***Ancient Chinese, Japanese, Korean architecture**

Class here ancient Oriental architecture

For ancient south and southeast Asian architecture, see 722.4; for ancient Middle Eastern architecture, see 722.5

.11	*Ancient Chinese architecture

Class ancient Tibetan architecture in 722.4

.12	*Ancient Japanese architecture
.13	*Ancient Korean architecture
.2	***Ancient Egyptian architecture**
.3	***Ancient Semitic architecture**

Class comprehensive works on Semitic architecture in 720.8992

.31	*Phoenician architecture

Class here architecture of Tyre, ancient Sidon

For colonial Phoenician, see 722.32

.32	*Colonial Phoenician architecture

Including architecture of Carthage, Utica, ancient Cyprus

.33	*Ancient Palestinian architecture

Including ancient Israelite, Judean, Jewish architecture

.4	***Ancient south and southeast Asian architecture**
.44	*Ancient Indian architecture
.5	***Ancient Middle Eastern architecture**

For ancient Egyptian architecture, see 722.2; for ancient Semitic architecture, see 722.3; for ancient Aegean architecture, see 722.61

.51	*Mesopotamian architecture
.52	*Ancient Persian architecture
.6	***Ancient western architecture**

For Roman architecture, see 722.7; for Greek (Hellenic) architecture, see 722.8; for other ancient western architecture, see 722.9

.61	*Aegean, Minoan, Mycenaean architecture

Subdivisions are added for any or all topics in heading

.62	*Etruscan architecture
.7	***Roman architecture**

*Add as instructed under 721–729

.709 37   Architecture of Italian Peninsula and adjacent territories

Class architecture of Roman empire in 722.7

.8   *Greek (Hellenic) architecture

Class here comprehensive works on Greek and Roman architecture

For Roman architecture, see 722.7

.809 38   Architecture of Greece

Class architecture of Hellenistic world in 722.8

.9   *Other ancient western architecture

723   †Architecture from ca. 300 to 1399

Class here medieval architecture

.1   †Early Christian architecture

.2   †Byzantine architecture

.3   †Saracenic architecture

Class here Moorish architecture

For Mudéjar architecture, see 720.9460902

.4   †Romanesque and Norman architecture

.5   †Gothic architecture

724   †Architecture from 1400

Class here modern architecture

.1   †1400–1800

Class here colonial styles

For colonial styles of a later period, see the period, e.g., 1800–1899 724.5

.12   †1400–1499

Class here Renaissance architecture

For Renaissance architecture of an earlier or later period, see the period, e.g., 1500–1599 724.14

.14   †1500–1599

.16   †1600–1699

Class here comprehensive works on baroque architecture

For baroque architecture of 1700–1799, see 724.19

---

*Add as instructed under 721–729
†Do not use notation 09 from Table 1; class architecture limited to a specific country or locality in 720.9, biography in 720.92

.19 †1700–1799

Class here Georgian, rococo architecture

.2 **†Classical revival architecture**

Class here neoclassical architecture

.22 †Roman revival architecture

.23 †Greek revival architecture

.3 **†Gothic revival architecture**

.5 **†1800–1899**

Class here eclecticism, revivals, Victorian architecture

> *For classical revival architecture, see 724.2; for gothic revival architecture,*
> *see 724.3. For eclecticism and revivals of another specific period, see the*
> *period, e.g., 1700–1799 724.19*

.52 †Italianate revivals

Including Renaissance revival, Romanesque revival architecture

.6 **†1900–1999**

Including art nouveau, expressionism, functionalism, international style

.7 **†2000–**

> ## 725–728 Specific types of structures

Class here development of architectural schools and styles, comprehensive
works on specific structures and their interior design and decorations,
interdisciplinary works on design and construction

Class comprehensive works in 720. Class structures rehabilitated to a single
new use with the new use, e.g., warehouses converted into apartments 728.314;
class structures rehabilitated to multiple new uses with the old use, e.g.,
warehouses converted into retail stores and apartments 725.35

> *For structural engineering, see 624.1; for engineering design and*
> *construction of specific types of habitable structures, see 690.5–690.8; for*
> *interior decoration, see 747*

725 ***Public structures**

> *For public structures used primarily for religious and related purposes,*
> *see 726; for public structures used primarily for educational and research*
> *purposes, see 727; for public structures used primarily for residential and*
> *related purposes, see 728*

---

*Add as instructed under 721–729
†Do not use notation 09 from Table 1; class architecture limited to a specific country or locality in
720.9, biography in 720.92

SUMMARY

.1 ***Government buildings**

> Class here international government, civic center buildings

.11 ***Legislative buildings**

> Class here capitols

.12 ***Executive buildings**

> Class here buildings containing branches of executive department

.13 ***Local government buildings**

> Regardless of specific kind of local jurisdiction

.14 ***Customs buildings**

.15 ***Court, record, archive buildings**

> Subdivisions are added for any or all topics in heading

.16 ***Post offices**

.17 ***Official residences**

> Including embassy, legation, consulate buildings
>
> Class here executive mansions, palaces of rulers

.18 ***Military and police buildings**

> Including armories, arsenals, barracks, castles, fortresses, forts
>
> Subdivisions are added for either or both topics in heading
>
> Class engineering of forts and fortresses in 623.1; class comprehensive works on castles in 728.81

.19 ***Fire stations**

.2 ***Commercial and communications buildings**

> Subdivisions are added for commercial and communications buildings together, for commercial buildings alone
>
> *For refreshment facilities, see 725.7*

---

*Add as instructed under 721–729

.21   *Retail trade buildings

      Class here bazaars, shopping malls, shops, stores

.23   *Office and communications buildings

      Including medical office buildings and clinics, radio and television buildings and towers

      Subdivisions are added for either or both topics in heading

.24   *Financial institutions

      For exchanges, see 725.25

.25   *Exchanges

      Including board of trade, chamber of commerce buildings, stock and commodity exchange

.3   *Transportation, storage, agricultural buildings

      Subdivisions are added for transportation, storage, agricultural buildings together; for transportation buildings alone

.31   *Railroad and rapid transit stations

      Class here passenger stations

      Subdivisions are added for either or both topics in heading

      For railroad freight stations, see 725.32

.32   *Railroad freight stations

.33   *Railroad and rapid transit buildings

      Including roundhouses

      Subdivisions are added for either or both topics in heading

      For railroad and rapid transit stations, see 725.31

.34   *Marine transportation facilities

      Including docks, piers

      Class engineering of naval facilities in 623.64; class engineering of harbors, ports, roadsteads in 627.2

      See also 725.4 for shipyards

.35   *Warehouses

      Class here comprehensive works on storage buildings

      For a specific kind of storage building other than warehouse, see the kind, e.g., storage elevators 725.36

.36   *Storage elevators

*Add as instructed under 721–729

.37   *Agricultural buildings

> Including comprehensive works on greenhouses [*formerly* 728.924]; shearing sheds

> Class here comprehensive works on agricultural structures [*formerly* 728.92], farm buildings

>> *For storage elevators, see 725.36; for farmhouses, see 728.6; for agricultural buildings associated with residential buildings, see 728.92*

.372   *Barns and sheds

> Class here comprehensive works on barns

> Subdivisions are added for either or both topics in heading

> Class shearing sheds in 725.37

>> *For barns and sheds associated with residential buildings, see 728.922*

.38   *Motor vehicle transportation buildings

> Including bus terminals, filling stations, garages, parking facilities

.39   *Air transportation buildings

> Including air terminals, hangars

> Class engineering of military air facilities in 623.66

.4   *Industrial buildings

> Including factories, mills, plants, shipyards

.5   *Welfare and health buildings

> Subdivisions are added for welfare and health buildings together, for welfare buildings alone

.51   *General hospital and sanatorium buildings

> Class here comprehensive works on health buildings

>> *For a specific kind of health building not provided for here, see the kind, e.g., medical office buildings and clinics 725.23, children's hospital buildings 725.57*

.52   *Mental health facility buildings

> Class here psychiatric hospital buildings

.53   *Buildings of institutions for people with mental disabilities

.54   *Buildings of institutions for people with physical disabilities

.55   *Buildings of institutions for poor people

> Class buildings of institutions for poor people in late adulthood in 725.56

.56   *Buildings of institutions for people in late adulthood

*Add as instructed under 721–729

.57   *Child welfare institutions and children's hospital buildings

       Subdivisions are added for either or both topics in heading

.59   Other types of welfare buildings

.592   *Veterinary hospitals and shelters

        Subdivisions are added for either or both topics in heading

.594   *Veterans' homes

.597   *Morgues and crematories

        Subdivisions are added for either or both topics in heading

.6   ***Correctional institutions**

      Class here prison and reformatory buildings

.7   ***Refreshment facilities and park structures**

.71   *Eating places

      Class here restaurants

.72   *Drinking places

      Class here bars, pubs, taverns

.73   *Bathhouses and saunas

      Class here comprehensive works on public and domestic bathhouses and saunas

      Subdivisions are added for either or both topics in heading

       For domestic bathhouses and saunas, see 728.96

.74   *Swimming pools

      Class here comprehensive works on public and domestic swimming pools

       For domestic swimming pools, see 728.962

.76   *Amusement park buildings and casinos

      Subdivisions are added for either or both topics in heading

.8   **Recreation buildings**

       For refreshment facilities and park structures, see 725.7

.804   General categories of recreation buildings

.804 2   *Multiple-purpose complexes

       Class here cultural centers

       Class community centers for adult education in 727.9

.804 3   *Sports complexes (Sports centers, Sports pavilions)

*Add as instructed under 721–729

.81   *Concert and music halls

         Subdivisions are added for either or both topics in heading

         For opera houses, see 725.822

.82   *Buildings for shows and spectacles

.822   *Theaters and opera houses

         Subdivisions are added for either or both topics in heading

.823   *Motion picture theaters (Cinemas)

.827   *Buildings for outdoor performances and for athletic and outdoor sports and games

         Including grandstands

         Class here amphitheaters, astrodomes, stadiums

         Subdivisions are added for any or all topics in heading

         For racetrack buildings, see 725.89

.83   *Auditoriums

         Class here performing arts centers

         For concert and music halls, see 725.81; for theaters and opera houses, see 725.822

.84   *Buildings for indoor games

         Including bowling alleys; pool halls; halls for card games, checkers, chess

         For gymnasiums, see 725.85

.85   *Athletic club buildings and gymnasiums

         Subdivisions are added for either or both topics in heading

.86   *Dance halls and rinks

         Subdivisions are added for either or both topics in heading

.87   *Boathouses and recreation pier buildings

         Subdivisions are added for either or both topics in heading

.88   *Riding-club buildings

.89   *Racetrack buildings

.9   **Other public structures**

         Including fountains with little or no sculptural decoration

         Class comprehensive works on fountains in 731.724

.91   *Convention centers

         Class here exhibition buildings

*Add as instructed under 721–729

.94   *Memorial buildings

Class memorial buildings for a specific purpose with the purpose, e.g., memorial library buildings 727.8

.96   Arches, gateways, walls

Standard subdivisions are added for any or all topics in heading

See also 721.2 for walls as structural elements; also 721 for arches as structural elements

.97   *Towers

Including bell, clock towers

See also 726.2 for minarets; also 726.597 for church towers

.98   Bridges, tunnels, moats

Class engineering of moats in 623.31; class engineering of tunnels in 624.193; class engineering of bridges in 624.2

726   *Buildings for religious and related purposes

SUMMARY

726.1	**Temples and shrines**
.2	**Mosques and minarets**
.3	**Synagogues and Jewish temples**
.4	**Accessory houses of worship**
.5	**Buildings associated with Christianity**
.6	**Cathedrals**
.7	**Monastic buildings**
.8	**Mortuary chapels and tombs**
.9	**Other buildings for religious and related purposes**

> **726.1–726.3 Buildings associated with non-Christian religions**

Class comprehensive works in 726. Class a specific kind of building for religious purposes associated with a specific religion with the building, e.g., Buddhist monasteries 726.7843

See also 726.5 for buildings associated with Christianity

.1   *Temples and shrines

Subdivisions are added for either or both topics in heading

.12–.19   Temples and shrines of a specific non-Christian religion

Add to base number 726.1 the numbers following 29 in 292–299, e.g., Buddhist temples and shrines 726.143; however, for mosques and minarets, see 726.2; for synagogues and Jewish temples, see 726.3

.2   *Mosques and minarets

Subdivisions are added for either or both topics in heading

*Add as instructed under 721–729

.3   ***Synagogues and Jewish temples**

> Subdivisions are added for either or both topics in heading

.4   ***Accessory houses of worship**

> For all religions
>
> Including chapels, parish houses, Sunday school buildings; comprehensive works on baptistries
>
> Class Christian chapels in 726.5
>
> > *For baptistries as a part of church buildings, see 726.596*
> >
> > *See also 726.9 for residential parish houses*

.5   ***Buildings associated with Christianity**

> Class here Christian chapels; church buildings
>
> Class side chapels in 726.595
>
> > *For mortuary chapels, see 726.8. For a specific kind of building not provided for here, see the building, e.g., cathedrals 726.6, Franciscan monasteries 726.773*

.51   Design, decoration, construction of structural elements

> Add to base number 726.51 the numbers following 721 in 721.1–721.8, e.g., design, decoration, construction of church vaulting 726.5143
>
> Class decoration of structural elements in specific mediums in 726.524–726.528

.52   Decoration in specific mediums, built-in church furniture, design and decoration of parts

.524–.528   Decoration in specific mediums

> Add to base number 726.52 the numbers following 729 in 729.4–729.8, e.g., decoration in relief 726.525
>
> Class decorations of built-in church furniture in 726.529. Class decoration in a specific medium not in an architectural context with the medium, e.g., sculpture 730

.529   Built-in church furniture

> Class built-in church furniture in a specific medium not in an architectural context with the medium, e.g., carved pew ends 731.54

.529 1   Sacramental furniture

> Including altars, baptismal fonts, confessionals, tabernacles

.529 2   Rostral furniture

> Including lecterns, prayer desks, pulpits

**Add as instructed under 721 729

.529 3	Seats and canopies
	Including baldachins, bishops' thrones, choir stalls, pews
.529 6	Screens and railings
	Including altar and rood screens, altar and chancel railings, reredoses
.529 7	Organ cases
.529 8	Lighting fixtures

.58 **Buildings of specific denominations**

Add to base number 726.58 the numbers following 28 in 281–289, e.g., Anglican church buildings 726.583; however, for geographic treatment of buildings of specific denominations, see 726.509

Class specific parts of church buildings of specific denominations in 726.59

.59 **Parts**

Class design and construction of parts in 726.51; class design and decoration of parts in 726.52

.591 Entrances and approaches

.592 Naves and transepts

.593 Chancels, choirs, sanctuaries, choir lofts, pulpit platforms

.594 Clerestories

.595 Side chapels

Class chapels as separate buildings in 726.5

.596 Sacristies and baptistries

Class comprehensive works on baptistries in 726.4

.597 Towers and steeples

.6 *Cathedrals

For details and parts of cathedrals, see 726.51–726.59

.62 Cathedrals of Eastern churches

For Orthodox cathedrals, see 726.63

.620 9 History and biography

Do not use for geographic treatment; class in 726.609

.63 Orthodox cathedrals

.630 9 History and biography

Do not use for geographic treatment; class in 726.609

.64 Roman Catholic cathedrals

*Add as instructed under 721–729

.640 9   History and biography

                        Do not use for geographic treatment; class in 726.609

.65   Anglican cathedrals

.650 9   History and biography

                        Do not use for geographic treatment; class in 726.609

.69   *Accessory structures

                        Including cathedral cloisters, chapter houses

                        Comprehensive works on cloisters relocated to 726.796

.7   *Monastic buildings

                        Class here abbeys, convents, friaries, monasteries, priories

                        Class monastic churches either as a place of public worship or as a separate church building in 726.5

.77   Monastic buildings of specific Christian orders

[.770 1–.770 9]   Standard subdivisions

                        Do not use; class in 726.701–726.709

.771–.779   Subdivisions of monastic buildings of specific Christian orders

                        Add to base number 726.77 the numbers following 271 in 271.1–271.9, e.g., Franciscan monasteries 726.773; however, for geographic treatment of buildings of specific orders, see 726.709

.78   Monastic buildings of orders of other religions

                        Add to base number 726.78 the numbers following 29 in 292–299, e.g., Buddhist monasteries 726.7843

.79   Parts and accessory structures

                        Including cells, refectories

                        Class monastic libraries in 727.8

.796   Cloisters

                        Class here comprehensive works on cloisters [*formerly* 726.69]

                        For cathedral cloisters, see 726.69; for collegiate cloisters, see 727.38

.8   *Mortuary chapels and tombs

                        Subdivisions are added for either or both topics in heading

.9   Other buildings for religious and related purposes

                        Including episcopal palaces, missions, parsonages, buildings of religious associations, buildings housing roadside shrines

*Add as instructed under 721 729

727   *Buildings for educational and research purposes

> Class here school buildings
>
> Subdivisions are added for buildings for educational and research purposes together, for buildings for educational purposes alone

---

> ## 727.1–727.3 Buildings for education at specific levels
>
> Class professional and technical school buildings at a specific level in 727.4; class comprehensive works in 727
>
> *For buildings for adult education, see 727.9*

.1   ***Primary school buildings**

.2   ***Secondary school buildings**

.3   ***College and university buildings**

> Subdivisions are added for either or both topics in heading
>
> Class specialized buildings of colleges and universities in 727.4–727.8

.38   Accessory structures

> Including dining halls, dormitories, student unions

.4   **Professional and technical school buildings**

.400 01–.400 09   Standard subdivisions

.400 1–.499 9   Specific types of professional and technical school buildings

> Add to base number 727.4 notation 001–999, e.g., law school buildings 727.434

.5   **Research buildings**

> Class here laboratory, observatory buildings

.500 01–.500 09   Standard subdivisions

.500 1–.599 9   Specific types of research buildings

> Add to base number 727.5 notation 001–999, e.g., conservatories (botanical research buildings) 727.558 [*formerly* 728.924], physics laboratories 727.553

.6   **Museum buildings**

.600 01–.600 09   Standard subdivisions

.600 1–.699 9   Specific types of museum buildings

> Add to base number 727.6 notation 001–999, e.g., science museum buildings 727.65; however, for art museum buildings, see 727.7

*Add as instructed under 721–729

.7   ***Art museum and gallery buildings**

> Subdivisions are added for either or both topics in heading

.8   ***Library buildings**

.82   *General libraries

.820 9   History and biography

> Do not use for geographic treatment; class in 727.809

.821–.828   Specific kinds of general libraries

> Add to base number 727.82 the numbers following 027 in 027.1–027.8, e.g., public library buildings 727.824; then add further as instructed under 721–729, e.g., energy conservation in public library buildings 727.8240472; however, for geographic treatment, see 727.809; for branch libraries, see 727.84

.83   *Libraries devoted to specific subjects

.830 9   History and biography

> Do not use for geographic treatment; class in 727.809

.84   *Branch libraries

.840 9   History and biography

> Do not use for geographic treatment; class in 727.809

.9   **Other buildings for educational and research purposes**

> Including community centers for adult education, learned society buildings

728   ***Residential and related buildings**

> Class here domestic architecture, conventional housing

> Subdivisions are added for residential and related buildings together, for residential buildings alone

> *For official residences, see 725.17; for episcopal palaces, parsonages, see 726.9; for residential educational buildings, see 727.1–727.3*

.1   ***Low-cost housing**

> Dwellings designed along simple lines to reduce construction costs

> Class specific types of low-cost housing in 728.3–728.7

.3   **Specific kinds of conventional housing**

[.301–.309]   Standard subdivisions

> Do not use; class in 728.01–728.09

.31   *Multiple dwellings

---

*Add as instructed under 721 729

| .312 | *Duplex houses and row houses |

Class here double houses, semi-detached houses, terrace houses, townhouses

Subdivisions are added for either or both topics in heading

| .314 | *Apartment houses |

Including apartment hotels, tenements

| .37 | *Separate houses |

Class here cottages

For farmhouses, see 728.6; for vacation houses, see 728.72; for large and elaborate private dwellings, see 728.8

| .372 | *Multistory houses |

| .373 | *Single-story houses |

Class here bungalows, ranch and split-level houses

> ### 728.4–728.7 Special-purpose housing

Class comprehensive works in 728

.4 *Club houses

Country, city, fraternal clubs

Class a type of club house not provided for here with the type, e.g., racetrack club houses 725.89

.5 *Hotels and motels

Subdivisions are added for either or both topics in heading

For apartment hotels, see 728.314

.6 *Farmhouses

Class here farm cottages

Class comprehensive works on farm buildings in 725.37

.7 *Vacation houses, cabins, hunting lodges, houseboats, mobile homes

| .72 | *Vacation houses |

| .73 | *Cabins |

Class vacation cabins in 728.72

| .78 | *Houseboats |

*Add as instructed under 721–729

.79   *Mobile homes

      Including campers, trailers

      For houseboats, see 728.78

      See Manual at 643.29, 690.879, 728.79 vs. 629.226

.8   ***Large and elaborate private dwellings**

      Class here chateaux, manor houses, mansions, plantation houses, villas

.81   *Castles

      Fortified residences

      Class here comprehensive works on architecture of castles

      For castles as military structures, see 725.18

.82   *Palaces

      Residences of nobility

      Class fortified palaces in 728.81

      See also 725.17 for palaces of rulers; also 726.9 for episcopal palaces

.9   ***Miscellaneous structures associated with residential buildings**

      Including gatehouses

.92   *Agricultural structures associated with residential buildings

      For farmhouses, see 728.6

      Comprehensive works on agricultural structures relocated to 725.37

.922   *Barns and sheds

      Subdivisions are added for either or both topics in heading

.924   *Greenhouses

      Class here conservatories

      Comprehensive works on greenhouses relocated to 725.37; conservatories (botanical research buildings) relocated to 727.558

.927   *Birdhouses

      Class here aviaries

.93   *Decks and patios

      Subdivisions are added for either or both topics in heading

.96   Swimming pools and related structures

      Including bathhouses, saunas

      Class comprehensive works on bathhouses and saunas in 725.73

*Add as instructed under 721–729

.962 *Swimming pools

> Class comprehensive works on swimming pools in 725.74

.98 *Garages

729 Design and decoration of structures and accessories

Class here interior architecture (the art or practice of planning and supervising the design and execution of architectural interiors and their furnishings)

Class design and decoration of structures and accessories of specific types of buildings in 725–728

For interior decoration, see 747

See Manual at 729

> ### 729.1–729.2 Design in specific planes

Class design of structural elements in specific planes in 721.1–721.8; class comprehensive works in 729. Class architectural drawings for one structure or a specific type of structure with the structure in 725–728, plus notation 0222 from table under 721–729, e.g., architectural drawings of palaces 728.820222

.1 **Design in vertical plane**

Including facades

Class here elevations, sections

.102 22 Pictures and related illustrations

Do not use for architectural drawings; class in 729.1

.11 Composition

.13 Proportion

.19 Inscriptions and lettering

Standard subdivisions are added for either or both topics in heading

.2 **Design in horizontal plane**

Class here modular design; floor plans

Class architectural plans as a set of drawings for a project in 720.222

.202 22 Pictures and related illustrations

Do not use for architectural drawings; class in 729.2

.23 Proportion

.24 *Interior arrangement

.25 *Lines of interior communication

*Add as instructed under 721–729

.28   Lighting

Including daylighting

.29   Acoustics

>   **729.4–729.8 Decoration in specific mediums**

Class comprehensive works in 729. Class decoration in a specific medium not in an architectural context with the medium, e.g., sculpture 730

.4   **Decoration in paint**

As an adjunct to architecture

.5   **Decoration in relief**

Including carved and sculptured decoration and ornament, Gothic tracery

.6   **Decoration in veneer and incrustation**

Use of wood, stone, metal, enamel in architectural decoration

.7   **Decoration in mosaic**

Class comprehensive works on mosaics in 738.5

.8   **Decoration in ornamental glass**

730   Sculpture and related arts

Standard subdivisions are added for sculpture and related arts together, for sculpture alone

Class here plastic arts

Class plastic arts covering all visual arts in 700

SUMMARY

730.1–.9	**Standard subdivisions of sculpture and related arts together, of sculpture alone**
731	**Processes, forms, subjects of sculpture**
732	**Sculpture from earliest times to ca. 500, sculpture of nonliterate peoples**
733	**Greek, Etruscan, Roman sculpture**
734	**Sculpture from ca. 500 to 1399**
735	**Sculpture from 1400**
736	**Carving and carvings**
737	**Numismatics and sigillography**
738	**Ceramic arts**
739	**Art metalwork**

[.01]   Philosophy and theory of plastic arts

Relocated to 730.1

[.02]   Miscellany of plastic arts

Relocated to 730.2

[.03–.08]	Standard subdivisions of plastic arts
	Relocated to 730.3–730.8
[.09]	Standard subdivisions of plastic arts
	Relocated to 730.9

.1 Philosophy and theory of sculpture and related arts together, of sculpture alone

Notation 01 from Table 1 as modified below

Class here philosophy and theory of plastic arts [*formerly* 730.01]

.11 Appreciative aspects

Do not use for systems; class in 730.1

Class psychological principles in 730.19

.117 Aesthetics

.118 Criticism and appreciation

Theory, technique, history

Class works of critical appraisal in 730.9

.18 Inherent features

Including color, composition, decorative values, form, movement, space, style, symmetry, vision

.2 Miscellany of sculpture and related arts together, of sculpture alone

Class here miscellany of plastic arts [*formerly* 730.02]

.28 Auxiliary techniques and procedures; apparatus, equipment, materials of sculpture and related arts

Notation 028 from Table 1 as modified below

Do not use for auxiliary techniques and procedures of sculpture alone; class in 731.028

Class here basic techniques and procedures, techniques of two or more of the plastic arts, e.g., firing of clays in sculpture and ceramics

.284 Apparatus, equipment, materials of sculpture and related arts

Do not use for materials for sculpture alone; class in 731.2. Do not use for apparatus and equipment for sculpture alone; class in 731.3

.3–.8 Standard subdivisions of sculpture and related arts together, of sculpture alone

Class here standard subdivisions of plastic arts [*formerly* 730.03–730.08]

.9 **History, geographic treatment, biography of sculpture and related arts together, of sculpture alone**

> Class here standard subdivisions of plastic arts [*formerly* 730.09], schools and styles limited to a specific country or locality

> Class sculpture of nonliterate peoples regardless of time or place in 732.2; class comprehensive works on specific schools and styles of sculpture not limited to country or locality in 732–735

.901–.905 Historical periods of sculpture and related arts

> Do not use for sculpture alone; class in 732–735

.92 Biography

> Class here description and critical appraisal of sculptors or plastic artists and their works regardless of process, representation, style or school, period, place; sculptors who also work in the other plastic arts

.922 Collected biography

> Including works of sculptors or plastic artists from several geographic areas

> Class works of more than one sculptor or plastic artist in the same geographic area, region, place in general (*not* limited by continent, country, locality) in 730.91

.922 3 Ancient world

> Class here works of more than one plastic artist

> Class works of more than one sculptor in 732–733

.922 4–.922 9 Specific continents, countries, localities in modern world

> Class works of more than one sculptor or plastic artist in 730.94–730.99

.93 Ancient world

> Do not use for sculpture alone; class in 732–733

.95 Asia

> Class here Buddhist, Oriental sculpture

> > For Buddhist sculpture in an area not provided for here, see the area, e.g., Buddhist sculpture in Hawaii 730.9969

.954 India and neighboring south Asian countries

> Class here Hindu, Jain sculpture

> > For Hindu sculpture in an area not provided for here, see the area, e.g., Hindu sculpture in Indonesia 730.9598

> **731–735 Sculpture**

> Class comprehensive works in 730

> *See Manual at 731–735 vs. 736–739*

731 Processes, forms, subjects of sculpture

Class processes, forms, subjects of specific periods and by specific schools in 732–735

.028 Auxiliary techniques and procedures

Class comprehensive works on basic and auxiliary techniques and procedures in 731.4

[.028 4] Apparatus, equipment, materials

Do not use for materials; class in 731.2. Do not use for apparatus and equipment; class in 731.3

[.028 8] Maintenance and repair

Do not use; class in 731.48

.092 Biography

Do not use for individual sculptors; class in 730.92

> ## 731.2–731.4 Techniques, procedures, apparatus, equipment, materials

Class forms employing techniques, procedures, apparatus, equipment, materials in 731.5; class subjects employing techniques, procedures, apparatus, equipment, materials in 731.8; class comprehensive works in 731.4

.2 ***Materials**

Including ceramic materials, found objects, metals, paper, papier-mâché, plastics, rope, stone, textiles, wax, wire, wood

Class use of materials in specific techniques in 731.4

.3 ***Apparatus and equipment**

Including tools, machines, accessories

Class use of apparatus and equipment in specific techniques in 731.4

.4 ***Techniques and procedures**

Class here comprehensive works on techniques, procedures, apparatus, equipment, materials together

For auxiliary techniques and procedures, see 731.028; for materials, see 731.2; for apparatus and equipment, see 731.3

.41 ***Direct-metal sculpture**

Including beating, bending, cutting, hammering, shaping, soldering, welding metals (including pipe and wire)

Class art metalwork in 739

.42 ***Modeling**

In clay, wax, other plastic materials with and without armatures

*Do not use notation 092 from Table 1 for individual sculptors; class in 730.92

.43		*Molding

             Preparation of molds and models

             Class use of molds in 731.45

.45	*Casting

             Including sand casting

.452	*Cement and plaster casting
.453	*Plastics casting
.456	*Casting in bronze

             Including lost-wax casting

             Class here casting in metals

                For casting in metals other than bronze, see 731.457

.457	*Casting in metals other than bronze

             Class comprehensive works on casting in metals in 731.456

.46	*Carving and chiseling techniques in sculpture

             Standard subdivisions are added for either or both topics in heading

.462	*Sculpturing in wood
.463	*Sculpturing in stone
.47	*Firing and baking

             Standard subdivisions are added for either or both topics in heading

             Including firing and baking clay models for molding

             Class techniques of firing and baking in ceramics in 738.143

.48	*Maintenance and repair

             Class here conservation, preservation, restoration

.5	***Forms**

             Development, description, critical appraisal, collections of works not limited by time or place

             For sculpture in the round, see 731.7

.54	*Sculpture in relief

             Class iconography of sculpture in relief in 731.8

.542	*Portals and doors

             Standard subdivisions are added for either or both topics in heading

.549	*Monumental reliefs

             For monumental brasses, see 739.522

*Do not use notation 092 from Table 1 for individual sculptors; class in 730.92

.55   *Mobiles and stabiles

.7   *Sculpture in the round

            Development, description, critical appraisal, collections of works

            Class iconography of sculpture in the round in 731.8

.72   *Decorative sculpture

            Including garden sculpture, sculptured vases and urns

.724   *Fountains

            Class here comprehensive works on fountains

                *For fountains as a water feature in landscape architecture, see 714;
                for public fountains with little or no sculptural decoration, see 725.9;
                for tabletop and indoor fountains, see 745.5946*

.74   *Busts

.75   *Masks

.76   *Monuments

            For monumental brasses, see 739.522

.77   *Totem poles

.8   *Iconography

            Development, description, critical appraisal, works not limited by time or place

.81   *Equestrian sculpture

.82–.89   Other specific subjects

            Add to base number 731.8 the numbers following 704.94 in
            704.942–704.949, e.g., mythology and legend 731.87; however, for
            individual sculptors, see 730.92; for busts, see 731.74; for masks, see 731.75

>   **732–735 Schools and styles of sculpture**

            Class comprehensive works in 730.9

**732   Sculpture from earliest times to ca. 500, sculpture of
           nonliterate peoples**

[.09]   History, geographic treatment, biography

            Do not use for biography; class in 730.92. Do not use for history and
            geographic treatment; class in 732

.2   †Sculpture of nonliterate peoples

            Regardless of time or place

*Do not use notation 092 from Table 1 for individual sculptors; class in 730.92
†Do not use notation 092 from Table 1; class biography in 730.92

.22   †Paleolithic sculpture

.23   †Rock art (sculpture)

>   **732.3–732.9 Ancient sculpture**

Class comprehensive works in 732

.3   **†Ancient Palestinian sculpture**

Including Israelite, Judean, Jewish sculpture

.4   **†Ancient south and southeast Asian sculpture**

.44   †Ancient Indian sculpture

.5   **†Mesopotamian and ancient Persian sculpture**

.6   **†Ancient British, Celtic, Germanic, Iberian, Slavic sculpture**

.7   **†Ancient Oriental sculpture**

For ancient Oriental sculpture of a specific place not provided for here, see the place, e.g., ancient Indian sculpture 732.44

.71   †Ancient Chinese sculpture

.72   †Ancient Japanese sculpture

.73   †Ancient Korean sculpture

.8   **†Ancient Egyptian sculpture**

.9   **Sculpture of other ancient areas**

Add to base number 732.9 the numbers following —39 in notation 392–398 from Table 2, e.g., Phoenician sculpture 732.944; however, for biography, see 730.92; for ancient sculpture of Greek Archipelago, see 733.309391

For Greek, Etruscan, Roman sculpture, see 733

733   †Greek, Etruscan, Roman sculpture

.3   **†Greek (Hellenic) sculpture**

Class comprehensive works on Greek and Roman sculpture in 733

.309 38   Sculpture of Greece

Class sculpture of Hellenistic world in 733.3

.4   **†Etruscan sculpture**

.5   **†Roman sculpture**

.509 37   Sculpture of Italian Peninsula and adjacent territories

Class sculpture of Roman Empire in 733.5

†Do not use notation 092 from Table 1; class biography in 730.92

734　　*Sculpture from ca. 500 to 1399

> Class here medieval sculpture

.2　　*Styles

.22　　　*Early Christian and Byzantine sculpture

.222　　　　*Early Christian sculpture

.224　　　　*Byzantine sculpture

.24　　　*Romanesque sculpture

.25　　　*Gothic sculpture

735　　*Sculpture from 1400

> Class here modern sculpture

.2　　Specific periods

.21　　　*1400–1799

> Including baroque, Renaissance sculpture

.22　　　*1800–1899

> Including classical revival sculpture, romanticism, realism

.23　　　*1900–1999

.230 4　　　Schools and styles

> Add to base number 735.2304 the numbers following 709.040 in 709.0401–709.0407, e.g., abstractionism in sculpture 735.230452; however, for assemblages, constructions, sound sculpture, land art, mixed media, composites, see 709.04; for geographic treatment, see 730.9; for biography, see 730.92

.231–.239　　Periods

> Add to base number 735.23 the numbers following —0904 in notation 09041–09049 from Table 1, e.g., sculpture of 1960–1969 735.236; however, for geographic treatment, see 730.9; for biography, see 730.92

.24　　　*2000–2099

> ## 736–739　Other plastic arts

> Processes and products

> Class comprehensive works in 730. Class a plastic art not provided for here with the art in 745–749, e.g., textile arts 746

> *See also 731–735 for sculpture*

> *See Manual at 731–735 vs. 736–739*

*Do not use notation 09 from Table 1; class geographic treatment in 730.9, biography in 730.92

736   Carving and carvings

Standard subdivisions are added for either or both topics in heading

.2   Precious and semiprecious stones (Glyptics)

Standard subdivisions are added for either or both topics in heading

Class engraved seals, stamps, signets in 737.6; class setting of precious and semiprecious stones in 739.27

.202 8   Lapidary work

Do not use for auxiliary techniques and procedures; apparatus, equipment, materials; class in 736.202

Including cutting, polishing, engraving gems

.22   Specific forms

Class carving in specific materials regardless of form in 736.23–736.28

For scarabs, see 736.20932

.222   Cameos

.223   Intaglios

.224   Figurines

> 736.23–736.28 Specific stones

Class comprehensive works in 736.2

.23   Diamonds

.24   Jade

See also 731–735 for jade sculpture

.25   Sapphires

.28   Obsidian

.4   Wood

Including butter prints and molds, whittling

See also 731–735 for wood sculpture; also 745.51 for wood handicrafts

.5   Stone

Including lettering, inscriptions, designs

Class here effigial and sepulchral slabs

See also 731–735 for stone sculpture

.6   Ivory, bone, horn, shell, amber

.62	Ivory

> Class netsukes of ivory in 736.68; class scrimshaws of ivory in 736.69
>
> *See also 731–735 for ivory sculpture*

.68	Netsukes
.69	Scrimshaws
.7	**Ornamental fans**

> Class fans of a specific material with the material, e.g., ivory fans 736.62

.9	**Other materials**
.93	Wax
.94	Ice and snow
.95	Soap
.96	Sand sculpture

> Class here sandcastles

.98	Paper cutting and folding
.980 952	Paper cutting and folding of Japan

> *For origami, see 736.982*

.982	Origami
.984	Silhouettes

> Class comprehensive works on drawing and cutting silhouettes in 741.7

737 Numismatics and sigillography

> Standard subdivisions are added for numismatics and sigillography together, for numismatics alone
>
> *For paper money, see 769.55*

.2	**Medals and related objects**
.22	Medals

> Class here medallions

.222	Commemorative medals
.223	Civilian and military medals

> Including decorations, orders

.224	Religious medals
.23	Amulets and talismans
.24	Buttons and pins

> Standard subdivisions are added for either or both topics in heading

.242   Political buttons and pins

> Standard subdivisions are added for either or both topics in heading

> Class here campaign buttons and pins

.243   Sports buttons and pins

> Standard subdivisions are added for either or both topics in heading

.3   **Counters and tokens**

> Standard subdivisions are added for either or both topics in heading

.4   **Coins**

> Class here counterfeit coins

.409 3–.409 9   Specific continents and localities

> Do not use for specific countries; class in 737.49

.43   Gold coins

.430 93–.430 99   Specific continents and localities

> Do not use for specific countries; class in 737.49

.49   Coins of specific countries

> By place of origin

> Add to base number 737.49 notation 3–9 from Table 2, e.g., Roman coins minted in Egypt 737.4932

.6   **Engraved seals, signets, stamps**

> Standard subdivisions are added for any or all topics in heading

> Class here sigillography

> Class interdisciplinary works on sigillography in 929.9

738   **Ceramic arts**

> Class here pottery

> Use 738 for pottery covering porcelain and earthenware or porcelain and stoneware. Use 738.3 for pottery limited to earthenware or stoneware. Because porcelain, which was invented in China, did not reach other parts of Asia until the 9th century and Europe before the 17th century, ancient pottery of a place other than China was either earthenware or stoneware and is classed in 738.309, e.g., pottery of ancient Italy 738.30937, Aztec pottery 738.09720902

> Class ceramic sculpture in 731–735

> *For glass, see 748*

SUMMARY

.028　　　　Auxiliary techniques and procedures

> Class comprehensive works on techniques and procedures in 738.14

[.028 4]　　　Apparatus, equipment, materials

> Do not use for materials; class in 738.12. Do not use for apparatus and equipment; class in 738.13

[.028 8]　　　Maintenance and repair

> Do not use; class in 738.18

.09　　　　History, geographic treatment, biography

> Class here brands of pottery

.092　　　　Biography

> Regardless of material or product

> Class here ceramic artists

> *For enamelers, see 738.4092; for mosaicists, see 738.5092*

.1　　　　**Techniques, procedures, apparatus, equipment, materials**

> Class techniques, procedures, apparatus, equipment, materials of specific products in 738.4–738.8

.12　　　　Materials

> Including clays, e.g., kaolin; color materials

> Class use of materials in specific techniques in 738.14

.127　　　　Glazes

.13　　　　Apparatus and equipment

> Including potter's wheels

> Class use of apparatus and equipment in specific techniques in 738.14

.136　　　　Kilns

.14　　　　Techniques and procedures

> *For auxiliary techniques and procedures, see 738.028; for decorative treatment, see 738.15; for conservation, preservation, restoration, see 738.18*

.142　　　　Modeling and casting

.143 Firing

Before and after glazing

.144 Glazing

.15 Decorative treatment

Including sgrafitto decoration, slip tracing, transfer painting, underglaze and overglaze painting

For glazing, see 738.144

.18 Maintenance and repair

Including expertizing

Class here conservation, preservation, restoration

> ## 738.2–738.8 Products

Development, description, critical appraisal, collections of works

Class comprehensive works in 738

.2 **Porcelain**

Class comprehensive works on porcelain, earthenware, stoneware in 738

For specialized porcelain products, see 738.4–738.8

[.202 8] Auxiliary techniques and procedures; apparatus, equipment, materials

Do not use for auxiliary techniques and procedures; class in 738.028

[.202 84] Apparatus, equipment, materials

Do not use for materials; class in 738.12. Do not use for apparatus and equipment; class in 738.13

.209 History and geographic treatment of porcelain

Class here brands

[.209 2] Biography

Do not use; class in 738.092

.27 Specific types and varieties of porcelain

Including blue and white transfer ware

[.270 1–.270 8] Standard subdivisions

Do not use; class in 738.201–738.208

[.270 9] History, geographic treatment, biography

Do not use for history and geographic treatment; class in 738.209. Do not use for biography; class in 738.092

.28 Tableware and vessels

> Standard subdivisions are added for either or both topics in heading

> Class tableware and vessels of specific types or varieties in 738.27

.280 9 History

> Do not use for geographic treatment; class in 738.209

[.280 92] Biography

> Do not use; class in 738.092

.3 Earthenware and stoneware

> Standard subdivisions are added for either or both topics in heading

> Use 738 for pottery covering porcelain and earthenware or porcelain and stoneware. Use 738.3 for pottery limited to earthenware or stoneware. Because porcelain, which was invented in China, did not reach other parts of Asia until the 9th century and Europe before the 17th century, ancient pottery of a place other than China was either earthenware or stoneware and is classed in 738.309, e.g., pottery of ancient Italy 738.30937, Aztec pottery 738.09720902

> *For specific earthenware and stoneware products, see 738.4–738.8*

[.302 8] Auxiliary techniques and procedures; apparatus, equipment, materials

> Do not use for auxiliary techniques and procedures; class in 738.028

[.302 84] Apparatus, equipment, materials

> Do not use for materials; class in 738.12. Do not use for apparatus and equipment; class in 738.13

.309 History and geographic treatment

> Class here brands

[.309 2] Biography

> Do not use; class in 738.092

.309 3 Ancient world

> *For ancient and classical Middle Eastern and western vessels, see 738.382*

.37 Specific types and varieties of earthenware and stoneware

> Including delftware, faience

[.370 1–.370 8] Standard subdivisions

> Do not use; class in 738.301–738.308

[.370 9] History, geographic treatment, biography

> Do not use for history and geographic treatment; class in 738.309. Do not use for biography; class in 738.092

.372 Majolica

.372 09	History
	Do not use for geographic treatment; class in 738.309
[.372 092]	Biography
	Do not use; class in 738.092
.38	Tableware and vessels

Standard subdivisions are added for either or both topics in heading

Class tableware and vessels of specific types and varieties in 738.37

| .380 9 | History |

Do not use for geographic treatment; class in 738.309. Do not use for biography; class in 738.092

| .382 | Middle Eastern and western vessels |

Standard subdivisions are added for a specific type of vessel, e.g., ancient Egyptian vases 738.3820932

Ancient and classical

| [.382 092] | Biography |

Do not use; class in 738.092

> **738.4–738.8 Specific products and techniques of making them**

Class ceramic sculpture in 731–735; class comprehensive works on porcelain products in 738.28; class comprehensive works on earthenware and stoneware products in 738.38; class comprehensive works in 738

For porcelain tableware and vessels, see 738.28; for earthenware and stoneware tableware and vessels, see 738.38

.4　　Enamels

Including basse-taille, champlevé, ronde bosse

For nielloing, see 739.15; for jewelry, see 739.27; for enameling glass, see 748.6

.42　　Cloisonné

.46　　Surface-painted enamels

.5　　Mosaics

Class here mosaic painting, comprehensive works on mosaics in all materials

For mosaics of a specific material not provided for here, see the material, e.g., mosaic glass 748.5

.52　　Mosaics used with architecture

Including floors, pavements, walls; fixed screens and panels

.56　　Mosaics applied to portable objects

Including mosaic jewelry, ornaments, ornamental objects, movable panels

.6 **Ornamental bricks and tiles**

Standard subdivisions are added for either or both topics in heading

.8 **Other products**

Including braziers, candlesticks, lamps, lighting fixtures, stoves

.82 Figurines

Including figure groups, animals, plants

See also 738.83 for dolls

.83 Dolls

Class comprehensive works on handicrafting dolls in 745.59221

739 Art metalwork

For numismatics, see 737

SUMMARY

739.028	Auxiliary techniques and procedures
.1	Techniques, procedures, apparatus, equipment, materials
.2	Work in precious metals
.3	Clocks and watches
.4	Ironwork
.5	Work in metals other than iron
.7	Arms and armor

.028 Auxiliary techniques and procedures

Class comprehensive works on techniques and procedures in 739.14

[.028 4] Apparatus, equipment, materials

Do not use for materials; class in 739.12. Do not use for apparatus and equipment; class in 739.13

.1 **Techniques, procedures, apparatus, equipment, materials**

Class techniques, procedures, apparatus, equipment, materials for a specific kind of metalwork with the kind, e.g., goldsmithing 739.22028

.12 Materials

Class use of materials in specific techniques in 739.14

.13 Apparatus and equipment

Including tools, machines, accessories

Class use of apparatus and equipment in specific techniques in 739.14

.14 Techniques and procedures

Including bending, casting, drawing, forging, rolling, shaping metals by hammering and beating (repoussé work), stamping, welding

For auxiliary techniques and procedures, see 739.028; for decorative treatment, see 739.15

.15 Decorative treatment

Including chasing, damascening, nielloing, painting, patinating

.2 **Work in precious metals**

Class clocks and watches in precious metals in 739.3

.209 2 Biography

Use 739.2092 for goldsmiths who work in gold and other materials, especially silver. Use 739.22092 for goldsmiths who work in gold alone

> 739.22–739.24 Work in specific metals

Class jewelry in specific metals in 739.27; class comprehensive works in 739.2

.22 Goldsmithing

Class comprehensive works on goldsmithing and silversmithing in 739.2

.220 28 Auxiliary techniques and procedures

Class here comprehensive works on techniques, procedures, apparatus, equipment, materials together

Class comprehensive works on basic and auxiliary techniques and procedures in 739.224

[.220 284] Apparatus, equipment, materials

Do not use for materials; class in 739.222. Do not use for apparatus and equipment; class in 739.223

.220 9 History, geographic treatment, biography

.220 92 Biography

Use 739.2092 for goldsmiths who work in gold and other materials, especially silver. Use 739.22092 for goldsmiths who work in gold alone

.222–.225 Techniques, procedures, apparatus, equipment, materials

Add to base number 739.22 the numbers following 739.1 in 739.12–739.15, e.g., decorative treatment 739.225; however, for history, geographic treatment, biography, see 739.2209

Class techniques, apparatus, equipment, materials for specific products in 739.228; class comprehensive works in 739.22028

.228 *Products

Gold and gold-plate

.228 2 *Religious articles

---

*Do not use notation 09 from Table 1; class in 739.209

.228 3   *Tableware

          Including flatware, hollow ware

          Class tableware for religious use in 739.2282

.228 4   *Receptacles

          Including boxes, loving cups, vases

          Class religious receptacles in 739.2282

.23   Silversmithing

.230 28   Auxiliary techniques and procedures

          Class here comprehensive works on techniques, procedures, apparatus, equipment, materials together

          Class comprehensive works on basic and auxiliary techniques and procedures in 739.234

[.230 284]   Apparatus, equipment, materials

          Do not use for materials; class in 739.232. Do not use for apparatus and equipment; class in 739.233

.232–.238   Techniques, procedures, apparatus, equipment, materials; products

          Add to base number 739.23 the numbers following 739.22 in 739.222–739.228, e.g., silver tableware 739.2383

.24   Platinumwork

.27   Jewelry

       Design of settings, mounting gems, repair work

       Class here interdisciplinary works on making fine and costume jewelry

       Class interdisciplinary works on jewelry in 391.7; class interdisciplinary works on making costume jewelry in 688.2

         For carving precious and semiprecious stones, see 736.2; for making handcrafted costume jewelry, see 745.5942. For jewelry made with little or no precious metal, see the specific material other than metal elsewhere in 700, e.g., mosaic jewelry 738.56, glass bead necklaces 748.85

.270 28   Auxiliary techniques and procedures

          Class here comprehensive works on techniques, procedures, apparatus, equipment, materials together

          Class comprehensive works on basic and auxiliary techniques and procedures in 739.274

[.270 284]   Apparatus, equipment, materials

          Do not use for materials; class in 739.272. Do not use for apparatus and equipment; class in 739.273

*Do not use notation 09 from Table 1; class in 739.209

.272–.275 Techniques, procedures, apparatus, equipment, materials

> Add to base number 739.27 the numbers following 739.1 in 739.12–739.15, e.g., decorative treatment 739.275

> Class techniques, apparatus, equipment, materials for specific products in 739.278; class comprehensive works in 739.27028

.278 Products

> Including belt buckles, shoe buckles, watch fobs

.278 2 Finger rings

.3 Clocks and watches

Standard subdivisions are added for either or both topics in heading

Class here clockcases regardless of material

Class clocks as furniture in 749.3; class interdisciplinary works on clocks in 681.113; class interdisciplinary works on watches in 681.114

.302 8 Auxiliary techniques and procedures

> Class here comprehensive works on techniques, procedures, apparatus, equipment, materials together

> Class comprehensive works on basic and auxiliary techniques and procedures in 739.34

[.302 84] Apparatus, equipment, materials

> Do not use for materials; class in 739.32. Do not use for apparatus and equipment; class in 739.33

.32–.35 Techniques, procedures, apparatus, equipment, materials

> Add to base number 739.3 the numbers following 739.1 in 739.12–739.15, e.g., decorative treatment 739.35; however, for history, geographic treatment, biography, see 739.309

> Class techniques, apparatus, equipment, materials for specific products in 739.38; class comprehensive works in 739.3028

> ### 739.4–739.5 Work in base metals

Class clocks and watches in base metals in 739.3; class comprehensive works in 739

For arms and armor, see 739.7

.4 Ironwork

Class here wrought iron, cast iron, stainless steel

.402 8 Auxiliary techniques and procedures

> Class here comprehensive works on techniques, procedures, apparatus, equipment, materials together

> Class comprehensive works on basic and auxiliary techniques and procedures in 739.44

[.402 84]	Apparatus, equipment, materials
	Do not use for materials; class in 739.42. Do not use for apparatus and equipment; class in 739.43
.42–.45	Techniques, procedures, apparatus, equipment, materials

Add to base number 739.4 the numbers following 739.1 in 739.12–739.15, e.g., decorative treatment 739.45; however, for history, geographic treatment, biography, see 739.409

Class techniques, apparatus, equipment, materials for specific products in 739.48; class comprehensive works in 739.4028

| .48 | Products |

Including balcony motifs, balustrades, grills, knockers, ornamental nails

| [.480 9] | History, geographic treatment, biography |
| | Do not use; class in 739.409 |

| **.5** | **Work in metals other than iron** |
| .51 | Copper and its alloys |

For brass, see 739.52

| .511 | Copper |
| .512 | Bronze |

See also 731–735 for bronze sculpture

| .52 | Brass |
| .522 | Monumental brasses |

Class here rubbing and rubbings for study and research of brasses

Class rubbings as art form in 760

| .53 | Tin and its alloys |

For bronze, see 739.512

.532	Tin
.533	Pewter
.54	Lead
.55	Zinc and its alloys

Subdivisions are added for zinc and its alloys together, for zinc alone

For brass, see 739.52

.56	Nickel
.57	Aluminum
.58	Chromium

.7   **Arms and armor**

> Standard subdivisions are added for arms and armor together, for arms alone
>
> Class here decorative treatment of shapes, handles, grips, metalwork
>
> Class interdisciplinary works on arms and armor in 623.44
>
> *See also 623.441 for stone weapons*

\>   739.72–739.74   Arms

> Class comprehensive works in 739.7

.72   Edged weapons

> Including axes, daggers, dirks, knives, spears
>
> Class edged arrows in 739.73; class interdisciplinary works on knives in 621.932

.722   Swords and sabers

> Standard subdivisions are added for either or both topics in heading

.723   Bayonets

.73   Missile-hurling weapons

> Including air guns, bows and arrows, spring guns
>
> *For firearms, see 739.74*

.74   Firearms

> Add to base number 739.74 the numbers following 623.4 in 623.42–623.44, e.g., pistols 739.74432
>
> Class interdisciplinary works on small firearms in 683.4

.75   Armor

.752   Shields

740   Graphic arts [*formerly* 760] and decorative arts

Standard subdivisions are added for graphic and decorative arts together, for graphic arts alone

Including copy art made with photoduplication equipment, rubbings, typewriter art, typographical designs; two-dimensional mixed-media art and composites

Class here digital images, two-dimensional art

Class comprehensive works on graphic and plastic arts in 701–709. Class rubbings used for study and research in a specific field with the field, e.g., monumental brasses 739.522

For painting and paintings, see 750; for printmaking and prints, see 760; for photography and photographs, see 770; for cinematography and videography, see 777

SUMMARY

.285   Computer applications

> Do not use for comprehensive works on digital images; class in 740; however use subdivisions of 740.285 for specific computer applications in graphic arts, e.g., application of computer programs to digital images 740.28553

.4   **Iconography of graphic arts [*formerly* 760.044], iconography of decorative arts**

> Add to base number 740.4 the numbers following 704.94 in 704.942–704.949, e.g., landscapes in graphic arts 740.436
> Subdivisions are added for either or both topics in heading

.9   **History, geographic treatment, biography of graphic arts [*formerly* 760.09]; history, geographic treatment, biography of graphic and decorative arts together**

.901–.905   Periods of development

> Not limited by country or locality

> Add to base number 740.90 the numbers following 709.0 in 709.01–709.05, e.g., graphic arts of the Renaissance 740.9024

741   Drawing and drawings

> Class comprehensive works on drawing and painting in 750; class comprehensive works on two-dimensional art in 760

> *For drawing and drawings by subject, see 743*

SUMMARY

.01   Philosophy and theory

> Notation 01 from Table 1 as modified below

.011   **Appreciative aspects**

> Do not use for systems; class in 741.01
>
> Class psychological principles in 741.019

.011 7   Aesthetics

.011 8   Criticism and appreciation

> Including theory, technique, history
>
> Class works of critical appraisal in 741.09

.018   Inherent features

> Including color, composition, decorative values, form, light, movement, space, style, symmetry, time
>
> Class perspective in 742

.02   **Miscellany**

.028   **Auxiliary techniques and procedures**

> Class comprehensive works on basic and auxiliary techniques and procedures in 741.2

[.028 4]   Apparatus, equipment, materials

> Do not use; class in 741.2

.028 8   Maintenance and repair

> Including expertizing
>
> Class identification of reproductions, copies, forgeries, alterations in 741.217

.07   **Education, research, related topics**

.074   **Museums and exhibits**

> *For collections of drawings, see 741.9*

.09   **History, geographic treatment, biography**

.090 1–.090 5   Historical periods

> *For collections of drawings from specific periods, see 741.92*

.092   **Biography**

> Regardless of medium, process, subject, period, place
>
> Class artists working in special applications in 741.5–741.7; class collections of drawings in 741.9

.093–.099   **Specific continents, countries, localities**

> *For collections of drawings from specific continents, countries, localities, see 741.93–741.99*

.2   ***Techniques, procedures, apparatus, equipment, materials**

Including one-color washes highlighting drawings

Class here comprehensive works on basic and auxiliary techniques and procedures

Class techniques, procedures, apparatus, equipment, materials used in special applications in 741.5–741.7; class techniques, procedures, apparatus, equipment, materials used in drawing specific subjects in 743.4–743.8; class collections of drawings regardless of medium or process in 741.9

> *For auxiliary techniques and procedures, see 741.028; for perspective, see 742*
>
> *See also 751.422 for watercolor*

.21   *Techniques of reproduction and conservation

.217   *Reproduction

        Execution and identification

.217 2   *Reproductions and copies

        Standard subdivisions are added for either or both topics in heading

.217 4   *Forgeries and alterations

>   741.22–741.29 Specific mediums

Class comprehensive works in 741.2

.22   *Charcoal

.23   *Chalk and crayon

.235   *Pastel

.24   *Pencil

.25   *Silverpoint

.26   *Ink

        Class here brush, marker, pen drawing

.29   *Scratchboard and airbrush drawing

>   **741.5–741.7 Special applications**

Class here works that began with drawing but use other techniques such as painting, printing, photography to create the final product

Class comprehensive works in 741.6

---

*Do not use notation 092 from Table 1 for individual artists; class in 741.092

.5   **Comic books, graphic novels, fotonovelas, cartoons, caricatures, comic strips**

> Standard subdivisions are added for comic books, graphic novels, fotonovelas, cartoons, caricatures, comic strips together; for comic books alone; for graphic novels alone; for fotonovelas alone
>
> Variant name for comic books: comics
>
> Class comic books, graphic novels, fotonovelas, cartoons, caricatures, comic strips whose purpose is to inform or persuade with the subject, e.g., political cartoons 320.0207
>
> *See Manual at 741.5; also at 741.5 vs. 741.56*

.502 8   Auxiliary techniques and procedures

> Class comprehensive works on basic and auxiliary techniques and procedures in 741.51

[.502 84]   Apparatus, equipment, materials

> Do not use; class in 741.51

.507 4   Museums and exhibits

> Do not use for collections; class in 741.59

[.509]   History, geographic treatment, biography

> History, geographic treatment, biography of cartoons, caricatures, comic strips relocated to 741.569; history, geographic treatment, biography of comic books, graphic novels, fotonovelas and comprehensive history, geographic treatment, biography of comic books, graphic novels, fotonovelas, cartoons, caricatures, comic strips relocated to 741.59

.51   Techniques, procedures, apparatus, equipment, materials

> Class here comprehensive works on basic and auxiliary techniques and procedures; comprehensive works on drawing and writing comic books, graphic novels, fotonovelas, cartoons, caricatures, comic strips
>
> Class techniques, procedures, apparatus, equipment, materials used for special aspects in 741.53; class techniques, procedures, apparatus, equipment, materials used for cartoon animation in 741.58
>
> *For auxiliary techniques and procedures, see 741.5028; for photographic techniques for fotonovelas, see 771; for writing comic books, graphic novels, fotonovelas, cartoons, caricatures, comic strips, see 808.06*

.53   Special aspects of comic books, graphic novels, fotonovelas, cartoons, caricatures, comic strips

> Class here critical appraisal and description of genres, techniques for creating works in specific genres
>
> Class single works and collections of cartoons, caricatures, comic strips regardless of genre in 741.569; class single works and collections of comic books, graphic novels, fotonovelas regardless of genre in 741.59

.531   **Comic books, graphic novels, fotonovelas, cartoons, caricatures, comic strips displaying specific qualities**

Add to base number 741.531 the numbers following —1 in notation 11–17 from Table 3C, e.g., critical appraisal of horror graphic novels 741.53164

Subdivisions are added for any or all topics in heading

.532–.539   **Comic books, graphic novels, fotonovelas, cartoons, caricatures, comic strips dealing with specific themes and subjects**

Add to base number 741.53 the numbers following —3 in notation 32–39 from Table 3C, e.g., history and critical appraisal of superhero graphic novels 741.5352, drawing cartoon animals 741.5362

Subdivisions are added for any or all topics in heading

.56   **Cartoons, caricatures, comic strips**

Standard subdivisions are added for any or all topics in heading

Variant name for comic strips: strip cartoons

See Manual at 741.5 vs. 741.56

.560 28   Auxiliary techniques and procedures

Class comprehensive works on basic and auxiliary techniques and procedures in 741.51

.560 74   Museums and exhibits

Do not use for collections; class in 741.569

[.560 9]   History, geographic treatment, biography

Do not use; class in 741.569

.569   **History, geographic treatment, biography of cartoons, caricatures, comic strips [*formerly* 741.509]**

Single works or collections of works

Class here collections of cartoons, caricatures, comic strips [*formerly* 741.59]; development, description, critical appraisal

Class cartoon animation in 741.58; class comprehensive works on history, geographic treatment, biography of comic books, graphic novels, fotonovelas, cartoons, caricatures, comic strips in 741.59. Class works of description and critical appraisal that focus on a specific aspect and are not limited to an individual artist or writer with the aspect in 741.53, e.g., critical appraisal of comic strips about animals 741.5362

.569 1   Treatment by areas, regions, places in general

Add to base number 741.5691 the numbers following —1 in notation 11–19 from Table 2, e.g., caricatures from Western Hemisphere 741.5691812

.569 3–.569 9   Specific continents, countries, localities

> Add to base number 741.569 notation 3–9 from Table 2, e.g., a collection of European cartoons 741.5694, a collection of cartoons by multiple artists from London 741.569421, a collection of comic strips by a single author first published in United States 741.56973
>> Single works, collections by individual artists or writers, biographies and critical appraisal of individual artists or writers are classed at country level only, without further addition. For example, a biography of an individual artist from London is classed in 741.56942 (*not* 741.569421, 741.56942092). Notation from Table 1 is added for works treating more than one artist or writer, e.g., general history of United States comic strips 741.5697309, collected biography of English caricature artists 741.569420922

> *See Manual at 741.593–741.599 and 741.5693–741.5699*

.58   Cartoon animation

> Class here animation cels; techniques for creating animated drawings

> Class photographic techniques in 777.7; class comprehensive works on animated films in 791.4334; class animated films themselves in 791.437; class comprehensive works on animated television programs in 791.453; class animated television programs themselves in 791.457

.59   History, geographic treatment, biography

> Single works or collections of works

> Class here history, geographic treatment, biography of comic books, graphic novels, fotonovelas and comprehensive history, geographic treatment, biography of comic books, graphic novels, fotonovelas, cartoons, caricatures, comic strips [*formerly* 741.509]; development, description, critical appraisal

> Class cartoon animation in 741.58. Class works of description and critical appraisal that focus on a specific aspect and are not limited to a single work or to an individual artist or writer with the aspect in 741.53, e.g., critical appraisal of superhero graphic novels 741.5352

> Collections of cartoons, caricatures, comic strips relocated to 741.569

.591   Treatment by areas, regions, places in general

> Add to base number 741.591 the numbers following —1 in notation 11–19 from Table 2, e.g., graphic novels from Western Hemisphere 741.591812

.593–.599	Specific continents, countries, localities

> Add to base number 741.59 notation 3–9 from Table 2, e.g., a collection of European comic books 741.594, a collection of comic books by multiple artists from London 741.59421, a single graphic novel first published in Japan 741.5952
>> Single works, collections by individual artists or writers, biographies and critical appraisal of individual artists or writers are classed at country level only, without further addition. For example, a biography of an individual graphic novelist from London is classed in 741.5942 (*not* 741.59421, 741.5942092). Notation from Table 1 is added for works treating more than one artist or writer, e.g., general history of Japanese comic books 741.595209, collected biography of Japanese comic artists 741.59520922
>
> *See Manual at 741.593–741.599 and 741.5693–741.5699*

.6 **Graphic design, illustration, commercial art**

> Standard subdivisions are added for any or all topics in heading
>
> Class here comprehensive works on special applications of drawing
>
> Class comprehensive works on graphic arts, comprehensive works on two-dimensional art in 740. Class a specific type of illustration, a specific form of graphic design, a specific form of commercial art, not provided for here with the type or form, e.g., original oil paintings for book jackets 759
>
> *See Manual at 741.6 vs. 800*

.64	Books and book jackets

> Standard subdivisions are added for either or both topics in heading
>
> Class illumination of manuscripts and books in 745.67

.642	Children's books
.65	Magazines and newspapers
.652	Magazines and magazine covers

> Standard subdivisions are added for either or both topics in heading

.66	Covers for sheet music and recordings
.67	Advertisements and posters

> Standard subdivisions are added for advertisements and posters together, for advertisements alone

.672	Fashion drawing

> Class fashion design in 746.92

.674	Commercial posters

> Class here comprehensive works on posters
>
> *For art posters (posters as a specific form of prints), see 769.5*

.68	Calendars, postcards, greeting and business cards
.682	Calendars

.683	Postcards

Class government-issued postcards without illustration in 769.566

.684	Greeting cards
.685	Business cards (Trade cards)
.69	Labels and match covers
.692	Labels
.694	Match covers

.7 **Silhouettes**

Class cut-out silhouettes in 736.984

.9 **Collections of drawings**

Regardless of medium or process

Class here exhibition catalogs, preliminary drawings as works of art in their own right

Class collections by artists devoted to special applications in 741.5–741.7; class collections of drawings by subject not from a specific period or place in 743.9. Class preliminary drawings not treated as works of art in their own right with the finished work, e.g., preliminary drawings for frescoes 751.73

.92	Specific periods

Not limited geographically

.921	Earliest times to 499
.922	500–1399
.923	1400–1799
.924	1800–
.924 1	1800–1899
.924 2	1900–1999
.924 3	2000–2099
.93–.99	Specific continents, countries, localities

Add to base number 741.9 notation 3–9 from Table 2, e.g., collections of drawings from London 741.9421
Collections by individual artists are classed at country level only. Notation 074 from Table 1 for collections is not added. For example, a collection of an individual artist from London is classed in 741.942 (*not* 741.9421, 741.942074421)

742   **Perspective in drawing**

Theory, principles, methods

Class perspective in special applications in 741.5–741.7; class perspective in drawing specific subjects in 743.4–743.8; class comprehensive works on perspective in the arts in 701.82

743 *Drawing and drawings by subject

Standard subdivisions are added for drawing and drawings by subject together, for drawing alone

.4 *Drawing human figures

Class here nudes

For fashion drawing, see 741.672

.42 *Portraiture

Class portraiture of specific kinds of people in 743.43–743.45

> 743.43–743.45 Specific kinds of people

Class anatomy of specific kinds of people in 743.49; class comprehensive works in 743.4

.43 *Men

.44 *Women

.45 *Children

.46 *Bones (Skeletal system)

.47 *Muscles (Muscular system)

.49 *Anatomy for artists

Including parts and regions of body, e.g., head, abdomen, hands

For bones, see 743.46; for muscles, see 743.47

.5 *Drawing draperies

.6 *Drawing animals

Add to base number 743.6 the numbers following 59 in 592–599, e.g., drawing birds 743.68; however, for artists, see 741.092

.7 *Drawing plants

Including fruits

.73 *Drawing flowers

.76 *Drawing trees

.8 Drawing other subjects

Add to base number 743.8 the numbers following 704.94 in 704.943–704.949, e.g., landscapes 743.836; however, for artists, see 741.092

*Do not use notation 092 from Table 1 for artists; class in 741.092

.9 **Collections of drawings by subject (Iconography)**

Not limited by period or by place of production

Add to base number 743.9 the numbers following 704.94 in 704.942–704.949, e.g., collections of drawings of buildings 743.94

Class collections of drawings by subject from a specific period or place in 741.92–741.99

[744] **[Unassigned]**

Most recently used in Edition 17

745 **Decorative arts**

Class here folk art

For a decorative art not provided for here, see the art in 736–739, 746–749, e.g., interior decoration 747

SUMMARY

745.1		Antiques
.2		Industrial art and design
.4		Pure and applied design and decoration
.5		Handicrafts
.6		Calligraphy, heraldic design, illumination
.7		Decorative coloring
.8		Cycloramas, dioramas, panoramas
.9		Other decorative arts

.1 **Antiques**

For a specific kind of antique, see the kind, e.g., brasses 739.52, passenger automobiles 629.222

See Manual at 745.1

.102 8   Auxiliary techniques and procedures; apparatus, equipment, materials

Notation 028 from Table 1 as modified below

Class here basic techniques and procedures

.102 87   Techniques of reproduction, execution, identification

Do not use for testing and measurement; class in 745.1028

.102 872   Reproductions and copies

.102 874   Forgeries and alterations

.102 88   Maintenance and repair

Including expertizing

Class identification of reproductions, copies, forgeries, alterations in 745.10287

.2 **Industrial art and design**

Creative design of mass-produced commodities

Standard subdivisions are added for either or both topics in heading

> *For design of a specific commodity, see the commodity, e.g., automobiles 629.231*

.4 **Pure and applied design and decoration**

Standard subdivisions are added for any or all topics in heading

Class here design source books

> *For industrial design, see 745.2. For design in a specific art form, see the form, e.g., design in architecture 729*

.5 **Handicrafts**

Creative work done by hand with aid of simple tools or machines

Including work in bread dough

Class home (amateur) workshops in 684.08; class interdisciplinary works on handicrafts in 680. Class the handicraft aspects of another form of art with the art, e.g., printmaking using rubber stamps 761

> *For decorative coloring, see 745.7; for floral arts, see 745.92*

> *See Manual at 680 vs. 745.5*

> 745.51–745.58 Specific materials

Class specific objects made from specific materials in 745.59; class comprehensive works in 745.5

> *For textile handicrafts, see 746; for glass handicrafts, see 748*

.51 Woods

Including bamboo; ornamental woodwork

Class treen (woodenware) in 674.88; class woodworking in 684.08; class cabinetmaking (wooden furniture making) in 684.104; class artistic aspects of furniture in 749

> *For ornamental woodwork in furniture, see 749.5*

.512 Marquetry

Class here inlaying

.513 Scrollwork

Class here work with jig saws (scroll saws)

.514 Woodburning (Pyrography)

.53 Leathers and furs

Class construction of clothing in 646.4

.531	Leathers
.537	Furs
.54	Papers

> Including endpapers, paper boxes, tissue papers, wallpapers; gift wrapping, quilling
>
> Class paper cutting and folding in 736.98

| .542 | Papier-mâché |

> Class papier-mâché used in sculpture in 731.2

| .546 | Decoupage |

> Including potichomania

| .55 | Shells |
| .56 | Metals |

> Class art metalwork in 739

.57	Rubber and plastics
.572	Plastics
.572 3	Polymer clay
.58	Beads, found and other objects

> Class specific objects made from other objects in 745.59

| .582 | Beads |

> *For bead embroidery, see 746.5*
>
> *See also 745.5942 for beaded costume jewelry*

| .584 | Found objects |

> Including cattails, hosiery, scrap, stones

| .59 | Making specific objects |

> Class here handicrafts in composite materials
>
> *For textile handicrafts, see 746; for glass handicrafts, see 748*

| .592 | Toys, models, miniatures, related objects |

> Standard subdivisions are added for toys, models, miniatures, related objects together; for toys alone
>
> Including paper airplanes
>
> Class interdisciplinary works on mass-produced and handcrafted toys in 688.72

>   745.592 2–745.592 4   Toys and related objects

Class comprehensive works in 745.592

For toy soldiers, see 745.59282

.592 2   Dolls, puppets, marionettes

Class here clothing

.592 21   Dolls

Class porcelain dolls in 738.83

.592 24   Puppets and marionettes

.592 3   Dollhouses and furniture

Standard subdivisions are added for either or both topics in heading

See also 749.0228 for miniature furniture

.592 4   Soft toys

Class here stuffed toys

For stuffed dolls, see 745.59221

.592 43   Teddy bears

.592 8   Models and miniatures

Standard subdivisions are added for either or both topics in heading

Including ships in bottles

Class here interdisciplinary works on handcrafted models and miniatures

Class models and miniatures produced by assembly-line or mechanized manufacturing, interdisciplinary works on models and miniatures in 688.1; class play with remote-control models in 796.15

For handcrafted models and miniatures of a specific object, models for technical and professional use, see the object or use, plus notation 0228 from Table 1, e.g., handcrafted models of space stations 629.4420228; for miniature and model educational exhibits, see the subject illustrated, plus notation 074 from Table 1, e.g., handcrafted miniature physical anthropology exhibits 599.9074

See Manual at 745.5928

.592 82   Military models and miniatures

Standard subdivisions are added for either or both topics in heading

Including toy soldiers

.593   Useful objects

For toys, models, miniatures, related objects, see 745.592

.593 2	Lampshades
.593 3	Candles and candlesticks
.593 32	Candles
.593 4	Snuffboxes
.593 6	Decoys

Class carved birds not used for hunting in 730

.593 8	Scrapbooks

.594   Decorative objects

.594 1   Objects for special occasions

Including weddings

Class here greeting cards

.594 12   Christmas

.594 16   Holidays

Add to base number 745.59416 the numbers following 394.26 in 394.261–394.267, e.g., Halloween 745.5941646, Easter 745.5941667; however, for Christmas, see 745.59412; for Easter eggs, see 745.5944

.594 2   Costume jewelry

Class interdisciplinary works on costume jewelry in 391.7; class interdisciplinary works on making costume jewelry in 688.2; class interdisciplinary works on making jewelry in 739.27

.594 3   Artificial flowers

Class arrangement of artificial flowers in 745.92

.594 4   Egg decorating

Including Easter eggs

Class comprehensive works on handicrafts for Easter in 745.5941667

.594 6   Fountains

Class here tabletop fountains

Class comprehensive works on fountains in 731.724

.6   **Calligraphy, heraldic design, illumination**

.61   Calligraphy

Class here artistic, decorative lettering

Class penmanship in 652.1; class typography in 686.22

.619   Styles

.619 7   Latin styles (Western styles)

.619 74   Carolingian calligraphy

.619 75	Black-letter and Gothic calligraphy
.619 77	Italic calligraphy
.619 78	Roman calligraphy
.619 8	Greek calligraphy
.619 9	Other styles

> Add to base number 745.6199 the numbers following —9 in notation 91–99 from Table 6, e.g., Chinese calligraphy 745.619951

.66	Heraldic design
.67	Illumination of manuscripts and books

> Standard subdivisions are added for either or both topics in heading

> Class here facsimiles of manuscripts reproduced for their illuminations

> Class development, description, critical appraisal of manuscripts in 091; class development, description, critical appraisal of illustrated books in 096.1

> *See also 741.64 for book illustration*

.674	Illuminated manuscripts and books by language

> Add to base number 745.674 notation 1–9 from Table 6, e.g., illuminated manuscripts in Byzantine Greek 745.67487; however, for illuminated manuscripts in Latin, see 745.67094

> Class illuminated manuscripts and books in specific languages produced in specific countries and localities in 745.67093–745.67099

.7	**Decorative coloring**

> Class printing, painting, dyeing textiles in 746.6

.72	Painting and lacquering
.723	Painting

> Including rosemaling, tolecraft

.726	Lacquering

> Class here japanning

.73	Stenciling
.74	Decalcomania
.75	Gilding

> Class gilding as an aspect of bookbinding in 686.36; class gilding as an aspect of illumination of manuscripts and books in 745.67

.8	**Cycloramas, dioramas, panoramas**
.9	**Other decorative arts**

.92   Floral arts

Flower arrangement: selection and arrangement of plant materials and appropriate accessories

Class here arrangement of artificial flowers, three-dimensional arrangements

Class making artificial flowers in 745.5943; class potted plants as interior decorations in 747.98

>   745.922–745.925 Three-dimensional arrangements with specific materials

Class arrangements with specific materials for special occasions in 745.926; class comprehensive works in 745.92

.922   Flower arrangements in containers

.922 4   Western flower arrangements

.922 5   Asian flower arrangements

.922 51   Chinese flower arrangements

.922 52   Japanese flower arrangements

.923   Flower arrangements without containers

Including boutonnieres, corsages, set floral pieces

.924   Fruit and vegetable arrangements

Including carving of vegetables to produce artificial flowers

.925   Arrangements with other plant materials

Including driftwood, pods and cones, dried and gilded grasses and leaves

.926   Three-dimensional arrangements for special occasions

Including arrangements for church services, funerals, holidays, weddings

.928   Two-dimensional arrangements

Use of seeds and other dried plant materials in pictures, hangings, trays, for other decorative purposes

746   Textile arts

Class here textile handicrafts

Add to each subdivision identified by * as follows:

028	Auxiliary techniques and procedures; apparatus, equipment, materials
0288	Maintenance and repair
	Including expertizing
	Class here conservation, preservation, restoration
	Class identification of reproductions, copies, forgeries, alterations in 048
04	Special topics
041	Patterns
	Class patterns for specific products in 043
042	Stitches
	Class stitches for specific products in 043
043	Products
	Use only with base numbers for techniques
	For laces and related fabrics, see 746.2; for rugs and carpets, see 746.7
0432	Costume
	Including sweaters
0433	Pictures, hangings, tapestries
	Standard subdivisions are added for any or all topics in heading
0434–0438	Interior furnishings
	Add to base number 043 the numbers following 746.9 in 746.94–746.98, e.g., bedclothes 0437
048	Reproductions, copies, forgeries, alterations
	Execution and identification

Class domestic sewing and related operations in 646.2. Class a specific textile product not provided for here with the product, e.g., stuffed animals 745.5924

SUMMARY

746.04	**Specific materials**
.1	**Yarn preparation and weaving**
.2	**Laces and related fabrics**
.3	**Pictures, hangings, tapestries**
.4	**Needlework and handwork**
.5	**Bead embroidery**
.6	**Printing, painting, dyeing**
.7	**Rugs**
.9	**Other textile products**

.04   Specific materials

Add to base number 746.04 the numbers following 677 in 677.1–677.7, e.g., silk 746.0439, string art 746.0471

Class products in a specific material with the product, e.g., string pictures 746.3

> ### 746.1–746.9 Products and processes

Unless other instructions are given, observe the following table of preference, e.g., embroidered rugs 746.74 (*not* 746.44):

Laces and related fabrics	746.2
Rugs	746.7
Yarn preparation and weaving	746.1
Needlework and handwork	746.4
Bead embroidery	746.5
Printing, painting, dyeing	746.6
Pictures, hangings, tapestries	746.3
Other textile products	746.9

Class home sewing and clothing in 646; class textile manufacturing in 677; class comprehensive works in 746

.1   Yarn preparation and weaving

.11   Carding and combing

.12   Spinning, twisting, reeling

Standard subdivisions are added for spinning, twisting, reeling together; for spinning alone

.13   Dyeing

.14   *Weaving

Including card weaving

For weaving unaltered vegetable fibers, see 746.41; for nonloom weaving, see 746.42

.2   Laces and related fabrics

.22   *Laces

Including crocheted, darned laces

For tatting, see 746.436

.222   *Bobbin laces

.224   *Needlepoint laces

.226   *Knitted laces

.27   Passementerie

Including braids, cords, fringes

.3   *Pictures, hangings, tapestries

Subdivisions are added for any or all topics in heading

---

*Add as instructed under 746

| [.309] | History, geographic treatment, biography |

Do not use; class in 746.39

| (.309 2) | Biography |

(Optional number; prefer 746.392)

| .39 | History, geographic treatment, biography |

| .390 01–.390 09 | Standard subdivisions |

Add to base number 746.3900 the numbers following —00 in notation 001–009 from Table 2, e.g., periodicals of the history of tapestries 746.39005

| .390 1–.390 5 | Historical periods |

Add to base number 746.390 the numbers following —090 in notation 0901–0905 from Table 1, e.g., tapestries from 20th century 746.3904

| .391–.399 | Geographic treatment, biography |

Add to base number 746.39 notation 1–9 from Table 2, e.g., artists 746.392
(Option: Class biography in 746.3092)

| **.4** | **Needlework and handwork** |

Standard subdivisions are added for either or both topics in heading

| .41 | Weaving, braiding, matting unaltered vegetable fibers |

Including raffia work, rushwork

| .412 | Basketry |

| .42 | Nonloom weaving and related techniques |

Including braiding, plaiting, twining

Class nonloom weaving of unaltered vegetable fibers in 746.41

For card weaving, see 746.14

| .422 | *Knotting |

| .422 2 | *Macramé |

| .422 4 | *Netting |

Including knotless netting, sprang

| .43 | *Knitting, crocheting, tatting |

| .432 | *Knitting |

Class comprehensive works on knitting and crocheting in 746.43

| .434 | *Crocheting |

| .436 | *Tatting |

*Add as instructed under 746

.44	*Embroidery
	Including couching, cutwork, drawn work, hardanger, smocking
.440 28	Auxiliary techniques and procedures; apparatus, equipment, materials
	Including machine embroidery
.442	*Canvas embroidery and needlepoint
	Including bargello
	Subdivisions are added for either or both topics in heading
	Class cross-stitch and counted thread embroidery in 746.443
.443	*Cross-stitch
	Class here counted thread embroidery
.445	*Appliqué
.446	*Crewelwork
.447	*Silk ribbon embroidery
.46	*Patchwork and quilting
	Class here quilts
	Subdivisions are added for either or both topics in heading
.460 437	Bedclothes
	Number built according to instructions under 746
	Class quilts in 746.46
.5	***Bead embroidery**
.6	***Printing, painting, dyeing**
	Including hand decoration, stenciling
.62	*Printing
	Block and silk-screen
.66	*Resist-dyeing
.662	*Batik
.664	*Tie-dyeing
.7	***Rugs**
	Class here carpets
[.709]	History, geographic treatment, biography
	Do not use; class in 746.79

*Add as instructed under 746

(.709 2)	Biography
	(Optional number; prefer 746.792)
.72	*Woven rugs

Class here Navajo rugs; Jacquard, plain, tapestry, twill weaves

For pile rugs, see 746.75

.73	*Crocheted, knitted, braided rugs
.74	*Hooked and embroidered rugs
.75	Pile rugs
.750 95	Asian pile rugs

Class here Oriental-style rugs

For styles from Caucasus region, see 746.759

[.750 951–.750 958]   Asian countries and localities other than southeast Asia

Do not use; class in 746.751–746.758

>   746.751–746.759   Oriental-style rugs

Class comprehensive works in 746.75095

.751–.758   Styles from specific Asian countries and localities other than southeast Asia

Add to base number 746.75 the numbers following —5 in notation 51–58 from Table 2, e.g., Chinese rugs 746.751

See also 746.750959 for styles from southeast Asia

.759	Styles from Caucasus region
.79	History, geographic treatment, biography
.790 01–.790 09	Standard subdivisions

Add to base number 746.7900 the numbers following —00 in notation 001–009 from Table 2, e.g., periodicals of the history of rugs 746.79005

.790 1–.790 5   Historical periods

Add to base number 746.790 the numbers following —090 in notation 0901–0905 from Table 1, e.g., rugs from 20th century 746.7904

.791–.799   Geographic treatment, biography

Add to base number 746.79 notation 1–9 from Table 2, e.g., artists 746.792
(Option: Class biography in 746.7092)

.9   **Other textile products**

*Add as instructed under 746

.92   Costume

Class here fashion design

Class interdisciplinary works on clothing in 391; class interdisciplinary works on clothing construction in 646.4

See Manual at 391 vs. 646.3, 746.92

.94   *Draperies

Class here curtains

.95   *Furniture covers

Class here antimacassars, kneelers, slipcovers, upholstery

.96   *Table linens

Class here doilies, mats, napkins (serviettes), scarves, tablecloths; fair linens

.97   *Bedclothes

Class here bedspreads, blankets; sheets, pillowcases

For afghans, see 746.430437; for quilts, see 746.46

.98   *Towels

Class here toweling

747   Interior decoration

Design and decorative treatment of interior furnishings

Class here interior decoration of residential buildings

Class interior architecture (interior design) in 729; class textile arts and handicrafts in 746; class interior decoration of specific types of residential buildings in 747.88

For furniture and accessories, see 749

.1   **Decoration under specific limitations**

Including decorating on a budget

Class a specific aspect of decoration under limitations with the aspect, e.g., decorating dining rooms on a budget 747.76

>   **747.3–747.4   Decoration of specific elements**

Class decoration of specific elements in specific rooms of residential buildings in 747.7; class decoration of specific elements in specific types of buildings in 747.8; class specific decorations of specific elements in 747.9; class comprehensive works in 747

---

*Add as instructed under 746

.3 **Ceilings, walls, doors, windows**

> Including decorative hangings, painting, paneling, woodwork

> Class here textile wall coverings, wallpapers

> *For draperies, see 747.5*

.4 **Floors**

> *For rugs and carpets, see 747.5*

.5 **Draperies, upholstery, rugs and carpets**

.7 **Decoration of specific rooms of residential buildings**

> Class specific decorations regardless of room in 747.9

.73 Studies

> Class here home libraries

.75 Living rooms, drawing rooms, parlors

> Standard subdivisions are added for any or all topics in heading

.76 Dining rooms

.77 Bedrooms

> Class here nurseries

.78 Bathrooms

> Including powder rooms

.79 Other rooms

.791 Recreation rooms

> Class here family rooms

.797 Kitchens

.8 **Decoration of specific types of buildings**

> Class specific decorations regardless of type of building in 747.9

.85–.87 Decoration of public, religious, educational, research buildings

> Add to base number 747.8 the numbers following 72 in 725–727, e.g., decoration of theaters 747.85822

.88 Decoration of specific types of residential buildings

> Add to base number 747.88 the numbers following 728 in 728.1–728.9, e.g., decoration of hotels 747.885

> Class decoration of residential buildings of institutions in 747.85–747.87; class comprehensive works on decoration of residential buildings in 747

> *For decoration of specific rooms of residential buildings, see 747.7*

.9   **Specific decorations**

Unless other instructions are given, observe the following table of preference, e.g., decorative lighting for Christmas 747.92 (*not* 747.93):

Decorating with houseplants	747.98
Decorative lighting	747.92
Decorating with color	747.94
Decorations for specific occasions	747.93

See also 747.5 for draperies, upholstery, rugs and carpets

.92   Decorative lighting

.93   Decorations for specific occasions

Including holidays, parties, weddings

.94   Decorating with color

.98   Decorating with houseplants

748   Glass

Class here glassware

For glass sculpture, see 730

.092   Biography

Class here glassmakers

.2   **Blown, cast, decorated, fashioned, molded, pressed glass**

Standard subdivisions are added for any or all topics in heading

Class here comprehensive works on tableware

Class stained glass in 748.5; class comprehensive works on glass made by a specific technique in 748

For methods of decoration, see 748.6; for stained, painted, leaded, mosaic tableware, see 748.5; for specific articles made from blown, cast, decorated, fashioned, molded, pressed glass, see 748.8

Use of this number for glassware discontinued; class in 748

.202 8   Auxiliary techniques and procedures; apparatus, equipment, materials

Notation 028 from Table 1 as modified below

Class here basic techniques and procedures

.202 82   Glassblowing

.202 86   Bottle and jar cutting

Do not use for green technology; class in 748.2028

Standard subdivisions are added for either or both topics in heading

.202 87	Reproductions, copies, forgeries, alterations

Do not use for testing and measurement; class in 748.2028

Execution and identification

.202 88	Maintenance and repair

Including expertizing

Class identification of reproductions, copies, forgeries, alterations in 748.20287

.5 Stained, painted, leaded, mosaic glass

Standard subdivisions are added for stained, painted, leaded, mosaic glass together; for stained glass alone; for painted glass alone; for leaded glass alone

Class comprehensive works on mosaics in 738.5; class comprehensive works on tableware in 748.2

For specific articles made from stained, painted, leaded, mosaic glass, see 748.8

.502 8	Auxiliary techniques and procedures; apparatus, equipment, materials

Notation 028 from Table 1 as modified below

Class here basic techniques and procedures

.502 82	Glass painting and staining
.502 84	Leaded glass craft

Do not use for apparatus, equipment, materials of stained, painted, leaded, mosaic glass together; class in 748.5028

.502 85	Mosaic glass craft

Do not use for computer applications; class in 748.5028

.6 Methods of decoration

Including cutting, enameling, sandblasting

Class methods of decoration of specific articles in 748.8

For painted glass, see 748.5

[.609 2]	Biography

Do not use; class in 748.2092

.62	Engraving
.63	Etching

.8 Specific articles

Including mirrors, ornaments

Class mirrors as furniture in 749.3; class glass lamps and lighting fixtures in 749.63

.82 Bottles

> Bottles of artistic interest regardless of use
>
> Class manufacture of glass bottles in 666.192

.83 Specific articles of tableware

> Class here drinking glasses
>
> Class works on more than one type of tableware, comprehensive works on tableware in 748.2

.84 Paperweights

.85 Glass beads

749 Furniture and accessories

> Standard subdivisions are added for furniture and accessories together, for furniture alone
>
> *For upholstery, see 747.5*

.1 Antique furniture

> Class specific kinds of antique furniture in 749.3

.102 8 Auxiliary techniques and procedures; apparatus, equipment, materials

> Notation 028 from Table 1 as modified below

.102 87 Reproductions, copies, forgeries, alterations

> Do not use for testing and measurement; class in 749.1028
>
> Execution and identification

.102 88 Maintenance and repair

> Including expertizing
>
> Class identification of reproductions, copies, forgeries, alterations in 749.10287

[.109] History, geographic treatment, biography

> Do not use; class in 749.09

.3 Specific kinds of furniture

> Including beds, cabinets, chests, clockcases, desks, mirrors, screens, tables
>
> Class outdoor furniture in 749.8
>
> *For built-in furniture, see 749.4; for heating and lighting fixtures and furniture, see 749.6; for picture frames, see 749.7*

[.301–.309] Standard subdivisions

> Do not use; class in 749.01–749.09

.32 Chairs

.4   **Built-in furniture**

> Class built-in church furniture in architectural design in 726.529
>
> *For heating and lighting fixtures and furniture, see 749.6*

.5   **Ornamental woodwork in furniture**

> Including inlay trim, lacquer work, marquetry, scrollwork
>
> Class ornamental woodwork in a specific kind of furniture with the kind, e.g., picture frames 749.7

.6   **Heating and lighting fixtures and furniture**

.62   Heating

> Including mantels, fireplace and inglenook fixtures and furniture

.63   Lighting

> Including chandeliers, lamps, sconces
>
> Class built-in church lighting fixtures in architectural design in 726.5298

.7   **Picture frames**

> Including shadow boxes
>
> Class here picture framing

.8   **Outdoor furniture**

> Class furniture used both indoors and outdoors in 749.3

750   Painting and paintings

> Class here comprehensive works on painting and drawing
>
> Unless other instructions are given, observe the following table of preference, e.g., an individual Canadian painter of landscapes 759.11 (*not* 758.10971), landscape painting in Canada 758.10971 (*not* 759.11):

Individual painters and their work	759.1–759.9
Techniques, procedures, apparatus, equipment, materials	751.2–751.6
Iconography	753–758
Specific forms	751.7
Geographic treatment	759.1–759.9
Periods of development	759.01–759.07
Color	752

> Class comprehensive works on graphic arts, two-dimensional art in 760. Class painting in a specific decorative art with the art, e.g., illumination of manuscripts and books 745.67
>
> *For drawing and drawings, see 741*

SUMMARY

750.1–.8	**Standard subdivisions**
751	**Techniques, procedures, apparatus, equipment, materials, forms**
752	**Color**
753	**Symbolism, allegory, mythology, legend**
754	**Genre paintings**
755	**Religion**
757	**Human figures**
758	**Nature, architectural subjects and cityscapes, other specific subjects**
759	**History, geographic treatment, biography**

.1   **Philosophy and theory**

Notation 01 from Table 1 as modified below

.11   Appreciative aspects

Do not use for systems; class in 750.1

Class psychological principles in 750.19

.117   Aesthetics

.118   Criticism and appreciation

Including theory, technique, history

Class works of critical appraisal in 759

.18   Inherent features

Including composition, decorative values, form, light, movement, perspective, space, style, symmetry, vision

For color, see 752

.28   Auxiliary techniques and procedures

For comprehensive works on basic and auxiliary techniques and procedures, see 751.4

[.284]   Apparatus, equipment, materials

Do not use for materials; class in 751.2. Do not use for apparatus and equipment; class in 751.3

[.288]   Maintenance and repair

Do not use; class in 751.6

[.9]   **History, geographic treatment, biography**

Do not use; class in 759

(.92)   Biography

(Optional number; prefer 759)

751 *Techniques, procedures, apparatus, equipment, materials, forms

.2 *Materials

Including coatings, fixatives, mediums, pigments, surfaces

Class use of materials in specific techniques in 751.4

.3 *Apparatus, equipment, artists' models

Class use of apparatus and equipment in specific techniques in 751.4

.4 *Techniques and procedures

Class here comprehensive works on basic and auxiliary techniques and procedures

For auxiliary techniques and procedures, see 750.28; for techniques of reproduction, see 751.5; for maintenance and repair, see 751.6

.42 *Use of water-soluble mediums

For tempera painting, see 751.43

.422 *Watercolor painting

Including casein painting, gouache

Class ink painting in color in 751.425

.422 4 Watercolor painting techniques by subject

Add to base number 751.4224 the numbers following 704.94 in 704.942–704.949, e.g., techniques of landscape painting in watercolor 751.422436; however, for individual painters, see 759.1–759.9

.425 *Ink painting

.425 1 *Chinese ink painting

.425 14 Chinese ink painting techniques by subject

Add to base number 751.42514 the numbers following 704.94 in 704.942–704.949, e.g., techniques of landscape painting in Chinese ink painting 751.4251436; however, for individual painters, see 759.1–759.9

.425 2 *Japanese ink painting

.426 *Acrylic painting

.426 4 Acrylic painting techniques by subject

Add to base number 751.4264 the numbers following 704.94 in 704.942–704.949, e.g., techniques of landscape painting in acrylics 751.426436; however, for individual painters, see 759.1–759.9

.43 *Tempera painting

.44 *Fresco painting

*Do not use notation 092 from Table 1 for individual painters; class in 759.1–759.9

.45   *Oil painting

.454   Oil painting techniques by subject

> Add to base number 751.454 the numbers following 704.94 in 704.942–704.949, e.g., techniques of landscape painting in oils 751.45436; however, for individual painters, see 759.1–759.9

.46   *Encaustic painting (Wax painting)

.49   *Other methods

> Including finger, polymer, roller (brayer), sand painting

> *For mosaic painting, see 738.5*

.493   *Collage

> With painting as the basic technique

.494   *Airbrush

.5   ***Techniques of reproduction**

> Execution, identification, determination of authenticity of reproductions, copies, forgeries, alterations

> *For printmaking and prints, see 760*

.58   *Forgeries and alterations

.6   ***Maintenance and repair**

.62   *Conservation, preservation, restoration

> Standard subdivisions are added for any or all topics in heading

> Including expertizing

> Class identification of reproductions, copies, forgeries, alterations in 751.5

.7   ***Specific forms**

.73   *Murals and frescoes

> Class here painted graffiti, street art

.74   *Panoramas, cycloramas, dioramas

> Standard subdivisions are added for any or all topics in heading

.75   *Scene paintings

> Including theatrical scenery

.76   *Glass underpainting

> Class glass underpainting as a technique of glass decoration in 748.6

.77   *Miniatures

> Class miniatures done as illuminations in manuscripts and books in 745.67

*Do not use notation 092 from Table 1 for individual painters; class in 759.1–759.9

752 ***Color**

> Class technology of color in 667; class comprehensive works on color in the fine and decorative arts in 701.85

> ### 753–758 Iconography

> Class here development, description, critical appraisal, works regardless of form

> A work with two or more subjects is classed with the subject that is the center of interest, e.g., cityscapes with incidental human figures 758.7 (*not* 757), church interiors displaying Stations of the Cross 755.4 (*not* 758.7)

> Class comprehensive works in 750

> *See Manual at 704.9 and 753–758*

753 ***Symbolism, allegory, mythology, legend**

  .6 ***Symbolism and allegory**

> Standard subdivisions are added for either or both topics in heading

> *For religious symbolism, see 755*

  .7 ***Mythology and legend**

> Class religious mythology in 755

754 ***Genre paintings**

755 ***Religion**

> Class here religious symbolism

> Add to base number 755 the numbers following 704.948 in 704.9482–704.9489, e.g., paintings of Holy Family 755.56; however, for individual painters, see 759.1–759.9

[756] **[Unassigned]**

> Most recently used in Edition 19

---

*Do not use notation 092 from Table 1 for individual painters; class in 759.1–759.9

757   *Human figures

Class here portraits

Unless other instructions are given, observe the following table of preference, e.g., groups of nude women 757.2 (*not* 757.4 or 757.6):

Erotica	757.8
Nudes	757.2
Miniature portraits	757.7
Specific groups of people	757.3–757.5
Groups of human figures	757.6

Class symbolism of human figures in 753.6. Class human figures engaged in a specific activity or occupation with the activity or occupation, e.g., farmers 758.5092, doctors 758.961092, circus clowns 758.979133

For human figures associated with mythology and legend, see 753.7; for human figures associated with religion, see 755

Human figures engaged in a specific activity relocated to the activity, e.g., ice skaters 758.979691092

.2   *Nudes

Class here nudes of men [*formerly* 757.3], nudes of women [*formerly* 757.4], nudes of children [*formerly* 757.5], groups of nudes [*formerly* 757.6]

[.22]   Nudes

Number discontinued; class in 757.2

[.23]   Draped figures

Number discontinued; class in 757

> ### 757.3–757.5   Specific groups of people

Class comprehensive works in 757

.3   *Men

Nudes of men relocated to 757.2

.4   *Women

Nudes of women relocated to 757.2

.5   *Children

Nudes of children relocated to 757.2

.6   *Groups of human figures

Groups of nudes relocated to 757.2; hunters relocated to 758.979929

.7   *Miniature portraits

*Do not use notation 092 from Table 1 for individual painters; class in 759.1–759 9

.8　　***Erotica**

Including pornography

758　　*Nature, architectural subjects and cityscapes, other specific subjects

Standard subdivisions are added for nature and other specific subjects together; for nature alone

---

> **758.1–758.5 Nature**

Class comprehensive works in 758

.1　　***Landscapes**

Add to base number 758.1 notation 1–9 from Table 2, e.g., landscapes of Utah 758.1792; however, for individual painters, see 759.1–759.9

.2　　***Marine scenes and seascapes**

Standard subdivisions are added for either or both topics in heading

.3　　***Animals**

Add to base number 758.3 the numbers following 59 in 592–599, e.g., eagles 758.38942

Class symbolism of animals in 753.6

For animals associated with mythology and legend, see 753.7; for animals associated with religion, see 755

.4　　***Still life**

Class symbolism of still life in 753.6

For still life associated with mythology and legend, see 753.7; for still life associated with religion, see 755

.42　　***Flowers**

.5　　***Plants**

Class here agriculture

Class symbolism of plants in 753.6; class landscapes in 758.1

For plants associated with mythology and legend, see 753.7; for plants associated with religion, see 755; for animals, see 758.3; for flowers, see 758.42

.7　　***Architectural subjects and cityscapes**

Standard subdivisions are added for either or both topics in heading

Add to base number 758.7 notation 1–9 from Table 2, e.g., cityscapes of England 758.742; however, for individual painters, see 759.1–759.9

---

*Do not use notation 092 from Table 1 for individual painters; class in 759.1–759.9

.9   **Other specific subjects**

Not provided for elsewhere

Add to base number 758.9 notation 001–999, e.g., paintings of scientific subjects 758.95, of hunters 758.979929 [*formerly* 757.6], of historical events 758.99; however, for individual painters, see 759.1–759.9

759   **History, geographic treatment, biography**

Class here development, description, critical appraisal, works

Class exhibitions of paintings not limited by place, period, or subject in 750.74

(Option: Class biography in 750.92)

>   759.01–759.07   Periods of development

Class here schools and styles not limited by country or locality, works on one or two periods of European painting

Class works on three or more periods of European painting in 759.94; class comprehensive works in 759. Class schools associated with a specific locality with the locality in 759.1–759.9, e.g., Florentine school of Italian painting 759.551

When classifying works of more than one painter, notation 074 and notation 075 from Table 1 for Museums, collections, exhibits and Museum activities, respectively, take preference over notation 0922 for Collected biography

See Manual at 704.9 and 753–758

.01   *Nonliterate peoples, and earliest times to 499

.011   *Nonliterate peoples

Regardless of time or place

Class paintings of both nonliterate and literate cultures in 759.1–759.9

.011 2   *Paleolithic painting and paintings

Standard subdivisions are added for either or both topics in heading

.011 3   *Rock art (painting and paintings)

.02   *500–1399

Class here medieval painting and paintings

.021   *500–1199

.021 2   *Early Christian painting and paintings

Standard subdivisions are added for either or both topics in heading

For early Christian painting and paintings before 500, see 759.01

---

*Do not use notation 092 from Table 1 for individual painters; class in 759.1–759.9

.021 4	*Byzantine painting and paintings

Standard subdivisions are added for either or both topics in heading

For Byzantine painting and paintings before 500, see 759.01

.021 6	*Romanesque painting and paintings

Standard subdivisions are added for either or both topics in heading

.022	*1200–1399

Class here Gothic painting and paintings

For Gothic painting and paintings of an earlier or later period, see the specific period, e.g., 500–1199 759.021

.03	*1400–1599

Class here Renaissance painting and paintings

For Renaissance painting and paintings before 1400, see 759.022

.04	*1600–1799
.046	*1600–1699

Class here baroque painting and paintings

For baroque painting and paintings of 1700–1799, see 759.047

.047	*1700–1799

Including rococo painting and paintings

.05	*1800–1899

Add to base number 759.05 the numbers following 709.034 in 709.0341–709.0349, e.g., romanticism in painting 759.052; however, for individual painters, see 759.1–759.9

.06	*1900–1999

Class here modern painting

Add to base number 759.06 the numbers following 709.040 in 709.0401–709.0407, e.g., surrealist painting 759.0663; however, for individual painters, see 759.1–759.9

For 1800–1899, see 759.05; for 2000–2099, see 759.07

.07	*2000–2099

*Do not use notation 092 from Table 1 for individual painters; class in 759.1–759.9

> **759.1–759.9 Geographic treatment**

Individual painters are classed in notation at country level only. Standard subdivisions —074, —075, and —092 from Table 1 are not added for individual painters, e.g., an exhibition of the work of a Canadian painter, collecting the person's works, and a biography of the painter 759.11 (*not* 759.11074, 759.11075, or 759.11092, respectively)

Class painting and paintings of nonliterate peoples in 759.011; class western painting of one or two specific periods in 759.02–759.07; class comprehensive works in 759

(Option: To give local emphasis and a shorter number to painting and paintings of a specific country, use one of the following:

(Option A: Place them first by use of a letter or other symbol for the country, e.g., Burmese painting and paintings 759.B [preceding 759.1]

(Option B: Class them in 759.1; in that case class painting and paintings of North America in 759.97)

.1   **North America**

For painting and paintings of Middle America, see 759.972

(Option: To give local emphasis and a shorter number to painting and paintings of a specific country other than United States and Canada, class them in this number; in that case class painting and paintings of North America in 759.97)

.11   Canada

Add to base number 759.11 the numbers following —71 in notation 711–719 from Table 2, e.g., painting and paintings of Toronto 759.113541

.13   United States

Class painting and paintings of specific states in 759.14–759.19

See also 759.97295 for painting and paintings of Puerto Rico

.14–.19   Specific states of United States

Add to base number 759.1 the numbers following —7 in notation 74–79 from Table 2, e.g., painting and paintings of San Francisco 759.19461

Class individual painters in 759.13

For painting and paintings of Hawaii, see 759.9969

> **759.2–759.8 Europe**

Class comprehensive works in 759.94

For countries and localities not provided for here, see the country or locality in 759.949, e.g., painting and paintings of Belgium 759.9493

.2 **British Isles**

Class here England

When classifying individual painters, England, Scotland, Wales, and Northern Ireland are considered to be separate countries. Therefore, an English painter is classed in 759.2, a Scottish painter in 759.2911, a Welsh painter in 759.2929, and a Northern Ireland painter in 759.2916

.21–.28 England

Add to base number 759.2 the numbers following —42 in notation 421–428 from Table 2, e.g., painting and paintings of Manchester 759.2733

.29 Scotland, Ireland, Wales

Add to base number 759.29 the numbers following —4 in notation 41–42 from Table 2, e.g., painting and paintings of Scotland 759.2911

.3–.8 **Miscellaneous parts of Europe**

Add to base number 759 the numbers following —4 in notation 43–48 from Table 2, e.g., painting and paintings of France 759.4

.9 **Other geographic areas**

.91 Areas, regions, places in general

Add to base number 759.91 the numbers following —1 in notation 11–19 from Table 2, e.g., Western Hemisphere 759.91812

Individual painters are classed in the notation for their respective countries, e.g., painters from Canada 759.11

.93–.99 Specific continents, countries, localities

Class here painting and paintings of specific periods, e.g., painting and paintings of 1800–1899 in South America 759.9809034

Add to base number 759.9 notation 3–9 from Table 2, e.g., comprehensive works on painting and paintings of Europe 759.94, Etruscan painting and paintings 759.9375, painting and paintings of Hawaii 759.9969; however, for individual Hawaiian painters, see 759.13

Class works on one or two periods of European painting in 759.02–759.07, e.g., painting and paintings of 1800–1899 in Europe 759.05 (*not* 759.9409034); class painting and paintings from parts of Europe in notation 41–48 from Table 2 in 759.2–759.8

760 **Printmaking and prints**

For printing, see 686.2

Graphic arts relocated to 740

SUMMARY

760.1–.8	**Standard subdivisions**
761	**Relief processes (Block printing)**
763	**Lithographic processes (Planographic processes)**
764	**Chromolithography and serigraphy**
765	**Metal engraving**
766	**Mezzotinting, aquatinting, related processes**
767	**Etching and drypoint**
769	**Prints**

[.044]   Iconography of graphic arts

> Relocated to 740.4

[.09]   History, geographic treatment, biography of graphic arts

> Relocated to 740.9

.1   **Philosophy and theory**

> Notation 01 from Table 1 as modified below

.11   Appreciative aspects

> Do not use for systems; class in 760.1

> Class psychological principles in 760.19

.117   Aesthetics

.118   Criticism and appreciation

> Including theory, technique, history

> Class works of critical appraisal in 769.9

.18   Inherent features

> Including color, composition, decorative values, form, light, movement, perspective, space, style, symmetry, vision

.2   **Miscellany**

.28   Auxiliary techniques and procedures; apparatus, equipment, materials

> Notation 028 from Table 1 as modified below

> Class here basic techniques and procedures

> Class techniques, procedures, apparatus, equipment, materials for making specific kinds of prints in 761–767

.7   **Education, research, related topics**

.75   Museum activities and services

> Do not use for collecting; class in 769.12

[.9]   **History, geographic treatment, biography**

> Do not use; class in 769.9

(.92)   Biography

> (Optional number; prefer 769.92)

> ## 761–767 Printmaking

Fine art of executing a printing block or plate representing a picture or design conceived by the printmaker or copied from another artist's painting or drawing or from a photograph

Techniques, procedures, equipment, materials

Class maintenance and repair in 769.0288; class techniques, procedures, apparatus, equipment, materials of reproduction in 769.1; class techniques, procedures, apparatus, equipment, materials employed by individual printmakers in 769.92; class comprehensive works in 760.28

761   Relief processes (Block printing)

Including raw potato printing, rubber-stamp printing

.2   **Wood engraving**

.3   **Linoleum-block printing**

.8   **Metal relief engraving**

[762]   [Unassigned]

Most recently used in Edition 14

763   Lithographic processes (Planographic processes)

For chromolithography, see 764.2

.2   **Surfaces**

.22   Stone lithography

.23   Aluminum lithography

.24   Zinc lithography

764   Chromolithography and serigraphy

.2   **Chromolithography**

.8   **Serigraphy**

Class here silk-screen printing

> ## 765–767 Intaglio processes

Class comprehensive works in 765

765 Metal engraving

Class here comprehensive works on metal relief and metal intaglio processes, on intaglio processes

For metal relief engraving, see 761.8; for mezzotinting and aquatinting, see 766; for etching and drypoint, see 767

.2 **Line engraving**

.5 **Stipple engraving**

.6 **Criblé engraving**

766 Mezzotinting, aquatinting, related processes

.2 **Mezzotinting**

.3 **Aquatinting**

.7 **Composite processes**

Use of two or more processes in a single print

767 Etching and drypoint

.2 **Etching**

.3 **Drypoint**

[768] [Unassigned]

Most recently used in Edition 14

769 Prints

Works produced using a printing block, screen, or plate

Class here description, critical appraisal, collections regardless of process

.075 Museum activities and services

Do not use for collecting; class in 769.12

[.09] History, geographic treatment, biography

Do not use; class in 769.9

.1 **Collecting and reproduction of prints**

Class collecting and reproduction of specific forms of prints in 769.5

.12 Collecting prints

.17 Techniques of reproduction

.172 Reproductions and copies

.174 Forgeries and alterations

.4 ***Iconography**

Add to base number 769.4 the numbers following 704.94 in 704.942–704.949, e.g., portrait prints 769.42; however, for individual printmakers, see 769.92

Class postage stamps by subject in 769.564; class printmakers regardless of subject in 769.92; class sports cards in 796.075

.5 ***Forms of prints**

Including lettering, inscriptions, designs on name cards, diplomas, decorative prints, art posters

Class prints other than postage stamps on a specific subject regardless of form in 769.4; class comprehensive works on posters in 741.674

For sports cards, see 796.075

.52 *Bookplates

.53 *Paper dolls

.55 Paper money

Class here counterfeit paper money

[.550 9] History, geographic treatment, biography

Do not use; class in 769.559

.559 History, geographic treatment, biography

.559 001–.559 009 Standard subdivisions

Add to base number 769.55900 the numbers following —00 in notation 001–009 from Table 2, e.g., periodicals of the history of paper money 769.559005

.559 01–.559 05 Historical periods

Add to base number 769.5590 the numbers following —090 in notation 0901–0905 from Table 1, e.g., paper money from 20th century 769.55904

.559 1–.559 9 Geographic treatment, biography

Add to base number 769.559 notation 1–9 from Table 2, e.g., paper money of France 769.55944; however, for individual printmakers, see 769.92

.56 Postage stamps and related devices

Standard subdivisions are added for postage stamps and related devices together, for postage stamps alone

Class here philately (study and collecting of stamps)

Unless other instructions are given, class a subject with aspects in two or more subdivisions of 769.56 in the number coming first, e.g., counterfeit stamps depicting plants 769.562 (*not* 769.56434)

Class stamps other than for prepayment of postage in 769.57

*Do not use notation 092 from Table 1 for individual printmakers; class in 769.92

[.560 9]	History, geographic treatment, biography
	Do not use; class in 769.569
.561	*United Nations postage stamps, postal stationery, covers
.562	*Counterfeit postage stamps, covers, cancellations
.563	*Postage stamps commemorating persons and events
.564	Postage stamps depicting various specific subjects (Iconography)

Add to base number 769.564 the numbers following 704.94 in 704.943–704.949, e.g., postage stamps of plants of the world 769.56434; however, for individual printmakers, see 769.92

For stamps commemorating persons and events, see 769.563

.565	*Covers
.566	*Postal stationery

Postal-service-issued stationery (e.g., letter sheets, envelopes, postcards) bearing imprinted stamps

Class illustrated postcards in 741.683

.567	*Postmarks, cancellations, cachets

Standard subdivisions are added for any or all topics in heading

See also 769.562 for counterfeit cancellations

.569	History, geographic treatment, biography
.569 001–.569 009	Standard subdivisions

Add to base number 769.56900 the numbers following —00 in notation 001–009 from Table 2, e.g., periodicals of the history of postage stamps 769.569005

.569 01–.569 05	Historical periods

Add to base number 769.5690 the numbers following —090 in notation 0901–0905 from Table 1, e.g., postage stamps from 20th century 769.56904

.569 1–.569 9	Geographic treatment, biography

Add to base number 769.569 notation 1–9 from Table 2, e.g., postage stamps from San Marino 769.5694549; however, for individual printmakers, see 769.92

.57	*Stamps other than for prepayment of postage

Including Christmas seals, officially sealed labels, ration coupons; postage-due, postal savings, and savings stamps

.572	*Revenue stamps

---

*Do not use notation 092 from Table 1 for individual printmakers; class in 769.92

.9 **History, geographic treatment, biography of printmaking and prints**

Class the history of a specific process with the process, e.g., history of lithography 763.09

See Manual at 769.9

.900 1–.900 9   Standard subdivisions

Add to base number 769.900 the numbers following —00 in notation 001–009 from Table 2, e.g., periodicals of the history of printmaking 769.9005

.901–.905   Historical periods

Add to base number 769.90 the numbers following —090 in notation 0901–0905 from Table 1, e.g., printmaking in 20th century 769.904

.91–.99   Geographic treatment, biography

Add to base number 769.9 notation 1–9 from Table 2, e.g., printmaking in England 769.942

.92   Biography

Number built according to instructions under 769.91–769.99

Class here engravers, printmakers

(Option: Class in 760.92)

770 Photography, computer art, cinematography, videography

Standard subdivisions are added for photography, computer art, cinematography, videography together; for photography alone

Class here conventional photography (photography using film), digital photography

Class technological photography in 621.367

See also 760 for hybrid photography

SUMMARY

.1   **Philosophy and theory**

Notation 01 from Table 1 as modified below

.11   Inherent features

        Do not use for systems; class in 770.1

        Including color, composition, decorative values, form, light, movement, perspective, space, style, symmetry, vision

.2   **Miscellany**

.23   Photography as a profession, occupation, hobby

.232   Photography as a profession and occupation

.233   Photography as a hobby

.28   Auxiliary techniques and procedures

        For comprehensive works on basic and auxiliary techniques and procedures, see 771

[.284]   Apparatus, equipment, materials

        Do not use; class in 771

.285   Computer applications

        Do not use for comprehensive works on digital photography; class in 770; however use subdivisions of 770.285 for specific computer applications in photography, e.g., application of computer programs to digital photography 770.28553

[.286]   Green technology (Environmental technology)

        Do not use; class in 771.40286

.9   **History, geographical treatment, biography**

.92   Biography

        Class here photographers regardless of type of artistic photography

        Class photographs in 779. Class photographers associated with a specific application with the application, e.g., photojournalists 070.49092

        For motion picture, television, video photographers, see 777.092

        See Manual at 779 vs. 770.92

771 *Techniques, procedures, apparatus, equipment, materials

Including techniques of pinhole photography, of photography without camera; comprehensive works on basic and auxiliary techniques and procedures

Class here interdisciplinary works on description, use, manufacture of apparatus, equipment, materials

Class techniques, procedures, apparatus, equipment, materials used in special processes in 772–774; class techniques, procedures, apparatus, equipment, materials used in specific fields and special kinds of photography in 778

For auxiliary techniques and procedures, see 770.28. For manufacture of a specific kind of apparatus, equipment, material, see the apparatus, equipment, or material, e.g., cameras 681.418

.1 **Studios, laboratories, darkrooms**

Class laboratory and darkroom practice in 771.4

.2 **Furniture and fittings**

.3 **Cameras and accessories**

Standard subdivisions are added for cameras and accessories, for cameras alone

Class here digital cameras

.31 Specific makes of cameras

Class here specific makes and brands of digital cameras [*both formerly* 771.33], specific brands of cameras

Arrange alphabetically by trade name

.32 Specific types of cameras that use film

Including 35mm, automatic, instant, large format, miniature, single-lens reflex

Class here specific types of digital cameras [*formerly* 771.33]

Class specific makes of specific types of cameras with film in 771.31

[.33] Digital cameras

Use of this number for comprehensive works on digital cameras discontinued; class in 771.3

Specific makes and brands of digital cameras relocated to 771.31; specific types of digital cameras relocated to 771.32

---

*Do not use notation 0285 from Table 1 for comprehensive works on digital photography; class in 770 and its subdivisions without use of notation 0285, e.g., digital trick photography 778.8; however, use subdivisions of notation 0285 for specific computer applications in photography, e.g., application of computer programs to digital trick photography 778.8028553. Do not use notation 092 from Table 1 for photographers; class in 770.92

.35   Optical parts of cameras

> Class optical parts of specific makes of cameras in 771.31

> *For shutters, see 771.36; for focusing and exposure apparatus, see 771.37*

.352   Lenses

.356   Filters

.36   Camera shutters

> Class shutters of specific makes of cameras in 771.31

.37   Focusing and exposure apparatus

> Including exposure meters, range finders, viewfinders

> Class focusing and exposure apparatus of specific makes of cameras in 771.31

.38   Accessories

> Including carrying cases, tripods

.4   *Processing of photographic images

> Photographic images: negatives, positives, digital images, photographs, prints, slides, transparencies

> Class here comprehensive works on laboratory practice of photography and cinematography

> Class comprehensive works on photographic images in 779

> *For chemical materials, see 771.5; for laboratory practice of cinematography, see 777.55*

.402 86   Green technology (Environmental technology)

> Including waste technology [*formerly also* 771.47]

.43   *Preparation and manipulation of negatives

> Standard subdivisions are added for either or both topics in heading

> Class here comprehensive works on negatives

> Class comprehensive works on darkroom practice in 771.44

> *For preservation and storage of negatives, see 771.45; for organization and distribution of negatives, see 771.48*

---

*Do not use notation 0285 from Table 1 for comprehensive works on digital photography; class in 770 and its subdivisions without use of notation 0285, e.g., digital trick photography 778.8; however, use subdivisions of notation 0285 for specific computer applications in photography, e.g., application of computer programs to digital trick photography 778.8028553. Do not use notation 092 from Table 1 for photographers; class in 770.92

.44 ***Preparation and manipulation of positives**

> Standard subdivisions are added for either or both topics in heading

> Including developing and printing apparatus [*formerly* 771.49]; contact printing, enlarging, developing, mounting

> Class here preparation and manipulation of photographic digital images [*formerly* 775]; preparation and manipulation of photographs, prints, slides, transparencies; comprehensive works on positives, on darkroom practice, on preparation and manipulation of photographic images

>> *For darkroom practice involving negatives, preparation and manipulation of negatives, see 771.43; for preservation and storage of positives, see 771.46; for organization and distribution of positives, see 771.48; for darkroom practice of cinematography, see 777.55*

.45 ***Preservation and storage of negatives**

> Standard subdivisions are added for either or both topics in heading

> Class here comprehensive works on preservation and storage of photographic images

>> *For preservation and storage of positives, see 771.46*

> Preservation and storage of slides and transparencies relocated to 771.46

.46 ***Preservation and storage of positives**

> Standard subdivisions are added for either or both topics in heading

> Class here preservation and storage of slides and transparencies [*both formerly* 771.45]; preservation and storage of photographic digital images, photographs, prints

>> *For mounting, see 771.44*

[.47] **Waste technology**

> Relocated to 771.40286

.48 ***Projection [*formerly* 778.2], organization, distribution of photographic images**

> Standard subdivisions are added for any or all topics in heading

>> *For motion picture projection, see 777.57; for stereoscopic projection, see 778.4*

[.49] **Developing and printing apparatus**

> Relocated to 771.44

.5 **Chemical materials**

---

*Do not use notation 0285 from Table 1 for comprehensive works on digital photography; class in 770 and its subdivisions without use of notation 0285, e.g., digital trick photography 778.8; however, use subdivisions of notation 0285 for specific computer applications in photography, e.g., application of computer programs to digital trick photography 778.8028553. Do not use notation 092 from Table 1 for photographers; class in 770.92

.52   Support materials

> Including backings of cellulose compounds, ceramics, glass, metal, paper

.53   Photosensitive surfaces

.532   Specific photosensitive surfaces

.532 2   Plates

.532 3   Papers

.532 4   Films

> Class here comprehensive works on film used in photography and cinematography
>
> *For film used in cinematography, see 777.38*

.54   Developing and printing supplies

> Including developing, fixing, intensifying, reducing, toning solutions

---

> ## 772–774 Special photographic processes
>
> Techniques, procedures, apparatus, equipment, materials
>
> Class processing techniques in specific fields and special kinds of photography in 778; class comprehensive works in 771
>
> *For photomechanical printing techniques, see 686.232*

772   *Metallic salt processes

.1   *Direct positive and printing-out processes

> Early photographic processes
>
> *For platinum printing-out process, see 772.3*

.12   *Daguerreotype process

.14   *Ferrotype, tintype, wet-collodion processes

*Do not use notation 0285 from Table 1 for comprehensive works on digital photography; class in 770 and its subdivisions without use of notation 0285, e.g., digital trick photography 778.8; however, use subdivisions of notation 0285 for specific computer applications in photography, e.g., application of computer programs to digital trick photography 778.8028553. Do not use notation 092 from Table 1 for photographers; class in 770.92

.16   *Kallitype processes

.3   ***Platinotype processes**

>   Including platinum printing-out process

.4   ***Silver processes**

>   Use of silver halides in principal light-sensitive photographic emulsions

773   ***Pigment processes of printing**

>   Early photographic printing processes

.1   ***Carbon and carbro processes**

>   Including Mariotype, ozotype, ozobrome

.2   ***Powder processes (Dusting-on processes)**

>   Class xerography in 686.44

.3   ***Imbibition processes**

.5   ***Gum-bichromate processes**

.6   ***Photoceramic and photoenamel processes**

.7   ***Diazotype processes**

.8   ***Oil processes**

>   Including bromoil process

774   ***Holography**

>   Class here holographic images

[775]   **Digital photography**

>   Use of this number for comprehensive works on digital photography discontinued; class in 770

>   Preparation and manipulation of photographic digital images relocated to 771.44

---

*Do not use notation 0285 from Table 1 for comprehensive works on digital photography; class in 770 and its subdivisions without use of notation 0285, e.g., digital trick photography 778.8; however, use subdivisions of notation 0285 for specific computer applications in photography, e.g., application of computer programs to digital trick photography 778.8028553. Do not use notation 092 from Table 1 for photographers; class in 770.92

776   Computer art (Digital art)

Art objects produced using computers for display using computer output devices

Including artistic aspects of virtual reality

Class here comprehensive works on computer art and computer applications in the arts

> For computer applications in the arts, see 700.285; for computer applications in fine and decorative arts, see 702.85; for computer music, see 786.76. For computer design of specific commodity, see the commodity, e.g., computer design of automobiles 629.231
>
> See Manual at 776 vs. 006.5–006.7

.2   **Graphics displayed on computer display devices**

.4   **Prints of computer graphics**

.6   **Animation and video**

> For animated cartoon cinematography and videography, see 777.7

.7   **Multimedia computer art**

> For web page design, see 006.7

777   Cinematography and videography

This schedule, which replaces that formerly appearing at 778.5, is new. A comparative table giving both old and new numbers for a substantial list of topics and equivalence tables showing the numbers in the old and new schedules appear in volume 1 in this edition

Standard subdivisions are added for either or both topics in heading

Class here conventional cinematography (cinematography using film), digital cinematography and videography, amateur and professional cinematography and videography; home video systems, television photography, video art

Unless other instructions are given, class a subject with aspects in two or more subdivisions of 777 in the number coming last, e.g., cameras used for special effects 777.9 (*not* 777.34)

Class comprehensive works on motion picture production and cinematography, interdisciplinary works on motion pictures in 791.43; class comprehensive works on television production in 791.45; class interdisciplinary works on television in 384.55. Class a specific application of cinematography, videography, or video art with the application, e.g., use of videography in diagnosis of diseases 616.075028, use of videos in performance art 709.04

> See also 006.7 for interactive video
>
> See Manual at 791.43, 791.45 vs. 777

.028 5   Computer applications

> Do not use for comprehensive works on digital cinematography and videography; class in 777; however use subdivisions of notation 0285 for specific computer applications in cinematography and videography, e.g., application of computer programs to digital cinematography 777.028553

.028 8   Maintenance and repair

                    Do not use for preservation; class in 777.58

.092   Biography

                  Class here cinematographers and videographers regardless of type of artistic cinematography and videography

                  Class cinematographers and videographers associated with a specific application with the application, e.g., photojournalists 070.49092

.3   **†Apparatus, equipment, materials**

                  Class here interdisciplinary works on use and manufacture of apparatus, equipment, materials

                  For manufacture of a specific kind of apparatus, equipment, materials, see the apparatus, equipment, or material, e.g., cameras 681.418

.34   †Cameras and camcorders

                  Standard subdivisions are added for either or both topic in heading

.36   †Recorders

.38   †Recording formats

                  Class here DVDs, film

.5   **†Elements and modes**

                  Including electronic field production (EFP)

                  See also 070.43 for electronic new gathering

.52   †Lighting

.53   †Sound

.55   †Editing and post-production

                  Standard subdivisions are added for either or both topics in heading

                  Including titling

                  Class here darkroom and laboratory practice

                  For animation, see 777.7; for special effects, see 777.9

.57   †Projection and display

Do not use notation 0285 from Table 1 for comprehensive works on digital cinematography and videography; class in 777 and its subdivisions without use of notation 0285, e.g., digital trick videography 777.9; however, use subdivisions of notation 0285 for specific computer applications in cinematography and videography, e.g., application of computer programs to digital trick videography 777.9028553. Do not use notation 092 from Table 1 for photographers; class in 770.92

.58   †Preservation and storage

        Standard subdivisions are added for either or both topics in heading

        Including restoration

        See also 025.1773 for archiving of motion picture films and video recordings

.6   **†Specific kinds and types of cinematography and videography**

        Including aerial, close-up, high-speed, infrared, macrography, micrography, panoramic, space, time-lapse, underwater cinematography and videography

.65   †Stereoscopic cinematography and videography

        Standard subdivisions are added for either or both topics in heading

.7   **†Animation**

        Including stop motion

        Class here animated cartoons

        Class comprehensive works on animated cartoons in 791.4334

.8   **Cinematography and videography of specific subjects**

        Add to base number 777.8 the numbers following 704.94 in 704.942–704.949, e.g., cinematography of animals 777.832, videography of landscapes 777.836; then, for either or both topics in heading, add further as follows:

01	Philosophy and theory
02	Miscellany
0285	Computer applications

                Do not use for comprehensive works on digital cinematography and videography; class in 777.82–777.89 without use of notation 0285 e.g., digital cinematography of animals 777.832; however, use subdivisions of notation 0285 for specific computer applications in cinematography and videography, e.g., application of computer programs to digital cinematography of animals 777.832028553

03–08	Standard subdivisions
09	History, geographic treatment, biography
092	Biography

                Do not use for cinematographers and videographers; class in 777.092

.9   **†Special effects**

        Class here trick cinematography and videography

---

†Do not use notation 0285 from Table 1 for comprehensive works on digital cinematography and videography; class in 777 and its subdivisions without use of notation 0285, e.g., digital trick videography 777.9; however, use subdivisions of notation 0285 for specific computer applications in cinematography and videography, e.g., application of computer programs to digital trick videography 777.9028553. Do not use notation 092 from Table 1 for photographers; class in 770.92

778   Specific fields and special kinds of photography

Class here interdisciplinary works on use and manufacture of apparatus, equipment, materials of specific fields and specific kinds of photography

Unless other instructions are given, observe the following table of preference, e.g., color aerial photography 778.35 (*not* 778.6):

Special effects and trick photography	778.8
Photography of specific subjects	778.9
Stereoscopic photography and projection	778.4
Special kinds of photography	778.3
Photography under specific conditions	778.7
Color photography	778.6

Class photographs created by a specific field or kind of photography in 779

For manufacture of a specific kind of apparatus, equipment, materials, see the apparatus, equipment, or material, e.g., cameras 681.418

SUMMARY

778.3	**Special kinds of photography**
.4	**Stereoscopic photography and projection**
.6	**Color photography**
.7	**Photography under specific conditions**
.8	**Special effects and trick photography**
.9	**Photography of specific subjects**

[.2]   Projection

Projection relocated to 771.48; comprehensive works on filmstrips, slides relocated to 779

.3   *Special kinds of photography

Not provided for elsewhere

Including Kirlian photography (high-voltage, high-frequency photopsychography)

Class a special kind of photography in relation to cinematography and videography in 777. Class a specific application of photography with the application, e.g., use of photography in astronomy 522.63

For technological photography and photo-optics, see 621.367

See also 133.892 for parapsychological aspects of Kirlian photography

Photography of specific subjects by special kinds of photography relocated to 778.9

.31   *Photomicrography

---

*Do not use notation 0285 from Table 1 for comprehensive works on digital photography; class in 770 and its subdivisions without use of notation 0285, e.g., digital trick photography 778.8; however, use subdivisions of notation 0285 for specific computer applications in photography, e.g., application of computer programs to digital trick photography 778.8028553. Do not use notation 092 from Table 1 for photographers; class in 770.92

.32   *Photography in terms of focus

.322   *Telephotography

> *For aerial and space photography, see 778.35; for panoramic photography, see 778.36*

.324   *Close-up photography

> Including photomacrography

.34   *Infrared photography

> Interdisciplinary works

> *For technological infrared photography, see 621.3672*

.35   *Aerial and space photography

> Including interpretation

> *For photogrammetry, see 526.982*

.36   *Panoramic photography

.37   *High-speed photography

> Including use of short-duration electronic flash

> Class use of normal photographic electronic flash (flashbulb photography) in 778.72

.4   *Stereoscopic photography and projection

> *For stereoscopic motion picture projection, see 777.57; for stereoscopic cinematography and videography, see 777.65*

> Stereoscopic photography and projection of specific subjects relocated to 778.9

[.5]   Cinematography and videography

> Relocated to 777

> **778.6–778.8   Specific topics in photography**

> Class specific topics in relation to cinematography and videography in 777; class comprehensive works in 770

.6   *Color photography

> Class here photography of colors

> Class color photomicrography in 778.31

> Color photography of specific subjects relocated to 778.9

---

*Do not use notation 0285 from Table 1 for comprehensive works on digital photography; class in 770 and its subdivisions without use of notation 0285, e.g., digital trick photography 778.8; however, use subdivisions of notation 0285 for specific computer applications in photography, e.g., application of computer programs to digital trick photography 778.8028553. Do not use notation 092 from Table 1 for photographers; class in 770.92

.602 8	Auxiliary techniques and procedures; apparatus, equipment, materials

For processing auxiliary techniques and procedures, apparatus, equipment, materials in color photography, see 778.66

.62	*Photography of colors in monochrome

Orthochromatic and panchromatic

.63	*Direct process reproduction in color photography

Including Lippmann process

.65	*Additive processes in color photography
.66	*Processing techniques, procedures, apparatus, equipment, materials in color photography

Class here subtractive processes, production of color films and prints by subtractive analysis and subtractive synthesis, respectively

Class direct process reproduction in color photography in 778.63; class additive processes in color photography in 778.65

.7	***Photography under specific conditions**

Photography of specific subjects under specific conditions relocated to 778.9

.71	*Outdoor photography
.712	*Photography in sunlight
.719	*Night photography

For infrared photography, see 778.34

.72	*Indoor photography and photography by artificial light

Class here use of normal photographic electronic flash (flashbulb photography)

Class short-duration flash in high-speed photography in 778.37

For infrared photography, see 778.34

.73	*Underwater photography
.75	*Photography under extreme climatic conditions
.76	*Available light photography

Class outdoor available light photography in 778.71; class indoor available light photography in 778.72

---

*Do not use notation 0285 from Table 1 for comprehensive works on digital photography; class in 770 and its subdivisions without use of notation 0285, e.g., digital trick photography 778.8; however, use subdivisions of notation 0285 for specific computer applications in photography, e.g., application of computer programs to digital trick photography 778.8028553. Do not use notation 092 from Table 1 for photographers; class in 770.92

.8　　***Special effects and trick photography**

> Standard subdivisions are added for either or both topics in heading
>
> Including composite, high-contrast, tabletop photography; photomontage; photography of specters, distortions, multiple images, silhouettes

.9　　**Photography of specific subjects**

> Class here photography of specific subjects by special kinds of photography [*formerly* 778.3]; stereoscopic photography and projection of specific subjects [*formerly* 778.4]; color photography of specific subjects [*formerly* 778.6]; photography of specific subjects under specific conditions [*formerly* 778.7]; comprehensive works on techniques of photographing, photographs of, and photographers of a specific subject
>
> Add to base number 778.9 the numbers following 704.94 in 704.942–704.949, e.g., portrait photography 778.92; then add further as follows:

01	Philosophy and theory
02	Miscellany
0285	Computer applications

> > Do not use for comprehensive works on digital photography in the topic; class in 778.92–778.99 without use of notation 0285, e.g., digital portrait photography 778.92; however, use subdivisions of notation 0285 for specific computer applications in photography, e.g., application of computer programs to digital portrait photography 778.92028553

03–08	Standard subdivisions
09	History, geographic treatment, biography
092	Biography

> > Do not use for photographers; class in 770.92

779　　**Photographic images**

> Collections, history, criticism
>
> Class here filmstrips, slides [*formerly* 778.2], transparencies; digital images, photographs, prints
>
> Add to base number 779 the numbers following 704.94 in 704.942–704.949, e.g., photographic images of children 779.25
>
> *For processing of photographic images, see 771.4; for holograhic images, see 774*
>
> *See Manual at 779 vs. 770.92*

---

*Do not use notation 0285 from Table 1 for comprehensive works on digital photography; class in 770 and its subdivisions without use of notation 0285, e.g., digital trick photography 778.8; however, use subdivisions of notation 0285 for specific computer applications in photography, e.g., application of computer programs to digital trick photography 778.8028553. Do not use notation 092 from Table 1 for photographers; class in 770.92

780 Music

After general topics (780 and 781) the basic arrangement of the schedule is based on the voice, instrument, or ensemble making the music. Any tradition of vocal music (e.g., classical, popular) is classed in 782–783; any tradition of instrumental music (e.g., classical, popular) is classed in 784–788

Unless other instructions are given, class a subject with aspects in two or more subdivisions of 780 in the number coming last, e.g., sacred vocal music 782.22 (*not* 781.7)

When instructed, add the indicator 0 or 1 and the notation from the subdivisions coming earlier in the schedule, e.g., rock songs 782.42166 (*not* 781.66). In building numbers, do not add by use of 0 or 1 (alone or in combination) more than twice, e.g., history of rock protest songs 782.421661592 (*not* 782.42166159209)
　(Option: Add as many times as desired)

This schedule does not distinguish scores, texts, or recordings
　(Option: To distinguish scores, texts, recordings, use one of the following:

　(Option A: Prefix a letter or other symbol to the number for treatises, e.g., scores for violin M787.2, violin recordings R787.2 or MR787.2; use a special prefix to distinguish miniature scores from other scores, MM787.2

　(Option B: Add to the number for treatises the numbers following 78 in 780.26–780.269, e.g., miniature scores of music for violin 787.20265

　(Option C: Class recordings in 789, e.g., recordings of folk music 789.2, recordings of violin folk music 789.2072)

See Manual at 780; also at 781.6 vs. 780, 780.9

SUMMARY

782	Vocal music
.001–.009	Standard subdivisions
.01–.08	[General principles of vocal music and musical forms]
.1	Operas and related dramatic vocal forms
.2	Nondramatic vocal forms
.3	Services (Liturgy and ritual)
.4	Secular forms
.5	Mixed voices
.6	Women's voices
.7	Children's voices
.8	Men's voices
.9	Other types of voices

783	Music for single voices
.001 .009	Standard subdivisions
.01–.09	[General principles of music for single voices, musical forms, nondramatic vocal forms]
.1	Single voices in combination
.2	Solo voice
.3	High voice
.4	Middle voice
.5	Low voice
.6–.8	Women's, children's, men's voices
.9	Other types of voice

784	Instruments and instrumental ensembles and their music
.01–.09	Standard subdivisions
.1	General principles, musical forms, instruments
.2	Full orchestra (Symphony orchestra)
.3	Chamber orchestra
.4	Light orchestra
.6	Keyboard, mechanical, electronic, percussion bands
.7	String orchestra
.8	Wind band
.9	Brass band

785	Ensembles with only one instrument per part
.001–.009	Standard subdivisions
.01–.09	[General principles of ensembles with only one instrument per part, musical forms, instruments]
.1	Ensembles by size
.2	Ensembles with keyboard
.3	Ensembles without electrophones and with percussion and keyboard
.4	Ensembles without keyboard
.5	Ensembles without keyboard and with percussion
.6	Keyboard, mechanical, aeolian, electrophone, percussion ensembles
.7	String ensembles
.8	Woodwind ensembles
.9	Brass ensembles

786	Keyboard, mechanical, electrophonic, percussion instruments
.2	Pianos
.3	Clavichords
.4	Harpsichords
.5	Organs
.6	Mechanical and aeolian instruments
.7	Electronic instruments (Electrophones)
.8	Percussion instruments
.9	Drums and devices used for percussive effects

787	**Stringed instruments (Chordophones)**
.2	**Violins**
.3	**Violas**
.4	**Cellos (Violoncellos)**
.5	**Double basses**
.6	**Viols and related instruments**
.7	**Plectral instruments**
.8	**Plectral lute family**
.9	**Harps and musical bows**

788	**Wind instruments (Aerophones)**
.2	**Woodwind instruments and free aerophones**
.3	**Flute family**
.4	**Reed instruments**
.5	**Double-reed instruments**
.6	**Single-reed instruments**
.7	**Saxophones**
.8	**Free reeds**
.9	**Brass instruments (Lip-reed instruments)**

.000 1–.099 9	Relation of music to other subjects

Works in which the focus is music

Add to base number 780.0 three-digit numbers 001–999 (but stop before any zero that follows a non-zero number), e.g., music and literature 780.08, music and Welsh literature 780.0891 (*not* 780.089166), music and the performing arts 780.079 (*not* 780.07902)

See Manual at 780.079 vs. 790.2

.1	**Philosophy and theory, analytical guides, program notes**

Notation 01 from Table 1 as modified below

For general principles, theory of music, see 781

.14	Communication, editing

Notation 014 from Table 1 as modified below

.148	Musical notation, abbreviations, acronyms, symbols

Including staff notation, neumes, tablature, tonic sol-fa; braille musical notation

Class transcription from one form of notation to another in 780.149

.149	Editing
.15	Analytical guides and program notes

Do not use for scientific principles; class in 781.2

(.16)	Bibliographies, catalogs, indexes

(Optional number; prefer 016.78)

(.162)	†Bibliographies and catalogs of music literature
(.164)	†Bibliographies and catalogs of scores and parts

Including bibliographies and catalogs of manuscript scores and parts

†(Optional number; prefer 016.78)

(.166)   †Discographies

> Bibliographies and catalogs of music recorded on phonorecords (cylinders, discs, wires, tapes, films)

> Including biodiscographies

[.19]   Psychological principles

> Do not use; class in 781.11

.2   **Miscellany; texts; treatises on music scores and recordings**

> Notation 02 from Table 1 as modified below

.202   Synopses and outlines

> *For synopses of stories and plots, see 782.00269*

.216   Lists, inventories, catalogs of music

> Class here thematic catalogs

> Class bibliographic catalogs of music in 016.78

> *For thematic catalogs of individual composers, see 780.92*

.26   Texts; treatises on music scores and recordings

> Standard subdivisions are added for a combination of two or more topics in heading, for scores alone

> In schedules other than 780, indicate scores, recordings, texts, and treatises about them by adding the numbers following 78 in 780.262–780.269, e.g., bibliography of music manuscripts 016.780262, bibliography of manuscripts of violin music 016.78720262, discography of violin music 016.78720266

> *See Manual at 780.26*

> (Option: To distinguish scores and recordings within 780, add to the number for treatises the numbers following 78 in 780.26–780.269, e.g., miniature scores of music for violin 787.20265. Other options are described at 780)

> (Option: Class here law of music; prefer appropriate subdivisions of 340)

> >   780.262–780.265   Scores

> Class comprehensive works in 780.26

> *For words and other vocal sounds to be sung or recited with music, see 780.268*

.262   *Manuscripts

> Including autograph scores, sketch books

---

*(Option: Use this standard subdivision to distinguish scores and recordings; see details in note under 780.26)

†(Optional number; prefer 016.78)

.263   *Printed music

        For performance scores, see 780.264; for study scores, see 780.265

        See also 070.5794 for music publishing; also 686.284 for music printing

.264   *Performance scores and parts

        Standard subdivisions are added for either or both topics in heading

        Including full scores, conducting scores, piano-vocal scores

.265   *Study scores (Miniature scores, Pocket scores)

.266   *Sound recordings of music

        Class here comprehensive works on music recordings

        For video recordings, see 780.267

        See also 781.49 for recording of music

.267   *Video recordings of music

.268   Words and other vocal sounds to be sung or recited with music

        Including librettos, lyrics, poems, screenplays

        Class here texts

        The words must be discussed in a musical context. If the words are presented as literature, folklore, or religious text, class the work in 800, 398, or 200, respectively, e.g., hymn texts presented as religious texts 264.23

        Use this number only for building other numbers, e.g., lyrics of songs 782.420268, texts of choral symphonies 784.221840268; never use it by itself

        Class comprehensive works in 782.00268

        For stories, plots, synopses, see 780.269

.269   Stories, plots, synopses

        Standard subdivisions are added for any or all topics in heading

        Including scenarios

        Use this number only for building other numbers, e.g., plots of operas 782.10269, synopses of choral symphonies 784.221840269; never use it by itself

        Class comprehensive works in 782.00269

.28   Auxiliary techniques and procedures; apparatus, equipment, materials

        See also 781.4 for techniques of music

---

*(Option: Use this standard subdivision to distinguish scores and recordings; see details in note under 780.26)

.284		Apparatus, equipment, materials

> Do not use for musical instruments; class in 784.19
>
> *See also 780.26 for scores; also 780.266 for recordings*

.285   Computer applications

> *For computer composition, see 781.34; for the computer as a musical instrument, see 786.76*

.7   **Education, research, related topics; performances**

> Notation 07 from Table 1 as modified below
>
> Including use of apparatus and equipment in study and teaching
>
> Class here special teaching and learning methods

.72   Research

.721   Research methods

> Class here musicology

.74   Museums, collections, exhibits

> Do not use for festivals; class in 780.78
>
> Exhibitions and fairs relocated to 780.78

.76   Review, exercises, examinations, works for self-instruction

.77   Special teaching and learning methods

> *For techniques for acquiring musical skills and learning a repertoire, see 781.42*

.78   Performances (Concerts and recitals)

> Do not use for use of apparatus and equipment in study and teaching; class in 780.7
>
> Class here exhibitions and fairs [*formerly* 780.74]; festivals [*formerly* 780.79]; performances at festivals and competitions
>
> Add to base number 780.78 notation 3–9 from Table 2, e.g., concerts in London 780.78421
>
> *See also 781.43 for performance techniques*

.79   Competitions, awards, financial support

> Add to base number 780.79 notation 3–9 from Table 2 for geographic eligibility only, e.g., music competitions open to contestants from Italy 780.7945, music awards open to entries from the United States 780.7973, music fellowships limited to residents of California 780.79794
>
> Class performances at competitions in 780.78
>
> Festivals relocated to 780.78

.8   **Groups of people**

.89   Ethnic and national groups

> *For folk music, see 781.62*
>
> *See Manual at 781.62 vs. 780.89*

.9   **History, geographic treatment, biography**

No distinction is made between the music of a place and music in a place, e.g., Viennese music and music played in Vienna are both classed in 780.943613

Class critical appraisal in analytical guides and program notes in 780.15

> *See Manual at 781.6 vs. 780, 780.9*

> 780.901–780.905   Periods of stylistic development of music

Even though the periods are those of western music, this does not limit the use of these numbers to western or European music only

Class here schools, styles, time periods not limited ethnically or by country or locality

Class comprehensive works in 780.9

.901   Ancient times through 499

.902   500–1449

Including Gothic style, ars antiqua, ars nova, medieval music

> *For 1450–1499, see 780.9031*

.903   1450–

Class here modern music

> *For 1900–1999, see 780.904; for 2000–2099, see 780.905*

.903 1   Ca. 1450–ca. 1600

Including Renaissance music

.903 2   Ca. 1600–ca. 1750

Including baroque music, nuove musiche

.903 3   Ca. 1750–ca. 1825

Including preclassicism, classicism, rococo style

Class here 18th century music

> *For rococo style of earlier period, music of 1700–1750, see 780.9032*

.903 4   Ca. 1825–ca. 1900

Including nationalism, romanticism

Class here 19th century music

> *For music of earlier part of 19th century, see 780.9033; for 20th century nationalism, see 780.904*

.904		1900–1999

> Including avant-garde music, impressionism, neoclassicism
>
> *For early impressionism, see 780.9034*

[.904 1–.904 9]   Individual decades

> Do not use; class in 780.904

.905   2000–2099

.92   Biography

> Class here composers, performers, critics; thematic catalogs of individual composers
>
> Class general thematic catalogs in 780.216
>
> *See Manual at 780.92; also at 780.92 and 791.092*
>
> (Option: Class individual composers in 789)

.94   Music of Europe

> Use only for works that stress that they are discussing the European origin and character of music in contrast to music from other sources

---

> ## 781–788 Principles, forms, ensembles, voices, instruments

Class here music of all traditions
(Option: 781–788 may be used for only one tradition of music; in that case, class all other traditions in 789. For example, if it is desired to emphasize western art music, class it here, and class all other traditions of music in 789, e.g., jazz 789.5; or, if it is desired to emphasize jazz, class it here, and class all other traditions of music in 789, e.g., western art music 789.8)

Unless other instructions are given, class a subject with aspects in two or more subdivisions of 781–788 in the number coming last, e.g., jazz mass 782.323165 (*not* 781.65), Johann Sebastian Bach's cello sonatas 787.4183 (*not* 784.183)

Class comprehensive works in 780

781 General principles and musical forms

Class here music theory

Use the subdivisions of 781 only when the subject is not limited to voice, instrument, or ensemble. If voice, instrument, or ensemble is specified, class with voice, instrument, or ensemble; and then add as instructed. For example, rehearsal of music 781.44, rehearsal of opera (a form for the voice) 782.1144, rock music (both vocal and instrumental) 781.66, rock songs 782.42166

See Manual at 780.92

SUMMARY

.01–.09   Standard subdivisions

> Notation from Table 1 as modified under 780.1–780.9, e.g., music theory during the Renaissance 781.09031

.1   Basic principles of music

.11   Psychological principles

> *For aesthetics, appreciation, taste, see 781.17*

.12   Religious principles

.17   Artistic principles

> Class here aesthetics, appreciation, taste

———————————

> ### 781.2–781.8 Other principles and musical forms

> Add to each subdivision identified by * as follows:
> 01–09   Standard subdivisions
>   Notation from Table 1 as modified under 780.1–780.9, e.g., performances 078
> 1   General principles
>   Add to 1 the numbers following 781 in 781.1–781.7, e.g., rock music 166, rehearsing rock music 166144

> In building numbers, do not add by use of 0 or 1 (alone or in combination) more than twice, e.g., history of rock protest songs 782.421661592 (*not* 782.42166159209)
>   (Option: Add as many times as desired)

> Class comprehensive works in 781

.2   *Elements of music

> Class here scientific principles

.22   *Time

> *For playing time, see 781.432*

.222   *Pulse

.224   *Rhythm

.226   *Meter

*Add as instructed under 781.2–781.8

.23	*Musical sound
.232	*Pitch
.233	*Volume
.234	*Timbre (Tone color)
.235	*Attack and decay

Subdivisions are added for either or both topics in heading

.236	*Silence

Including rests

.237	*Intervals

For consonance, see 781.238; for dissonance, see 781.239

.238	*Consonance
.239	*Dissonance
.24	*Melody
.246	*Scales and scalic formations

Subdivisions are added for either or both topics in heading

Class comprehensive works on modes in 781.263

.247	*Ornaments

Including embellishments, trills

.248	*Themes

Including subject, countersubject, idée fixe, leitmotif

See also 780.216 for thematic catalogs

.25	*Harmony

Class here harmonic organization, comprehensive works on harmony and counterpoint

Class intervals in 781.237; class figured bass in 781.47

For homophony, see 781.285; for counterpoint, see 781.286

.252	*Chords

Including arpeggios

.254	*Cadences
.256	*Harmonic rhythm
.258	*Tonality

Key relationships

For tonal systems, see 781.26

*Add as instructed under 781.2–781.8

.26	*Tonal systems
.262	*Diatonicism
.263	*Medieval church modes

Class here comprehensive works on modes, modes of western folk music

For other modes, see 781.264

| .264 | Other modes |

Including ancient Greek modes, Byzantine echoi, Indian rāgas

Class modes of western folk music in 781.263

| .265 | *Macrotonality |

Tonality based on units larger than the diatonic whole tone

Including pentatonicism

| .266 | *Whole tonality |

Tonality based on scales of diatonic whole tones

| .267 | *Atonality |

Music with no fixed tonic or key center

For dodecaphony, see 781.268

| .268 | *Dodecaphony (Twelve-tone system, Note rows) |

Class comprehensive works on serialism in 781.33

| .269 | *Microtonality |

Tonality based on melodic units smaller than the diatonic semitone

| .28 | *Texture |
| .282 | *Monody |

Music with a single melodic line

| .283 | *Heterophony |

Music with a single melodic line simultaneously varied by two or more performers

| [.284] | Polyphony |

Relocated to 781.286

| .285 | *Homophony |

A dominant melodic line over chordal accompaniment

---

*Add as instructed under 781.2–781.8

.286　　　　　　　　*Counterpoint

Two or more independent melodic lines

Class here polyphony [*formerly* 781.284]

Class comprehensive works on harmony and counterpoint in 781.25

.3　　　*Composition

.302 85　　　　　　　Computer applications

Do not use for computer composition; class in 781.34

.32　　　　　　　*Indeterminacy and aleatory composition

Forms of composition based on chance

.33　　　　　　　Serialism

.330 1–.330 9　　　　Standard subdivisions

Notation from Table 1 as modified under 780.1–780.9, e.g., performances of serial music 781.33078

.331　　　　　　　Basic principles of serialism

.331 1　　　　　　Psychological principles

For aesthetics, appreciation, taste, see 781.3317

.331 2　　　　　　Religious principles

.331 7　　　　　　Artistic principles

Class here aesthetics, appreciation, taste

.332–.338　　　　Specific elements of serialism

Add to base number 781.33 the numbers following 781.2 in 781.22–781.28, e.g., serialized rhythm 781.3324; however, for atonality, see 781.267

.34　　　　　　　*Computer composition

See also 786.76 for computers as a musical instrument

.344–.346　　　　Computer science aspects

Unless it is redundant, add to base number 781.34 the numbers following 00 in 004–006, e.g., use of digital personal computers 781.34416, but use of digital computers 781.34 (*not* 781.344)

.36　　　　　　　*Extemporization (Improvisation)

.37　　　　　　　*Arrangement

Including transcription

For arrangements, see 781.38

.374　　　　　　　*Orchestration

*Add as instructed under 781.2–781.8

.377	*Paraphrase and parody
.38	*Arrangements

See Manual at 781.38

.382–.388	Original voice, instrument, ensemble of the arrangements

Add to base number 781.38 the numbers following 78 in 782–788, e.g., arrangements of violin music 781.3872

Use these numbers only for building other numbers; never use them by themselves

.4 *Techniques of music

For techniques of composition, see 781.3

.42	*Techniques for acquiring musical skills and learning a repertoire
.423	*Sight and score reading

Subdivisions are added for either or both topics in heading

.424	*Listening and ear training

Subdivisions are added for either or both topics in heading

.426	*Memorizing
.43	*Performance techniques

For extemporization, see 781.36; for specific performance techniques, see 781.44–781.48

See also 784.193 for techniques for playing instruments

.432	*Playing time
.434	*Harmonization
.436	*Transposition
.438	*Ensemble technique

> 781.44–781.48 Specific performance techniques

Class comprehensive works in 781.43

.44	*Rehearsal and practice

Subdivisions are added for either or both topics in heading

.45	*Conducting
.46	*Interpretation

Including rubato

*Add as instructed under 781.2–781.8

.47   *Accompaniment

             Including continuo (figured bass, thorough bass)

             See Manual at 781.47

.48   *Breathing and resonance

             Subdivisions are added for either or both topics in heading

             Class breathing and resonance associated with instrumental performance in 784.1932

.49   *Recording of music

             See also 006.5 for computer hardware and software used in digital sound recording; also 621.3893 for sound recording and reproducing equipment; also 780.266 for treatises on music recordings

.5   *Kinds of music

.52   *Music for specific times

.522   *Music for days of week

.522 2   *Sunday

.522 8   *Saturday

.523   *Music for times of day

.524   *Music for the seasons

.524 2   *Spring

.524 4   *Summer

.524 6   *Fall (Autumn)

                       Including harvest

.524 8   *Winter

.53   *Music in specific settings

.532   *Outdoor music

                  Including street music

.534   *Indoor music

                  For specific indoor settings, see 781.535–781.539

             ──────────────

>   781.535–781.539 Specific indoor settings

             Class music in religious settings in 781.7; class comprehensive works in 781.534

.535   *Domestic setting

.536   *Court setting

*Add as instructed under 781.2–781.8

.538	*Theater setting
.539	*Concert hall setting
.54	*Music for specific media

        Background or mood music

.542	*Film music

          See also 777.53 for sound synchronization of motion pictures

.544	*Radio music
.546	*Television music

          See also 777.53 for sound synchronization of television programs

.55	*Music accompanying public entertainments
.552	*Dramatic music

        Class here incidental music

        Class incidental music for specific media in 781.54; class dramatic vocal music in 782.1

.554	*Dance music

          For ballet music, see 781.556

.556	*Ballet music
.56	*Program music

        Music depicting nonmusical concepts, e.g., music depicting the sea

        Class musical forms depicting nonmusical concepts in 784.18, e.g., nocturnes 784.18966

.57	*Music accompanying activities

        Including inaugurations, initiations

        Class music accompanying stages of the life cycle in 781.58; class music reflecting other themes and subjects regardless of activity in 781.59

          See also 781.55 for music accompanying public entertainments

.58	*Music accompanying stages of the life cycle
.582	*Birth and infancy

        Including music for infant baptism and circumcision

        Class here music for confinement

.583	*Attainment of puberty

        Including music for bar or bat mitzvahs

.584	*Attainment of majority

        Including music for debuts

*Add as instructed under 781.2–781.8

.586	*Courtship and engagement
.587	*Weddings and marriage
	Subdivisions are added for either or both topics in heading
.588	*Dying and death
	Including music for burials, cremations, funerals, mourning
.59	*Music reflecting other themes and subjects
.592	*Protest
.593	*Work
.594	*Sports and recreation
.595	*Sea life
.599	*Patriotic, political, military music

Class here music commemorating historical events

Subdivisions are added for any or all topics in heading

.6   *Traditions of music

Works emphasizing a specific tradition

See Manual at 781.6; also at 781.6 vs. 780, 780.9

(Option: If 781–788 is used for only one tradition of music, class all other traditions in 789)

.62	Folk music

Music originating within and associated with an ethnic or national group

Class folk rock in 781.66172. Class a specific style of music provided for in 781.64–781.66 with the style, e.g., reggae 781.646, Afro-Cuban jazz 781.6572687291

See also 780.9 for music of and performed in a specific location

See Manual at 781.62 vs. 780.89; also at 781.62 vs. 781.63–781.66

.620 01–.620 07	Standard subdivisions

Notation from Table 1 as modified under 780.1–780.9, e.g., performances of folk music 781.620078

.620 08	Groups of people
[.620 089]	Specific ethnic and national groups

Do not use; class in 781.621–781.629

.620 09	History, geographic treatment, biography

*Add as instructed under 781.2–781.8

.620 090 1–.620 090 3	Historical periods to 1900
	Add to base number 781.620090 the numbers following 780.90 in 780.901–780.903, e.g., folk music of the Renaissance 781.62009031
.620 090 4–.620 090 5	1900–2099
	Add to base number 781.620090 the numbers following —090 in notation 0904–0905 from Table 1, e.g., folk music of the 1970s 781.62009047
.620 091	Areas, regions, places in general
	For geographic treatment of folk music of specific ethnic and national groups, see 781.621–781.629
.620 092	Biography
	Class here composers, performers, critics; thematic catalogs of individual composers
	See Manual at 780.92; also at 780.92 and 791.092
	(Option: Class individual composers in 789)
.620 093–.620 099	Specific continents, countries, localities; extraterrestrial worlds
	For geographic treatment of folk music of specific ethnic and national groups, see 781.621–781.629
.620 1–.620 5	General principles of folk music
	Add to base number 781.620 the numbers following 781 in 781.1–781.5, e.g., folk music for springtime 781.6205242, rehearsing folk music for springtime 781.6205242144
.620 6	Influence of other traditions of music
	Add to base number 781.6206 the numbers following 781.6 in 781.63–781.69, e.g., influence of jazz on folk music 781.62065, performances of folk music influenced by jazz 781.62065078

.621–.629   Folk music of specific ethnic and national groups

Add to base number 781.62 notation 1–9 from Table 5, e.g., Spanish folk
music 781.6261; then add further as follows:

001–008   Standard subdivisions
                     Notation from Table 1 as modified under
                     780.1–780.9, e.g., performances of Spanish folk music
                     781.62610078
009   History, geographic treatment, biography
00901–00903   Historical periods to 1900
                     Add to base number 0090 the numbers following
                     780.90 in 780.901–780.903, e.g., Spanish folk
                     music of the Renaissance 781.6261009031
00904–00905   1900–2099
                     Add to base number 0090 the numbers following
                     —090 in notation 0904–0905 from Table
                     1, e.g., Spanish folk music of the 1970s
                     781.6261009047
[0093–0099]   Specific continents, countries, localities
                     Do not use; class in 03–09
01   General principles
                     Add to 01 the numbers following 781 in 781.1–781.5,
                     e.g., Spanish folk music for springtime 781.6261015242,
                     rhythm in Spanish folk music for springtime
                     781.62610152421224
02   Influence of other traditions of music
                     Add to 02 the numbers following 781.6 in 781.63–781.69,
                     e.g., influence of jazz on Spanish folk music
                     781.6261025, performances of Spanish folk music
                     influenced by jazz 781.6261025078
03–09   Specific continents, countries, localities
                     Add to 0 notation 3–9 from Table 2, e.g., Spanish folk
                     music in New York City 781.626107471

In building numbers, do not add by use of 0 or 1 (alone or in
combination) more than twice, e.g., history of Spanish protest folk-songs
782.421626101592 (*not* 782.42162610159209)
(Option: Add as many times as desired)

> 781.63–781.69 Other traditions of music

Add to each subdivision identified by † as follows:
01–08   Standard subdivisions
          Notation from Table 1 as modified under 780.1–780.8, e.g.,
          performances 078
09   History, geographic treatment, biography
0901–0903   Historical periods to 1900
          Add to base number 090 the numbers following 780.90 in
          780.901–780.903, e.g., music of the Renaissance 09031
0904–0905   1900–2099
          Add to base number 090 the numbers following —090 in
          notation 0904–0905 from Table 1, e.g., music of the 1970s
          09047
1   General principles, influence of other traditions of music, hybrid styles
11–15   General principles
          Add to 1 the numbers following 781 in 781.1–781.5, e.g.,
          springtime music 15242, melody in springtime music 15242124
16   Influence of other traditions of music
          Add to 16 the numbers following 781.6 in 781.62–781.69, e.g.,
          influence of folk music 162, performances of music influenced
          by folk music 162078
          See also 17 for hybrid styles
17   Hybrid styles
          Fusion of two or more styles from different traditions of music
          to create a new style
          Add to 17 the numbers following 781.6 in 781.62–781.69, e.g.,
          fusion with folk music 172, folk rock 781.66172
          See Manual at 781.6: Hybrid styles
          See also 16 for influence of other traditions of music

In building numbers, do not add by use of 0 or 1 (alone or in combination)
more than twice, e.g., history of rock protest songs 782.421661592 (*not*
782.42166159209)
(Option: Add as many times as desired)

Class comprehensive works in 781.6

.63   †Popular music

Class popular music originating within and associated with an ethnic or
national group in 781.62

For western popular music, see 781.64

See Manual at 781.62 vs. 781.63–781.66

.64   †Western popular music

Class western popular music originating within and associated with an ethnic
or national group in 781.62; class country music in 781.642

For jazz, see 781.65; for rock, see 781.66

See Manual at 781.62 vs. 781.63–781.66

†Add as instructed under 781.63–781.69

.642	†Country music

    Class here bluegrass music; specific country music styles

.643	†Blues

    Class here traditional rhythm and blues; specific blues styles

    Comprehensive works on rhythm and blues relocated to 781.644

.644	†Soul

    Class here comprehensive works on rhythm and blues [*formerly* 781.643], R&B; specific soul styles

    For traditional rhythm and blues, see 781.643

.645	†Ragtime
.646	†Reggae

    Class here specific reggae styles

.648	†Electronica

    Class here specific electronica styles

    Class comprehensive works on electronic music in 786.7

[.648 155 4]	Dance music

    Do not use; class in 781.648

.649	†Rap

    Class here specific rap styles

    Class comprehensive works on rap in 782.421649

.65	†Jazz

    See Manual at 781.62 vs. 781.63–781.66

[.651 7]	Hybrid styles

    Do not use; class in 781.657

.652	†Early jazz

    Class here origins of jazz

.653	†Traditional jazz

    Including New Orleans, Dixieland, Southwest and Kansas City, Harlem, white New York styles; Chicago breakdown

.654	†Mainstream jazz

    Including swing

†Add as instructed under 781.63–781.69

.655	†Modern jazz

> Including bop (bebop), hard bop, cool jazz, progressive jazz
>
> *For avant-garde jazz, see 781.656*

.656	†Avant-garde jazz
.657	Hybrid styles

> Add to base number 781.657 the numbers following 781.6 in 781.62–781.69, e.g., Afro-Cuban 781.6572687291, Indo-jazz 781.657291411
>
> Third stream relocated to 781.68175

.66	†Rock (Rock'n' roll)

> Class here specific rock styles
>
> *See Manual at 781.62 vs. 781.63–781.66*

.68	†Western art music (Classical music)

> Limited to classical music as a tradition in contrast to other traditions
>
> Class here comprehensive works on traditions of art music
>
> Class classical music in general in 780
>
> *For nonwestern art music, see 781.69*

.681 75	Hybrid styles

> Number built according to instructions under 781.63–781.69
>
> Class here third stream [*formerly* 781.657]

.69	†Nonwestern art music
.7	**Sacred music**

> Class sacred music accompanying stages of life cycle in 781.58; class works about church music that are limited to Christian church music in 781.71; class sacred vocal music in 782.22

.700 1–.700 9	Standard subdivisions

> Notation from Table 1 as modified under 780.1–780.9, e.g., performances of sacred music 781.70078

.701–.706	General principles of sacred music

> Add to base number 781.70 the numbers following 781 in 781.1–781.6, e.g., harmonic rhythm in sacred music 781.70256, appreciation of harmonic rhythm in sacred music 781.70256117

.71	Christian sacred music

> *For music of Christian church year, see 781.72*

†Add as instructed under 781.63–781.69

.710 01–.710 09	Standard subdivisions

Notation from Table 1 as modified under 780.1–780.9, e.g., performances of Christian sacred music 781.70078

.710 1–.710 6	General principles of Christian sacred music

Add to base number 781.710 the numbers following 781 in 781.1–781.6, e.g., harmonic rhythm in Christian sacred music 781.710256, appreciation of harmonic rhythm in Christian sacred music 781.710256117

.711–.719	Christian sacred music of specific denominations and sects

Add to base number 781.71 the numbers following 28 in 281–289 for the denomination or sect only, e.g., Lutheran sacred music 781.7141; then add further as follows:

001–009   Standard subdivisions
Notation from Table 1 as modified under 780.1–780.9, e.g., performances of Lutheran sacred music 781.71410078

01–06   General principles
Add to 0 the numbers following 781 in 781.1–781.6, e.g., harmonic rhythm in Lutheran sacred music 781.71410256, appreciation of harmonic rhythm in Lutheran sacred music 781.71410256117

.72	*Music of Christian church year
.722	*Advent
.723	*Christmas day

Class here Christmas season

For Epiphany, see 781.724

.724	*Epiphany
.725	*Lent
.725 5	*Passiontide

For Holy Week, see 781.726

.726	*Holy Week

Including Palm Sunday, Maundy Thursday, Good Friday

.727	*Easter Sunday

Class here Eastertide (Easter season)

For Ascensiontide, see 781.728

.728	*Ascensiontide
.729	*Pentecost and Trinity Sunday
.729 3	*Pentecost (Whitsunday)
.729 4	*Trinity Sunday

*Add as instructed under 781.2–781.8

.73	*Sacred music of classical (Greek and Roman) and Germanic religions

.74–.79   Sacred music of other religions and sects

> Add to base number 781.7 the numbers following 29 in 294–299 for the religion or sect only, e.g., Jewish sacred music 781.76; then add further as follows:
>
> 001–009   Standard subdivisions
>> Notation from Table 1 as modified under 780.1–780.9, e.g., performances of Jewish sacred music 781.760078
>
> 01–06   General principles
>> Add to base number 0 the numbers following 781 in 781.1–781.6, e.g., harmonic rhythm in Jewish sacred music 781.760256, appreciation of harmonic rhythm in Jewish sacred music 781.760256117

.8   ***Musical forms**

> Class here formal analysis; works that do not specify voice, instrument, or ensemble
>
> Class works for specific voice, instrument, or ensemble with the voice, instrument, or ensemble, e.g., Brahms' Variations on a theme by Schumann 786.21825 (*not* 781.825)
>
> *For vocal forms, see 782.1–782.4; for instrumental forms, see 784.183–784.189*

.82   Specific musical forms

[.820 1–.820 9]   Standard subdivisions

> Do not use; class in 781.801–781.809

.822   *Binary, ternary, da capo forms

> Subdivisions are added for a combination of two or more forms

.822 2   *Binary form

.822 3   *Ternary form

.822 5   *Da capo form

.823   *Strophic form

.824   *Rondos

> Including sonata-rondos

.825   *Variations

> Including theme and variations

.826   *Paraphrase forms

> Including musical parody

.827   *Ground bass (Ostinato)

> Including chaconnes, passacaglias

*Add as instructed under 781.2–781.8

.828   *Cantus firmus

782   Vocal music

Class orchestral music with vocal parts in 784.22

For music for single voices, see 783

See Manual at 782; also at 782: Flow chart

SUMMARY

782.001–.009	**Standard subdivisions**
.01–.08	**[General principles of vocal music and musical forms]**
.1	**Operas and related dramatic vocal forms**
.2	**Nondramatic vocal forms**
.3	**Services (Liturgy and ritual)**
.4	**Secular forms**
.5	**Mixed voices**
.6	**Women's voices**
.7	**Children's voices**
.8	**Men's voices**
.9	**Other types of voices**

.001–.009   Standard subdivisions

Notation from Table 1 as modified under 780.1–780.9, e.g., performances of vocal music 782.0078

.01–.07   General principles of vocal music

Add to base number 782.0 the numbers following 781 in 781.1–781.7, e.g., patriotic vocal music 782.0599, rhythm in patriotic vocal music 782.05991224

.08   Musical forms

Add to base number 782.08 the numbers following 784.18 in 784.182–784.189, e.g., vocal music in waltz form 782.08846

For vocal forms, see 782.1–782.4

*Add as instructed under 781.2–781.8

>   **782.1–782.4 Vocal forms**

Class here treatises about and recordings of vocal forms for specific voices and ensembles

Add to each subdivision identified by * as follows:
    01–09   Standard subdivisions
                  Notation from Table 1 as modified under 780.1–780.9, e.g., performances 078
    1   General principles and musical forms
   11–17   General principles
                  Add to 1 the numbers following 781 in 781.1–781.7, e.g., rock music 166, rehearsing rock music 166144
    18   Musical forms
                  Add to 18 the numbers following 784.18 in 784.182–784.189, e.g., da capo form 1822, composition in da capo form 182213

In building numbers, do not add by use of 0 or 1 (alone or in combination) more than twice, e.g., history of rock protest songs 782.421661592 (*not* 782.42166159209)
    (Option: Add as many times as desired)

Class comprehensive works in 782

.1   ***Operas and related dramatic vocal forms**

Regardless of type of voice or vocal group

Subdivisions are added for operas and related dramatic vocal forms together, for operas alone

Class here concert versions

See Manual at 782.1 vs. 792.5, 792.6

.109 2   Biography

Class here biographies of singers known equally well as opera and recital singers, of conductors known primarily as opera conductors

Class biographies of singers known primarily as recital singers in 782.42168092; class biographies of conductors known equally well for conducting operas and orchestral music in 784.2092

.109 4   European opera

Use only for works that stress that they are discussing European opera in contrast to operas from all other sources

.12   ***Operettas**

Class here zarzuelas

.13   ***Singspiels**

*Add as instructed under 782.1–782.4

.14 ***Musical plays**

Musical plays differ from other dramatic musical forms by the fact that in them the action is predominantly outside the music, while in the other dramatic forms the action is predominantly in the music

Class here ballad operas, musicals, revues

For masques, see 782.15

See Manual at 782.1 vs. 792.5, 792.6

.15 ***Masques**

.2 ***Nondramatic vocal forms**

For secular forms, see 782.4

.22 ***Sacred vocal forms**

For specific sacred vocal forms, see 782.23–782.29

> 782.23–782.29 **Specific sacred vocal forms**

Class comprehensive works in 782.22

For services, see 782.3

.23 ***Oratorios**

Including passions

.24 ***Large-scale vocal forms**

Class here comprehensive works on cantatas

For oratorios, see 782.23; for secular cantatas, see 782.48

.25 ***Small-scale vocal forms**

Class here anthems [*formerly* 782.265], sacred songs

Unless otherwise indicated, if the forms are called motets, class them in 782.26; if called hymns, class them in 782.27; if called carols, class them in 782.28; otherwise, class them here

Class comprehensive works on songs in 782.42

See also 782.421599 for national anthems

.253 ***Spirituals**

.254 ***Gospel music**

.26 ***Motets**

Motets composed after 1600 limited to those using imitative polyphony in the style of Palestrina

---

*Add as instructed under 782.1–782.4

[.265]	Anthems

> Relocated to 782.25

.27	*Hymns

> *For carols, see 782.28*

.28	*Carols
.29	*Liturgical forms
.292	*Chant

> Including responses, e.g., litanies, suffrages
>
> Class here plainsong
>
> Class Gregorian chant in 782.3222; class Anglican chant in 782.3223

> 782.294–782.298 Specific texts

> Class comprehensive works in 782.29

.294	*Psalms
.295	*Biblical texts

> Including amens, canticles
>
> *For psalms, see 782.294*

.296	*Non-Biblical texts

> Class parts of the mass in 782.323

.297	*Tropes

> Accretions to the liturgy
>
> *For liturgical drama, see 782.298*

.298	*Liturgical drama
.3	***Services (Liturgy and ritual)**

> Musical settings of prescribed texts of specific religions
>
> Class texts used by a specific religion with the religion, e.g., liturgy and ritual of a Christian church 264

.32	*Christian services
.322	Services of specific denominations
[.322 01–.322 09]	Standard subdivisions

> Do not use; class in 782.3201–782.3209

*Add as instructed under 782.1–782.4

.322 1–.322 9   Subdivisions for services of specific denominations

Add to base number 782.322 the numbers following 28 in 281–289, e.g., music for Lutheran services 782.32241; then add further as follows:

001–009   Standard subdivisions

Notation from Table 1 as modified under 780.1–780.9, e.g., performances of music for Lutheran services 782.322410078

01–07   General principles

Add to 0 the numbers following 781 in 781.1–781.7, e.g., music for Lutheran Easter Sunday services 782.322410727, composition of music for Lutheran Easter Sunday services 782.32241072713

08   Musical forms

Add to 08 the numbers following 784.18 in 784.182–784.189, e.g., preludes for Lutheran services 782.3224108928, composition of preludes for Lutheran services 782.322410892813

Class specific liturgies of specific denominations in 782.323–782.326

>   782.323–782.326   Specific liturgies

Class comprehensive works in 782.32

.323   *Mass (Communion service)

This number is used for music including both the common and the proper of the mass. Masses written from 1350 to today are usually limited to the common and are thus classed in 782.3232. The major exception is the requiem mass, which is classed in 782.3238. Music for an individual part of the mass is classed with that part, e.g., gradual 782.3235

.323 2   *Common of the mass (Ordinary of the mass)

Including Kyrie, Gloria, Credo, Sanctus, Benedictus, Agnus Dei

For common of requiem mass, see 782.3238

.323 5   *Proper of the mass

Including introit, gradual, tract, sequence, offertory, communion

For proper of requiem mass, see 782.3238

.323 8   *Requiem mass

.324   *Divine office

Including matins, lauds, prime, terce, sext, none, vespers, compline

See also 782.325 for morning prayer; also 782.326 for evening prayer

.325   *Morning prayer

Including matins of the Anglican church

---

*Add as instructed under 782.1 782.4

.326   *Evening prayer

           Including evensong of the Anglican church

.33   *Services of classical (Greek and Roman) and Germanic religions

.34–.39   Services of other specific religions and sects

           Add to base number 782.3 the numbers following 29 in 294–299 for the
           religion or sect only, e.g., music for Jewish services 782.36; then add further
           as follows:
           001–009   Standard subdivisions
                      Notation from Table 1 as modified under 780.1–780.9,
                      e.g., performances of music for Jewish services
                      782.360078
           01–07   General principles
                      Add to 0 the numbers following 781 in 781.1–781.7, e.g.,
                      music for Jewish spring services 782.3605242, composition
                      of music for Jewish spring services 782.360524213
           08   Musical form
                      Add to 08 the numbers following 784.18 in
                      784.182–784.189, e.g., preludes for Jewish services
                      782.3608928, composition of preludes for Jewish services
                      782.360892813

.4   *Secular forms

.42   *Songs

           Class here comprehensive works on songs

           For sacred songs, see 782.25

.421 599   National anthems

               Number built according to instructions under 782.1–782.4

               See also 782.25 for sacred anthems

.421 64   Western popular songs

               Number built according to instructions under 782.1–782.4

               Class comprehensive works on western popular music in 781.64

               For jazz songs, see 782.42165; for rock songs, see 782.42166

.421 649   Rap songs

               Number built according to instructions under 782.1–782.4

               Class here comprehensive works on rap music

               *For rap music limited to instrumental tracks, see the
               instrument, e.g., drum rap beats 786.91649*

*Add as instructed under 782.1–782.4

.421 65	Jazz songs

> Number built according to instructions under 782.1–782.4

> Class comprehensive works on jazz in 781.65; class comprehensive works on western popular songs in 782.42164

.421 66	Rock (Rock'n' roll) songs

> Number built according to instructions under 782.1–782.4

> Class comprehensive works on rock music in 781.66; class comprehensive works on western popular songs in 782.42164

.421 68	Art songs

> Number built according to instructions under 782.1–782.4

> Class here lieder

.421 680 92	Biography

> Number built according to instructions under 782.1–782.4

> Class here biographies of singers known primarily as recital singers

> Class biographies of singers known equally well as opera and recital singers in 782.1092

.43	*Forms derived from poetry

> Including ballads, balletts, chansons, frottole, villancicos

> Class here madrigals

> *For villancicos that are Christmas carols, see 782.281723*

.47	*Song cycles
.48	*Secular cantatas

*Add as instructed under 782.1 782.4

> **782.5–782.9 Vocal executants**

Add to each subdivision identified by † as follows:
```
01–09    Standard subdivisions
             Notation from Table 1 as modified under 780.1–780.9, e.g.,
             performances 078
1        General principles and musical forms
11–17    General principles
             Add to 1 the numbers following 781 in 781.1–781.7, e.g., rock
             music 166, rehearsing rock music 166144
18       Musical forms
             Add to 18 the numbers following 784.18 in 784.182–784.189,
             e.g., da capo form 1822, composition in da capo form 182213
             Class dramatic vocal forms in 782.1
                 For nondramatic vocal forms, see 2–4
2–4      Nondramatic vocal forms
             Add the numbers following 782 in 782.2–782.4, e.g., secular
             cantatas 48
```

In building numbers, do not add by use of 0 or 1 (alone or in combination) more than twice, e.g., texts of rock protest songs for mixed voices 782.5421661592 (*not* 782.54216615920268)
(Option: Add as many times as desired)

Use 782.5–782.9 for scores and parts of vocal forms for specific kinds of vocal ensembles, e.g., mixed-voice choirs 782.5, children's choirs 782.7. Use 782.1–782.4 for treatises about and recordings of vocal forms for specific kinds of vocal ensembles. Class performance techniques for a specific ensemble or form with the ensemble or form, e.g., breathing techniques for choral music 782.5148, for opera 782.1148

Class comprehensive works in 782

> *See Manual at 782*

.5   †**Mixed voices**

Class here choral music, music intended equally for choral or part-song performance, choral music with solo parts, unison voices

> *For part songs, see 783.1*

> **782.6–782.9 Types of voices**

Class comprehensive works in 782

.6   †**Women's voices**

Class here music intended equally for women's or children's voices

Class music for children's voices in 782.7

.66   †Soprano voices (Treble voices)

.67   †Mezzo-soprano voices

†Add as instructed under 782.5–782.9

.68	†Contralto voices (Alto voices)

.7 †Children's voices

Class music intended equally for women's or children's voices in 782.6

.76	†Soprano voices (Treble voices)
.77	†Mezzo-soprano voices
.78	†Contralto voices (Alto voices)
.79	†Changing voices

.8 †Men's voices

.86	†Treble and alto voices

Class here countertenor, falsetto, castrato voices

Subdivisions are added for either or both topics in heading

.87	†Tenor voices
.88	†Baritone voices
.89	†Bass voices

.9 †Other types of voices

.96	†Speaking voices (Choral speech)
.97	†Sprechgesang
.98	†Whistle

783 Music for single voices

Class here the voice

Use 783 for scores and parts of vocal forms for specific kinds or ensembles of single voice. Use 782.1–782.4 for treatises about and recordings of vocal forms for specific kinds or ensembles of single voice. Class performance techniques for a specific kind or ensemble of single voice or for a specific form with the kind, ensemble, or form, e.g., breathing techniques for part songs 783.1148, for opera 782.1148

See Manual at 782

.001–.009	Standard subdivisions

Notation from Table 1 as modified under 780.1–780.9, e.g., performances of music for single voice 783.0078

.01–.07	General principles of music for single voices

Add to base number 783.0 the numbers following 781 in 781.1–781.7, e.g., patriotic music for single voices 783.0599, rhythm in patriotic music for single voices 783.05991224

†Add as instructed under 782.5–782.9

.08 Musical forms

> Add to base number 783.08 the numbers following 784.18 in 784.182–784.189, e.g., vocal music in waltz form for the single voice 783.08846

> > *For dramatic vocal forms, see 782.1; for nondramatic vocal forms, see 783.09*

.09 Nondramatic vocal forms

> Add to base number 783.09 the numbers following 782 in 782.2–782.4, e.g., carols for single voices 783.0928

.1 Single voices in combination

> Class here part songs

> Class music intended equally for choral or part-song performance in 782.5

.101–.109 Standard subdivisions

> Notation from Table 1 as modified under 780.1–780.9, e.g., performances of part songs 783.1078

.11 General principles and musical forms

.111–.117 General principles of single voices in combination

> Add to base number 783.11 the numbers following 781 in 781.1–781.7, e.g., patriotic part songs 783.11599, rehearsing patriotic part songs 783.11599144

.118 Musical forms

> Add to base number 783.118 the numbers following 784.18 in 784.182–784.189, e.g., part songs in waltz form 783.118846, rehearsing part songs in waltz form 783.118846144

> > *For dramatic vocal forms, see 782.1; for nondramatic vocal forms, see 783.119*

.119 Nondramatic vocal forms

> Add to base number 783.119 the numbers following 782 in 782.2–782.4, e.g., carols for single voices in combination 783.11928

\>   783.12–783.19   Ensembles by size

Add to each subdivision identified by † as follows:

01–09   Standard subdivisions

Notation from Table 1 as modified under 780.1–780.9, e.g., performances 078

1   General principles and musical forms

11–17   General principles

Add to 1 the numbers following 781 in 781.1–781.7, e.g., rock music 166, rehearsing rock music 166144

18   Musical forms

Add to 18 the numbers following 784.18 in 784.182–784.189, e.g., da capo form 1822, composition in da capo form 182213

Class dramatic vocal forms in 782.1

For nondramatic vocal forms, see 2–4

2–4   Nondramatic vocal forms

Add the numbers following 782 in 782.2–782.4, e.g., secular cantatas 48

6–9   Types of voices

Add the numbers following 782 in 782.6–782.9, e.g., female voices 6; then add notation 01–09 and 1–4 from this table, e.g., secular cantatas for female voice 648

In building numbers, do not add by use of 0 or 1 (alone or in combination) more than twice, e.g., texts of rock protest songs for two singers 783.12421661592 (*not* 783.124216615920268)

(Option: Add as many times as desired)

Class comprehensive works in 783.1

.12   †Duets

.13   †Trios

.14   †Quartets

.15   †Quintets

.16   †Sextets

.17   †Septets

.18   †Octets

.19   †Nonets and larger combinations

†Add as instructed under 783.12–783.19

> **783.2–783.9 Solo voices**

Add to each subdivision identified by ‡ as follows:
01–09　Standard subdivisions
　　　　Notation from Table 1 as modified under 780.1–780.9, e.g.,
　　　　performances 078
1　　　General principles and musical forms
11–17　General principles
　　　　Add to 1 the numbers following 781 in 781.1–781.7, e.g., rock
　　　　music 166, rehearsing rock music 166144
18　　　Musical forms
　　　　Add to 18 the numbers following 784.18 in 784.182–784.189,
　　　　e.g., da capo form 1822, composition in da capo form 182213
　　　　Class dramatic vocal forms in 782.1
　　　　For nondramatic vocal forms, see 2–4
2–4　　Nondramatic vocal forms
　　　　Add the numbers following 782 in 782.2–782.4, e.g., secular
　　　　cantatas 48

In building numbers, do not add by use of 0 or 1 (alone or in combination) more than twice, e.g., history of rock protest songs for high voice 783.3421661592 (*not* 783.342166159209)
(Option: Add as many times as desired)

Class comprehensive works in 783.2

.2　　　‡**Solo voice**

Class here comprehensive works on types of single voices

For specific types of single voices, see 783.3–783.9

> **783.3–783.9 Specific types of single voices**

Class single voices in ensembles in 783.12–783.19; class comprehensive works in 783.2

.3　　　‡**High voice**

Class woman's soprano voice in 783.66; class child's soprano voice in 783.76; class man's treble voice and alto voice in 783.86; class tenor voice in 783.87

.4　　　‡**Middle voice**

Class woman's mezzo-soprano voice in 783.67; class child's mezzo-soprano voice in 783.77; class baritone voice in 783.88

.5　　　‡**Low voice**

Class woman's contralto voice in 783.68; class child's contralto voice in 783.78; class bass voice in 783.89

.6–.8　　**Women's, children's, men's voices**

Add to base number 783 the numbers following 782 in 782.6–782.8, e.g., bass voice 783.89

‡Add as instructed under 783.2–783.9

.9   ‡**Other types of voice**

.96   ‡Speaking voice

.97   ‡Sprechgesang

.98   ‡Whistle

.99   ‡Voice instruments

> Including didjeridu, mirliton (kazoo), roarers, voice disguisers (sympathetic instruments relying on the human voice for their sound production)

> ### 784–788 Instruments and their music

Add to each subdivision identified by * as follows:
>
> 01–09   Standard subdivisions
>> Notation from Table 1 as modified under 780.1–780.9, e.g., performances 078
>>> *See Manual at 784–788: Add table: 092*
>
> 1   General principles, musical forms, instruments
> 11–17   General principles
>> Add to 1 the numbers following 781 in 781.1–781.7, e.g., performance techniques 143
>>> *For techniques for playing instruments, see 193*
>
> 18–19   Musical forms and instruments
>> Add to 1 the numbers following 784.1 in 784.18–784.19, e.g., sonata form 183, techniques for playing instruments 193

In building numbers, do not add by use of 0 or 1 (alone or in combination) more than twice, e.g., history of atonality in piano sonatas 786.21831267 (*not* 786.2183126709)
> (Option: Add as many times as desired)

Class comprehensive works in 784

> *See Manual at 784–788*

784   Instruments and instrumental ensembles and their music

> *For ensembles with only one instrument per part, see 785; for specific instruments and their music, see 786–788*
>
> *See also 787 for music for unspecified melody instrument*
>
> *See Manual at 784–788*

SUMMARY

784.01–.09	**Standard subdivisions**
.1	**General principles, musical forms, instruments**
.2	**Full orchestra (Symphony orchestra)**
.3	**Chamber orchestra**
.4	**Light orchestra**
.6	**Keyboard, mechanical, electronic, percussion bands**
.7	**String orchestra**
.8	**Wind band**
.9	**Brass band**

---

‡Add as instructed under 783.2–783.9

.01–.09 Standard subdivisions

> Notation from Table 1 as modified under 780.1–780.9, e.g., performances 784.078

.1 General principles, musical forms, instruments

SUMMARY

.11–.17 General principles of instruments and instrumental ensembles and their music

> Add to base number 784.1 the numbers following 781 in 781.1–781.7, e.g., performance techniques 784.143

> *For techniques for playing instruments, see 784.193*

.18 †Musical forms

784.182–784.189 Specific musical forms

> Add to each subdivision identified by † as instructed under 781.2–781.8, e.g., composing waltzes 784.1884613

> Class comprehensive works in 784.18

SUMMARY

.182 †General musical forms

.182 2 †Binary, ternary, da capo forms

> Subdivisions are added for a combination of two or more forms

.182 3 †Strophic form

.182 4 †Rondos

> Including sonata-rondos

.182 5 †Variations

> Including theme and variations

†Add as instructed under 781.2–781.8

.182 6	†Paraphrase forms

Including musical parody

.182 7	†Ground bass (Ostinato)

Including chaconnes, passacaglias

>   784.183–784.189 Instrumental forms

Except for concerto form, comprehensive works on an instrumental form regardless of the executant are classed here, e.g., symphony form 784.184. Individual works and works for a specific executant are classed with the executant, e.g., Camille Saint-Saëns' Symphony No. 3 (for full orchestra including an organ) 784.2184, Charles Marie Widor's Symphony No. 5 (for solo organ) 786.5184

Class comprehensive works in 784.18

.183	†Sonata form and sonatas

Subdivisions are added for either or both topics in heading

Class sonata-rondos in 784.1824

.183 2	†Sonatinas
.184	†Symphonies

Including sinfoniettas

Class symphonies, sinfoniettas for full orchestras in 784.2184

.184 3	†Symphonic poems

Class symphonic poems for full orchestras in 784.21843

.184 5	†Sinfonia concertantes
.185	†Suites and related forms

Including cassations

Subdivisions are added for a combination of two or more forms

.185 2	†Divertimentos
.185 4	†Partitas
.185 6	†Serenades
.185 8	†Suites
.186	†Concerto form

Use this subdivision only for concerto as a form other than solo instruments with full orchestra, e.g., concerto forms for wind bands 784.8186, Bartok's Concerto for orchestra 784.2186

Including cadenzas, concertantes

Class comprehensive works on concertos in 784.23

---

†Add as instructed under 781.2–781.8

.186 2	†Concertinos
.187	†Contrapuntal forms
.187 2	†Fugues
.187 4	†Inventions
.187 5	†Canzonas
.187 6	†Fancies and ricercares

Including innomines, tientos

Subdivisions are added for either or both topics in heading

See also 784.1894 for fantasias (an improvisatory form)

.187 8	†Canons
.188	†Dance forms
.188 2	†European dance forms

Including galliards, saltarellos

For dances of the classical suite, see 784.1883; for European dance forms of the 19th and later centuries, see 784.1884

.188 23	†Pavans
.188 3	†Dances of the classical suite

Including gavottes, sicilianas

.188 35	†Minuets
.188 4	†European dance forms of the 19th and later centuries

Including galops, mazurkas, polonaises

.188 44	†Polkas
.188 46	†Waltzes
.188 5	†Asian dance forms
.188 6	†African dance forms
.188 7	†North American dance forms

Including cakewalks, hoedowns, square dances

For Latin-American dance forms, see 784.1888

.188 8	†Latin-American dance forms

Including rumbas, sambas

.188 85	†Tangos
.188 9	†Dance forms of the Pacific Ocean islands and other parts of the world

Add as instructed under 781.2–781.8

.189	†Other instrumental forms
	Class here small-scale and character instrumental forms
.189 2	†Introductory forms
	Music preceding other music or other activities
.189 24	†Fanfares
.189 26	†Overtures
	Class here concert overtures
	Class overtures for full orchestras in 784.218926
.189 28	†Preludes
.189 3	†Intermediate forms
	Music for between or after other activities
	Including interludes, intermezzos, postludes, voluntaries
	Class voluntaries for organs in 786.51893
	For incidental music, see 781.552
.189 4	†Forms of music of an improvisatory or virtuoso nature
	Including arabesques, fantasias, impromptus
	See also 784.1876 for fancies (a contrapuntal form)
.189 45	†Rhapsodies
.189 47	†Toccatas
.189 49	†Artistic études
.189 6	†Romantic and descriptive forms
	Including ballades, meditations, songs without words
.189 64	†Elegies
.189 66	†Nocturnes
.189 68	†Romances
.189 7	†Marches
.189 9	†Forms derived from vocal music
.189 92	†Forms derived from sacred music
	Including chorale preludes
	Class chorale preludes for organs in 786.518992
	For instrumental forms derived from liturgical forms, see 784.18993
.189 925	†Chorales

†Add as instructed under 781.2–781.8

.189 93	†Instrumental forms derived from liturgical forms
.19	Instruments

Class here acoustic form of instruments, electric form of instruments

For specific instruments, see 786–788

.190 28	Auxiliary techniques and procedures
[.190 284]	Apparatus, equipment, materials

Do not use; class in 784.19

[.190 287]	Testing and measurement

Do not use; class in 784.1927

[.190 288]	Maintenance and repair

Do not use; class in 784.1928

[.190 94–.190 99]	Specific continents, countries, localities in modern world

Do not use; class in 784.194–784.199

.192	Techniques and procedures for instruments themselves

See also 784.193 for techniques for playing instruments

.192 2	Description and design
.192 3	Construction

For construction by machine, see 681.8

.192 7	Testing, measurement, verification
.192 8	Maintenance, tuning, repair

Including temperament

.193	†Techniques for playing instruments

Class comprehensive works on performance techniques in 784.143

.193 2	†Breathing and resonance
.193 4	†Embouchure

Including lipping, tonguing

.193 6	†Arm techniques
.193 62	†Forearm techniques
.193 64	†Wrist techniques
.193 65	†Hand techniques

For left-hand techniques, see 784.19366; for right-hand techniques, see 784.19367

.193 66	†Left-hand techniques

†Add as instructed under 781.2–781.8

.193 67	†Right-hand techniques	
.193 68	†Finger techniques	
	Including fingering, touch, vibrato	
.193 69	†Bowing techniques	
.193 8	†Leg techniques	
	Including pedaling	

.194–.199   Specific continents, countries, localities in modern world

> Add to base number 784.19 notation 4–9 from Table 2, e.g., instruments of Germany 784.1943

.2   ***Full orchestra (Symphony orchestra)**

> Class here comprehensive works on orchestral combinations, music intended equally for orchestral or chamber performance
>
> *For other orchestral combinations, see 784.3–784.9; for chamber music, see 785*

.209 2   Biography

> Class here biographies of conductors known equally well for conducting operas and orchestral music
>
> Class biographies of conductors known primarily as opera conductors in 782.1092

.22   *Orchestra with vocal parts

.23   *Orchestra with one or more solo instruments

> Class here comprehensive works on concertos
>
> *For concerto form, see 784.186; for orchestra with more than one solo instrument, see 784.24; for orchestra with one solo instrument, see 784.25*

.24   *Orchestra with more than one solo instrument

> Including concerti grossi

.25   *Orchestra with one solo instrument

> Class here comprehensive works on solo concertos
>
> *For specific solo instruments, see 784.26–784.28*

.26–.28   Specific solo instruments with orchestra

> Add to base number 784.2 the numbers following 78 in 786–788, e.g., orchestra with solo piano 784.262, rehearsing orchestra with solo piano 784.262144

---

*Add as instructed under 784–788
†Add as instructed under 781.2–781.8

> ### 784.3–784.9 Other orchestral and band combinations

Add to each subdivision identified by † as follows:
- 01–09   Standard subdivisions
  - Notation from Table 1 as modified under 780.1–780.9, e.g., performances 078
- 1   General principles, musical forms, instruments
- 11–17   General principles
  - Add to 1 the numbers following 781 in 781.1–781.7, e.g., sacred music 17, rehearsing sacred music 17044
- 18–19   Musical forms and instruments
  - Add to 1 the numbers following 784.1 in 784.18–784.19, e.g., waltz form 18846, bowing techniques 19369
- · 2   Featured voices, instruments, ensembles
  - Add to 2 the numbers following 78 in 782–788, e.g., flutes 2832

Class comprehensive works on orchestral and band combinations, on band in 784; class comprehensive works on orchestral combinations in 784.2

.3   **†Chamber orchestra**

> *For chamber music, see 785*

.4   **†Light orchestra**

> Class here salon orchestra

.44   †School orchestra

.46   †Orchestra with toy instruments

.48   †Dance orchestra (Dance band)

> Class here big bands

.6   **†Keyboard, mechanical, electronic, percussion bands**

.68   †Percussion band

> Class here rhythm band

.7   **†String orchestra**

.8   **†Wind band**

> Band consisting of woodwind instruments, brass instruments, or both

> *For brass band, see 784.9*

.83   †Marching band

.84   †Military band

.89   †Woodwind band

.9   **†Brass band**

---

†Add as instructed under 784.3–784.9

785   Ensembles with only one instrument per part

Class here chamber music

Class works for solo melody instrument with keyboard or other accompaniment in 786–788

See Manual at 784–788

SUMMARY

785.001–.009		**Standard subdivisions**
	.01–.09	**[General principles of ensembles with only one instrument per part, musical forms, instruments]**
	.1	**Ensembles by size**
	.2	**Ensembles with keyboard**
	.3	**Ensembles without electrophones and with percussion and keyboard**
	.4	**Ensembles without keyboard**
	.5	**Ensembles without keyboard and with percussion**
	.6	**Keyboard, mechanical, aeolian, electrophone, percussion ensembles**
	.7	**String ensembles**
	.8	**Woodwind ensembles**
	.9	**Brass ensembles**

.001–.009   Standard subdivisions

Notation from Table 1 as modified under 780.1–780.9, e.g., performances of chamber music 785.0078

.01–.07   General principles of ensembles with only one instrument per part

Add to base number 785.0 the numbers following 781 in 781.1–781.7, e.g., performance techniques 785.043, jazz ensembles 785.065

For techniques for playing instruments, see 785.093

.08–.09   Musical forms and instruments

Add to base number 785.0 the numbers following 784.1 in 784.18–784.19, e.g., waltz form 785.08846, techniques for playing instruments 785.093

.1   Ensembles by size

These provisions, when applied throughout 785, refer to the number of instruments, except when percussion instruments are involved; in that case they refer to the number of performers

.12   *Duets

.13   *Trios

.14   *Quartets

.15   *Quintets

.16   *Sextets

.17   *Septets

.18   *Octets

*Add as instructed under 784–788

.19   *Nonets and larger ensembles

>   **785.2–785.9   Specific kinds of ensembles**

Add to each subdivision identified by † as follows:
01–09   Standard subdivisions
         Notation from Table 1 as modified under 780.1–780.9, e.g.,
         performances 078
1   General principles, musical forms, size of ensemble
11–17   General principles
         Add to 1 the numbers following 781 in 781.1–781.7, e.g., sacred
         music 17, conducting sacred music 17045
         Class instrumental techniques for mixed ensembles in 784.193.
         Class instrumental techniques for a specific instrument with
         the instrument in 786–788, e.g., bowing techniques for violins
         787.219369
18   Musical forms
         Add to 18 the numbers following 784.18 in 784.182–784.189,
         e.g., waltz form 18846
19   Size of ensemble
         Add to 19 the numbers following 785.1 in 785.12–785.19, e.g.,
         octets 198

In building numbers, do not add by use of 0 or 1 (alone or in combination)
more than twice, e.g., history of atonality in piano duets 785.621921267 (*not*
785.62192126709)
    (Option: Add as many times as desired)

Class comprehensive works in 785

>   **785.2–785.5   Ensembles consisting of two or more instrumental groups**

Class comprehensive works in 785

.2   **†Ensembles with keyboard**

*For ensembles without electrophones and with percussion and keyboard, see
785.3*

.22   †Ensembles of woodwind, brass, strings, keyboard

.23   †Ensembles of woodwind, brass, keyboard

.24   †Ensembles of woodwind, strings, keyboard

.25   †Ensembles of brass, strings, keyboard

.26   †Ensembles of woodwind and keyboard

Three or more instruments

See also 788.2 for ensembles of one woodwind instrument and keyboard

---

*Add as instructed under 784–788
†Add as instructed under 785.2–785.9

.27	†Ensembles of brass and keyboard
	Three or more instruments
	See also 788.9 for ensembles of one brass instrument and keyboard
.28	†Ensembles of strings and keyboard
	Three or more instruments
	See also 787 for ensembles of one stringed instrument and keyboard
.29	†Ensembles with electrophones, percussion, keyboard
.292	†Ensembles of woodwind, brass, strings, electrophones, percussion, keyboard
.293	†Ensembles of woodwind, brass, electrophones, percussion, keyboard
.294	†Ensembles of woodwind, strings, electrophones, percussion, keyboard
.295	†Ensembles of brass, strings, electrophones, percussion, keyboard
.296	†Ensembles of woodwind, electrophones, percussion, keyboard
.297	†Ensembles of brass, electrophones, percussion, keyboard
.298	†Ensembles of strings, electrophones, percussion, keyboard
.299	†Ensembles with electrophones and keyboard
.299 2	†Ensembles of woodwind, brass, strings, electrophones, keyboard
.299 3	†Ensembles of woodwind, brass, electrophones, keyboard
.299 4	†Ensembles of woodwind, strings, electrophones, keyboard
.299 5	†Ensembles of brass, strings, electrophones, keyboard
.299 6	†Ensembles of woodwind, electrophones, keyboard
.299 7	†Ensembles of brass, electrophones, keyboard
.299 8	†Ensembles of strings, electrophones, keyboard
.299 9	†Ensembles of electrophones and keyboard
	Two or more electrophones
	See also 786.7 for ensembles of one electrophone and keyboard
.3	**†Ensembles without electrophones and with percussion and keyboard**
.32	†Ensembles of woodwind, brass, strings, percussion, keyboard
.33	†Ensembles of woodwind, brass, percussion, keyboard
.34	†Ensembles of woodwind, strings, percussion, keyboard
.35	†Ensembles of brass, strings, percussion, keyboard
.36	†Ensembles of woodwind, percussion, keyboard

†Add as instructed under 785.2–785.9

.37	†Ensembles of brass, percussion, keyboard
.38	†Ensembles of strings, percussion, keyboard
.39	†Ensembles of keyboard and percussion

.4 **†Ensembles without keyboard**

For ensembles without keyboard and with percussion, see 785.5

.42	†Ensembles of woodwind, brass, strings
.43	†Ensembles of woodwind and brass (Wind ensembles)
.44	†Ensembles of woodwind and strings
.45	†Ensembles of brass and strings
.46	†Ensembles with electrophones
.462	†Ensembles of woodwind, brass, strings, electrophones
.463	†Ensembles of woodwind, brass, electrophones
.464	†Ensembles of woodwind, strings, electrophones
.465	†Ensembles of brass, strings, electrophones
.466	†Ensembles of woodwinds and electrophones
.467	†Ensembles of brass and electrophones
.468	†Ensembles of strings and electrophones

.5 **†Ensembles without keyboard and with percussion**

.52	†Ensembles of woodwind, brass, strings, percussion
.53	†Ensembles of woodwind, brass, percussion
.54	†Ensembles of woodwind, strings, percussion
.55	†Ensembles of brass, strings, percussion
.56	†Ensembles of woodwind and percussion
.57	†Ensembles of brass and percussion
.58	†Ensembles of strings and percussion
.59	†Ensembles with electrophones and percussion
.592	†Ensembles of woodwind, brass, strings, electrophones, percussion
.593	†Ensembles of woodwind, brass, electrophones, percussion
.594	†Ensembles of woodwind, strings, electrophones, percussion
.595	†Ensembles of brass, strings, electrophones, percussion
.596	†Ensembles of woodwind, electrophones, percussion
.597	†Ensembles of brass, electrophones, percussion

†Add as instructed under 785.2–785.9

.598   †Ensembles of strings, electrophones, percussion

.599   †Ensembles of electrophones and percussion

>   **785.6–785.9 Ensembles consisting of only one instrumental group**

The inclusion of "only one kind" in the 785.6–785.9 headings limits the subdivisions to individual kind of instruments, not to family of instruments. For example, a string quartet, which usually consists of two violins, a viola, and a cello is classed in 785.7194 string quartets, not 785.72194 violin quartets

When adding from 786–788 to indicate the instrument, add only the notation for the instrument; do not follow the footnote leading to add instructions. After indicating the instrument, add as instructed under 785.2–785.9, where notation 19 is used to indicate size of ensemble. For example, 785.7194 means string quartets, not string instruments of Europe (the meaning that would result from following the footnote instruction). The correct number for string quartets of Europe is 785.7194094

Class comprehensive works in 785

.6   **†Keyboard, mechanical, aeolian, electrophone, percussion ensembles**

.62–.65   Keyboard ensembles

Add to base number 785.6 the numbers following 786 in 786.2–786.5 for the instrument only, e.g., music for piano ensembles 785.62; then add further as instructed under 785.2–785.9, e.g., music for three pianos 785.62193
  Notation 19 from table under 785.2–785.9 for size of ensemble can mean either number of instruments or, when only one instrument is used, number of performers. For example, 785.62192 can mean either music for two pianos or music for piano (four hands)

.66   †Ensembles of mechanical and aeolian instruments

Subdivisions are added for ensembles of mechanical and aeolian instruments together, for ensembles of mechanical instruments alone

.664–.668   Ensembles with only one kind of mechanical instrument

Add to base number 785.66 the numbers following 786.6 in 786.64–786.68 for the instrument only, e.g., music for carillons 785.664

.669   †Aeolian ensembles

.67   †Electrophone ensembles

For ensembles of a specific kind or group of electrically amplified or modified standard instruments, see the instrument or group of instruments, e.g., electric guitar ensembles 785.787

See also 786.7 for electronic music for one performer

.673–.676   Ensembles with only one type of electrophone instrument

Add to base number 785.67 the numbers following 786.7 in 786.73–786.76 for the instrument only, e.g., music for synthesizers 785.674; then add further as instructed under 785.2–785.9, e.g., sextets for synthesizers 785.674196

---

†Add as instructed under 785.2–785.9

.68   †Percussion ensembles

> Class here ensembles for more than one performer; see note under 785.1

> *See also 786.8 for percussion music for one performer*

.7   †String ensembles

> Class here bowed string ensembles

.72–.79   Ensembles of only one kind of stringed instrument

> Add to base number 785.7 the numbers following 787 in 787.2–787.9 for the instrument only, e.g., music for guitar 785.787; then add further as instructed under 785.2–785.9, e.g., quartet for guitars 785.787194

.8   †Woodwind ensembles

.83–.88   Ensembles of only one kind of woodwind instrument

> Add to base number 785.8 the numbers following 788 in 788.3–788.8 for the instrument only, e.g., music for saxophones 785.87; then add further as instructed under 785.2–785.9, e.g., quartet for saxophones 785.87194

.9   †Brass ensembles

.92–.99   Ensembles of only one kind of brass instrument

> Add to base number 785.9 the numbers following 788.9 in 788.92–788.99 for the instrument only, e.g., music for trombones 785.93; then add further as instructed under 785.2–785.9, e.g., quartet for trombones 785.93194

> ## 786–788 Specific instruments and their music

> Class here music for solo instrument, music for solo instrument accompanied by one other instrument when the accompanying instrument clearly has a subsidiary role; acoustic form of instruments, electric form of instruments

> Unless the forerunner of a modern instrument has its own notation, class it with the modern instrument. For example, the shawm, a forerunner of the oboe and an instrument without its own number, is classed with the oboe in 788.52; however, the vihuela, the forerunner of the guitar, is classed in 787.86 (its own number), not with the guitar in 787.87

> Class chamber music in 785; class comprehensive works in 784

> *For voice instruments, see 783.99*

786   *Keyboard, mechanical, electrophonic, percussion instruments*

> Class here comprehensive works on keyboard instruments, on keyboard stringed instruments; music for unspecified keyboard instrument

> *See Manual at 784–788*

*Add as instructed under 784–788
†Add as instructed under 785.2–785.9

SUMMARY

786.2	**Pianos**
.3	**Clavichords**
.4	**Harpsichords**
.5	**Organs**
.6	**Mechanical and aeolian instruments**
.7	**Electronic instruments (Electrophones)**
.8	**Percussion instruments**
.9	**Drums and devices used for percussive effects**

> ### 786.2–786.5 Keyboard instruments

Class mechanical keyboard instruments in 786.66; class keyboard idiophones in 786.83; class comprehensive works in 786. Class music for more than one performer on one keyboard instrument as an ensemble with the ensemble in 785.62–785.65, e.g., piano (four hands) 785.62192

> ### 786.2–786.4 Keyboard stringed instruments

Class comprehensive works in 786

.2   *Pianos

.28   *Prepared pianos

.3   *Clavichords

.4   *Harpsichords

Class here spinets, virginals

.5   *Organs

Class here keyboard wind instruments

Class concertinas in 788.84; class accordions in 788.86

.55   *Reed organs and regals

Variant names for reed organs: American organs, cabinet organs, harmoniums

Subdivisions are added for either or both topics in heading

.59   *Electronic organs

Class here comprehensive works on keyboard electrophones

Class a keyboard instrument whose sound is generated by conventional means, even though amplified or modified electronically, with the instrument, e.g., electric piano 786.2

See also 786.74 for synthesizers

*Add as instructed under 784–788

.6 ***Mechanical and aeolian instruments**

> Subdivisions are added for mechanical and aeolian instruments together, for mechanical instruments alone

---

> 786.64–786.68 Mechanical instruments

Class comprehensive works in 786.6

.64 ***Mechanical struck idiophones**

Including carillons, mechanized bells

Class here comprehensive works on mechanical idiophones

For mechanical plucked idiophones, see 786.65

.65 ***Mechanical plucked idiophones**

Including music boxes, symphonions

.66 ***Mechanical keyboard instruments**

Mechanical instruments with attached functional keyboard

Including player pianos (pianolas)

Class mechanical wind keyboard instruments in 786.68

.67 ***Mechanical stringed instruments**

Class mechanical stringed keyboard instruments in 786.66

.68 ***Mechanical wind instruments**

Including fair organs

.69 ***Aeolian instruments**

Instruments activated by the blowing of the wind

.7 ***Electronic instruments (Electrophones)**

Class here electronic music in the sense of music with a focus on electronically produced or manipulated sounds; comprehensive works on electronic music

Class keyboard electrophones in 786.59. Class a specific electrically amplified or modified acoustic instrument with the instrument, e.g., electric guitar 787.87

For electronica, see 781.648

.73 ***Monophonic electrophones**

Electronic sound producers capable of producing only one pitch at a time

Including ondes martenot, theremins

*Add as instructed under 784–788

.74   *Synthesizers

> *For tapes, see 786.75; for computers, see 786.76*

> Use of this number for comprehensive works on electronic music discontinued; class in 786.7

.75   Tapes

> Class here musique concrète (concrete music)

.76   Computers

> *See also 781.34 for using computers to compose music*

.8   ***Percussion instruments**

> *For drums, see 786.92–786.98; for struck stringed instruments, see 787.7*

.82   *Idiophones (Vibrating sonorous solids)

> Class here comprehensive works on percussion instruments of definite pitch

> Class percussion instruments of indefinite pitch in 786.88

> > *For mechanical idiophones, see 786.64; for keyboard idiophones, see 786.83; for set idiophones, see 786.84–786.87; for single idiophones, see 786.88*

.83   *Keyboard idiophones

> Class here celestas

>   786.84–786.87   Set idiophones

> Class comprehensive works in 786.84

.84   *Percussed idiophones

> Sonorous solids struck by or against nonsonorous objects, e.g., sticks struck on ground

> Class here comprehensive works on set idiophones (similar sonorous solids combined to form one instrument)

> > *For plucked idiophones, see 786.85; for friction idiophones, see 786.86; for concussion idiophones, see 786.87*

.842–.848   Sonorous solids of specific shapes

> Add to base number 786.84 the numbers following 786.884 in 786.8842–786.8848, e.g., bar idiophones 786.843, performances on bar idiophones 786.843078

.85   *Plucked idiophones

> Elastic bars or rods, usually of metal, fixed at one end and vibrated by plucking the free end

> Including sanzas (thumb pianos)

*Add as instructed under 784–788

.86   *Friction idiophones

      Objects rubbed to produce sounds of definite pitch

.862–.868   Sonorous solids of specific shapes

      Add to base number 786.86 the numbers following 786.884 in 786.8842–786.8848, e.g., vessels 786.866, rehearsing on vessels 786.866144

.87   *Concussion idiophones

      Two or more similar sonorous objects struck together to make both vibrate

.872–.878   Sonorous objects of specific shapes

      Add to base number 786.87 the numbers following 786.884 in 786.8842–786.8848, e.g., blocks 786.873, rehearsing playing of blocks 786.873144

.88   *Single idiophones

      Idiophones consisting of a single sonorous object

      Class here comprehensive works on percussion instruments of indefinite pitch

      For a specific percussion instrument of indefinite pitch not provided for here, see the instrument, e.g., cymbals 786.873

.884   *Percussed idiophones

.884 2   *Sticks and rods

      Including triangles

      Subdivisions are added for either or both topics in heading

.884 3   *Bars, plates, blocks

      Including anvils, gongs

      Subdivisions are added for any or all topics in heading

.884 4   *Troughs

.884 5   *Tubes

.884 6   *Vessels

      For bells, see 786.8848

.884 8   *Bells

.884 85   *Hand bells

.885   *Rattled idiophones

      Including maracas, sistrums

*Add as instructed under 784–788

.886   *Scraped idiophones

> Idiophones consisting of two objects, a notched one being scraped by the other to create vibrations in one or the other

> Including football rattles, washboards

.887   *Plucked idiophones

> Including jew's harps

.888   *Friction idiophones

> Including musical saws

.9   ***Drums and devices used for percussive effects**

> Subdivisions are added for drums and devices used for percussive effects together, for drums alone

---

>   786.92–786.98 Drums (Membranophones, Vibrating stretched membranes)

> Class comprehensive works in 786.9

.92   *Struck drums

> *For kettle-shaped drums, see 786.93; for tubular drums, see 786.94; for frame-shaped drums, see 786.95*

.93   *Kettle-shaped drums

> Including timpani (kettledrums), nakers (naqara), tabla

.94   *Tubular drums

> Including snare drums (side drums)

.95   *Frame-shaped drums

> Drums with depth of body not exceeding radius of membrane

> Including bass drums, tambourines

.96   *Rattle drums

> Drums whose membrane or membranes are struck by pellets or pendants

.97   *Plucked drums

> Drums each with a string that when plucked transmits a vibration to the membrane through which the string passes

.98   *Friction drums

> Drums whose membrane is made to vibrate by being rubbed either directly or by an attached stick or cord

> Including quicas, rommelpots

*Add as instructed under 784 788

.99   *Devices used for percussion effects

             Including motor horns, popguns, sirens, whips

787   *Stringed instruments (Chordophones)

Class here bowed string instruments, music for unspecified melody instrument, comprehensive works on the lute family (instruments whose strings run from the resonating belly to the neck)

Class keyboard stringed instruments in 786; class mechanical stringed instruments in 786.67

See Manual at 784–788

.2   *Violins

Class here comprehensive works on violin family

For violas, see 787.3; for cellos, see 787.4; for double basses, see 787.5

.3   *Violas

.4   *Cellos (Violoncellos)

.5   *Double basses

.6   *Viols and related instruments

Subdivisions are added for viols and related instruments together, for viols alone

For double basses, see 787.5

.62   *Descant viols

.63   *Treble viols

.64   *Tenor viols

.65   *Bass viols (Viola da gambas)

.66   *Viola d'amores

.69   *Hurdy-gurdies (Vielles)

.7   *Plectral instruments

Class here zithers, comprehensive works on struck stringed instruments

For plectral lute family, see 787.8; for harps and musical bows, see 787.9

>   787.72–787.75 Zithers

Class comprehensive works in 787.7

.72   *Stick, tube, trough zithers

Subdivisions are added for any or all topics in heading

*Add as instructed under 784–788

.73   *Frame, ground, harp, raft zithers

> Subdivisions are added for any or all topics in heading

.74   *Board zithers

> Including cimbaloms, dulcimers, santirs, yang ch'ins

> Class here struck board zithers

> *For plucked board zithers, see 787.75*

.75   *Plucked board zithers

> Including Appalachian dulcimers, autoharps, concert zithers, psalteries, Tyrolean zithers

.78   *Lyres

.8   *Plectral lute family

> Class here long-necked, short-necked lutes

.82   *Round-backed lute family

> Including sitars, tamburas

> *For lutes, see 787.83; for mandolins, see 787.84*

.83   *Lutes

.84   *Mandolins

.85   *Flat-backed lute family

> Including biwas, citterns, shamisens

> *For vihuelas, see 787.86; for guitars, see 787.87; for banjos, see 787.88; for ukuleles, see 787.89*

.86   *Vihuelas

.87   *Guitars

.875   *Balalaikas

.88   *Banjos

.89   *Ukuleles

.9   *Harps and musical bows

> Subdivisions are added for harps and musical bows together, for harps alone

.92   *Musical bows

> Stringed instruments each with one or more strings stretched across a single flexible string bearer

> Class pluriarcs in 787.93

> *See also 787.19 for the bow of bowed instruments*

---

*Add as instructed under 784 788

.93   *Pluriarcs (Compound musical bows)

> Stringed instruments with strings stretched across several string bearers

---

> 787.94–787.98 Harps

Class comprehensive works in 787.9

.94   *Bow harps (Arched harps) and angle harps

> Harps with neck forming an arch with the resonator

> Subdivisions are added for either or both topics in heading

.95   *Frame harps

> Harps with pillar joining end of neck to resonator

> Including Celtic harps, orchestral harps

.98   *Bridge harps (Harp-lutes)

> Lute-bodied harps with strings that are perpendicular to body of the harp and that pass through a bridge

> Including koras

788   *Wind instruments (Aerophones)

Class keyboard wind instruments in 786.5; class mechanical wind instruments in 786.68

See Manual at 784–788

.2   *Woodwind instruments and free aerophones

Subdivisions are added for woodwind instruments and free aerophones together, for woodwind instruments alone

For specific woodwind instruments, see 788.3–788.8

.29   *Free aerophones

> Aerophones in which the airstream is not directed into or through a cavity or tube but directly into the outer air, or the air remains static and the instrument when moved vibrates through friction with the air

> Including bull-roarers

> Class free aerophones used for percussion effects in 786.99

> ## 788.3–788.8 Specific woodwind instruments

Class comprehensive works in 788.2

.3   *Flute family

> Including nose flutes

*Add as instructed under 784–788

.32	*Transverse flutes (Side-blown flutes)

Variant name: flutes

For piccolos and fifes, see 788.33; for bass flutes, see 788.34

.33	*Piccolos and fifes

Subdivisions are added for either or both topics in heading

.34	*Bass flutes
.35	*Duct, end-blown, notched flutes

Including flageolets, penny whistles, shakuhachis

Subdivisions are added for any or all topics in heading

For recorders, see 788.36

.36	*Recorders
.363	*Sopranino recorders
.364	*Descant recorders (Soprano recorders)
.365	*Treble recorders (Alto recorders)
.366	*Tenor recorders
.367	*Bass recorders
.37	*Multiple flutes

Several flutes formed into one instrument

Class here pan pipes

.38	*Vessel flutes

Including ocarinas

.4	***Reed instruments**

For double-reed instruments, see 788.5; for single-reed instruments, see 788.6; for free reeds, see 788.8

.49	*Bagpipes

Including cornemuses; Northumbrian, uillean (union) pipes

Class here single-reed and double-reed bagpipes

.5	***Double-reed instruments**

Including crumhorns, racketts

For bagpipes, see 788.49

.52	*Oboes
.53	*Cors anglais (English horns)

*Add as instructed under 784–788

.58	*Bassoons

> *For double bassoons, see 788.59*

.59	*Double bassoons (Contrabassoons)

.6   *Single-reed instruments

> *For bagpipes, see 788.49; for saxophones, see 788.7*

.62	*Clarinets

> *For bass clarinets, see 788.65*

.65	*Bass clarinets

.7   *Saxophones

.72	*Soprano saxophones
.73	*Alto saxophones
.74	*Tenor saxophones
.75	*Bass saxophones

.8   *Free reeds

Instruments consisting of sets of individual free reeds

.82	*Mouth organs

Including shengs

Class here harmonicas

.84	*Concertinas

Including bandoneons

.86	*Accordions
.863	*Button accordions

Class here melodeons

.865	*Piano accordions

.9   *Brass instruments (Lip-reed instruments)

.92	*Trumpets
.93	*Trombones
.94	*French horns (Horns)

> *See also 788.53 for English horns*

.95	*Bugles
.96	*Cornets
.97	*Flugelhorns (Saxhorns)

Add as instructed under 784–788

.974   *Tenor horns

Including B-flat horns (also called baritones in United Kingdom and Germany), E-flat horns (also called alto horns in North America and France)

.975   *Euphoniums and baritones (American)

Subdivisions are added for either or both topics in heading

.98   *Tubas

.99   *Other brass instruments

Including cornetts, ophicleides, serpents

(789)   Composers and traditions of music

(Optional number and subdivisions; prefer 780 for music as a whole; prefer 781–788 for principles, forms, ensembles, voices, instruments)

(Option A: Arrange treatises about all composers at 789 plus an alphabeting mark; then to the result add further as follows:
01–09   Music as a whole
            Add the numbers following 78 in 780.1–780.9, e.g., manuscripts 0262
1–8   Principles, forms, ensembles, voices, instruments
            Add the numbers following 78 in 781–788, e.g., vocal music 2

(Option B: Use 789 and its subdivisions for traditions of music

(Option C: Use 789 and its subdivisions for recordings of music

(If option A is used with either option B or C, class comprehensive works on traditions of music in 789.1)

Unless other instructions are given, class a subject with aspects in two or more subdivisions of 789 in the number coming last, e.g., Spanish folk music for springtime 789.261015242 (*not* 789.2015242)

(.1)   †General principles of traditions of music

Add to base number 789.1 the numbers following 781 in 781.1–781.5, e.g., treatment of springtime music in various traditions 789.15242

(If Option A is used with either Option B or C, class here comprehensive works on traditions of music)

(.2)   †Folk music

Music originating within and associated with an ethnic or national group

Class folk rock in 789.6172. Class a specific style of music provided for in 789.4–789.6 with the style, e.g., reggae 789.46, Afro-Cuban jazz 789.572687291

*Add as instructed under 784–788
†(Optional number; prefer 781–788)

(.200 1–.200 7)	†Standard subdivisions

Notation from Table 1 as modified under 780.1–780.9, e.g., performances of folk music 789.20078

(.200 8)	†Groups of people
[.200 89]	Specific ethnic and national groups

Do not use; class in 789.21–789.29

(.200 9)	†History, geographic treatment, biography
(.200 901–.200 903)	†Historical periods to 1900

Add to base number 789.20090 the numbers following 780.90 in 780.901–780.903, e.g., folk music of the Renaissance 789.2009031

(.200 904–.200 905)	†1900–2099

Add to base number 789.20090 the numbers following —090 in notation 0904–0905 from Table 1, e.g., folk music of the 1970s 781.62009047

(.200 91–.200 99)	†Geographic treatment and biography

For geographic treatment of folk music of specific ethnic and national groups, see 789.21–789.29

(.201)	†General principles, influence of other traditions, musical forms
(.201 1–.201 5)	†General principles

Add to base number 789.201 the numbers following 781 in 781.1–781.5, e.g., folk music for springtime 789.2015242, rhythm in folk music for springtime 789.20152421224

(.201 6)	†Influence of other traditions of music

Add to base number 789.2016 the numbers following 789 in 789.3–789.9, e.g., influence of jazz on folk music 789.20165, performances of folk music influenced by jazz 789.20165078

(.201 8)	†Musical forms

Add to base number 789.2018 the numbers following 784.18 in 784.182–784.189, e.g., march form in folk music 789.201897

(.202–.208)	†Voices, instruments, ensembles

Add to base number 789.20 the numbers following 78 in 782–788, e.g., folk songs for women singers 789.202642

†(Optional number; prefer 781–788)

(.21–.29)   †Folk music of specific ethnic and national groups

> Add to base number 789.2 notation 1–9 from Table 5, e.g., Spanish folk music 789.261; then add further as follows:

001–008   Standard subdivisions

> Notation from Table 1 as modified under 780.1–780.9, e.g., performances of Spanish folk music 789.2610078

009   History, geographic treatment, biography

00901–00903   Historical periods to 1900

> Add to base number 0090 the numbers following 780.90 in 780.901–780.903, e.g., Spanish folk music of the Renaissance 789.261009031

00904–00905   1900–2099

> Add to base number 0090 the numbers following —090 in notation 0904–0905 from Table 1, e.g., Spanish folk music of the 1970s 789.261009047

[0093–0099]   Specific continents, countries, localities

> Do not use; class in 03–09

01   General principles, influence of other traditions of music, musical forms

011–015   General principles

> Add to 01 the numbers following 781 in 781.1–781.5, e.g., Spanish folk music for springtime 789.261015242, rhythm in Spanish folk music for springtime 789.2610152421224

016   Influence of other traditions of music

> Add to 016 the numbers following 789 in 789.3–789.9, e.g., influence of jazz on Spanish folk music 789.2610165, performances of Spanish folk music influenced by jazz 789.2610165078

018   Musical forms

> Add to 018 the numbers following 784.18 in 784.182–784.189, e.g., march form in Spanish folk music 789.26101897

02   Voices, instruments, ensembles

> Add to 02 the numbers following 78 in 782–788, e.g., Spanish folk music for the guitar 789.26102787

03–09   Specific continents, countries, localities

> Add to 0 notation 3–9 from Table 2, e.g., Spanish folk music in New York City 789.26107471

---

†(Optional number; prefer 781 788)

> **(789.3–789.9) Other traditions of music**

Add to each subdivision identified by * as follows:

001–008   Standard subdivisions
       Notation from Table 1 as modified under 780.1–780.8, e.g., performance 0078

009   History, geographic treatment, biography

00901–00903   Historical periods to 1900
       Add to base number 0090 the numbers following 780.90 in 780.901–780.903, e.g., music of the Renaissance 009031

00904–00905   1900–2099
       Add to base number 0090 the numbers following —090 in notation 0904–0905 from Table 1, e.g., music of the 1970s 009047

01   General principles, influence of other traditions of music, hybrid styles, musical forms

011–015   General principles
       Add to 01 the numbers following 781 in 781.1–781.5, e.g., springtime music 015242, melody in springtime music 015242124

016   Influence of other traditions of music
       Add to 016 the numbers following 789 in 789.2–789.9, e.g., influence of folk music 0162, performances of music influenced by folk music 0162078
       See also 017 for hybrid styles

017   Hybrid styles
       Fusion of two or more styles from different traditions of music to create a new style
       Add to 017 the numbers following 789 in 789.2–789.9, e.g., fusion with folk music 0172, folk rock 789.60172
       See also 016 for influence of other traditions of music

018   Musical forms
       Add to 018 the numbers following 784.18 in 784.182–784.189, e.g., march form 01897

1   Voices, instruments, ensembles
       Add to 1 the numbers following 78 in 782–788, e.g., guitar music 1787

Class comprehensive works in 789

(.3)   †*Popular music**

Class popular music originating within and associated with an ethnic or national group in 789.2

For western popular music, see 789.4

(.4)   †*Western popular music**

Class western popular music originating within and associated with an ethnic or national group in 789.2; class country music in 789.42

For jazz, see 789.5; for rock, see 789.6

---

*Add as instructed under 789.3–789.9
†(Optional number; prefer 781–788)

(.42)	†*Country music

           Class here bluegrass music; specific country music styles

(.43)	†*Blues

           Class here traditional rhythm and blues; specific blues styles

           Comprehensive works on rhythm and blues relocated to 789.44

(.44)	†*Soul

           Class here comprehensive works on rhythm and blues [*formerly* 789.43], R&B; specific soul styles

           For traditional rhythm and blues, see 789.43

(.45)	†*Ragtime
(.46)	†*Reggae

           Class here specific reggae styles

(.48)	†*Electronica

           Class here specific electronica styles

(.49)	†*Rap

           Class here specific rap styles

(.5)	**†*Jazz**
[.501 7]	Hybrid styles

           Do not use; class in 789.57

(.52)	†*Early jazz

           Class here origins of jazz

(.53)	†*Traditional jazz

           Including New Orleans, Dixieland, Southwest and Kansas City, Harlem, white New York styles; Chicago breakdown

(.54)	†*Mainstream jazz

           Including swing

(.55)	†*Modern jazz

           Including bop (bebop), hard bop, cool jazz, progressive jazz

           For avant-garde jazz, see 789.56

(.56)	†*Avant-garde jazz

*Add as instructed under 789.3–789.9
†(Optional number; prefer 781–788)

(.57)	†Hybrid styles

Add to 789.57 the numbers following 781.6 in 781.62–781.69, e.g., Afro-Cuban 789.572687291, Indo-jazz 789.57291411

Third stream relocated to 789.80175

(.6)   †*Rock (Rock'n' roll)

Class here specific rock styles

(.7)   †Sacred music

(.700 1–.700 9)	†Standard subdivisions

Notation from Table 1 as modified under 780.1–780.9, e.g., performances of sacred music 789.70078

(.701)	†General principles, influence of other traditions of music, musical forms

Add to base number 789.701 the numbers following 01 in notation 011–018 from table under 789.3–789.9, e.g., influence of folk music 789.70162

(.702)	†Voices, instruments, ensembles

Add to base number 789.702 the numbers following 78 in 782–788, e.g., sacred music for the guitar 789.702787

(.71)	†*Christian sacred music

For music of Christian church year, see 789.72

(.72)	†*Music of Christian church year

(.722–.729)	†Sacred music of specific parts of Christian church year

Add to base number 789.72 the numbers following 781.72 in 781.722–781.729, e.g., Christmas music 789.723; then add further as instructed under 789.3–789.9, e.g., Christmas music for the guitar 789.7231787

(.73)	†*Sacred music of classical (Greek and Roman) and Germanic religions

(.74–.79)	†Sacred music of other specific religions

Add to base number 789.7 the numbers following 29 in 294–299, e.g., Jewish sacred music 789.76; then add further as instructed under 789.3–789.9, e.g., Jewish sacred music for the guitar 789.761787

(.8)   †*Western art music (Classical music)

Limited to classical music as a tradition in contrast to other traditions

Class here comprehensive works on traditions of art music

For nonwestern art music, see 789.9

---

*Add as instructed under 789.3–789.9
†(Optional number; prefer 781–788)

(.801 75)	†Hybrid styles

> Number built according to instructions under 789.3–789.9
>
> Class here third stream [*formerly* 789.57]

(.9)   †*Nonwestern art music

790   Recreational and performing arts

Class here government policy on recreation; interdisciplinary works on recreation

For sociology of recreation, see 306.48; for music, see 780

SUMMARY

*Add as instructed under 789.3–789.9
†(Optional number; prefer 781–788)

794		**Indoor games of skill**
	.1	**Chess**
	.2	**Checkers (Draughts)**
	.3	**Darts**
	.4	**Go**
	.6	**Bowling**
	.7	**Ball games**
	.8	**Electronic games**
795		**Games of chance**
	.01	**Philosophy and theory**
	.1	**Games with dice**
	.2	**Wheel and top games**
	.3	**Games dependent on drawing numbers or counters**
	.4	**Card games**
796		**Athletic and outdoor sports and games**
	.01–.09	**Standard subdivisions and general kinds of sports and games**
	.1	**Miscellaneous games**
	.2	**Activities and games requiring equipment**
	.3	**Ball games**
	.4	**Weight lifting, track and field, gymnastics**
	.5	**Outdoor life**
	.6	**Cycling and related activities**
	.7	**Driving motor vehicles**
	.8	**Combat sports**
	.9	**Ice and snow sports**
797		**Aquatic and air sports**
	.028 9	**Safety measures**
	.1	**Boating**
	.2	**Swimming and diving**
	.3	**Other aquatic sports**
	.5	**Air sports**
798		**Equestrian sports and animal racing**
	.2	**Horsemanship**
	.4	**Horse racing**
	.6	**Driving and coaching**
	.8	**Dog racing**
799		**Fishing, hunting, shooting**
	.1	**Fishing**
	.2	**Hunting**
	.3	**Shooting other than game**

.01–.05   Standard subdivisions of recreation

.06   Organizations and management of recreation; recreation centers

         Notation 06 from Table 1 as modified below

.068   Recreation centers

         Do not use for management of recreation; class in 790.069

         Indoor and outdoor

         Including parks and community centers as recreation centers

         Add to base number 790.068 notation 1–9 from Table 2, e.g., recreation centers of California 790.068794

.069   Management of recreation

> Add to base number 790.069 the numbers following —068 in notation 0681–0688 from Table 1, e.g., personnel management 790.0693

.07   Education, research, related topics of recreation

.08   Recreation for groups of people

> Do not use for activities and programs for specific classes of people; class in 790.19

.09   History, geographic treatment, biography of recreation

.1   **General kinds of recreational activities**

> Class here leisure

>> *For a specific activity, see the activity, e.g., paper cutting and folding 736.98, piano playing 786.2143, outdoor sports 796*

[.101–.109]   Standard subdivisions

> Do not use; class in 790.01–790.09

.13   Activities generally engaged in by individuals

> Class here interdisciplinary works on hobbies

>> *For a hobby, see the subject of the hobby, plus notation 023 from Table 1, e.g., knitting as a hobby 746.432023*

.132   Collecting

> Class collecting a specific kind of object with the object, plus notation 075 from Table 1, e.g., coin collecting 737.4075, sports cards 796.075

.133   Play with toys

> Including electric trains

>> *For play with a specific toy not provided for here, see the toy, e.g., flying model airplanes 796.154*

.134   Participation in contests

>> *See also 659.17 for advertising by means of contests*

.138   Passive activities (Spectator activities)

> Including listening, reading, watching

.15   Activities generally engaged in by groups

.18   Travel and tourism

> Standard subdivisions are added for either or both topics in heading

.19   Activities and programs for specific groups of people

> Class activities generally engaged in by individuals in 790.13; class activities generally engaged in by groups other than families in 790.15

.191   Activities and programs for families

.192	Activities and programs by age level

Class activities for specific sexes regardless of age in 790.194; class activities for people with physical illnesses, people with disabilities regardless of age in 790.196

.192 2	Children

.192 6	Adults aged 65 and over

.194	Activities and programs for groups by sex

Class activities for people with physical illnesses, people with disabilities regardless of sex in 790.196

.196	Activities and programs for people with physical illnesses, people with disabilities

See also 615.85153 for recreational therapy

.2   The performing arts in general

Use for works that treat athletic and outdoor sports and games as well as public performances

Class comprehensive works on public performances in 791; class comprehensive works on athletic and outdoor sports and games in 796

For sociology of performing arts, see 306.484. For a specific performing art, see the art, e.g., symphony orchestra performances 784.2078, motion pictures 791.43; for a specific sport, see the sport, e.g., basketball 796.323, swimming 797.21

See Manual at 780.079 vs. 790.2

791   Public performances

Other than sport and game performances

Class here performances at fairs

For musical performances other than stage presentations, see 780; for stage presentations, see 792; for musical stage presentations, see 792.5; for magic, see 793.8; for speech as a type of performance, see 808.54

See also 793–796 for sport and game performances

SUMMARY

791.01–.09	Standard subdivisions and amusement parks
.1	**Traveling shows**
.3	**Circuses**
.4	**Motion pictures, radio, television**
.5	**Puppetry and toy theaters**
.6	**Pageantry**
.8	**Animal performances**

.06	Organizations and management; amusement parks

Notation 06 from Table 1 as modified below

.068   Amusement parks

Do not use for management; class in 791.069

Add to base number 791.068 notation 1–9 from Table 2, e.g., amusement parks of United States 791.06873

.069   Management

Add to base number 791.069 the numbers following —068 in notation 0681–0688 from Table 1, e.g., marketing 791.0698

.09   History, geographic treatment, biography

.092   Biography

See Manual at 780.92 and 791.092

.1   **Traveling shows**

Including medicine shows

For circuses, see 791.3; for showboats, see 792.022

.12   Minstrel shows and skits

See also 792.7 for vaudeville

.3   **Circuses**

Class here amateur circuses

.32   Animal performances

.33   Clowns

.34   Acrobatics and trapeze work

.35   Freaks and sideshows

.38   Parades

.4   **Motion pictures, radio, television**

Unless other instructions are given, class a subject with aspects in two or more subdivisions of 791.4 in the number coming last, e.g., critical appraisal of a specific film 791.4372 (*not* 791.433)

See also 302.234 for social aspects of motion pictures, radio, and television as mass media

See Manual at 363.31 vs. 303.376, 791.4; also at 384.54, 384.55, 384.8 vs. 791.4

.43   **Motion pictures**

Regardless of distribution medium or method

Class here made-for-television movies, video recordings of motion pictures [*both formerly* 791.45]; direct-to-video and direct-to-DVD releases of motion pictures; dramatic films, entertainment films; films developed originally for Internet transmission; comprehensive works on dramatic, entertainment, documentary, educational, news films

Class photographic aspects of motion pictures in 777

For documentary, educational, news films, see 070.18

See also 384.8 for communication aspects of motion pictures

See Manual at 780.92 and 791.092; also at 791.43 vs. 791.45; also at 791.43, 791.45 vs. 777

.430 1–.430 8   Standard subdivisions

Notation from Table 1 as modified under 792.01–792.02, e.g., makeup for motion pictures 791.43027; however, for programming (scheduling), see 384.84; for types of presentation, see 791.433

.430 9   History, geographic treatment, biography

Class here description, critical appraisal of specific companies and studios

For description, critical appraisal of specific films, see 791.437

.430 92   Biography

Do not use for people associated with only one aspect of motion pictures; class in 791.4302 e.g., actors 791.43028092

.433   **Types of presentation**

Including home and amateur films

Class a specific genre or type of film with a specific type of presentation in 791.436; class specific films in 791.437

.433 4   Animated films

Including cartoon films, computer animated films, puppet films

Class comprehensive works on puppetry in 791.53

For animation of cartoon films, see 741.58; for time-lapse cinematography, see 776.6; for photographic techniques of cartoon films, see 777.7

.433 402 85   Computer applications

Do not use for computer animated films; class in 791.4334

.436   **Special aspects of films**

Class here film adaptations, film genres

.436 1	Films displaying specific qualities

Add to base number 791.4361 the numbers following —1 in notation 11–17 from Table 3C, e.g., comedies 791.43617

.436 2–.436 9	Films dealing with specific themes and subjects

Add to base number 791.436 the numbers following —3 in notation 32–39 from Table 3C, e.g., films of the West and westerns 791.4365878

.437	Films

Class here screenplays

Class texts of plays in 800. Class subject-oriented films themselves with the subject, e.g., films on flower gardening 635.9

See Manual at 791.437 and 791.447, 791.457, 792.9; also at 808.82 vs. 791.437, 791.447, 791.457, 792.9

.437 2	Single films

Arrange alphabetically by title of film

.437 5	Two or more films

Class here collections of film reviews

Class works which focus on a specific aspect of films with the aspect in 791.436, e.g., westerns 791.4365878; class critical appraisal of films associated with a specific person with the person, e.g., films of a motion-picture photographer 777.092, of a director 791.430233092

.44	Radio

Regardless of distribution medium or method

Class here dramatic programs, entertainment programs; radio programs developed originally for Internet transmission; comprehensive works on dramatic, entertainment, documentary, educational, news programs

For documentary, educational, news programs, see 070.194

See also 384.54 for communication aspects of radio

See Manual at 780.92 and 791.092

.440 1–.440 8	Standard subdivisions

Notation from Table 1 as modified under 792.01–792.02, e.g., value of radio 791.44013; however, for programming (scheduling), see 384.5442; for types of presentation, see 791.443

.440 9	History, geographic treatment, biography

Class here description, critical appraisal of specific companies and stations

For description, critical appraisal of specific programs, see 791.447

.440 92   Biography

> Do not use for people associated with only one aspect of radio; class in 791.4402 e.g., actors 791.44028092

.443   Types of presentation

> Including commercials, live or recorded programs, network programs

> Class a specific genre or type of program with a specific type of presentation in 791.446; class specific programs in 791.447

.446   Special aspects of radio programs

> Class here radio adaptations, radio genres, types of programs

.446 1   Programs displaying specific qualities

> Add to base number 791.4461 the numbers following —1 in notation 11–17 from Table 3C, e.g., comedies 791.44617

.446 2–.446 9   Programs dealing with specific themes and subjects

> Add to base number 791.446 the numbers following —3 in notation 32–39 from Table 3C, e.g., programs of the West and westerns 791.4465878

.447   Radio programs

> Class here radio plays

> Class texts of plays in 800. Class subject-oriented programs themselves with the subject, e.g., programs on flower gardening 635.9

> *See Manual at 791.437 and 791.447, 791.457, 792.9; also at 808.82 vs. 791.437, 791.447, 791.457, 792.9*

.447 2   Single programs

> Arrange alphabetically by name of program

.447 5   Two or more programs

> Class here collections of program reviews

> Class works which focus on a specific aspect of programs with the aspect in 791.446, e.g., westerns 791.4465878; class critical appraisal of programs associated with a specific person with the person, e.g., programs of a director 791 440233092

.45	Television

Regardless of distribution medium or method

Class here dramatic programs, entertainment programs; mini-series, extended pilots of television series; television-like programs developed originally for Internet transmission; comprehensive works on dramatic, entertainment, documentary, educational, news programs

Class use of video recordings not provided for here with the use, e.g., video recordings of rock music 781.66

> *For documentary, educational, news programs, see 070.195*

> *See also 384.55 for communication aspects of television; also 791.43 for direct-to-video and direct-to-DVD releases of motion pictures*

> *See Manual at 780.92 and 791.092; also at 791.43 vs. 791.45; also at 791.43, 791.45 vs. 777*

Made-for-television movies, video recordings of motion pictures relocated to 791.43

.450 1–.450 8	Standard subdivisions

> Notation from Table 1 as modified under 792.01–792.02, e.g., scenery and lighting for television 791.45025; however, for programming (scheduling), see 384.5531; for types of presentation, see 791.453

.450 9	History, geographic treatment, biography

Class here description, critical appraisal of specific companies, stations, networks

> *For description, critical appraisal of specific programs, see 791.457*

.450 92	Biography

Do not use for people associated with only one aspect of television; class in 791.4502 e.g., actors 791.45028092

.453	Types of presentation

Including commercials, live or recorded programs, network programs

Class a specific genre or type of program with a specific type of presentation in 791.456; class specific programs in 791.457

.456	Special aspects of television programs

Class here television adaptations, television genres, types of programs

.456 1	Programs displaying specific qualities

Add to base number 791.4561 the numbers following —1 in notation 11–17 from Table 3C, e.g., comedies 791.45617

.456 2–.456 9	Programs dealing with specific themes and subjects

Add to base number 791.456 the numbers following —3 in notation 32–39 from Table 3C, e.g., programs of the West and westerns 791.4565878

.457   Programs

> Class here television plays

> Class texts of plays in 800. Class subject-oriented programs themselves with the subject, e.g., programs on flower gardening 635.9

>> *See Manual at 791.437 and 791.447, 791.457, 792.9; also at 808.82 vs. 791.437, 791.447, 791.457, 792.9*

.457 2   Single programs

> Arrange alphabetically by name of program

.457 5   Two or more programs

> Class here collections of program reviews

> Class works which focus on a specific aspect of programs with the aspect in 791.456, e.g., westerns 791.456278; class critical appraisal of programs associated with a specific person with the person, e.g., programs of a television photographer 777.092, of a director 791.450233092

.5   **Puppetry and toy theaters**

.53   Puppetry

> Class here marionettes, shadow puppets

> Class puppet films in 791.4334

.538   Production scripts of puppet plays

> Class texts of plays in 800

.6   **Pageantry**

> Including parades, floats for parades

> Class interdisplinary works on pageants, processions, parades in 394.5

>> *For circus parades, see 791.38; for water pageantry, see 797.203*

>> *See also 794.17 for living chess*

.62   Pageants

>> *See also 791.66 for beauty pageants*

.622   Religious pageants

.624   Historical and patriotic pageants

.64   Cheerleading

> Add to base number 791.64 the numbers following 796.3 in 796.31–796.35, e.g., cheerleading at American football games 791.6432

.66   Beauty contests

> Class here beauty pageants

.8　　　**Animal performances**

Including cockfighting

For circus animal performances, see 791.32; for equestrian sports and animal racing, see 798

.82　　　Bullfighting

.84　　　Rodeos

Class here Wild West shows

792　　Stage presentations

Class here dramatic presentation, theater

Class texts of plays in 800

For motion pictures, radio, television, see 791.4; for puppetry and toy theaters, see 791.5

See Manual at 780.92 and 791.092

SUMMARY

792.01–.09	**Standard subdivisions and types of stage presentation**
.1	**Tragedy and serious drama**
.2	**Comedy and melodrama**
.3	**Pantomime**
.5	**Opera**
.6	**Musical plays**
.7	**Variety shows and theatrical dancing**
.8	**Ballet and modern dance**
.9	**Stage productions**

.01　　　Philosophy and theory

Notation 01 from Table 1 as modified below

Do not use for value; class in 792.013

.013　　　Value, influence, effect

Class influence and effect on a specific subject with the subject, e.g., influence and effect on crime 364.254

.015　　　Criticism and appreciation

Do not use for scientific principles; class in 792.01

Standard subdivisions are added for either or both topics in heading

.02　　　Techniques, procedures, apparatus, equipment, materials, miscellany

Do not use for miscellany; class in 792.029

>   792.022–792.028   Specific techniques, procedures, apparatus, equipment, materials

Use notation 01–09 (*except* —028 for apparatus, equipment, materials) from Table 1 under each subdivision identified by *, e.g., periodicals on amateur theater 792.022205, computer applications for special effects 792.0240285

Class comprehensive works in 792.02

.022	*Types of stage presentation

Including showboats, street theater, tent shows

.022 2	*Amateur theater
.022 3	*Little theater
.022 4	*Summer theater
.022 6	*Children's theater
.022 8	*Arena theater (Theater-in-the-round)
.023	*Supervision
.023 2	*Production
.023 3	*Direction
.023 6	*Programming
.024	*Special effects

Including sound effects, visual effects

.025	*Setting

Including lighting, scenery

.026	*Costuming
.027	*Makeup and hair

Standard subdivisions are added for makeup and hair together, for makeup alone

Including wigs

.028	*Acting and performance

Including impersonation, improvisation, use of expression and gestures

.029	Miscellany

Do not use for commercial miscellany; class in 792.0299

.029 07	Humorous treatment
.029 08	Audiovisual treatment

*Add as instructed under 792.022–792.028

.029 1–.029 8		Miscellaneous works

Add to base number 792.029 the numbers following —02 in notation 021–028 from Table 1, e.g., stage as a profession 792.0293; however, for specific techniques, procedures, apparatus, equipment, materials, see 792.022–792.028

.029 9   Commercial miscellany

Including price lists, prospectuses, trade catalogs

.09   History, geographic treatment, biography

Class here description, critical appraisal of specific theaters and companies

For specific productions in specific theaters or by specific companies, see 792.9

.092   Biography

Do not use for people associated with only one aspect of stage presentations; class in 792.02 e.g., actors 792.028092

> ### 792.1–792.8 Specific kinds of performances

Add to each subdivision identified by † the numbers following 792 in 792.01–792.09, e.g., costuming for ballet 792.8026

Class comprehensive works in 792

.1   **†Tragedy and serious drama**

.12   †Tragedy

.14   †Historical drama

.16   †Religious and morality plays

Including miracle, mystery, passion plays

See also 792.09 for treatment of religious concepts in the theater; also 792.27 for modern mystery plays

.2   **†Comedy and melodrama**

.23   †Comedy

For panto, see 792.38; for stand-up comedy, see 792.76

.27   †Melodrama

Including modern mystery (suspense) drama

See also 792.16 for religious mystery-plays

.3   **†Pantomime**

Class here mime, silent pantomime

---

†Add as instructed under 792.1–792.8

.38　　†Panto

> Pantomime in the nonsilent British tradition, usually performed around Christmas time

.5　†**Opera**

> Class here dramatic vocal forms
>
> Class interdisciplinary works on dramatic vocal forms, on opera in 782.1
>
> *For musical plays, see 792.6; for variety shows, see 792.7*
>
> *See Manual at 782.1 vs. 792.5, 792.6*

.509　　History, geographic treatment, biography

> Class here description, critical appraisal of specific theaters and companies
>
> *For specific productions in specific theaters or by specific companies, see 792.54*

.54　　Opera productions

> Class here production and stage guides

.542　　Single operas

> Arrange alphabetically by title

.545　　Two or more operas

> Class here collections of reviews
>
> Class critical appraisal of operas associated with a specific person other than the composer or librettist with the person, e.g., operas associated with a singer 782.1092, with a director 792.50233092

.6　†**Musical plays**

> Class here ballad operas, musicals, revues
>
> Class interdisciplinary works on musical plays in 782.14
>
> *See Manual at 782.1 vs. 792.5, 792.6*

.609　　History, geographic treatment, biography

> Class here description, critical appraisal of specific theaters and companies
>
> *For specific productions in specific theaters or by specific companies, see 792.64*

.62　　Dancing

> Including choreography
>
> Class comprehensive works on theatrical dancing in 792.78; class comprehensive works on choreography in 792.82

†Add as instructed under 792.1–792.8

.64		Musical play productions

Class here production and stage guides

.642   Single musical plays

Arrange alphabetically by name

.645   Two or more musical plays

Class here collections of reviews

Class critical appraisal of musical plays associated with a specific person other than the composer or librettist with the person, e.g., musical plays associated with a singer 782.14092, with a director 792.60233092

.7 †Variety shows and theatrical dancing

Class here burlesque, cabaret, vaudeville, music hall and nightclub presentations

Subdivisions are added for variety shows and theatrical dancing together, for variety shows alone

Class stage productions in 792.9

> *For magic shows, see 793.8; for juggling, see 793.87; for ventriloquism, see 793.89*

> *See also 791.12 for minstrel shows and skits*

.76   †Stand-up comedy

.78   †Theatrical dancing

Including tap dancing

Class stage productions in 792.9

> *For dancing in musical plays, see 792.62*

.8 †Ballet and modern dance

Class here comprehensive works on dancing

Subdivisions are added for either or both topics in heading

> *For dancing in musical plays, see 792.62; for theatrical and tap dancing, see 792.78; for social, folk, national dancing, see 793.3*

> *See Manual at 780.92 and 791.092*

.809   History, geographic treatment, biography

Class here description, critical appraisal of specific theaters and companies

> *For specific productions in specific theaters or by specific companies, see 792.84*

.809 2   Biography

Do not use for people associated with only one aspect of ballet and modern dance; class in 792.802 e.g., dancers 792.8028092

---

†Add as instructed under 792.1 792.8

.82   Choreography

> Class here choreology, e.g., Labanotation, Benesh

.84   Ballet productions

> Class here stories, plots, analyses, librettos, production scripts, stage guides

.842   Single ballets

> Arrange alphabetically by title

.845   Two or more ballets

> Class here collections of reviews

> Class critical appraisal of ballets associated with a specific person with the person, e.g., ballets associated with a director 792.80233092

.9   **Stage productions**

> Class here production scripts, stage guides; description, critical appraisal of specific productions in specific theaters and companies

> Class description, critical appraisal, production scripts of operas in 792.54; class description, critical appraisal, production scripts of musical plays in 792.64; class description, critical appraisal, production scripts of ballets in 792.84

> *See Manual at 791.437 and 791.447, 791.457, 792.9; also at 808.82 vs. 791.437, 791.447, 791.457, 792.9*

.92   Single productions

> Arrange alphabetically by title

.95   Two or more productions

> Class here collections of reviews

> Class critical appraisal of productions associated with a specific person other than the playwright with the person, e.g., productions associated with a director 792.0233092

793   **Indoor games and amusements**

> *For indoor games of skill, see 794; for games of chance, see 795*

.01   Philosophy and theory; activities and programs for specific groups of people

> Notation 01 from Table 1 as modified below

.019   Activities and programs for specific groups of people

> Do not use for psychological principles; class in 793.01

> Add to base number 793.019 the numbers following 790.19 in 790.191–790.196, e.g., indoor games and amusements for children 793.01922

.08   Groups of people

> *For activities and programs for specific groups of people, see 793.019*

.2   **Parties and entertainments**

.21	Children's parties
.22	Seasonal parties

> Class children's seasonal parties in 793.21

.24	Charades and tableaux
.3	**Social, folk, national dancing**

> Standard subdivisions are added for social, folk, national dancing together; for social dancing alone

> Including belly, jazz dancing

.31	Folk and national dancing

> Standard subdivisions are added for either or both topics in the heading

[.310 9]	History, geographic treatment, biography

> Do not use; class in 793.319

.319	History, geographic treatment, biography
.319 001–.319 009	Standard subdivisions

> Add to base number 793.31900 the numbers following —00 in notation 001–009 from Table 2, e.g., periodicals of the history of folk dancing 793.319005

.319 01–.319 05	Historical periods

> Add to base number 793.3190 the numbers following —090 in notation 0901–0905 from Table 1, e.g., folk dances of 20th century 793.31904

.319 1–.319 9	Geographic treatment, biography

> Add to base number 793.319 notation 1–9 from Table 2, e.g., folk dances of Germany 793.31943

.32	Clog dancing
.33	Ballroom dancing (Round dances)

> Including disco dancing, fox trot, jitterbug, waltz

.34	Square dancing
.35	Dances with accessory features

> Including cotillions, germans, sword dances

.36	Line dancing
.38	Balls

> Class ballroom dancing in 793.33

.4	**Games of action**
.5	**Forfeit and trick games**

.7 **Games not characterized by action**

> *For charades and tableaux, see 793.24*

.73 Puzzles and puzzle games

> Standard subdivisions are added for either or both topics in heading

> Including acrostics, quizzes, rebuses; jigsaw puzzles

> Class puzzles as formal instructional devices for the teaching of a specific subject with the subject, plus notation 07 from Table 1, e.g., puzzles teaching the use of the Bible 220.07

> *For mathematical games and recreations, see 793.74*

.732 Crossword puzzles

.734 Word games

> Including anagrams, palindromes

.735 Riddles

> Class riddles as folk literature in 398.6; class riddles as jokes by known authors, interdisciplinary works on riddles in 808.882

> *See Manual at T3A—8 + 02, T3B—802, T3B—8 + 02 vs. 398.6, 793.735*

.738 Maze puzzles

.74 Mathematical games and recreations

.8 **Magic and related activities**

> Standard subdivisions are added for magic and related activities together, for magic alone

> Including scientific recreations

> Class here conjuring

.85 Card tricks

.87 Juggling

.89 Ventriloquism

.9 **Other indoor diversions**

.92 War games (Battle games)

> *See also 355.48 for military use of war games; also 796.1 for outdoor war games*

.93 Adventure games

> Class here fantasy, mystery games, role-playing games

> *See also 793.92 for war games (battle games)*

[.930 285] Computer applications

> Do not use; class in 793.932

.932   Computer adventure games

> Class here computer fantasy, video adventure, video fantasy games
>
> Unless it is redundant, add to base number 793.932 the numbers following 00 in 004–006, e.g., programs for digital personal computers 793.932536, but use of digital computers 793.932 (*not* 793.9324)
>
> Class comprehensive works on computer games in 794.8
>
> *See Manual at 793.932 vs. 794.822*

.96   String games

> Including making cat's cradles

794   Indoor games of skill

> Class here board games
>
> Class war games in 793.92; class adventure, fantasy, mystery games in 793.93; class games combining skill and chance in 795
>
> *For backgammon, see 795.15*

.1   **Chess**

[.102 85]   Computer applications

> Do not use; class in 794.172

.12   Strategy and tactics

> Including specific strategies and tactics, e.g., combinations, sacrifices, traps, pitfalls, attack, counterattack, defense
>
> Class specific strategies and tactics applied during a specific portion of a game in 794.122–794.124; class strategy and tactics with individual chessmen in 794.14

.122   Openings

.123   Middle games

.124   End games

.14   Individual chessmen

> Including specific attributes, e.g., position, moves, power, value
>
> Class specific attributes of a specific piece in 794.142–794.147

.142   Pawns

.143   Rooks (Castles)

.144   Knights

.145   Bishops

.146   Queen

.147   King

.15   Collections of games

.152   Master matches

> Class master matches by individual players in 794.159

.157   Tournaments and championships

> Class tournaments and championships of individual players in 794.159

.159   Games, matches, tournaments, championships of individual players

.17   Special forms of chess

> Including living chess, simultaneous play

.172   Computer chess

> Unless it is redundant, add to base number 794.172 the numbers following 00 in 004–006, e.g., use of digital personal computers 794.172416, but use of digital computers 794.172 (*not* 794.1724)

.18   Variants of chess

> Including fairy chess, shogi

.2   **Checkers (Draughts)**

.3   **Darts**

.4   **Go**

.6   **Bowling**

> Class here variants of bowling, e.g., ninepins (skittles), tenpins
>
> *See also 796.315 for lawn bowling*

.7   **Ball games**

> Class athletic ball games, comprehensive works on ball games in 796.3
>
> *For bowling, see 794.6*

.72   Billiards

> Class here carom billiards
>
> *For pocket billiards, see 794.73*

.73   Pocket billiards

> Including English billiards

.733   Pool (American pocket billiards)

.735   Snooker

.75   Pinball games

.8   **Electronic games**

> Class here computer, video games
>
> Class computerized forms of a specific indoor game or amusement with the game or amusement in 793–795, plus notation 0285 from Table 1, e.g., computerized checkers 794.20285

[.802 85]   Computer applications

> Do not use; class in 794.81

.81   Computer applications

> Class here data processing

> Unless it is redundant, add to base number 794.81 the numbers following 00 in 004–006, e.g., programs for digital personal computers 794.81536, but use of digital computers as a whole 794.81 (*not* 794.814)

> Class data processing for specific genres of computer games in 794.82; class data processing for computerized athletic and outdoor sports and games in 794.86–794.89

.82   Specific genres of computer games

> Class computerized war games (battle games) in 793.920285; class computerized adventure, fantasy, mystery games in 793.932; class computerized athletic and outdoor sports and games in 794.86–794.89

.822   Arcade games

> Unless it is redundant, add to base number 794.822 the numbers following 00 in 004–006, e.g., programs for digital personal computers 794.822536, but use of digital computers 794.822 (*not* 794.8224)

> *See Manual at 793.932 vs. 794.822*

.86–.89   Computerized athletic and outdoor sports and games

> Add to base number 794.8 the numbers following 79 in 796–799, e.g., computerized baseball 794.86357

795   Games of chance

> Class here gambling

> Class gambling on a specific activity with the activity, e.g., on horse racing 798.401

> *See also 364.172 for gambling as a crime; also 616.85841 for compulsive gambling*

.01   Philosophy and theory

> Including betting systems

.015 192   Probabilities

> Class here probabilities of winning

> *See Manual at 795.015192 vs. 519.27*

.1   **Games with dice**

.12   Craps

.15   Backgammon

.2   **Wheel and top games**

.23   Roulette

.27	Slot machines
.3	**Games dependent on drawing numbers or counters**
.32	Dominoes
.34	Mah jong
.36	Bingo
.38	Lotteries

Including lotto

.4	**Card games**
.41	Games in which skill is a major element
.411	Cribbage
.412	Poker
.413	Whist and bridge whist
.414	Auction bridge
.415	Contract bridge

Class here comprehensive works on bridge

For bridge whist, see 795.413; for auction bridge, see 795.414

.415 2	Bidding
.415 3	Play of the hand
.415 4	Scoring systems
.415 8	Collections of games and matches
.416	Pinochle
.418	Rummy and its variants

Including canasta

.42	Games based chiefly on chance

Including baccarat, faro

.423	Blackjack (Twenty-one)
.43	Games in which card position is a major element

Including solitaire, patience

796   Athletic and outdoor sports and games

Standard subdivisions are added for any or all topics in heading

Including modern pentathlon

Class here government policy on sports

Use 796 for athletics covering sports as a whole. Use 796.42 for athletics limited to track and field

Class exercise and sports activities as means of improving physical fitness in 613.71; class computerized athletic and outdoor sports and games in 794.86

> *For aquatic and air sports, see 797; for equestrian sports and animal racing, see 798; for fishing, hunting, shooting, see 799. For a specific sport of modern pentathlon, see the sport, e.g., pistol shooting 799.312*

> *See also 617.1027 for sports medicine*

SUMMARY

796.01–.09	**Standard subdivisions and general kinds of sports and games**
.1	**Miscellaneous games**
.2	**Activities and games requiring equipment**
.3	**Ball games**
.4	**Weight lifting, track and field, gymnastics**
.5	**Outdoor life**
.6	**Cycling and related activities**
.7	**Driving motor vehicles**
.8	**Combat sports**
.9	**Ice and snow sports**

.04   General kinds of sports and games

> *See Manual at 796.08 vs. 796.04*

>   796.042–796.044   Amateur and professional sports

> Class variants of amateur and professional sports in 796.045; class extreme amateur and professional sports in 796.046; class comprehensive works in 796.04

.042   Amateur sports

> Class here intramural sports

> *For college sports, see 796.043*

.043   College sports

> Intercollegiate and intramural sports

.044   Professional sports

.045   Variant sports and games

> Versions of sports and games developed by modifying the basic version of the original sports and games

> Class variants of extreme sports and games in 796.046

.045 6		Wheelchair sports

Class here sports and games modified for participation of people with physical disabilities

.046	Extreme sports
.06	Organizations, facilities, management

Notation 06 from Table 1 as modified below

.068	Facilities

Do not use for management; class in 796.069

Class here field houses, physical education facilities, playgrounds, stadiums

Add to base number 796.068 notation 1–9 from Table 2, e.g., playgrounds of London 796.068421

See also 725.8 for architecture of recreational buildings

.069	Management

Add to base number 796.069 the numbers following —068 in notation 0681–0688 from Table 1, e.g., financial management 796.0691

.07	Education, research, related topics

Notation 07 from Table 1 as modified below

.071	Education

Do not use for teaching; class in 796.077

.077	Coaching

Class here teaching

.08	Groups of people

Class general kinds of sports and games for specific groups of people in 796.04

See Manual at 796.08 vs. 796.04

.087	People with disabilities and illnesses, gifted people

Class sports and games modified for participation of people with physical disabilities in 796.0456

.092	Biography

See Manual at 796.092

.1	**Miscellaneous games**

Not provided for elsewhere

.13	Singing and dancing games
.14	Active games

For activities and games requiring equipment, see 796.2

.15   Play with remote-control vehicles; play with kites

Toy or model vehicles

Standard subdivisions are added for play with remote-control vehicles and play with kites together; for play with remote-control vehicles alone

Class here control line vehicles; comprehensive works on model vehicles

Class comprehensive works on play with toys in 790.133

See Manual at 796.15 vs. 629.0460228

Play with robots relocated to 796.16

>   796.152–796.156 Play with remote-control vehicles

Class comprehensive works in 796.15

.152   Remote-control ships

Class here comprehensive works on model ships

.154   Remote-control aircraft

Class here remote-control airplanes; comprehensive works on model aircraft, on model airplanes

Class paper airplanes in 745.592

.156   Remote-control land vehicles

Including remote-control racing cars

Class here model automobiles; comprehensive works on model land vehicles

For play with model trains, play with remote-control trains, see 790.133

.158   Play with kites

.16   Play with robots [*formerly* 796.15]

.2   Activities and games requiring equipment

Not provided for elsewhere

Including flying discs, marbles, Yo-Yos

.21   Roller skating

Class here in-line skating (rollerblading)

Class a specific sport using roller skates or rollerblades with the sport, e.g., roller hockey 796.3566

.22   Skateboarding

.24   Pitching games

Including horseshoes, quoits

.3 Ball games

Class here comprehensive works on outdoor and indoor ball games

For indoor ball games, see 794.7

SUMMARY

.31 Ball thrown or hit by hand

Including boccie, pétanque

For inflated ball thrown or hit by hand, see 796.32

.312 Court handball

Variant name: handball

See also 796.327 for team handball

.315 Lawn bowling

See also 794.6 for indoor bowling

.32 Inflated ball thrown or hit by hand

.323 Basketball

.323 01–.323 09 Standard subdivisions

Notation from Table 1 as modified under 796.3320202–796.332077, e.g., basketball courts 796.323068

.323 2 Strategy and tactics

.323 3 Refereeing

.323 6 Specific types of basketball

Class strategy and tactics regardless of type in 796.3232; class refereeing of specific types of basketball in 796.3233

See Manual at 796.08 vs. 796.04

[.323 601–.323 609] Standard subdivisions

Do not use; class in 796.32301–796.32309

.323 62 Precollege basketball

.323 63 College basketball

.323 64 Professional and semiprofessional basketball

.323 8		Variants of basketball

Including wheelchair basketball, women's rules

See also 796.323082 for women playing by standard rules

See Manual at 796.08 vs. 796.04

.324	Netball	
.325	Volleyball	
.325 02		Miscellany
.325 020 2		Handbooks and guides

Use of this number for synopses and outlines discontinued; class in 796.32502

.325 020 22	Official rules
.325 020 24	Spectators' guides
.325 06	Organizations, facilities, management

Notation 06 from Table 1 as modified below

Including clubs, leagues

.325 068	Grounds and their layout

Add to base number 796.325068 notation 1–9 from Table 2, e.g., volleyball courts in Miami Beach 796.325068759381

Management relocated to 796.325069

.325 069	Management [*formerly* 796.325068]

Add to base number 796.325069 the numbers following —068 in notation 0681–0688 from Table 1, e.g., financial management 796.3250691

.325 07	Education, research, related topics

Notation 07 from Table 1 as modified below

.325 071	Education

Teaching relocated to 796.325077

.325 075	Museum activities and services Collecting

Class here collectibles, e.g., volleyball cards

.325 077	Coaching

Class here teaching [*formerly* 796.325071]

.325 2	Strategy and tactics
.325 3	Refereeing and umpiring

.325 6	Specific types of volleyball

Class strategy and tactics regardless of type in 796.3252; class refereeing and umpiring of specific types of volleyball in 796.3253

See Manual at 796.08 vs. 796.04

[.325 601–.325 609]	Standard subdivisions

Do not use; class in 796.32501–796.32509

.325 62	Precollege volleyball
.325 63	College volleyball
.325 64	Professional and semiprofessional volleyball
.325 8	Variants of volleyball

See Manual at 796.08 vs. 796.04

.325 82	Beach volleyball
.327	Team handball

Variant names: field handball, fieldball, handball

See also 796.312 for court handball

.33	Inflated ball driven by foot

Including Gaelic football

SUMMARY

796.332	American football
.333	Rugby
.334	Soccer (Association football)
.335	Canadian football
.336	Australian-rules football

.332	American football
.332 02	Miscellany
.332 020 2	Handbooks and guides

Do not use for synopses and outlines; class in 796.33202

.332 020 22	Official rules
.332 020 24	Spectators' guides
.332 06	Organizations, facilities, management

Notation 06 from Table 1 as modified below

Including clubs, leagues

.332 068	Grounds and their layout

Do not use for management; class in 796.332069

Add to base number 796.332068 notation 1–9 from Table 2, e.g., football fields of Washington, D.C. 796.332068753

.332 069	Management
	Add to base number 796.332069 the numbers following —068 in notation 0681–0688 from Table 1, e.g., financial management 796.3320691
.332 07	Education, research, related topics
	Notation 07 from Table 1 as modified below
.332 071	Education
	Do not use for teaching; class in 796.332077
.332 075	Museum activities and services
	Class here collectibles, e.g., football cards
.332 077	Coaching
	Class here teaching
.332 08	Groups of people
	See Manual at 796.08 vs. 796.04
.332 2	Strategy and tactics
.332 22	Formations
.332 23	Line play
.332 24	Backfield play
.332 25	Passing
.332 26	Blocking and tackling
.332 27	Kicking
.332 3	Refereeing and umpiring
.332 6	Specific types of American football
	Class strategy and tactics regardless of type in 796.3322; class refereeing and umpiring of specific types of American football in 796.3323
	See Manual at 796.08 vs. 796.04
[.332 601–.332 609]	Standard subdivisions
	Do not use; class in 796.33201–796.33209
.332 62	Precollege football
.332 63	College football
	Including bowl games
	See also 796.332648 for Super Bowl
.332 64	Professional and semiprofessional football
.332 648	Super Bowl

.332 8	Variants of American football
	Including six-man football, touch football
	See Manual at 796.08 vs. 796.04
.333	Rugby
	Class here Rugby Union
.333 01–.333 09	Standard subdivisions
	Notation from Table 1 as modified under 796.3320202–796.332077, e.g., official rules 796.33302022
.333 2	Strategy and tactics
.333 23	Forward play
.333 24	Halfback play
.333 25	Three-quarter play
.333 26	Back play
.333 3	Refereeing and umpiring
.333 6	Specific types of rugby
	Class strategy and tactics regardless of type in 796.3332; class refereeing and umpiring of specific types of rugby in 796.3333
	See Manual at 796.08 vs. 796.04
[.333 601–.333 609]	Standard subdivisions
	Do not use; class in 796.33301–796.33309
.333 62	Clubs
	Including college and university
.333 63	County cup competition
.333 64	Tours
.333 65	International rugby
.333 8	Rugby League
.334	Soccer (Association football)
	See also 796.33 for Gaelic football
.334 01–.334 09	Standard subdivisions
	Notation from Table 1 as modified under 796.3320202–796.332077, e.g., coaching 796.334077
.334 2	Strategy and tactics
.334 22	Formations
.334 23	Forward play
.334 24	Halfback play

.334 25	Back play
.334 26	Goalkeeping
.334 3	Refereeing and umpiring
.334 6	Specific types of soccer

Class strategy and tactics regardless of type in 796.3342; class refereeing and umpiring of specific types of soccer in 796.3343

See Manual at 796.08 vs. 796.04

[.334 601–.334 609]	Standard subdivisions

Do not use; class in 796.33401–796.33409

.334 62	Amateur soccer
.334 63	League soccer
.334 64	Cup competition

For World Cup competition, see 796.334668

.334 66	International soccer
.334 668	World Cup competition
.334 8	Variants of soccer

See Manual at 796.08 vs. 796.04

.335	Canadian football
.335 01–.335 09	Standard subdivisions

Notation from Table 1 as modified under 796.3320202–796.332077, e.g., coaching 796.335077

.335 2	Strategy and tactics
.335 3	Refereeing and umpiring
.335 6	Specific types of Canadian football

Class strategy and tactics regardless of type in 796.3352; class refereeing and umpiring of specific types of Canadian football in 796.3353

See Manual at 796.08 vs. 796.04

[.335 601–.335 609]	Standard subdivisions

Do not use; class in 796.33501–796.33509

.335 62	Precollege Canadian football
.335 63	College Canadian football
.335 64	Professional and semiprofessional Canadian football
.335 648	Grey Cup

.335 8   Variants of Canadian football

                Including touch football

                   See Manual at 796.08 vs. 796.04

.336   Australian-rules football

.34   Racket games

                Including court tennis (royal tennis), paddle tennis

                   See also 796.24 for deck tennis

.342   Tennis (Lawn tennis)

.342 01–.342 09   Standard subdivisions

                Notation from Table 1 as modified under
                796.3320202–796.332077, e.g., layout of tennis courts 796.342068

.342 2   Strategy and tactics

.342 21   Service

.342 22   Forehand

.342 23   Backhand

.342 27   Singles

.342 28   Doubles

.342 3   Refereeing

.343   Squash

                Class here rackets, racquetball

.345   Badminton

.346   Table tennis

.347   Lacrosse

.35   Ball driven by club, mallet, bat

                Including hurling

.352   Golf

.352 01–.352 09   Standard subdivisions

                Notation from Table 1 as modified under
                796.3320202–796.332077, e.g., official rules 796.35202022

                   See also 712.5 for design and construction of golf courses

.352 2   Variants of golf

                Including miniature golf

                   See Manual at 796.08 vs. 796.04

.352 3   Tactics of play

                Class here grip, swing, adapting to specific golf courses

.352 32	Play with woods
.352 33	Play with distance irons

Class here comprehensive works on play with irons

For play with chipping or pitching irons, see 796.35234

.352 34	Play with chipping or pitching irons
.352 35	Putting
.352 4	Refereeing
.352 6	Specific types of golf

Class tactics of play regardless of type in 796.3523; class refereeing of specific types of golf in 796.3524

See Manual at 796.08 vs. 796.04

[.352 601–.352 609]	Standard subdivisions

Do not use; class in 796.35201–796.35209

.352 62	Amateur golf

Class open games and matches in 796.35266

.352 64	Professional golf

Class open games and matches in 796.35266

.352 66	Open games and matches

Including British Open, Masters Tournament

.353	Polo
.354	Croquet
.355	Field hockey

Including indoor field hockey

Class comprehensive works on hockey in 796.356

.356	Hockey

Using ball, puck, or ring

For field hockey, see 796.355; for hockey games played on ice, see 796.96; for hockey games played underwater, see 797.25

.356 2	Floorball
.356 4	Street hockey

Class here ball hockey, dek hockey

.356 6	Roller hockey

Including skater hockey (inline skater hockey)

See also 796.35662 for inline hockey

.356 62	Inline hockey
	See also 796.3566 for skater hockey
.356 64	Rink hockey
	Variant names: hardball hockey, quad roller hockey
.357	Baseball
.357 01–.357 09	Standard subdivisions
	Notation from Table 1 as modified under 796.3320202–796.332077, e.g., coaching 796.357077
.357 2	Strategy and tactics
.357 22	Pitching
.357 23	Catching
.357 24	Infield play
	Class here comprehensive works on fielding
	For outfield play, see 796.35725
.357 25	Outfield play
.357 26	Batting
.357 27	Base running
.357 3	Umpiring
.357 6	Specific types of baseball
	Class strategy and tactics regardless of type in 796.3572; class umpiring of specific types of baseball in 796.3573
	See Manual at 796.08 vs. 796.04
[.357 601–.357 609]	Standard subdivisions
	Do not use; class in 796.35701–796.35709
.357 62	Precollege baseball
	Class here Little league
.357 63	College baseball
.357 64	Professional and semiprofessional baseball
.357 646	World series games
.357 648	All-star games
.357 8	Variants of baseball
	Including softball
	See Manual at 796.08 vs. 796.04
.358	Cricket

.358 01–.358 09	Standard subdivisions
	Notation from Table 1 as modified under 796.3320202–796.332077, e.g., coaching 796.358077
.358 2	Strategy and tactics
.358 22	Bowling
.358 23	Fielding
.358 24	Wicketkeeping
.358 26	Batting
.358 3	Umpiring
.358 6	Specific types of cricket
	Class strategy and tactics regardless of type in 796.3582; class umpiring of specific types of cricket in 796.3583
	See Manual at 796.08 vs. 796.04
[.358 601–.358 609]	Standard subdivisions
	Do not use; class in 796.35801–796.35809
.358 62	Amateur cricket
	Including school, college and university
.358 63	County cricket
.358 65	International cricket
.358 8	Variants of cricket
	Including single-wicket cricket
	See Manual at 796.08 vs. 796.04
.4	**Weight lifting, track and field, gymnastics**
.406	Organizations, facilities, management
	Notation 06 from Table 1 as modified below
.406 8	Gymnasiums and stadiums
	Do not use for management; class in 796.4069
	Add to base number 796.4068 notation 1–9 from Table 2, e.g., gymnasiums of Japan 796.406852
.406 9	Management
	Add to base number 796.4069 the numbers following —068 in notation 0681–0688 from Table 1, e.g., financial management 796.40691
.407	Education, research, related topics
	Notation 07 from Table 1 as modified below

.407 1	Education

> Do not use for teaching; class in 796.4077

.407 7	Coaching

> Class here teaching

.41	Weight lifting

Including bodybuilding for contests

Class weight training for fitness and interdisciplinary works on weight training, bodybuilding for fitness and interdisciplinary works on bodybuilding in 613.713

.42	Track and field *Used for running/sprinting*

Class here decathlon, heptathlon; running

Use 796 for athletics covering sports as a whole. Use 796.42 for athletics limited to track and field

> *For field events, see 796.43; for orienteering, see 796.58*

> *See also 613.7172 for running as an exercise*

.420 6	Organizations, facilities, management

> Notation 06 from Table 1 as modified below

.420 68	Athletic fields

> Do not use for management; class in 796.42069

> Add to base number 796.42068 notation 1–9 from Table 2, e.g., athletic fields of Russia 796.4206847

.420 69	Management

> Add to base number 796.42069 the numbers following —068 in notation 0681–0688 from Table 1, e.g., personnel management 796.420693

.422	Sprints *use 796.4*

> Class sprint relays in 796.427

.423	Middle-distance races

> Class middle-distance relay races in 796.427

.424	Distance races

> Class distance relay races in 796.427

>> *For marathon, see 796.4252; for triathlon, see 796.4257; for cross-country races, see 796.428*

.425	Non-track races

> Class here road running

>> *For cross-country races, see 796.428; for race walking, see 796.429*

.425 2	Marathon

.425 7		Triathlon
.426		Hurdles and steeplechase

> Class hurdle and steeplechase relay races in 796.427

.427		Relay races
.428		Cross-country races
.429		Race walking (Heel-and-toe races)
.43		Jumping and throwing

> Class here field events

.432		Jumping

> Including long jump (broad jump), triple jump (hop, step, and jump), high jump
>
> *For pole vaulting, see 796.434*

.434		Pole vaulting

> *See also 796.442 for gymnastic vaulting*

.435		Throwing

> Including boomerang and discus throwing, javelin hurling, shot-putting
>
> *See also 796.24 for throwing games*

.44		Gymnastics

> Including aerobic gymnastics (sports aerobics)
>
> Class interdisciplinary works on aerobic exercise in 613.71
>
> *For trapeze work, rope climbing, tightrope walking, see 796.46; for tumbling, trampoling, acrobatics, contortion, see 796.47*
>
> *See also 613.714 for gymnastic exercises*

.440 92		Biography

> Class biography of a specific type of gymnast with the type, e.g., artistic gymnast 796.442092

.442		Artistic gymnastics

> Gymnastics whose routines use the following apparatus: floor [*formerly* 796.47], balance beam, high bar, parallel bars, pommel horse, still rings, uneven bars, vault

.443		Rhythmic gymnastics

> Gymnastics whose routines use the following apparatus: ball, clubs, hoop, ribbon rope

.46		Trapeze work, rope climbing, tightrope walking

> *See also 791.34 for trapeze work and tightrope walking as circus acts*

.47   Tumbling, trampolining, acrobatics, contortion

> Floor as an apparatus in artistic gymnastics relocated to 796.442

.472   Tumbling

> Class tumbling as part of artistic gymnastics in 796.442; class tumbling as part of rhythmic gymnastics in 796.443; class tumbling as part of trampolining in 796.474

.474   Trampolining

> Class here trampoline, synchronized trampoline, double mini-trampoline

.476   Acrobatics

> Class here acrobatic gymnastics (sports acrobatics)

> *For acrobatics as circus acts, see 791.34*

.48   Olympic games

> Arrange specific games chronologically

> Class Paralympics in 796.0456; class Special Olympics in 796.0874. Class a specific activity with the activity, e.g., basketball 796.323, swimming 797.21

> *For winter Olympic games, see 796.98*

.480 93–.480 99   Geographic treatment

> Do not use for specific games; class in 796.48

.5   **Outdoor life**

> Class a specific activity of outdoor life not provided for here with the activity, e.g., fishing 799.1

.51   Walking

> Class here backpacking, hiking

> *For walking by kind of terrain, see 796.52*

> *See also 796.58 for orienteering*

> *See Manual at 913–919 vs. 796.51*

.52   Walking and exploring by kind of terrain

.522   Mountains, hills, rocks

> Class here mountaineering

.522 3   Rock climbing

> Class sport and indoor rock climbing in 796.5224

.522 4   Sport climbing

> Class here indoor climbing

.524   Canyons and other depressions

> Class here a sport regardless of type of depression, e.g., canyoning (canyoneering), gorge walking

.525	Caves
	Class here spelunking
	See also 797.2 for cave swimming
.53	Beach activities
	For aquatic sports, see 797.1–797.3
.54	Camping
	Including snow camping
.542	Kinds of camps
	Class here camps operated for profit
	Class activities in specific kinds of camps in 796.545
.542 2	Institutional camps
	Including church, school, scouts, YMCA camps
	Class institutional day camps in 796.5423
.542 3	Day camps
.545	Activities
	Including campfires, games, woodcraft
	For beach activities, see 796.53
.56	Dude ranching and farming
.58	Orienteering
	Class orientation in 912.014

.6   **Cycling and related activities**

Use of wheeled vehicles not driven by motor or animal power

Including soapbox racing

For roller skating, see 796.21; for skateboarding, see 796.22

>   796.62–796.64 Cycling

Class comprehensive works in 796.6

.62	Bicycle racing
	Class triathlon in 796.4257; class racing on mountain bikes in 796.63
	See also 796.75 for motorcycle racing
.622	BMX (Bicycle motocross)
.624	Cyclo-cross
.626	Road cycling
.628	Track cycling

.63   Mountain biking (All-terrain cycling)

.64   Bicycle touring for pleasure

> *See also 796.62 for touring as a form of racing*

.67   Street luge racing

> *See also 796.954 for lugeing*

.68   Landsailing (Sand yachting)

.7   **Driving motor vehicles**

> *For snowmobiling, see 796.94*

>   796.72–796.76   Driving for competition

Class comprehensive works in 796.7

.72   Automobile racing

> Class here driving sports cars [*formerly* 796.77]

> *See also 796.156 for toy car racing*

.720 6   Organizations, facilities, management

> Notation 06 from Table 1 as modified below

.720 68   Racetracks and speedways

> Do not use for management; class in 796.72069

> Add to base number 796.72068 notation 1–9 from Table 2, e.g., Indianapolis Motor Speedway 796.7206877252

.720 69   Management

> Add to base number 796.72069 the numbers following —068 in notation 0681–0688 from Table 1, e.g., financial management 796.720691

.73   Automobile rallies

.75   Motorcycle and motor scooter racing

.756   Motocross and supercross

> Standard subdivisions are added for either or both topics in heading

.76   Karting and midget car racing

> Standard subdivisions are added for karting and midget car racing together, for karting alone

[.77]   Driving sports cars

> Relocated to 796.72

[.78]   Travel by private passenger automobile

> Relocated to 910

[.79]	Travel by motor homes, recreational vehicles, trailers
	Relocated to 910
.8	**Combat sports**
	Class here interdisciplinary works on martial arts
	Class combat with animals in 791.8; class Oriental martial arts forms in 796.815
	For martial arts as exercises for physical fitness, see 613.7148
.81	Unarmed combat
	For boxing, see 796.83
.812	Wrestling
	Including arm wrestling
.812 2	Greco-Roman wrestling
.812 3	Freestyle wrestling (Catch-as-catch-can wrestling)
.812 5	Sumo
.815	Oriental martial arts forms
	Class martial arts forms including both Oriental forms and other military forms, e.g., boxing, fencing, in 796.8
.815 2	Judo
	Class here jujitsu
.815 3	Karate
.815 4	Aikido
.815 5	Chinese forms of martial arts
	For kempo and kung fu, see 796.8159
.815 7	Taekwondo
.815 9	Kempo and kung fu
.83	Boxing
.86	Fencing
	Including bojutsu, kendo
	Class here sword fighting
.9	**Ice and snow sports** — use for all snow sports
	For sled dog racing, see 798.83; for ice fishing, see 799.122
	See also 796.54 for snow camping; also 798.6 for horse-drawn sleighing
.91	Ice skating
.912	Figure skating
	Class here ice dancing, pair skating

.914   Speed skating

> Class here long track speed skating, short track speed skating

.92   Snowshoeing

.93   Skiing and snowboarding

> Standard subdivisions are added for skiing and snowboarding together, for skiing alone

.930 92   Biography

> Class biography of a specific type of skier with the type, e.g., alpine skier 796.935092

.932   Cross-country skiing

> Class here Nordic combination, Nordic skiing

> *For jumping, see 796.933*

.932 2   Biathlon

.933   Jumping

.935   Alpine skiing (Downhill skiing)

> Class here downhill, giant slalom, slalom, supergiant slalom racing

.937   Freestyle skiing

> Including aerial and mogul skiing; ski cross

.939   Snowboarding

> Including big air, halfpipe, slopestyle snowboarding; snowboard cross (boardercross), parallel giant slalom racing

> Class here alpine and freestyle snowboarding

.94   Snowmobiling

.95   Sledding and coasting

> Including tobogganing

.952   Bobsleigh

954   Luge

> *See also 796.67 for street luge racing*

.956   Skeleton

.96   Ice games

.962   Ice hockey

> Class comprehensive works on hockey in 796.356

.962 01–.962 09   Standard subdivisions

> Notation from Table 1 as modified under 796.3320202–796.332077, e.g., coaching 796.962077

.962 2	Strategy and tactics
	Including skating
.962 27	Goalkeeping
.962 3	Refereeing
.962 6	Specific types of ice hockey
	Class strategy and tactics regardless of type in 796.9622
	See Manual at 796.08 vs. 796.04
[.962 601–.962 609]	Standard subdivisions
	Do not use; class in 796.96201–796.96209
.962 62	Junior hockey
.962 63	College hockey
.962 64	Professional hockey
.962 648	Stanley Cup
.962 66	International hockey
	Class here specific tournaments
.963	Bandy
	Including rink bandy
.964	Curling
.965	Broomball
.966	Ringette
	See also 796.356 for gym ringette, inline ringette
.97	Iceboating
.98	Winter Olympic games
	Arrange specific games chronologically
	Class a specific activity with the activity, e.g., skating 796.91
.980 93–.980 99	Geographic treatment
	Do not use for specific games; class in 796.98

797   Aquatic and air sports

Standard subdivisions are added for aquatic and air sports together, for aquatic sports alone

Class computerized aquatic and air sports in 794.87

.028 9	Safety measures
	Class comprehensive works on water safety in aquatic sports in 797.200289

> **797.1–797.3 Aquatic sports**

Class comprehensive works in 797

For fishing, see 799.1

.1   **Boating**

.12   Types of vessels

Class seamanship for specific types of vessels in 623.882; class boat racing with specific types of vessels in 797.14

.121   Rafting

.122   Canoeing

.122 4   Kayaking

.123   Rowing

.124   Sailing

See also 796.68 for landsailing; also 797.33 for sailboarding

.124 6   Yachting

Class here comprehensive works on yachting

For motor yachting, see 797.1256

See also 643.29 for yachts permanently docked as dwellings

.125   Motorboating

.125 6   Yachting

.129   Houseboating

See also 643.29 for houseboats permanently docked as dwellings

.14   Boat racing and regattas

Standard subdivisions are added for any type of racing, e.g., yacht racing in Britain 797.140941

.2   **Swimming and diving**

Standard subdivisions are added for swimming and diving together, for diving alone

Class here water parks

.200 1–.200 9   Standard subdivisions

.203   Water pageantry

See also 797.21 for synchronized swimming

.21   Swimming

Class triathlon in 796.4257

For underwater swimming, see 797.23

.217   Synchronized swimming

.23   Underwater swimming

> *For a specific underwater game, see the game, e.g., underwater hockey 797.25*

.232   Skin diving and snorkeling

> Standard subdivisions are added for either or both topics in heading

.234   Scuba diving

.24   Springboard and platform diving

> Standard subdivisions are added for either or both topics in heading

.25   Water games

> Including underwater hockey

.252   Water polo

.3   **Other aquatic sports**

> Including wakeboarding

.32   Surfing (Surf riding)

.33   Windsurfing (Boardsailing, Sailboarding)

.35   Water skiing

.37   Jet skiing

.5   **Air sports**

> Including bungee jumping

.51   Balloon flying

> 797.52–797.54 Flying motor-driven aircraft

> Class comprehensive works in 797.5

> *See also 797.55 for paramotoring*

.52   Racing

.53   Flying for pleasure

.54   Stunt flying

> Class here display aerobatics

.55   Gliding and soaring

> Including hang gliding, paramotoring

.56   Parachuting (Skydiving)

> Including skysurfing

798   Equestrian sports and animal racing

Standard subdivisions are added for equestrian sports and animal racing together, for equestrian sports alone

Class computerized equestrian sports and animal racing in 794.88

>   **798.2–798.6   Equestrian sports**

Class rodeos in 791.84; class hunting with aid of horses in 799.23; class comprehensive works in 798

For polo, see 796.353

See also 636.108971027 for equine sports medicine

.2   Horsemanship

For horse racing, see 798.4

.23   Riding

Class here training of both horse and rider, dressage

Class training of only the horse in 636.1088

For jumping, see 798.25

.230 74   Museums, collections, exhibits

Do not use for riding exhibitions; class in 798.24

[.230 79]   Competitions and awards

Do not use; class in 798.24

.24   Riding exhibitions and competitions

Class jumping in 798.25

.242   Eventing

Class here three-day events

.25   Jumping

.4   Horse racing

Class here flat racing

.400 1–.400 5   Standard subdivisions

.400 6   Organizations, facilities, management

Notation 06 from Table 1 as modified below

.400 68   Racetracks

Do not use for management; class in 798.40069

Add to base number 798.40068 notation 1–9 from Table 2, e.g., racetracks of England 798.4006842

.400 69		Management

Add to base number 798.40069 the numbers following —068 in notation 0681–0688 from Table 1, e.g., management of marketing 798.400698

.400 7–.400 8		Standard subdivisions
.400 9		History, geographic treatment, biography

Class here specific races

.401		Betting

Including pari-mutuel

.45		Steeplechasing (National Hunt racing)
.46		Harness racing
.6		**Driving and coaching**

Including horse-drawn sleighing

For harness racing, see 798.46

.8		**Dog racing**
.83		Sled dog racing
.85		Greyhound racing
799		**Fishing, hunting, shooting**

Class computerized fishing, hunting, shooting games in 794.89

See also 688.79 for the manufacture of both mass-produced and handcrafted equipment

SUMMARY

799.1	**Fishing**
.2	**Hunting**
.3	**Shooting other than game**

.1	**Fishing**

Class shellfishing in 799.254; class interdisciplinary works on fishing in 639.2

.11	Freshwater fishing

Class here coarse fishing

Class fishing for specific kinds of freshwater fishes in 799.17

>   799.12–799.14   Specific methods of fishing

Class specific methods of freshwater fishing in 799.11; class specific methods of saltwater fishing in 799.16; class specific methods of fishing for specific kinds of fish in 799.17; class comprehensive works in 799.1

.12   Angling

> Class here game, pan fishing

> Class game fishing is the sense of fishing for salmon, trout, graylings in 799.1755

.122   Bait fishing

> Variant names: bottom, still fishing

> Including ice fishing

.124   Fly fishing

> Class here casting

> *For bait-casting, see 799.126*

> *See also 688.79124 for making artificial flies*

.126   Bait-casting (Spin-fishing)

.128   Trolling

.13   Net fishing

.14   Other methods of fishing

> Including spearfishing

.16   Saltwater fishing

> Class fishing for specific kinds of saltwater fishes in 799.17

.17   Specific kinds of fishes

> Class comprehensive works on fishing for freshwater fishes in 799.11; class comprehensive works on fishing for saltwater fishes in 799.16

[.170 1–.170 9]   Standard subdivisions

> Do not use; class in 799.101–799.109

.172–.177   Subdivisions for specific kinds of fishes

> Add to base number 799.17 the numbers following 597 in 597.2–597.7, e.g., trout fishing 799.1757

> Class coarse fishing, game fishing in sense of sports fishing in 799.12; class game fishing in sense of fishing for salmon, trout, graylings in 799.1755

.2   **Hunting**

> Class here sports trapping; comprehensive works on hunting and shooting sports, on commercial and sports hunting

> *For commercial, subsistence hunting, see 639.1; for shooting other than game, see 799.3*

.202   Miscellany

.202 8	Auxiliary techniques and procedures; apparatus, equipment, materials
	Notation 028 from Table 1 as modified below
	Class here basic techniques and procedures
.202 82	Blowpipes, bolas, boomerangs, lassos, nets, slings, spears
.202 83	Guns
.202 832	Rifles
.202 833	Pistols
.202 834	Shotguns
.202 85	Bows and arrows
	Do not use for computer applications; class in 799.2028
[.209]	History, geographic treatment, biography
	Do not use; class in 799.29

>   799.21–799.23   Methods

Class methods of hunting specific kinds of animals in 799.24–799.27; class comprehensive works in 799.2

.21	Shooting game
.213	Shooting game with guns
.215	Shooting game with bows and arrows
.23	Hunting with aid of animals
.232	Hunting with falcons
.234	Hunting with dogs

>   799.24–799.27   Hunting specific kinds of animals

Class comprehensive works in 799.2

.24	Birds

Class here fowling, game birds, wildfowling

Class waterfowling in 799.244

.244	Waterfowl

Class here ducks, lowland game birds

Add to base number 799.244 the numbers following 598.41 in 598.412–598.418, e.g., geese 799.2447

.246	Upland game birds

Class here Galliformes

Add to base number 799.246 the numbers following 598.6 in 598.62–598.65, e.g., turkeys 799.24645

.248	Specific kinds of birds other than waterfowl and upland game birds
[.248 01–.248 09]	Standard subdivisions

Do not use; class in 799.2401–799.2409

.248 3–.248 9	Subdivisions for specific kinds of birds other than waterfowl and upland game birds

Add to base number 799.248 the numbers following 598 in 598.3–598.9, e.g., shore birds 799.24833

Class comprehensive works in 799.24

.25	Small game hunting

For birds, see 799.24

.252–.259	Specific kinds of small game

Add to base number 799.25 the numbers following 59 in 592–599, e.g., shellfishing 799.254, fox hunting 799.259775

.26	Big game hunting

Class here comprehensive works on hunting big game mammals

For specific kinds, see 799.27

.27	Specific kinds of big game

For birds, see 799.24

[.270 1–.270 9]	Standard subdivisions

Do not use; class in 799.2601–799.2609

.271–.278	Specific kinds of big game mammals

Add to base number 799.27 the numbers following 599 in 599.1–599.8, e.g., white-tailed deer 799.27652; however, for comprehensive works on big game, on big game mammals, see 799.26

.279	Reptiles

Add to base number 799.279 the numbers following 597.9 in 597.92–597.98, e.g., crocodiles 799.27982

.29	History, geographic treatment, biography
.290 01–.290 09	Standard subdivisions

Add to base number 799.2900 the numbers following —00 in notation 001–009 from Table 2, e.g., periodicals of the history of hunting 799.29005

.290 1–.290 5	Historical periods

Add to base number 799.290 the numbers following —090 in notation 0901–0905 from Table 1, e.g., hunting in 20th century 799.2904

.291–.299	Geographic treatment, biography

Add to base number 799.29 notation 1–9 from Table 2, e.g., hunting in Germany 799.2943

.3 Shooting other than game

For ballistic devices, see 799.20282–799.20285

.31	Shooting with guns
.312	Shooting at stationary targets

For biathlon, see 796.932

.313	Shooting at moving targets
.313 2	Trapshooting

Class here skeet shooting

.32	Shooting with bow and arrow (Archery)

800 Literature (Belles-lettres) and rhetoric

Class here works of literature, works about literature

After general topics (800–809) the basic arrangement is literature by language, then literature of each language by form, then each form by historical period; however, miscellaneous writings are arranged first by historical period, then by form. More detailed instructions are given at the beginning of Table 3

Unless other instructions are given, observe the following table of preference, e.g., collections of drama written in poetry from more than two literatures 808.82 (*not* 808.81):

> Drama
> Poetry
>   Class epigrams in verse with miscellaneous writings
> Fiction
> Essays
> Speeches
> Letters
> Miscellaneous writings
> Humor and satire

Class folk literature in 398.2; class librettos, poems, words written to be sung or recited with music in 780.268; class interdisciplinary works on language and literature in 400; class interdisciplinary works on the arts in 700

> *See Manual at 800; also at 080 vs. 800; also at 741.6 vs. 800; also at 800 vs. 398.2; also at 800, T3C—362 vs. 398.245, 590, 636*

SUMMARY

820	**English and Old English (Anglo-Saxon) literatures**
.1–.9	Standard subdivisions; collections in more than one form; history, description, critical appraisal of works in more than one form of English literature
821	English poetry
822	English drama
823	English fiction
824	English essays
825	English speeches
826	English letters
827	English humor and satire
828	English miscellaneous writings
829	Old English (Anglo-Saxon) literature
830	**German literature and literatures of related languages**
.01–.09	Standard subdivisions of literatures of Germanic languages
.1–.9	Standard subdivisions; collections in more than one form; history, description, critical appraisal of works in more than one form of German literature
831	German poetry
832	German drama
833	German fiction
834	German essays
835	German speeches
836	German letters
837	German humor and satire
838	German miscellaneous writings
839	Other Germanic literatures
840	**French literature and literatures of related Romance languages**
.01–.09	Standard subdivisions of literatures of Romance languages
.1–.9	Standard subdivisions; collections in more than one form; history, description, critical appraisal of works in more than one form of French literature
841	French poetry
842	French drama
843	French fiction
844	French essays
845	French speeches
846	French letters
847	French humor and satire
848	French miscellaneous writings
849	Occitan, Catalan, Franco-Provençal literatures
850	**Literatures of Italian, Dalmatian, Romanian, Rhaetian, Sardinian, Corsican languages**
.1–.9	Standard subdivisions; collections in more than one form; history, description, critical appraisal of works in more than one form of Italian literature
851	Italian poetry
852	Italian drama
853	Italian fiction
854	Italian essays
855	Italian speeches
856	Italian letters
857	Italian humor and satire
858	Italian miscellaneous writings
859	Literatures of Romanian, Rhaetian, Sardinian, Corsican languages

860	Literatures of Spanish, Portuguese, Galician languages
.01–.09	Standard subdivisions of literatures of Spanish, Portuguese, Galician languages
.1–.9	Standard subdivisions; collections in more than one form; history, description, critical appraisal of works in more than one form of Spanish literature
861	Spanish poetry
862	Spanish drama
863	Spanish fiction
864	Spanish essays
865	Spanish speeches
866	Spanish letters
867	Spanish humor and satire
868	Spanish miscellaneous writings
869	Literatures of Portuguese and Galician languages
870	Latin literature and literatures of related Italic languages
.01–.09	Standard subdivisions of literatures of Italic languages
.1–.9	Standard subdivisions; collections in more than one form; history, description, critical appraisal of works in more than one form of Latin literature
871	Latin poetry
872	Latin dramatic poetry and drama
873	Latin epic poetry and fiction
874	Latin lyric poetry
875	Latin speeches
876	Latin letters
877	Latin humor and satire
878	Latin miscellaneous writings
879	Literatures of other Italic languages
880	Classical Greek literature and literatures of related Hellenic languages
.01–.09	Standard subdivisions of classical (Greek and Latin) literatures
.1–.9	Standard subdivisions; collections in more than one form; history, description, critical appraisal of works in more than one form of classical Greek literature
881	Classical Greek poetry
882	Classical Greek dramatic poetry and drama
883	Classical Greek epic poetry and fiction
884	Classical Greek lyric poetry
885	Classical Greek speeches
886	Classical Greek letters
887	Classical Greek humor and satire
888	Classical Greek miscellaneous writings
889	Modern Greek literature
890	Literatures of other specific languages and language families
891	East Indo-European and Celtic literatures
892	Afro-Asiatic literatures
893	Non-Semitic Afro-Asiatic literatures
894	Literatures of Altaic, Uralic, Hyperborean, Dravidian languages; literatures of miscellaneous languages of south Asia
895	Literatures of East and Southeast Asia
896	African literatures
897	Literatures of North American native languages
898	Literatures of South American native languages
899	Literatures of non-Austronesian languages of Oceania, of Austronesian languages, of miscellaneous languages

801 Philosophy and theory

> Notation 01 from Table 1 as modified below
>
> Do not use for value; class in 801.3. Do not use for techniques and principles of criticism; class in 801.95

.3 Value, influence, effect

.9 Nature and character

> Notation 019 from Table 1 as modified below
>
> Do not use for psychological principles; class in 801.92

.92 Psychology

> Including literature as a product of imagination

.93 Aesthetics

.95 Criticism

> Class here theory, technique, history of literary criticism
>
> Class textual criticism of specific literary forms in 801.959; class theory, technique, history of literary criticism of specific literary forms in 808.1–808.7; class works of critical appraisal in 809
>
> *See Manual at 800: Literary criticism*

.959 Textual criticism

802 Miscellany

803 Dictionaries, encyclopedias, concordances

[804] [Unassigned]

> Most recently used in Edition 16

805 Serial publications

> Class collections of literary texts in serial form in 808.80005; class history, description, critical appraisal in serial form in 809.005

806 Organizations and management

807 Education, research, related topics

808 Rhetoric and collections of literary texts from more than two literatures

Rhetoric: effective use of language

Standard subdivisions are added for rhetoric and collections of literary texts from more than two literatures, for rhetoric alone

Do not use for literature with respect to groups of people; class in 808.89

Class here composition

Class general treatment of standard usage of language (prescriptive linguistics) in 418; class theory, technique, history of literary criticism in 801.95. Class treatment of standard usage in a specific language with the specific language, plus notation 8 from Table 4, e.g., English usage 428

SUMMARY

808.001–.009	**Standard subdivisions**
.02–.06	**General topics in rhetoric**
.1	**Rhetoric of poetry**
.2	**Rhetoric of drama**
.3	**Rhetoric of fiction**
.4	**Rhetoric of essays**
.5	**Rhetoric of speech**
.6	**Rhetoric of letters**
.7	**Rhetoric of humor and satire**
.8	**Collections of literary texts from more than two literatures**

.001–.009   Standard subdivisions

> 808.02–808.06 General topics in rhetoric

Class comprehensive works in 808

.02   Authorship techniques, plagiarism, editorial techniques

Writing in publishable form

Class here comprehensive works on preparation and submission of manuscripts, on preparation and submission of scholarly manuscripts

Class authorship and editorial techniques for a specific kind of composition with the kind in 808.06, e.g., 808.066378 academic theses and dissertations

For submission of manuscripts to agents and publishers, see 070.52

See also 001.4 for research

.025   Plagiarism

Class here works that focus on avoiding unintentional plagiarism, interdisciplinary works on plagiarism

Class citation style in 808.027

For a specific aspect of plagiarism, see the aspect, e.g., plagiarism in the context of copyright law 346.0482, plagiarism as a kind of student cheating 371.58, plagiarism in the work of an American fiction writer of the late 20th century 813.54

.027 Editorial techniques

> Preparation of manuscripts in publishable form

> Including proofreading

> Class here style manuals

.03 Specific elements of rhetoric

> Class preparation of manuscripts using specific elements in 808.02; class specific kinds of writing using specific elements in 808.06

.032 Figures of speech

> Including metaphor, simile

.036 Narration

.04 Rhetoric in specific languages

> Class preparation of manuscripts in specific languages in 808.02; class specific elements of rhetoric in specific languages in 808.03; class rhetoric of specific kinds of composition in specific languages in 808.06

.042 Rhetoric in English

.042 7 Study of rhetoric through critical reading

> Including collections and single works for critical reading

> Class here readers used in the study of composition

> > *For readers limited to a particular literary form, see the form, e.g., short stories 808.31*

.042 8 Rhetoric in English for those whose native language is different

.043–.049 Rhetoric in other languages

> Add to base number 808.04 notation 3–9 from Table 6, e.g., German rhetoric 808.0431; then to the result add the numbers following 808.042 in 808.04201–808.0428, e.g., study of German rhetoric through critical reading 808.04317

.06 Rhetoric of specific kinds of writing

> Class rhetoric in specific literary forms in 808.1–808.7

.062 Abstracts and summaries

.066   Professional, technical, expository literature

> Add to base number 808.066 three-digit numbers 001–999 (but stop before any zero that follows a non-zero number), e.g., legal writing 808.06634, writing about natural history 808.0665 (*not* 808.066508), writing on bridge engineering 808.066624 (*not* 808.0666242); then, for writing in a foreign language, add 0 and to the result add notation 2–9 from Table 6, e.g., legal writing in Spanish for speakers of another language 808.06634061; however, for résumé writing, writing cover letters for job hunting, see 650.142

> *For abstracts and summaries, see 808.062; for expository adult easy literature, see 808.067; for expository writing for children, see 808.0688*

> *See Manual at 005.15 vs. 808.066005; also at 340 vs. 808.06634; also at 658.45 vs. 651.7, 808.06665*

.066 378   Writing for and about higher education

> Number built according to instructions under 808.066

> Class here authorship and editorial techniques for academic theses and dissertations

> Class comprehensive works on authorship and editorial techniques for scholarly writing in 808.02. Class authorship and editorial techniques for academic theses and dissertations about a specific subject other than higher education with the subject in 808.066, e.g., psychology 808.06615

.067   Adult easy literature

> Works for adults learning to read or for adult beginners in foreign languages

.068   Children's literature

.068 1–.068 7   Specific literary forms

> Add to base number 808.068 the numbers following 808 in 808.1–808.7, e.g., drama 808.0682

.068 8   Expository writing

> ## 808.1–808.7 Rhetoric in specific literary forms

> Class here aesthetics, appreciation, character and nature, composition, theory of specific literary forms; technique, theory, history of criticism of specific literary forms

> Observe table of preference under 800

> Class theory, technique, history of textual criticism of specific literary forms in 801.959; class specific forms for children in 808.0681–808.0687; class works of critical appraisal of specific literary forms in 809.1–809.7; class comprehensive works on theory, technique, history of literary criticism in 801.95; class comprehensive works on rhetoric in specific literary forms in 808

> *See Manual at 800: Literary criticism*

.1   **Rhetoric of poetry**

         Class here prosody

         Add to base number 808.1 the numbers following —10 in notation 102–107 from Table 3B, e.g., lyric poetry 808.14

         Class linguistic studies of prosody across several languages and from the linguist's viewpoint in 414.6. Class prosodic studies of a particular language as a whole from the linguist's viewpoint with the intonation for the specific language, plus notation 16 from Table 4, e.g., prosodic studies of the Italian language 451.6

.2   **Rhetoric of drama**

         Add to base number 808.2 the numbers following —20 in notation 202–205 from Table 3B, e.g., one-act plays 808.241

.3   **Rhetoric of fiction**

         Class here rhetoric of novelettes and novels

.31–.38   Fiction of specific scope and kinds

         Add to base number 808.3 the numbers following —30 in notation 301–308 from Table 3B, e.g., science fiction 808.38762

.39   Fiction displaying specific elements

         Add to base number 808.39 the numbers following —2 in notation 22–27 from Table 3C, e.g., characters in fiction 808.397

         Class fiction of specific scope and kinds displaying specific elements in 808.31–808.38

.4   **Rhetoric of essays**

.5   **Rhetoric of speech**

         Art or technique of oral expression

         Class here voice, expression, gesture

.51   Public speaking (Oratory)

         Including public speaking for broadcast media

         For preaching, see 251; for debating, see 808.53

.512   Toasts and after-dinner speeches

         Standard subdivisions are added for either or both topics in heading

.53   Debating

         Class here public discussion of opposing views regardless of format

.54   Recitation

         Class here oral interpretation

         Class choral speaking in 808.55

.543   Storytelling

.545	Oral interpretation of poetry

Class here poetry slams

Use of this number for reading aloud other kinds of materials discontinued; class in 808.54

.55	Choral speaking
.56	Conversation
.6	**Rhetoric of letters**
.7	**Rhetoric of humor and satire**

Class here rhetoric of parody

.8	**Collections of literary texts from more than two literatures**

Texts by more than one author in more than two languages not from the same language family

Class here texts in more than two literatures from two or more language families

Class works that are limited to a specific topic found in subdivisions of 808.8 and consist equally of literary texts and history, description, critical appraisal of literature with the topic in 808.8, e.g., texts and criticism of literature of the 18th century 808.80033, texts and criticism of drama 808.82; class collections of texts from more than two literatures in the same language with the literature of that language, e.g., collections of works from English, American, and Australian literatures in English (more than one literary form) 820.8; class collections of texts from literatures in more than two languages from the same family with the literature of that family, e.g., French, Italian, and Spanish literatures 840

See Manual at 808.8; also at 080 vs. 800

SUMMARY

808.800 01–.800 07	**Standard subdivisions**
.800 1–.800 5	**Collections from specific periods**
.801–.803	**Collections displaying specific features**
.81	**Collections of poetry**
.82	**Collections of drama**
.83	**Collections of fiction**
.84	**Collections of essays**
.85	**Collections of speeches**
.86	**Collections of letters**
.87	**Collections of humor and satire**
.88	**Collections of miscellaneous writings**
.89	**Collections for and by groups of people**

.800 01–.800 07	Standard subdivisions
[.800 08]	Groups of people

Do not use; class in 808.89

[.800 09] History, geographic treatment, biography

Do not use for collections of literature for and by people resident in specific regions, continents, countries, localities; class in 808.89. Do not use for history, description, critical appraisal; class in 809

.800 1–.800 5 Collections from specific periods

Add to base number 808.800 the numbers following —090 in notation 0901–0905 from Table 1, e.g., collections of 18th century literature 808.80033

.801–.803 Collections displaying specific features

Add to base number 808.80 notation 1–3 from Table 3C, e.g., collections of literature featuring classicism 808.80142, on death 808.803548

> 808.81–808.88 Collections in specific forms

Observe table of preference under 800

Class comprehensive works in 808.8

See Manual at 808.81–808.88 and 809.1–809.7

.81 Collections of poetry

Class here folk poetry

For anonymous nursery rhymes and related rhymes and rhyming games from the oral tradition, see 398.8

.810 01–.810 07 Standard subdivisions

[.810 08] Groups of people

Use of this number for comprehensive works discontinued; class in 808.81

[.810 081–.810 088] Poetry for and by groups of people with specific attributes

Relocated to 808.81992

[.810 089] Poetry for and by ethnic and national groups

Relocated to 808.8198

.810 09 History and geographic treatment

[.810 090 1–.810 090 5] Historical periods

Do not use; class in 808.8101–808.8105

.810 091 Areas, regions, places in general

Poetry for and by people resident in specific regions relocated to 808.81991

[.810 092] Biography

Do not use; class in 808.81 without adding notation from Table 1

.810 093–.810 099	Specific continents, countries, localities

Poetry for and by people resident in specific continents, countries, localities relocated to 808.81993–808.81999

.810 1–.810 5	Historical periods

Add to base number 808.810 the numbers following —090 in notation 0901–0905 from Table 1, e.g., 18th century poetry 808.81033

.812–.817	Specific kinds of poetry

Add to base number 808.81 the numbers following —10 in notation 102–107 from Table 3B, e.g., collections of narrative poetry 808.813

.819	Poetry displaying specific features, poetry for and by specific groups of people

Class poetry of specific kinds displaying specific features, poetry of specific kinds for and by specific groups of people in 808.812–808.817

.819 1–.819 3	Poetry displaying specific features

Add to base number 808.819 notation 1–3 from Table 3C, e.g., collections of poetry about animals 808.819362

.819 8	Poetry for and by ethnic and national groups [*formerly* 808.810089]

Observe table of preference under —8–9 in Table 3C

.819 805–.819 809	Poetry for and by ethnic and national groups with ethnic origins from more than one continent, of European descent

Add to base number 808.8198 notation 05–09 from Table 5, e.g., poetry by people of mixed African and European descent 808.81980596009

.819 81–.819 89	Poetry for and by specific ethnic and national groups

Add to base number 808.8198 notation 1–9 from Table 5, e.g., poetry by people of African ancestry 808.819896

.819 9	Poetry for and by groups of people with specific attributes, residents of specific areas

Add to base number 808.8199 the numbers following —9 in notation 91–99 from Table 3C, e.g., poetry for and by groups of people resident in specific regions 808.81991 [*formerly* 808.810091]; poetry for and by groups of people with specific attributes 808.81992 [*formerly* 808.810081–808.810088]; poetry for and by groups of people resident in specific continents, countries, localities 808.81993–808.81999 [*formerly* 808.810093–808.810099]

Observe table of preference under —8–9 in Table 3C

.82	Collections of drama

Class here folk drama

See Manual at 808.82 vs. 791.437, 791.447, 791.457, 792.9

.820 01–.820 07	Standard subdivisions

[.820 08]   Groups of people

Use of this number for comprehensive works discontinued; class in 808.82

[.820 081–.820 088]   Drama for and by groups of people with specific attributes

Relocated to 808.82992

[.820 089]   Drama for and by ethnic and national groups

Relocated to 808.8298

.820 09   History and geographic treatment

[.820 090 1–.820 090 5]   Historical periods

Do not use; class in 808.8201–808.8205

.820 091   Areas, regions, places in general

Drama for and by people resident in specific regions relocated to 808.82991

[.820 092]   Biography

Do not use; class in 808.82 without adding notation from Table 1

.820 093–.820 099   Specific continents, countries, localities

Drama for and by people resident in specific continents, countries, localities relocated to 808.82993–808.82999

.820 1–.820 5   Historical periods

Add to base number 808.820 the numbers following —090 in notation 0901–0905 from Table 1, e.g., 18th century drama 808.82033

.822–.825   Specific media, scope, kinds of drama

Add to base number 808.82 the numbers following —20 in notation 202–205 from Table 3B, e.g., collections of tragedies 808.82512

.829   Drama displaying specific features, drama for and by specific groups of people

Class drama of specific media, scope, kinds displaying specific features, drama of specific media, scope, kinds for and by specific groups of people in 808.822–808.825

.829 1–.829 3   Drama displaying specific features

Add to base number 808.829 notation 1–3 from Table 3C, e.g., collections of plays about Faust 808.829351

.829 8   Drama for and by ethnic and national groups [*formerly* 808.820089]

Observe table of preference under —8–9 in Table 3C

.829 805–.829 809	Drama for and by ethnic and national groups with ethnic origins from more than one continent, of European descent
	Add to base number 808.8298 notation 05–09 from Table 5, e.g., drama by people of mixed Asian and European descent 808.82980595009
.829 81–.829 89	Drama for and by specific ethnic and national groups
	Add to base number 808.8298 notation 1–9 from Table 5, e.g., drama by people of Asian ancestry 808.829895
.829 9	Drama for and by groups of people with specific attributes, residents of specific areas
	Add to base number 808.8299 the numbers following —9 in notation 91–99 from Table 3C, e.g., drama for and by people resident in specific regions 808.82991 [*formerly* 808.820091]; drama for and by groups of people with specific attributes 808.82992 [*formerly* 808.820081–808.820088]; drama for and by people resident in specific continents, countries, localities 808.82993–808.82999 [*formerly* 808.820093–808.820099]
	Observe table of preference under —8–9 in Table 3C

.83   Collections of fiction

.830 01–.830 07	Standard subdivisions
[.830 08]	Groups of people
	Use of this number for comprehensive works discontinued; class in 808.83
[.830 081–.830 088]	Fiction for and by groups of people with specific attributes
	Relocated to 808.83992
[.830 089]	Fiction for and by ethnic and national groups
	Relocated to 808.8398
.830 09	History and geographic treatment
[.830 090 1–.830 090 5]	Historical periods
	Do not use; class in 808.8301–808.8305
.830 091	Areas, regions, places in general
	Fiction for and by people resident in specific regions relocated to 808.83991
[.830 092]	Biography
	Do not use; class in 808.83 without adding notation from Table 1
.830 093–.830 099	Specific continents, countries, localities
	Fiction for and by people resident in specific continents, countries, localities relocated to 808.83993–808.83999

.830 1–.830 5	Historical periods

Add to base number 808.830 the numbers following —090 in notation 0901–0905 from Table 1, e.g., 18th century fiction 808.83033

.831–.838	Specific scope and types of fiction

Add to base number 808.83 the numbers following —30 in notation 301–308 from Table 3B, e.g., collections of love stories 808.8385

.839	Fiction displaying specific features, fiction for and by specific groups of people

Class fiction of specific scope and types displaying specific features, fiction of specific scope and types for and by specific groups of people, in 808.831–808.838

.839 1–.839 3	Fiction displaying specific features

Add to base number 808.839 notation 1–3 from Table 3C, e.g., collections of fiction about animals 808.839362

.839 8	Fiction for and by ethnic and national groups [*formerly* 808.830089]

Observe table of preference under —8–9 in Table 3C

.839 805–.839 809	Fiction for and by ethnic and national groups with ethnic origins from more than one continent, of European descent

Add to base number 808.8398 notation 05–09 from Table 5, e.g., fiction by people of mixed African and European descent 808.83980596009

.839 81–.839 89	Fiction for and by specific ethnic and national groups

Add to base number 808.8398 notation 1–9 from Table 5, e.g., fiction by people of African ancestry 808.839896

.839 9	Fiction for and by groups of people with specific attributes, residents of specific areas

Add to base number 808.8399 the numbers following —9 in notation 91–99 from Table 3C, e.g., fiction for and by people resident in specific regions 808.83991 [*formerly* 808.830091]; fiction for and by groups of people with specific attributes 808.83992 [*formerly* 808.830081–808.830088]; fiction for and by people resident in specific continents, countries, localities 808.83993–808.83999 [*formerly* 808.830093–808.830099]

Observe table of preference under —8–9 in Table 3C

.84	Collections of essays
.840 01–.840 07	Standard subdivisions
[.840 08]	Groups of people

Use of this number for comprehensive works discontinued; class in 808.84

[.840 081–.840 088]	Essays for and by groups of people with specific attributes

Relocated to 808.84992

[.840 089]		Essays for and by ethnic and national groups
		Relocated to 808.8498
.840 09		History and geographic treatment
[.840 090 1–.840 090 5]		Historical periods
		Do not use; class in 808.8401–808.8405
.840 091		Areas, regions, places in general
		Essays for and by people resident in specific regions relocated to 808.84991
[.840 092]		Biography
		Do not use; class in 808.84 without adding notation from Table 1
.840 093–.840 099		Specific continents, countries, localities
		Essays for and by people resident in specific continents, countries, localities relocated to 808.84993–808.84999
.840 1–.840 5	Historical periods	
	Add to base number 808.840 the numbers following —090 in notation 0901–0905 from Table 1, e.g., 18th century essays 808.84033	

.849 Essays displaying specific features, essays for and by specific groups of people

.849 1–.849 3	Essays displaying specific features	
	Add to base number 808.849 notation 1–3 from Table 3C, e.g., collections of descriptive essays 808.84922	
.849 8	Essays for and by ethnic and national groups [*formerly* 808.840089]	
	Observe table of preference under —8–9 in Table 3C	
.849 805–.849 809		Essays for and by ethnic and national groups with ethnic origins from more than one continent, of European descent
		Add to base number 808.8498 notation 05–09 from Table 5, e.g., essays by people of mixed African and European descent 808.84980596009
.849 81–.849 89		Essays for and by specific ethnic and national groups
		Add to base number 808.8498 notation 1–9 from Table 5, e.g., essays by people of African ancestry 808.849896

.849 9   Essays for and by groups of people with specific attributes, residents of specific areas

> Add to base number 808.8499 the numbers following —9 in notation 91–99 from Table 3C, e.g., essays for and by people resident in specific regions 808.84991 [*formerly* 808.840091]; essays for and by groups of people with specific attributes 808.84992 [*formerly* 808.840081–808.840088]; essays for and by people resident in specific continents, countries, localities 808.84993–808.84999 [*formerly* 808.840093–808.840099]

> Observe table of preference under —8–9 in Table 3C

.85   Collections of speeches

.850 01–.850 07   Standard subdivisions

[.850 08]   Groups of people

> Use of this number for comprehensive works discontinued; class in 808.85

[.850 081–.850 088]   Speeches for and by groups of people with specific attributes

> Relocated to 808.85992

[.850 089]   Speeches for and by ethnic and national groups

> Relocated to 808.8598

.850 09   History and geographic treatment

[.850 090 1–.850 090 5]   Historical periods

> Do not use; class in 808.8501–808.8505

.850 091   Areas, regions, places in general

> Speeches for and by people resident in specific regions relocated to 808.85991

[.850 092]   Biography

> Do not use; class in 808.85 without adding notation from Table 1

.850 093–.850 099   Specific continents, countries, localities

> Speeches for and by people resident in specific continents, countries, localities relocated to 808.85993–808.85999

.850 1–.850 5   Historical periods

> Add to base number 808.850 the numbers following —090 in notation 0901–0905 from Table 1, e.g., 18th century speeches 808.85033

.851–.856   Specific kinds of speeches

> Add to base number 808.85 the numbers following —50 in notation 501–506 from Table 3B, e.g., debates 808.853

.859   Speeches displaying specific features, speeches for and by specific groups of people

Class speeches of specific kinds displaying specific features, speeches of specific kinds for and by specific groups of people in 808.851–808.856

.859 1–.859 3   Speeches displaying specific features

Add to base number 808.859 notation 1–3 from Table 3C, e.g., collections of descriptive speeches 808.85922

.859 8   Speeches for and by ethnic and national groups [*formerly* 808.850089]

Observe table of preference under —8–9 in Table 3C

.859 805–.859 809   Speeches for and by ethnic and national groups with ethnic origins from more than one continent, of European descent

Add to base number 808.8598 notation 05–09 from Table 5, e.g., speeches by people of mixed Asian and European descent 808.85980595009

.859 81–.859 89   Speeches for and by specific ethnic and national groups

Add to base number 808.8598 notation 1–9 from Table 5, e.g., speeches by people of African ancestry 808.859896

.859 9   Speeches for and by groups of people with specific attributes, residents of specific areas

Add to base number 808.8599 the numbers following —9 in notation 91–99 from Table 3C, e.g., speeches for and by people resident in specific regions 808.85991 [*formerly* 808.850091]; speeches for and by groups of people with specific attributes 808.85992 [*formerly* 808.850081–808.850088]; speeches for and by people resident in specific continents, countries, localities 808.85993–808.85999 [*formerly* 808.850093–808.850099]

Observe table of preference under —8–9 in Table 3C

.86   Collections of letters

.860 01–.860 07   Standard subdivisions

[.860 08]   Groups of people

Use of this number for comprehensive works discontinued; class in 808.86

[.860 081–.860 088]   Letters for and by groups of people with specific attributes

Relocated to 808.86992

[.860 089]   Letters for and by ethnic and national groups

Relocated to 808.8698

.860 09   History and geographic treatment

[.860 090 1–.860 090 5]   Historical periods

Do not use; class in 808.8601–808.8605

.860 091	Areas, regions, places in general
	Letters for and by people resident in specific regions relocated to 808.86991
[.860 092]	Biography
	Do not use; class in 808.86 without adding notation from Table 1
.860 093–.860 099	Specific continents, countries, localities
	Letters for and by people resident in specific continents, countries, localities relocated to 808.86993–808.86999
.860 1–.860 5	Historical periods
	Add to base number 808.860 the numbers following —090 in notation 0901–0905 from Table 1, e.g., 18th century letters 808.86033

.869   **Letters displaying specific features, letters for and by specific groups of people**

.869 1–.869 3   Letters displaying specific features

> Add to base number 808.869 notation 1–3 from Table 3C, e.g., collections of letters displaying classicism 808.869142

.869 8   Letters for and by ethnic and national groups [*formerly* 808.860089]

> Observe table of preference under —8–9 in Table 3C

.869 805–.869 809   Letters for and by ethnic and national groups with ethnic origins from more than one continent, of European descent

> Add to base number 808.8698 notation 05–09 from Table 5, e.g., letters by people of mixed African and European descent 808.86980596009

.869 81–.869 89   Letters for and by specific ethnic and national groups

> Add to base number 808.8698 notation 1–9 from Table 5, e.g., letters by people of African ancestry 808.869896

.869 9   Letters for and by groups of people with specific attributes, residents of specific areas

> Add to base number 808.8699 the numbers following —9 in notation 91–99 from Table 3C, e.g., letters for and by people resident in specific regions 808.86991 [*formerly* 808.860091]; letters for and by groups of people with specific attributes 808.86992 [*formerly* 808.860081–808.860088]; letters for and by people resident in specific continents, countries, localities 808.86993–808.86999 [*formerly* 808.860093–808.860099]

> Observe table of preference under —8–9 in Table 3C

.87	Collections of humor and satire

Limited to collections (or texts and criticism) of works in two or more literary forms including both verse and prose

Class here parody

See also 808.888 for humor and satire in two or more prose forms

(Option: Give preference to humor and satire over all other literary forms)

.870 01–.870 07	Standard subdivisions
[.870 08]	Groups of people

Use of this number for comprehensive works discontinued; class in 808.87

[.870 081–.870 088]	Humor and satire for and by groups of people with specific attributes

Relocated to 808.87992

[.870 089]	Humor and satire for and by ethnic and national groups

Relocated to 808.8798

.870 09	History and geographic treatment
[.870 090 1–.870 090 5]	Historical periods

Do not use; class in 808.8701–808.8705

.870 091	Areas, regions, places in general

Humor and satire for and by people resident in specific regions relocated to 808.87991

[.870 092]	Biography

Do not use; class in 808.87 without adding notation from Table 1

.870 093–.870 099	Specific continents, countries, localities

Humor and satire for and by people resident in specific continents, countries, localities relocated to 808.87993–808.87999

.870 1–.870 5	Historical periods

Add to base number 808.870 the numbers following —090 in notation 0901–0905 from Table 1, e.g., 18th century literary humor 808.87033

.879	**Humor and satire displaying specific features, humor and satire for and by specific groups of people**
.879 1–.879 3	Humor and satire displaying specific features

Add to base number 808.879 notation 1–3 from Table 3C, e.g., collections of literary humor about holidays 808.879334

.879 8	Humor and satire for and by ethnic and national groups [*formerly* 808.870089]

Observe table of preference under —8–9 in Table 3C

.879 805–.879 809   Humor and satire for and by ethnic and national groups with ethnic origins from more than one continent, of European descent

> Add to base number 808.8798 notation 05–09 from Table 5, e.g., humor and satire by people of mixed African and European descent 808.87980596009

.879 81–.879 89   Humor and satire for and by specific ethnic and national groups

> Add to base number 808.8798 notation 1–9 from Table 5, e.g., humor and satire by people of African ancestry 808.879896

.879 9   Humor and satire for and by groups of people with specific attributes, residents of specific areas

> Add to base number 808.8799 the numbers following —9 in notation 91–99 from Table 3C, e.g., humor and satire for and by people resident in specific regions 808.87991 [*formerly* 808.870091]; humor and satire for and by groups of people with specific attributes 808.87992 [*formerly* 808.870081–808.870088]; humor and satire for and by people resident in specific continents, countries, localities 808.87993–808.87999 [*formerly* 808.870093–808.870099]

> Observe table of preference under —8–9 in Table 3C

.88   Collections of miscellaneous writings

> Limited to kinds of miscellaneous writings provided for below

.880 01–.880 08   Standard subdivisions

.880 09   History and geographic treatment

[.880 090 1–.880 090 5]   Historical periods

> Do not use; class in 808.8801–808.8805

[.880 092]   Biography

> Do not use; class in 808.88 without adding notation from Table 1

.880 1–.880 5   Historical periods

> Add to base number 808.880 the numbers following —090 in notation 0901–0905 from Table 1, e.g., 18th century miscellaneous writings 808.88033

.882   Anecdotes, epigrams, graffiti, jokes, jests, quotations, riddles, tongue twisters

> Standard subdivisions are added for any or all topics in heading

> Class here interdisciplinary works on riddles [*formerly* 398.6]; interdisciplinary works on tongue twisters [*formerly* 398.8]; riddles as jokes by known authors; tongue twisters by known authors; jokes and jests by known authors, interdisciplinary works on jokes and jests

> Class humor and satire in two or more literary forms, including both verse and prose, in 808.87

>> *For anonymous riddles from the oral tradition, see 398.6; for anonymous jokes and jests from the oral tradition, see 398.7; for anonymous tongue twisters from the oral tradition, see 398.8; for riddles as a type of puzzle similar to logic puzzles, see 793.735*

.883   Diaries, journals, notebooks, reminiscences

> Class interdisciplinary collections of diaries in 900. Class diaries, journals, notebooks, reminiscences of nonliterary authors with the appropriate subject, e.g., diaries of astronomers 520.922

.887   Works without identifiable form

> Class here experimental and nonformalized works

> Class experimental works with an identifiable literary form with the form, e.g., experimental novels 808.83

.888   Prose literature

> Class prose without identifiable form in 808.887. Class a specific form of prose literature with the form, e.g., essays 808.84

.89   Collections for and by groups of people

> Class here comprehensive works consisting equally of literary texts and history, description, critical appraisal of literature with respect to groups of people

> Add to base number 808.89 notation 8–9 from Table 3C, e.g., collections of literature in more than one language by people of African descent 808.89896

> Class literature displaying specific features for and by groups of people in 808.801–808.803; class literature in specific forms for and by groups of people in 808.81–808.88; class literatures of specific languages for and by groups of people in 810–890

>> *For history, description, critical appraisal of literature with respect to groups of people, see 809.8*

809 **History, description, critical appraisal of more than two literatures**

Notation 09 from Table 1 as modified below

Do not use for geographic treatment; class in 809.89

History, description, critical appraisal of works by more than one author in more than two languages not from the same language family

Class here collected biography of authors, individual and collected biography of critics; history, description, critical appraisal of works in more than two literatures from two or more language families

Class theory, technique, history of literary criticism in 801.95. Class history, description, critical appraisal of more than two literatures in the same language with the literature of that language, e.g., history of English, American, and Australian literatures in English (more than one literary form) 820.9; class history, description, critical appraisal of literatures in more than two languages from the same family with the literature of that family, e.g., French, Italian, and Spanish literatures 840

See Manual at 808.8

.001–.007 Standard subdivisions

[.008] Groups of people

Do not use; class in 809.8

[.009] History, geographic treatment, biography

Do not use for history without subdivision, biography; class in 809. Do not use for historical periods; class in 809.01–809.05. Do not use for geographic treatment; class in 809.89

.01–.05 Literature from specific periods

Add to base number 809.0 the numbers following —090 in notation 0901–0905 from Table 1, e.g., history, description, critical appraisal of 18th century literature 809.033

.1–.7 **Literature in specific forms other than miscellaneous writings**

Add to base number 809 the numbers following 808.8 in 808.81–808.87, e.g., history, description, critical appraisal of poetry 809.1, of poetry about animals 809.19362

Class theory, technique, history of literary criticism of specific literary forms other than miscellaneous writings in 808.1–808.7; class miscellaneous writings in 809.98

See Manual at 800: Literary criticism; also at 808.81–808.88 and 809.1–809.7

.8   **Literature for and by groups of people**

Class here history and description of literature with respect to groups of people

Unless other instructions are given, observe the following table of preference, e.g., history, description, critical appraisal of literature for or by American Roman Catholic girls 809.892827 (*not* 809.813, 809.8921282, or 809.8973):

People by age group	809.89282–809.89285
People by gender or sex	809.89286–809.89287
People by relationships, people by miscellaneous social attributes, people with disabilities and illnesses, gifted people	809.89205–809.89207
Occupational and religious groups	809.8921
Ethnic and national groups except for groups with ethnic origins from more than one continent, of European descent	809.81–809.88
Ethnic and national groups with ethnic origins from more than one continent, of European descent	809.805–809.809
Residents of specific continents, countries, localities	809.893–809.899
Residents of specific regions	809.891

Class literature in specific forms for and by groups of people in 809.1–809.7; class literature displaying specific features for and by groups of people in 809.9; class literatures of specific languages for and by groups of people in 810–890

.805–.809   **Literature for and by ethnic and national groups with ethnic origins from more than one continent, of European descent**

Add to base number 809.80 the numbers following —0 in notation 05–09 from Table 5, e.g., Europeans 809.809

>   **809.81–809.88**   Literature for and by ethnic and national groups except for groups with ethnic origins from more than one continent, of European descent

Class comprehensive works in 809.8

.81–.87   **Literature for and by larger western ethnic and national groups**

Add to base number 809.8 notation 1–7 from Table 5, e.g., North Americans 809.81

.88   **Literature for and by ancient Greeks, modern Greeks and Cypriots, other ethnic and national groups**

.881   **Ancient Greeks**

.888   **Modern Greeks and Cypriots**

.889   **Other ethnic and national groups**

Add to base number 809.889 the numbers following —9 in notation 91–99 from Table 5, e.g., Jewish literature 809.88924

.89   **Literature for and by other groups of people**

Add to base number 809.89 the numbers following —9 in notation 91–99 from Table 3C, e.g., literature in more than one language by painters 809.892175, literature by residents of Canada 809.8971

.9   **Literature displaying specific features, miscellaneous writings**

> Class literature in specific forms other than miscellaneous writings displaying specific features in 809.1–809.7

.91–.92   Literature displaying specific qualities and elements

> Add to base number 809.9 notation 1–2 from Table 3C, e.g., history, description, critical appraisal of literature displaying tragedy and horror 809.916
>
> Class literature dealing with specific themes and subjects and displaying specific qualities and elements in 809.933

.93   Literature displaying other aspects

.933   Literature dealing with specific themes and subjects

> Add to base number 809.933 the numbers following —3 in notation 32–39 from Table 3C, e.g., history, description, critical appraisal of literature dealing with marriage 809.933543

.935   Literature emphasizing subjects

> Works not basically belletristic discussed as literature, in which the real interest is in the literary quality of the text rather than the subject of the text
>
> Add to base number 809.935 notation 001–999, e.g., religious works as literature 809.9352, biography and autobiography as literature 809.93592
>
> Class literary examination of texts in which the real interest is in the subject of the texts with the texts, e.g., literary examination of sacred books in order to reach conclusions about meaning, structure, authorship, date 208.2

.98   Miscellaneous writings

> Add to base number 809.98 the numbers following 808.88 in 808.882–808.887, e.g., history, description, critical appraisal of jokes 809.982
>
> Class theory, technique, history of literary criticism of miscellaneous writings in 808

> ## 810–890 Literatures of specific languages and language families

Literature is classed by the language in which originally written
(Option: Class translations into a language requiring local emphasis with the literature of that language)

Class here collections of texts from literatures of two languages; history, description, critical appraisal of literatures of two languages

Unless there is a specific provision for a dialect, literature in a dialect is classed with the literature of the basic language. Subdivisions are added for literature in a dialect if subdivisions can be added for literature of the basic language, e.g., poetry by early 20th-century author writing in Swiss German dialect 831.912

Literature in a pidgin or creole is classed with the source language from which more of its vocabulary comes than from its other source language(s). Subdivisions are added for literature in a pidgin or creole if subdivisions can be added for literature of the source language, e.g., poetry by late 20th-century author writing in French creole 841.914

Under each literature identified by *, add to designated base number notation 1–8 from Table 3A for works by or about individual authors, notation 01–09 or notation 1–8 from Table 3B for works by or about more than one author. If the base number is not identified in a note, it is the number given for the literature, e.g., for Dutch 839.31. Full instructions for building numbers are given at the start of Table 3

Use the same literary period table for all works of or about literature in the same language, regardless of country of origin, except for special provisions for American literature in English under 810. If option C below is followed, optional period tables may be used for affiliated literatures (literatures in the same language, but from countries other than the traditional homeland)

The numbers used in this schedule for literatures of individual languages do not necessarily correspond exactly with those in 420–490 or with the notation in Table 6. Use notation from Table 6 only when so instructed, e.g., at 899

Unless other instructions are given, class a work containing or discussing literatures of two languages in 810–890 in the number coming first, e.g., a collection of English and French texts 820.8 (*not* 840.8), but a collection of classical Greek and Latin texts 880

Class texts by more than one author in more than two languages not from the same language family in 808.8; class history, description, critical appraisal of works by more than one author in more than two languages not from the same language family in 809; class comprehensive works in 800

(Option: For any group of literatures, add notation 04 from Table 1 and then add notation 01–09 or notation 1–8 from Table 3B, e.g., collections of literary texts written in Ethiopian languages 892.80408. Other options for specific groups of literatures are found at 891.4, 894.8, 896, 897, 898)

(Option: To give preferred treatment to, or make available more and shorter numbers for the classification of, literature of any specific language that it is desired to emphasize, use one of the following options:

(Option A: Class in 810, where full instructions appear
(continued)

> ## 810–890 Literatures of specific languages and language families (continued)

> (Option B: Give preferred treatment by placing before 810 through use of a letter or other symbol, e.g., literature of Arabic language 8A0, for which the base number is 8A

> (Option C: Where two or more countries share the same language, either [1] use initial letters to distinguish the separate countries, or [2] use the special number designated for literatures of those countries that are not preferred. Full instructions appear under 811–818, 819, 821–828, 828.99, 841–848, 848.99, 861–868, 868.99, 869, 869.899)

810   American literature in English

English-language literature of North America, South America, Hawaii, and geographically associated islands

Class comprehensive works on American literature in English and English literature in 820

(Option: To give local emphasis and a shorter number to a specific literature other than American literature in English, e.g., Afrikaans literature, class it here; in that case class American literature in English in 820. Other options are described under 810–890)

.1–.9   Standard subdivisions; collections in more than one form; history, description, critical appraisal of works in more than one form of American literature in English

Add to base number 810 the numbers following —0 in notation 01–09 from Table 3B, e.g., a collection of American literature in English 810.8

Use period table under 811–818

> ## 811–818 Subdivisions for specific forms of American literature in English

Except for modifications shown below, add to base number 81 as instructed at beginning of Table 3, e.g., American poetry in English 811

Use the following period table for English-language literature from any part of North America, South America, Hawaii, and geographically associated islands; for comprehensive works on English-language literature from all these areas

PERIOD TABLE FOR AMERICAN LITERATURE IN ENGLISH
```
1      Colonial period, 1607–1776
2      1776–1829
3      1830–1861
          Class here 19th century
              For 1800–1829, see 2; for 1861–1899, see 4
4      1861–1899
5      1900–1999
52        1900–1945
54        1945–1999
6      2000–
```

Class comprehensive works in 810

(Option: Distinguish English-language literatures of specific countries by initial letters, e.g., literature of Canada C810, of Jamaica J810, of United States U810; or class literatures not requiring local emphasis in 819. Other options are described under 810–890)

(OPTIONAL PERIOD TABLE FOR AMERICAN LITERATURE IN ENGLISH
```
(For Canada
   (3      Colonial period to 1867 in Canada
              Class here 19th century
                  For 1867–1899, see 4
   (4      1867–1899 in Canada
   (5      1900–1999 in Canada
   (52        1900–1945 in Canada
   (54        1945–1999 in Canada
   (6      2000 to present in Canada)
```

811   American poetry in English

Number built according to instructions under 811–818 and at beginning of Table 3

812   American drama in English

Number built according to instructions under 811–818 and at beginning of Table 3

813   American fiction in English

Number built according to instructions under 811–818 and at beginning of Table 3

814   American essays in English

Number built according to instructions under 811–818 and at beginning of Table 3

815   **American speeches in English**

> Number built according to instructions under 811–818 and at beginning of Table 3

816   **American letters in English**

> Number built according to instructions under 811–818 and at beginning of Table 3

817   **American humor and satire in English**

> Number built according to instructions under 811–818 and at beginning of Table 3

818   **American miscellaneous writings in English**

> Number built according to instructions under 811–818 and at beginning of Table 3

(819)   **American literatures in English not requiring local emphasis**

> (Optional number; prefer 810 for all American literatures in English. Other options are described under 810–890)
>
> Class here English-language literatures of specific American countries other than the country requiring local emphasis, e.g., libraries emphasizing United States literature may class here Canadian literature, and libraries emphasizing Canadian literature may class here United States literature

(.1)   *†**Canada**

(.3)   *†**United States**

(.5)   *†**Mexico**

(.7)   **Central America**

> (Optional number; prefer 810)

(.700 1–.700 9)   Standard subdivisions; collections in more than one form; history, description, critical appraisal of works in more than one form of Central American literature in English

> (Optional numbers; prefer 810.1–810.9)
>
> Add to base number 819.700 the numbers following —0 in notation 01–09 from Table 3B, e.g., a collection of Central American literature in English 819.7008

(.701–.708)   Subdivisions for specific forms of Central American literature in English

> (Optional numbers; prefer 811–818)
>
> Add to base number 819.70 as instructed at beginning of Table 3, e.g., Central American poetry in English 819.701

---

*Add to base number as instructed at beginning of Table 3
†(Optional number; prefer 810 for comprehensive works; prefer 810.1–810.9 for standard subdivisions; collections in more than one form; history, description, critical appraisal of works in more than one form; prefer 811–818 for specific forms)

(.71–.77)   Specific countries

> (Optional numbers; prefer 810)

> Add to base number 819.7 the numbers following —728 in notation 7281–7287 from Table 2, e.g., English-language literature of Costa Rica 819.76; then add further as instructed at beginning of Table 3, e.g., a collection of English-language literature of Costa Rica 819.7608

(.8)   West Indies (Antilles) and Bermuda

> (Optional number; prefer 810)

(.800 1–.800 9)   Standard subdivisions; collections in more than one form; history, description, critical appraisal of works in more than one form of English-language literatures of West Indies (Antilles) and Bermuda

> > (Optional numbers; prefer 810.1–810.9)

> > Add to base number 819.800 the numbers following —0 in notation 01–09 from Table 3B, e.g., a collection of English-language literature of West Indies 819.8008

(.801–.808)   Subdivisions for specific forms of English-language literatures of West Indies (Antilles) and Bermuda

> (Optional numbers; prefer 811–818)

> Add to base number 819.80 as instructed at beginning of Table 3, e.g., English-language poetry of West Indies 819.801

(.81)   *†Cuba

(.82)   *†Jamaica

(.83)   *†Dominican Republic

(.84)   *†Haiti

(.85)   *†Puerto Rico

(.86)   *†Bahama Islands

(.87)   *†Leeward Islands

(.88)   *†Windward and other southern islands

(.89)   *†Bermuda

(.9)   South America

> (Optional number; prefer 810)

---

*Add to base number as instructed at beginning of Table 3
†(Optional number; prefer 810 for comprehensive works; prefer 810.1–810.9 for standard subdivisions; collections in more than one form; history, description, critical appraisal of works in more than one form; prefer 811–818 for specific forms)

(.900 1–.900 9)   Standard subdivisions; collections in more than one form; history, description, critical appraisal of works in more than one form of English-language literatures of South America

> (Optional numbers; prefer 810.1–810.9)

> Add to base number 819.900 the numbers following —0 in notation 01–09 from Table 3B, e.g., a collection of English-language literature from South America 819.9008

(.901–.908)   Subdivisions for specific forms of English-language literatures of South America

> (Optional numbers; prefer 811–818)

> Add to base number 819.90 as instructed at beginning of Table 3, e.g., English-language poetry from South America 819.901

(.91–.99)   Specific countries

> (Optional numbers; prefer 810)

> Add to base number 819.9 the numbers following —8 in notation 81–89 from Table 2, e.g., English-language literature of Brazil 819.91; then add further as instructed at beginning of Table 3, e.g., a collection of English-language literature of Brazil 819.9108

820   English and Old English (Anglo-Saxon) literatures

Subdivisions are added for English literature alone

For American literature in English, see 810

.1–.9   Standard subdivisions; collections in more than one form; history, description, critical appraisal of works in more than one form of English literature

> Add to base number 820 the numbers following —0 in notation 01–09 from Table 3B, e.g., a collection of English literature 820.8

> Use period table under 821–828

> ## 821–828 Subdivisions for specific forms of English literature

Except for modifications shown under specific entries, add to base number 82 as instructed at beginning of Table 3, e.g., a collection of English literature 820.8

Use the following period table for literature from all countries and continents except North America, South America, Hawaii, and associated islands; for comprehensive works on literature in English language

PERIOD TABLE FOR ENGLISH

1	Early English period, 1066–1400
	Class here medieval period
2	1400–1558
3	Elizabethan period, 1558–1625
	Class here 16th century; Renaissance and Jacobean periods
	For 1500–1558, the pre-Elizabethan part of the Renaissance, see 2
4	1625–1702
	Class here Caroline and Restoration periods
5	Queen Anne period, 1702–1745
	Class here 18th century
	For 1700–1702, see 4; for 1745–1799, see 6
6	1745–1799
7	1800–1837
	Class here romantic period
8	Victorian period, 1837–1899
	Class here 19th century
	For 1800–1837, see 7
9	1900–
91	1900–1999
912	1900–1945
914	1945–1999
92	2000–

Class comprehensive works in 820

(Option: Distinguish English-language literatures of specific countries by initial letters, e.g., literature of England E820, of Ireland Ir820, of Scotland S820, of Wales W820, or of all British Isles B820, of Australia A820, of India In820; or class literatures not requiring local emphasis in 828.99. If literatures are identified by one of these methods, assign optional period numbers given below for literature of Ireland, Africa, Asia, Australia, and New Zealand; otherwise, assign the period numbers given above for all English-language literatures except American literature. Other options are described under 810–890

(continued)

> **821–828 Subdivisions for specific forms of English literature (continued)**

(OPTIONAL PERIOD TABLES FOR ENGLISH

(For Ireland

(1 Medieval and early modern to 1659 in Ireland
     Class here 17th century
     For 1660–1699, see 2

(2 1660–1799 in Ireland

(3 1800–1899 in Ireland

(4 1900–1945 in Ireland
     Class here Irish literary revival, 20th century
     For Irish literary revival in 19th century, see 3; for 1945–1999, see 5

(5 1945–1999 in Ireland

(6 2000 to present in Ireland

(For African countries other than South Africa

(1 Early period to 1959 in African countries other than South Africa

(2 1960–1999 in African countries other than South Africa
     Class here 20th century
     For 1900–1959, see 1

(3 2000 to present in African countries other than South Africa

(For Asian countries

(1 Early period to 1858 in Asian countries
     Class here 19th century
     For 1858–1899, see 2

(2 1858–1947 in Asian countries

(3 1947–1999 in Asian countries
     Class here 20th century
     For 1900–1947, see 2

(4 2000 to present in Asian countries

(For Australia

(1 Early period to 1889 in Australia

(2 1890–1945 in Australia

(3 1945–1999 in Australia
     Class here 20th century
     For 1900–1945, see 2

(4 2000 to present in Australia

(For New Zealand

(1 Early period to 1907 in New Zealand

(2 1907–1999 in New Zealand

(3 2000 to present in New Zealand

(continued)

> ### 821–828   Subdivisions for specific forms of English literature (continued)

(For South Africa
   (1   Early period to 1909 in South Africa
   (2   1909–1961 in South Africa
           Class here 20th century
             For 1900–1909, see 1; for 1961–1994, see 3; for 1994–1999, see 4
   (3   1961–1994 in South Africa
   (4   1994 to present in South Africa)

821   English poetry

Number built according to instructions under 821–828 and at beginning of Table 3

822   English drama

Number built according to instructions under 821–828 and at beginning of Table 3

.3   Drama of Elizabethan period, 1558–1625

Number built according to instructions under 821–828 and at beginning of Table 3

.33 William Shakespeare

(Option: Subarrange works about and by Shakespeare according to the following table, which may be adapted for use with any specific author:

A Authorship controversies
(Option: Class here bibliography; prefer 016.82233)
B Biography
D Critical appraisal
Class critical appraisal of individual works in O-Z
E Textual criticism
Class textual criticism of individual works in O-Z
F Sources, allusions, learning
G Societies, concordances, miscellany
H Quotations, condensations, adaptations
I Complete works in English without notes
J Complete works in English with notes
K Complete works in translation
L Partial collections in English without notes
M Partial collections in English with notes
N Partial collections in translation
>O-Z Individual works
Use the first number of each pair for texts, the second for description and critical appraisal
Class poems in 821.3
>O-R Comedies
O1–2 All's well that ends well
O3–4 As you like it
O5–6 The comedy of errors
O7–8 Love's labour's lost
P1–2 Measure for measure
P3–4 The merchant of Venice
P5–6 The merry wives of Windsor
P7–8 A midsummer night's dream
Q1–2 Much ado about nothing
Q3–4 The taming of the shrew
Q5–6 The tempest
Q7–8 Twelfth night
R1–2 The two gentlemen of Verona
R3–4 The winter's tale
>S-V Tragedies
S1–2 Antony and Cleopatra
S3–4 Coriolanus
S5–6 Cymbeline
S7–8 Hamlet
T1–2 Julius Caesar
T3–4 King Lear
T5–6 Macbeth
T7–8 Othello
U1–2 Pericles
U3–4 Romeo and Juliet
U5–6 Timon of Athens
U7–8 Titus Andronicus
V1–2 Troilus and Cressida

(continued)

.33 William Shakespeare (continued)

    >W-X Histories
    W1–2 Henry IV, parts 1–2
    W3–4 Henry V
    W5–6 Henry VI, parts 1–3
    W7–8 Henry VIII
    X1–2 King John
    X3–4 Richard II
    X5–6 Richard III
    Y   Poems
        (Optional numbers; prefer 821.3)
    Y1–2 General works
    Y3–4 Venus and Adonis
    Y5–6 The rape of Lucrece
    Y7–8 Sonnets
    Z   Spurious and doubtful works)

823   English fiction

Number built according to instructions under 821–828 and at beginning of Table 3

824   English essays

Number built according to instructions under 821–828 and at beginning of Table 3

825   English speeches

Number built according to instructions under 821–828 and at beginning of Table 3

826   English letters

Number built according to instructions under 821–828 and at beginning of Table 3

827   English humor and satire

Number built according to instructions under 821–828 and at beginning of Table 3

828   English miscellaneous writings

Number built according to instructions under 821–828 and at beginning of Table 3

(.99)   English-language literatures not requiring local emphasis

(Optional number; prefer 820 for all non-American English-language literatures. Other options are described under 810–890)

Class here English-language literatures of specific non-American countries other than the country requiring local emphasis, e.g., libraries emphasizing British literature may class here Australian, Indian, other literatures, and libraries emphasizing Indian literature may class here British literature

(.991)	†Scotland and Ireland

> (Option: Class here all English-language literature of United Kingdom, of Great Britain, of British Isles. Add to base number 828.991 as instructed at beginning of Table 3 for United Kingdom, for Great Britain, for British Isles, e.g., a collection of English-language literature from the British Isles 828.99108)

(.991 1)	*†Scotland
(.991 5)	*†Ireland
(.992)	*†England and Wales
(.992 9)	*†Walcs
(.993)	†New Zealand, Australia, India, South Africa
(.993 3)	*†New Zealand
(.993 4)	*†Australia
(.993 5)	*†India
(.993 6)	*†South Africa
(.994–.999)	Other parts of the world

> (Optional numbers; prefer 820)

> English-language literature except of British Isles, North America, South America, Hawaii, New Zealand, Australia, India, South Africa, and associated islands

> Add to base number 828.99 notation 4–9 from Table 2, e.g., English-language literature of Israel 828.995694; then add 0 and to the result add further as instructed at beginning of Table 3, e.g., English-language poetry of Israel 828.99569401

829   Old English (Anglo-Saxon) literature

.01–.09	Standard subdivisions; collections in more than one form; history, description, critical appraisal of works in more than one form of Old English (Anglo-Saxon) literature

> Limited to works by or about more than one author

> Add to base number 829 notation 01–09 from Table 3B, e.g., history, description, critical appraisal of works in more than one form 829.09

.1   Poetry

> *For Caedmon, see 829.2; for Beowulf, see 829.3; for Cynewulf, see 829.4*

---

*Add to base number as instructed at beginning of Table 3
†(Optional number; prefer 820 for comprehensive works; prefer 820.1–820.9 for standard subdivisions; collections in more than one form; history, description, critical appraisal of works in more than one form; prefer 821–828 for specific forms)

.100 1–.100 9 Standard subdivisions; collections; history, description, critical appraisal

Limited to works by or about more than one author

Add to base number 829.100 the numbers following —100 in notation 1001–1009 from Table 3B, e.g., collections of Old English poetry 829.1008

.2   **Caedmon**

.3   **Beowulf**

.4   **Cynewulf**

.8   **Prose literature**

.800 1–.800 9 Standard subdivisions; collections; history, description, critical appraisal

Limited to works by or about more than one author

Add to base number 829.800 the numbers following —100 in notation 1001–1009 from Table 3B, e.g., collections of Old English prose 829.8008

830   German literature and literatures of related languages

Class here literatures of Germanic languages

For English and Old English (Anglo-Saxon) literatures, see 820

.01–.09 Standard subdivisions of literatures of Germanic languages

.1–.9   **Standard subdivisions; collections in more than one form; history, description, critical appraisal of works in more than one form of German literature**

Class here literature in Alsatian, Franconian, Pennsylvania Dutch (Pennsylvania German), Swabian, Swiss-German dialects

Add to base number 830 the numbers following —0 in notation 01–09 from Table 3B, e.g., a collection of German literature 830.8

Use period table under 031–838

See also 839.1 for Yiddish (Judeo-German) literature; also 839.4 for low German (Plattdeutsch) literature

> ## 831–838 Subdivisions for specific forms of German literature

Class here specific forms of literature in Alsatian, Franconian, Pennsylvania Dutch (Pennsylvania German), Swabian, Swiss-German dialects

Add to base number 83 as instructed at beginning of Table 3, e.g., German poetry 831

PERIOD TABLE

1	Early period to 1099
	Class here Old High German literature
2	1100–1349
	Class here medieval period, 750–1349; Middle High German literature
	For 750–1099, see 1
21	1100–1249
	Class here 13th century, Blütezeit
	For 1250–1299, see 22
22	1250–1349
	Class here 14th century
	For 1350–1399, see 3
3	1350–1517
4	Reformation period, 1517–1625
5	1625–1749
	Class here baroque period
6	1750–1832
	Class here 18th century, classical period, romantic period
	For 1700–1749, see 5; for later romantic period, see 7
7	1832–1856
	Class here 19th century
	For 1800–1832, see 6; for 1856–1899, see 8
8	1856–1899
9	1900–
91	1900–1990
912	1900–1945
914	1945–1990
92	1990–

Class comprehensive works in 830

See also 839.1 for Yiddish (Judeo-German) literature; also 839.4 for low German (Plattdeutsch) literature

831 German poetry

Number built according to instructions under 831–838 and at beginning of Table 3

832 German drama

Number built according to instructions under 831–838 and at beginning of Table 3

833 German fiction

Number built according to instructions under 831–838 and at beginning of Table 3

834 German essays

Number built according to instructions under 831–838 and at beginning of Table 3

835 German speeches

Number built according to instructions under 831–838 and at beginning of Table 3

836 German letters

Number built according to instructions under 831–838 and at beginning of Table 3

837 German humor and satire 838

Number built according to instructions under 831–838 and at beginning of Table 3

838 German miscellaneous writings

Number built according to instructions under 831–838 and at beginning of Table 3

839 Other Germanic literatures

SUMMARY

.1 *Yiddish literature

PERIOD TABLE
1   Early period to 1699
2   Period of enlightenment, 1700–1859
        Class here 19th century
            For 1860–1899, see 3
3   1860–1945
        Class here 20th century
            For 1945–1999, see 4
4   1945–

> 839.2–839.4 Low Germanic literatures

Class comprehensive works in 839

*Add to base number as instructed at beginning of Table 3

.2 ***Frisian literature**

Including Old Frisian literature

PERIOD TABLE
1	Early period to 1609
2	1609–1799
3	1800–1899
4	1900–1999
5	2000–

.3 **Netherlandish literatures**

.31 *Dutch literature

Including Old Low Franconian literature

Class here Flemish literature

PERIOD TABLE
1	Medieval period to 1449
	Class here 15th century
	For 1450–1499, see 2
2	Renaissance period, 1450–1599
3	1600–1699
4	1700–1799
5	1800–1899
6	1900–1999
62	1900–1945
64	1945–1999
7	2000–

.36 *Afrikaans literature

PERIOD TABLE
1	Early period to 1875
2	1875–1904
3	1904–1924
4	1924–1961
	Class here 20th century
	For 1900–1904, see 2; for 1904–1924, see 3; for 1961–1994, see 5; for 1994–1999, see 6
5	1961–1994
6	1994–

.4 ***Low German (Plattdeutsch) literature**

Including Old Low German literature, Old Saxon literature

PERIOD TABLE
1	Early period to 1599
2	1600–1899
3	1900–1999
4	2000–

*Add to base number as instructed at beginning of Table 3

.5   **North Germanic literatures (Nordic literatures)**

> Class here comprehensive works on East Scandinavian literatures, West Scandinavian literatures, modern West Scandinavian literatures; comprehensive works on literatures of the Nordic countries

> *For specific North Germanic literatures, see 839.6–839.8; for Finnic literatures, see 894.54; for Sámi literatures, see 894.57*

> **839.6–839.8 Specific North Germanic literatures**

> Class comprehensive works in 839.5

.6   **Old Norse (Old Icelandic), Icelandic, Faroese literatures**

.600 1–.600 9   Standard subdivisions of comprehensive works on Old Norse (Old Icelandic), Icelandic, Faroese literatures

.601–.609   Standard subdivisions; collections in more than one form; history, description, critical appraisal of works in more than one form of Old Norse (Old Icelandic) literature

> Add to base number 839.60 the numbers following —0 in notation 01–09 from Table 3B, e.g., a collection of Old Norse literature 839.608

.61–.68   Subdivisions for specific forms of Old Norse (Old Icelandic) literature

> Add to base number 839.6 as instructed at beginning of Table 3, e.g., Old Norse poetry 839.61

.69   Icelandic and Faroese literatures

.690 01–.690 09   Standard subdivisions of comprehensive works on Icelandic and Faroese literatures

.690 1–.690 9   Standard subdivisions; collections in more than one form; history, description, critical appraisal of works in more than one form of Icelandic literature

> Add to base number 839.690 the numbers following —0 in notation 01–09 from Table 3B, e.g., a collection of Icelandic literature 839.6908

> Use period table under 839.691–839.698

.691–.698   Subdivisions for specific forms of Icelandic literature

> Add to base number 839.69 as instructed at beginning of Table 3, e.g., Icelandic poetry 839.691

> PERIOD TABLE
> 1   Early period, 1500–1719
> 2   Age of enlightenment, 1720–1835
> 3   1835–1899
>   Class here 19th century
>   *For 1800–1835, see 2*
> 4   1900–1999
> 5   2000–

.699   *Faroese literature

.7   *Swedish literature

PERIOD TABLE

1	Medieval period to 1519
2	Reformation period, 1520–1639
3	1640–1739
	Class here 17th century
	For 1600–1639, see 2
4	1740–1779
	Class here 18th century
	For 1700–1739, see 3; for 1780–1799, see 5
5	Age of Gustavus, 1780–1809
	Including 1800–1809 [*formerly* 6]
6	1809–1909
	1800–1809 relocated to 5
62	1809–1830
	Class here period of romanticism
64	1830–1879
	Class here period of liberalism
67	1879–1909
	Including 1900–1909 [*formerly* 72]
	Class here period of realism
7	1909–1999
72	1909–1945
	1900–1909 relocated to 67
74	1945–1999
8	2000–

.8   Danish and Norwegian literatures

.81   *Danish literature

PERIOD TABLE

1	Medieval period to 1499
2	Reformation period, 1500–1559
	Class here 16th century
	For 1560–1599, see 3
3	Learned period, 1560–1699
4	Age of Holberg, 1700–1749
	Class here 18th century
	For 1750–1799, see 5
5	Period of enlightenment, 1750–1799
6	1800–1899
7	1900–1999
72	1900–1945
74	1945–1999
8	2000–

Class Dano-Norwegian literature in 839.82

*Add to base number as instructed at beginning of Table 3

.82   *Norwegian literature

Class here Dano-Norwegian, New Norwegian, Bokmål, Landsmål, Riksmål
literature

PERIOD TABLE
1   Medieval period to 1499
2   Reformation period, 1500–1559
Class here 16th century
For 1560–1599, see 3
3   Learned period, 1560–1699
4   1700–1749
Class here 18th century
For 1750–1799, see 5
5   Period of enlightenment, 1750–1799
6   1800–1899
7   1900–1999
72   1900–1945
74   1945–1999
8   2000–

.9   **East Germanic literatures**

840   French literature and literatures of related Romance languages

Class here literatures of Romance languages

Class comprehensive works on literatures of Italic languages in 870

*For literatures of Italian, Dalmatian, Romanian, Rhaetian, Sardinian, Corsican
languages, see 850; for literatures of Spanish, Portuguese, Galician languages,
see 860*

.01–.09   Standard subdivisions of literatures of Romance languages

.1–.9   **Standard subdivisions; collections in more than one form; history,
description, critical appraisal of works in more than one form of
French literature**

Add to base number 840 the numbers following —0 in notation 01–09 from
Table 3B, e.g., a collection of French literature 840.8

Use period table under 841–848

See also 849 for Occitan literature

*Add to base number as instructed at beginning of Table 3

> ## 841–848 Subdivisions for specific forms of French literature

Except for modifications shown under specific entries, add to base number 84 as instructed at beginning of Table 3, e.g., French poetry 841

Use the following period table for literature in French language from all countries and continents, for comprehensive works on literature in French language

PERIOD TABLE FOR FRENCH

1	Early period to 1399
	Class here medieval period
2	1400–1499
3	Renaissance period, 1500–1599
4	Classical period, 1600–1715
5	1715–1789
	Class here 18th century, Enlightenment, Age of Reason
	For 1700–1715, see 4; for 1789–1799, see 6
6	Revolution and Empire, 1789–1815
7	Constitutional monarchy, 1815–1848
	Class here 19th century
	For 1800–1815, see 6; for 1848–1899, see 8
8	1848–1899
9	1900–
91	1900–1999
912	1900–1945
914	1945–1999
92	2000–

Class comprehensive works in 840

See also 849 for Occitan literature

(Option: Distinguish French-language literatures of specific countries by initial letters, e.g., literature of Canada C840, of France F840; or class literatures not requiring local emphasis in 848.99. If literatures are identified by one of these methods, assign the optional period numbers given below for Belgium and non-European countries; otherwise, assign the period numbers given above for all French-language literatures. Other options are described under 810–890

(continued)

841–848 Subdivisions for specific forms of French literature (continued)

> (OPTIONAL PERIOD TABLES FOR FRENCH

(For Asian and African countries

(1	Early period to 1959 in Asian and African countries
(2	1960–1999 in Asian and African countries
	Class here 20th century
	For 1900–1959, see 1
(3	2000 to present in Asian and African countries

(For Belgium

(1	Early period to 1829 in Belgium
(2	1830–1899 in Belgium
	Class here 19th century
	For 1800–1829, see 2
(3	1900–1999 in Belgium
(32	1900–1945 in Belgium
(34	1945–1999 in Belgium
(4	2000 to present in Belgium

(For Canada

(3	Colonial period to 1867 in Canada
	Class here 19th century
	For 1867–1899, see 4
(4	1867–1899 in Canada
(5	1900–1999 in Canada
(52	1900–1945 in Canada
(54	1945–1999 in Canada
(6	2000 to present in Canada)

841 French poetry

Number built according to instructions under 841–848 and at beginning of Table 3

842 French drama

Number built according to instructions under 841–848 and at beginning of Table 3

843 French fiction

Number built according to instructions under 841–848 and at beginning of Table 3

844 French essays

Number built according to instructions under 841–848 and at beginning of Table 3

845 French speeches

Number built according to instructions under 841–848 and at beginning of Table 3

846 French letters

Number built according to instructions under 841–848 and at beginning of Table 3

847 French humor and satire

Number built according to instructions under 841–848 and at beginning of Table 3

848   French miscellaneous writings

(.99)   Number built according to instructions under 841–848 and at beginning of Table 3

(.99)   French-language literatures not requiring local emphasis

> (Optional number; prefer 840 for all French-language literatures. Other options are described under 810–890)

> Class here literatures of specific countries, e.g., libraries emphasizing literature of France may class here Belgian and Canadian literatures, libraries emphasizing Canadian literature may class here literature of France

(.991)   *†France

(.992)   *†Canada

(.993)   *†Belgium

(.994–.999)   Other parts of the world

> (Optional numbers; prefer 840)

> French-language literature except of France, Belgium, Canada

> Add to base number 848.99 notation 4–9 from Table 2, e.g., French-language literature of Tahiti 848.9996211; then add 0 and to the result add further as instructed at beginning of Table 3, e.g., French-language drama of Tahiti 848.999621102

849   Occitan, Catalan, Franco-Provençal literatures

Subdivisions are added for Occitan literature alone

.01–.09   Standard subdivisions; collections in more than one form; history, description, critical appraisal of works in more than one form of Occitan literature

> Class here Langue d'oc literature; literature in Auvergnat, Gascon, Languedocien, Limousin, Provençal dialects

> Add to base number 849.0 the numbers following —0 in notation 01–09 from Table 3B, e.g., a collection of Occitan literature 849.08

> Use period table under 849.1–849.8

> Class Franco-Provençal literature in 849 without further addition

---

*Add to base number as instructed at beginning of Table 3
†(Optional number; prefer 840 for comprehensive works; prefer 840.1–840.9 for standard subdivisions; collections in more than one form; history, description, critical appraisal of works in more than one form; prefer 821–848 for specific forms)

.1–.8 **Subdivisions for specific forms of Occitan literature**

Class here specific forms of Langue d'oc literature; specific forms of literature in Auvergnat, Gascon, Languedocien, Limousin, Provençal dialects

Add to base number 849 as instructed at beginning of Table 3, e.g., Occitan poetry 849.1

PERIOD TABLE
1	Early period to 1099
2	Golden age, 1100–1299
3	1300–1499
4	1500–1899
5	1900–1999
52	1900–1945
54	1945–1999
6	2000–

Class Franco-Provençal literature in 849 without further addition

.9 ***Catalan literature**

PERIOD TABLE
1	Early period to 1349
	Class here 14th century
	For 1350–1399, see 2
2	1350–1449
3	Golden age, 1450–1499
	Class here 15th century
	For 1400–1449, see 2
4	1500–1899
5	1900–1999
52	1900–1945
54	1945–1999
6	2000–

850 Literatures of Italian, Dalmatian, Romanian, Rhaetian, Sardinian, Corsican languages

Subdivisions are added for Italian literature alone

Class comprehensive works on literatures of Romance languages in 840; class comprehensive works on literatures of Italic languages in 870

.1–.9 **Standard subdivisions; collections in more than one form; history, description, critical appraisal of works in more than one form of Italian literature**

Add to base number 850 the numbers following —0 in notation 01–09 from Table 3B, e.g., a collection of Italian literature 850.8

Use period table under 851–858

---

*Add to base number as instructed at beginning of Table 3

> ### 851–858 Subdivisions for specific forms of Italian literature

> Add to base number 85 as instructed at beginning of Table 3, e.g., Italian poetry 851

> PERIOD TABLE
> | | |
> |---|---|
> | 1 | Early period to 1375 |
> | 2 | Period of classical learning, 1375–1492 |
> | | Class here Renaissance period |
> | | *For later Renaissance period, see 3* |
> | 3 | 1492–1542 |
> | 4 | 1542–1585 |
> | | Class here 16th century |
> | | *For 1500–1542, see 3; for 1585–1599, see 5* |
> | 5 | 1585–1748 |
> | 6 | 1748–1814 |
> | | Class here 18th century |
> | | *For 1700–1748, see 5* |
> | 7 | 1814–1859 |
> | | Class here 19th century, romantic period |
> | | *For 1800–1814, see 6; for 1859–1899, see 8* |
> | 8 | 1859–1899 |
> | 9 | 1900– |
> | 91 | 1900–1999 |
> | 912 | 1900–1945 |
> | 914 | 1945–1999 |
> | 92 | 2000– |

> Class comprehensive works in 850

851   Italian poetry

Number built according to instructions under 851–858 and at beginning of Table 3

852   Italian drama

Number built according to instructions under 851–858 and at beginning of Table 3

853   Italian fiction

Number built according to instructions under 851–858 and at beginning of Table 3

854   Italian essays

Number built according to instructions under 851–858 and at beginning of Table 3

855   Italian speeches

Number built according to instructions under 851–858 and at beginning of Table 3

856   Italian letters

Number built according to instructions under 851–858 and at beginning of Table 3

857   Italian humor and satire

Number built according to instructions under 851–858 and at beginning of Table 3

858 **Italian miscellaneous writings**

> Number built according to instructions under 851–858 and at beginning of Table 3

859 **Literatures of Romanian, Rhaetian, Sardinian, Corsican languages**

> Subdivisions are added for Romanian literature alone

.01–.09 Standard subdivisions; collections in more than one form; history, description, critical appraisal of works in more than one form of Romanian literature

> Add to base number 859.0 the numbers following —0 in notation 01–09 from Table 3B, e.g., a collection of Romanian literature 859.08
>
> Use period table under 859.1–859.8

.1–.8 **Subdivisions for specific forms of Romanian literature**

> Add to base number 859 as instructed at beginning of Table 3, e.g., Romanian poetry 859.1

> PERIOD TABLE
> | | |
> |---|---|
> | 1 | Early period to 1799 |
> | 2 | 1800–1899 |
> | 3 | 1900– |
> | 32 | 1900–1945 |
> | 34 | 1945–1989 |
> | 35 | 1989– |

.9 **Literatures of Rhaetian, Sardinian, Corsican languages**

.92 *Friulian literature

.94 *Ladin literature

.96 *Romansch literature

.98 Sardinian and Corsican literatures

.982 *Sardinian literature

.984 *Corsican literature

860 **Literatures of Spanish, Portuguese, Galician languages**

> Class comprehensive works on literatures of Romance languages in 840

.01–.09 Standard subdivisions of literatures of Spanish, Portuguese, Galician languages

---

*Add to base number as instructed at beginning of Table 3

.1–.9   **Standard subdivisions; collections in more than one form; history, description, critical appraisal of works in more than one form of Spanish literature**

Class here Judeo-Spanish (Ladino), Papiamento literature

Add to base number 860 the numbers following —0 in notation 01–09 from Table 3B, e.g., a collection of Spanish literature 860.8

Use period table under 861–868

See also 849.9 for Catalan literature

> ### 861–868 Subdivisions for specific forms of Spanish literature

Except for modifications shown under specific entries, add to base number 86 as instructed at beginning of Table 3, e.g., Spanish poetry 861

Class here specific forms of Judeo-Spanish (Ladino), Papiamento literature

Use the following period table for literature in Spanish language from all countries and continents, for comprehensive works on literature in Spanish language

PERIOD TABLE FOR SPANISH

1	Early period to 1369
	Class here 14th century
	For 1369–1399, see 2
2	1369–1516
3	Golden Age, 1516–1699
4	1700–1799
5	1800–1899
6	1900–1999
62	1900–1945
64	1945–1999
7	2000–

Class comprehensive works in 860

See also 849.9 for Catalan literature

(Option: Distinguish Spanish-language literatures of specific countries by initial letters, e.g., literature of Chile Ch860, of Colombia Co860, of Mexico M860 [or, of all American countries A860], of Spain S860; or class literatures not requiring local emphasis in 868.99. If literatures are identified by one of these methods, assign the optional period numbers given below for literature of American countries; otherwise, assign the period numbers given above for all Spanish-language literatures. Other options are described under 810–890

(OPTIONAL PERIOD TABLE FOR SPANISH

(For American countries	
(1	Colonial and revolutionary period, 1519–1826, in American countries
(2	1826–1888 in American countries
	Class here 19th century
	For 1800–1826, see 1; for 1888–1899, see 3
(3	1888–1909 in American countries
(4	1910–1999 in American countries
(42	1910–1945 in American countries
(44	1945–1999 in American countries
(5	2000 to present in American countries)

861   Spanish poetry

Number built according to instructions under 861–868 and at beginning of Table 3

862   Spanish drama

Number built according to instructions under 861–868 and at beginning of Table 3

863   **Spanish fiction**

> Number built according to instructions under 861–868 and at beginning of Table 3

864   **Spanish essays**

> Number built according to instructions under 861–868 and at beginning of Table 3

865   **Spanish speeches**

> Number built according to instructions under 861–868 and at beginning of Table 3

866   **Spanish letters**

> Number built according to instructions under 861–868 and at beginning of Table 3

867   **Spanish humor and satire**

> Number built according to instructions under 861–868 and at beginning of Table 3

868   **Spanish miscellaneous writings**

> Number built according to instructions under 861–868 and at beginning of Table 3

(.99)   Spanish-language literatures not requiring local emphasis

> (Optional number; prefer 860 for all Spanish-language literatures. Other options are described under 810–890)
>
> Class here literatures of specific countries other than the country requiring local emphasis, e.g., libraries emphasizing literature of Spain may class here Hispanic-American literatures, and libraries emphasizing literature of Mexico may class here literatures of other Hispanic-American countries and of Spain

(.991)   *†Spain

(.992)   Hispanic North America

> (Optional number; prefer 860)
>
> Class here comprehensive works on Spanish-language literature of Hispanic America
>
> *For Hispanic South America, see 868.993*

(.992 001–.992 009)   Standard subdivisions; collections in more than one form; history, description, critical appraisal of works in more than one form of Spanish-language literatures of Hispanic North America

> (Optional numbers; prefer 860.1–860.9)
>
> Add to base number 868.9920 the numbers following —0 in notation 01–09 from Table 3B, e.g., a collection of Spanish-language literature of Hispanic North America 868.992008

---

*Add to base number as instructed at beginning of Table 3
†(Optional number; prefer 860 for comprehensive works; prefer 860.1–860.9 for standard subdivisions; collections in more than one form; history, description, critical appraisal of works in more than one form; prefer 861–868 for specific forms)

(.992 01–.992 08)		Subdivisions for specific forms of Spanish-language literatures of Hispanic North America

        (Optional numbers; prefer 861–868)

        Add to base number 868.9920 as instructed at beginning of Table 3, e.g., Spanish-language poetry of Hispanic North America 868.99201

(.992 1)   *†Mexico

(.992 2)   Central America

        (Optional number; prefer 860)

(.992 200 1–.992 200 9)   Standard subdivisions; collections in more than one form; history, description, critical appraisal of works in more than one form of Spanish-language literatures of Central America

        (Optional numbers; prefer 860.1–860.9)

        Add to base number 868.992200 the numbers following —0 in notation 01–09 from Table 3B, e.g., a collection of Spanish-language literature of Central America 868.9922008

(.992 201–.992 208)   Subdivisions for specific forms of Spanish-language literatures of Central America

        (Optional numbers; prefer 861–868)

        Add to base number 868.99220 as instructed at beginning of Table 3, e.g., Spanish-language poetry of Central America 868.992201

(.992 21–.992 27)   Specific countries

        (Optional numbers; prefer 860)

        Add to base number 868.9922 the numbers following —728 in notation 7281–7287 from Table 2, e.g., Spanish-language literature of Costa Rica 868.99226; then add further as instructed at beginning of Table 3, e.g., collections of Spanish-language literature of Costa Rica 868.9922608

(.992 3)   West Indies (Antilles)

        (Optional number; prefer 860)

---

*Add to base number as instructed at beginning of Table 3
†(Optional number; prefer 860 for comprehensive works; prefer 860.1–860.9 for standard subdivisions; collections in more than one form; history, description, critical appraisal of works in more than one form; prefer 861–868 for specific forms)

(.992 300 1–.992 300 9)	Standard subdivisions; collections in more than one form; history, description, critical appraisal of works in more than one form of Spanish literatures of West Indies

(Optional numbers; prefer 860.1–860.9)

Add to base number 868.992300 the numbers following —0 in notation 01–09 from Table 3B, e.g., a collection of Spanish-language literature of West Indies 868.9923008

(.992 301–.992 308)	Subdivisions for specific forms of Spanish-language literatures of West Indies

(Optional numbers; prefer 861–868)

Add to base number 868.99230 as instructed at beginning of Table 3, e.g., Spanish-language poetry of West Indies 868.992301

(.992 31)	*†Cuba
(.992 33)	*†Dominican Republic
(.992 35)	*†Puerto Rico
(.993)	Hispanic South America

(Optional number; prefer 860)

(.993 001–.993 009)	Standard subdivisions; collections in more than one form; history, description, critical appraisal of works in more than one form of Spanish-language literatures of Hispanic South America

(Optional numbers; prefer 860.1–860.9)

Add to base number 868.99300 the numbers following —0 in notation 01–09 from Table 3B, e.g., a collection of Spanish-language literature of Hispanic South America 868.993008

(.993 01–.993 08)	Subdivisions for specific forms of Spanish-language literatures of Hispanic South America

(Optional numbers; prefer 861–868)

Add to base number 868.9930 as instructed at beginning of Table 3, e.g., Spanish-language poetry of Hispanic South America 868.99301

---

*Add to base number as instructed at beginning of Table 3
†(Optional number; prefer 860 for comprehensive works; prefer 860.1–860.9 for standard subdivisions; collections in more than one form; history, description, critical appraisal of works in more than one form; prefer 861–868 for specific forms)

(.993 2–.993 7)   Argentina, Chile, Bolivia, Peru, Colombia, Ecuador, Venezuela

(Optional numbers; prefer 860)

Add to base number 868.993 the numbers following —8 in notation 82–87 from Table 2, e.g., Spanish-language literature of Chile 868.9933; then add further as instructed at beginning of Table 3, e.g., history and critical appraisal of Spanish-language literature of Chile 868.993309

(.993 9)   Paraguay and Uruguay

(Optional numbers; prefer 860)

Add to base number 868.9939 the numbers following —89 in notation 892–895 from Table 2, e.g., Spanish-language literature of Uruguay 868.99395; then add further as instructed at beginning of Table 3, e.g., history and critical appraisal of Spanish-language literature of Uruguay 868.9939509

(.994–.999)   Other parts of the world

(Optional numbers; prefer 860)

Spanish-language literature except of Spain, Hispanic America

Add to base number 868.99 notation 4–9 from Table 2, e.g., Spanish-language literature of the United States 868.9973; then add 0 and to the result add further as instructed at beginning of Table 3, e.g., Spanish-language poetry of the United States 868.997301

869 *Literatures of Portuguese and Galician languages

Subdivisions are added for literature of Portuguese language alone

Use the following period table for literature in Portuguese language from all countries and continents, for comprehensive works on literature in Portuguese language

PERIOD TABLE FOR PORTUGUESE

1	Early period to 1499
2	1500–1799
	Class here classical period
3	1800–1899
4	1900–1999
41	1900–1945
42	1945–1999
5	2000–

See also 860 for Papiamento literature

(Option: Distinguish Portuguese-language literatures of specific countries by initial letters, e.g., literature of Brazil B869, of Portugal P869; or class literatures not requiring local emphasis in 869.899. If literatures are identified by one of these methods, assign the optional period numbers given below for literature of Brazil; otherwise, assign the period numbers given above for all Portuguese-language literatures. Other options are described under 810–890)

(OPTIONAL PERIOD TABLE FOR PORTUGUESE
  (For Brazil

(1	Period of formation, 1500–1749, in Brazil
	Class here 18th century
	For 1750–1799, see 2
(2	Period of transformation, 1750–1829, in Brazil
(3	1830–1921 in Brazil
	Class here 19th century
	For 1800–1829, see 2
(4	1921–1999 in Brazil
(5	2000 to present in Brazil)

(.899)   Portuguese-language literatures not requiring local emphasis

(Optional number; prefer 869 for all Portuguese-language literatures. Other options are described under 810–890)

Class here literatures of specific countries other than the country requiring local emphasis, e.g., libraries emphasizing literature of Portugal may class here Brazilian literature, and libraries emphasizing Brazilian literature may class here literature of Portugal

(.899 1)   *‡Portugal

(.899 2)   *‡Brazil

*Add to base number as instructed at beginning of Table 3
‡(Optional number; prefer 869 for comprehensive works; prefer 869.01–869.09 for standard subdivisions; collections in more than one form; history, description, critical appraisal of works in more than one form; prefer 869.1–869.8 for specific forms)

(.899 4–.899 9)   ‡Other parts of world

Portuguese-language literature except of Portugal, Brazil

Add to base number 869.899 notation 4–9 from Table 2, e.g., Portuguese-language literature of India 869.89954; then add 0 and to the result add further as instructed at beginning of Table 3, e.g., Portuguese-language drama of India 869.8995402

.9   *Galician literature

Class here Gallegan literature

Use the following period table for literature in Galician language from all countries and continents, for comprehensive works on literature in Galician language

PERIOD TABLE
1	Early period to 1499
2	1500–1799
3	1800–1899
	Class here period of revival
4	1900–1999
5	2000–

870   Latin literature and literatures of related Italic languages

Class here literatures of Italic languages

Class comprehensive works of or on literatures of classical (Greek and Latin) languages in 880

For literatures of Romance languages, see 840

.01–.09   Standard subdivisions of literatures of Italic languages

.1–.9   Standard subdivisions; collections in more than one form; history, description, critical appraisal of works in more than one form of Latin literature

Add to base number 870 the numbers following —0 in notation 01–09 from Table 3B, e.g., a collection of Latin literature 870.8

Use period table under 871–878

---

*Add to base number as instructed at beginning of Table 3
‡(Optional number; prefer 869 for comprehensive works; prefer 869.01–869.09 for standard subdivisions; collections in more than one form; history, description, critical appraisal of works in more than one form; prefer 869.1–869.8 for specific forms)

> ### 871–878 Subdivisions for specific forms of Latin literature

Add to base number 87 as instructed at beginning of Table 3, e.g., Latin letters 876; however, observe the special interpretations of and exceptions to notation from Table 3 that appear below, e.g., Latin poetry of the Roman period 871.01, Latin epic poetry and fiction of the Roman period 873.01

PERIOD TABLE

1	Roman period to ca. 499
2	Pre-Carolingian period, ca. 500–ca. 749
	Class here 8th century
	For 750–799, see 3
3	Medieval period, ca. 750–1349
	Class here 14th century
	For 1350–1399, see 4
4	Modern period, 1350–

Class comprehensive works in 870

871   †Latin poetry

For dramatic poetry, see 872; for epic poetry, see 873; for lyric poetry, see 874

.01–.04   Specific periods

Add to base number 871.0 notation 1–4 from the period table under 871–878, e.g., Latin poetry of the Roman period 871.01; then, for works by or about more than one author, add the numbers following —10 in notation 1001–1009 from Table 3B, e.g., collections of Latin poetry from the Roman period 871.0108

Do not use 871.02–871.07 for specific kinds

872   †Latin dramatic poetry and drama

Subdivisions are added for either or both topics in heading

.01–.04   Specific periods

Add to base number 872.0 notation 1–4 from the period table under 871–878, e.g., Latin drama of the Roman period 872.01; then, for works by or about more than one author, add the numbers following —10 in notation 1001–1009 from Table 3B, e.g., collections of Latin drama from the Roman period 872.0108

Do not use 872.02–872.05 for specific media, scope, kinds

873   †Latin epic poetry and fiction

Subdivisions are added for either or both topics in heading

---

†Add as instructed under 871–878 and at beginning of Table 3

.01–.04 Specific periods

> Add to base number 873.0 notation 1–4 from the period table under 871–878, e.g., Latin epic poetry of the Roman period 873.01; then, for works by or about more than one author, add the numbers following —10 in notation 1001–1009 from Table 3B, e.g., collections of Latin epic poetry from the Roman period 873.0108

> Do not use 873.01–873.08 for specific scope and kinds

874 †Latin lyric poetry

.01–.04 Specific periods

> Add to base number 874.0 notation 1–4 from the period table under 871–878, e.g., Latin lyric poetry of the Roman period 874.01; then, for works by or about more than one author, add the numbers following —10 in notation 1001–1009 from Table 3B, e.g., collections of Latin lyric poetry from the Roman period 874.0108

875 †Latin speeches

.01–.04 Specific periods

> Add to base number 875.0 notation 1–4 from the period table under 871–878, e.g., Latin speeches of the Roman period 875.01; then, for works by or about more than one author, add the numbers following —10 in notation 1001–1009 from Table 3B, e.g., collections of Latin speeches from the Roman period 875.0108

> Do not use 875.01–875.06 for specific kinds

876 †Latin letters

.01–.04 Specific periods

> Add to base number 876.0 notation 1–4 from the period table under 871–878, e.g., Latin letters of the Roman period 876.01; then, for works by or about more than one author, add the numbers following —10 in notation 1001–1009 from Table 3B, e.g., collections of Latin letters from the Roman period 876.0108

877 †Latin humor and satire

.01–.04 Specific periods

> Add to base number 877.0 notation 1–4 from the period table under 871–878, e.g., Latin humor and satire of the Roman period 877.01; then, for works by or about more than one author, add the numbers following —10 in notation 1001–1009 from Table 3B, e.g., collections of Latin humor and satire from the Roman period 877.0108

878 †Latin miscellaneous writings

.000 1–.000 9 Standard subdivisions

†Add as instructed under 871–878 and at beginning of Table 3

.002–.008   Specific kinds of miscellaneous writings

> Numbers built according to instructions under 871–878 and at beginning of Table 3

.01–.04   Specific periods

> Add to base number 878.0 notation 1–4 from the period table under 871–878, e.g., Latin miscellaneous writings of the Roman period 878.01; then, for works by or about more than one author, add the numbers following —10 in notation 1001–1009 from Table 3B, e.g., collections of Latin miscellaneous writings from the Roman period 878.0108

879   Literatures of other Italic languages

.4   **Latinian literatures other than Latin**

.7   **Literatures of Sabellian languages**

.9   **Osco-Umbrian literatures**

880   Classical Greek literature and literatures of related Hellenic languages

> Class here literatures of Hellenic languages, comprehensive works of or on literatures of classical (Greek and Latin) languages

> *For Latin literature, see 870*

.01–.09   Standard subdivisions of classical (Greek and Latin) literatures

.1–.9   **Standard subdivisions; collections in more than one form; history, description, critical appraisal of works in more than one form of classical Greek literature**

> Add to base number 880 the numbers following —0 in notation 01–09 from Table 3B, e.g., a collection of Greek literature 880.8

> Use period table under 881–888

> ## 881–888 Subdivisions for specific forms of classical Greek literature

> Add to base number 88 as instructed at beginning of Table 3, e.g., a collection of classical Greek speeches 885; however, observe the special interpretations of and exceptions to notation from Table 3 that appear below, e.g., classical Greek poetry of the ancient period 881.01, classical Greek epic poetry and fiction of the ancient period 883.01

> PERIOD TABLE
> 1   Ancient period to ca. 499
> 2   Medieval and Byzantine periods, ca. 500–1599
> 3   Modern period, 1600–

> Class comprehensive works in 880

881   ‡Classical Greek poetry

> *For dramatic poetry, see 882; for epic poetry, see 883; for lyric poetry, see 884*

.01–.03   Specific periods

> Add to base number 881.0 notation 1–3 from the period table under 881–888, e.g., classical Greek poetry of the ancient period 881.01; then, for works by or about more than one author, add the numbers following —10 in notation 1001–1009 from Table 3B, e.g., collections of classical Greek poetry of the ancient period 881.0108
>
> Do not use 881.02–881.07 for specific kinds

882   ‡Classical Greek dramatic poetry and drama

> Subdivisions are added for either or both topics in heading

.01–.03   Specific periods

> Add to base number 882.0 notation 1–3 from the period table under 881–888, e.g., classical Greek drama of the ancient period 882.01; then, for works by or about more than one author, add the numbers following —10 in notation 1001–1009 from Table 3B, e.g., collections of classical Greek drama of the ancient period 882.0108
>
> Do not use 882.02–882.05 for specific media, scope, kinds

883   ‡Classical Greek epic poetry and fiction

> Subdivisions are added for either or both topics in heading

.01–.03   Specific periods

> Add to base number 883.0 notation 1–3 from the period table under 881–888, e.g., classical Greek epic poetry of the ancient period 883.01; then, for works by or about more than one author, add the numbers following —10 in notation 1001–1009 from Table 3B, e.g., collections of classical Greek epic poetry of the ancient period 883.0108
>
> Do not use 883.01–883.08 for specific scope and kinds

884   ‡Classical Greek lyric poetry

.01–.03   Specific periods

> Add to base number 884.0 notation 1–3 from the period table under 881–888, e.g., classical Greek lyric poetry of the ancient period 884.01; then, for works by or about more than one author, add the numbers following —10 in notation 1001–1009 from Table 3B, e.g., collections of classical Greek lyric poetry of the ancient period 884.0108

885   ‡Classical Greek speeches

‡Add as instructed under 881–888 and at beginning of Table 3

.01–.03   Specific periods

> Add to base number 885.0 notation 1–3 from the period table under
> 881–888, e.g., classical Greek speeches of the ancient period 885.01; then,
> for works by or about more than one author, add the numbers following
> —10 in notation 1001–1009 from Table 3B, e.g., collections of classical
> Greek speeches of the ancient period 885.0108
>
> Do not use 885.01–885.06 for specific kinds

886   ‡Classical Greek letters

.01–.03   Specific periods

> Add to base number 886.0 notation 1–3 from the period table under
> 881–888, e.g., classical Greek letters of the ancient period 886.01; then, for
> works by or about more than one author, add the numbers following —10
> in notation 1001–1009 from Table 3B, e.g., collections of classical Greek
> letters of the ancient period 886.0108

887   ‡Classical Greek humor and satire

.01–.03   Specific periods

> Add to base number 887.0 notation 1–3 from the period table under
> 881–888, e.g., classical Greek humor and satire of the ancient period
> 887.01; then, for works by or about more than one author, add the numbers
> following —10 in notation 1001–1009 from Table 3B, e.g., collections of
> classical Greek humor and satire of the ancient period 887.0108

888   ‡Classical Greek miscellaneous writings

.000 1–.000 9   Standard subdivisions

.002–.008   Specific kinds of miscellaneous writings

> Numbers built according to instructions under 881–888 and at beginning
> of Table 3

.01–.03   Specific periods

> Add to base number 888.0 notation 1–3 from the period table under
> 881–888, e.g., classical Greek miscellaneous writings of the ancient period
> 888.01; then, for works by or about more than one author, add the numbers
> following —10 in notation 1001–1009 from Table 3B, e.g., collections of
> classical Greek miscellaneous writings of the ancient period 888.0108

‡Add as instructed under 881–888 and at beginning of Table 3

889 *Modern Greek literature

Class here Katharevusa and Demotic literature

PERIOD TABLE
1	Early period to 1821
2	1821–1899
3	1900–1999
32	1900–1945
34	1945–1999
4	2000–

890 Literatures of other specific languages and language families

Class texts by more than one author in more than two languages not from the same language family in 808.8; class history, description, critical appraisal of works by more than one author in more than two languages not from the same language family in 809

SUMMARY

891	**East Indo-European and Celtic literatures**
892	**Afro-Asiatic literatures**
893	**Non-Semitic Afro-Asiatic literatures**
894	**Literatures of Altaic, Uralic, Hyperborean, Dravidian languages; literatures of miscellaneous languages of south Asia**
895	**Literatures of East and Southeast Asia**
896	**African literatures**
897	**Literatures of North American native languages**
898	**Literatures of South American native languages**
899	**Literatures of non-Austronesian languages of Oceania, of Austronesian languages, of miscellaneous languages**

891 East Indo-European and Celtic literatures

Standard subdivisions are added for East Indo-European and Celtic literatures together, for East Indo-European literatures alone

SUMMARY

891.1	**Indo-Iranian literatures**
.2	**Sanskrit literature**
.3	**Middle Indo-Aryan literatures**
.4	**Modern Modern Indo-Aryan literatures**
.5	**Iranian literatures**
.6	**Celtic literatures**
.7	**Russian literature and related East Slavic literatures**
.8	**Slavic (Slavonic) literatures**
.9	**Baltic and other Indo-European literatures**

.1 Indo-Iranian literatures

For Indo-Aryan literatures, see 891.2–891.4; for Iranian literatures, see 891.5

*Add to base number as instructed at beginning of Table 3

> ### 891.2–891.4 Indo-Aryan literatures

> Class comprehensive works in 891.1

.2   ***Sanskrit literature**

Class here classical Sanskrit literature

.29   Vedic (Old Indo-Aryan) literature

.3   **Middle Indo-Aryan literatures**

Former heading: Middle Indic literatures

Class here comprehensive works on Prakrit literatures

For modern Prakrit literatures, see 891.4

.37   *Pali literature

.4   **Modern Indo-Aryan literatures**

Former heading: Modern Indic literatures

PERIOD TABLE FOR SPECIFIC MODERN INDO-ARYAN LITERATURES
```
1      Early period to 1345
2      1345–1645
          Class here 14th century
              For 1300–1345, see 1
3      1645–1845
          Class here 17th century
              For 1600–1645, see 2
4      1845–1895
          Class here 19th century
              For 1800–1845, see 3; for 1895–1899, see 5
5      1895–1919
6      1920–1939
7      1940–
71        1940–1999
              Class here 20th century
                  For 1900–1919, see 5; for 1920–1939, see 6
72        2000–
```

Class comprehensive works on Prakrit literatures in 891.3

(Option: Treat literatures of all modern Indo-Aryan languages as literature of one language, with base number 891.4. Add to base number 891.4 as instructed at beginning of Table 3, e.g., a collection of literary texts in modern Indo-Aryan languages 891.408)

.41   Sindhi and Lahnda literatures

Subdivisions are added for Sindhi literature alone

*Add to base number as instructed at beginning of Table 3

.410 1–.410 9	Standard subdivisions; collections in more than one form; history, description, critical appraisal of works in more than one form of Sindhi literature

> Add to base number 891.410 the numbers following —0 in notation 01–09 from Table 3B, e.g., a collection of Sindhi literature 891.4108

> Use period table under 891.4

.411–.418	Subdivisions for specific forms of Sindhi literature

> Add to base number 891.41 as instructed at beginning of Table 3, e.g., Sindhi poetry 891.411

> Use period table under 891.4

.419	*Lahnda literature

> Use period table under 891.4

.42	*Panjabi literature

> Use period table under 891.4

.43	Hindi literature and related Western Hindi literatures

Class here Western Hindi literatures

> *For languages of east central zone of Indo-Aryan languages (Eastern Hindi languages), see 891.492*

.430 01–.430 09	Standard subdivisions of Western Hindi literatures
.430 1–.430 9	Standard subdivisions; collections in more than one form; history, description, critical appraisal of works in more than one form of Hindi literature

> Add to base number 891.430 the numbers following —0 in notation 01–09 from Table 3B, e.g., a collection of Hindi literature 891.4308

> Use period table under 891.4

.431–.438	Subdivisions for specific forms of Hindi literature

> Add to base number 891.43 as instructed at beginning of Table 3, e.g., Hindi poetry 891.431

> Use period table under 891.4

.439	*Urdu literature

> Use period table under 891.4

.44	*Bengali literature

> Use period table under 891.4

.45	Assamese, Bihari, Oriya literatures
.451	*Assamese literature

> Use period table under 891.4

*Add to base number as instructed at beginning of Table 3

.454   *Bihari literature

> Class here literatures in Bhojpuri, Magahi, Maithili

> Use period table under 891.4

.456   *Oriya literature

> Use period table under 891.4

.46   Marathi and Konkani literatures

> Subdivisions are added for Marathi literature alone

.460 1–.460 9   Standard subdivisions; collections in more than one form; history, description, critical appraisal of works in more than one form of Marathi literature

> > Add to base number 891.460 the numbers following —0 in notation 01–09 from Table 3B, e.g., a collection of Marathi literature 891.4608

> > Use period table under 891.4

.461–.468   Subdivisions for specific forms of Marathi literature

> Add to base number 891.46 as instructed at beginning of Table 3, e.g., Marathi poetry 891.461

> Use period table under 891.4

.469   *Konkani literature

> Use period table under 891.4

.47   Gujarati, Bhili, Rajasthani literatures

> Subdivisions are added for Gujarati literature alone

.470 1–.470 9   Standard subdivisions; collections in more than one form; history, description, critical appraisal of works in more than one form of Gujarati literature

> > Add to base number 891.470 the numbers following —0 in notation 01–09 from Table 3B, e.g., a collection of Gujarati literature 891.4708

> > Use period table under 891.4

.471–.478   Subdivisions for specific forms of Gujarati literature

> Add to base number 891.47 as instructed at beginning of Table 3, e.g., Gujarati poetry 891.471

> Use period table under 891.4

.479   *Rajasthani literature

> Class here Jaipuri, Marwari literatures

> Use period table under 891.4

.48   Sinhalese-Maldivian literatures

> Class here Sinhalese (Sinahala) literature

*Add to base number as instructed at beginning of Table 3

.480 1–.480 9	Standard subdivisions; collections in more than one form; history, description, critical appraisal of works in more than one form of Sinhalese (Sinhala) literature

> Add to base number 891.480 the numbers following —0 in notation 01–09 from Table 3B, e.g., a collection of Sinhalese literature 891.4808

> Use period table under 891.4

.481–.488	Subdivisions for specific forms of Sinhalese (Sinhala) literature

> Add to base number 891.48 as instructed at beginning of Table 3, e.g., Sinhalese poetry 891.481

> Use period table under 891.4

.489	*Divehi (Maldivian) literature

> Use period table under 891.4

.49	Other Indo-Aryan literatures

> Including Nuristani (Kafiri) literature

> *See also 894.8 for Dravidian literatures; also 895.4 for Tibeto-Burman literatures; also 895.95 for Munda literatures*

.492	Literatures of east central zone of Indo-Aryan languages (Eastern Hindi literatures)

> Including Awadhi, Bagheli, Chattisgarhi, Fijian Hindustani (Fiji Hindi) literatures

> Class comprehensive works on Hindi literatures in 891.43

.495	*Nepali literature
.496	Pahari literatures

> Including Garhwali literature

> Class here literatures of northern zone of Indo-Aryan languages

> *For Nepali literature, see 891.495*

.497	*Romani literature
.499	Dardic (Pisacha) literatures

> Including Kashmiri, Khowar, Kohistani, Shina literatures

.5	**Iranian literatures**
.51	*Old Persian literature

> Class here ancient West Iranian literatures

> *See also 891.52 for Avestan literature*

.52	*Avestan literature

> Class here ancient East Iranian literatures

*Add to base number as instructed at beginning of Table 3

.53 Middle Iranian literatures

> Including Khotanese (Saka), Pahlavi (Middle Persian), Sogdian literatures

.55 *Modern Persian (Farsi) literature

> PERIOD TABLE
> 1   Period of formal development, ca. 1000–1389
> 2   1389–1899
> 3   1900–1999
> 4   2000–

> *See also 891.56 for Dari literature; also 891.57 for Tajik literature*

.56 *Dari literature

.57 *Tajik literature

.59 Other modern Iranian literatures

> Including Pamir literatures, Ossetic literature

.593 *Pashto (Afghan) literature

.597 Kurdish literatures and literatures of related languages

> Including central and southern Kurdish

> Class here Kurdish (Kurmanji, northern Kurdish) literature

.597 01–.597 09 Standard subdivisions; collections in more than one form; history, description, critical appraisal of works in more than one form of Kurdish (Kurmanji, northern Kurdish) literature

> Add to base number 891.5970 the numbers following —0 in notation 01–09 from Table 3B, e.g., a collection of Kurdish literature 891.59708

.597 1–.597 8 Subdivisions for specific forms of Kurdish (Kurmanji, northern Kurdish) literature

> Add to base number 891.597 as instructed at beginning of Table 3, e.g., Kurdish poetry 891.5971

.598 *Baluchi literature

.6   Celtic literatures

> Including Gaulish

---

*Add to base number as instructed at beginning of Table 3

.62   *Irish Gaelic literature

        PERIOD TABLE
           1   Early period to 1171
                  Class here 12th century
                    For 1171–1199, see 2
           2   1171–1599
           3   1600–1875
           4   1875–1999
           42   1875–1922
                  Class here Irish literary revival
           43   1922–1999
           5   2000–

.63   *Scottish Gaelic literature

        PERIOD TABLE
           1   Early period to 1599
           2   1600–1829
           3   1830–1999
           32   1830–1899
                  Class here 19th century
                    For 1800–1829, see 2
           34   1900–1999
           4   2000–

.64   *Manx literature

.66   *Welsh (Cymric) literature

        PERIOD TABLE
           1   Early period to 1599
           12   Early period to 1299
           14   1300–1599
           2   1600–1999
           22   1600–1799
           24   1800–1899
           26   1900–1945
                  Class here 20th century
                    For 1945–1999, see 28
           28   1945–1999
           3   2000–

.67   *Cornish literature

.68   *Breton literature

        PERIOD TABLE
           1   Early period to 1799
           2   1800–1899
           3   1900–1999
           4   2000–

*Add to base number as instructed at beginning of Table 3

.7   Russian literature and related East Slavic literatures

Class here East Slavic literatures

Class comprehensive works on Slavic (Slavonic) literatures in 891.8

.700 1–.700 9   Standard subdivisions of East Slavic literatures

.701–.709   Standard subdivisions; collections in more than one form; history, description, critical appraisal of works in more than one form of Russian literature

Add to base number 891.70 the numbers following —0 in notation 01–09 from Table 3B, e.g., a collection of Russian literature 891.708

Use period table under 891.71–891.78

.71–.78   Subdivisions for specific forms of Russian literature

Add to base number 891.7 as instructed at beginning of Table 3, e.g., Russian poetry 891.71

PERIOD TABLE
1	Early period to 1699
2	1700–1799
3	1800–1917
4	1917–1991
	Class here 20th century
	For 1900–1917, see 3; for 1991–1999, see 5
42	1917–1945
44	1945–1991
5	1991–

.79   Ukrainian and Belarusian literatures

Subdivisions are added for Ukrainian literature alone

.790 1–.790 9   Standard subdivisions; collections in more than one form; history, description, critical appraisal of works in more than one form of Ukrainian literature

Add to base number 891.790 the numbers following —0 in notation 01–09 from Table 3B, e.g., a collection of Ukrainian literature 891.7908

Use period table under 891.791–891.798

.791–.798   Subdivisions for specific forms of Ukrainian literature

Add to base number 891.79 as instructed at beginning of Table 3, e.g., Ukrainian poetry 891.791

PERIOD TABLE
1	Early period to 1798
2	1798–1917
3	1917–1991
	Class here 20th century
	For 1900–1917, see 2; for 1991–1999, see 4
32	1917–1945
34	1945 1991
4	1991–

.799   *Belarusian literature

> PERIOD TABLE
> | | |
> |---|---|
> | 1 | Early period to 1798 |
> | 2 | 1798–1917 |
> | 3 | 1917–1991 |
> | | Class here 20th century |
> | | *For 1900–1917, see 2; for 1991–1999, see 4* |
> | 4 | 1991– |

.8   Slavic (Slavonic) literatures

> Class here comprehensive works on literatures of Balto-Slavic languages

> *For East Slavic literatures, see 891.7; for Baltic literatures, see 891.91–891.93*

.81   Bulgarian literature and related South Slavic literatures

> Class here South Slavic literatures

> *For Serbian literature, see 891.82; for Croatian and Bosnian literatures, see 891.83; for Slovenian literature, see 891.84*

.810 01–.810 09   Standard subdivisions of South Slavic literatures

.810 1–.810 9   Standard subdivisions; collections in more than one form; history, description, critical appraisal of works in more than one form of Bulgarian literature

> Add to base number 891.810 the numbers following —0 in notation 01–09 from Table 3B, e.g., a collection of Bulgarian literature 891.8108

> Use period table under 891.811–891.818

.811–.818   Subdivisions for specific forms of Bulgarian literature

> Add to base number 891.81 as instructed at beginning of Table 3, e.g., Bulgarian poetry 891.811

> PERIOD TABLE
> | | |
> |---|---|
> | 1 | Early period to 1849 |
> | | Class here 19th century |
> | | *For 1850–1899, see 2* |
> | 2 | 1850–1899 |
> | 3 | 1900–1991 |
> | 4 | 1991– |

.819   *Macedonian literature

*Add to base number as instructed at beginning of Table 3

.82   *Serbian literature

Class here Serbo-Croatian literature; comprehensive works on Serbian, Croatian, Bosnian literatures

PERIOD TABLE
1		Early period to ca. 1549
		Class here 16th century
		For 1550–1599, see 2
2		Period of renaissance, ca. 1550–1699
3		1700–1799
4		1800–1899
5		1900–1991
52		1900–1945
54		1945–1991
6		1991–

Croatian literature relocated to 891.83; Bosnian literature relocated to 891.839

.83   Croatian literature [*formerly* 891.82] and Bosnian literature

Subdivisions are added for Croatian literature alone

.830 1–.830 9   Standard subdivisions; collections in more than one form; history, description, critical appraisal of works in more than one form of Croatian literature

Add to base number 891.830 the numbers following —0 in notation 01–09 from Table 3B, e.g., a collection of Croatian literature 891.8308

Use period table under 891.831–891.838

.831–.838   Subdivisions for specific forms of Croatian literature

Add to base number 891.83 as instructed at beginning of Table 3, e.g., Croatian poetry 891.831

PERIOD TABLE
1		Early period to ca. 1549
		Class here 16th century
		For 1550–1599, see 2
2		Period of renaissance, ca. 1550–1699
3		1700–1799
4		1800–1899
5		1900–1991
52		1900–1945
54		1945–1991
6		1991–

*Add to base number as instructed at beginning of Table 3

.839   *Bosnian literature [*formerly* 891.82]

PERIOD TABLE
>1   Early period to ca. 1549
>   Class here 16th century
>   *For 1550–1599, see 2*
>2   Period of renaissance, ca. 1550–1699
>3   1700–1799
>4   1800–1899
>5   1900–1991
>52   1900–1945
>54   1945–1991
>6   1991–

.84   *Slovenian literature

PERIOD TABLE
>1   Early period to ca. 1549
>   Class here 16th century
>   *For 1550–1599, see 2*
>2   Period of renaissance, ca. 1550–1699
>3   1700–1799
>4   1800–1899
>5   1900–1991
>6   1991–

.85   Polish literature and related West Slavic literatures

Including Kashubian literature

Class here West Slavic literatures

For Czech literature, see 891.86; for Slovak literature, see 891.87; for Wendish literature, see 891.88; for Polabian literature, see 891.89

.850 01–.850 09   Standard subdivisions of West Slavic literatures

.850 1–.850 9   Standard subdivisions; collections in more than one form; history, description, critical appraisal of works in more than one form of Polish literature

Add to base number 891.850 the numbers following —0 in notation 01–09 from Table 3B, e.g., a collection of Polish literature 891.8508

Use period table under 891.851–891.858

---

*Add to base number as instructed at beginning of Table 3

.851–.858   Subdivisions for specific forms of Polish literature

Add to base number 891.85 as instructed at beginning of Table 3, e.g.,
Polish poetry 891.851

PERIOD TABLE
1	Early period to 1399
2	1400–1499
3	Golden age, 1500–1599
4	1600–1699
5	1700–1795
6	1795–1919
7	1919–1989

Class here 20th century
For 1900–1919, see 6; for 1989–1999, see 8

72	1919–1945
73	1945–1989
8	1989–

.86   *Czech literature

Class here literature in Moravian dialects

PERIOD TABLE
1	Early period to 1399
2	1400–1449

Class here 15th century
For 1450–1499, see 3

3	Humanist period, 1450–1620
4	1620–1899

Class here 17th century
For 1600–1620, see 3

5	1900–1989
52	1900–1945
54	1945–1989
6	1989–

.87   *Slovak literature

.88   *Wendish (Lusatian, Sorbian) literature

.89   *Polabian literature

.9   Baltic and other Indo-European literatures

>   891.91–891.93 Baltic literatures

Class comprehensive works in 891.9

.91   Old Prussian literature

*Add to base number as instructed at beginning of Table 3

.92   *Lithuanian literature

           PERIOD TABLE
               1   Early period to 1799
               2   1800–1899
               3   1900–1991
               4   1991–

.93   *Latvian (Lettish) literature

           PERIOD TABLE
               1   Early period to 1799
               2   1800–1899
               3   1900–1991
               4   1991–

.99   Other Indo-European literatures

           Add to base number 891.99 the numbers following —9199 in notation
           91991–91998 from Table 6, e.g., Armenian literature 891.992, Hittite
           literature 891.998; then to the number given for each literature listed below
           add further as instructed at beginning of Table 3, e.g., a collection of
           Armenian literature 891.99208

           891.991 Albanian

           891.992 Armenian

           PERIOD TABLE FOR ARMENIAN
               1   Early period to 599
               2   600–999
               3   1000–1399
               4   1400–1849
               5   1850–1991
                     Class here 19th century
                         For 1800–1849, see 4
               6   1991–

892   Afro-Asiatic literatures

           Class here Semitic literatures

           For non-Semitic Afro-Asiatic literatures, see 893

.1   Akkadian (Assyro-Babylonian) literature

           Class here East Semitic literatures; literatures in Assyrian, Babylonian dialects
           of Akkadian

           For Eblaite literature, see 892.6

           See also 899.95 for Sumerian literature

*Add to base number as instructed at beginning of Table 3

>   **892.2–892.9 West Semitic literatures**

       Class comprehensive works in 892

.2   **Aramaic literatures**

       For Eastern Aramaic literatures, see 892.3

.29   Western Aramaic literatures

       Including Samaritan literature

.3   **Eastern Aramaic literatures**

       Class here Syriac literature

.4   ***Hebrew literature**

       PERIOD TABLE

1	Early period to 699
2	700–1699
	Class here medieval period
3	1700–1819
4	1820–1885
	Class here 19th century
	For 1800–1819, see 3; for 1885–1899, see 5
5	1885–1947
6	1947–1999
	Class here 20th century
	For 1900–1947, see 5
7	2000–

       Class comprehensive works on Canaanitic literatures in 892.6

.6   **Canaanite literatures**

       Including Eblaite literature

       Class here comprehensive works on Canaanitic literatures

       For Hebrew, see 892.4

.67   Ugaritic literature

.7   **Arabic and Maltese literatures**

       Class here classical Arabic literature, modern standard Arabic literature, Judeo-Arabic literature; literatures of Arabic and Maltese languages

       See also 892.9 for South Arabian literatures

---

*Add to base number as instructed at beginning of Table 3

.701–.709   Standard subdivisions; collections in more than one form; history, description, critical appraisal of works in more than one form of Arabic literatures

> Add to base number 892.70 the numbers following —0 in notation 01–09 from Table 3B, e.g., a collection of Arabic literature 892.708
>
> Use period table under 892.71–892.78

.71–.78   Subdivisions for specific forms of Arabic literatures

> Add to base number 892.7 as instructed at beginning of Table 3, e.g., Arabic poetry 892.71
>
> PERIOD TABLE
>   1   Pre-Islamic period to 622
>   2   Early Islamic and Mukhadrami period, 622–661
>   Class here 7th century
>   *For 600–622, see 1; for 661–699, see 32*
>   3   661–1258
>   32   Umayyad period, 661–749
>   Class here 8th century
>   *For 750–799, see 34*
>   34   Abbasid period, 750–1258
>   Class here 13th century
>   *For 1258–1299, see 4*
>   4   1258–1799
>   5   1800–1945
>   6   1945–1999
>   Class here 20th century
>   *For 1900–1945, see 5*
>   7   2000–

.79   *Maltese literature

.8   Ethiopian literatures

> Including Gurage, Harari literatures
>
> Class here comprehensive works on South Semitic literatures
>
> *For South Arabian literatures, see 892.9*

.81   Geʻez literature

.82   *Tigré literature

.83   *Tigrinya (Tigrigna) literature

.87   *Amharic literature

.9   South Arabian literatures

> Including Mahri, Sokotri literatures
>
> Class comprehensive works on South Semitic literatures in 892.8
>
> *See also 892.7 for North Arabic literatures*

---

*Add to base number as instructed at beginning of Table 3

893   Non-Semitic Afro-Asiatic literatures

Add to base number 893 the numbers following —93 in notation 931–937 from
Table 6, e.g., Berber literatures 893.3, Somali literature 893.54; then to the number
given for each literature listed below add further as instructed at beginning of Table
3, e.g., a collection of Somali literature 893.5408

893.1 Egyptian

893.2 Coptic

893.33 Tamazight

893.34 Kabyle

893.38 Tamashek

893.54 Somali

893.55 Oromo

893.72 Hausa

894   Literatures of Altaic, Uralic, Hyperborean, Dravidian languages; literatures of miscellaneous languages of south Asia

SUMMARY

894.1–.3	Altaic literatures
.4	Samoyedic literatures
.5	Finno-Ugric literatures
.6	Hyperborean (Paleosiberian) literatures
.8	Dravidian literatures and literatures of miscellaneous languages of south Asia

.1–.3   **Altaic literatures**

Add to base number 894 the numbers following —94 in notation 941–943 from Table 6, e.g., Mongolian literature 894.23, Altai literature 894.33; then to the number given for each literature listed below add further as instructed at beginning of Table 3, e.g., a collection of Mongolian literature 894.2308

894.23 Mongolian proper, Halh Mongolian (Khalkha Mongolian)

894.315 Chuvash

894.323 Uighur

894.325 Uzbek

894.332 Yakut

894.345 Kazakh

894.347 Kyrgyz

894.35 Turkish (Osmanli), Ottoman Turkish

PERIOD TABLE FOR TURKISH (OSMANLI), OTTOMAN TURKISH
1	Early period to 1499
2	1500–1849
3	1850–1999
	Class here 19th century, 20th century
	For 1800–1849, see 2
4	2000–

894.361 Azerbaijani

894.364 Turkmen

894.387 Tatar

894.388 Crimean Tatar

Class comprehensive works in 894

For Ainu literature, see 894.6; for Japanese literature, see 895.6; for Korean literature, see 895.7

.4   **Samoyedic literatures**

.5   **Finno-Ugric literatures**

Class here comprehensive works on Uralic literatures, on Uralic and Yukaghir literatures

For Samoyedic literatures, see 894.4; for Yukaghir literatures, see 894.6

.51   Ugric literatures

Including Ostyak (Khanty), Vogul literatures

.511   *Hungarian (Magyar) literature

> PERIOD TABLE
> 1   Early period to 1799
> 2   1800–1899
> 3   1900–1989
> 32   1900–1945
> 34   1945–1989
> 4   1989–

.53   Permic literatures

> Including Votyak (Udmurt), Zyrian (Komi) literatures

.54   Finnic literatures

> Including Karelian, Kven Finnish, Livonian, Tornedalen Finnish, Veps literatures

> *For Permic literatures, see 894.53; for Middle Volga literatures, see 894.56; for Sámi literatures, see 894.57*

.541   *Finnish (Suomi) literature

> PERIOD TABLE
> 1   Early period to 1799
> 2   1800–1899
> 3   1900–1999
> 4   2000–

> Class Kven Finnish literature, Tornedalen Finnish literature in 894.54

.545   *Estonian literature

> PERIOD TABLE
> 1   Early period to 1861
>   Class here 19th century
>   *For 1861–1899, see 2*
> 2   1861–1991
> 3   1991–

[.55]   Sámi (Saami) literatures

> Relocated to 894.57

.56   Middle Volga literatures

> Including Mari, Mordvin literatures

*Add to base number as instructed at beginning of Table 3

.57   Sámi (Saami) literatures [*formerly* 894.55]

Add to base number 894.57 the numbers following —9457 in notation 94572–94576 from Table 6, e.g., Eastern Sámi literatures 894.576, North Sámi literature 894.5745; then to the number given for each literature listed below add further as instructed at beginning of Table 3, e.g., a collection of North Sámi literature 894.574508

894.5722 South Sámi

894.5743 Lule Sámi

894.5745 North Sámi

.6   **Hyperborean (Paleosiberian) literatures**

Including Ainu literature, Yukaghir literatures

Class comprehensive works on Uralic and Yukaghir literatures in 894.5

.8   **Dravidian literatures and literatures of miscellaneous languages of south Asia**

Standard subdivisions are added for Dravidian literatures and literatures of miscellaneous languages of south Asia together, for Dravidian literatures alone

PERIOD TABLE FOR SPECIFIC DRAVIDIAN LITERATURES
```
1        Early period to 1345
2        1345–1645
             Class here 14th century
                 For 1300–1345, see 1
3        1645–1845
             Class here 17th century
                 For 1600–1645, see 2
4        1845–1895
             Class here 19th century
                 For 1800–1845, see 3; for 1895–1899, see 5
5        1895–1919
6        1920–1939
7        1940–
71           1940–1999
                 Class here 20th century
                     For 1900–1919, see 5; for 1920–1939, see 6
72           2000–
```

(Option: Treat literatures of all Dravidian languages as literature of one language, with base number 894.8. Add to base number 894.8 as instructed at beginning of Table 3, e.g., a collection of literature in Dravidian languages 894.808)

.81   South Dravidian literatures

Including Kota, Toda literatures

Class here literatures of the Dravida group

.811   *Tamil literature

                 Use period table under 894.8

.812   *Malayalam literature

                 Use period table under 894.8

.814   *Kannada (Kanarese) literature

                 Use period table under 894.8

.82   Central Dravidian literatures

.823   *Gondi literature

                 Use period table under 894.8

.824   *Kui (Khond, Kandh) literature

                 Use period table under 894.8

.827   *Telugu literature

                 Use period table under 894.8

.83   Brahui literature and related North Dravidian literatures

                 Class here North Dravidian literatures

.830 01–.830 09   Standard subdivisions of North Dravidian literatures

.830 1–.830 9   Standard subdivisions; collections in more than one form; history, description, critical appraisal of works in more than one form of Brahui literature

                 Add to base number 894.830 the numbers following —0 in notation 01–09 from Table 3B, e.g., a collection of Brahui literature 894.8308

                 Use period table under 894.8

.831–.838   Subdivisions for specific forms of Brahui literature

                 Add to base number 894.83 as instructed at beginning of Table 3, e.g., Brahui poetry 894.831

                 Use period table under 894.8

.89   Literatures of miscellaneous languages of south Asia

                 Only those literatures provided for below

                 Class literatures of languages of south Asia closely related to languages of east and southeast Asia in 895; class literatures of Indo-Iranian languages of south Asia and comprehensive works on literatures of south Asia in 891.1

.892   *Burushaski literature

---

*Add to base number as instructed at beginning of Table 3

895   Literatures of East and Southeast Asia

Class here Sino-Tibetan literatures

Here are classed literatures of South Asian languages closely related to the languages of East and Southeast Asia

For literature of Austronesian languages of East and Southeast Asia, see 899.2

.1   *Chinese literature

PERIOD TABLE

1	Origins, 15th century to 221 B.C.
	Class here classical age
2	221 B.C.–618 A.D.
	Class here middle epoch
22	Period of Qin (Ch'in) and Han dynasties, 221 B.C.–220 A.D.
24	Period of Six dynasties and Sui dynasty, 220–618 A.D.
3	Period of Tang dynasty, Five dynasties, Ten kingdoms, 618–960
	Class here renaissance and neoclassicism
4	960–1912
42	Period of Song dynasty, 960–1279
44	Period of Yuan (Mongol) dynasty, 1271–1368
	For period of Yuan dynasty during 1271–1279, see 42
46	Period of Ming dynasty, 1368–1644
48	Period of Qing (Manchu) dynasty, 1644–1912
5	1912–2009
51	1912–1949
52	1949–2009
6	2010–

.4   Tibetan literature and related Tibeto-Burman literatures

Class here Tibeto-Burman literatures

For Burmese literature, see 895.8

.400 1–.400 9   Standard subdivisions of Tibeto-Burman literatures

.401–.409   Standard subdivisions; collections in more than one form; history, description, critical appraisal of works in more than one form of Tibetan literature

Add to base number 895.40 the numbers following —0 in notation 01–09 from Table 3B, e.g., a collection of Tibetan literature 895.408

.41–.48   Subdivisions for specific forms of Tibetan literature

Add to base number 895.4 as instructed at beginning of Table 3, e.g., Tibetan poetry 895.41

.49   Literatures of Eastern Himalayan languages

Including Newari literature

Class here literatures of Kiranti languages, of Mahakiranti languages

See also 891.495 for Nepali literature

---

*Add to base number as instructed at beginning of Table 3

.6   ***Japanese literature**

     PERIOD TABLE

1	Early period to 1185
14	Heian period, 794–1185
2	Medieval period, 1185–1603
22	Kamakura period, 1185–1334
24	1334–1603

           Class here 14th century, Muromachi period
           For 1300–1334, see 22

3	Tokugawa (Edo) period, 1603–1868
32	1603–1769

           Class here 18th century, Genroku period
           For 1770–1799, see 34

34	1770–1868

           Class here Bunka-Bunsei period (1804–1829), 19th century
           For 1868–1899, see 4

4	1868–1945
42	Meiji period, 1868–1912
44	1912–1945

           Class here 20th century
           For 1900–1912, see 42; for 1945–1999, see 5

5	1945–1999
6	2000–

.7   ***Korean literature**

     PERIOD TABLE

1	Early period to 1392
2	Yi period, 1392–1910
28	1894–1910
3	1910–1945
4	1945–1999

           Class here 20th century
           For 1900–1910, see 28; for 1910–1945, see 3

5	2000–

.8   ***Burmese literature**

     PERIOD TABLE

1	Early period to 1799
2	1800–1899
3	1900–1999
4	2000–

*Add to base number as instructed at beginning of Table 3

.9   Literatures of miscellaneous languages of Southeast Asia; Munda literatures

> Limited to the literatures provided for below
>
> Including literatures of Kadai languages, Kam-Sui languages
>
> Class here literatures of Daic languages
>
> Class literatures in Austroasiatic languages in 895.93
>
> *For literatures in Austronesian languages, see 899.2*

.91   Thai (Siamese) literature and Tai literatures

> Class here Tai literatures

.910 01–.910 09   Standard subdivisions of literatures of Tai languages

.910 1–.910 9   Standard subdivisions; collections in more than one form; history, description, critical appraisal of works in more than one form of Thai (Siamese) literature

> Add to base number 895.910 the numbers following —0 in notation 01–09 from Table 3B, e.g., a collection of Thai literature 895.9108
>
> Use period table under 895.911–895.918

.911–.918   Subdivisions for specific forms of Thai (Siamese) literature

> Add to base number 895.91 as instructed at beginning of Table 3, e.g., Thai poetry 895.911
>
> PERIOD TABLE
> 1   Early period to 1799
> 2   1800–1899
> 3   1900–1999
> 4   2000–

.919   Other Tai literatures

> Including Shan literature
>
> *For Viet-Muong literatures, see 895.92*

.919 1   *Lao literature

*Add to base number as instructed at beginning of Table 3

.92–.97   Viet-Muong, Austroasiatic, Munda, Hmong-Mien (Miao-Yao) literatures

> Add to base number 895.9 the numbers following —959 in notation 9592–9597 from Table 6, e.g., Vietnamese literature 895.922, Mundari literature 895.95; then to the number given for each literature listed below add further as instructed at beginning of Table 3, e.g., a collection of Vietnamese literature 895.92208

895.922 Vietnamese

PERIOD TABLE FOR VIETNAMESE
1   Early period to 1799
2   1800–1899
3   1900–1999
32   1900–1945
        Class here 20th century
        For 1945–1999, see 34
34   1945–1999
4   2000–

895.932 Khmer (Cambodian)

895.972 Hmong (Miao)

895.978 Yao

896   African literatures

Add to base number 896 the numbers following —96 in notation 961–965 from Table 6, e.g., Songhai literature 896.5, Swahili literature 896.392; then to the number given for each literature listed below add further as instructed at beginning of Table 3, e.g., a collection of Swahili literature 896.39208

896.3214 Wolof

896.322 Fula (Fulani)

896.332 Ibo (Igbo)

896.333 Yoruba

896.3374 Ewe

896.3378 Gã

896.3385 Akan, Fante, Twi

896.3452 Bambara

896.348 Mende

896.3616 Sango

896.3642 Efik

896.3915 Bemba

(continued)

896   African literatures (continued)

896.3918 Nyanja, Chichewa (Chewa)

896.392 Swahili

896.3931 Kongo (Koongo)

896.3932 Mbundu (Kimbundu)

896.39461 Rwanda (Kinyarwanda)

896.39465 Rundi

896.3954 Kikuyu

896.3957 Ganda (Luganda)

896.3962 Duala

896.39686 Lingala

896.3975 Shona

896.3976 Venda (Tshivenda)

896.39771 Northern Sotho

896.39772 Southern Sotho

896.39775 Tswana

896.3978 Tsonga

896.3985 Xhosa

896.3986 Zulu

896.3987 Swazi (siSwati)

896.3989 Ndebele (South Africa)

PERIOD TABLE FOR SPECIFIC AFRICAN LITERATURES
1   Early period to 1959
2   1960–1999
            Class here 20th century
               For 1900–1959, see 1
3   2000–

Class Afrikaans literature in 839.36; class Malagasy literature in 899.3. Class literature in an African creole having a non-African primary source language with the source language, e.g., Krio literature 820

For Ethiopian literatures, see 892.8; for non-Semitic Afro-Asiatic literatures, see 893

(Option: Treat literatures of all African languages as literature of one language, with base number 896. Add to base number 896 as instructed at beginning of Table 3, e.g., a collection of literature in African languages 896.08)

897   Literatures of North American native languages

Class here comprehensive works on literatures of North and South American native languages

Add to base number 897 the numbers following —97 in notation 971–979 from Table 6, e.g., Zoque literature 897.43, Nahuatl literature 897.452; then to the number given for each literature listed below add further as instructed at beginning of Table 3, e.g., a collection of Nahuatl literature 897.45208

897.124 Eastern Canadian Inuktitut

897.19 Aleut

897.26 Navajo (Diné)

897.28 Haida

897.323 Cree

897.333 Ojibwa, Chippewa

897.422 Cakchikel

897.423 Quiché

897.427 Maya, Yucatec Maya

897.4287 Tzotzil

897.452 Nahuatl (Aztec)

897.4542 Yaqui

897.4544 Huichol

897.4552 Tohono O'Odham

897.45529 Akimel O'Odham

897.4574 Shoshoni

897.458 Hopi

897.492 Kiowa

897.494 Tewa

897.5243 Dakota

897.557 Cherokee

897.68 Zapotec

897.83 San Blas Kuna (San Blas Cuna)

897.933 Pawnee

(continued)

897   Literatures of North American native languages (continued)

897.9435 Kalispel, Pend d'Oreille

897.994 Zuni

For literatures of South American native languages, see 898

(Option: Treat literatures of all North American native languages as literature of one language, with base number 897. Add to base number 897 as instructed at beginning of Table 3, e.g., a collection of literary texts in North American native languages 897.08)

898   Literatures of South American native languages

Add to base number 898 the numbers following —98 in notation 982–984 from Table 6, e.g., Quechua literature 898.323, Tucano literature 898.35; then to the number given for each literature listed below add further as instructed at beginning of Table 3, e.g., a collection of Quechua literature 898.32308

898.323 Quechua (Kechua)

898.324 Aymara

898.372 Shuar

898.3822 Paraguayan Guaraní

898.3832 Tupí (Nhengatu)

898.72 Mapudungun (Mapuche)

Class comprehensive works on literatures of North and South American native languages in 897

(Option: Treat literatures of all South American native languages as literature of one language, with base number 898. Add to base number 898 as instructed at beginning of Table 3, e.g., a collection of literature in South American Native languages 898.08)

899   Literatures of non-Austronesian languages of Oceania, of Austronesian languages, of miscellaneous languages

Add to base number 899 the numbers following —99 in notation 991–999 from Table 6, e.g., Polynesian literatures 899.4, Maori literature 899.442, literature originally composed and presented in sign languages 899.98, American Sign Language literature 899.987; then to the number given for each literature listed below add further as instructed at beginning of Table 3, e.g., a collection of Maori literature 899.44208

899.211 Tagalog (Filipino)

PERIOD TABLE FOR TAGALOG (FILIPINO)
1   Early period to 1799
2   1800–1899
3   1900–1999
4   2000–

(continued)

899   **Literatures of non-Austronesian languages of Oceania, of Austronesian languages, of miscellaneous languages (continued)**

899.221 Indonesian (Bahasa Indonesia)

PERIOD TABLE FOR INDONESIAN (BAHASA INDONESIA)
1   Early period to 1899
2   1900–1999
3   2000–

899.222 Javanese

899.2232 Sunda (Sundanese)

899.2234 Madura (Madurese)

899.2238 Bali (Balinese)

899.2242 Aceh (Achinese)

899.2244 Minangkabau

899.22462 Batak Toba

899.22466 Batak Dairi

899.2248 Lampung

899.2256 Banjar (Banjarese)

899.2262 Bugis (Buginese)

899.2264 Makasar

899.28 Malay (Bahasa Malaysia, Standard Malay)

899.3 Malagasy

899.42 Hawaiian

899.442 Maori

899.444 Tahitian

899.462 Samoan

899.482 Tongan (Tonga)

899.484 Niue (Niuean)

899.59 Fijian

899.92 Basque

899.95 Sumerian

(continued)

899 **Literatures of non-Austronesian languages of Oceania, of Austronesian languages, of miscellaneous languages (continued)**

899.9623 Abkhaz

899.9625 Adyghe

899.969 Georgian

899.992 Esperanto

900 History, geography, and auxiliary disciplines

Class here social situations and conditions; general political history; military, diplomatic, political, economic, social, welfare aspects of specific wars

Class interdisciplinary works on ancient world, on specific continents, countries, localities in 930–990. Class history and geographic treatment of a specific subject with the subject, plus notation 09 from Table 1, e.g., history and geographic treatment of natural sciences 509, of economic situations and conditions 330.9, of purely political situations and conditions 320.9, history of military science 355.009

See also 303.49 for future history (projected events other than travel)

See Manual at 900

SUMMARY

940	**History of Europe**
.01–.09	**Standard subdivisions**
.1–.5	**[Historical periods]**
941	**British Isles**
942	**England and Wales**
943	**Germany and neighboring central European countries**
944	**France and Monaco**
945	**Italy, San Marino, Vatican City, Malta**
946	**Spain, Andorra, Gibraltar, Portugal**
947	**Russia and neighboring east European countries**
948	**Scandinavia**
949	**Other parts of Europe**
950	**History of Asia**
.01–.09	**Standard subdivisions**
.1–.4	**[Historical periods]**
951	**China and adjacent areas**
952	**Japan**
953	**Arabian Peninsula and adjacent areas**
954	**India and neighboring south Asian countries**
955	**Iran**
956	**Middle East (Near East)**
957	**Siberia (Asiatic Russia)**
958	**Central Asia**
959	**Southeast Asia**
960	**History of Africa**
.01–.09	**Standard subdivisions**
.1–.3	**[Historical periods]**
961	**Tunisia and Libya**
962	**Egypt and Sudan**
963	**Ethiopia and Eritrea**
964	**Morocco, Ceuta, Melilla, Western Sahara, Canary Islands**
965	**Algeria**
966	**West Africa and offshore islands**
967	**Central Africa and offshore islands**
968	**Republic of South Africa and neighboring southern African countries**
969	**South Indian Ocean islands**
970	**History of North America**
.001–.009	**Standard subdivisions**
.01–.05	**Historical periods**
971	**Canada**
972	**Mexico, Central America, West Indies, Bermuda**
973	**United States**
974	**Northeastern United States (New England and Middle Atlantic states)**
975	**Southeastern United States (South Atlantic states)**
976	**South central United States**
977	**North central United States**
978	**Western United States**
979	**Great Basin and Pacific Slope region of United States**

980		History of South America
	.001–.009	Standard subdivisions
	.01–.04	Historical periods
981		Brazil
982		Argentina
983		Chile
984		Bolivia
985		Peru
986		Colombia and Ecuador
987		Venezuela
988		Guiana
989		Paraguay and Uruguay

990		History of Australasia, Pacific Ocean islands, Atlantic Ocean islands, Arctic islands, Antarctica, extraterrestrial worlds
	.01–.09	Standard subdivisions of Australasia, Pacific Ocean islands, Atlantic Ocean islands, Arctic islands, Antarctica, extraterrestrial worlds together; of Australasia alone; of Pacific Ocean islands alone
993		New Zealand
994		Australia
995		New Guinea and neighboring countries of Melanesia
996		Polynesia and other Pacific Ocean islands
997		Atlantic Ocean islands
998		Arctic islands and Antarctica
999		Extraterrestrial worlds

.1–.9   **Standard subdivisions of history and geography**

901   Philosophy and theory of history

902   Miscellany of history

[.23]   Maps, plans, diagrams

Do not use; class in 911

903   Dictionaries, encyclopedias, concordances of history

904   Collected accounts of events

Class here adventure

Class travel in 910; class collections limited to a specific period in 909; class collections limited to a specific area or region but not limited by continent, country, locality in 909.09; class collections limited to a specific continent, country, locality in 930–990. Class history of a specific kind of event with the event, e.g., geological history of California earthquakes 551.2209794

See Manual at 900: Historic events vs. nonhistoric events

.5   **Events of natural origin**

.7   **Events induced by human activity**

905   Serial publications of history

906   Organizations and management of history

907   Education, research, related topics of history

.2   **Historical research**

Including oral history

Class here interdisciplinary works on historical research [*formerly* 001.432], on historiography

Class writing of history in 808.0669

.201–.209   Geographic treatment and biography

Add to base number 907.20 notation 1–9 from Table 2, e.g., historians and historiographers 907.202

Class historians and historiographers who specialize in a specific area with the area in 930–990, plus notation 007202 from table under 930–990, e.g., the biography of a German who specializes in French history in general 944.007202; class historians and historiographers who specialize in specific historical periods of a specific area with the historical period for the area studied, plus notation 092 from Table 1, e.g., biography of a German historian who specializes in the French Revolutionary period 944.04092

908   History with respect to groups of people

[.9]   **Ethnic and national groups**

Do not use; class in 909.04

909   World history

Civilization and events not limited by continent, country, locality

Class collected accounts of events not limited by period, area, region, subject in 904

See Manual at 306 vs. 305, 909, 930–990; also at 324 vs. 320.5, 320.9, 909, 930–990; also at 909, 930–990 vs. 320; also at 909, 930–990 vs. 320.4, 321, 321.09; also at 909, 930–990 vs. 910

(Option: Class primary textbooks on general history in 372.89045)

[.001–.008]   Standard subdivisions

Do not use; class in 901–908

[.009]   History

Do not use for historiography; class in 907.2. Do not use for general works on history; class in 909

[.009 01–.009 05]   Historical periods

Do not use; class in 909.1–909.8

[.009 1]   Areas, regions, places in general

Do not use; class in 909.09

[.009 2]   Biography

Do not use; class in 920

[.009 3–.009 9]　　　Specific continents, countries, localities; extraterrestrial worlds

　　　　　　　　　　Do not use; class in 930–990

.04　　　　　History with respect to ethnic and national groups

　　　　See also 920.0092 for general collections of biography of members of a specific ethnic or national group

　　　　See Manual at 920.008 vs. 305–306, 362

.040 5–.040 9　　　People of mixed ancestry with ethnic origins from more than one continent, people of European descent

　　　　Add to base number 909.04 notation 05–09 from Table 5, e.g., world history of people of European descent 909.0409; then add 0* and to the result add the numbers following 909 in 909.1–909.8, e.g., world history of people of European descent in 18th century 909.040907

　　　　(Option: Class here general history of specific ethnic and national groups with ethnic origins from more than one continent, of European descent in a specific continent, country, locality; prefer subdivision 004 from table under 930–990. If option is chosen, add notation 05–09 from Table 5 as above; then add 00 instead of 0 as above for world history by period, e.g., world history of people of European descent in 18th century 909.0409007; for specific areas add 0 and to the result add notation 3–9 from Table 2, e.g., history of people of European descent in United States 909.0409073)

.041–.049　　　Specific ethnic and national groups

　　　　Add to base number 909.04 notation 1–9 from Table 5, e.g., world history of Jews 909.04924; then add 0* and to the result add the numbers following 909 in 909.1–909.8, e.g., world history of Jews in 18th century 909.0492407

　　　　(Option: Class here general history of specific ethnic and national groups in a specific continent, country, locality; prefer subdivision 004 from table under 930–990. If option is chosen, add notation 1–9 from Table 5 as above; then add 00 instead of 0 as above for world history by period, e.g., world history of Jews in 18th century 909.04924007; for specific areas add 0 and to the result add notation 3–9 from Table 2, e.g., history of Jews in Germany 909.04924043)

———————

>　　　909.07–909.08　General historical periods

　　　　Class here general histories covering three or more continents (or three or more countries if not on the same continent)

　　　　Class specific historical periods in 909.1–909.8; class comprehensive works in 909

　　　　For ancient history, see 930

*Add 00 for standard subdivisions; see instructions at beginning of Table 1

.07	Ca. 500–1450/1500

Including comprehensive works on Crusades

Class here Middle Ages

Class history of a place during the period of the Crusades with the history of the place, e.g., history of Europe during the period of Crusades 940.18

> *For comprehensive works on a specific Crusade, see the history of the country or region in which most of the fighting took place, e.g., First Crusade 956.014, Fourth Crusade 949.503*

> *See also 940.1 for history of Europe during Middle Ages*

.08	Modern history, 1450/1500–
.09	Areas, regions, places in general

Not limited by continent, country, locality

Class here interdisciplinary works on areas, regions, places in general (other than landforms, oceans, seas)

Class general collections of biography by areas, regions, places in general in 920.0091; class interdisciplinary works on landforms, oceans, seas in 551.4

> *For geography of and travel in areas, regions, places in general, see 910.91*

> *See Manual at T1—092: Comprehensive biography: Public figures; also at 920.009, 920.03–920.09 vs. 909.09, 909.1–909.8, 930–990; also at 930–990: Biography*

.090 1–.090 9	Standard subdivisions
.091–.099	Specific areas, regions, places in general

Add to base number 909.09 the numbers following —1 in notation 11–19 from Table 2, e.g., history of tropical regions 909.093, of Caribbean Sea 909.096365, of western civilization 909.09821; then add 0* and to the result add the numbers following 909 in 909.1–909.8, e.g., history of tropical regions in 20th century 909.093082

> ### 909.1–909.8 Specific historical periods

Class general historical periods in 909.07–909.08; class general biographies limited to a specific historical period in 920.00901–920.00905; class comprehensive works in 909

> *For historical periods through 5th century, see 930.1–930.5*

> *See Manual at T1—092: Comprehensive biography: Public figures; also at 920.009, 920.03–920.09 vs. 909.09, 909.1–909.8, 930–990; also at 930–990: Biography*

*Add 00 for standard subdivisions; see instructions at beginning of Table 1; however, class historical atlases in 911.1

.1	**6th–12th centuries, 500–1199**

Class comprehensive works on Middle Ages in 909.07

.2	**13th century, 1200–1299**
.3	**14th century, 1300–1399**
.4	**15th century, 1400–1499**
.5	**16th century, 1500–1599**
.6	**17th century, 1600–1699**
.7	**18th century, 1700–1799**
.8	**1800–**
.81	19th century, 1800–1899

Class here industrial revolution

.82	20th century, 1900–1999
.821	1900–1919

Class here early 20th century

For World War I, see 940.3. For a part of early 20th century not provided for here, see the part, e.g., 1930–1939 909.823

.822	1920–1929
.823	1930–1939
.824	1940–1949

For World War II, see 940.53

.825	1950–1959

Class here late 20th century, post World War II period

For a part of late 20th century, post World War II period not provided for here, see the part, e.g., 1980–1989 909.828

.826	1960–1969
.827	1970–1979
.828	1980–1989
.829	1990–1999
.83	21st century, 2000–2099

See also 303.49 for futurology

.831	2000–2019
.831 1	2000–2009
.831 2	2010–2019

910 Geography and travel

Class here travel by private passenger automobile [*formerly* 796.78]; travel by motor homes, recreational vehicles, trailers [*all formerly* 796.79]; interdisciplinary works on tourism, on travel

Class general works on civilization, other than accounts of travel, in 909; class works on civilization, other than accounts of travel, in ancient world and specific places in modern world in 930–990. Class geographic treatment of a specific subject with the subject, plus notation 09 from Table 1, e.g., geographic treatment of religion 200.9, of geomorphology 551.4109

> For a specific aspect of tourism, see the aspect, e.g., tourist industry 338.4791, travel and tourism in Mexico 917.204

> See Manual at 550 vs. 910; also at 578 vs. 304.2, 508, 910; also at 909, 930–990 vs. 910

(Option: Class primary textbooks on general geography in 372.891045)

SUMMARY

910.01–.02	**[Philosophy and theory of geography and travel; the earth (physical geography)]**
.2–.9	**Standard subdivisions, world travel guides, accounts of travel and facilities for travelers**
911	**Historical geography**
912	**Graphic representations of surface of earth and of extraterrestrial worlds**
913–919	**Geography of and travel in specific continents, countries, localities; extraterrestrial worlds**

.01 Philosophy and theory of geography and travel

.014 Communication

Class here discursive works on place names and their origin, history, meaning

Class dictionaries and gazetteers of place names in 910.3

.02 The earth (Physical geography)

Class physical geography of a specific geological feature with the feature in 550, e.g., glaciers 551.312

> See also 551.41 for geomorphology

> See Manual at 550 vs. 910

.020 9 History and biography

[.020 91] Areas, regions, places in general

Do not use; class in 910.021

[.020 93–.020 99] Specific continents, countries, localities; extraterrestrial worlds

Do not use; class in 913–919 plus notation 02 from table under 913–919

.021	Physical geography of areas, regions, places in general

Add to base number 910.021 the numbers following —1 in notation 11–18 from Table 2, e.g., physical geography of forests 910.02152

(.1)	**Topical geography**

(Optional number; prefer specific subject, e.g., economic geography 330.91–330.99)

Do not use for philosophy and theory of geography and travel; class in 910.01

Add to base number 910.1 notation 001–899, e.g., economic geography 910.133; then add 0* and to the result add notation 1–9 from Table 2, e.g., economic geography of British Isles 910.133041

.2	**Miscellany; world travel guides**

Notation 02 from Table 1 as modified below

.202	World travel guides

Do not use for synopses and outlines; class in 910.2

Class here guidebooks and tour books providing tourists updated information about places in many areas of the globe: how to travel, what to see, where to stay, how to plan a vacation

Class guides to areas, regions, places in general in 910.91; class guides to specific continents, countries, localities in 913–919, plus notation 04 from table under 913–919

.22	Illustrations, models, miniatures
.223	Diagrams

Do not use for maps and plans; class in 912

.25	Directories of persons and organizations

Class here city directories, telephone books

Class city directories, telephone books of a specific place in 913–919, plus notation 0025 from table under 913–919

See also 910.46 for directories of facilities for travelers

See Manual at T1—025 vs. T1—029

.28	Auxiliary techniques and procedures; apparatus, equipment, materials

*Add 00 for standard subdivisions; see instructions at beginning of Table 1

.285   Computer applications

Class here interdisciplinary works on geographic information systems (GIS), global positioning systems (GPS), real-time locating systems (RTLS)

Class real-time locating systems that use radio frequency identification in 910.2856245

For an application of geographic information systems (GIS), global positioning systems (GPS), or real-time locating systems (RTLS) to a subject, see the subject, plus notation 0285 from Table 1, e.g., GIS applications in mathematical geography 526.0285

.3   **Dictionaries, encyclopedias, concordances, gazetteers**

Class here works on place names systematically arranged for ready reference

Class discursive works on place names in 910.014; class historical material associated with place names in general in 909; class historical material associated with place names of specific places in 930–990

.4   **Accounts of travel and facilities for travelers**

Standard subdivisions are added for accounts of travel and facilities for travelers together, for accounts of travel alone

Not geographically limited

For travel accounts that emphasize civilization of places visited, see 909; for discovery and exploration, see 910.9

See also 508 for scientific exploration and travel; also 910.202 for world travel guides

.41   Trips around the world

.45   Ocean travel and seafaring adventures

Including pirates' expeditions

Class how to plan a cruise vacation in 910.202; class ocean trips around the world in 910.41; class travel in specific oceans in 910.9163–910.9167

.452   Shipwrecks

Class here comprehensive works on ocean and inland waterway shipwrecks

Class water transportation safety in 363.123

For ocean shipwrecks, see the location of the wrecks in 910.9163–910.9167, e.g., sinking of Titanic 910.91634, shipwrecks of Alaskan waters of the Pacific Ocean 910.916434; for inland waterway shipwrecks, see the location of the wrecks in 913–919, plus notation 04 from table under 913–919, e.g., shipwrecks of Mississippi River 917.704, shipwrecks of Lake Superior 917.74904

See Manual at 900: Historic events vs. nonhistoric events

.46 Facilities for travelers

Class here directories of lodging for temporary residents; interdisciplinary and descriptive works on lodging for temporary residents, hotels, inns, motels

For a specific kind of facility for travelers other than lodging, see the kind of facility, e.g., transportation facilities 388.04, eating and drinking places 647.95; for a specific aspect of lodging for temporary residents, see the aspect, e.g., household management 647.94

[.460 25] Directories of persons and organizations

Do not use for general directories of persons and organizations; class in 910.46. Do not use for directories of persons and organizations limited to specific continents, countries, localities; class in 913–919 plus notation 06 from table under 913–919

.460 9 History and biography

[.460 93–.460 99] Specific continents, countries, localities

Do not use; class in 913–919 plus notation 06 from table under 913–919

.462 Resorts

Class here park and safari lodges, directories

[.462 025] Directories of persons and organizations

Do not use for general directories of persons and organizations; class in 910.462. Do not use for directories of persons and organizations limited to specific continents, countries, localities; class in 913–919 plus notation 062 from table under 913–919

.462 09 History and biography

[.462 093–.462 099] Specific continents, countries, localities

Do not use; class in 913–919 plus notation 062 from table under 913–919

.464 Bed and breakfast accommodations

Class here boarding and rooming houses, directories

[.464 025] Directories of persons and organizations

Do not use for general directories of persons and organizations; class in 910.464. Do not use for directories of persons and organizations limited to specific continents, countries, localities; class in 913–919 plus notation 064 from table under 913–919

.464 09 History and biography

[.464 093–.464 099] Specific continents, countries, localities

Do not use; class in 913–919 plus notation 064 from table under 913–919

.466 Hostels

Class here elder, youth hostels; directories

[.466 025] Directories of persons and organizations

Do not use for general directories of persons and organizations; class in 910.466. Do not use for directories of persons and organizations limited to specific continents, countries, localities; class in 913–919 plus notation 066 from table under 913–919

.466 09 History and biography

[.466 093–.466 099] Specific continents, countries, localities

Do not use; class in 913–919 plus notation 066 from table under 913–919

.468 Campsites

Class here recreation vehicle (RV), trailer camps; directories

Class trailer camps for long-term residents in 647.92; class travel by motor homes, recreational vehicles, trailers in 910

[.468 025] Directories of persons and organizations

Do not use for general directories of persons and organizations; class in 910.468. Do not use for directories of persons and organizations limited to specific continents, countries, localities; class in 913–919 plus notation 068 from table under 913–919

.468 09 History and biography

[.468 093–.468 099] Specific continents, countries, localities

Do not use; class in 913–919 plus notation 068 from table under 913–919

.5–.8 **Standard subdivisions**

.9 **History, geographic treatment, biography**

Class here discovery, exploration, growth of geographic knowledge

.91 Geography of and travel in areas, regions, places in general

Class physical geography of areas, regions, places in general in 910.02; class interdisciplinary works on landforms, oceans, seas in 551.4

(Option: Class primary geography textbooks on specific areas, regions, places in general in 372.8911)

.92 Geographers, travelers, explorers regardless of country of origin

.93–.99   Discovery and exploration by specific countries

> Do not use for geography of and travel in specific continents, countries, localities; extraterrestrial worlds; class in 913–919
>
> Add to base number 910.9 notation 3–9 from Table 2 for the country responsible, e.g., explorations by Great Britain 910.941
>
> Class discovery and exploration by a specific country in areas, regions, places in general in 910.91; class discovery and exploration by a specific country in specific continents, countries, localities, extraterrestrial worlds in 913–919, plus notation 04 from table under 913–919; class periods of discovery and exploration in history in 930–990

911   Historical geography

> Growth and changes in political divisions
>
> Class here historical atlases

.09   History

[.091–.099]   Geographic treatment and biography

> Do not use; class in 911.1–911.9

.1–.9   Geographic treatment and biography

> Add to base number 911 notation 1–9 from Table 2, e.g., historical geography of China 911.51

912   Graphic representations of surface of earth and of extraterrestrial worlds

> Class here atlases, maps, charts, plans, road maps (highway maps)
>
> Class map drawing in 526
>
> *For graphic representation of a specific subject other than geography, travel, and roads, see the subject, plus notation 0223 from Table 1, e.g., railroad atlases 385.0223*

.01   Philosophy and theory; map reading

> Notation 01 from Table 1 as modified below

.014   Map reading

> Do not use for communication; class in 912.01
>
> Class here orientation
>
> Class orienteering in 796.58

.014 8   Map scales, symbols, abbreviations, acronyms

.09   History and biography of maps and map making

[.091]   Maps and map making of specific areas, regions, places in general

> Do not use; class in 912.19

[.093–.099]   Maps and map making of specific continents, countries, localities,
                   extraterrestrial worlds

> Do not use; class in 912.3–912.9

.1   Areas, regions, places in general

.19   Specific areas, regions, places in general

> Add to base number 912.19 the numbers following —1 in notation 11–19
> from Table 2, e.g., maps of Western Hemisphere 912.19812

.3–.9   Specific continents, countries, localities; extraterrestrial worlds

> Class here land atlases of countries, tax maps that provide general descriptions
> of assessed land and structures

> Add to base number 912 notation 3–9 from Table 2, e.g., maps of Du Page
> County, Illinois 912.77324

913–919   Geography of and travel in specific continents, countries, localities; extraterrestrial worlds

Class here comprehensive works on ancient and modern geography of and travel in specific continents, countries, localities

Add to base number 91 notation 3–9 from Table 2, e.g., geography of England 914.2, of Norfolk, England 914.261; then add further as follows:

001	Philosophy and theory
0014	Communication
	Class here discursive works on place names and their origin, history, and meaning
	Class dictionaries and gazetteers of place names in 003
002	Miscellany
0022	Illustrations, models, miniatures
00222	Pictures and related illustrations
	Including aerial photographs
	Class photographs reflecting the civilization of places in 930–990
[00223]	Maps, plans, diagrams
	Do not use; class in 912
0025	Directories of persons and organizations
	Class here city directories, telephone books
0028	Auxiliary techniques and procedures; apparatus, equipment, materials
00285	Computer applications
	Class here geographic information systems (GIS), global positioning systems (GPS), real-time locating systems (RTLS)
	Class real-time locating systems that use radio frequency identification in 002856245
003	Dictionaries, encyclopedias, concordances, gazetteers
	Class here works on place names systematically arranged for ready reference
	Class discursive works on place names in 0014; class historical material associated with place names in 930–990
005–008	Standard subdivisions
[009]	History, geographic treatment, biography
	Do not use; class in 913–919 without adding from this table
01	Prehistoric geography
	Do not add to notation 4–6 from Table 2 if there is a corresponding notation 3 from Table 2, e.g., prehistoric geography of Greece 913.801 (*not* 914.9501), of Russia 914.701
	Class prehistoric physical geography in 02; class prehistoric geography of areas, regions, places in general in 09
02	The earth (Physical geography)
	Class physical geography of a specific geological feature with the feature in 550, e.g., glaciers of Canada 551.3120971
	See also 551.41 for geomorphology
	See Manual at 550 vs. 910

(continued)

913–919   Geography of and travel in specific continents, countries, localities; extraterrestrial worlds (continued)

04   Travel

Class here discovery, exploration; guidebooks

Class world travel guides in 910.202; class travel accounts that emphasize the civilization of country visited in 930–990

> *For facilities for travelers, see 06*
>
> *See Manual at 913–919: Add table: 04; also at 913–919 vs. 796.51*

040901–040905   Historical periods for regions

Do not use for historical periods of continents countries, localities; for historical periods for regions sharing the same historical period numbers as a country; class in 041–049

Limited to regions not sharing the same historical period numbers as a country, e.g., travel in central Europe during 19th century 914.30409034

041–049   Historical periods

Add to 04 the historical period numbers following 0 that appear in subdivisions of 930–990, e.g., travel in England during period of House of Tudor 914.2045; however, for historical periods of United States as a whole, see 917.3041–917.3049

> *For historical periods for regions not sharing the same historical period numbers as a country, see 040901–040905*

06   Facilities for travelers

Class here lodging for travelers; directories of facilities for travelers; interdisciplinary and descriptive works on lodging for temporary residents, hotels, motels, inns in specific continents, countries, localities

> *For a specific kind of facility for travelers other than lodging, see the kind of facility, e.g., transportation facilities 388.04, eating and drinking places 647.953–647.959; for a specific aspect of lodging for temporary residents, see the aspect, e.g., household management 647.94093–647.94099*

[06025]   Directories of persons and organizations

Do not use; class in 06

0609   History and biography

060901–060905   Historical periods for regions

Do not use for historical periods of continents countries, localities; for historical periods for regions sharing the same historical period numbers as a country; class in 061

Limited to regions not sharing the same historical period numbers as a country, e.g., facilities for travelers in central Europe during 19th century 914.30609034

061   Historical periods

Add to 061 the historical period numbers following 0 that appear in subdivisions of 930–990, e.g., facilities for travelers in England in 2011 914.20618612; however, for historical periods of United States as a whole, see 917.3061

> *For historical periods for regions not sharing the same historical period numbers as a country, see 060901–060905*

(continued)

913–919 Geography of and travel in specific continents, countries, localities; extraterrestrial worlds (continued)

062   Resorts

Class here park and safari lodges

06201–06209   Standard subdivisions

As modified under 0602–0609

0621–0629   Historical periods

Add to 062 the historical period numbers following 0 that appear in subdivisions of 930–990, e.g., resorts in England in 2011 914.20628612; however, for historical periods of United States as a whole, see 917.30621–917.30629

For historical periods for regions not sharing the same historical period numbers as a country, see 0620901–0620905

064   Bed and breakfast accommodations

Class here boarding and rooming houses, directories

06401–06409   Standard subdivisions

As modified under 0602–0609

0641–0649   Historical periods

Add to 064 the historical period numbers following 0 that appear in subdivisions of 930–990, e.g., bed and breakfast accommodations in England in 2011 914.20648612; however, for historical periods of United States as a whole, see 917.30641–917.30649

For historical periods for regions not sharing the same historical period numbers as a country, see 0640901–0640905

066   Hostels

Class here elder, youth hostels; directories

06601–06609   Standard subdivisions

As modified under 0602–0609

0661–0669   Historical periods

Add to 066 the historical period numbers following 0 that appear in subdivisions of 930–990, e.g., hostels in England in 2011 914.20668612; however, for historical periods of United States as a whole, see 917.30661–917.30669

For historical periods for regions not sharing the same historical period numbers as a country, see 0660901–0660905

068   Campsites

Class here recreation vehicle (RV), trailer camps; directories; interdisciplinary and descriptive works on lodging for campsites in specific continents, countries, localities

Class trailer camps for long-term residents in 647.92

(continued)

913–919 Geography of and travel in specific continents, countries, localities; extraterrestrial worlds (continued)

06801–06809	Standard subdivisions As modified under 0602–0609
0681–0689	Historical periods Add to 068 the historical period numbers following 0 that appear in subdivisions of 930–990, e.g., campsites in England in 2011 914.20688612; however, for historical periods of United States as a whole, see 917.30681–917.30689 *For historical periods for regions not sharing the same historical period numbers as a country, see 0680901–0680905*
09	Areas, regions, places in general Add to 09 the numbers following —1 in notation 11–18 from Table 2, e.g., geography of urban regions of England 914.209732 Class physical geography of areas, regions, places in 02; class travel in 04; class civilization in 930–990, plus notation 0091–0098 from Table under 930–990

Class historical geography in 911; class graphic representations in 912; class area studies in 940–990; class comprehensive works, geography of and travel in more than one continent in 910; class interdisciplinary works on geography and history of ancient world, of specific continents, countries, localities in 930–990

> See Manual at 913–919; also at 333.7–333.9 vs. 508, 913–919, 930–990; also at 520 vs. 500.5, 523.1, 530.1, 919.9

(Option: Class primary geography textbooks on ancient world, on specific continents, countries, localities in 372.8913–372.8919)

913   Geography of and travel in ancient world

Number built according to instructions under 913–919

914   Geography of and travel in Europe

Number built according to instructions under 913–919

915   Geography of and travel in Asia

Number built according to instructions under 913–919

916   Geography of and travel in Africa

Number built according to instructions under 913–919

917   Geography of and travel in North America

Number built according to instructions under 913–919

.3   Geography of and travel in United States

Number built according to instructions under 913–919

> *For geography of and travel in specific states of United States, see 917.4–917.9*

.304   Travel

Number built according to instructions under 913–919

.304 1–.304 9	Historical periods

> Add to 04 the numbers following 973 in 973.1–973.9, e.g., travel in United States during the Clinton administration 917.304929

.306	Facilities for travelers

> Number built according to instructions under 913–919

.306 1	Historical periods

> Add to base number 917.3061 the numbers following 973 in 973.1–973.9, e.g., facilities for travelers in United States in 1993–2001 917.3061929

.306 2	Resorts

> Number built according to instructions under 913–919

.306 21–.306 29	Historical periods

> Add to base number 917.3062 the numbers following 973 in 973.1–973.9, e.g., resorts in United States in 1993–2001 917.3062929

.306 4	Bed and breakfast accommodations

> Number built according to instructions under 913–919

.306 41–.306 49	Historical periods

> Add to base number 917.3064 the numbers following 973 in 973.1–973.9, e.g., bed and breakfast accommodations in United States in 1993–2001 917.3064929

.306 6	Hostels

> Number built according to instructions under 913–919

.306 61–.306 69	Historical periods

> Add to base number 917.3066 the numbers following 973 in 973.1–973.9, e.g., hostels in United States in 1993–2001 917.3066929

.306 8	Campsites

> Number built according to instructions under 913–919

.306 81–.306 89	Historical periods

> Add to base number 917.3068 the numbers following 973 in 973.1–973.9, e.g., campsites in United States in 1993–2001 917.3068929

.4–.9 Geography of and travel in specific states of United States

> Add to base number 91 notation 74–79 from Table 2, e.g., geography of and travel in California 917.94; then add further as instructed under 913–919, e.g., travel in California 917.9404, travel in California in 2001 917.940454

> *For geography of and travel in specific states of Hawaii, see 919.69*

918   Geography of and travel in South America

> Number built according to instructions under 913–919

919   Geography of and travel in Australasia, Pacific Ocean islands, Atlantic Ocean islands, Arctic islands, Antarctica and on extraterrestrial worlds

> Number built according to instructions under 913–919

.904   Travel on extraterrestrial worlds

> Number built according to instructions under 913–919

> Class here accounts of projected flights

> *See Manual at 629.43, 629.45 vs. 559.9, 919.904*

.920 4   Travel in planets of solar system and their satellites

> Number built according to instructions under 913–919

> Class here accounts of projected planetary flights

> Class accounts of projected flights to a specific planet with the planet in 919.921–919.929, plus notation 04 from table under 913–919, e.g., projected accounts of flights to Mars 919.92304

920   Biography, genealogy, insignia

> Class here autobiographies, diaries, reminiscences, correspondence; biography as a discipline

> Class biography of people associated with a specific subject with the subject, plus notation 092 from Table 1, e.g., biography of chemists 540.92

> (Option A: For biography of people associated with a specific subject, use subdivisions identified by *, then, for each number identified by †, add notation 3–9 from Table 2, e.g., Baptists from Louisiana 922.6763

> (Option B: Class individual biography in 92 or B; class collected biography in 92 or 920 undivided

> (Option C: Class individual biography of men in 920.71; class individual biography of women in 920.72)

> *See Manual at T1—092*

.001–.002   Standard subdivisions of biography as a discipline

.003   Dictionaries, encyclopedias, concordances of biography as a discipline

> *See also 920.02 for biographical dictionaries*

.005–.007   Standard subdivisions of biography as a discipline

.008   Biography as a discipline with respect to groups of people; general collections of biography by groups of people with specific attributes

> *See Manual at 920.008 vs. 305–306, 362*

[.008 1]	People by gender or sex
	Do not use; class in 920.7

[.008 2]	Women
	Do not use; class in 920.72

[.008 8]	Occupational and religious groups
	Do not use; class with the specific group plus notation 092 from Table 1, e.g., biography of Lutherans 284.1092

[.008 9]	Ethnic and national groups
	Do not use; class in 920.0092

.009 **History and geographic treatment of biography as a discipline; general collections of biography by period, region, group**

> Subdivisions are added for biography as a discipline, for general collections of biography, or for both

> *See Manual at T1—092: Comprehensive biography: Public figures; also at 920.009, 920.03–920.09 vs. 909.09, 909.1–909.8, 930–990; also at 930–990: Biography*

.009 01–.009 05 Historical periods

> Add to base number 920.0090 the numbers following —090 in notation 0901–0905 from Table 1, e.g., general biography of 19th century 920.009034

.009 1 Areas, regions, places in general

> Add to base number 920.0091 the numbers following —1 in notation 11–19 from Table 2, e.g., biographies of suburbanites 920.0091733

.009 2 Ethnic and national groups

> Do not use for biography of biography as a discipline; class in 920 without subdivision

> *See Manual at 920.008 vs. 305–306, 362*

.009 205–.009 209 People of mixed ancestry with ethnic origins from more than one continent, people of European descent

> Add to base number 920.0092 notation 05–09 from Table 5, e.g., biographies of people of European descent 920.009209

.009 21–.009 29 Specific ethnic and national groups

> Add to base number 920.0092 notation 1–9 from Table 5, e.g., biographies of Swedes 920.0092397

.009 3–.009 9 Biography as a discipline by specific continents, countries, localities

> Do not use for general collections of biography by specific continents, countries, localities; class in 920.03–920.09

.02	General collections of biography

> *For a collection limited by period, place, group, or subject, see the period, place, group, or subject, e.g., collections of biographies of people resident in England 920.042, collections of biographies of scientists 509.22*

[.020 3]	Dictionaries, encyclopedias, concordances

Do not use; class in 920.02

[.020 8]	General collections of biography with respect to groups of people

Do not use; class in 920.008

[.020 81]	People by gender or sex

Do not use; class in 920.7

[.020 82]	Women

Do not use; class in 920.72

[.020 88]	Occupational and religious groups

Do not use; class with the specific group plus notation 092 from Table 1, e.g., biography of Lutherans 284.1092

[.020 89]	Ethnic and national groups

Do not use; class in 920.0092

.03–.09	General collections of biography by specific continents, countries, localities

Not associated with a specific subject

Add to base number 920.0 notation 3–9 from Table 2, e.g., collections of biographies of people resident in England 920.042

Class collections by sex regardless of continent, country, locality in 920.7

> *For collected biography of public figures who had a significant impact upon general history of a specific continent, country, or locality, see the history of the continent, country, or locality in 930–990, plus 0099 from table under 930–990, e.g., collected biography of kings and queens of England 942.0099*

> *See Manual at T1—092: Comprehensive biography: Public figures; also at 920.009, 920.03–920.09 vs. 909.09, 909.1–909.8, 930–990; also at 930–990: Biography*

(.1)	***Bibliographers**
(.2)	***Librarians and book collectors**
(.3)	***Encyclopedists**

Class lexicographers in 924

(.4)	***Publishers and booksellers**

*(Optional number; prefer specific subject, as described under 920)

(.5)	*Journalists and news commentators

.7   People by gender or sex

Class here individual biography of people not associated with a specific subject, collected biography of people by gender or sex

Class general collections of biography in 920.02

For collected biography of transgender or intersex people, see 920.00867

(Option: Class here all individual biography; prefer specific subject, plus notation 092 from Table 1, e.g., biography of a female scientist 509.2)

.71   Men

See Manual at 920.008 vs. 305–306, 362

.72   Women

See Manual at 920.008 vs. 305–306, 362

(.9)   *People associated with other subjects

Not provided for in 920.1–920.5, 921–928

Add to base number 920.9 notation 001–999, e.g., astrologers 920.91335

(921)   *Philosophers and psychologists

> **(921.1–921.8) Modern western philosophers and psychologists**

Class comprehensive works in 921

(.1)   *United States and Canadian philosophers and psychologists

(.2)   *British philosophers and psychologists

Including English, Scottish, Irish, Welsh philosophers and psychologists

(.3)   *German and Austrian philosophers and psychologists

(.4)   *French philosophers and psychologists

(.5)   *Italian philosophers and psychologists

(.6)   *Spanish and Portuguese philosophers and psychologists

(.7)   *Russian philosophers and psychologists

(.8)   *†Other modern western philosophers and psychologists

(.9)   *Ancient, medieval, eastern philosophers and psychologists

Add to base number 921.9 the numbers following 18 in 181–189, e.g., Aristotelian philosophers 921.95

---

*(Optional number; prefer specific subject, as described under 920)
†Add as instructed under 920

(922) *Religious leaders, thinkers, workers

>   **(922.1–922.8) Christians**

       Class comprehensive works in 922

(.1) ***†Early church and Eastern churches**

       Subdivisions are added for either or both topics in heading

(.2) ***Roman Catholics**

(.21)   *Popes

(.22)   *Saints

(.24–.29) ***Roman Catholics from specific continents, countries, localities in modern world**

       Add to base number 922.2 notation 4–9 from Table 2, e.g., Roman Catholics from the City of Montréal 922.271428

       For popes, see 922.21; for saints, see 922.22

(.3) ***†Anglicans**

(.4) ***†Lutherans, Huguenots, continental Protestants**

       Subdivisions are added for any or all topics in heading

(.5) ***†Presbyterians, Congregationalists, American Reformed**

       Subdivisions are added for any or all topics in heading

(.6) ***†Baptists, Disciples of Christ, Adventists**

       Subdivisions are added for any or all topics in heading

(.7) ***†Methodists**

(.8) ***Members of other Christian denominations and sects**

(.81)   *†Unitarians and Universalists

       Subdivisions are added for either or both topics in heading

(.83)   *†Latter-Day Saints

(.84)   *†Swedenborgians

(.85)   *†Christian Scientists

(.86)   *†Friends (Quakers)

(.87)   *†Mennonites

(.88)   *†Shakers

---

*(Optional number; prefer specific subject, as described under 920)
†Add as instructed under 920

(.89) *Other Christian denominations and sects

Not provided for elsewhere

(.9) *Adherents of other religions

(.91) *Atheists and Deists

(.94) *Adherents of Indic religions

(.943) *Buddhists

(.944) *Jains

(.945) *Hindus

(.946) *Sikhs

(.95) *Zoroastrians (Parsees)

(.96) *Adherents of Judaism

(.97) *Adherents of Islam

(.99) *Other religions

Not provided for elsewhere

(923) *People in social sciences

(.1) *†Heads of state

Class here kings, queens, presidents

(.2) *†People in political science and politics

Class here legislators, governors, politicians, statesmen, diplomats, nobility; political scientists

For heads of state, see 923.1

(.3) *People in economics

(.31) *†Labor leaders

(.33–.39) *People in economics from specific continents, countries, localities

Add to base number 923.3 notation 3–9 from Table 2, e.g., people in economics from Chicago 923.377311

For labor leaders, see 923.31

(.4) *Criminals and people in law

(.41) *†Criminals

(.43–.49) *People in law

Add to base number 923.4 notation 3–9 from Table 2, e.g., people in law from Sydney 923.49441

*(Optional number; prefer specific subject, as described under 920)
†Add as instructed under 920

(.5)   *†**Public administrators and military personnel**

> Subdivisions are added for either or both topics in heading
>
> *For heads of state, see 923.1; for governors, politicians, statesmen, see 923.2*

(.6)   *†**Philanthropists, humanitarians, social reformers**

> Subdivisions are added for any or all topics in heading

(.7)   *†**Educators**

(.8)   *†**People in commerce, communications, transportation**

> Subdivisions are added for any or all topics in heading

(.9)   ***Explorers, geographers, pioneers**

(924)   *Philologists and lexicographers

> Add to base number 924 notation 1–9 from Table 6, e.g., lexicographers of Chinese 924.951

(925)   *Scientists

> Add to base number 925 the numbers following 5 in 510–590, e.g., botanists 925.8

(926)   *People in technology

> Add to base number 926 the numbers following 6 in 610–690, e.g., engineers 926.2
>
> *See also 920.4 for booksellers*

(927)   *People in the arts and recreation

> Add to base number 927 the numbers following 7 in 710–790, e.g., baseball players 927.96357
>
> *For people in literature, see 928*

(928)   *People in literature, history, biography, genealogy

> Including historians, writers and critics of belles-lettres
>
> *See also 923.9 for explorers, geographers, pioneers*

(.1)   ***Americans**

(.2–.9)   ***Writers in literature, history, biography, genealogy by language**

> Add to base number 928 notation 2–9 from Table 6 for language in which person has written, e.g., writers in Italian 928.51
>
> Class Americans in 928.1

929   Genealogy, names, insignia

---

*(Optional number; prefer specific subject, as described under 920)
†Add as instructed under 920

.1   **Genealogy**

> *For family histories, see 929.2; for sources, see 929.3*

[.102 84]   Apparatus, equipment, materials

> Do not use; class in 929.3

.107 2   Research

> Class here the specific techniques and procedures involved in doing genealogical research in a specific area
>
> Class comprehensive works on genealogical research in 929.1

[.109 4–.109 9]   Specific continents, countries, localities in modern world

> Do not use; class in 929.107204–929.107209

.2   **Family histories**

> Class family histories emphasizing the contributions of the members of the family to a specific occupation with the occupation, e.g., the Rothschilds as a family of bankers 332.10922; class family histories of a prominent person that emphasize the person's life with the biography number for the person, e.g., forebears, family, and life of John Fitzgerald Kennedy 973.922092
>
> *For royal houses, peerage, see 929.7*
>
> *See Manual at 929.2*
>
> (Option: Arrange alphabetically by name)

.202 8   Auxiliary techniques and procedures; apparatus, equipment, materials

> Do not use for the techniques of compiling family histories; class in 929.1

.3   **Genealogical sources**

> Standard subdivisions are added for miscellaneous collections and individual sources
>
> Class here census records, court records, tax lists, wills
>
> Use only for sources published by a genealogical organization or compiled by a genealogist. Sources published or compiled by other agencies are normally classed with the subject of the publication, e.g., United States population census records 304.60973; however, if the source has been either enhanced or rearranged to emphasize the genealogical content, the source is classed here, e.g., United States population census records with name indexes added 929.373
>
> Class how to use sources in 929.1; class cemetery records used as genealogical sources in 929.5
>
> *For epitaphs, see 929.5*

[.309 3–.309 9]   Specific continents, countries, localities

> Do not use; class in 929.33–929.39

.33–.39	Specific continents, countries, localities

Regardless of form

Add to base number 929.3 notation 3–9 from Table 2, e.g., sources from New York 929.3747

.4   **Personal names**

See also 929.97 for names of houses, pets, ships

.42   Surnames

.44   Forenames

Class here lists of names for babies

.5   **Cemetery records**

Regardless of form

Including epitaphs

.6   **Heraldry**

Including crests

Class here armorial bearings, coats of arms

For royal houses, peerage, orders of knighthood, see 929.7

.7   **Royal houses, peerage, orders of knighthood**

Class here rank, precedence, titles of honor; genealogies tracing or establishing titles of honor; works emphasizing lineage or descent with respect to royalty or the peerage; history and genealogy of royal families

Class histories of a royal family that include general historical events or biographies of members of the royal family in 930–990. Class family histories of a prominent person that emphasize the person's life with the biography number for the person, e.g., forebears, family, and life of Winston Churchill 941.084092

[.709 41–.709 49]   Specific countries of Europe

Do not use; class in 929.72–929.79

.71   Orders of knighthood

Class Christian orders of knighthood in 255.791; class Christian orders of knighthood in church history in 271.791

>   929.72–929.79 Treatment of royal houses, peerage, gentry by specific countries of Europe

Class comprehensive works in 929.7094

.72   Great Britain and Ireland

.73–.79   Other countries of Europe

Add to base number 929.7 the numbers following —4 in notation 43–49 from Table 2, e.g., royal houses of France 929.74

.8   **Orders, decorations, autographs**

.81   Orders and decorations

> Add to base number 929.81 notation 1–9 from Table 2, e.g., orders of Germany 929.8143
> > Subdivisions are added for either or both topics in heading
>
> *For armorial bearings, see 929.6*

.88   Autographs

> Class autographs associated a specific subject with the subject, plus notation 075 from Table 1, e.g., American football autographs 796.332075

.9   **Forms of insignia and identification**

> Including identification cards, motor vehicle registration plates, seals
>
> Class seals with armorial bearings in 929.6. Class forms of insignia and identification not provided for here with the form, e.g., coats of arms 929.6; class a specific aspect of identification cards not provided for here with the aspect, e.g., forgery of identification cards 364.163; class identification marks in a specific subject with the subject, plus notation 027 from Table 1, e.g., airline insignia 387.70275
>
> *See also 737.6 for artistic aspects of seals*

.92   Flags and banners

> Standard subdivisions are added for either or both topics in heading
>
> Including ship, ownership flags and banners
>
> Class here national, state, provincial flags and banners
>
> Class military use in 355.15

.95   Service marks and trademarks

> Standard subdivisions are added for either or both topics in heading

.97   Names

> Including names of houses, ships, pets
>
> Class here interdisciplinary works on onomastics (study of origin, history, use of proper names)
>
> *For place names, see 910.014; for personal names, see 929.4*

.970 14   Communication

> Do not use for etymology; class in 412

> ## 930–990   History of specific continents, countries, localities; extraterrestrial worlds

Civilization and events

Class here interdisciplinary works on geography and history of ancient world, of specific continents, countries, localities

Add to base number 9 notation 3–9 from Table 2, e.g., general history of Europe 940, of England 942, of Norfolk, England 942.61; then add further as follows:

001	Philosophy and theory
002	Miscellany
00223	Maps, plans, diagrams
	Do not use for historical atlases; class in 911.1–911.9
003	Dictionaries, encyclopedias, concordances
004	Ethnic and national groups
	(Option: Class in 909.04)
00405–00409	Specific ethnic and national groups with ethnic origins from more than one continent, of European descent
	Add to 0040 the numbers following —0 in notation 05–09 from Table 5, e.g., history and civilization of people of European descent in New York 974.700409
	Class relation of ethnic and national groups with ethnic origins from more than one continent, of European descent to a war with the war, plus notation 089 from Table 1, e.g., relation of Europeans to World War II 940.5308909
0041–0049	Specific ethnic and national groups
	Add to 004 notation 1–9 from Table 5, e.g., history and civilization of North American native peoples in New York 974.700497
	Class indigenous groups in the prehistoric period with the period, e.g., Inca empire before Spanish conquest 985.019; class relation of ethnic and national groups to a war with the war, plus notation 089 from Table 1, e.g., relation of Arabs to World War II 940.53089927
005–006	Standard subdivisions
007	Education, research, related topics
0072	Historical research
007202	Historians and historiographers
	Class historians and historiographers specializing in a specific historical period of a specific area with the historical period for the area studied, plus notation 092 from Table 1, e.g., the biography of a Canadian historian who specializes in United States Revolutionary War 973.3092
	See Manual at 930–990: Biography
008	Groups of people
[0089]	Ethnic and national groups
	Do not use; class in 004

(continued)

> ## 930–990 History of specific continents, countries, localities; extraterrestrial worlds (continued)

009	Areas, regions places in general; collected biography
	Notation 09 from Table 1 as modified below
	Do not use for history, geographic treatment, biography together; class in 930–990 without adding from this table. Do not use for historical periods; class in 01–09. Do not use for individual biography; class in 01–09, plus notation 092 from Table 1. Do not use for specific continents, countries, localities; class in 930–990 without adding from this table
0091–0098	Areas, regions, places in general
	Add to 009 the numbers following —1 in notation 11–18 from Table 2, e.g., urban regions 009732
0099	Collected biography
	Description, critical appraisal, biography of people associated with the history of the continent, country, locality but limited to no specific period
	Class collected biography of a specific period in 01–09, plus notation 0922 from Table 1; class historians and historiographers in 007202; class comprehensive works on collected biography of a specific continent, country, or locality in 920.03–920.09

> *See Manual at T1—092: Comprehensive biography: Public figures; also at 920.009, 920.03–920.09 vs. 909.09, 909.1–909.8, 930–990; also at 930–990: Biography*

01–09	Historical periods
	Class here indigenous groups in the prehistoric period, e.g., Inca empire before Spanish conquest 985.019 (*not* 985.00498323)
	Add to 0 the period division numbers following 0 from the appropriate continent, country, locality in 930–990, e.g., period of 1760–1820 in British history 073 (from 941.073), period of 1815–1847 in German history 073 (from 943.073), period of 1815–1847 in Austrian history 042 (from 943.6042)
	Unless other period notation is specified, add to each geographic subdivision of an area the period notation for the area as a whole, e.g., period of Ottoman Empire in Saudi Arabia 953.803 (based on period of Ottoman Empire in Arabian Peninsula 953.03)
	Class areas, regions, places in general in a specific period in 0091–0098; class ethnic and national groups in a specific period in 004. Class relation of ethnic and national groups to a war with the war, plus notation 089 from Table 1, e.g., relation of Arabs to World War II 940.53089927

> *See Manual at 930–990: Biography; also at 930–990: Add table: 01–09*

The schedules that follow do not enumerate all the countries and localities that appear in Table 2; however, the foregoing instructions apply to history of any place in notation 3–9 from Table 2, e.g., period of 1815–1847 in Viennese history 943.613042

(continued)

> ## 930–990   History of specific continents, countries, localities; extraterrestrial worlds (continued)

Class sociology of war in 303.66; class sociology of military institutions in 306.27; class social factors affecting war in 355.02; class social causes of war in 355.0274; class historical geography in 911; class geography of ancient world, of specific continents, countries, localities in 913–919; class comprehensive works in 909

See Manual at 930–990; also at 306 vs. 305, 909, 930–990; also at 324 vs. 320.5, 320.9, 909, 930–990; also at 333.7–333.9 vs. 508, 913–919, 930–990; also at 909, 930–990 vs. 320; also at 909, 930–990 vs. 320.4, 321, 321.09; also at 909, 930–990 vs. 910; also at 930–990 vs. 355.009, 355–359

(Option: Class primary history textbooks on ancient world, on specific continents, countries, localities in 372.893–372.899)

930   History of ancient world to ca. 499

SUMMARY

930.01–.09	**Standard subdivisions**
.1–.5	**[Archaeology and historical periods]**
931	**China to 420**
932	**Egypt to 640**
933	**Palestine to 70**
934	**South Asia to 647**
935	**Mesopotamia to 637 and Iranian Plateau to 637**
936	**Europe north and west of Italian Peninsula to ca. 499**
937	**Italian Peninsula to 476 and adjacent territories to 476**
938	**Greece to 323**
939	**Other parts of ancient world**

.01–.09   Standard subdivisions

As modified under 930–990; however, for archaeology, see 930.1

.1   **Archaeology**

Study of past civilizations through discovery, collection, interpretation of material remains

Class here early history to 4000 B.C.; prehistoric archaeology; interdisciplinary works on archaeology

For industrial archaeology, see 609; for archaeology of specific oceans and seas, see 909.0963–909.0967; for archaeology of continents, countries, localities provided for in notation 3 from Table 2, see 931–939; for archaeology of modern period, ancient and prehistoric archaeology of continents, countries, localities not provided for in notation 3 from Table 2, see 940–990

See also 700 for artistic aspects of archaeological objects

.102   Miscellany

.102 8	Auxiliary techniques and procedures; apparatus, equipment, materials
	Notation 028 from Table 1 as modified below
	Class here basic techniques and procedures
.102 804	Underwater archaeology
	For archaeology of specific oceans and seas, see 909.0963–909.0967
.102 82	Discovery of remains
.102 83	Excavation of remains
.102 85	Interpretation of remains
	Including dating techniques

> 930.11–930.16 Specific prehistoric ages

Class comprehensive works in 930.1

[.11]	Eolithic Age
	Relocated to 930.124
.12	Paleolithic Age (Old Stone Age)
	Class here comprehensive works on Stone Ages
	For Mesolithic Age, see 930.13; for Neolithic Age, see 930.14
.124	Lower Paleolithic Age
	Including Acheulian culture
	Class here Eolithic Age [*formerly* 930.11]
.126	Middle Paleolithic Age
	Including Mousterian culture
.128	Upper Paleolithic Age
	Including Aurignacian culture, Solutrean culture
.13	Mesolithic Age (Middle Stone Age)
.14	Neolithic Age (New Stone Age)
.15	Copper Age and Bronze Age
	Class here 3999–1000 B.C.
	For 1200–1000 B.C., see 930.16
.153	Copper Age (Chalcolithic Age)
.156	Bronze Age

.16	Iron Age

Class here 999–1 B.C.

See also 938.08 for Hellenistic period

.5   **1st–5th centuries, 1–499**

\>   **931–939   Specific places**

Class archaeology and history of specific oceans and seas in 909.0963–909.0967; class archaeology and history of modern period, ancient and prehistoric archaeology and history of continents, countries, localities not provided for in notation 3 from Table 2 in 940–990; class comprehensive works in 930

931   ***China to 420**

(Option: Class in 951.01)

.01	Early history to ca. 1523 B.C.
.02	Period of Shang (Yin) dynasty, ca. 1523–ca. 1028 B.C.
.03	Period of Zhou (Chou) dynasty and warring states, ca. 1028–221 B.C.
.04	Period of Qin (Ch'in) to Jin (Chin) dynasties, 221 B.C.–420 A.D.

Including Han dynasty, 202 B.C.–220 A.D.

932   ***Egypt to 640**

(Option: Class in 962.01)

.01	Early history to 332 B.C.
.011	Prehistoric period to ca. 3100 B.C.
.012	Protodynastic, Old Kingdom, first intermediate periods, ca. 3100–2052 B.C.

Including 1st–11th dynasties

.013	Middle Kingdom and second intermediate periods, 2052–1570 B.C.

Including 12th–17th dynasties

.014	Period of New Kingdom, 1570–1075 B.C.

Including 18th–20th dynasties

.015	Late and Saite periods, 1075–525 B.C.

Including 21st–26th dynasties, period of sovereignty of Cush

.016	Persian periods and last Egyptian kingdom, 525–332 B.C.

Including 27th–31st dynasties

.02	Hellenistic, Roman, Byzantine periods, 332 B.C.–640 A.D.

*Add as instructed under 930–990

.021	Hellenistic period, 332–30 B.C.
.022	Roman period, 30 B.C.–324 A.D.
.023	Byzantine (Coptic) period, 324–640

933   *Palestine to 70

See also 220.93 for Biblical archaeology; also 220.95 for history of Biblical events

(Option: Class Palestine, Israel in 956.9401; class Jordan, West Bank in 956.9501)

.01	Early history to return of Jews from bondage in Egypt, ca. 1225 B.C.
.02	Great age of Twelve Tribes, ca. 1225–922 B.C.

Including rule of Judges, Saul, David, Solomon

.03	Periods of partition, conquest, foreign rule, 922–168 B.C.

Including periods of Assyrian, Babylonian, Persian, Hellenistic rule

.04	168–63 B.C.

Including Hasmonean (Maccabean) period

.05	Period of Roman protectorate and rule to destruction of Jerusalem, 63 B.C.–70 A.D.

934   *South Asia to 647

Class here India to 647

(Option: Class in 954.01)

.01	Pre-Aryan civilizations to ca. 1500 B.C.
.02	Indo-Aryan (Vedic) period, ca. 1500–ca. 600 B.C.

Including Iron Age culture in south India

.03	Ca. 600–ca. 322 B.C.
.04	Period of Maurya dynasty, ca. 322–185 B.C.
.043	Ca. 322–ca. 274 B.C.
.045	Reign of Aśoka, ca. 274–ca. 237 B.C.
.047	Ca. 237–185 B.C.
.05	Period of changing dynasties, 185 B.C.–318 A.D.
.06	Period of Gupta dynasty, 318–500
.07	500–647

Including reign of Harsha, 606–647

*Add as instructed under 930–990

.9   **Other jurisdictions to 647**

Class here Pakistan (West and East, 1947–1971) to 647

(Option: Class in 954.901)

.91   *Pakistan to 647

(Option: Class in 954.9101)

.92   *Bangladesh to 647

(Option: Class in 954.9201)

935   *Mesopotamia to 637 and Iranian Plateau to 637

Subdivisions are added for Mesopotamia and Iranian Plateau together, for Mesopotamia alone

(Option: Class in 956.701)

.01   Early history to ca. 1900 B.C.

.02   Ca. 1900–ca. 900 B.C.

.03   Period of Assyrian Empire, ca. 900–625 B.C.

.04   625–539 B.C.

Including reign of Nebuchadnezzar II, 605–562 B.C.

Class here Neo-Babylonian (Chaldean) Empire

.05   Period of Persian Empire, 539–332 B.C.

For Persian Wars, see 938.03

.06   Hellenistic period, 332 B.C.–226 A.D.

.062   332–ca. 250 B.C.

Class here period of Seleucid Empire, 323–ca. 250 B.C.

.064   Period of Parthian Empire, ca. 250 B.C.–226 A.D.

.07   Period of Neo-Persian (Sassanian) Empire, 226–637

>   **935.2–935.5 Mesopotamia to 637**

Class here Iraq to 637

Class comprehensive works in 935

.2   **Kurdish Autonomous Region of Iraq to 637**

Add to base number 935.2 the numbers following 935 in 935.01–935.07, e.g., period of Persian Empire 935.205

(Optional number; prefer 956.7201)

*Add as instructed under 930–990

.4**Upper Mesopotamia to 637**

Including Upper Mesopotamian portion of Arabia Deserta to 637 [*formerly* 939.47]

Add to base number 935.4 the numbers following 935 in 935.01–935.07, e.g., Kingdom of Mitanni 935.402

(Option: Class in 956.7401)

.5**Lower Mesopotamia to 637**

Including Lower Mesopotamian portion of Arabia Deserta to 637 [*formerly* 939.47]

Class here Babylonia

(Option: Class in 956.7501)

.501Early history to ca. 1900 B.C.

Class here Akkadian, Sumerian, Ur periods

.502Period of Babylonian Empire, ca. 1900–ca. 900 B.C.

Including reign of Hammurabi, ca. 1792–ca. 1750 B.C.

.503–.507Ca. 900 B.C.–637 A.D.

Add to base number 935.5 the numbers following 935 in 935.03–935.07, e.g., period of Neo-Babylonian Empire 935.504

.7**Iranian Plateau to 637**

Class here Iran to 637, Persia to 637

(Option: Class in 955.01)

.701–.707Historical periods of Iranian Plateau to 637

Add to base number 935.7 the numbers following 935 in 935.01–935.07, e.g., period of Persian Empire 935.705

.71–.79Provinces of Iran to 637

Add to 935.7 the numbers following —55 in notation 551–559 from Table 2, e.g., Media 935.75, Elam 935.76; then add 0† and to the result add the numbers following 935.0 in 935.01–935.07, e.g., Median Empire 935.7504, Media province of Persian Empire 935.7504, Elamite Kingdom 935.7601, Elam province of Persian Empire 935.7605

(Option: Class Media, Ecbatana in 955.501; class Elam, Susa in 955.601; class Persis, Pasargadae, Persepolis in 955.7201)

†Add 00 for standard subdivisions; see instructions at beginning of Table 1

936   *Europe north and west of Italian Peninsula to ca. 499

Including western Mediterranean region

Class here Europe, western Europe

For a specific part of ancient Europe not provided for here, see the part, e.g., Italy 937; Eastern Europe 947.000901, Russia 947.01

(Option: Class western Mediterranean region in 909.098221; class Europe, Europe north and west of Italian Peninsula, western Europe in 940.11)

.01   Early history to ca. 1000 B.C.

(Option: Class in 940.111)

.02   Ca. 1000–ca. 200 B.C.

(Option: Class in 940.112)

.03   Ca. 200 B.C.–ca. 499 A.D.

(Option: Class in 940.113)

.1   *British Isles to 410

For England to 410 and Wales to 410, see 936.2

(Option: Class in 941.012)

.101–.104   Historical periods of British Isles to 410

Add to base number 936.10 the numbers following 936.20 in 936.201–936.204, e.g., Roman period 936.104

.11   *Scotland to 410

(Option: Class in 941.1012)

.110 1   Early history to ca. 600 B.C.

(Option: Class in 941.10121)

.110 2   Ca. 600–79 B.C.

Class here Celtic period

(Option: Class in 941.10122)

.110 3   79 B.C.–410 A.D.

Class here period of Roman contacts

(Option: Class in 941.10123)

.12   *Northeastern Scotland to 410

(Option: Class in 941.2012)

.120 1   Early history to ca. 600 B.C.

(Option: Class in 941.20121)

*Add as instructed under 930–990

.120 2	Ca. 600–79 B.C.
	(Option: Class in 941.20122)
.120 3	79 B.C.–410 A.D.
	(Option: Class in 941.20123)
.13	*Southeastern Scotland to 410
	(Option: Class in 941.3012)
.130 1	Early history to ca. 600 B.C.
	(Option: Class in 941.30121)
.130 2	Ca. 600–79 B.C.
	(Option: Class in 941.30122)
.130 3	79 B.C.–410 A.D.
	(Option: Class in 941.30123)
.14	*Southwestern Scotland to 410
	(Option: Class in 941.4012)
.140 1	Early history to ca. 600 B.C.
	(Option: Class in 941.40121)
.140 2	Ca. 600–79 B.C.
	(Option: Class in 941.40122)
.140 3	79 B.C.–410 A.D.
	(Option: Class in 941.40123)
.15	*Ireland to 433
	(Option: Class in 941.5012)
.150 1	Early history to ca. 400 B.C.
	(Option: Class in 941.50121)
.150 2	Celtic period, ca. 400 B.C.–433 A.D.
	Including 410–433 [*formerly* 941.501]
	(Option: Class in 941.50122)
.16	*Northern Ireland to 433; Donegal, Monaghan, Cavan counties of Republic of Ireland to 433
	Subdivisions are added for Northern Ireland, Donegal, Monaghan, Cavan counties together; for Northern Ireland alone
.160 1	Early history to ca. 400 B.C.
	(Option: Class in 941.60121)

*Add as instructed under 930–990

.160 2	Celtic period, ca. 400 B.C.–433 A.D.
	Including 410–433 [*formerly* 941.601]
	(Option: Class in 941.60122)
.17	*Republic of Ireland to 433
	(Option: Class in 941.7012)
.170 1	Early history to ca. 400 B.C.
	(Option: Class in 941.70121)
.170 2	Celtic period, ca. 400 B.C.–433 A.D.
	Including 410–433 [*formerly* 941.701]
	(Option: Class in 941.70122)
.18	*Leinster to 433
	(Option: Class in 941.8012)
.180 1	Early history to ca. 400 B.C.
	(Option: Class in 941.80121)
.180 2	Celtic period, ca. 400 B.C.–433 A.D.
	Including 410–433 [*formerly* 941.801]
	(Option: Class in 941.80122)
.19	*Munster to 433
	(Option: Class in 941.9012)
.190 1	Early history to ca. 400 B.C.
	(Option: Class in 941.90121)
.190 2	Celtic period, ca. 400 B.C.–433 A.D.
	Including 410–433 [*formerly* 941.901]
	(Option: Class in 941.90122)

.2 ***England to 410 and Wales to 410**

Subdivisions are added for England to 410 and Wales to 410 together, for England to 410 alone

(Option: Class England to 410 in 942.012; class Wales to 410 in 942.9012)

.201	Early history to ca. 600 B.C.
.201 1–.201 5	Early history to ca. 1000 B.C.
	Add to base number 936.201 the numbers following 930.1 in 930.11–930.15, e.g., Bronze Age 936.20156
.201 6	Ca. 1000–ca. 600 B.C.

*Add as instructed under 930–990

.202	Celtic period, ca. 600–55 B.C.
.203	Period of early Roman contacts, 55 B.C.–43 A.D.
.204	Roman period, 43–410

.3   ***Germanic regions to 481 and Pannonia**

> *For British Isles to 410, see 936.1*

> (Option: Class Germanic regions, Germany in 943.012)

> Scandinavia to 481 relocated to 936.8; Norway to 481 relocated to 936.81; Sweden to 481 relocated to 936.85; Denmark to 481 relocated to 936.89; Germanic regions in Netherlands to 481 relocated to 936.921; Germanic regions in Switzerland to 481 relocated to 936.947

.301   Early history to 113 B.C.

> (Option: Class in 943.0121)

.301 1–.301 5   Early history to ca. 1000 B.C.

> Add to base number 936.301 the numbers following 930.1 in 930.11–930.15, e.g., Bronze Age 936.30156

.301 6   Ca. 1000–113 B.C.

.302   Period of contacts with Roman Republic and Empire, 113 B.C.–481 A.D.

> (Option: Class in 943.0122)

.36   *Austria and Liechtenstein to 476

> Class here Noricum

> Subdivisions are added for Austria and Liechtenstein together, for Austria alone

> (Option: Class in 943.601)

.360 1   Early history to ca. 390 B.C.

> (Option: Class in 943.6011)

.360 2   Celtic period, ca. 390–15 B.C.

> (Option: Class in 943.6012)

.360 3   Roman period, ca. 15 B.C.–476 A.D.

> (Option: Class in 943.6013)

.364   *Western Austria, and Liechtenstein

> Subdivisions are added for Western Austria and Liechtenstein together, for Western Austria alone

.364 8   *Liechtenstein to 476

> (Option: Class in 943.648)

---

*Add as instructed under 930–990

.364 801	Early history to ca. 390 B.C.
.364 802	Celtic period, ca. 390–15 B.C.
.364 803	Roman period, ca. 15 B.C.–476 A.D.
.39	*Pannonia [*formerly* 939.8]

         Class here Hungary to ca. 640 [*formerly* 939.8]

         (Option: Class in 943.9011)

.4   *Celtic regions to 486

         For British Isles, see 936.1

         (Option: Class Celtic regions, France in 944.012)

         Netherlands to 486 relocated to 936.92; Belgium to 486 relocated to 936.93; Luxembourg to 486 relocated to 936.935; Switzerland to 486 relocated to 936.94

.401	Early history to 125 B.C.

         (Option: Class in 944.0121)

.401 1–.401 5	Early history to ca. 1000 B.C.

         Add to base number 936.401 the numbers following 930.1 in 930.11–930.15, e.g., Bronze Age 936.40156

.401 6	Ca. 1000–125 B.C.
.402	Gallo-Roman period, 125 B.C.–486 A.D.

         (Option: Class in 944.0122)

.6   *Iberian Peninsula to 415 and adjacent islands to 415

         (Option: Class Iberian Peninsula and adjacent islands in 946.000901; class Spain in 946.012)

.601	Early history to ca. 1000 B.C.

         (Option: Class Iberian Peninsula and adjacent islands to 4000 B.C. in 946.0009012; Iberian Peninsula and adjacent islands, 3999–1000 B.C., in 946.0009013; class Spain in 946.0121)

.602	Period of Greek, Phoenician, and early Celtic and Germanic contacts, ca. 1000–218 B.C.

         (Option: Class Iberian Peninsula and adjacent islands in 946.0009014; class Spain in 946.0122)

.603	Roman period, 218 B.C.–415 A.D.

         (Option: Class Iberian Peninsula and adjacent islands to 999–1 B.C. in 946.0009014; Iberian Peninsula and adjacent islands, 1–415, in 946.0009015; class Spain in 946.0123)

---

*Add as instructed under 930–990

.69   *Portugal to 415

    (Option: Class in 946.9012)

.690 1   Early history to ca. 1000 B.C.

    (Option: Class in 946.90121)

.690 2   Period of Greek, Phoenician, and early Celtic and Germanic contacts, ca. 1000–218 B.C

    (Option: Class in 946.90122)

.690 3   Roman period, 218 B.C.–415 A.D.

    (Option: Class in 946.90123)

.8   ***Scandinavia to 481 [*formerly* 936.3]***

    For Finland to 481, see 948.9701

    (Option: Class in 948.012)

.81   *Norway to 481 [*formerly* 936.3]

    (Option: Class in 948.1012)

.85   *Sweden to 481 [*formerly* 936.3]

    (Option: Class in 948.5012)

.89   *Denmark to 481 [*formerly* 936.3]

    (Option: Class in 948.9012)

.9   **†Netherlands to 486, Belgium to 486, Luxembourg to 486, Switzerland to 486**

.92   *Netherlands to 486 [*formerly* 936.4]

    Class here Celtic regions of Netherlands to 486, comprehensive works on Low Countries to 486

    For southern Low Countries to 486, see 936.93

    (Option: Class in 949.2012)

.920 1   Early history to 125 B.C.

    (Option: Class in 949.20121)

.920 2   Gallo-Roman period, 125 B.C.–486 A.D.

    (Option: Class in 949.20122)

.921   *Northeastern provinces of Netherlands to 481

    Class here Germanic regions of Netherlands to 481 [*formerly* 936.3]

    For Flevoland to 481, see 936.922

    (Option: Class in 949.21012)

*Add as instructed under 930–990

†Add as instructed under 930–990; however, do not add historical periods

.921 01	Early history to 113 B.C.
	(Option: Class in 949.210121)
.921 02	Period of contacts with Roman Republic and Empire, 113 B.C.–481 A.D.
	(Option: Class in 949.210122)
.93	*Belgium to 486 [*formerly* 936.4]
	(Option: Class in 949.3012)
.930 1	Early history to 125 B.C.
	(Option: Class in 949.30121)
.930 2	Gallo-Roman period, 125 B.C.–486 A.D.
	(Option: Class in 949.30122)
.935	*Luxembourg to 486 [*formerly* 936.4]
	(Option: Class in 949.35012)
.935 01	Early history to 125 B.C.
	(Option: Class in 949.350121)
.935 02	Gallo-Roman period, 125 B.C.–486 A.D.
	(Option: Class in 949.350122)
.94	*Switzerland to 486 [*formerly* 936.4]
	(Option: Class in 949.4012)
.940 1	Early history to 125 B.C.
	(Option: Class in 949.40121)
.940 2	Gallo-Roman period, 125 B.C.–486 A.D.
	(Option: Class in 949.40122)
.947	*Alpine region cantons to 481
	Class here Germanic regions of Switzerland to 481 [*formerly* 936.3]
	(Option: Class in 949.47012)
.947 01	Early history to 113 B.C.
	(Option: Class 949.470121)
.947 02	Period of contacts with Roman Republic and Empire, 113 B.C.–481 A.D.
	(Option: Class 949.47012)

*Add as instructed under 930–990

937   *Italian Peninsula to 476 and adjacent territories to 476

Class here Mediterranean region

Subdivisions are added for Italian Peninsula and adjacent territories together, for Italian Peninsula alone

(Option: Class Mediterranean region in 909.1822; class Italian Peninsula and adjacent territories in 945.012)

.01   Early history to 510 B.C.

Class here Roman Kingdom, 753–510 B.C.

.02   Period of Roman Republic, 510–31 B.C.

For specific periods, see 937.03–937.05

>   937.03–937.05   Specific periods under the Republic

Class comprehensive works in 937.02

.03   Period of unification of Italy, 510–264 B.C.

.04   Period of Punic Wars, 264–146 B.C.

.05   Period of civil strife, 146–31 B.C.

.06   Period of Roman Empire, 31 B.C.–476 A.D.

For specific periods, see 937.07–937.09

>   937.07–937.09   Specific periods under the Empire

Class comprehensive works in 937.06

.07   Early and middle periods, 31 B.C.–284 A.D.

.08   Period of absolutism, 284–395

.09   Final period, 395–476

.9   ***Sardinia to 453 and Corsica to 453**

Subdivisions are added for Sardinia and Corsica together; for Sardinia alone

(Option: Class in 945.9012)

.901–.908   Early history to 395

Add to base number 937.90 the numbers following 937.0 in 937.01–937.08, e.g., Sardinia during period of Roman Empire 937.906

.909   Final period of Roman Empire, 395–453

453–476 relocated to 945.901

.99   *Corsica

(Option: Class in 945.99012)

*Add as instructed under 930–990

.990 1–.990 8   Early history to 395

Add to base number 937.990 the numbers following 937.0 in
937.01–937.08, e.g., Corsica during period of Roman Empire
937.9906

.990 9   Final period of Roman Empire, 395–453

453–476 relocated to 944.9901

938   *Greece to 323

Class here the Hellenistic World; the eastern Mediterranean region; southern
Europe

(Option: Class eastern Mediterranean region in 909.098224; class southern Europe
in 940.11; class Greece in 949.5012)

.01   Early history to 775 B.C.

.02   775–500 B.C.

.03   Persian Wars, 500–479 B.C.

.04   Period of Athenian supremacy, 479–431 B.C.

.05   Period of Peloponnesian War, 431–404 B.C.

.06   Period of Spartan and Theban supremacy, 404–362 B.C.

.07   Period of Macedonian supremacy, 362–323 B.C.

.08   Hellenistic period, 323–146 B.C.

.09   Roman era, 146 B.C.–323 A.D.

939   *Other parts of ancient world

.1   *Aegean Islands to 323

(Option: Class in 949.58012)

.101–.109   Historical periods

Add to base number 939.10 the numbers following 938.0 in
938.01–938.09, e.g., Hellenistic period 939.108

.18   *Crete to 323

(Option: Class in 949.59012)

.2   †Diocese of Asia (Dioecesis Asiana)

Class here western Asia Minor to 640, comprehensive works on Asia Minor to
640

For eastern Asia Minor to 640, see 939.3

(Option: Class in 956.1012)

*Add as instructed under 930–990
†Add as instructed under 930–990; however, do not add historical periods

.3   †**Eastern Asia Minor to 640 and Cyprus to 640**

(Option: Class eastern Asia Minor in 956.1012)

.37   †Cyprus to 640

(Option: Class in 956.93012)

.4   ***Middle East to 640**

Class a specific part of Middle East not provided for here with the part, e.g., Egypt 932, Palestine 933

(Option: Class in 956.012)

.401   Early history to ca. 1900 B.C.

.402   Period of Babylonian and Assyrian Empires, ca. 1900–539 B.C.

.403   Period of Persian Empire, 539–332 B.C.

.404   Hellenistic period, 332–30 B.C.

.405   Roman period, 30 B.C.–ca. 640 A.D.

.43   *Syria to 640

(Option: Class in 956.9101)

.431   *Hatay Province of modern Turkey to 640

Including Antioch

(Option: Class in 956.48)

.44   *Phoenicia

Class here Lebanon to 640

(Option: Class in 956.9202)

.46   Moab and Edom

.462   *Moab

(Option: Class in 956.95601)

.464   *Edom

(Option: Class in 956.94901)

[.47]   Arabia Deserta

Upper Mesopotamian portion of Arabia Deserta to 637 relocated to 935.4; Lower Mesopotamian portion of Arabia Deserta to 637 relocated to 935.5; Arabia Deserta to 622 relocated to 939.49; Arabia Deserta, 622–637 relocated to 953.02

---

*Add as instructed under 930–990
†Add as instructed under 930–990; however, do not add historical periods

.48   *Arabia Petraea

Including Sinai Peninsula to 622; Petra

(Option: Class Arabia Petraea in 953.01; class Sinai Peninsula in 953.101; class Petra in 956.957701)

.49   *Arabian Peninsula to 622

Including Bahrain to 622, Kuwait to 622, Oman to 622, Persian Gulf States to 622, Qatar to 622, Saudi Arabia to 622, United Arab Emirates to 622, Yemen to 622

Class here Arabia Deserta to 622 [*formerly* 939.47]; Arabia Felix

For Upper Mesopotamian portion of Arabia Deserta to 637, see 935.4; for Lower Mesopotamian portion of Arabia Deserta to 637, see 935.5; for Arabia Petraea, see 939.48

(Option: Class Arabia Felix, Arabia to 622 in 953.01; class Yemen to 622 in 953.301; class Oman to 622 in 953.53; class United Arab Emirates to 622 in 953.57; class Persian Gulf States to 622 in 953.6; class Qatar to 622 in 953.63; class Bahrain to 622 in 953.65; class Kuwait to 622 in 953.67; class Saudi Arabia to 622 in 953.801)

.5   †**Black Sea region to 640 and Caucasus to 640**

Subdivisions are added for Black Sea region to 640 and Caucasus to 640 together, for Black Sea region to 640 alone

(Option: Class Black Sea region to 640 in 909.098229)

.51   †Scythia

Class here Black Sea area of Romania to 640

(Option: Class in 949.83)

.52   †Sarmatia

Class here Ukraine to 640

(Option: Class in 947.7)

.53   †Caucasus

(Option: Class in 947.5)

.534   †Albania

(Option: Class in 947.54)

.536   †Iberia

Class here Georgia to 640

(Option: Class in 947.58)

.538   †Colchis

(Option: Class in 947.58)

*Add as instructed under 930–990
†Add as instructed under 930–990; however, do not add historical periods

.55   †Armenia

Class here Armenia region to 640

(Option: Class modern country of Armenia in 947.56; class Armenia region to 640, Armenia [ancient kingdom] in 956.62012)

.6   †Central Asia to ca. 640

Including Afghanistan to ca. 640, Māzandarān province of Iran to 637, Tajikistan to ca. 640, Turkmenistan to ca. 640, Uzbekistan to ca. 640; Ariana, Bactria, Hyrcania, Margiana, Parthia, Sogdiana

For Kyrgyzstan to ca. 640, see 958.43; for Kazakhstan to ca. 640, see 958.45

(Option: Class Māzandarān province of Iran to 637, Hyrcania in 955.23; class Central Asia to ca. 640 in 958; class Afghanistan to ca. 640, Ariana, Bactria, Parthia in 958.101; class Turkmenistan to ca. 640, Margiana in 958.507; class Tajikistan to ca. 640 in 958.607; class Uzbekistan to ca. 640, Sogdiana in 958.707)

.7   *North Africa to ca. 640

For Egypt to 640, see 932

(Option: Class in 961.01)

.701   Early history to ca. 800 B.C.

.702   Carthaginian period, ca. 800–146 B.C.

.703   Roman period, 146 B.C.–429 A.D.

Vandal period, 429–534 relocated to 939.704; Byzantine period, 534–ca. 640 relocated to 939.705

.704   Vandal period, 429–534 [*formerly* 939.703]

.705   Byzantine period, 534–ca. 640 [*formerly* 939.703]

.71   *Mauretania

(Option: Class in 965.01)

.710 1   Early history to ca. 800 B.C.

(Option: Class in 965.011)

.710 2   Carthaginian period, ca. 800–146 B.C.

(Option: Class in 965.012)

.710 3   Period of Kingdom of Mauretania, 146 B.C.–42 A.D.

(Option: Class in 965.013)

.710 4   Roman period, 42–ca. 435 A.D.

(Option: Class in 965.014)

---

*Add as instructed under 930–990
†Add as instructed under 930–990; however, do not add historical periods

.710 5	Vandal period, ca. 435–534
	(Option: Class in 965.015)
.710 6	Byzantine period, 534–647
	(Option: Class in 965.016)
.712	*Mauretania Tingitana
	Class here Morocco to 647
	(Option: Class in 964.01)
.712 01	Early history to ca. 800 B.C.
	(Option: Class in 964.011)
.712 02	Carthaginian period, ca. 800–146 B.C.
	(Option: Class in 964.012)
.712 03	Period of Kingdom of Mauretania, 146–25 B.C.
	(Option: Class in 964.013)
.712 04	Roman period, 25 B.C.–429 A.D.
	(Option: Class in 964.014)
.712 05	Vandal period, 429–534
	(Option: Class 964.015)
.712 06	Byzantine period, 534–647
	(Option: Class in 964.016)
.714	*Mauretania Caesariensis
	Class here Algeria to 647
	(Option: Class in 965.01)
.714 01–.714 06	Historical periods of Mauretania Caesariensis
	Add to base number 939.7140 the numbers following 939.710 in 939.7101 939.7106, e.g., Roman period 939.71404
.72	*Numidia
	Class here northeastern provinces of Algeria to 647
	(Option: Class in 965.501)
.720 1	Early history to ca. 800 B.C.
	(Option: Class 965.5011)
.720 2	Carthaginian period, ca. 800–146 B.C.
	(Option: Class 965.5012)

*Add as instructed under 930–990

.720 3	Period of Kingdom of Numidia, 146–46 B.C.	
	(Option: Class 965.5013)	
.720 4	Roman period, 46 B.C.–439 A.D.	
	(Option: Class 965.5014)	
.720 5	Vandal period, 439–534	
	(Option: Class 965.5015)	
.720 6	Byzantine period, 534–647	
	(Option: Class 965.5016)	
.73	*Carthage	
	Class here Tunisia to 647	
	(Option: Class in 961.101)	
.730 1	Early history to ca. 800 B.C.	
	(Option: Class in 961.1011)	
.730 2	Carthaginian period, ca. 800–146 B.C.	
	(Option: Class in 961.1012)	
.730 3	Roman period, 146 B.C.–439 A.D.	
	(Option: Class in 961.1013)	
.730 4	Vandal period, 439–534	
	(Option: Class in 961.1014)	
.730 5	Byzantine period, 534–647	
	(Option: Class in 961.1015)	
.74	*Tripolis	
	(Option: Class in 961.201)	
.740 1	Early history to ca. 800 B.C.	
	(Option: Class in 961.2011)	
.740 2	Carthaginian period, ca. 800–146 B.C.	
	(Option: Class in 961.2012)	
.740 3	Roman period, 146 B.C.–439 A.D.	
	(Option: Class in 961.2013)	
.740 4	Vandal period, 439–534	
	(Option: Class in 961.2014)	
.740 5	Byzantine period, 534–644	
	(Option: Class in 961.2015)	

*Add as instructed under 930–990

.75   *Cyrenaica

      (Option: Class in 961.201)

.750 1   Early history to ca. 940 B.C.

      (Option: Class in 961.201)

.750 2   Egyptian period, ca. 940–ca. 630 B.C.

      (Option: Class in 961.201)

.750 3   Greek period, ca. 630–ca. 500 B.C.

      (Option: Class in 961.201)

.750 4   Persian period, ca. 500–323 B.C.

      (Option: Class in 961.201)

.750 5   Hellenistic period, 323–96 B.C.

      (Option: Class in 961.201)

.750 6   Roman period, 96 B.C.–330 A.D.

      (Option: Class in 961.201)

.750 7   Byzantine period, 330–642

      (Option: Class in 961.201)

.76   *Marmarica to 642

      (Option: Class in 961.201)

.760 1   Early history to ca. 940 B.C.

      (Option: Class in 961.201)

.760 2   Egyptian period, ca. 940–ca. 630 B.C.

      (Option: Class in 961.201)

.760 3   Greek period, ca. 630–ca. 500 B.C.

      (Option: Class in 961.201)

.760 4   Persian period, ca. 500–323 B.C.

      (Option: Class in 961.201)

.760 5   Hellenistic period, 323–96 B.C.

      (Option: Class in 961.201)

.760 6   Roman period, 96 B.C.–330 A.D.

      (Option: Class in 961.201)

.760 7   Byzantine period, 330–642

      (Option: Class in 961.201)

*Add as instructed under 930–990

.77   *Gaetulia

Class here Sahara provinces of Algeria to 647

(Option: Class in 965.701)

.78   *Nubia

Class here northern states of Sudan to 500, Ethiopia (a part of what is now modern Sudan, not modern Ethiopia), Kush

Class comprehensive works on the Sudan to 500 in 962.401

(Option: Class in 962.501)

.8   †Southeastern Europe to ca. 640

See also 939.5 for Black Sea region to 640

(Option: Class Thrace to 323 in 949.57012; class southeastern Europe to ca. 640 in 949.601; class Turkey in Europe [Eastern Thrace] to 323 in 949.61012; class İstanbul Province to 323, Constantinople to 323 in 949.618012; class Albania to 640 in 949.65012; class former Yugoslavia to ca. 640, Illyria, Illyricum in 949.7012; class Serbia to ca. 640 in 949.71011; class Croatia to ca. 640 in 949.72012; class Slovenia to ca. 640 in 949.73012; class Bosnia and Hercegovina to ca. 640 in 949.742012; class Montenegro to ca. 640 in 949.745012; class Macedonia to ca. 640 in 949.76012; class Bulgaria to ca. 640, Moesia in 949.9012)

Hungary to ca. 640, Pannonia relocated to 936.39

.88   Dacia

Number built according to instructions under 939.8

Including Moldova to ca. 640 [*formerly* 947.6]

Class here Romania to ca. 640

(Option: Class Moldova to ca. 640 in 947.6; class Romania to ca. 640, Dacia in 949.8012)

*Add as instructed under 930–990
†Add as instructed under 930–990; however, do not add historical periods

> ## 940–990 History of specific continents, countries, localities in modern world; extraterrestrial worlds

Class here area studies; comprehensive works on ancient and modern history of specific continents, countries, localities

Except for modifications shown under specific entries, add to each subdivision identified by ‡ as follows:

08   Groups of people
       Do not use for enemy sympathizers, pacifists; class in 1
[086914]   Displaced persons
          Relocated to 1
09   History, geographic treatment, biography
       Do not use for participation of specific groups of countries; class in 3
[094–099]   Specific continents, countries, localities
       Do not use for specific continents; class in 3. Do not use for specific countries and localities; class in 34–39
1   Social, political, economic history
       Standard subdivisions are added for any or all topics in heading
       Including displaced persons [*formerly* 086914], consequences, e.g., movement of people; causes, results, efforts to preserve or restore peace
       Class general diplomatic history in 2; class prisoner-of-war camps in 7. Class results in and effects on a specific country with the history of the country, e.g., effect of Vietnamese War on United States 973.923 (*not* 959.70431)
2   Diplomatic history
       Class diplomatic causes, efforts to preserve or restore peace, diplomatic results in 1
3   Participation of specific groups of countries and of specific countries, localities
       Class military participation of specific groups of countries, of specific countries, localities in 409. Class participation in a specific activity with the activity, e.g., efforts to preserve or restore peace 1
34–39   Participation of specific countries and localities
       Add to 3 notation 4–9 from Table 2, e.g., participation by France 344
4   Military operations and units
       Standard subdivisions are added for either or both topics in heading
       Class here military history
       Class units engaged in a specific type of service with the service, e.g., medical units 7
       For an aspect of military history not provided for here, see the aspect, e.g., prisoner-of-war camps 7
42   Land operations
45   Naval operations
48   Air operations

(continued)

> ## 940–990 History of specific continents, countries, localities in modern world; extraterrestrial worlds (continued)

<table>
<tr><td>6</td><td>Celebrations, commemorations, memorials
Including decorations and awards, rolls of honor, cemeteries, monuments</td></tr>
<tr><td>7</td><td>Prisoners of war, medical and social services
Including prisoner-of-war camps</td></tr>
<tr><td>8</td><td>Other military topics
Including deserters; military life and customs; military personnel missing in action; unconventional warfare, propaganda</td></tr>
</table>

Class comprehensive works in 909

For general history of ancient world, see 930

See Manual at 930–990: Wars

940   History of Europe

SUMMARY

944	**France and Monaco**
.01–.08	Historical periods of France and Monaco together, of France alone
.9	Provence-Côte d'Azur, Monaco, Corsica
945	**Italy, San Marino, Vatican City, Malta**
.01–.09	Historical periods of Italy, San Marino, Vatican City, Malta together; of Italy alone
.1	Northwestern Italy
.2	Lombardy (Lombardia) region
.3	Northeastern Italy
.4	Emilia-Romagna region and San Marino
.5	Tuscany (Toscana) region
.6	Central Italy and Vatican City
.7	Southern Italy
.8	Sicily and adjacent islands
.9	Sardinia
946	**Spain, Andorra, Gibraltar, Portugal**
.000 1–.000 9	Standard subdivisions of Spain, Andorra, Gibraltar, Portugal
.001–.009	Standard subdivisions of Spain
.01–.08	Historical periods of Spain
.7	Eastern Spain and Andorra
.8	Andalusia autonomous community and Gibraltar
.9	Portugal
947	**Russia and neighboring east European countries**
.000 1–.000 9	Standard subdivisions of eastern Europe
.001–.009	Standard subdivisions of Russia
.01–.08	Historical periods of Russia
.5	Caucasus
.6	Moldova
.7	Ukraine
.8	Belarus
.9	Lithuania, Latvia, Estonia
948	**Scandinavia**
.01–.07	Historical periods of northern Europe, of Scandinavia
.1	Norway
.2	Southeastern Norway (Østlandet)
.3	Southwestern Norway (Sørlandet and Vestlandet)
.4	Central and northern Norway (Trøndelag and Nord-Norge)
.5	Sweden
.6	Southern Sweden (Götaland)
.7	Central Sweden (Svealand)
.8	Northern Sweden (Norrland)
.9	Denmark and Finland
949	**Other parts of Europe**
.1	Northwestern islands
.2	Netherlands
.3	Belgium and Luxembourg
.4	Switzerland
.5	Greece
.6	Balkan Peninsula
.7	Serbia, Croatia, Slovenia, Bosnia and Hercegovina, Montenegro, Macedonia
.8	Romania
.9	Bulgaria

.01–.09   Standard subdivisions

        As modified under 930–990

.1	**Early history to 1453**
	Class here Middle Ages, 476–1453
	For ancient history to ca. 499, see 936
(.11)	Early history to ca. 499
	(Optional number; prefer 936)
(.111)	Early history to ca. 1000 B.C.
	(Optional number; prefer 936.01)
(.112)	Ca. 1000–ca. 200 B.C.
	(Optional number; prefer 936.02)
(.113)	Ca. 200 B.C.–ca. 499 A.D.
	(Optional number; prefer 936.03)
.12	Ca. 500–799
	Class here Early Middle Ages (Dark Ages), 476–999
	For 800–899, see 940.142; for 900–999, see 940.144
.14	Age of feudalism, 800–1099
.142	800–899
.144	900–999
.146	1000–1099
	For period of First Crusade, see 940.18
.17	1100–1453
	For period of Crusades, 1100–1299, see 940.18; for 1300–1453, see 940.19
.18	Period of Crusades, 1100–1299
	Including period of First Crusade, 1096–1099
	Class here High Middle Ages, 1000–1299
	Class comprehensive works on Crusades in 909.07. Class comprehensive works on a specific Crusade with the history of the country or region in which most of the fighting took place, e.g., First Crusade 956.014
	For 1000–1099, see 940.146
.182	1100–1199
.184	1200–1299
.19	1300–1453
	Class here Late Middle Ages
.192	1300 1399
	Including period of Black Death

.193	1400–1453

.2 **1453–**

For World War I, see 940.3; for 1918 to present, see 940.5

.21 Renaissance period, 1453–1517

Class here 15th century

For 1400–1453, see 940.193

See also 945.05 for Renaissance period in Italy

.22 1517–1789

For Reformation period, 1517–1648, see 940.23; for 1648–1789, see 940.25

.23 Reformation period, 1517–1648

For Thirty Years' War, see 940.24

.232 1517–1618

.24 ‡Thirty Years' War, 1618–1648

.25 1648–1789

.252 1648–1715

Class here 17th century

For 1600–1648, see 940.23

.252 3 1648–1688

.252 5 1688–1701

Class here War of the League of Augsburg (War of the Grand Alliance), 1688–1697

For North American aspects of War of the League of Augsburg, see 973.25

.252 6 1701–1715

Class here War of the Spanish Succession, 1701–1714

For North American aspects of War of the Spanish Succession, see 973.25

.253 1715–1789

Class here 18th century

For 1700–1715, see 940.252; for 1789–1799, see 940.27

.253 1 1715–1740

‡Add as instructed under 940–990

.253 2	War of the Austrian Succession, 1740–1748
	Class Silesian Wars in 943.054
	For North American aspects of War of the Austrian Succession, see 973.26
.253 3	1748–1756
.253 4	Seven Years' War, 1756–1763
	For North American aspects of Seven Years' War, see 973.26
.253 5	1763–1789
.27	‡Period of French Revolution and Napoleon I, 1789–1815
	Class here Napoleonic Wars in specific European countries, e.g., war in Spain (Peninsular War), 1807–1814
.271	Social, political, economic history
	Number built according to instructions under 940–990
.271 4	Congress of Vienna
	Class results in and effects on a specific country with the history of the country, e.g., effect on France 944.061
.28	1815–1914
	Class here comprehensive works on 19th–20th centuries
	For comprehensive works on 20th century, see 940.5
.282	1815–1829
.283	1830–1848
	For revolutions of 1848, see 940.284
.284	Revolutions of 1848
.285	1849–1859
.286	1860–1869
.287	1870–1899
.288	1900–1914
.3	**World War I, 1914–1918**
	For military history, see 940.4
.308	Groups of people
	Do not use for noncombatants, pacifists, enemy sympathizers; class in 940.316

‡Add as instructed under 940–990

.308 991 992	Armenians

> Do not use for Armenian massacres, 1915–1916; class in 956.620154

.309	History, geographic treatment, biography

> Do not use for participation of specific groups of countries; class in 940.33

[.309 4–.309 9]	Specific continents, countries, localities in modern world

> Do not use; class in 940.34–940.39

.31	Social, political, economic history

> Add to base number 940.31 the numbers following 940.531 in 940.5311–940.5317, e.g., internment camps 940.317

> *For diplomatic history, see 940.32*

.32	Diplomatic history

> *For diplomatic causes, see 940.3112; for efforts to preserve or restore peace, see 940.312; for diplomatic results, see 940.314*

.322	Allies and associated powers

[.322 094–.322 099]	Specific continents, countries, localities in modern world

> Do not use; class in 940.3224–940.3229

.322 4–.322 9	Specific continents, countries, localities in modern world

> Add to base number 940.322 notation 4–9 from Table 2, e.g., diplomatic history of Great Britain 940.32241

.324	Central Powers

[.324 094–.324 099]	Specific continents, countries, localities in modern world

> Do not use; class in 940.3244–940.3249

.324 4–.324 9	Specific continents, countries, localities in modern world

> Add to base number 940.324 notation 4–9 from Table 2, e.g., diplomatic history of Germany 940.32443

.325	Neutrals

[.325 094–.325 099]	Specific continents, countries, localities in modern world

> Do not use; class in 940.3254–940.3259

.325 4–.325 9	Specific continents, countries, localities in modern world

> Add to base number 940.325 notation 4–9 from Table 2, e.g., diplomatic history of Switzerland 940.325494

.33	Participation of specific groups of countries

> Class a specific activity with the activity, e.g., diplomatic history among neutrals 940.325

> *For participation of specific countries and localities, see 940.34–940.39*

.332	Allies and associated powers
.334	Central Powers
.335	Neutrals
.34–.39	Participation of specific countries and localities

> Class here mobilization in specific countries and localities

> Add to base number 940.3 notation 4–9 from Table 2, e.g., participation of Great Britain 940.341

> Class a specific activity with the activity, e.g., efforts by a specific country to preserve or restore peace 940.312

.4   **Military history of World War I**

SUMMARY

940.400 1–.400 9	**Standard subdivisions**
.401–.409	**[General aspects]**
.41	**Operations and units**
.42	**Land campaigns and battles of 1914–1916**
.43	**Land campaigns and battles of 1917–1918**
.44	**Air operations**
.45	**Naval operations**
.46–.48	**Celebrations, commemorations, memorials; prisoners of war; medical and social services; other military topics**

.400 1–.400 8	Standard subdivisions
.400 9	History, geographic treatment, biography

> Do not use for military campaigns; class in 940.41–940.45

.400 92	Biography

> Do not use for personal narratives; class in 940.481–940.482

[.400 94–.400 99]	Specific continents, countries, localities in modern world

> Do not use for military participation of specific countries; class in 940.4094–940.4099. Do not use for land operations; class in 940.41

.401	Strategy
.401 2	Allies and associated powers
.401 3	Central Powers
.402	Mobilization
[.402 094–.402 099]	Specific continents, countries, localities in modern world

> Do not use; class in 940.34–940.39

.403	Ethnic minorities as troops
.405	Repressive measures and atrocities

> Class internment camps in 940.317; class Armenian massacres, 1915–1916, in 956.620154

.409   Military participation of specific countries

> Add to base number 940.409 notation 4–9 from Table 2, e.g., military participation of Germany 940.40943

.41   Operations and units

> Standard subdivisions are added for either or both topics in heading

> Class here land operations

> *For land campaigns and battles of 1914–1916, see 940.42; for land campaigns and battles of 1917–1918, see 940.43; for air operations, see 940.44; for naval operations, see 940.45*

[.410 94–.410 99]   Specific continents, countries, localities in modern world

> Do not use; class in 940.449

>   940.412–940.413   Military units and their operations

> Class here organization, history, rosters, service records

> Class comprehensive works in 940.41. Class units engaged in a special service with the service, e.g., ambulance companies 940.4753

> *For operations in Europe, see 940.414; for operations in Asia, see 940.415; for operations in Africa, see 940.416; for rolls of honor and lists of dead, see 940.467*

.412   Military units of Allies and associated powers

[.412 094–.412 099]   Specific continents, countries, localities in modern world

> Do not use; class in 940.4124–940.4129

.412 4–.412 9   Specific continents, countries, localities in modern world

> Add to base number 940.412 notation 4–9 from Table 2, e.g., French units 940.41244

.413   Military units of Central Powers

[.413 094–.413 099]   Specific continents, countries, localities in modern world

> Do not use; class in 940.4134–940.4139

.413 4–.413 9   Specific continents, countries, localities in modern world

> Add to base number 940.413 notation 4–9 from Table 2, e.g., Austrian units 940.413436

.414   Operations in Europe

.414 4   Western front

> Class here German western front, French front

.414 5   Austro-Italian front

.414 7   Eastern front

> Class here German eastern front, Russian front

.415	Operations in Asia
.416	Operations in Africa
.42	Land campaigns and battles of 1914–1916
.421	1914, western front
.422	1914, eastern front
.423	1914, other areas
.424	1915, western and Austro-Italian fronts
.425	1915, eastern front
.426	1915, other areas

Including Gallipoli Campaign

.427	1916, European fronts
.427 2	Western and Austro-Italian fronts
.427 5	Eastern front
.429	1916, other areas
.429 1	Asia Minor
.43	Land campaigns and battles of 1917–1918
.431	1917, western and Austro-Italian fronts
.432	1917, eastern front
.433	1917, other areas
.434	1918, western and Austro-Italian fronts

Including final German offensives

Class final allied offensives in 940.435–940.436

>   **940.435–940.436 Final allied offensives**

Class comprehensive works in 940.434

.435	Allied offensives of July 18–September 24, 1918
.436	Allied offensives of September 25–November 11, 1918
.437	1918, eastern front
.438	1918, other areas
.439	Armistice, November 11, 1918
.44	Air operations

Including antiaircraft defenses

Class here combined air and naval operations

For naval operations, see 940.45

[.440 94–.440 99]	Specific continents, countries, localities in modern world
	Do not use; class in 940.449
.442	Air raids
	Class specific events by year in 940.444–940.448
.443	Air bases

> 940.444–940.448 Events by year

Class comprehensive works in 940.44

.444	Events of 1914
.445	Events of 1915
.446	Events of 1916
.447	Events of 1917
.448	Events of 1918
.449	Operations of specific countries

Class here aircraft, crews, units

Add to base number 940.449 notation 4–9 from Table 2, e.g., air operations of Germany 940.44943

Class events by year regardless of country in 940.444–940.448

.45	Naval operations
[.450 94–.450 99]	Specific continents, countries, localities in modern world
	Do not use; class in 940.459
.451	Submarine warfare
.451 2	German use
	Class events by year in 940.4514
.451 3	Allied use
	Class events by year in 940.4514
[.451 309 4–.451 309 9]	Specific continents, countries, localities in modern world
	Do not use; class in 940.45134–940.45139
.451 34–.451 39	Specific continents, countries, localities in modern world

Add to base number 940.4513 notation 4–9 from Table 2, e.g., United States use of submarines 940.451373

.451 4	Specific events
.451 6	Antisubmarine warfare
	Class events by year in 940.4514

.452	Blockades and blockade running

> Class events by year in 940.454–940.458

.453	Naval bases

> **940.454–940.458 Events by year**

> Class events in submarine warfare by year in 940.4514; class comprehensive works in 940.45

.454	Events of 1914
.455	Events of 1915
.456	Events of 1916
.457	Events of 1917
.458	Events of 1918
.459	Naval operations of specific countries

> Class here ships, crews, units

> Add to base number 940.459 notation 4–9 from Table 2, e.g., naval operations of Italy 940.45945

> Class events by year regardless of country in 940.454–940.458

.46–.48	Celebrations, commemorations, memorials; prisoners of war; medical and social services; other military topics

> Add to base number 940.4 the numbers following 940.54 in 940.546–940.548, e.g., prisoners of war 940.472

.5	**1918–**

SUMMARY

940.51	1918–1929
.52	1930–1939
.53	World War II, 1939–1945
.54	Military history of World War II
.55	1945–1999
.56	2000–

.51	1918–1929
.52	1930–1939

> Class Holocaust in 940.5318

.53	World War II, 1939–1945

> Class here Sino-Japanese Conflict, 1937–1945

> *For military history, see 940.54; for Sino-Japanese Conflict during 1937–1941, see 951.042*

SUMMARY

940.530 1–.530 9	**Standard subdivisions**
.531	**Social, political, economic history; Holocaust**
.532	**Diplomatic history**
.533	**Participation of specific groups of countries**
.534–.539	**Participation of specific countries and localities**

.530 8   Groups of people

> Do not use for noncombatants, pacifists, enemy sympathizers; class in 940.5316

> *See also 940.5318 for Holocaust*

[.530 869 14]   Displaced persons

> Relocated to 940.53145

.530 9   History, geographic treatment, biography

> Do not use for participation of specific groups of countries; class in 940.533

[.530 94–.530 99]   Specific continents, countries, localities in modern world

> Do not use; class in 940.534–940.539

.531   Social, political, economic history; Holocaust

> *For diplomatic history, see 940.532*

SUMMARY

940.531 1	**Causes**
.531 2	**Efforts to preserve or restore peace**
.531 4	**Political, diplomatic, economic results**
.531 6	**Noncombatants, pacifists, enemy sympathizers**
.531 7	**Concentration and related camps**
.531 8	**Holocaust**

.531 1   Causes

531 12   Political and diplomatic causes

.531 13   Economic causes

.531 14   Social and psychological causes

.531 2   Efforts to preserve or restore peace

.531 4   Political, diplomatic, economic results

> Class here consequences

> Class results in and effects on a specific country with the history of the country, e.g., on Norway 948.1043

.531 41   Conferences and treaties

> *For consequences of conferences and treaties, see 940.53142*

.531 42	Consequences of conferences and treaties

> *For movement of people, see 940.53145*

.531 422	Reparations
.531 424	Territorial questions
.531 425	Establishment of new nations
.531 426	Establishment of mandates
.531 44	Reconstruction
.531 45	Movement of people

Class here displaced persons [*formerly* 940.53086914]; forced repatriation, population transfers

> *For emigration of Jews in relation to Holocaust, see 940.5318142*

.531 6	Noncombatants, pacifists, enemy sympathizers
.531 61	Noncombatants

Including children

.531 62	Pacifists
.531 63	Enemy sympathizers
.531 7	Concentration and related camps

Class here internment camps

Class camps as a part of the Holocaust in 940.53185; class prisoner-of-war camps in 940.5472

.531 709	History, geographic treatment, biography

Use area notation to indicate country maintaining the camps, e.g., internment camps maintained by the United States 940.53170973

> *For camps by location, see 940.53174–940.53179*

.531 709 4	Camps maintained by countries in Europe

Do not use for camps maintained by Axis Powers; class in 940.53185

.531 74–.531 79	Camps by location

Add to base number 940.5317 notation 4–9 from Table 2, e.g., Manzanar internment camp for Japanese-Americans 940.531779487; however, for specific European concentration camps maintained by Axis Powers, see 940.531853–940.531859

Class extermination camps in 940.53185

.531 8	Holocaust

Class here Holocaust, 1933–1945; Holocaust with respect to Jews

[.531 808 992 4]	Holocaust with respect to Jews
	Do not use; class in 940.5318
.531 809 2	Biography
	Class here life of persons in a specific ghetto or extermination camp
.531 81	General topics of Holocaust
[.531 810 1–.531 810 9]	Standard subdivisions
	Do not use; class in 940.531801–940.531809
.531 811	Causes
.531 813	Economic history
.531 813 2	Economic actions against businesses and property
	Class here boycott, confiscation
	Class indemnification and restitution of confiscated and stolen property in 940.5318144
.531 813 4	Forced labor
	Class general works on forced labor during World War II in 940.5405
.531 814	Consequences
	Class long-term welfare services to Holocaust survivors and their descendants in 362.87
	For war crime trials, see 341.690268
.531 814 2	Emigration of Jews
	Class here emigration to Palestine
	For emigration of Jews to Palestine as part of the history of Israel, see 956.9404
.531 814 4	Indemnification and restitution of confiscated and stolen property
	Standard subdivisions are added for any or all topics in heading
	Class comprehensive works on confiscated and stolen property in 940.5318132
	See also 341.67 for law of enemy aliens and their property, war victims
.531 818	Holocaust denial
	Class here denial of extermination camps
.531 83	Resistance movements and rescue operations

.531 832	Resistance movements

Class resistance movements associated with a specific ghetto or extermination camp in 940.53185; class general works on resistance movements during World War II in 940.5336

.531 835	Rescue operations

Class here Righteous Gentiles

.531 84	Specific events

Class a specific event associated with a specific ghetto or extermination camp in 940.53185

.531 842	Events of 1933–1938

Class here Nuremberg laws, Kristallnacht

.531 844	Events of 1939–1945

Class here Wannsee-Konferenz

.531 844 5	Babi Yar Massacre

.531 846	Events of 1945

Class here liberation of extermination camps

.531 85	Ghettos and extermination camps maintained by Axis Powers

Standard subdivisions are added for either or both topics in heading

Class here European concentration camps maintained by Axis Powers

Class denial of extermination camps in 940.531818; class Wannsee-Konferenz in 940.531844; class comprehensive works on concentration camps in 940.5317

[.531 850 92]	Biography

Do not use; class in 940.5318092

[.531 850 943–.531 850 949]	Geographic treatment

Do not use; class in 940.531853–940.531859

.531 853–.531 859	Specific ghettos and extermination camps

Class here specific European concentration camps maintained by Axis Powers

Add to base number 940.53185 the numbers following —4 in notation 43–49 from Table 2, e.g., Warsaw Ghetto 940.531853841, Auschwitz 940.531853858; however, do not add notation 092 from Table 1 for biography; class in 940.5318092
> Subdivisions are added for either or both topics in heading

.531 86	Commemorations and memorials

Class commemorations and memorials associated with a specific ghetto or extermination camp in 940.53185

.531 862	Commemorations
	Class here remembrance days
.531 864	Memorials
	Class museums that are also memorials in 940.5318074
.531 87	Welfare services to Holocaust victims
	Services provided during and immediately after the Holocaust
	Class long-term welfare services to Holocaust survivors and their descendants in 362.87; class rescue operations in 940.531835
.532	Diplomatic history

For diplomatic causes, see 940.53112; for efforts to preserve or restore peace, see 940.5312; for diplomatic results, see 940.5314

.532 2	Allies
[.532 209 4–.532 209 9]	Specific continents, countries, localities in modern world
	Do not use; class in 940.53224–940.53229
.532 24–.532 29	Specific continents, countries, localities in modern world
	Add to base number 940.5322 notation 4–9 from Table 2, e.g., diplomatic history of Great Britain 940.532241
.532 4	Axis Powers
[.532 409 4–.532 409 9]	Specific continents, countries, localities in modern world
	Do not use; class in 940.53244–940.53249
.532 44–.532 49	Specific continents, countries, localities in modern world
	Add to base number 940.5324 notation 4–9 from Table 2, e.g., diplomatic history of Japan 940.532452
.532 5	Neutrals
	Add to base number 940.5325 notation 4–9 from Table 2, e.g., diplomatic history of Switzerland 940.5325494
[.532 509 4–.532 509 9]	Specific continents, countries, localities in modern world
	Do not use; class in 940.53254–940.53259
.532 54–.532 59	Specific continents, countries, localities in modern world
	Add to base number 940.5325 notation 4–9 from Table 2, e.g., diplomatic history of Switzerland 940.5325494
.533	Participation of specific groups of countries

Class here national groups, anti-Axis and pro-Axis national groups, mobilization

Class a specific activity with the activity, e.g., diplomatic history among Axis Powers 940.5324

For participation of specific countries, see 940.534–940.539

.533 2	Allies
.533 4	Axis Powers
.533 5	Neutrals
.533 6	Occupied countries

Class here governments-in-exile; resistance, underground movements

Class resistance movements as part of Holocaust in 940.531832

For countries occupied by Axis Powers, see 940.5337; for countries occupied by Allies, see 940.5338

.533 7	Countries occupied by Axis Powers
.533 8	Countries occupied by Allies
.534–.539	Participation of specific countries and localities

Add to base number 940.53 notation 4–9 from Table 2, e.g., participation of Great Britain 940.5341

Class a specific activity with the activity, e.g., efforts by a specific country to preserve or restore peace 940.5312

.54	Military history of World War II

SUMMARY

940.540 01–.540 09	**Standard subdivisions**
.540 1–.540 9	**[General aspects]**
.541	**Operations and units**
.542	**Campaigns and battles by theater**
.544	**Air operations**
.545	**Naval operations**
.546	**Celebrations, commemorations, memorials**
.547	**Prisoners of war; medical and social services**
.548	**Other military topics**

.540 01–.540 08	Standard subdivisions
.540 09	History, geographic treatment, biography

Do not use for military campaigns; class in 940.541–940.545

.540 092	Biography

Do not use for personal narratives; class in 940.5481–940.5482

[.540 094–.540 099]	Specific continents, countries, localities in modern world

Do not use for military participation of specific countries; class in 940.54094–940.54099. Do not use for land operations; class in 940.541

.540 1	Strategy
.540 12	Allies
.540 13	Axis Powers
.540 2	Mobilization

[.540 209 4–.540 209 9]   Specific continents, countries, localities in modern world

Do not use; class in 940.534–940.539

.540 3   African Americans and American native peoples as troops

.540 4   Ethnic minorities as troops

> *For African Americans and American native peoples as troops, see 940.5403*

.540 5   Repressive measures and atrocities

Including forced labor

Class concentration and related camps in 940.5317; class Holocaust in 940.5318; class forced labor as part of Holocaust in 940.5318134

.540 9   Military participation of specific countries

Add to base number 940.5409 notation 4–9 from Table 2, e.g., military participation of Germany 940.540943

.541   Operations and units

> *For air operations, see 940.544; for naval operations, see 940.545*

[.541 094–.541 099]   Specific continents, countries, localities in modern world

Do not use for operations of specific countries; class in 940.5412–940.5413. Do not use for specific campaigns and battles by theater; class in 940.542

> 940.541 2–940.541 3 Military units and their operations

Class here organization, history, rosters, service records; comprehensive works on units whose operations were limited to a specific theater

Class comprehensive works in 940.541. Class units engaged in a special service with the service, e.g., ambulance companies 940.54753

> *For units engaged in a specific campaign or battle not equal to a theater, see 940.542; for rolls of honor and lists of dead, see 940.5467*

.541 2   Military units of Allies

[.541 209 4–.541 209 9]   Specific continents, countries, localities in modern world

Do not use; class in 940.54124–940.54129

.541 24–.541 29   Specific continents, countries, localities in modern world

Add to base number 940.5412 notation 4–9 from Table 2, e.g., French units 940.541244

.541 3   Military units of Axis Powers

[.541 309 4–.541 309 9]   Specific continents, countries, localities in modern world

Do not use; class in 940.54134–940.54139

.541 34–.541 39	Specific continents, countries, localities in modern world
	Add to base number 940.5413 notation 4–9 from Table 2, e.g., Japanese units 940.541352
.542	Campaigns and battles by theater
.542 1	European theater
	Add to base number 940.5421 the numbers following —4 in notation 41–49 from Table 2, e.g., battles in France 940.54214
.542 3	African theater
	Add to base number 940.5423 the numbers following —6 in notation 61–69 from Table 2, e.g., battles in North Africa 940.54231
.542 4	Middle East theater
	Class African countries of the Middle East in 940.5423
.542 5	East and South Asian theaters
	Standard subdivisions are added for East and South Asian theaters together, for East Asian theater alone
.542 51–.542 52	Battles in China, Korea, Japan, adjacent areas
	Add to base number 940.5425 the numbers following —5 in notation 51–52 from Table 2, e.g., battles in China 940.54251
	Class Sino-Japanese Conflict during 1937–1941 in 951.042
.542 59	Southeast Asian theater
	Add to base number 940.54259 the numbers following —59 in notation 591–599 from Table 2, e.g., battles in Philippines 940.542599
	For battles in western New Guinea, see 940.542651
.542 6	Pacific Ocean theater
	Add to base number 940.5426 the numbers following —9 in notation 93–96 from Table 2, e.g., battles in western New Guinea 940.542651, battle of Midway 940.5426699, attack on Pearl Harbor 940.5426693
	For Southeast Asian theater, see 940.54259
	See also 940.54252 for Japan; also 940.542599 for Philippines
.542 8	American theater
.542 9	Other areas
.542 93	Atlantic Ocean
	Class here battle of the Atlantic, 1939–1945
.544	Air operations
	Including antiaircraft defenses
	Class here combined air and naval operations
	For naval operations, see 940.545

[.544 094–.544 099]	Specific continents, countries, localities in modern world

Do not use for campaigns and battles by theater; class in 940.542. Do not use for operations of specific countries; class in 940.5449

.544 2	Campaigns and battles
.544 209 4–.544 209 9	Specific continents, countries, localities in modern world

Class here comprehensive works on campaigns and battles by a specific country

Do not use for a specific campaign or battle; class in 940.542 e.g., battle of Britain 940.54211, attack on Pearl Harbor 940.5426693

.544 3	Air bases
[.544 309 4–.544 309 9]	Specific continents, countries, localities in modern world

Do not use; class in 940.54434–940.54439

.544 34–.544 39	Specific continents, countries, localities in modern world

Add to base number 940.5443 notation 4–9 from Table 2, e.g., air bases in England 940.544342

.544 9	Operations of specific countries

Class here aircraft, crews, units

Add to base number 940.5449 notation 4–9 from Table 2, e.g., operations of Germany 940.544943

For comprehensive works on campaigns and battles by a specific country, see 940.5442. For a specific campaign or battle, see the campaign or battle in 940.5421–940.5429, e.g., battle of Britain 940.54211, attack on Pearl Harbor 940.5426693

.545	Naval operations

Class here campaigns and battles

[.545 094–.545 099]	Specific continents, countries, localities in modern world

Do not use for campaigns and battles by theater; class in 940.542. Do not use for operations of specific countries; class in 940.5459

.545 1	Submarine warfare
.545 16	Antisubmarine warfare
.545 2	Blockades and blockade running

Standard subdivisions are added for either or both topics in heading

.545 3	Naval bases

.545 9	Operations of specific countries

Class here ships, crews, units; comprehensive works on campaigns and battles by a specific country

Add to base number 940.5459 notation 4–9 from Table 2, e.g., Australian naval operations 940.545994

Class a specific kind of operation with the operation, e.g., blockades 940.5452

For a specific campaign or battle, see the campaign or battle in 940.5421–940.5429, e.g., battle of Midway 940.5426699, battle of the Atlantic 940.54293

.546	Celebrations, commemorations, memorials

Standard subdivisions are added for any or all topics in heading

Including commemorative meetings, decorations and awards

For celebrations, commemorations, memorials of a specific event, see the event, e.g., Normandy Invasion 940.5421421

.546 5	Monuments and cemeteries

Standard subdivisions are added for either or both topics in heading

[.546 509 4–.546 509 9]	Specific continents, countries, localities in modern world

Do not use; class in 940.54654–940.54659

.546 54–.546 59	Specific continents, countries, localities in modern world

Add to base number 940.5465 notation 4–9 from Table 2, e.g., monuments and cemeteries in France 940.546544

.546 7	Rolls of honor and lists of dead

Standard subdivisions are added for either or both topics in heading

[.546 709 4–.546 709 9]	Specific continents, countries, localities in modern world

Do not use; class in 940.54674–940.54679

.546 74–.546 79	Specific continents, countries, localities in modern world

Add to base number 940.5467 notation 4–9 from Table 2, e.g., lists of Japanese dead 940.546752

.547	Prisoners of war; medical and social services
.547 2	Prisoner-of-war camps

Class here prisoners of war

For prisoners exchange, see 940.5473

[.547 209 4–.547 209 9]	Specific continents, countries, localities in modern world

Do not use; class in 940.54724–940.54729

.547 24–.547 29	Specific continents, countries, localities in modern world

Add to base number 940.5472 notation 4–9 from Table 2, e.g., prisoner-of-war camps maintained by Germany 940.547243

.547 3	Prisoners exchange
.547 5	Medical services

> *For hospitals, see 940.5476*

.547 509 4–.547 509 9	Specific continents and localities in modern world

> Do not use for services of specific countries; class in 940.54754–940.54759

.547 52	Sanitary affairs
.547 53	Ambulance services
.547 54–.547 59	Services of specific countries

> Add to base number 940.5475 notation 4–9 from Table 2, e.g., French medical services 940.547544

.547 6	Hospitals
[.547 609 4–.547 609 9]	Specific continents, countries, localities in modern world

> Do not use for hospitals in specific places; class in 940.54763. Do not use for hospitals maintained by specific countries; class in 940.54764–940.54769

.547 63	Hospitals in specific places

> Add to base number 940.54763 notation 4–9 from Table 2, e.g., hospitals in Rome 940.5476345632

> Class hospitals maintained in specific places by specific countries in 940.54764–940.54769.

.547 64–.547 69	Hospitals maintained by specific countries

> Add to base number 940.5476 notation 4–9 from Table 2, e.g., hospitals maintained by Italy 940.547645

.547 7	Relief and welfare services

> Standard subdivisions are added for either or both topics in heading

[.547 709 4–.547 709 9]	Specific continents, countries, localities in modern world

> Do not use for activities conducted by specific countries; class in 940.54778. Do not use for activities in specific places; class in 940.54779

.547 71	Activities of Red Cross
.547 78	Activities conducted by specific countries

> Add to base number 940.54778 notation 4–9 from Table 2, e.g., activities conducted by Switzerland 940.54778494

> Class Red Cross activities conducted by specific countries in 940.54771

.547 79	Activities in specific places

Add to base number 940.54779 notation 4–9 from Table 2, e.g., welfare activities in Paris 940.5477944361

Class activities of Red Cross in specific places in 940.54771; class welfare activities conducted in specific places by specific countries in 940.54778

.547 8	Religious life and chaplain services

Standard subdivisions are added for either or both topics in heading

.548	Other military topics

Including deserters, military personnel missing in action

.548 1	Personal narratives of individuals from Allies

Class here comprehensive works on personal narratives

Class personal narratives on a specific subject with the subject, plus notation 092 from Table 1, e.g., on blockade running 940.5452092

For personal narratives of individuals from Axis Powers, see 940.5482

[.548 109 4–.548 109 9]	Specific continents, countries, localities in modern world

Do not use; class in 940.54814–940.54819

.548 14–.548 19	Specific continents, countries, localities in modern world

Add to base number 940.5481 notation 4–9 from Table 2, e.g., personal narratives of Britons 940.548141

.548 2	Personal narratives of individuals from Axis Powers

Class personal narratives on a specific subject with the subject, plus notation 092 from Table 1, e.g., on blockade running 940.5452092

[.548 209 4–.548 209 9]	Specific continents, countries, localities in modern world

Do not use; class in 940.54824–940.54829

.548 24–.548 29	Specific continents, countries, localities in modern world

Add to base number 940.5482 notation 4–9 from Table 2, e.g., personal narratives of Germans 940.548243

.548 3	Military life and customs of Allies

Class here comprehensive works on military life and customs

For celebrations, commemorations, memorials, see 940.546; for military life and customs of Axis Powers, see 940.5484

[.548 309 4–.548 309 9]	Specific continents, countries, localities in modern world

Do not use; class in 940.54834–940.54839

.548 34–.548 39	Specific continents, countries, localities in modern world

Add to base number 940.5483 notation 4–9 from Table 2, e.g., military life in United States Navy 940.548373

.548 4	Military life and customs of Axis Powers

> *For celebrations, commemorations, memorials, see 940.546*

[.548 409 4–.548 409 9]	Specific continents, countries, localities in modern world

> Do not use; class in 940.54844–940.54849

.548 44–.548 49	Specific continents, countries, localities in modern world

> Add to base number 940.5484 notation 4–9 from Table 2, e.g., military life in Luftwaffe 940.548443

.548 5	Unconventional warfare

> Class here counterintelligence, intelligence, psychological warfare, sabotage, subversion

> *For propaganda, see 940.5488*

.548 509 4–.548 509 9	Specific continents, countries, localities in modern world

> Do not use for unconventional warfare of Allies; class in 940.5486. Do not use for unconventional warfare of Axis Powers; class in 940.5487

.548 6	Unconventional warfare of Allies
[.548 609 4–.548 609 9]	Specific continents, countries, localities in modern world

> Do not use; class in 940.54864–940.54869

.548 64–.548 69	Specific continents, countries, localities in modern world

> Add to base number 940.5486 notation 4–9 from Table 2, e.g., intelligence operation of United States 940.548673

.548 7	Unconventional warfare of Axis Powers
[.548 709 4–.548 709 9]	Specific continents, countries, localities in modern world

> Do not use; class in 940.54874–940.54879

.548 74–.548 79	Specific continents, countries, localities in modern world

> Add to base number 940.5487 notation 4–9 from Table 2, e.g., intelligence operations of Germany 940.548743

.548 8	Propaganda
[.548 809 4–.548 809 9]	Specific continents, countries, localities in modern world

> Do not use for propaganda by Allies; class in 940.54886. Do not use for propaganda by Axis Powers; class in 940.54887. Do not use for propaganda in specific places; class in 940.54889

.548 86	Propaganda by Allies
[.548 860 94–.548 860 99]	Specific continents, countries, localities in modern world

> Do not use; class in 940.548864–940.548869

.548 864–.548 869	Specific continents, countries, localities in modern world

Add to base number 940.54886 notation 4–9 from Table 2, e.g., propaganda by United States 940.5488673

.548 87	Propaganda by Axis Powers

[.548 870 94–.548 870 99]	Specific continents, countries, localities in modern world

Do not use; class in 940.548874–940.548879

.548 874–.548 879	Specific continents, countries, localities in modern world

Add to base number 940.54887 notation 4–9 from Table 2, e.g., propaganda by Germany 940.5488743

.548 89	Propaganda in specific places

Add to base number 940.54889 notation 4–9 from Table 2, e.g., propaganda in United States 940.5488973

Class propaganda by one side or one country regardless of location in 940.54886–940.54887

.55	1945–1999
.554	1945–1949
.555	1950–1959
.556	1960–1969
.557	1970–1979
.558	1980–1989
.559	1990–1999
.56	2000–
.561	2000–2019
.561 1	2000–2009
.561 2	2010–2019

941 *British Isles

Class here Great Britain, United Kingdom

See Manual at 941

*Add as instructed under 930–990

SUMMARY

941.01–.08	**[Historical periods]**
.1	**Scotland**
.2	**Northeastern Scotland**
.3	**Southeastern Scotland**
.4	**Southwestern Scotland**
.5	**Ireland**
.6	**Northern Ireland; Donegal, Monaghan, Cavan counties of Republic of Ireland**
.7	**Republic of Ireland**
.8	**Leinster**
.9	**Munster**

.01   Early history to 1066

> *For ancient history to 410, see 936.1*

(.012)   Ancient history to 410

> (Optional number; prefer 936.1)

> Add to base number 941.012 the numbers following 936.20 in 936.201–936.204, e.g., 4th century 941.0124

.013–.019   Pre-Anglo-Saxon period through reign of Saxon kings, 410–1066

> Add to base number 941.01 the numbers following 942.01 in 942.013–942.019, e.g., period of Danish kings 941.018

.02–.05   Norman period through House of Tudor period, 1066–1603

> Add to base number 941.0 the numbers following 942.0 in 942.02–942.05, e.g., reign of Henry VIII 941.052

.06   House of Stuart and Commonwealth periods, 1603–1714

> (Option: Class here Anglo-Dutch Wars; prefer 949.204)

.061   Reign of James I, 1603–1625

.062   Reign of Charles I, 1625–1649

> Class Civil War in 942.062

.063   Period as Commonwealth and Protectorate, 1649–1660

> *For Protectorate of Oliver Cromwell, see 941.064; for Protectorate of Richard Cromwell, see 941.065*

.064   Protectorate of Oliver Cromwell, 1653–1658

.065   Protectorate of Richard Cromwell, 1658–1659

.066   Reign of Charles II, 1660–1685 (Restoration)

.067   1685–1689

> Class here reign of James II, 1685–1688

.068   Reigns of William III (of Orange) and Mary II, 1689–1702

.069   Reign of Anne, 1702–1714

.07   Period of House of Hanover, 1714–1837

.071   Reign of George I, 1714–1727

.072   Reign of George II, 1727–1760

       (Option: Class here War of Jenkins' Ear; prefer 946.055)

.073   Reign of George III, 1760–1820

       Including formation of United Kingdom

.074   Reign of George IV, 1820–1830

.075   Reign of William IV, 1830–1837

.08   Period of Victoria and House of Windsor, 1837–

.081   Reign of Victoria, 1837–1901

       Class here 19th century

       For 1800–1820, see 941.073; for 1820–1830, see 941.074; for 1830–1837, see 941.075

       (Option: Class here Crimean War; prefer 947.0738. Class here South African [Second Anglo-Boer] War; prefer 968.048)

.082   1901–1999

       For reign of George V, see 941.083; for 1936–1945, see 941.084; for 1945–1999, see 941.085

.082 3   Reign of Edward VII, 1901–1910

.083   Reign of George V, 1910–1936

.084   1936–1945

       Class here reigns of Edward VIII, 1936, and George VI, 1936–1952; period of World War II, 1939–1945

       For reign of George VI during 1945–1949, see 941.0854; for reign of George VI during 1950–1952, see 941.0855

.085   1945–1999

       Class here reign of Elizabeth II, 1952 to present

       For 2000 to present, see 941.086

.085 4   1945–1949

.085 5   1950–1959

.085 6   1960–1969

.085 7   1970–1979

.085 8   1980–1989

.085 9   1990–1999

.086   2000–

.086 1   2000–2019

.086 11   2000–2009

.086 12	2010–2019

.1   ***Scotland**

> *For northeastern Scotland, see 941.2; for southeastern Scotland, see 941.3; for southwestern Scotland, see 941.4*

.101   Early history to 1057

> Including 11th century

> *For ancient history to 410, see 936.11; for 1057–1099, see 941.102*

(.101 2)   Ancient history to 410

> (Optional number; prefer 936.11)

(.101 21)   Early history to ca. 600 B.C.

> (Optional number; prefer 936.11)

(.101 22)   Celtic period, ca. 600–79 B.C.

> (Optional number; prefer 936.1102)

(.101 23)   Period of Roman contacts, 79 B.C.–410 A.D.

> (Optional number; prefer 936.1103)

.102   1057–1314

> Including Battle of Bannockburn, 1314

.103   1314–1424

.104   Reigns of James I through James V, 1424–1542

.105   Reformation period, 1542–1603

> Class here 16th century

> *For 1500–1542, see 941.104*

.106–.108   Personal union with England to present, 1603–

> Add to base number 941.10 the numbers following 941.0 in 941.06–941.08, e.g., reign of Edward VII 941.10823

.2   ***Northeastern Scotland**

.201–.208   Historical periods

> Add to base number 941.20 the numbers following 941.10 in 941.101–941.108, e.g., Reformation period 941.205

.3   ***Southeastern Scotland**

.301–.308   Historical periods

> Add to base number 941.30 the numbers following 941.10 in 941.101–941.108, e.g., Reformation period 941.305

.4   ***Southwestern Scotland**

*Add as instructed under 930–990

.401–.408	Historical periods

> Add to base number 941.40 the numbers following 941.10 in 941.101–941.108, e.g., Reformation period 941.405

.5   ***Ireland**

.501	Early history to 1086

> Including Battle of Clontarf, 1014

> *For ancient history to 433, see 936.15*

> 410–433 relocated to 936.1502

(.501 2)	Ancient history to 433

> (Optional number; prefer 936.15)

(.501 21)	Early history to ca. 400 B.C.

> (Optional number; prefer 936.1501)

(.501 22)	Celtic period, ca. 400 B.C.–433 A.D.

> (Optional number; prefer 936.1502)

.502	1086–1171
.503	Period under House of Plantagenet, 1171–1399
.504	Period under Houses of Lancaster and York, 1399–1485
.505	Period under House of Tudor, 1485–1603
.506	Period under House of Stuart, 1603–1691
.507	1691–1799
.508	1800–
.508 1	1800–1899
.508 2	1900–1999
.508 21	1900–1921

> Including Sinn Fein Rebellion (Easter Rebellion), 1916; Anglo-Irish War, 1919–1921

.508 22	1921–1949
.508 23	1950–1969
.508 24	1970–1999
.508 3	2000–

.6   ***Northern Ireland; Donegal, Monaghan, Cavan counties of Republic of Ireland**

> Subdivisions are added for Northern Ireland, Donegal, Monaghan, Cavan counties together; for Northern Ireland alone

*Add as instructed under 930–990

.601–.607	Early history to 1800

Add to base number 941.60 the numbers following 941.50 in 941.501–941.507, e.g., period under House of Tudor 941.605; however, 410–433 relocated from 941.601 to 936.1602

.608	1800–
.608 1	1800–1899
.608 2	1900–1999
.608 21	1900–1920

Including Government of Ireland Act, 1920

.608 22	1921–1949
.608 23	1949–1968
.608 24	1969–1999
.608 3	2000–

.7   *Republic of Ireland

For Leinster, see 941.8; for Munster, see 941.9

.701–.707	Early history to 1800

Add to base number 941.70 the numbers following 941.50 in 941.501–941.507, e.g., period under House of Tudor 941.705; however, 410–433 relocated from 941.701 to 936.1702

.708	1800–
.708 1	1800–1899
.708 2	1900–1999
.708 21	1900–1921
.708 22	1922–1949

Including period as Irish Free State, 1922–1937; as Eire, 1937–1949

.708 23	1949–1969
.708 24	1970–1999
.708 3	2000–

.8   *Leinster

.801–.807	Early history to 1800

Add to base number 941.80 the numbers following 941.50 in 941.501–941.507, e.g., period under House of Tudor 941.805; however, 410–433 relocated from 941.801 to 936.1802

*Add as instructed under 930–990

.808	1800–

> Add to base number 941.808 the numbers following 941.708 in 941.7081–941.7083, e.g., 1949–1969 941.80823

.9   ***Munster**

.901–.907	Early history to 1800

> Add to base number 941.90 the numbers following 941.50 in 941.501–941.507, e.g., period under House of Tudor 941.905; however, 410–433 relocated from 941.901 to 936.1902

.908	1800–

> Add to base number 941.908 the numbers following 941.708 in 941.7081–941.7083, e.g., 1949–1969 941.90823

942   *England and Wales

> Subdivisions are added for England and Wales together, for England alone
>
> *See Manual at 941*

> 942.01–942.08   Historical periods of England and Wales together, of England alone
>
> Class comprehensive works in 942

.01	Early history to 1066

> *For ancient history to 410, see 936.2*

(.012)	Ancient history of southern Britain to 410

> (Optional number; prefer 936.2)
>
> Add to base number 942.012 the numbers following 936.20 in 936.201–936.204, e.g., Celtic period 942.0122

.013	Pre-Anglo-Saxon period, 410–449
.014	449–ca. 600

> Including reign of King Arthur

.015	Period of Heptarchy, ca. 600–829

> Class supremacy of Wessex in 942.016

.015 3	Supremacy of Northumbria, 603–685
.015 7	Supremacy of Mercia, 757–796
.016	Supremacy of Wessex, 829–924

> Class here 9th century
>
> *For 800–829, see 942.015*

.016 1	Reign of Egbert, 829–839

*Add as instructed under 930–990

.016 2	Reign of Ethelwulf, 839–858
.016 3	Reigns of Ethelbald, Ethelbert, Ethelred I, 858–871
.016 4	Reign of Alfred the Great, 871–899
.016 5	Reign of Edward the Elder, 899–924
.017	Reigns of Saxon kings of England, 924–1016
.017 1	Reign of Athelstan, 924–940
.017 2	Reigns of Edmund I, Edred, Edwy, 940–959
.017 3	Reigns of Edgar and Edward the Martyr, 959–978
.017 4	Reigns of Ethelred II and Edmund II, 978–1016
.018	Reigns of Danish kings, 1016–1042

Class here 11th century

For 1000–1016, see 942.0174; for 1042–1066, see 942.019; for 1066–1099, see 942.02

.018 1	Reign of Canute, 1016–1035
.018 2	Reign of Harold I, 1035–1040
.018 3	Reign of Hardecanute, 1040–1042
.019	1042–1066

Including reign of Harold II, 1066

Class here reign of Edward the Confessor, 1042–1066

.02	Norman period, 1066–1154

Class here 12th century

For 1154–1199, see 942.03

.021	Reign of William I, 1066–1087

Including Battle of Hastings, 1066

.022	Reign of William II, 1087–1100
.023	Reign of Henry I, 1100–1135
.024	Reign of Stephen, 1135–1154
.03	Period of House of Plantagenet, 1154–1399

Class here medieval period

For 1066–1154, see 942.02; for 1399–1485, see 942.04

.031	Reign of Henry II, 1154–1189
.032	Reign of Richard I, 1189–1199
.033	Reign of John, 1199–1216

.034	Reign of Henry III, 1216–1272

         Class here 13th century

           For 1200–1216, see 942.033; for 1272–1299, see 942.035

.035	Reign of Edward I, 1272–1307
.036	Reign of Edward II, 1307–1327
.037	Reign of Edward III, 1327–1377

         Class here 14th century

           For 1300–1307, see 942.035; for 1307–1327, see 942.036; for 1377–1399, see 942.038

         (Option: Class here Hundred Years' War; prefer 944.025)

.038	Reign of Richard II, 1377–1399
.04	Period of Houses of Lancaster and York, 1399–1485

         Class here Wars of the Roses, 1455–1485

.041	Reign of Henry IV, 1399–1413
.042	Reign of Henry V, 1413–1422
.043	Reign of Henry VI, 1422–1461
.044	Reign of Edward IV, 1461–1483
.045	Reign of Edward V, 1483
.046	Reign of Richard III, 1483–1485
.05	Period of House of Tudor, 1485–1603
.051	Reign of Henry VII, 1485–1509
.052	Reign of Henry VIII, 1509–1547
.053	Reign of Edward VI, 1547–1553
.054	Reign of Mary I, 1553–1558
.055	Reign of Elizabeth I, 1558–1603

         Including Spanish Armada, 1588

.06–.08	House of Stuart and Commonwealth periods to present, 1603–

         Add to base number 942.0 the numbers following 941.0 in 941.06–941.08, e.g., reign of Victoria 942.081

.062	‡Reign of Charles I, 1625–1649

         Number built according to instructions under 942.06–942.08

         Class here Civil War, 1642–1649

‡Add as instructed under 940–990

943   Germany and neighboring central European countries

Class here central Europe

SUMMARY

943.000 1–.000 9	**Standard subdivisions of central Europe**
.001–.009	**Standard subdivisions of Germany**
.01–.08	**Historical periods of Germany**
.1	**Northeastern Germany**
.6	**Austria and Liechtenstein**
.7	**Czech Republic and Slovakia**
.8	**Poland**
.9	**Hungary**

.000 1–.000 8   Standard subdivisions of central Europe

As modified under 930–990

.000 9   Historical periods; areas, regions, places; biography of central Europe

.000 901–.000 905   Historical periods

Add to base number 943.00090 the numbers following —090 in notation 0901–0905 from Table 1, e.g., central Europe during the Middle Ages 943.000902

Class specific periods of Holy Roman Empire in 943.02–943.05; class comprehensive works on Holy Roman Empire in 943

.000 91–.000 99   Areas, regions, places in general; biography

As modified under 930–990

.001–.009   Standard subdivisions of Germany

As modified under 930–990

SUMMARY

943.01	**Early history to 843**
.02	**843–1519**
.03	**Period of Reformation and Counter-Reformation, 1519–1618**
.04	**1618–1705**
.05	**1705–1790**
.06	**Period of Napoleonic Wars, 1790–1815**
.07	**Period of German Confederation, 1815–1866**
.08	**1866–**

> 943.01–943.08 Historical periods of Germany

Class comprehensive works in 943

.01   Early history to 843

For ancient history to 481, see 936.3

(.012)   Ancient history to 481

(Optional number; prefer 936.3)

(.012 1)	Early history to 113 B.C.
	(Optional number; prefer 936.301)
(.012 2)	Period of contacts with Roman Republic and Empire, 113 B.C.–481 A.D.
	(Optional number; prefer 936.302)
.013	Period of Merovingian dynasty in Germany, 481–751

Including 8th century

Class comprehensive works on Merovingian dynasty in France and Germany in 944.013

For 751–800, see 943.014

.014	751–843

Class here Carolingian dynasty in Germany, 751–911; reign of Charlemagne in Germany, 768–814

Class comprehensive works on Carolingian dynasty in 944.014; class comprehensive works on reign of Charlemagne in France and Germany in 944.0142

For 843–911, see 943.021

>   943.02–943.05 Specific periods of Holy Roman Empire

Class comprehensive works in 943.02

.02	843–1519

After Treaty of Verdun, 843

Class here medieval period; comprehensive works on period of Holy Roman Empire, 962–1806

For later part of period of Holy Roman Empire, see 943.03–943.06

.021	843–911

Class here 9th century

For 800–843, see 943.014

.022	Period of Conrad I and House of Saxony, 911–1024
.023	1024–1137

Including reign of Lothair II, Holy Roman Emperor, 1125–1137

Class here period of Salian (Franconian) emperors, 1024–1125

.024	1138–1198

Class here period of Hohenstaufen dynasty, 1138–1254; reign of Frederick I Barbarossa, 1152–1190; 12th century

For 1100–1137, see 943.023; for later period of Hohenstaufen dynasty, see 943.025

.025 Later period of Hohenstaufen dynasty and Interregnum, 1198–1273

    Including reign of Frederick II, 1215–1250

    Class here 13th century

      For 1273–1299, see 943.026

.026 1273–1346

.027 1346–1438

    Including reign of Charles IV, 1346–1378; 14th century

    Class here period of House of Luxemburg

      For 1300–1346, reign of Henry VII, 1273–1313, see 943.026

.028 Reigns of Albert II and Frederick III, 1438–1493

    Class here 15th century

      For 1400–1438, see 943.027; for 1493–1499, see 943.029

.029 Reign of Maximilian I, 1493–1519

.03 Period of Reformation and Counter-Reformation, 1519–1618

    Class here period of House of Habsburg, 1493–1806

      For the reign of a specific Habsburg not provided for here, see the reign, e.g., reign of Leopold I 943.044

.031 Reign of Charles V, 1519–1556

    Including Peasants' War, 1524–1525; Schmalkaldic War, 1546–1547

    Campaigns and battles of wars between France and Holy Roman Empire fought outside of Italy, 1521–1599, relocated to 944.028; campaigns and battles of wars between France and Holy Roman Empire fought in Italy, comprehensive works on campaigns and battles of wars between France and Holy Roman Empire, 1521–1599, relocated to 945.06

.032 Reign of Ferdinand I, 1556–1564

.033 Reign of Maximilian II, 1564–1576

.034 Reign of Rudolf II, 1576–1612

.035 Reign of Matthias, 1612–1619

.04 1618–1705

.041 Period of Thirty Years' War, 1618–1648

    Class comprehensive works on Thiry Years' War in 940.24

      For reign of Matthias during Thirty Years' War, see 943.035; for reign of Ferdinand II during Thirty Years' War, see 943.042; for reign of Ferdinand III during Thirty Years' War, see 943.043

.042 Reign of Ferdinand II, 1619–1637

.043 Reign of Ferdinand III, 1637–1657

.044 Reign of Leopold I, 1658–1705

.05   1705–1790

.051   Reign of Joseph I, 1705–1711

.052   Reign of Charles VI, 1711–1740

.053   1740–1786

                         Class here reign of Frederick the Great, King of Prussia, 1740–1786

                             *For 1742–1745, see 943.054; for 1745–1765, see 943.055; for
                             1765–1786, see 943.057*

.054   Period of First and Second Silesian Wars, 1740–1745

                         Class here First Silesian War, 1740–1742; Second Silesian War,
                         1744–1745; reign of Charles VII, 1742–1745

                         Class War of the Austrian Succession in 940.2532

                             See also 940.2534 for Seven Years' War (Third Silesian War)

.055   Reign of Francis I, 1745–1765

                         Including period of Seven Years' War, 1756–1763

                         Class comprehensive works on Seven Years' War in 940.2534

.057   Reign of Joseph II, 1765–1790

.06   Period of Napoleonic Wars, 1790–1815

                     Including Confederation of the Rhine

                     Class comprehensive works on Napoleonic Wars in 940.27

.07   Period of German Confederation, 1815–1866

                     Class here 19th century, comprehensive works on Prussia

                         *For 1800–1815, see 943.06; for 1866–1899, see 943.08. For a specific
                         period of history of Prussia not provided for here, see the period, e.g.,
                         reign of Frederick the Great 943.053*

.073   1815–1847

.074   Revolution of 1848–1849

.076   1849–1866

                         Including Schleswig-Holstein War, 1864; Austro-Prussian War (Seven
                         Weeks' War), 1866
                             (Option: Class Schleswig-Holstein War in 948.904)

.08   1866–

.081   1866–1871

                         Class here period of North German Confederation

                             For Franco-German War, see 943.082

.082	‡Franco-German War, 1870–1871
	(Option: Class in 944.07)
.083	Reign of William I, 1871–1888

Class here comprehensive works on administrations of Otto von Bismarck, 1862–1890; German Empire, 1871–1918

For reigns of Frederick III and William II, see 943.084. For a specific part of administrations of Otto von Bismarck not provided for here, see the part, e.g., administration during period of North German Confederation 943.081

.084	Reigns of Frederick III and William II, 1888–1918
.084 9	Period of World War I, 1914–1918
.085	Period of Weimar Republic, 1918–1933
.085 1	Revolution of 1918
.086	Period of Third Reich, 1933–1945

Class Holocaust in 940.5318

.086 2	1933–1939
.086 4	Period of World War II, 1939–1945
.087	1945–1990

Class here 20th century; Federal Republic, 1949 to present; comprehensive works on Federal and Democratic Republics

For 1900–1918, see 943.084; for period of Weimar Republic, see 943.085; for period of Third Reich, 1933–1945, see 943.086; for 1990 to present, see 943.088; for German Democratic Republic, see 943.1087

.087 4	1945–1949
.087 5	Administration of Konrad Adenauer, 1949–1962
.087 6	1962–1969

Including administrations of Ludwig Erhard, 1962–1966; Kurt Georg Kiesinger, 1966–1969

.087 7	1969–1982

Including administrations of Willy Brandt, 1969–1974; Helmut Schmidt, 1974–1982

.087 8	1982–1990

Class here administration of Helmut Kohl, 1982–1998

Including period of reunification, 1989–1990

For administration of Helmut Kohl during 1990–1998, see 943.0881

‡Add as instructed under 940–990

.088	1990–
.088 1	Later half of administration of Helmut Kohl, 1990–1998
.088 2	Administration of Gerhard Schröder, 1998–2005
.088 3	Administration of Angela Merkel, 2005–

.1 *Northeastern Germany

For Saxony and Thuringia, see 943.2

.101–.107   Early history to 1866

Add to base number 943.10 the numbers following 943.0 in 943.01–943.07, e.g., northeastern Germany during period of German Confederation 943.107

.108   1866–

.108 1–.108 6   1866–1945

Add to base number 943.108 the numbers following 943.08 in 943.081–943.086, e.g., northeastern Germany during period of German Empire 943.1083

.108 7   Period of East Germany, 1945–1990

Class here period of German Democratic Republic, 1949–1990

.108 74   1945–1949

.108 75   Administration of Walter Ulbricht, 1949–1971

.108 77   Administration of Erich Honecker, 1971–1989

.108 79   1989–1990

Class comprehensive works on reunification of Germany in 943.0878

Class here fall of Berlin Wall, 1989

.108 8   Period as part of Federal Republic, 1990–

.108 81   1990–1998

.108 82   1998–2005

.108 83   2005–

.2 *Saxony and Thuringia

.201–.208   Historical periods

Add to base number 943.20 the numbers following 943.10 in 943.101–943.108, e.g., period as part of East Germany 943.2087

.6 *Austria and Liechtenstein

Subdivisions are added for Austria and Liechtenstein together, for Austria alone

For ancient history to 476, see 936.36

*Add as instructed under 930–990

(.601)	Ancient history to 476
	(Optional number; prefer 936.36)

> 943.602–943.605 Historical periods of Austria and Liechtenstein together, of Austria alone

Class comprehensive works in 943.6

.602	Medieval period, 476–1526
.602 2	476–976
.602 3	Period of House of Babenberg, 976–1246

Including 13th century

For 1246–1273, see 943.6024; for 1273–1299, see 943.6025

.602 4	1246–1273
.602 5	1273–1526
.603	1526–1815

Class here comprehensive works on period of House of Habsburg, 1273–1919

For a specific part of the period of House of Habsburg, see the part, e.g., period of Austro-Hungarian Monarchy 943.6044, period of House of Habsburg in Spain 946.04

.603 1	1526–1740
.603 2	1740–1815

Class here 18th century

For 1700–1740, see 943.6031

See also 940.2532 for War of the Austrian Succession

.604	1815–1918

Class here Austrian Empire, 1804–1918

For Austrian Empire during 1804–1815, see 943.6032

.604 2	1815–1848
.604 3	1848–1867
.604 4	Period of Austro-Hungarian Monarchy, 1867–1918
.604 41	1867–1914
.604 42	Period of World War I, 1914–1918
.605	1918–
.605 1	Period of First Republic, 1918–1938
.605 11	1918–1933
.605 12	1933–1938

.605 2	1938–1955
.605 22	Anschluss and World War II periods, 1938–1945
	Standard subdivisions are added for either or both topics in heading
.605 23	1945–1955
.605 3	1955–
	Class here period of Second Republic, 1945–
	For 1945–1955, see 943.60523
.605 32	1955–1970
.605 33	1970–1983
.605 34	1983–1999
.605 35	2000–
.64	*Western Austria, and Liechtenstein
	Subdivisions are added for Western Austria and Liechtenstein together, for Western Austria alone
.648	†Liechtenstein
	For ancient history to 476, see 936.36

.7   *Czech Republic and Slovakia

.702	Early history to 1918
.702 1	Early history to 907
	Including Great Moravian Empire
.702 2	907–1526
.702 23	Period of Přemyslid dynasty, 907–1306
.702 24	Period of House of Luxemburg, 1306–1526
	Including Hussite Wars, 1419–1436
.702 3	1526–1815
.702 32	1526–1620
.702 33	1620–1800
.702 34	1800–1815
.702 4	1815–1918

*Add as instructed under 930–990
†Add as instructed under 930–990; however, do not add historical periods

.703	1918–1992
	Class here Czechoslovakia
	For 1945–1992, see 943.704
.703 2	Period of Czechoslovak Republic, 1918–1939
.703 3	1939–1945
	Class here Protectorate of Bohemia and Moravia
.704	1945–1992
.704 2	1945–1968
	Including reform and repression, 1968
.704 3	1968–1992
.705	1993–
	Period of two sovereign nations
.71	*Czech Republic
	For Moravia, see 943.72
.710 2–.710 4	Early history to 1992
	Add to base number 943.710 the numbers following 943.70 in 943.702–943.704, e.g., Kingdom of Bohemia 943.7102
.710 5	Period of Republic, 1993–
.710 51	1993–
.710 511	Administration of Václav Havel, 1993–2003
.710 512	Administration of Václav Klaus, 2003–
.72	*Moravia
.720 2–.720 5	Historical periods
	Add to base number 943.720 the numbers following 943.70 in 943.702–943.705, e.g., period as a part of Czech Republic 943.7205
.73	*Slovakia
.730 2–.730 4	Early history to 1992
	Add to base number 943.730 the numbers following 943.70 in 943.702–943.704, e.g., Slovak Republic, 1939–1945, 943.73033
.730 5	Period of Slovak Republic, 1993–
.730 51	1993–
.730 511	1993–1999
	Class here administration of Michal Kováč, 1993–1998
.730 512	Administration of Rudolf Schuster, 1999–2004

Add as instructed under 930–990

.730 513	Administration of Ivan Gašparovič, 2004–

.8   ***Poland**

.802	Early history to 1795
.802 2	Early history to 1370
	Including period of Piast dynasty
.802 3	Period of Jagellon dynasty, 1370–1572
	Including 16th century
	For 1572–1599, see 943.8024
.802 4	Period of elective kings, 1572–1697
.802 5	1697–1795
	Including partitions of 1772, 1793, 1795
.803	Period of foreign rule, 1795–1918
.803 2	1795–1862
.803 3	1863–1918
.804	Period of Republic, 1918–1939
.805	1939–
	Class here 20th century
	For 1900–1918, see 943.8033; for 1918–1939, see 943.804
.805 3	1939–1945
.805 4	1945–1956
.805 5	1956–1980
.805 6	1980–1989
.805 7	1989–
.805 71	1989–1995
	Class here administration of Lech Wałęsa, 1990–1995
.805 72	Administration of Aleksander Kwaśniewski, 1995–2005
.805 73	Administration of Lech Kaczyński, 2005–2010
.805 74	Administration of Bronisław Komorowski, 2010–

.9   ***Hungary**

.901	Early history to 894
	For ancient history to ca. 640, see 939.8

*Add as instructed under 930–990

(.901 1)	Ancient history to ca. 640
	(Optional number; prefer 939.8)
.902	Period of House of Árpád, 894–1301
.903	Period of elective kings, 1301–1526
.904	Turkish and House of Habsburg periods, 1526–1918
.904 1	Turkish period, 1526–1686
	Including 16th century
	For 1500–1526, see 943.903
.904 2	Period of House of Habsburg, 1686–1918
	For period of Austro-Hungarian Monarchy, see 943.9043
.904 3	Period of Austro-Hungarian Monarchy, 1867–1918
.905	1918–
.905 1	1918–1941
.905 2	1942–1956
	Including uprising and suppression, 1956
.905 3	1956–1989
.905 4	1989–
.905 41	1989–2000
	Class here administration of Árpád Göncz, 1990–2000
.905 42	Administration of Ferenc Mádl, 2000–2005
.905 43	Administration of László Sólyom, 2005–2010
.905 44	Administration of Pál Schmitt, 2010–

944 *France and Monaco

Subdivisions are added for France and Monaco together, for France alone

SUMMARY

944.01	**Early history to 987**
.02	**Medieval period, 987–1589**
.03	**Period of House of Bourbon, 1589–1789**
.04	**Revolutionary period, 1789–1804**
.05	**Period of First Empire, 1804–1815**
.06	**Period of Restoration, 1815–1848**
.07	**Period of Second Republic and Second Empire (period of Napoleon III), 1848–1870**
.08	**1870–**
.9	**Provence-Côte d'Azur, Monaco, Corsica**

*Add as instructed under 930–990

>   **944.01–944.08 Historical periods of France and Monaco together, of France alone**

     Class comprehensive works in 944

.01   **Early history to 987**

     For ancient history to 486, see 936.4

(.012)   Ancient history to 486

     (Optional number; prefer 936.4)

(.012 1)   Early history to 125 B.C.

     (Optional number; prefer 936.401)

(.012 2)   Gallo-Roman period, 125 B.C.–486 A.D.

     (Optional number; prefer 936.402)

.013   **Period of Merovingian dynasty, 486–751**

     Including 8th century

     Class here comprehensive works on Merovingian dynasty in France and Germany

     For Merovingian dynasty in Germany, see 943.013; for 751–800, see 944.014

.014   **Period of Carolingian dynasty, 751–987**

     Class here comprehensive works on Carolingian dynasty in France, Germany, and Italy

     For Carolingian dynasty in Germany, see 943.014; for Carolingian dynasty in Italy, see 945.02

.014 2   Reign of Charlemagne, 768–814

.02   **Medieval period, 987–1589**

.021   **Period of Capetian dynasty, 987–1328**

     Including reigns of Hugh Capet, Robert II, Henry I, 987–1060; 11th century

     For reigns of other Capetian kings, see 944.022–944.024; for 1060–1099, see 944.022

.022   **Reigns of Philip I, Louis VI, Louis VII, 1060–1180**

.023   **Reigns of Philip II, Louis VIII, Louis IX, 1180–1270**

     Class here 13th century

     For 1270–1299, see 944.024

.024   **Reigns of Philip III, Philip IV, Louis X, Jean I, Philip V, Charles IV, 1270–1328**

.025	‡Period of House of Valois, 1328–1589

Including reigns of Philip VI, Jean II, Charles V, 1328–1380

Class here Hundred Years' War, 1337–1453; 14th century
(Option: Class Hundred Years' War in 942.037)

For 1300–1328, see 944.024; for reigns of other Valois kings, see 944.026–944.029

.026	Reigns of Charles VI and Charles VII, 1380–1461

Class here 15th century

For 1461–1499, see 944.027

.027	Reigns of Louis XI, Charles VIII, Louis XII, 1461–1515

French invasions of Italy, 1494–1559, relocated to 945.06

.028	Period of House of Angoulême, 1515–1589

Including reigns of Francis I and Henry II, 1515–1559

Class here campaigns and battles of wars between France and Holy Roman Empire fought outside of Italy, 1521–1599 [*both formerly* 943.031]; 16th century

For 1500–1515, see 944.027; for reigns of Francis II, Charles IX, Henry III, see 944.029; for 1589–1600, see 944.031

French invasions of Italy during period of House of Angoulême relocated to 945.06

.029	Reigns of Francis II, Charles IX, Henry III, 1559–1589
.03	Period of House of Bourbon, 1589–1789
.031	Reign of Henry IV, 1589–1610
.032	Reign of Louis XIII, 1610–1643
.033	Reign of Louis XIV, 1643–1715

Including War of Devolution, 1667–1668

Class here 17th century

For 1600–1610, see 944.031; for 1610–1643, see 944.032

.034	Reign of Louis XV, 1715–1774

Class here 18th century

For a specific part of 18th century not provided for here, see the part, e.g., Reign of Terror 944.044

.035	1774–1789

Class here period of Louis XVI, 1774–1792

For period of Louis XVI during 1789–1792, see 944.041

‡Add as instructed under 940–990

.04	Revolutionary period, 1789–1804
.041	Period of Estates-General, National Assembly, Legislative Assembly, 1789–1792
.042	Period of First Republic, 1792–1799

Including Vendean War, 1793–1800

For period of National Convention, see 944.043; for period of Directory, see 944.045

.043	Period of National Convention, 1792–1795

For Reign of Terror, see 944.044

.044	Period of Reign of Terror, 1793–1794
.045	Period of Directory, 1795–1799
.046	Period of Consulate, 1799–1804
.05	Period of First Empire, 1804–1815

Including reign of Louis XVIII, 1814–1815; Hundred Days, 1815

Class here reign of Napoleon I, 1804–1814

Class Napoleonic Wars in 940.27

.06	Period of Restoration, 1815–1848

Class here 19th century

For a specific part of 19th century not provided for here, see the part, e.g., Second Empire 944.07

.061	Reign of Louis XVIII, 1815–1824
.062	Reign of Charles X, 1824–1830
.063	Period of Louis Philippe, 1830–1848 (July Monarchy)
.07	Period of Second Republic and Second Empire (period of Napoleon III), 1848–1870

(Option: Class here Franco-German War; prefer 943.082)

.08	1870–
.081	Period of Third Republic, 1870–1945

Class here 20th century

For 1945–1958, see 944.082; for 1958–1999, see 944.083

.081 2	1870–1899

Including Paris Commune, 1871

.081 3	1900–1914
.081 4	Period of World War I, 1914–1918
.081 5	1918–1939

.081 6	Period of World War II, 1939–1945
.082	Period of Fourth Republic, 1945–1958
.083	Period of Fifth Republic, 1958–

For 2000 to present, see 944.084

.083 6	1958–1969
.083 7	1970–1979
.083 8	1980–1989
.083 9	1990–1999
.084	2000–
.084 1	2000–2019
.084 11	2000–2009
.084 12	2010–2019

.9   ***Provence-Côte d'Azur, Monaco, Corsica**

Subdivisions are added for Provence-Côte d'Azur, Monaco, Corsica together; for Provence-Côte d'Azur alone

.94   ***Alpes-Maritimes department and Monaco**

.949   †Monaco

For ancient history to 486, see 936.4

.99   *Corsica (Corse)

.990 1   Early history to 1077

Including 453–476 [*formerly* 937.9909], 987–1060 [*formerly* 944.99021], 1060–1077 [*formerly* 944.99022]

For ancient history to 453, see 937.99

(.990 12)   Ancient history to 453

(Optional number; prefer 937.99)

[.990 13–.990 14]   486–987

Numbers discontinued; class in 944.9901

.990 2   Pisan period, 1077–1347

Including assumption of sovereignty by Pope Gregory VII, 1077

[.990 21]   987–1060

Relocated to 944.9901

---

*Add as instructed under 930–990

†Add as instructed under 930–990; however, do not add historical periods

[.990 22]	1060–1180	
	Use of this number for 1077–1180 discontinued; class in 944.9902	
	1060–1077 relocated to 944.9901	
[.990 23–.990 24]	1180–1328	
	Numbers discontinued; class in 944.9902	
[.990 25]	1328–1380	
	Use of this number for 1328–1347 discontinued; class in 944.9902	
	1347–1380 relocated to 944.9903	
[.990 26–.990 29]	1380–1589	
	Relocated to 944.9903	
.990 3	Genoan period, 1347–1768	

Including 1347–1380 [*formerly* 944.99025], 1380–1589 [*formerly* 944.99026–944.99029]; 14th century, 18th century

For 1300–1347, see 944.9902; for 1768–1799, see 944.9904

[.990 31–.990 33]	1589–1715	
	Numbers discontinued; class in 944.9903	
[.990 34]	1715–1774	
	Use of this number for 1715–1768 discontinued; class in 944.9903	
	1768–1774 relocated to 944.9904	
[.990 35]	1774–1789	
	Relocated to 944.9904	
.990 4	1768–1804	

Including 1768–1774 [*formerly* 944.99034], 1774–1789 [*formerly* 944.99035]; British period, 1794–1796

Class here periods as part of France, 1768–1794, 1796–1804

.990 5–.990 8	1804–	

Add to base number 944.990 the numbers following 944.0 in 944.05–944.08, e.g., period of Third Republic 944.99081

945   *Italy, San Marino, Vatican City, Malta

Subdivisions are added for Italy, San Marino, Vatican City, Malta together; for Italy alone

---

*Add as instructed under 930–990

SUMMARY

> 945.01–945.09 Historical periods of Italy, San Marino, Vatican City, Malta together; of Italy alone

Class comprehensive works in 945

.01 Early history to 774

Including Gothic and Lombard kingdoms, 476–774

Class here comprehensive works on medieval period (Middle Ages) [*formerly* 945.03]

For ancient history to 476, see 937; for Early Middle Ages, see 945.02; for Late Middle Ages, see 945.04

(.012) Ancient history to 476

(Optional number; prefer 937)

Add to base number 945.012 the numbers following 937.0 in 937.01–937.09, e.g., Punic Wars 945.0124

.02 Period of Carolingian dynasty, 774–962

Including 10th century

Class here comprehensive works on Early Middle Ages (Dark Ages)

Class comprehensive works on Carolingian dynasty in 944.014

For Early Middle Ages during 476–774, see 945.01; for Early Middle Ages during 962–1122, see 945.03

.03 Period of German emperors, 962–1122

Comprehensive works on medieval period (Middle Ages) relocated to 945.01

.04 1122–1348

Including 1300–1348 [*formerly* 945.05]

Class here comprehensive works on Late Middle Ages [*formerly* 945.05]

For Late Middle Ages during 1348–1492, see 945.05

.05   **Period of Black Death to invasion of Charles VIII, 1348–1494**

        Including 14th century

        Class here Renaissance period

        1300–1348, comprehensive works on Late Middle Ages relocated to 945.04

.06   **1494–1527**

        Class here campaigns and battles of wars between France and Holy Roman Empire fought in Italy, comprehensive works on campaigns and battles of wars between France and Holy Roman Empire, 1521–1599 [*all formerly* 943.031]; French invasions of Italy, 1494–1559 [*formerly* 944.027]; French invasions of Italy during period of House of Angoulême [*formerly* 944.028]; comprehensive works on Italian Wars, 1494–1559

           For campaigns and battles of wars between France and Holy Roman Empire fought outside of Italy, 1521–1599, see 944.028; for Italian Wars during 1527–1559, see 945.07

.07   **Spanish and Austrian period, 1527–1796**

        Including 16th century

        For 1500–1527, see 945.06

.08   **1796–1900**

.082   **Napoleonic period, 1796–1815**

        Including 1814–1815 [*formerly* 945.083]; Kingdom of Italy, 1805–1814

.083   **Period of Risorgimento, 1815–1861**

        Napoleonic period during 1814–1815 relocated to 945.082

.084   **Reigns of Victor Emmanuel II and Umberto I, 1861–1900**

        Class here Roman question; period of House of Savoy in Kingdom of Italy, 1861–1946; comprehensive works on period of House of Savoy in Italy, 1343–1946

           For comprehensive works on period of House of Savoy in Piedmont, see 945.105; for reign of Victor Emmanuel III, see 945.091

.09   **1900–**

.091   **Reign of Victor Emmanuel III, 1900–1946**

        Including Fascist period, 1922–1943

        Class here 20th century

        For 1946–1999, see 945.092

.092   **Period of Republic, 1946–**

        For 2000 to present, see 945.093

.092 4   1946–1949

.092 5   1950–1959

.092 6   1960–1969

.092 7	1970–1979
.092 8	1980–1989
.092 9	1990–1999
.093	2000–
.093 1	2000–2019
.093 11	2000–2009
.093 12	2010–2019

.1   *Northwestern Italy

Class here Piedmont (Piemonte) region

.101   Early history to 774

Class here comprehensive works on medieval period (Middle Ages) [*formerly* 945.103]

> *For ancient history to 476, see 937.222; for Early Middle Ages, see 945.102; for Late Middle Ages, see 945.104*

(.101 2)   Ancient history to 476

(Optional number; prefer 937.222)

Add to base number 945.1012 the numbers following 937.0 in 937.01–937.09, e.g., Punic Wars 945.10124

.102   Period of Carolingian dynasty, 774–962

Including 10th century

Class here comprehensive works on Early Middle Ages (Dark Ages)

> *For Early Middle Ages during 476–774, see 945.101; for Early Middle Ages during 962–1122, see 945.103*

.103   Period of German emperors, 962–1122

Class here Margravate of Ivrea

Comprehensive works on medieval period (Middle Ages) relocated to 945.101

.104   1122–1343

Including 1300–1343 [*formerly* 945.105]

Class here comprehensive works on Late Middle Ages [*formerly* 945.105]

> *For Late Middle Ages during 1343–1492, see 945.105*

*Add as instructed under 930–990

.105   Period of House of Savoy to death of Philibert II, 1343–1504

> Including 1494–1504 [*formerly* 945.106], 14th century
>
> Class here comprehensive works on period of House of Savoy in Piedmont, 1343–1861
>
> Class comprehensive works on period of House of Savoy in Italy, 1343–1946, in 945.084
>
>> *For a specific part of the period of House of Savoy in Piedmont, see the part, e.g., House of Savoy during Napoleonic period 945.1082*
>
> 1300–1343, comprehensive works on Late Middle Ages relocated to 945.104

.106   Period of Charles III, 1504–1553

> Including 1527–1553 [*formerly* 945.107]
>
> Class here 16th century [*formerly* 945.107]
>
>> *For 1553–1600, see 945.107*
>
> 1494–1504 relocated to 945.105

.107   Period of Emmanuel Philibert through Victor Amadeus III, 1553–1796

> Including comprehensive works on Kingdom of Sardinia, 1718–1861
>
>> *For Kingdom of Sardinia during 1796–1815, see 945.1082; for Kingdom of Sardinia during 1815–1861, see 945.1083; for Kingdom of Sardinia in Sardinia, see 945.907*
>
> Period of Charles III during 1527–1553, 16th century relocated to 945.106

.108   1796–1900

.108 2   Napoleonic period, 1796–1815

> Including 1814–1815 [*formerly* 945.1083]
>
> Class here reign of Victor Emmanuel I, 1802–1821
>
>> *For reign of Victor Emmanuel I during 1815–1821, see 945.1083*

.108 3   Period of Risorgimento, 1815–1861

> Napoleonic period during 1814–1815 relocated to 945.1082

.108 4   Reigns of Victor Emmanuel II and Umberto I, 1861–1900

.109   1900–

> Add to base number 945.109 the numbers following 945.09 in 945.091–945.093, e.g., Piedmont during the Fascist period 945.1091

.11   *Valle d'Aosta region

---

*Add as instructed under 930–990

.110 1–.110 9   Historical periods

> Add to base number 945.110 the numbers following 945.0 in 945.01–945.09, e.g., Valle d'Aosta during the Fascist period 945.11091

> *For ancient history to 476, see 937.221*

.18   *Liguria region

> Class here period of Republic of Genoa, 1056–1797

.180 1–.180 9   Historical periods

> Add to base number 945.180 the numbers following 945.0 in 945.01–945.09, e.g., Ligurian Republic, 1797–1805 945.18082

> *For ancient history to 476, see 937.1*

.2   *Lombardy (Lombardia) region

.201   Early history to 774

> Class here comprehensive works on medieval period (Middle Ages) [*formerly* 945.203]

>> *For ancient history to 476, see 937.22; for Early Middle Ages, see 945.202; for Late Middle Ages, see 945.204*

(.201 2)   Ancient history to 476

> (Optional number; prefer 937.22)

> Add to base number 945.2012 the numbers following 937.0 in 937.01–937.09, e.g., Punic Wars 945.20124

.202   Period of Carolingian dynasty, 774–962

> Including 10th century

> Class here comprehensive works on Early Middle Ages (Dark Ages)

>> *For Early Middle Ages during 476–774, see 945.201; for Early Middle Ages during 962–1122, see 945.203*

.203   Period of German emperors, 962–1122

> Comprehensive works on medieval period (Middle Ages) relocated to 945.201

.204   1122–1277

> Period of House of Visconti during 1277–1300 relocated to 945.205

.205   Period of House of Visconti, 1277–1447

> Including 1277–1300 [*formerly* 945.204]

> Class here comprehensive works on Late Middle Ages

> Period of House of Sforza during 1447–1494 relocated to 945.206

*Add as instructed under 930–990

.206	Period of House of Sforza, 1447–1535

Including 1447–1494 [*formerly* 945.205], 1527–1535 [*formerly* 945.207]; 15th century

For 1400–1447, see 945.205

.207	Spanish and Austrian period, 1535–1796

Including 16th century

For 1500–1527, see 945.206

Period of House of Sforza during 1527–1535 relocated to 945.206

.208	1796–1900
.208 2	Napoleonic period, 1796–1815

Including 1814–1815 [*formerly* 945.2083]; Cisalpine Republic, 1797–1802

.208 3	Period of Risorgimento, 1815–1861

Napoleonic period during 1814–1815 relocated to 945.2082

.208 4	Reigns of Victor Emmanuel II and Umberto I, 1861–1900
.209	1900–

Add to base number 945.209 the numbers following 945.09 in 945.091–945.093, e.g., Lombardy during the Fascist period 945.2091

.3	***Northeastern Italy**

Class here Veneto region; period of Republic of Venice, 810–1797

.301	Early history to 774

Class here comprehensive works on medieval period (Middle Ages) [*formerly* 945.303]

For ancient history to 476, see 937.3; for Early Middle Ages, see 945.302; for Late Middle Ages, see 945.304

(.301 2)	Ancient history to 476

(Optional number; prefer 937.3)

Add to base number 945.3012 the numbers following 937.0 in 937.01–937.09, e.g., Punic Wars 945.30124

.302	Period of Carolingian dynasty, 774–962

Including 10th century

Class here comprehensive works on Early Middle Ages (Dark Ages)

For Early Middle Ages during 476–774, see 945.301; for Early Middle Ages during 962–1122, see 945.303

---

*Add as instructed under 930–990

.303   Period of German emperors, 962–1122

> Comprehensive works on medieval period (Middle Ages) relocated to 945.301

.304   1122–1339

> Including 1300–1339 [*formerly* 945.305]; period of House of Scaliger, 1259–1339

> Class here comprehensive works on Late Middle Ages [*formerly* 945.305]

> > *For Late Middle Ages during 1339–1494, see 945.305*

.305   Period after defeat of House of Scaliger to invasion of Charles VIII, 1339–1494

> Including 14th century

> 1300–1339, comprehensive works on Late Middle Ages relocated to 945.304

.306   Period of invasion of Charles VIII to Treaty of Noyon, 1494–1516

> 1516–1527 relocated to 945.307

.307   Period after Treaty of Noyon to Treaty of Campo Formio, 1516–1797

> Including 1516–1527 [*formerly* 945.306], 1796–1797 [*formerly* 945.3082]

> > *For wars between Venice and Ottoman Empire, see 949.505*

.308   1797–1900

.308 2   Napoleonic period, 1797–1815

> Including 1814–1815 [*formerly* 945.3083]

> 1796–1797 relocated to 945.307

.308 3   Period of Risorgimento, 1815–1866

> Including Venetian Republic, 1849

> Napoleonic period during 1814–1815 relocated to 945.3082

.308 4   Reigns of Victor Emmanuel II and Umberto I, 1866–1900

.309   1900–

> Add to base number 945.309 the numbers following 945.09 in 945.091–945.093, e.g., Veneto region during the Fascist period 945.3091

.38   *Trentino-Alto Adige region

---

*Add as instructed under 930–990

.380 1–.380 9   Historical periods

> Add to base number 945.380 the numbers following 945.0 in 945.01–945.09, e.g., Trentino-Alto Adige region during the Fascist period 945.38091

> *For ancient history to 476, see 937.37*

.39   *Friuli-Venezia Giulia region

.390 1–.390 9   Historical periods

> Add to base number 945.390 the numbers following 945.0 in 945.01–945.09, e.g., Friuli-Venezia Giulia region during the Fascist period 945.39091

> *For ancient history to 476, see 937.38*

.4   *Emilia-Romagna region and San Marino

> Subdivisions are added for Emilia-Romagna region and San Marino together, for Emilia-Romagna region alone

.49   †San Marino

> *For ancient history to 476, see 937.269*

.5   *Tuscany (Toscana) region

> Class here period of city-state of Florence, ca. 1100–1569

.501   Early history to 774

> Class here comprehensive works on medieval period (Middle Ages) [*formerly* 945.503]

> > *For ancient history to 476, see 937.5; for Early Middle Ages, see 945.502; for Late Middle Ages, see 945.504*

(.501 2)   Ancient history to 476

> (Optional number; prefer 937.5)

> Add to base number 945.5012 the numbers following 937.0 in 937.01–937.09, e.g., Punic Wars 945.50124

.502   Period of Carolingian dynasty, 774–962

> Including 10th century

> Class here comprehensive works on Early Middle Ages (Dark Ages)

> > *For Early Middle Ages during 476–774, see 945.501; for Early Middle Ages during 962–1122, see 945.503*

.503   Period of House of Attoni, 962–1115

> Comprehensive works on medieval period (Middle Ages) relocated to 945.501; 1115–1122 relocated to 945.504

---

*Add as instructed under 930–990

†Add as instructed under 930–990; however, do not add historical periods

.504 1115–1348

Including 1115–1122 [*formerly* 945.503], 1300–1348 [*formerly* 945.505]

Class here comprehensive works on Late Middle Ages [*formerly* 945.505]

For Late Middle Ages during 1348–1492, see 945.505

.505 Period of Black Death to invasion of Charles VIII, 1348–1494

Including 14th century

Class here period of House of Medici during 1434–1494; comprehensive works on period of House of Medici

For period of House of Medici during 1512–1527, see 945.506; for period of Ducal Medici, see 945.507

1300–1348, comprehensive works on Late Middle Ages relocated to 945.504

.506 1494–1531

Including 1527–1531 [*formerly* 945.507]; period of invasion of Charles VIII, 1494–1495; period of House of Medici during 1512–1527

Class here periods of Florence as a republic, 1494–1512 and 1527–1530

Class comprehensive works on period of House of Medici in 945.505

.507 1531–1801

Including 1796–1801 [*formerly* 945.5082]; period of Ducal Medici, 1531–1737; 16th century; period of House of Lorraine, 1737–1801, comprehensive works on House of Lorraine

Class here Grand Duchy of Tuscany during 1569–1801, comprehensive works on Grand Duchy of Tuscany

For 1500–1531, see 945.506; for Grand Duchy of Tuscany and House of Lorraine during 1814–1860, see 945.5083

1527–1531 relocated to 945.506

.508 1801–1900

.508 2 Napoleonic period, 1801–1814

Class here Kingdom of Etruria, 1801–1807

1796–1801 relocated to 945.507

.508 3 Period of Risorgimento, 1814–1861

Class here Grand Duchy of Tuscany and House of Lorraine during 1814–1860

Class comprehensive works on Grand Duchy of Tuscany and House of Lorraine in 945.507

.508 4 Reigns of Victor Emmanuel II and Umberto I, 1861–1900

.509   1900–

> Add to base number 945.509 the numbers following 945.09 in 945.091–945.093, e.g., Tuscany during the Fascist period 945.5091

.6   *Central Italy and Vatican City

> Class here Papal States (States of the Church), 728–1870
>
> Subdivisions are added for central Italy and Vatican City together, for central Italy alone
>
> > *For a specific part of Papal States, see the part, e.g., Tuscany 945.5, Marches 945.67*

.601–.609   Historical periods

> Add to base number 945.60 the numbers following 945.0 in 945.01–945.09, e.g., Central Italy during the Fascist period 945.6091
>
> *For ancient history to 476, see 937.6*

.63   *Rome (Roma) province and Vatican City

> Subdivisions are added for Rome province and Vatican City together, for Rome province alone

.634   †Vatican City

[.634 01–.634 09]   Historical periods

> Numbers discontinued; class in 945.634

.7   *Southern Italy

> Class here period of Kingdom of Naples, 1266–1815
>
> *For ancient history to 476, see 937.7; for Sicily, see 945.8*

.701   Early history to 774

> Including comprehensive works on Byzantine period, 553–1071, on Lombardic period, 568–1076
>
> Class here comprehensive works on medieval period (Middle Ages) [*formerly 945.703*]
>
> > *For ancient history to 476, see 937.7; for Early Middle Ages, see 945.702; for Late Middle Ages, see 945.704. For a part of Byzantine or Lombardic period not provided for here, see the part, e.g., Byzantine or Lombardic period during 1030–1071 945.703*

(.701 2)   Ancient history to 476

> (Optional number; prefer 937.7)
>
> Add to base number 945.7012 the numbers following 937.0 in 937.01–937.09, e.g., Punic Wars 945.70124

---

*Add as instructed under 930–990
†Add as instructed under 930–990; however, do not add historical periods

.702 Period of conflict between Byzantines and Arabs to start of Norman period, 774–1030

Including 962–1030 [*formerly* 945.703]

Class here comprehensive works on Early Middle Ages (Dark Ages)

For Early Middle Ages during 476–774, see 945.701; for Early Middle Ages during 962–1111, see 945.703

.703 Norman period, 1030–1186

Including 1122–1186 [*formerly* 945.704], 11th century

Comprehensive works on medieval period (Middle Ages) relocated to 945.701; 962–1030 relocated to 945.702

.704 Period of Swabian dynasties, 1186–1266

Class here comprehensive works on Late Middle Ages [*formerly* 945.705], 13th century; period of House of Hohenstaufen, 1194–1266

For Late Middle Ages during 1266–1442, see 945.705; for Late Middle Ages during 1442–1492, see 945.706

1122–1186 relocated to 945.703; 1266–1300 relocated to 945.705

.705 Period of House of Anjou, 1266–1442

Including 1266–1300 [*formerly* 945.704]

Comprehensive works on Late Middle Ages relocated to 945.704; 1442–1494 relocated to 945.706

.706 Period as part of Kingdom of Aragon, 1442–1516

Including 1442–1494 [*formerly* 945.705]

Class here 15th century

For 1400–1442, see 945.705

1516–1527 relocated to 945.707

.707 Spanish and Austrian period to Parthenopaean Republic, 1516–1799

Including 1516–1527 [*formerly* 945.706], 1796–1799 [*formerly* 947.7082], comprehensive works on period of House of Bourbon

For period of House of Bourbon during 1815–1860, see 945.7083

.708 1799–1900

.708 2 Napoleonic period, 1799–1815

Including 1814–1815 [*formerly* 945.7083]

1796–1799 relocated to 945.707

.708 3 1815–1861

Class here period of Kingdom of the Two Sicilies, 1816–1860

For period of Kingdom of the Two Sicilies in Sicily, see 945.8083

Napoleonic period during 1814–1815 relocated to 945.7082

.708 4	Reigns of Victor Emmanuel II and Umberto I, 1861–1900
.709	1900–

Class here questione meridionale (Southern question)

Add to base number 945.709 the numbers following 945.09 in 945.091–945.093, e.g., Southern Italy during the Fascist period 945.7091

.8 *Sicily and adjacent islands

Standard subdivisions are added for Sicily and adjacent islands together, for Sicily alone

Class here period of Kingdom of Sicily, 1130–1815

.801	Early history to 827

Including 774–827 [*formerly* 945.802]; period of Gothic kingdom, 476–535; period of Byzantine Empire, 535–827

Class here comprehensive works on medieval period (Middle Ages) [*formerly* 945.803]

> *For ancient history to 476, see 937.8; for Early Middle Ages, see 945.802; for Late Middle Ages, see 945.804*

(.801 2)	Ancient history to 476

(Optional number; prefer 937.8)

Add to base number 945.8012 the numbers following 937.0 in 937.01–937.09, e.g., Punic Wars 945.80124

.802	Arabic period, 827–1061

Including 962–1061 [*formerly* 945.803]; 9th century, 11th century

Class here comprehensive works on Early Middle Ages (Dark Ages)

> *For Early Middle Ages during 476–827, see 945.801; for Early Middle Ages during 1061–1189, see 945.803*

774–827 relocated to 945.801

.803	Norman period, 1061–1189

Including 1122–1189 [*formerly* 945.804]

Comprehensive works on medieval period (Middle Ages) relocated to 945.801; 962–1061 relocated to 945.802

*Add as instructed under 930–990

.804	Period of Swabian dynasties and House of Anjou, 1189–1302

Including 1300–1302 [*formerly* 945.805]; period of House of Hohenstaufen, 1194–1266

Class here comprehensive works on Late Middle Ages [*formerly* 945.805]

> *For Late Middle Ages during 1302–1412, see 945.805; for Late Middle Ages during 1412–1492, see 945.806*

1122–1189 relocated to 945.803

.805	Period as part of Kingdom of Aragon, 1302–1412

1300–1302, comprehensive works on Late Middle Ages relocated to 945.804; 1412–1494 relocated to 945.806

.806	Spanish period, 1412–1712

Including 1412–1494 [*formerly* 945.805]

Class here 1527–1712 [*formerly* 945.807]

.807	First period of House of Bourbon, 1712–1799

Including 1796–1799 [*formerly* 945.8082]

Class here comprehensive works on period of House of Bourbon

> *For period of House of Bourbon during 1815–1860, see 945.8083*

1527–1712 relocated to 945.806

.808	1799–1900
.808 2	Napoleonic period, 1799–1815

Including 1814–1815 [*formerly* 945.8083]

1796–1799 relocated to 945.807

.808 3	1815–1861

Class here period of Kingdom of the Two Sicilies in Sicily, 1816–1860

Class comprehensive works on Kingdom of the Two Sicilies in 945.7083

Napoleonic period during 1814–1815 relocated to 945.8082

.808 4	Reigns of Victor Emmanuel II and Umberto I, 1861–1900
.809	1900–

Add to base number 945.809 the numbers following 945.09 in 945.091–945.093, e.g., Sicily during the Fascist period 945.8091

.85	*Malta

*Add as instructed under 930–990

.850 1   Early history to 1530

         For ancient history to 476, see 937.85

(.850 12)   Ancient history to 476

         (Optional number; prefer 937.85)

         Add to base number 945.85012 the numbers following 937.0 in 937.01–937.09, e.g., early period of Roman Empire 945.850127

.850 2   Period of Knights of Malta, 1530–1798

         Including 16th century

         For 1500–1530, see 945.8501

.850 3   1798–1964

         Including French period, 1798–1800

         Class here British period, 1800–1964; 20th century

         For 1964 to present, see 945.8504

.850 4   1964–

.9   ***Sardinia**

.901   Early history to 534

         Including 453–476 [*formerly* 937.909]; Vandal kingdom, 476–534; 5th century

         For ancient history to 534, see 937.9

         534–774 relocated to 945.902

(.901 2)   Ancient history to 453

         (Optional number; prefer 937.9)

         Add to base number 945.9012 the numbers following 937.0 in 937.01–937.09, e.g., Punic Wars 945.90124

.902   Byzantine period, 534–900

         Including 534–774 [*formerly* 945.901]; 6th century

         Class here comprehensive works on medieval period (Middle Ages) [*formerly* 945.903]; comprehensive works on Early Middle Ages (Dark Ages)

         For Early Middle Ages during 453–534, see 945.901; for Late Middle Ages, see 945.903

         900–962 relocated to 945.903

*Add as instructed under 930–990

.903   Period of Giudicati, 900–1323

> Including 900–962 [*formerly* 945.902], 1122–1300 [*formerly* 945.904], 1300–1323 [*formerly* 945.905]

> Class here comprehensive works on Late Middle Ages [*formerly* 945.905]

>> For Late Middle Ages during 1323–1479, see 945.905; for Late Middle Ages during 1479–1492, see 945.906

> Comprehensive works on medieval period (Middle Ages) relocated to 945.902

[.904]   1122–1300

> Relocated to 945.903

.905   Period as part of Kingdom of Aragon, 1323–1479

> 1300–1323, comprehensive works on Late Middle Ages relocated to 945.903; 1479–1494 relocated to 945.906

.906   Spanish period, 1479–1717

> Including 1479–1494 [*formerly* 945.905], 1527–1717 [*formerly* 945.907]

.907   1717–1793

> Class here Kingdom of Sardinia in Sardinia, 1718–1861

> Class comprehensive works on Kingdom of Sardinia in 945.107

>> For Kingdom of Sardinia in Sardinia during 1793–1848, see 945.9082; for Kingdom of Sardinia in Sardinia during 1848–1861, see 945.9083

> 1527–1717 relocated to 945.906; 1793–1796 relocated to 945.9082

.908   1793–1900

.908 2   Period of antifeudal movements prior to Albertine Statute, 1793–1848

> Including 1793–1796 [*formerly* 945.907], 1814–1848 [*formerly* 945.9083]

.908 3   Period of proclamation of Albertine Statute to the start of Kingdom of Italy, 1848–1861

> 1814–1848 relocated to 945.9082

.908 4   Reigns of Victor Emmanuel II and Umberto I, 1861–1900

.909   1900–

> Add to base number 945.909 the numbers following 945.09 in 945.091–945.093, e.g., Sardinia during the Fascist period 945.9091

946   Spain, Andorra, Gibraltar, Portugal

.000 1–.000 8   Standard subdivisions of Spain, Andorra, Gibraltar, Portugal together

> As modified under 930–990

.000 9	Historical periods; areas, regions, places; biography of Spain, Andorra, Gibraltar, Portugal together
.000 901–.000 905	Historical periods

> Add to base number 946.00090 the numbers following —090 in notation 0901–0905 from Table 1, e.g., Spain, Andorra, Gibraltar, Portugal together during the Middle Ages 946.000902

.000 91–.000 99	Areas, regions, places in general; biography

> As modified under 930–990

.001–.009	Standard subdivisions of Spain

> As modified under 930–990

>   946.01–946.08 Historical periods of Spain

> Class comprehensive works in 946

.01	Early history to 711

> Class here period of Visigothic domination, 415–711

> *For ancient history to 415, see 936.6*

(.012)	Ancient history to 415

> (Optional number; prefer 936.6)

(.012 1)	Early history to ca. 1000 B.C.

> (Optional number; prefer 936.601)

(.012 2)	Period of Greek, Phoenician, early Celtic and Germanic contacts, ca. 1000–218 B.C.

> (Optional number; prefer 936.602)

(.012 3)	Roman period, 218 B.C.–415 A.D.

> (Optional number; prefer 936.603)

.02	Period of Moorish dynasties and reconquest, 711–1479
.03	Reign of Ferdinand V and Isabella I, 1479–1516

> Including union of Castile and Aragon

.04	Period of House of Habsburg, 1516–1700

> Class here 16th century

> *For 1500–1516, see 946.03; for 1598–1599, later period of House of Habsburg, see 946.051*

.042	Reign of Charles I, 1516–1556
.043	Reign of Philip II, 1556–1598
.05	Later period of House of Habsburg and period of House of Bourbon, 1598–1808

.051	Later period of House of Habsburg, 1598–1700
	Including reign of Philip III, 1598–1621
	For reign of Philip IV, see 946.052; for reign of Charles II, see 946.053
.052	Reign of Philip IV, 1621–1665
.053	Reign of Charles II, 1665–1700
.054	1700–1808
	Class here comprehensive works on House of Bourbon in Spain
	For the reign of a specific Bourbon ruler, see the reign, e.g., reign of Isabella II 946.072
.055	Reign of Philip V, 1700–1746
	Including Anglo-Spanish War (War of Jenkins' Ear), 1739–1741 (Option: Class War of Jenkins' Ear in 941.072)
	See also 940.2526 for War of the Spanish Succession
.056	Reign of Ferdinand VI, 1746–1759
.057	Reign of Charles III, 1759–1788
.058	Reign of Charles IV, 1788–1808
.06	Period of Peninsular War and rule of Joseph Bonaparte, 1808–1814
	Class comprehensive works on Peninsular War in 940.27
.07	1814–1931
.072	Reigns of Ferdinand VII and Isabella II, 1814–1868
	Including first Bourbon Restoration
	(Option: Class here Spanish-Moroccan War; prefer 964.03)
.073	1868–1874
	Including revolution 1868–1871; second Bourbon Restoration, 1871–1873; First Republic, 1873–1874
.074	Reigns of Alfonso XII and Alfonso XIII, 1874–1931
	(Option: Class here Spanish-American War; prefer 973.89)
.08	1931–
	Class here 20th century
	For 1900–1931, see 946.074
.081	‡Period of Second Republic, 1931–1939
	Class here Civil War, 1936–1939
.082	Period of Francisco Franco, 1939–1975

Add as instructed under 940–990

.082 4	1939–1949
.082 5	1950–1959
.082 6	1960–1969
.082 7	1970–1975
.083	Reign of Juan Carlos I, 1975–

.7 ***Eastern Spain and Andorra**

> Subdivisions are added for eastern Spain and Andorra together, for eastern Spain alone

.79 †Andorra

> *For ancient history to 415, see 936.6*

.8 ***Andalusia autonomous community and Gibraltar**

> Subdivisions are added for Andalusia autonomous community and Gibraltar together, for Andalusia autonomous community alone

.89 †Gibraltar

> *For ancient history to 415, see 936.6*

.9 ***Portugal**

.901 Early history to 1143

> *For ancient history to 415, see 936.6*

(.901 2) Ancient history to 415

> (Optional number; prefer 936.6)

> Add to base number 946.9012 the numbers following 946.012 in 946.0121–946.0123, e.g., period of Greek contacts 946.90122

.902 1143–1640

> Including 12th century

> *For 1100–1143, see 946.901*

.903 Period of House of Braganza, 1640–1910

.903 2 1640–1750

> Including restoration of Portuguese monarchy; 17th century, 18th century

> *For 1600–1640, see 946.902; for 1750–1799, see 946.9033*

.903 3 1750–1807

> Including Pombaline reforms

---

*Add as instructed under 930–990
†Add as instructed under 930–990; however, do not add historical periods

.903 4	Period of monarchy in exile, 1807–1820
	Including period of Peninsular War
	Class comprehensive works on Peninsular War in 940.27
.903 5	1820–1847
.903 6	1847–1910
	Class here 19th century

For a specific part of 19th century not provided for here, see the part, e.g., 1807–1820 946.9034

.904	1910–
.904 1	Period of Republic, 1910–1926
.904 2	1926–1968
	Including period of Salazar, 1933–1968
	Class here Novo Estado, 1933–1974

For Novo Estado during 1968–1974, see 946.9043

.904 3	1968–1974
.904 4	1974–

947   Russia and neighboring east European countries

Class here eastern Europe

Subdivisions are added for Russia and neighboring east European countries together, for Russia alone

SUMMARY

947.000 1–.000 9	**Standard subdivisions of eastern Europe**
.001–.009	**Standard subdivisions of Russia**
.01–.08	**Historical periods of Russia**
.5	**Caucasus**
.6	**Moldova**
.7	**Ukraine**
.8	**Belarus**
.9	**Lithuania, Latvia, Estonia**

.000 1–.000 8	Standard subdivisions of eastern Europe
	As modified under 930–990
.000 9	Historical periods; areas, regions, places; biography of eastern Europe
.000 901–.000 905	Historical periods

Add to base number 947.00090 the numbers following —090 in notation 0901–0905 from Table 1, e.g., eastern Europe during the Middle Ages 947.000902

.000 91–.000 99	Areas, regions, places in general; biography
	As modified under 930–990

.001–.009   Standard subdivisions of Russia

               As modified under 930–990

>   947.01–947.08 Historical periods of Russia

               Class comprehensive works in 947

.01   Early history to 862

               Including 9th century

                 For 862–899, see 947.02

.02   Period of Kievan Rus, 862–1240

.03   Period of Tatar suzerainty, 1240–1462

               Including 13th century, 15th century

               Class here 14th century

                 For 1200–1240, see 947.02; for 1462–1499, see 947.041

.04   1462–1689

.041   Reign of Ivan III, 1462–1505

.042   Reign of Basil III, 1505–1533

.043   Reign of Ivan IV (the Terrible), 1533–1584

               Including Livonian War, 1557–1582
                 (Option: Class Livonian War in 948.50322)

               Class here 16th century

                 For a specific part of 16th century not provided for here, see the part, e.g., 1505–1533 947.042

.044   Reigns of Theodore I and Boris Godunov, 1584–1605

.045   Time of Troubles, 1605–1613

               Including reigns of False Dmitri I and False Dmitri II

.046   Period of House of Romanov, 1613–1917

                 For reigns of specific Romanovs, see 947.047–947.083

.047   Reign of Michael, 1613–1645

               Class here 17th century

                 For a specific part of 17th century not provided for here, see the part, e.g., 1689–1699 947.05

.048   Reign of Alexis, 1645–1676

.049   Reigns of Theodore III and regent Sophia, 1676–1689

.05   Reign of Peter I (the Great), 1689–1725

               Including Great Northern War, 1700–1721
                 (Option: Class Great Northern War in 948.04 or 948.50345)

.06	1725–1796

Class here 18th century

For 1700–1725, see 947.05; for 1796–1799, see 947.071

.061	Reigns of Catherine I, Peter II, Anna, Ivan VI, 1725–1741
.062	Reigns of Elizabeth and Peter III, 1741–1762
.063	Reign of Catherine II (the Great), 1762–1796
.07	1796–1855

Class here 19th century

For 1855–1900, see 947.08

.071	Reign of Paul I, 1796–1801
.072	Reign of Alexander I, 1801–1825

Including period of invasion by Napoleon, 1812

.073	Reign of Nicholas I, 1825–1855
.073 8	‡Crimean War, 1853–1856

(Option: Class in 941.081)

.08	1855–
.081	Reign of Alexander II, 1855–1881

Russo-Turkish War, 1877–1878, relocated to 949.60387

.082	Reign of Alexander III, 1881–1894
.083	Reign of Nicholas II, 1894–1917

(Option: Class here Russo-Japanese War; prefer 952.031)

.084	1917–1991

Class here 20th century; Communist period; comprehensive works on Union of Soviet Socialist Republics, 1923–1991

For 1900–1917, see 947.083; for 1953–1991, see 947.085. For a specific part of Union of Soviet Socialist Republics, see the part, e.g., Ukraine 947.7085

.084 1	Period of revolutions, Alexander Kerensky, Vladimir Il´ich Lenin, 1917–1924
.084 2	Period of Joseph Stalin, 1924–1953

(Option: Class here Russo-Finnish War; prefer 948.97032)

.085	1953–1991
.085 2	Periods of Georgi Malenkov, Nikolay Aleksandrovich Bulganin, Nikita Sergeevich Khrushchev, 1953–1964

‡Add as instructed under 940–990

.085 3	Period of Leonid Il´ich Brezhnev and Aleksey Nikolayevich Kosygin, 1964–1982
.085 4	Periods of ĪŪ. V. Andropov, K. U. Chernenko, and Mikhail Sergeevich Gorbachev, 1982–1991
.086	1991–

Class here comprehensive works on Commonwealth of Independent States, 1991–

For a specific part of Commonwealth of Independent States, see the part, e.g., Ukraine 947.7086

.086 1	Administration of Boris Nikolayevich Yeltsin, 1991–1999
.086 2	Administration of Vladimir Vladimirovich Putin, 1999–2008
.086 3	Administration of Dmitry Medvedev, 2008–

> **947.5–947.9 European countries of former Soviet Union other than Russia; Caucasus area of Russia**

Except for modifications shown under specific entries, add to each subdivision identified by † as follows:

07	1796–1855
	Class here period as part of Russia
	Add to 07 the numbers following 947.07 in 947.071–947.073, e.g., reign of Paul I 071
	For a period as part of Russia not provided for here, see the period, e.g., period during reign of Alexander II 081
08	1855–
081	Reign of Alexander II, 1855–1881
082	Reign of Alexander III, 1881–1894
083	Reign of Nicholas II, 1894–1917
084	1917–1953
	Class here 20th century
	For 1900–1917, see 083; for 1953–1991, see 085; for 1991–1999, see 086
0841	1917–1940
	Class here period of independent countries, ca. 1917–ca. 1920
0842	Period of Joseph Stalin, 1940–1953
085	1953–1991
	Class here period as part of Soviet Union, ca. 1920–1991
	For ca. 1920–1940, see 0841; for period of Joseph Stalin, 1940–1953, see 0842
0852	Periods of Georgi Malenkov, Nikolay Aleksandrovich Bulganin, Nikita Sergeevich Khrushchev, 1953–1964
0853	Period of Leonid Il´ich Brezhnev and Aleksey Nikolayevich Kosygin, 1964–1982
0854	Periods of ĪŪ. V. Andropov, K. U. Chernenko, and Mikhail Sergeevich Gorbachev, 1982–1991
086	1991–

Class comprehensive works in 947

.5   ***†Caucasus**

> (Option: Class here ancient Caucasus; prefer 939.53)

.52   *Caucasus area of Russia

.520 1–.520 8   Historical periods

> Add to base number 947.520 the numbers following 947.0 in 947.01–947.08, e.g., later 20th century 947.52085

.54   *†Azerbaijan

> (Option: Class here ancient Albania; prefer 939.534)

.56   *†Armenia

> Class comprehensive works on Armenia region in 956.62

.58   *†Georgia

> (Options: Class here ancient Iberia; prefer 939.536. Class here ancient Colchis; prefer 939.538)

.6   ***†Moldova**

> Moldova to ca. 640 relocated to 939.88

.7   ***†Ukraine**

> (Options: Class here ancient Black Sea region; prefer 939.5. Class here ancient Sarmatia; prefer 939.52)

.8   ***†Belarus**

.9   ***†Lithuania, Latvia, Estonia**

> Class here Baltic States

.93   *Lithuania

.930 6   Period of union with Poland, 1569–1795

.930 7–.930 8   †1795–

.96   *Latvia

.960 5–.960 6   1721–1796

> Add to base number 947.960 the numbers following 947.0 in 947.05–947.06, e.g., reign of Peter I 947.9605

.960 7–.960 8   †1796–

.98   *Estonia

.980 5–.980 6   1721–1796

> Add to base number 947.980 the numbers following 947.0 in 947.05–947.06, e.g., reign of Peter I 947.9805

---

*Add as instructed under 930–990

†Add historical periods as instructed under 947.5–947.9

.980 7–.980 8   †1796–

948   *Scandinavia

Class here northern Europe

SUMMARY

948.01–.07	**Historical periods**
.1	**Norway**
.2	**Southeastern Norway (Østlandet)**
.3	**Southwestern Norway (Sørlandet and Vestlandet)**
.4	**Central and northern Norway (Trøndelag and Nord-Norge)**
.5	**Sweden**
.6	**Southern Sweden (Götaland)**
.7	**Central Sweden (Svealand)**
.8	**Northern Sweden (Norrland)**
.9	**Denmark and Finland**

> 948.01–948.07 Historical periods

Class comprehensive works in 948

.01   Early history to ca. 800

For ancient history to 481, see 936.8

(.012)   Ancient history to 481

(Optional number; prefer 936.8)

.02   Medieval period, ca. 800–1523

For 1387–1523, see 948.03

.022   Viking period, ca. 800–ca. 1050

Including 11th century

For ca. 1050–1099, see 948.023

.023   Ca. 1050–1387

.03   1387–1523

Class here period of Union of Kalmar, 1397–1523

.04   1523–1814

(Option: Class here Great Northern War; prefer 947.05)

.05   1814–1905

.06   1905–1999

.061   1905–1939

.062   1940–1945

*Add as instructed under 930–990
†Add historical periods as instructed under 947.5–947.9

.063	1945–1969
.064	1970–1999
.07	2000–
.071	2000–2019
.071 1	2000–2009
.071 2	2010–2019

.1 ***Norway**

> *For southeastern Norway, see 948.2; for southwestern Norway, see 948.3; for central and northern Norway, see 948.4*

.101 Early history to 1536

> Including period of Union of Kalmar, 1397–1523

> Class here medieval period

> *For ancient history to 481, see 936.81*

(.101 2) Ancient history to 481

> (Optional number; prefer 936.81)

.101 4 Viking period, ca. 800–ca. 1050

> Including 11th century

> *For ca. 1050–1099, see 948.101*

.102 Period of union with Denmark, 1536–1814

> Including 16th century

> *For 1500–1536, see 948.101*

.103 Period of union with Sweden, 1814–1905

.103 1	1814–1884
.103 6	1884–1905
.104	1905 1999
.104 1	1905–1945
.104 3	1945–1969
.104 4	1970–1999
.105	2000–
.105 1	2000–2019
.105 11	2000–2009
.105 12	2010–2019

*Add as instructed under 930–990

.2 ***Southeastern Norway (Østlandet)**

.201–.205   Historical periods

> Add to base number 948.20 the numbers following 948.10 in
> 948.101–948.105, e.g., Viking period 948.2014

.3 ***Southwestern Norway (Sørlandet and Vestlandet)**

.301–.305   Historical periods

> Add to base number 948.30 the numbers following 948.10 in
> 948.101–948.105, e.g., Viking period 948.3014

.4 ***Central and northern Norway (Trøndelag and Nord-Norge)**

.401–.405   Historical periods

> Add to base number 948.40 the numbers following 948.10 in
> 948.101–948.105, e.g., Viking period 948.4014

.5 ***Sweden**

> *For southern Sweden, see 948.6; for central Sweden, see 948.7; for northern
> Sweden, see 948.8*

.501   Early history to 1523

> Class here medieval period
>
> *For ancient history to 481, see 936.85*

(.501 2)   Ancient history to 481

> (Optional number; prefer 936.85)

.501 4   Viking period, ca. 800–ca. 1050

> Including 11th century
>
> *For ca. 1050–1099, see 948.5018*

.501 8   Ca. 1050–1523

.501 81   Ca. 1050–1397

.501 82   Period of Union of Kalmar, 1397–1523

.503   1523–1809

.503 2   Period of Vasa, 1523–1611

> Class here comprehensive works on period of House of Vasa,
> 1523–1654
>
> *For 1611–1654, see 948.5034*

.503 21   Reign of Gustav I Vasa, 1523–1560

.503 22   Reign of Erik XIV, 1560–1568

> (Option: Class here Livonian War; prefer 947.043)

*Add as instructed under 930–990

.503 23	Reign of John III, 1568–1592
.503 24	Reign of Sigismund III, 1592–1599
.503 25	Reign of Charles IX, 1599–1611
.503 4	Age of Greatness, 1611–1718
.503 41	Reign of Gustav II Adolf, 1611–1632
.503 42	Reign of Christina, 1632–1654
.503 43	Reign of Charles X Gustav, 1654–1660
.503 44	Reign of Charles XI, 1660–1697
.503 45	Reign of Charles XII, 1697–1718

(Option: Class here Great Northern War; prefer 947.05)

.503 6	Age of Freedom, 1718–1772

Class here 18th century

For 1700–1718, see 948.5034; for 1772–1799, see 948.5038

.503 61	Reign of Ulrika Eleonora, 1719–1720
.503 62	Reign of Fredrik I, 1720–1751
.503 63	1751–1772

Class here reign of Adolf Fredrik, 1751–1771

.503 8	Gustavian Period, 1772–1809
.503 81	Reign of Gustav III, 1772–1792
.503 82	Reign of Gustav IV Adolf, 1792–1809
.504	1809–1905
.504 1	1809–1872

Including reigns of Charles XIII, 1809–1818; Charles XIV John, 1818–1844; Oscar I, 1844–1859; Charles XV, 1859–1872; Riksdag Act, 1866

.504 2	Reign of Oscar II, 1872–1907

For reign of Oscar II during 1905–1907, see 948.5051

.505	1905–1999
.505 1	1905–1945

Class here reign of Gustav V, 1907–1950

For reign of Gustav V during 1945–1950, see 948.5053

.505 3	1945–1969

Class here reign of Gustav VI Adolf, 1950–1973

For reign of Gustav VI Adolf during 1970–1973, see 948.5054

.505 4   1970–1999

> Class here Carl XVI Gustaf, 1973 to present

> *For reign of Carl XVI Gustaf, 2000 to present, see 948.506*

.506   2000–

.6   *Southern Sweden (Götaland)

.601–.606   Historical periods

> Add to base number 948.60 the numbers following 948.50 in 948.501–948.506, e.g., period of House of Vasa 948.6032

.7   *Central Sweden (Svealand)

.701–.706   Historical periods

> Add to base number 948.70 the numbers following 948.50 in 948.501–948.506, e.g., period of House of Vasa 948.7032

.8   *Northern Sweden (Norrland)

.801–.806   Historical periods

> Add to base number 948.80 the numbers following 948.50 in 948.501–948.506, e.g., period of House of Vasa 948.8032

.9   Denmark and Finland

.900 1–.900 9   Standard subdivisions of Denmark

> As modified under 930–990

>   948.901–948.906   Historical periods of Denmark

> Class comprehensive works in 948.9

.901   Early history to 1387

> Class here medieval period

> *For ancient history to 481, see 936.89; for 1387–1536, see 948.902*

(.901 2)   Ancient history to 481

> (Optional number; prefer 936.89)

.901 3   481–ca. 800

.901 4   Viking period, ca. 800–ca. 1050

> Including 11th century

> *For ca. 1050–1099, see 948.9015*

---

*Add as instructed under 930–990

.901 5	Ca. 1050–1387
	Class here period of Estrith dynasty, 1047–1448
	For 1387–1448, see 948.902
.902	Period of union with Norway and Sweden, 1387–1536
	Class here period of Union of Kalmar, 1397–1523
.903	Period of union with Norway, 1536–1814
	Including 16th century
	For Great Northern War, see 947.05; for 1500–1536, see 948.902
.904	1814–1906
	(Option: Class here Schleswig-Holstein War; prefer 943.076)
.905	1906–1999
.905 1	1906–1945
.905 3	1945–1969
.905 4	1970–1999
.906	2000–
.906 1	2000–2019
.906 11	2000–2009
.906 12	2010–2019
.97	*Finland
.970 1	Early history to end of Swedish rule, 1809
	For Great Northern War, see 947.05
.970 2	Period of Russian rule, 1809–1917
.970 3	1917–
.970 31	1917–1939
.970 32	1939–1945
	Including Russo-Finnish War, 1939–1940
	(Option: Class Russo-Finnish War in 947.0842)
.970 33	1945–1982
.970 34	1982–

949   Other parts of Europe

*Add as instructed under 930–990

SUMMARY

.1   ***Northwestern islands**

.12   *Iceland

.120 1   Early history to 1262

Including 13th century

For 1262–1299, see 949.1202

.120 2   Medieval period, 1262–1550

Including 16th century

For 1550–1599, see 949.1203

.120 3   1550–1874

Including 19th century

For 1874–1899, see 949.1204

.120 4   Period of Governors, 1874–1904

.120 5   1904–1999

Including independence under Danish crown, 1918–1944; period of Republic, 1944–1999

.120 6   2000–

Class here comprehensive works on period of Republic, 1944 to present

For period of Republic, 1944–1999, see 949.1205

.15   †Faeroes

.2   ***Netherlands**

Class here comprehensive works on Low Countries, on Benelux countries

For southern Low Countries, see 949.3

.201   Early history to 1477

For ancient history to 486, see 936.92

---

*Add as instructed under 930–990
†Add as instructed under 930–990; however, do not add historical periods

(.201 2)	Ancient history to 486
	(Optional number; prefer 936.92)
.202	Period of House of Habsburg, 1477–1568
	Including 16th century
	For 1568–1599, see 949.203
.203	Period of struggle for independence, 1568–1648
.204	Period of Dutch Republic, 1648–1795
	Including Anglo-Dutch Wars, 1652–1653, 1665–1667; Great Wars against England, France, and allies, 1672–1678; Coalition War, 1690–1697; 17th century (Option: Class Anglo-Dutch Wars in 941.06)
	For 1600–1648, see 949.203
.205	1795–1830
	Including Batavian Republic, 1795–1806; Kingdom of Holland, 1806–1813
	Class here Napoleonic era
.206	1830–1901
	Class here 19th century
	For 1800–1830, see 949.205
.207	1901–
.207 1	Reign of Wilhelmina, 1890–1948
	For reign of Wilhelmina during 1890–1901, see 949.206
.207 2	Reign of Juliana, 1948–1980
.207 3	Reign of Beatrix, 1980–
.3	***Belgium and Luxembourg**
	Subdivisions are added for Belgium and Luxembourg together, for Belgium alone
.301	Early history to 1477
	For ancient history to 486, see 936.93
(.301 2)	Ancient history to 486
	(Optional number; prefer 936.93)
.302	Period of foreign rule, 1477–1830

*Add as instructed under 930–990

.303	1830–1909

Class here 19th century

For 1800–1830, see 949.302

.304	1909–
.304 1	Reign of Albert I, 1909–1934
.304 2	Reign of Léopold III, 1934–1951
.304 3	Reign of Baudouin I, 1951–1993
.304 4	Reign of Albert II, 1993–
.35	*Luxembourg
.350 1	Early history to 1482

For ancient history to 486, see 936.935

(.350 12)	Ancient history to 486

(Optional number; prefer 936.935)

.350 2	Period of foreign rule, 1482–1830
.350 3	1830–1890

Class here 19th century

For 1800–1830, see 949.3502; for 1890–1899, see 949.35041

.350 4	1890–
.350 41	1890–1918
.350 42	1918–1945
.350 43	1945–1999

Class here 20th century

For 1900–1918, see 949.35041; for 1918–1945, see 949.35042

.350 44	2000–
.4	***Switzerland**
.401	Early history to 1291

For ancient history to 486, see 936.94

(.401 2)	Ancient history to 486

(Optional number; prefer 936.94)

.402	1291–1499
.403	1499–1648

*Add as instructed under 930–990

.404		1648–1798
		Including 17th century
		For 1600–1648, see 949.403
.405		Napoleonic period, 1798–1815
		Class here Helvetic Republic, 1798–1803
.406		1815–1900
.406 2		Period of restoration, 1815–1848
.406 3		1848–1900
.407		1900–
.407 1		1900–1918
.407 2		1918–1945
.407 3		1945–1999
		Class here 20th century
		For 1900–1918, see 949.4071; for 1918–1945, see 949.4072
.407 4		2000–
.5	***Greece**	
.501		Early history to 717
		For ancient history to 323, see 938
(.501 2)		Ancient history to 323
		(Optional number; prefer 938)
		Add to base number 949.5012 the numbers following 938.0 in 938.01–938.09, e.g., Persian Wars 949.50123
.501 3		Early Byzantine period, 323–717
		Including wars against Avars and Persians
		Class here Eastern Roman (Byzantine) Empire, 323–717
.502		Middle Byzantine period, 717–1081
		Class here comprehensive works on Byzantine Empire
		For early Byzantine period, see 949.5013; for late Byzantine period, see 949.503. For a specific part of Byzantine Empire, see the part, e.g., Byzantine Empire in Egypt 932.023
.503		Late Byzantine period, 1081–1204
		Including Fourth Crusade, 1202–1204

*Add as instructed under 930–990

.504	Period of Latin and Greek states and Turkish conquest, 1204–1453
	Including 15th century
	For 1453–1499, see 949.505
.505	Period of Turkish domination, 1453–1821
.506	War of Independence, 1821–1830
.507	1830–
.507 1	1830–1833
.507 2	Period of monarchy, 1833–1924
	Including Greco-Turkish War, 1896–1897
	Class here 19th century
	For Balkan Wars, see 949.6039. For a specific part of 19th century not provided for here, see the part, e.g., 1821–1830 949.506
.507 3	Period of Republic, 1924–1935
.507 4	The period of the restoration of the monarchy, 1935–1967
	Class here 20th century
	For a specific part of 20th century not provided for here, see the part, e.g., 1974–1999 949.5076
.507 5	Period of military junta, 1967–1974
.507 6	Period of restoration of democratic rule, 1974–
.58	*Former Aegean Islands region (Aigaio Nēsoi periphereia)
.580 1	Early history to 717
	Number built according to instructions under 930–990
	For ancient history to 323, see 939.1
(.580 12)	Ancient history to 323
	(Optional number; prefer 939.1)
	Add to base number 949.58012 the numbers following 938.0 in 938.01–938.09, e.g., mythical age to 775 B.C. 949.580121
.59	*Crete region (Krētē periphereia)
.590 1	Early history to 827
	For ancient history to 323, see 939.18

*Add as instructed under 930–990

(.590 12)	Ancient history to 323
	(Optional number; prefer 939.18)
	Add to base number 949.59012 the numbers following 938.0 in 938.01–938.09, e.g., mythical age to 775 B.C. 949.590121
.590 13	First Byzantine period, 323–827
.590 2	Period of Arab rule, 827–961
	Including 9th century, 10th century
	For 800–827, see 949.59013; for 961–999, see 949.5903
.590 3	Second Byzantine period, 961–1206
.590 4	Period of Venetian rule, 1206–1669
	Including 17th century
	For 1669–1699, see 949.5905
.590 5	Period of Turkish domination, 1669–1898
.590 6	Period of autonomy, 1898–1913
.590 7	1913–
.590 72	Period of incorporation into Greece, 1913–1924
.590 73–.590 76	1924–
	Add to base number 949.5907 the numbers following 949.507 in 949.5073–949.5076, e.g., restoration of monarchy 949.59074

.6 ***Balkan Peninsula**

For ancient history to ca. 640, see 939.8

(.601)	Ancient history to ca. 640
	(Optional number; prefer 939.8)
.602	Ca. 640–1362
	Class here 14th century
	For 1362–1399, see 949.6031
.603	Period of Ottoman Empire, 1362–1913
.603 1	Period of conquest by Ottoman Empire, 1362–1529
.603 8	Period of national liberation, 1804–1912
.603 87	‡Russo-Turkish War, 1877–1878 [*formerly* 947.081]
.603 9	‡Balkan Wars, 1912–1913
.604	1913–1991

*Add as instructed under 930–990
‡Add as instructed under 940–990

.604 8	Communist period, 1945–1991
.605	1991–
.61	*Turkey in Europe (Eastern Thrace)
.610 1	Early history to 1918
.610 11–.610 14	Early history to 1453

> Add to base number 949.6101 the numbers following 949.50 in 949.501–949.504, e.g., period of Byzantine prosperity, 717–1081 949.61012
>
> *For ancient history to 323, see 939.8*

.610 15	1453–1918

> Class here period of Ottoman empire, 1453–1922
>
> *For 1918–1922, see 949.61023*

.610 2–.610 4	1918–

> Add to base number 949.610 the numbers following 956.10 in 956.102–956.104, e.g., 1918–1923 949.61023

.65	*Albania
.650 1	Early history to 1912

> *For ancient history to 323, see 939.8*

(.650 12)	Ancient history to 323

> (Optional number; prefer 939.8)

.650 2	1912–1946
.650 3	1946–1992

> Class here period of People's Republic, 1946–1991; 20th century
>
> *For a specific part of 20th century not provided for here, see the part, e.g., 1912–1946 949.6502*

.650 4	1992–
.7	***Serbia, Croatia, Slovenia, Bosnia and Hercegovina, Montenegro, Macedonia**
.701	Early history to 1918

> *For ancient history to ca. 640, see 939.87; for Balkan Wars, see 949.6039*

(.701 2)	Ancient history to ca. 640

> (Optional number; prefer 939.87)

*Add as instructed under 930–990

.702	Yugoslavia, 1918–1991
	Class here comprehensive works on former Yugoslavia, 20th century
	For 1900–1918, see 949.701; for 1991–1999, see 949.703; for Yugoslavia (1991–2003), see 949.7103
.702 1	Period of Kingdom, 1918–1939
	Class 1939–1941 in 949.7022
.702 2	Period of World War II, 1939–1945
.702 3	Administration of Josip Broz Tito, 1945–1980
.702 4	1980–1991
.703	Period as sovereign nations, 1991–
	See also 949.71031 for Yugoslavia (1991–2003)
.71	*Serbia
.710 1	Early history to 1918
	For ancient history to ca. 640, see 939.87
(.710 11)	Ancient history to ca. 640
	(Optional number; prefer 939.87)
.710 12	Ca. 640–1389
.710 13	Turkish period, 1389–1878
	For 1804–1878, see 949.71014
.710 14	Period of revolt and autonomy, 1804–1878
	Class here 19th century
	For 1800–1804, see 949.71013; for 1878–1899, see 949.71015
.710 15	Period of independence, 1878–1918
.710 2	1918–1991
	Class here 20th century
	Add to base number 949.7102 the numbers following 949.702 in 949.7021–949.7024, e.g., period of World War II 949.71022
	For 1900–1918, see 949.71015; for 1991–1999, see 949.7103
.710 3	1991–
.710 31	1991–2006
	Class here Yugoslavia (1991–2003), Serbia and Montenegro (2003–2006)
	Class Yugoslavia (1918–1991) in 949.702
	For Montenegro, see 949.745

*Add as instructed under 930–990

| .710 315 | ‡Kosovo Civil War, 1998–1999 |
| .710 32 | 2006– |

| .72 | *Croatia |
| .720 1–.720 3 | Historical periods |

> Add to base number 949.720 the numbers following 949.70 in 949.701–949.703, e.g., period of World War II 949.72022

| .73 | *Slovenia |
| .730 1–.730 3 | Historical periods |

> Add to base number 949.730 the numbers following 949.70 in 949.701–949.703, e.g., period of World War II 949.73022

.74	*Bosnia and Hercegovina, Montenegro
.742	*Bosnia and Hercegovina
.742 01–.742 03	Historical periods

> Add to base number 949.7420 the numbers following 949.70 in 949.701–949.703, e.g., period of World War II 949.742022

| .745 | *Montenegro |
| .745 01–.745 02 | Historical periods |

> Add to base number 949.7450 the numbers following 949.70 in 949.701–949.702, e.g., period of World War II 949.745022

| .745 03 | 1991– |
| .745 031 | 1991–2006 |

> Class here period as part of Yugoslavia (1991–2003), Serbia and Montenegro (2003–2006)

> Class comprehensive works on Yugoslavia (1991–2003), on Serbia and Montenegro (2003–2006) in 949.71031

| .745 032 | 2006– |

| .76 | *Macedonia |
| .760 1–.760 3 | Historical periods |

> Add to base number 949.760 the numbers following 949.70 in 949.701–949.703, e.g., period of World War II 949.76022

| **.8** | ***Romania** |
| .801 | Early history to 1861 |

> *For ancient history to ca. 640, see 939.88*

| (.801 2) | Ancient history to ca. 640 |

> (Optional number; prefer 939.88)

---

*Add as instructed under 930–990
‡Add as instructed under 940–990

.801 3	Ca. 640–1250
	Including 13th century
	For 1250–1299, see 949.8014
.801 4	Period of Wallachia and Moldavia principalities, 1250–ca. 1500
.801 5	Turkish period, ca. 1500–1821
	Including reign of Michael the Brave, 1593–1601; Phanarist period, 1711–1821
.801 6	1821–1861
	Class here 19th century
	For 1800–1821, see 949.8015; for 1861–1899, see 949.802
.802	Period of monarchy, 1861–1947
	Class here period of Kingdom, 1881–1947; 20th century
	For Balkan Wars, see 949.6039; for 1947–1999, see 949.803
.803	1947–
.803 1	Period of People's Republic, 1947–1989
.803 2	1989–
.83	*Black Sea area
	For early history to 640, see 939.51
.9	***Bulgaria**
.901	Early history to 1878
	For ancient history to ca. 640, see 939.89
(.901 2)	Ancient history to ca. 640
	(Optional number; prefer 939.89)
.901 3	Ca. 640–1018
	Class here First Bulgarian Empire, ca. 680–1014
.901 4	Period of Byzantine rule and Second Bulgarian Empire, 1018–1396
.901 5	Turkish period, 1396–1878
.902	1878–1946
	Class here 20th century
	For 1946–1999, see 949.903
.902 2	1878–1918
	For Balkan Wars, see 949.6039
.902 3	1918–1946

*Add as instructed under 930–990

.903	1946–

.903 1   Period of People's Republic, 1946–1991

.903 2   1991–

950   History of Asia

SUMMARY

950.01–.09	Standard subdivisions
.1–.4	[Historical periods]
951	China and adjacent areas
952	Japan
953	Arabian Peninsula and adjacent areas
954	India and neighboring south Asian countries
955	Iran
956	Middle East (Near East)
957	Siberia (Asiatic Russia)
958	Central Asia
959	Southeast Asia

.01–.09   Standard subdivisions

As modified under 930–990

.1   **Early history to 1162**

Including 12th century

For 1162–1199, see 950.21

.2   **1162–1480**

Class here Mongol Empire

.21   1162–1227

Class here reign of Genghis Khan, ca. 1200–1227

.22   1227–1294

Class here reign of Kublai Khan, ca. 1259–1294; 13th century

For 1200–1227, see 950.21; for 1294–1299, see 950.23

.23   1294–1336

.24   1336–1405

Class here reign of Timur (Tamerlane), ca. 1358–1405; 14th century

For 1300–1336, see 950.23

.25   1405–1480

Class here 15th century

For 1400–1405, see 950.24; for 1480–1499, see 950.3

.3   **Period of European exploration and penetration, 1480–1905**

.4   **1905–**

.41	1905–1945
.42	1945–1999

Class here 20th century

For 1900–1905, see 950.3; for 1905–1945, see 950.41

.424	1945–1949
.425	1950–1959
.426	1960–1969
.427	1970–1979
.428	1980–1989
.429	1990–1999
.43	2000–
.431	2000–2019
.431 1	2000–2009
.431 2	2010–2019

951   *China and adjacent areas

Subdivisions are added for China and adjacent areas together, for China alone

---

>   951.01–951.06 Historical periods of China and adjacent areas together, of China alone

Class comprehensive works in 951

.01	Early history to 960

For ancient history to 420, see 931

(.011–.014)	Ancient history to 420

(Optional numbers; prefer 931)

Add to base number 951.01 the numbers following 931.0 in 931.01–931.04, e.g., Shang dynasty 951.012

.015	Period of Northern and Southern dynasties, 420–581
.016	Period of Sui dynasty, 581–618
.017	Period of Tang dynasty, 618–907
.018	Period of Five dynasties and Ten kingdoms, 907–960

Class here 10th century

For 900–907, see 951.017; for 960–999, see 951.024

.02	960–1644

*Add as instructed under 930–990

.024	Period of Song dynasty, 960–1279
.025	1279–1368

Class here period of Yuan (Mongol) dynasty, 1271–1368; 14th century

For period of Yuan dynasty during 1271–1279, see 951.024; for 1368–1399, see 951.026

.026	Period of Ming dynasty, 1368–1644
.03	Period of Qing (Manchu) dynasty, 1644–1912
.032	1644–1795

Including 17th century

For 1600–1644, see 951.026

.033	1796–1850

Including Opium War, 1840–1842

Class here 19th century

For 1850–1864, see 951.034; for 1864–1899, see 951.035

.034	Period of Taiping Rebellion, 1850–1864
.035	1864–1911

Including Sino-Japanese War, 1894–1895; Boxer Rebellion, 1899–1901 (Option: Class Sino-Japanese War in 952.031)

.036	Period of Revolution of 1911–1912
.04	Period of Republic, 1912–1949
.041	1912–1927
.042	Period of nationalist government, 1927–1949

Including Sino-Japanese Conflict during 1937–1941 (Option: Class Sino-Japanese Conflict during 1937–1941 in 952.033)

Class comprehensive works on Sino-Japanese Conflict, 1937–1945, in 940.53

.05	Period of People's Republic, 1949–

Class here 20th century

For 2000 to present, see 951.06. For a specific part of 20th century not provided for here, see the part, e.g., Revolution of 1911–1912 951.036

.055	1949–1959
.056	1960–1969

Including Cultural Revolution

.057	1970–1979
.058	1980–1989
.059	1990–1999

.06	2000–
.061	2000–2019
.061 1	2000–2009
.061 2	2010–2019
.2	***Southeastern China and adjacent areas**
.24	*East China Sea area
.249	*Taiwan (Formosa) and adjacent islands
.249 02	Early history to 1683

For ancient history to 420, see 931.249

.249 03	Chinese period, 1683–1895
.249 04	Japanese period, 1895–1945
.249 05	Period of Republic of China (Nationalist China), 1945–

Including 20th century

For 1900–1945, see 951.24904

.25	*Hong Kong
.250 1–.250 3	Chinese period to 1843

Add to base number 951.250 the numbers following 951.0 in 951.01–951.03, e.g., period of Ming dynasty 951.25026

.250 4	Period as a British dependency, 1843–1997

Including 19th century

For 1800–1843, see 951.25033; for 1945–1997, see 951.2505

.250 5	1945–1997
.250 6	Period as part of People's Republic, 1997–
.26	*Macau

For ancient history to 420, see 931

.260 1–.260 3	Chinese period to 1849

Add to base number 951.260 the numbers following 951.0 in 951.01–951.03, e.g., period of Ming dynasty 951.26026

.260 4	Period as an overseas territory of Portugal, 1849–1999
.260 6	Period as part of People's Republic, 1999–
.7	***Mongolia**
.73	†Outer Mongolia (Mongolian People's Republic)

*Add as instructed under 930–990
†Add as instructed under 930–990; however, do not add historical periods

.9   ***Korea**

.901   Early history to 1392

.902   Period of Yi dynasty, 1392–1910

.903   Japanese period, 1910–1945

.904   1945–1999

       Class here 20th century

        For 1900–1910, see 951.902; for 1910–1945, see 951.903

.904 1   1945–1950

.904 2   ‡Korean War, 1950–1953

.904 3   1953–1999

.905   2000–

.93   ***North Korea (People's Democratic Republic of Korea)**

.930 1   Early history to 1392

.930 2   Period of Yi dynasty, 1392–1910

.930 3   Japanese period, 1910–1945

.930 4   1945–1994

       Class here 20th century

        For 1900–1910, see 951.9302; for 1910–1945, see 951.9303; for 1994–1999, see 951.93051

.930 41   1945–1950

.930 42   Period of Korean War, 1950–1953

.930 43   Administration of Kim Il-sŏng, 1948–1994

        For administration of Kim Il-sŏng during 1948–1950, see 951.93041; for administration of Kim Il-sŏng during 1950–1953, see 951.93042

.930 5   1994–

.930 51   Administration of Kim Chŏng-il, 1994–

.95   ***South Korea (Republic of Korea)**

.950 1   Early history to 1392

.950 2   Period of Yi dynasty, 1392–1910

.950 3   Japanese period, 1910–1945

---

*Add as instructed under 930–990
‡Add as instructed under 940–990

.950 4	1945–1998
	Class here 20th century
	For 1900–1910, see 951.9502; for 1910–1945, see 951.9503; for 1998–1999, see 951.9505
.950 41	1945–1950
.950 42	Period of Korean War, 1950–1953
.950 43	1953–1979
	Class here administration of Park Chung Hee, 1962–1979
.950 44	1979–1998
.950 5	1998–
	Including administration of Kim Dae Jung, 1998–2003

952 *Japan

.01	Early history to 1185
.02	Feudal period, 1185–1868
	Class here chūsei period
.021	Kamakura period, 1185–1334
.022	Namboku period, 1334–1392
	Class here 14th century
	For 1300–1334, see 952.021; for 1392–1399, see 952.023
.023	Muromachi period, 1392–1573
	Including 16th century
	For 1573–1599, see 952.024
.024	Momoyama period, 1573–1603
.025	Tokugawa (Edo) period, 1603–1868
	Including 19th century
	Class here kinsei period
	For 1868–1899, see 952.031. For a specific part of kinsei period not provided for here, see the part, e.g., 1945–1999 952.04
.03	1868–1945
.031	Meiji period, 1868–1912
	Including Russo-Japanese War, 1904–1905 (Option: Class Russo-Japanese War in 947.083)
	(Option: Class here Sino-Japanese War, 1894–1895; prefer 951.035)

*Add as instructed under 930–990

| .032 | Taishō period, 1912–1926 |
| .033 | Shōwa period, 1926–1989 |

Class here 20th century

For Shōwa period during 1945–1989, see 952.04. For a specific part of 20th century not provided for here, see the part, e.g., Russo-Japanese War, 1904–1905 952.031

(Option: Class here Sino-Japanese Conflict, 1937–1941; prefer 951.042)

.04	1945–1999
.044	1945–1949
.045	1950–1959
.046	1960–1969
.047	1970–1979
.048	1980–1989
.049	1990–1999

Class here Heisei period, 1989 to present

For Heisei period in 1989, see 952.048; for 2000 to present, see 952.05

.05	2000–
.051	2000–2019
.051 1	2000–2009
.051 2	2010–2019

953   *Arabian Peninsula and adjacent areas

For ancient history to 622, see 939.49

| (.01) | Ancient history to 622 |

(Optional number; prefer 939.49)

>   953.02–953.05 Historical periods of Arabian Peninsula and adjacent areas together, of Arabian Peninsula alone

Class comprehensive works in 953

| .02 | 622–1517 |

Including Arabia Deserta, 622–637 [*formerly* 939.47]

| .03 | Period of Ottoman Empire, 1517–1740 |

Class period of struggles to overthrow Turks in 953.04

*Add as instructed under 930–990

.04	1740–1926

         Including 18th century

         Class here period of struggles to overthrow Turks, 1740–1918

            For 1700–1740, see 953.03

.05	1926–
.052	1926–1964

         Class here 20th century

            For 1900–1926, see 953.04; for 1964–1999, see 953.053

.053	1964–1999
.054	2000–
.1	***Sinai Peninsula**
.101–.105	Historical periods

         Add to base number 953.10 the numbers following 962.0 in 962.01–962.05, e.g., period of Ottoman Empire 953.103

         For ancient history to 622, see 939.48

.3	***Yemen**

         For ancient history to 622, see 939.49

(.301)	Ancient history to 622

         (Optional number; prefer 939.49)

.302	622–1517
.303	Period of Ottoman Empire, 1517–1740

         Class period of struggles to overthrow Turks in 953.304

.304	1740–1918

         Including 18th century

            For 1700–1740, see 953.303

.305	1918–
.305 2	1918–1990

         Class here 20th century

            For 1900–1918, see 953.304; for 1990–1999, see 953.3053

.305 3	Period as Republic of Yemen, 1990–
.32	***Northern Yemen**

         For ancient history to 622, see 939.49

*Add as instructed under 930–990

(.320 1)		Ancient history to 622
		(Optional number; prefer 939.49)
.320 2–.320 4		622–1918

Add to base number 953.320 the numbers following 953.30 in 953.302–953.304, e.g., 1740–1918 953.3204

.320 5		1918–
.320 52		1918–1990

Including Yemen Arab Republic, 1962–1990

Class here 20th century

For 1900–1918, see 953.3204; for 1990–1999, see 953.32053

.320 53   Period as part of Republic of Yemen, 1990–

.35   *Southern Yemen

For ancient history to 622, see 939.49

(.350 1)   Ancient history to 622

(Optional number; prefer 939.49)

.350 2   622–1517

.350 3   1517–1839

.350 4   British period, 1839–1967

Including 19th century, 20th century

For 1800–1839, see 953.3503; for 1967–1990, see 953.35052; for 1900–1999, see 953.35053

.350 5   1967–

.350 52   1967–1990

Class here People's Democratic Republic of Yemen, 1970–1990

.350 53   Period as part of Republic of Yemen, 1990–

.5   **†Oman and United Arab Emirates**

For ancient history to 622, see 939.49

.53   †Oman

For ancient history to 622, see 939.49

(Option: Class here Oman to 622; prefer 939.49)

---

*Add as instructed under 930–990
†Add as instructed under 930–990; however, do not add historical periods

.57	†United Arab Emirates

For ancient history to 622, see 939.49

(Option: Class here United Arab Emirates to 622; prefer 939.49)

.6	**†Persian Gulf States**

For ancient history to 622, see 939.49; for Oman and United Arab Emirates, see 953.5

(Option: Class here Persian Gulf States to 622; prefer 939.49)

.63	†Qatar

For ancient history to 622, see 939.49

(Option: Class here Qatar to 622; prefer 939.49)

.65	†Bahrain

For ancient history to 622, see 939.49

(Option: Class here Bahrain to 622; prefer 939.49)

.67	†Kuwait

For ancient history to 622, see 939.49

(Options: Class here Kuwait to 622; prefer 939.49. Class here Persian Gulf Crisis and War, 1990–1991; prefer 956.70442)

.8	***Saudi Arabia**

For ancient history to 622, see 939.49

(.801)	History to 622

(Optional number; prefer 939.49)

.802–.805	622–

Add to base number 953.80 the numbers following 953.0 in 953.02–953.05, e.g., 1740–1926 953.804

.805 3	1964–1999

Number built according to instructions under 953.802–953.805

Class military operations in Saudia Arabia during Persian Gulf Crisis and War, 1990–1991, in 956.704424

954   *India and neighboring south Asian countries

Class here south Asia

Subdivisions are added for India and neighboring south Asian countries together, for India alone

For history of India to 647, see 934

---

*Add as instructed under 930–990

†Add as instructed under 930–990; however, do not add historical periods

SUMMARY

954.02	**647–1785**	
.03	**Period of British rule, 1785–1947**	
.04	**1947–1971**	
.05	**1971–**	
.9	**Other jurisdictions**	

(.01)   Ancient history to 647

(Optional number; prefer 934)

Add to base number 954.01 the numbers following 934.0 in 934.01–934.07, e.g., reign of Aśoka 954.0145

.02   647–1785

.021   647–997

Including 7th century

For 600–647, see 934.07

.022   Period of Muslim conquests, 997–1206

.022 3   Period of Ghazni dynasty, 997–1196

.022 5   Period of Ghor dynasty, 1196–1206

.023   1206–1414

.023 2   Period of slave kings of Delhi, 1206–1290

.023 4   Period of Khalji dynasty, 1290–1320

.023 6   Period of Tughluk dynasty, 1320–1414

.024   1414–1526

.024 2   Period of Sayyid dynasty, 1414–1451

.024 5   Period of Lodi dynasty, 1451–1526

.025   Period of Mogul Empire, 1526–1707

.025 2   Reign of Babur, 1526–1530

.025 3   Reign of Humayun, 1530–1556

.025 4   Reign of Akbar, 1556–1605

Class here 16th century

For a specific part of 16th century not provided for here, see the part, e.g., 1500–1526 954.0236

.025 6   Reign of Jahangir, 1605–1627

.025 7   Reign of Shahjahan, 1628–1658

.025 8	Reign of Aurangzeb, 1658–1707
	Class here 17th century
	For a specific part of 17th century not provided for here, see the part, e.g., 1605–1627 954.0256
.029	Period of European penetration, 1707–1785
.029 2	1707–1744
.029 4	Period of Anglo-French conflict, 1744–1757
	Including Battle of Plassey, 1757
.029 6	1757–1772
	Including governorship of Lord Clive, 1757–1767
.029 8	Governorship of Warren Hastings, 1772–1785
.03	Period of British rule, 1785–1947
	For governorship of Lord Clive, see 954.0296; for governorship of Warren Hastings, see 954.0298
.031	Period of East India Company, 1785–1858
	Class here 19th century
	For 1858–1899, see 954.035
.031 1	Governorships of Sir John Macpherson, Marquis Cornwallis (first term), John Shore (Lord Teignmouth), 1785–1798
.031 2	Governorships of Marquess Wellesley, Marquess Cornwallis (second term), Sir George Barlow, 1798–1807
.031 3	Governorships of 1st Earl of Minto, Marquess of Hastings, Earl Amherst, 1807–1828
.031 4	Governorships of Lord Bentinck, Baron Metcalfe, Earl of Auckland, 1828–1842
.031 5	Governorships of Earl of Ellenborough and Viscount Hardinge, 1842–1848
.031 6	Governorship of Marquis of Dalhousie, 1848–1856
.031 7	Governorship of Earl Canning, 1856–1862
	Including Sepoy Mutiny, 1857–1858
	For governorship of Earl Canning during 1858–1862, see 954.0351
.035	Period of control by crown, 1858–1947
	Class here period of Indian national movement, 1885–1947; 20th century
	For 1947–1971, see 954.04; for 1971–1999, see 954.05
.035 1	Governorships of Earl Canning, 8th Earl of Elgin, Baron Lawrence, 1858–1868

.035 2	Governorships of Earl of Mayo and Earl of Northbrook, 1869–1876
.035 3	Governorships of Earl of Lytton and Marquess of Ripon, 1876–1884
.035 4	Governorships of Marquis of Dufferin and Marquess of Lansdowne, 1884–1894
.035 5	Governorships of 9th Earl of Elgin and Marquis of Curzon, 1894–1905
.035 6	Governorships of 4th Earl of Minto and Baron Hardinge, 1905–1916
.035 7	Governorships of Viscount Chelmsford and Marquess of Reading, 1916–1926
.035 8	Governorships of Earl of Halifax and Marquess of Willingdon, 1926–1936
.035 9	Governorships of Marquess of Linlithgow, Earl of Wavell, Earl Mountbatten, 1936–1947

.04   1947–1971

.042   Prime ministership of Jawaharlal Nehru, 1947–1964

.043   Prime ministership of Lal Bahadur Shastri, 1964–1966

         (Option: Class here Indo-Pakistan War, 1965; prefer 954.9045)

.045   First prime ministership of Indira Gandhi, 1966–1977

         For first prime ministership of Indira Gandhi during 1971–1977, see 954.051

.05   1971–

.051   Later half of first prime ministership of Indira Gandhi, 1971–1977

         (Option: Class here Indo-Pakistan War, 1971; prefer 954.92051)

.052   1977–1999

         Including prime ministerships of Morarji Desai, 1977–1979; of Charan Singh, 1979; of Rajiv Gandhi, 1984–1989; of Vishwanath Pratap Singh, 1989–1990; of Chandra Shekhar, 1990–1991; of P. V. Narasimha Rao, 1991–1999; second prime ministership of Indira Gandhi, 1980–1984

.053   1999–

.053 1   Prime ministership of Atal Bihari Vajpayee, 1999–2004

.053 2   2004–

         Including prime ministership of Manmohan Singh, 2004–

.9   **Other jurisdictions**

         Class here Pakistan (West and East, 1947–1971)

.900 1–.900 9   Standard subdivisions of Pakistan (West and East, 1947–1971)

         As modified under 930–990

(.901)	History of Pakistan (West and East, 1947–1971) to 647

(Optional number; prefer 934.9)

Add to base number 954.901 the numbers following 934.0 in 934.01–934.07, e.g., reign of Aśoka 954.90145

> 954.902–954.905 Historical periods of Pakistan (West and East, 1947–1971)

Class comprehensive works in 954.9

For ancient history to 647, see 934.9

(Option: Class early history to 647 in 954.901; prefer 934.9)

.902–.903	647–1947

Add to base number 954.90 the numbers following 954.0 in 954.02–954.03, e.g., period of East India Company 954.9031

.904	1947–1971
.904 2	Administration of Mahomed Ali Jinnah, 1947–1948
.904 3	1948–1958
.904 5	Administration of Mohammad Ayub Khan, 1958–1969

Including Indo-Pakistan War, 1965
(Option: Class Indo-Pakistan War, 1965, in 954.043)

.904 6	Administration of Aga Muhammad Yahya Khan, 1969–1971
.905	1971–
.91	*Pakistan
(.910 1)	Ancient history to 647

(Optional number; prefer 934.91)

Add to base number 954.9101 the numbers following 934.0 in 934.01–934.07, e.g., reign of Aśoka 954.910145

> 954.910 2–954.910 5 Historical periods of Pakistan

Class comprehensive works in 954.91

For ancient history to 647, see 934.91

(Option: Class early history to 647 in 954.9101; prefer 934.91)

.910 2–.910 3	647–1947

Add to base number 954.910 the numbers following 954.0 in 954.02–954.03, e.g., period of East India Company 954.91031

*Add as instructed under 930–990

.910 4	1947–1971
	Add to base number 954.9104 the numbers following 954.904 in 954.9042–954.9046, e.g., administration of Mahomed Ali Jinnah 954.91042
.910 5	1971–
	For Indo-Pakistan War, 1971, see 954.9205
.910 51	1971–1988
.910 52	1988–1999
.910 53	1999–
.92	*Bangladesh
(.920 1)	Ancient history to 647
	(Optional number; prefer 934.92)
	Add to base number 954.9202 the numbers following 934.0 in 934.01–934.07, e.g., reign of Aśoka 954.920145

>   954.920 2–954.920 5   Historical periods of Bangladesh

Class comprehensive works in 954.92

For ancient history to 647, see 934.92

(Option: Class early history to 647 in 954.9201; prefer 934.92)

.920 2–.920 3	647–1947
	Add to base number 954.920 the numbers following 954.0 in 954.02–954.03, e.g., period of East India Company 954.92031
.920 4	1947–1971
	Add to base number 954.9204 the numbers following 954.904 in 954.9042–954.9046, e.g., administration of Mahomed Ali Jinnah 954.92042
.920 5	1971–
.920 51	‡Indo-Pakistan War, 1971
	(Option: Class Indo-Pakistan War, 1971, in 954.051)
.93	*Sri Lanka
.930 1	Early history to 1795
.930 2	British period, 1795–1948
	Including 20th century
	For 1948–1972, see 954.93031; for 1972–1999, see 954.93032

*Add as instructed under 930–990
‡Add as instructed under 940–990

.930 3	1948–
.930 31	Period as independent Commonwealth state, 1948–1972
.930 32	Period as republic, 1972–
.95	†Maldives
.96	†Nepal
.98	†Bhutan

955   *Iran

For early history to 637, see 935.7

(.01)   Early history to 637

          (Optional number; prefer 935.7)

          Add to base number 955.01 the numbers following 935.0 in 935.01–935.07, e.g., period of Sassanian Empire 955.017

.02   637 1499

.022   Period of Arab domination, 637–1055

          Including 7th century, 11th century

              For 600–637, see 935.07; for 1055–1099, see 955.024

              See Manual at 930–990: Add table: Centuries

.024   Period of Turkish domination, 1055–1219

.026   Period of Mongol domination, 1219–1335

.028   1335–1499

          Including 14th century

          Class here period of Turkoman domination, 1405–1499

              For 1300–1335, see 955.026

.03   Period of Persian dynasties, 1499–1794

.04   1794–1906

.05   1906–2005

.051   1906–1925

.052   Reign of Reza Shah Pahlavi, 1925–1941

.053   Reign of Mohammed Reza Pahlavi, 1941–1979

.054   1979–2005

*Add as instructed under 930–990
†Add as instructed under 930–990; however, do not add historical periods

.054 2	‡Period of Ruhollah Khomeini, 1979–1989
	Class here Iraqi-Iranian Conflict, 1980–1988
	(Option: Class Iraqi-Iranian Conflict in 956.70441)
.054 3	1989–1997
.054 4	Administration of Muḥammad Khātamī, 1997–2005
.06	2005–
.061	Administration of Mahmoud Ahmadinejad, 2005–
.23	*Māzandarān province
	For early history to 637, see 939.6
(.230 1)	Early history to 637
	(Optional number; prefer 939.6)
	Class here Hyrcania

956   *Middle East (Near East)

SUMMARY

956.01–.05	[Historical periods]
.1	Turkey
.2	Western Turkey
.3	North central Turkey
.4	South central Turkey
.5	East central Turkey
.6	Eastern Turkey
.7	Iraq
.9	Syria, Lebanon, Cyprus, Israel, Jordan

.01	Early history to 1900
	For ancient history to ca. 640, see 939.4
(.012)	Ancient history to ca. 640
	(Optional number; prefer 939.4)
	Add to base number 956.012 the numbers following 939.40 in 939.401–939.405, e.g., Hellinistic period 956.0124
.013	640–1000
	Including 7th century
	For 600–640, see 939.405
.014	Period of Seljuk supremacy, 1000–1300
	Including First Crusade, 1096–1099; Second Crusade, 1147–1149; Third Crusade, 1189–1192

*Add as instructed under 930–990
‡Add as instructed under 940–990

.015	1300–1900

Class here Ottoman Empire, ca. 1300–1922

*For 1900–1918, see 956.02; for 1918–1922, see 956.03. For a
specific part of the Ottoman Empire, see the part, e.g., Ottoman
Empire in Turkey 956.1015*

.02	1900–1918
.03	1918–1945
.04	1945–1980

Class here 20th century

*For 1900–1918, see 956.02; for 1918–1945, see 956.03; for 1980–1999,
see 956.05*

.042	Israel-Arab War, 1948–1949
.044	Sinai Campaign, 1956
.046	Israel-Arab War, 1967 (Six Days' War)
.048	Israel-Arab War, 1973 (Yom Kippur War)
.05	1980–
.052	Israel-Lebanon-Syria Conflict, 1982–1985
.053	1985–1999
.054	2000–
.1	***Turkey**

For divisions of Turkey, see 956.2–956.6

.101	Early history to 1918

For ancient history to ca. 640, see 939.2

(.101 2)	Ancient history to ca. 640

(Optional number; prefer 939.2)

.101 3	640–1100

Including 7th century

For 600–640, see 939.2

.101 4	Period of Seljuk dynasty, 1100–1300
.101 5	1300–1918

Class here period of Ottoman Empire, 1300–1922

For 1918–1922, see 956.1023

*Add as instructed under 930–990

.101 51	1300–1451
	Including 15th century
	For 1451–1499, see 956.10152
.101 52	1451–1566
	Including 16th century
	For 1566–1599, see 956.10153
.101 53	1566–1774
	Including 18th century
	For 1774–1799, see 956.10154
.101 54	1774–1918
	For Russo-Turkish War, 1877–1878, see 949.60387
.102	1918–1950
	Class here 20th century; period of Republic, 1923 to present
	For 1900–1918, see 956.1015; for 1950–1999, see 956.103
.102 3	1918–1923
.102 4	Administration of Kemal Atatürk, 1923–1938
.102 5	Administration of İsmet İnönü, 1938–1950
.103	1950–1999
.103 5	1950–1959
.103 6	1960–1969
.103 7	1970–1979
.103 8	1980–1989
.103 9	1990–1999
.104	2000–
.104 1	2000–2019
.104 11	2000–2009
.104 12	2010–2019

>   **956.2–956.6 Divisions of Turkey**

Class comprehensive works in 956.1

For Turkey in Europe, see 949.61

.2   *Western Turkey

> *For history of western Turkey to 640, see 939.2. For history of a specific part of western Turkey to 640, see the part in 939, e.g., history of Troy 939.21*

(Option: Class history of a specific part of western Turkey to 640 with the part in 956.2, e.g., history of Troy 956.22)

.201–.204   Historical periods

> Add to base number 956.20 the numbers following 956.10 in 956.101–956.104, e.g., period of Ottoman Empire 956.2015

.3   *North central Turkey

> *For history of north central Turkey to 640, see 939.3. For history of a specific part of western Turkey to 640, see the part in 939, e.g., history of Paphlagonia 939.317*

(Option: Class history of a specific part of north central Turkey to 640 with the part in 956.3, e.g., history of Paphlagonia 956.37)

.301–.304   Historical periods

> Add to base number 956.30 the numbers following 956.10 in 956.101–956.104, e.g., period of Ottoman Empire 956.3015

.4   *South central Turkey

> *For history of south central Turkey to 640, see 939.2. For history of a specific part of south central Turkey to 640, see the part in 939, e.g., history of Cappadocia to 640 939.34*

(Option: Class history of a specific part of south central Turkey to 640 with the part in 956.4, e.g., history of Cappadocia to 640 956.41)

.401–.404   Historical periods

> Add to base number 956.40 the numbers following 956.10 in 956.101–956.104, e.g., period of Ottoman Empire 956.4015

.5   *East central Turkey

> *For history of east central Turkey to 640, see 939.33. For history of a specific part of east central Turkey to 640, see the part in 939, e.g., history of Commagene 939.36*

(Option: Class history of a specific part of east central Turkey to 640 with the part in 956.5, e.g., history of Commagene 956.52)

.501–.504   Historical periods

> Add to base number 956.50 the numbers following 956.10 in 956.101–956.104, e.g., period of Ottoman Empire 956.5015

*Add as instructed under 930–990

.6   ***Eastern Turkey**

> *For history of eastern Turkey to 640, see 939.42. For history of a specific part of eastern Turkey to 640, see the part in 939, e.g., history of ancient kingdom of Armenia 939.55*

> (Option: Class history of a specific part of eastern Turkey to 640 with the part in 956.6, e.g., history of ancient kingdom of Armenia 956.62012)

.601–.604   Historical periods

> Add to base number 956.60 the numbers following 956.10 in 956.101–956.104, e.g., period of Ottoman Empire 956.6015

.62   Northeastern Turkey

> Number built according to instructions under 930–990

> Class here comprehensive works on Armenia region

> *For country of Armenia, see 947.56*

(.620 12)   Ancient history to 640

> (Optional number; prefer 939.55)

.620 154   1774–1918

> Number built according to instructions under 930–990

> Including Armenian massacres, 1894–1896, 1915–1916

.620 23   1918–1923

> Number built according to instructions under 930–990

> Class here Republic of Armenia, 1918–1920

.7   ***Iraq**

> *For history to 637, see 935*

(.701)   Ancient history to 637

> (Optional number; prefer 935)

> Add to base number 956.701 the numbers following 935.0 in 935.01–935.07, e.g., Hellenistic period 956.7016

.702   637–1553

> Including 7th century, 16th century

> *For 600–637, see 935.07; for 1553–1600, see 956.703*

> *See Manual at 930–990: Add table: Centuries*

.703   Period of Ottoman Empire, 1553–1920

.704   1920–

---

*Add as instructed under 930–990

.704 1	Period of mandate, 1920–1932
	Class here reign of Faysal I, 1921–1933
	For reign of Faysal I during 1932–1933, see 956.7042
.704 2	Period of independent monarchy, 1932–1958
	Including reigns of Ghazi I, Faisal II
.704 3	Period of Republic, 1958–
	For administration of Saddam Hussein, see 956.7044
.704 4	1979–
	Class here administration of Saddam Hussein, 1979–2003
.704 41	1979–1990
	(Option: Class here Iraqi-Iranian Conflict, 1980–1988; prefer 955.0542)
.704 42	‡Persian Gulf Crisis and War, 1990–1991
	Class here Iraq-Kuwait Crisis, 1990–1991, Persian Gulf War, 1991
	(Option: Class in 953.67)
.704 423 1	Participation of specific groups of countries
	Number built according to instructions under 940–990
	For participation of specific countries, see 956.7044234–956.7044239
.704 423 12	Participation of Arab countries
.704 43	‡1991–
	Class here Iraq War, 2003 to present; period of occupation and reconstruction, 2003 to present

.9   *Syria, Lebanon, Cyprus, Israel, Jordan

.901–.905	Early history to present
	Add to base number 956.90 the numbers following 956.0 in 956.01–956.05, e.g., 1945–1980 956.904
.91	*Syria
	For early history to ca. 640, see 939.43
(.910 1)	Early history to ca. 640
	(Optional number; prefer 939.43)

*Add as instructed under 930–990
‡Add as instructed under 940–990

.910 2	640–1516
	Including 7th century
	For 600–640, see 939.43
.910 3	Period of Ottoman Empire, 1516–1920
.910 4	1920–
.910 41	Period of mandate, 1920–1945
.910 42	Period of Republic, 1945–
	Including period as a part of United Arab Republic, 1958–1961
	Class Israel-Arab War, 1948–1949, in 956.042; class Israel-Arab War, 1967, in 956.046; class Israel-Arab War, 1973, in 956.048; class Israel-Lebanon-Syria Conflict, 1982–1985, in 956.052; class comprehensive works on United Arab Republic in 962.053
.92	*Lebanon
	For early history to ca. 640, see 939.44
(.920 2)	Early history to ca. 640
	Class here Phoenicia
	(Optional number; prefer 939.44)
.920 3	640–1926
.920 32	640–1517
	Including 7th century
	For 600–640, see 939.44
.920 34	Period of Ottoman Empire, 1517–1920
	Including period of autonomy, 1861–1918
.920 35	Period of mandate, 1920–1941
	For 1926–1941, see 956.92042
.920 4	1926–
	Class here 20th century
	For 1900–1920, see 956.92034; for 1920–1926, see 956.92035
.920 42	1926–1941
.920 43	1941–
	Class Israel-Arab War, 1948–1949, in 956.042
	For 1975 to present, see 956.92044

*Add as instructed under 930–990

.920 44	‡Period of civil war and religious strife, 1975–1990
	Class here Civil War, 1975–1990
	Class Israel-Lebanon-Syria Conflict, 1982–1985, in 956.052
.920 45	1990–
.920 451	1990–2006
.920 452	‡Lebanon War, 2006
.920 453	2006–
.93	*Cyprus
.930 1	Early history to 1571
	Including 16th century
	For ancient history to ca. 640, see 939.37; for 1571–1599, see 956.9302
(.930 12)	Ancient history to ca. 640
	(Optional number; prefer 939.37)
.930 2	1571–1878
.930 3	British period, 1878–1960
	Class here 20th century
	For 1960–1999, see 956.9304
.930 4	1960–
.94	*Palestine; Israel
	For early history of Palestine to 70, see 933; for early history of Israel to 70, see 933.4
	See also 320.54095694 for Zionism; also 909.04924 for world history of Jews
(.940 1)	Early history to 70
	(Optional number; prefer 933 for Palestine to 70; prefer 933.4 for Israel to 70)
	Add to base number 956.9401 the numbers following 933.0 in 933.01–933.05, e.g., age of Solomon 956.94012
.940 2	Mishnaic and Talmudic periods, 70–640
.940 3	640–1917
.940 31	640–1096
	Including 7th century
	For 600–640, see 956.9402

*Add as instructed under 930–990
‡Add as instructed under 940–990

.940 32	Period of Crusades, 1096–1291
.940 33	Mameluke period, 1291–1517
.940 34	Period of Ottoman Empire, 1517–1917
.940 4	Period of British control, 1917–1948
.940 5	1948–

Class here 20th century

For 1900–1917, see 956.9403; for 1917–1948, see 956.9404

.940 52	1948–1967

Class Israel-Arab War, 1948–1949, in 956.042; class Sinai Campaign, 1956, in 956.044; class Israel-Arab War, 1967, in 956.046

.940 53	1967–1974

Class Israel-Arab War, 1973, in 956.048

.940 54	1974–

Class Israel-Lebanon-Syria Conflict, 1982–1985, in 956.052

.949	*Darom district

For early history of Judah, Judaea portion of Darom district to 70, see 933.49; for early history of Edom portion of Darom district to 70, see 939.464

(.949 01)	Early history to 70

(Optional number; prefer 933.49 for Judah, Judaea; prefer 939.464 for Edom)

Including Edom, Judah, Judaea

.95	*Jordan and West Bank

Subdivisions are added for Jordan and West Bank together, for Jordan alone

For early history to 70, see 933.5

(.950 1)	Early history to 70

(Optional number; prefer 933.5)

Add to base number 956.9501 the numbers following 933.0 in 933.01–933.05, e.g., Roman period 956.95015

.950 2	70–640
.950 3	640–1923

Including 7th century, period of Ottoman Empire

For 600–640, see 956.9502

.950 4	1923–

*Add as instructed under 930–990

.950 42	Period of mandate, 1923–1946
.950 43	Period of Hashemite Kingdom, 1946–

 Class Israel-Arab War, 1948–1949, in 956.042; class Israel-Arab War, 1967, in 956.046

 For 1967 to present, see 956.95044

.950 44	1967–
.953	*Nablus district

 Class here comprehensive works on West Bank

 For a part of West Bank not provided for here, see the part, e.g., Hebron district 956.951

.956 3	*Karak Province

 For early history to 70, see 939.462

(.956 301)	Early history to 70

 (Optional number; prefer 939.462)

 Class here Moab

.957 7	*Ma'ān Province

 For early history to 70, see 939.48

(.957 701)	Early history to 70

 (Optional number; prefer 939.48)

 Class here Petra

957 *Siberia (Asiatic Russia)

.03	Pre-Russian period to 1581
.07	1581–1855
.08	1855–

 Add to base number 957.08 the numbers following 947.08 in 947.081–947.086, e.g., period of Siberia under Stalin 957.0842

958 *Central Asia

 For early history to ca. 640, see 939.6

 (Option: Class here early history to ca. 640; prefer 939.6)

.01–.04	Historical periods

 Add to base number 958.0 the numbers following 950 in 950.1–950.4, e.g., period of Mongol Empire 958.02

.1	*Afghanistan

*Add as instructed under 930–990

.101	Early history to 1221

For early history to ca. 640, see 939.6

(Option: Class here early history to ca. 640; prefer 939.6)

.102	1221–1709
.103	1709–1919
.104	1919–
.104 2	1919–1933
.104 3	Reign of Muhammad Zahir Shah, 1933–1973
.104 4	Period of Republic, 1973–1978
.104 5	Period of Democratic Republic, 1978–1992

Including 1991–1992 [*formerly* 958.1046]

.104 6	1992–2001

Class here Taliban period, 1996–2001

Period of Democratic Republic during 1991–1992 relocated to 958.1045

.104 7	‡2001–

Class here Afghan War, 2001 to present

.4   *Turkestan

For Turkmenistan, see 958.5; for Tajikistan, see 958.6; for Uzbekistan, see 958.7

.407	Pre-Russian period to 1855

Including 19th century

For early history to ca. 640, see 939.6; for 1855–1899, see 958.408

(Option: Class here early history to ca. 640; prefer 939.6)

.408	1855–

Add to base number 958.408 the numbers following 947.08 in 947.081–947.086, e.g., later 20th century 958.4085

.43	*Kyrgyzstan
.430 7	Pre-Russian period to 1855

Including 19th century

For 1855–1899, see 958.4308

*Add as instructed under 930–990
‡Add as instructed under 940–990

.430 8	1855–
	Add to base number 958.4308 the numbers following 947.08 in 947.081–947.086, e.g., later 20th century 958.43085
.45	*Kazakhstan
.450 7	Pre-Russian period to 1855
	Including 19th century
	For 1855–1899, see 958.4508
.450 8	1855–
	Add to base number 958.4508 the numbers following 947.08 in 947.081–947.086, e.g., later 20th century 958.45085

.5   *Turkmenistan

.507	Pre-Russian period to 1855
	Including 19th century
	For early history to ca. 640, see 939.6; for 1855–1899, see 958.508
	(Option: Class here early history to ca. 640; prefer 939.6)
.508	1855–
.508 1–.508 5	1855–1991
	Add to base number 958.508 the numbers following 947.08 in 947.081–947.085, e.g., later 20th century 958.5085
.508 6	1991–
.508 61	Administration of Saparmurad Niyazov, 1991–2006
.508 62	2006–

.6   *Tajikistan

.607	Pre-Russian period to 1855
	Including 19th century
	For early history to ca. 640, see 939.6; for 1855–1899, see 958.608
	(Option: Class here early history to ca. 640; prefer 939.6)
.608	1855–
	Add to base number 958.608 the numbers following 947.08 in 947.081–947.086, e.g., later 20th century 958.6085

.7   *Uzbekistan

*Add as instructed under 930–990

.707   Pre-Russian period to 1855

         Including 19th century

            For early history to ca. 640, see 939.6; for 1855–1899, see 958.708

         (Option: Class here early history to ca. 640; prefer 939.6)

.708   1855–

         Add to base number 958.708 the numbers following 947.08 in 947.081–947.086, e.g., later 20th century 958.7085

959   *Southeast Asia

SUMMARY

959.01–.05	**[Historical periods]**
.1	**Myanmar**
.3	**Thailand**
.4	**Laos**
.5	**Malaysia, Brunei, Singapore**
.6	**Cambodia**
.7	**Vietnam**
.8	**Indonesia and East Timor**
.9	**Philippines**

.01   Early history to 1499

.02   1500–1699

.03   1700–1799

.04   1800–1899

.05   1900–

.051   1900–1941

         Class here 20th century

            For 1941–1945, see 959.052; for 1945–1999, see 959.053

.052   Period of Japanese occupation, 1941–1945

.053   1945–1999

.054   2000–

.1   *Myanmar

.102   Early history to 1826

.103   Period of British conquest, 1826–1885

         Class here 19th century

            For 1800–1826, see 959.102; for 1886–1899, see 959.104

---

*Add as instructed under 930–990

.104	Period of British rule, 1886–1948
	Class here 20th century
	For 1948–1999, see 959.105
.105	1948–
.105 1	1948–1962
.105 2	1962–1989
.105 3	1989–
.3	***Thailand**
.302	Early history to 1782
.302 1	Early history to 1219
.302 2	Period as Sukhothai, 1219–1350
	Including 14th century
	For 1350–1399, see 959.3023
.302 3	Period as Ayutthaya, 1350–1767
	Including 18th century
	For 1767–1782, see 959.3024; for 1782–1799, see 959.3031
.302 4	Reign of Tāk Sin, 1767–1782
.303	1782–1910
.303 1	Reign of Phutthayǭtfā Čhulālōk (Rama I), 1782–1809
.303 2	Reign of Phutthalœtlā Naphālai (Rama II), 1809–1824
.303 3	Reign of Nangklao (Rama III), 1824–1851
.303 4	Reign of Mongkut (Rama IV), 1851–1868
.303 5	Reign of Chulalongkorn (Rama V), 1868–1910
.304	1910–
.304 1	Reign of Vajiravudh (Rama VI), 1910–1925
.304 2	Reign of Prajadhipok (Rama VII), 1925–1935
.304 3	Reign of Ananda Mahidol (Rama VIII), 1935–1946
.304 4	Reign of Bhumibol Adulyadej (Rama IX), 1946–
.4	***Laos**
.403	Early history to 1949
	Including period as a part of French Indochina, 1893–1954
	For 1949–1954, see 949.4041

*Add as instructed under 930–990

.404	1949–

Class here 20th century

For 1900–1949, see 959.403

.404 1	1949–1975

Class military operations in Laos during Vietnamese War in 959.70434

.404 2	Period as People's Democratic Republic, 1975–
.5	***Malaysia, Brunei, Singapore**

Subdivisions are added for Malaysia, Brunei, Singapore together; for Malaysia alone

.503	Early history to 1946
.504	1946–1963
.505	Period of federation, 1963–

Class here 20th century

For 1900–1946, see 959.503; for 1946–1963, see 959.504; for 2003 to present, see 959.506

.505 1	Prime ministership of Tunku Abdul Rahman Putra Al-Haj, 1963–1970

Including separation of Singapore, 1965

.505 2	Prime ministership of Tun Haji Abdul Razak bin Dato' Hussein, 1971–1976
.505 3	Prime ministership of Datuk Hussein Onn, 1976–1981
.505 4	Prime ministership of Mahathir bin Mohamad, 1981–2003
.506	2003–
.506 1	Prime ministership of Abdullah bin Ahmad Haji Badawi, 2003–2009
.506 2	Prime ministership of Datuk Najib Tun Razak, 2009–
.55	*Brunei
.550 3	Early history to 1888
.550 4	Period as British protectorate, 1888–1983
.550 5	1984–
.57	*Singapore
.570 3	Early history to 1946
.570 4	1946–1963

*Add as instructed under 930–990

.570 5	1963–

.570 5 | 1963–

Class here 20th century; period as separate nation, 1965–

For 1900–1946, see 959.5703; for 1946–1963, see 959.5704

.570 51 | 1963–1990

Including period of federation with Malaysia, 1963–1965

Class here prime ministership of Lee Kuan Yew, 1959–1990

For prime ministership of Lee Kuan Yew during 1959–1963, see 959.5704

.570 52 | Prime ministership of Goh Chok Tong, 1990–2004

.570 53 | Prime ministership of Lee Hsien Loong, 2004–

.6   *Cambodia

.601 | Early history to 802

.602 | Period of Khmer Empire, 802–1431

.603 | 1431–1949

Including period as a part of French Indochina, 1863–1949; 15th century

.604 | 1949–

Class here 20th century

For 1900–1949, see 959.603

.604 1 | 1949–1970

Class military operations in Cambodia during Vietnamese War in 959.70434

.604 2 | 1970–1993

Including period as Khmer Republic, 1970–1979

Class here period as Kampuchea, 1979–1993

.604 3 | 1993–

.7   *Vietnam

.701 | Early history to 939 [*formerly* 959.703]

.702 | 939–1883 [*formerly* 959.703]

*Add as instructed under 930–990

.703	French period, 1883–1945

Class here comprehensive works on French Indochina

For Laos as a part of French Indochina, see 959.403; for Cambodia as a part of French Indochina, see 959.603; for Indochinese War, 1946–1954, see 959.7041

Early history to 939 relocated to 959.701; 939–1883 relocated to 959.702; 1945–1949 relocated to 959.7041

.704	1945–

Class here 20th century

For 1900–1945, see 959.703

.704 1	‡1945–1954

Class here 1945–1949 [*formerly* 959.703]; Indochinese War, 1946–1954

.704 2	1954–1961

Class comprehensive works on period of North Vietnam and South Vietnam, 1954–1975, in 959.7043

.704 3	‡Vietnamese War, 1961–1975

Class here comprehensive works on period of North Vietnam and South Vietnam, 1954–1975

For 1954–1961, see 959.7042

.704 33	Participation of specific groups of countries, of specific countries, localities, groups

Number built according to instructions under 940–990

Class military participation of specific countries, localities, groups in 959.70434. Class a specific activity with the activity, e.g., efforts to preserve or restore peace 959.70431

.704 331	North Vietnam
.704 332	South Vietnam
.704 332 2	National Liberation Front

Class here Vietcong

.704 332 5	Government forces
.704 334–.704 339	Participation of specific countries and localities

Number built according to instructions under 940–990

Add to base number 959.70433 notation 4–9 from Table 2, e.g., United States participation 959.7043373; however, for North Vietnam, see 959.704331; for South Vietnam, see 959.704332

.704 4	1975–

‡Add as instructed under 940–990

.8   ***Indonesia and East Timor**

> Subdivisions are added for Indonesia and East Timor together, for Indonesia alone

---

\>   959.801–959.804 Historical periods for Indonesia and East Timor together, for Indonesia alone

> Class comprehensive works in 959.8

.801   Early history to 1602

.801 1   Early history to 358 [*formerly* 959.8012]

.801 2   Period of Hindu kingdoms, 358–1478

> Early history to 358 relocated to 959.8011

.801 5   Period of Muslim rule, 1478–1602

.802   1602–1945

.802 1   Period of Dutch East India Company, 1602–1800

> Including 1798–1800 [*formerly* 959.8022]

.802 2   Periods under control of British and Netherlands governments, 1800–1945

> 1798–1800 relocated to 959.8021

.802 21   1800–1808

.802 22   Administration of Herman Willem Daendels, 1808–1811

.802 23   1811–1942

> Including Java War, 1825–1830

.802 24   Period of Japanese occupation, 1942–1945

.803   1945–1998

> Class here 20th century; period of Republic, 1950 to present
>
> *For 1900–1942, see 959.80223; for 1942–1945, see 959.80224; for 1998 to present, see 959.804*

.803 5   Administration of Soekarno, 1945–1967

> Including 1960–1967 [*formerly* 959.8036]; period as United States of Indonesia, 1949–1950

[.803 6]   1960–1969

> 1960–1967 relocated to 959.8035; 1967–1969 relocated to 959.8037

.803 7   Administration of Soeharto, 1967–1998

> Including 1967–1969 [*formerly* 959.8036]; 1980–1989 [*formerly* 959.8038]; 1990–1998 [*formerly* 959.8039]

*Add as instructed under 930–990

[.803 8]	1980–1989
	Relocated to 959.8037
[.803 9]	1990–1999
	1990–1998 relocated to 959.8037; administration of B. J. Habibie, 1998–1999 relocated to 959.8041
.804	1998–
.804 1	1998–2004
	Including administration of B. J. Habibie, 1998–1999 [*formerly* 959.8039]; administration of Abdurrahman Wahid, 1999–2001
	Class here administration of Megawati Soekarnoputri, 2001–2004
.804 2	Administration of Susilo Bambang Yudhoyono, 2004–
.86	*Lesser Sunda Islands (Nusa Tenggara)
.87	*East Timor
.870 1	Early history to 1520
.870 2	1520–1945
.870 3	1945–1999
	Class here 20th century
	For 1900–1945, see 959.8702
.870 31	1945–1975
.870 32	1975–1999
.870 4	1999–
	Class here period as Democratic Republic of East Timor, 2002–

.9   *Philippines

.901	Early history to 1564
	Including 16th century
	For 1564–1599, see 959.902
.902	Spanish period, 1564–1898
.902 7	Period of insurrection against Spanish, 1896–1898
.903	United States period, 1898–1946
	Class here 20th century
	For 1946–1999, see 959.904
.903 1	Philippine-American War, 1898–1901
.903 2	Period of United States rule, 1901–1935

*Add as instructed under 930–990

.903 5	Period of Commonwealth, 1935–1946
.904	Period of Republic, 1946–

For 2001 to present, see 959.905

.904 1	Administration of Manuel Roxas, 1946–1948
.904 2	Administration of Elpidio Quirino, 1948–1954
.904 3	Administration of Ramon Magsaysay, 1954–1957
.904 4	Administration of Carlos Garcia, 1957–1961
.904 5	Administration of Diosdado Macapagal, 1961–1965
.904 6	Administration of Ferdinand Marcos, 1965–1986
.904 7	Administration of Corazon Cojuangco Aquino, 1986–1992
.904 8	Administration of Fidel V. Ramos, 1992–1998
.904 9	Administration of Joseph Ejercito Estrada, 1998–2001
.905	2001–
.905 1	Administration of Gloria Macapagal-Arroyo, 2001–2010
.905 2	Administration of Benigno S. Aquino III, 2010–

960　History of Africa

SUMMARY

960.01–.09	**Standard subdivisions**
.1–.3	**[Historical periods]**
961	**Tunisia and Libya**
962	**Egypt and Sudan**
963	**Ethiopia and Eritrea**
964	**Morocco, Ceuta, Melilla, Western Sahara, Canary Islands**
965	**Algeria**
966	**West Africa and offshore islands**
967	**Central Africa and offshore islands**
968	**Republic of South Africa and neighboring southern African countries**
969	**South Indian Ocean islands**

.01–.09	Standard subdivisions

As modified under 930–990

.1	**Early history to 640**
.2	**640–1885**
.21	640–1450

Including 7th century, 15th century

For 600–640, see 960.1; for 1450–1499, see 960.22

See Manual at 930–990: Add table: Centuries

.22	1450–1799

.23	1800–1885
.3	**1885–**
.31	1885–1945

Class here 20th century

For 1945–1999, see 960.32

.312	1885–1914
.314	1914–1918
.316	1918–1945
.32	1945–1999
.324	1945–1949
.325	1950–1959
.326	1960–1969
.327	1970–1979
.328	1980–1989
.329	1990–1999
.33	2000–
.331	2000–2019
.331 1	2000–2009
.331 2	2010–2019

961   *Tunisia and Libya

Class here North Africa

For early history to ca. 640, see 939.7

(.01)	Early history to ca. 640

(Optional number; prefer 939.7)

Add to base number 961.01 the numbers following 939.70 in 939.701–939.705, e.g., Carthaginian periond 961.012

.02	Periods of Arab rule and Ottoman Empire, ca. 640–1830
.022	Period of Arab rule, ca. 640–ca. 1520

Including 7th century

For 600–ca. 640, see 939.705

.023	Period of Ottoman Empire, ca. 1520–1830

(Option: Class here Tripolitan War with the United States; prefer 973.47. Class here United States War with Algiers; prefer 973.53)

*Add as instructed under 930–990

.03	Period of European conquest and hegemony, 1830–1950

Including 19th century, 20th century

For 1800–1830, see 961.023; for 1950–1999, see 961.04

.04	1950–1999
.045	1950–1959
.046	1960–1969
.047	1970–1979
.048	1980–1989
.049	1990–1999
.05	2000–
.051	2000–2019
.051 1	2000–2009
.051 2	2010–2019
.1	***Tunisia**

For early history to 647, see 939.73

(.101)	Early history to 647

(Optional number; prefer 939.73)

Add to base number 961.101 the numbers following 939.730 in 939.7301–939.7305, e.g., Carthaginian period 961.1012

.102	Period of Arab rule, 647–1516

Including 7th century

For 600–647, see 939.7305

.103	Period of Ottoman Empire, 1516–1881
.104	1881–1956

Class here 20th century

For 1956–1999, see 961.105

.105	1956–
.105 1	Administration of Habib Bourguiba, 1956–1987
.105 2	Administration of Zayn al-ʿĀbidīn Bin ʿAlī, 1987–2011
.105 3	2011–
.2	***Libya**

For early history to 644, see 939.74; for Cyrenaica to 642, see 939.75; for Marmarica to 642, see 939.76

*Add as instructed under 930–990

(.201)	Early history to 644

(Optional number; prefer 939.74)

Add to base number 961.201 the numbers following 939.740 in 939.7401–939.7405, e.g., Carthaginian period 961.2012; however, for Cyrenaica, Marmarica to 642, see 961.2

.202	644–1911
.202 2	Period of Arab rule, 644–1551

Including 7th century, 16th century

For 600–644, see 939.7405; for 1551–1599, see 961.2024

See Manual at 930–990: Add table: Centuries

.202 4	Period of Ottoman Empire, 1551–1911
.203	Period of Italian rule, 1911–1952
.204	1952–

Class here 20th century

For 1900–1911, see 961.2024; for 1911–1952, see 961.203

.204 1	Reign of Idris I, 1952–1969
.204 2	Period of Muammar Qaddafi, 1969–

962   Egypt and Sudan

.000 1–.000 8	Standard subdivisions of Egypt and Sudan

As modified under 930–990

.000 9	Historical periods; areas, regions, places; collected biography of Egypt and Sudan
.000 901–.000 905	Historical periods

Add to base number 962.00090 the numbers following —090 in notation 0901–0905 from Table 1, e.g., Egypt and Sudan during 20th century 962.000904

.000 91–.000 99	Areas, regions, places in general; collected biography

As modified under 930–990

.001–.009	Standard subdivisions of Egypt

As modified under 930–990

(.01)	Early history to 640

(Optional number; prefer 932)

Add to base number 962.01 the numbers following 932.0 in 932.01–932.02, e.g., period of New Kingdom 962.0114

> 　　　　　　　962.02–962.05　Historical periods of Egypt

　　　　　　　　　Class comprehensive works in 962

　　　　　　　　　　For early history to 640, see 932

　　　　　　　　　　(Option: Class early history to 640 in 962.01; prefer 932)

.02　　　　　　　Period of Arab rule, 640–1517

　　　　　　　　　　Including 7th century

　　　　　　　　　　For 600–640, see 932.023

.024　　　　　　　Mameluke period, 1250–1517

.03　　　　　　　Period of Ottoman Empire, 1517–1882

.04　　　　　　　Period of British occupation and protectorate, 1882–1922

.05　　　　　　　1922–

.051　　　　　　　Reign of Fu'ād I, 1922–1936

.052　　　　　　　1936–1953

　　　　　　　　　　Class here reign of Faruk I, 1936–1952

　　　　　　　　　　Class Israel-Arab War, 1948–1949, in 956.042

.053　　　　　　　1953–1970

　　　　　　　　　　Including administration of Mohammed Naguib, 1953–1954; period of United Arab Republic, 1958–1961

　　　　　　　　　　Class here administration of Gamal Abdel Nasser, 1954–1970

　　　　　　　　　　Class Sinai Campaign, 1956, in 956.044; class Israel-Arab War, 1967, in 956.046

　　　　　　　　　　For Syrian part of United Arab Republic, see 956.91042

.054　　　　　　　Administration of Anwar Sadat, 1970–1981

　　　　　　　　　　Class Israel-Arab War, 1973, in 956.048

.055　　　　　　　Administration of Muḥammad Ḥusnī Mubārak, 1981–2011

.056　　　　　　　2011–

.4　　　*Sudan

　　　　　　　　　　For parts of Sudan, see 962.5–962.9

.401　　　　　　　Early history to 500

.402　　　　　　　500–1820

.402 2　　　　　　　Period of Christian kingdoms, 500–1504

.402 3　　　　　　　Period of Funj Sultanate, 1504–1820

*Add as instructed under 930–990

.403   Period as Anglo-Egyptian Sudan, 1820–1956

Including 20th century

Class here period of Egyptian and British rule

For 1956–1999, see 962.404

.404   1956–

.404 1   1956–1969

Class here Civil War of 1955–1972

.404 2   Administration of Ja'far Muḥammad Numayrī, 1969–1985

.404 3   1985–

Class here administration of Omar Hassan Ahmad al-Bashir, 1996 to present

---

> ### 962.5–962.9 Parts of Sudan

Class comprehensive works in 962.4

.5   ***Eastern and Northern regions of Sudan**

For early history to 500, see 939.78

(.501)   Early history to 500

(Optional number; prefer 939.78)

Class here ancient Ethiopia (a part of what is now modern Sudan, not modern Ethiopia), Nubia, Kush

See also 963.01 for ancient history of modern Ethiopia

.502–.504   500–

Add to base number 962.50 the numbers following 962.40 in 962.402–962.404, e.g., period of Christian kingdoms 962.5022

.6   ***Khartoum province and Central region of Sudan**

.601–.604   Historical periods

Add to base number 962.60 the numbers following 962.40 in 962.401–962.404, e.g., period as a part of Anglo-Egyptian Sudan 962.603

.7   ***Darfur region of Sudan**

.701–.704   Historical periods

Add to base number 962.70 the numbers following 962.40 in 962.401–962.404, e.g., period as a part of Anglo-Egyptian Sudan 962.703

.8   ***Kordofan region of Sudan**

*Add as instructed under 930–990

.801–.804   Historical periods

> Add to base number 962.80 the numbers following 962.40 in 962.401–962.404, e.g., period as a part of Anglo-Egyptian Sudan 962.803

.9   *Southern regions of Sudan

.901–.904   Historical periods

> Add to base number 962.90 the numbers following 962.40 in 962.401–962.404, e.g., period as a part of Anglo-Egyptian Sudan 962.903; however, for Civil War of 1955–1972, see 962.4041

963   *Ethiopia and Eritrea

> Subdivisions are added for Ethiopia and Eritrea together, for Ethiopia alone

---

> 963.01–963.07   Historical periods for Ethiopia and Eritrea together, for Ethiopia alone

> Class comprehensive works in 963

.01   Early history to 640

> *See also 939.78 for ancient Ethiopia (a part of what is now modern Sudan, not modern Ethiopia)*

.02   640–1543

> Including 7th century

> *For 600–640, see 963.01*

.03   1543–1855

> Including 16th century, 19th century

> *For 1500–1543, see 963.02; for 1855–1899, see 963.04*

> *See Manual at 930–990: Add table: Centuries*

.04   1855–1913

.041   Reign of Theodore II, 1855–1868

.042   1868–1889

> Class here reign of John IV, 1872–1889

.043   Reign of Menelik II, 1889–1913

> Including Ethiopian War, 1895–1896

.05   1913–1941

> Class here 20th century

> *For 1900–1913, see 963.043; for 1941–1974, see 963.06; for 1974–1999, see 963.07*

*Add as instructed under 930–990

.053	Reign of Lij Yasu, 1913–1916
.054	Period of Jah Rastafari (Haile Selassie) as regent and king, 1917–1930
.055	Reign of Haile Selassie (Jah Rastafari) as emperor, 1930–1974

> *For reign during 1935–1936, see 963.056; for reign during 1936–1941, see 963.057; for reign during 1941–1974, see 963.06*

.056	Italo-Ethiopian War, 1935–1936
.057	Period of Italian rule, 1936–1941
.06	1941–1974

Including deposition of Haile Selassie, 1974

.07	1974–
.071	1974–1991

Including Ogaden War, 1977–1978

Class here chairmanship of Mengistu Haile-Mariam, 1977–1991; Somali-Ethiopian conflicts, 1978–1991

1991–1993 relocated to 963.0721

.072	1991–
.072 1	1991–

Including 1991–1993 [*formerly* 963.071]

Class here prime ministership of Malas Zénāwi, 1995 to present

Class Somalia Civil War, 1991 to present, in 967.73053

.4 *Northern provinces

Number built according to instructions under 930–990

Including period of kingdom of Aksum

> *For period of kingdom of Aksum in Eritrea, see 963.501*

.5 *Eritrea

.501	Early history to 640
.502	640–1543

Including 7th century

> *For 600–640, see 963.501*

*Add as instructed under 930–990

.503	1543–1855

Including 16th century, 19th century

For 1500–1543, see 963.502; for 1855–1889, see 963.504; for 1889–1899, see 963.505

See Manual at 930–990: Add table: Centuries

.504	1855–1889
.504 1	Reign of Theodore II, 1855–1868
.504 2	1868–1889

Including reign of John IV, 1872–1889

.505	Period of Italian control, 1889–1941

Class here 20th century

For 1941–1952, see 963.506; for 1952–1999, see 963.507

.506	Period of British control, 1941–1952
.507	1952–
.507 1	Period of union with Ethiopia, 1952–1993
.507 2	1993–

964 *Morocco, Ceuta, Melilla, Western Sahara, Canary Islands

Subdivisions are added for Morocco, Ceuta, Melilla, Western Sahara, Canary Islands together; for Morocco alone

(.01)	Ancient history to 647

(Optional number; prefer 939.712)

Add to base number 964.01 the numbers following 939.7120 in 939.71201–939.71206, e.g., Roman period 964.014

> 964.02–964.05 Historical periods of Morocco

Class comprehensive works in 964

For early history to 647, see 939.712

(Option: Class early history to 647 in 964.01; prefer 939.712)

.02	Periods of Arab and Berber rule, 647–1830
.021	647–ca. 1050

Including 7th century, 11th century

For 600–647, see 939.71206; for ca. 1050–1099, see 964.023

See Manual at 930–990: Add table: Centuries

*Add as instructed under 930–990

.023	Ca. 1050–ca. 1550
	Including 16th century
	For ca. 1550–1599, see 964.025
.025	Ca. 1550–1830
.03	1830–1899
	Including Spanish-Moroccan War, 1859–1860 (Option: Class Spanish-Moroccan War in 946.072)
	Class here 19th century
	For 1800–1830, see 964.02
.04	1900–1956
	Class here 20th century; period of French and Spanish protectorates, 1912–1956; reign of Muḥammad V, 1927–1961
	For 1956–1999, see 964.05; for reign of Muḥammad V during 1956–1961, see 964.051
.05	1956–
.051	Later portion of reign of Muḥammad V, 1956–1961
.052	Reign of Hassan II, 1961–1999
.053	Reign of Mohammed VI, 1999–
.8	***Western Sahara**
.801	Early history to 1888
.802	Spanish period, 1888–1976
.803	Moroccan period, 1976–
	Including Moroccan and Mauritanian period, 1976–1979
.9	***Canary Islands**
.906	Early history to 1402
.907	Periods of French, Portuguese, Spanish rule, 1402–1927
.908	Period as Provinces of Spain, 1927–
	Class here 20th century
	For 1900–1927, see 964.907
.908 1	1927–1939
.908 2	Period of Francisco Franco, 1939–1975
	Add to base number 964.9082 the numbers following 946.082 in 946.0824–946.0827, e.g., 1960–1969 964.90826
.908 3	Reign of Juan Carlos I, 1975–

*Add as instructed under 930–990

965 *Algeria

For early history to 647, see 939.714

(.01) Early history to 647

(Optional number; prefer 939.714)

Add to base number 965.01 the numbers following 939.710 in 939.7101–939.7105, e.g., Roman period 965.014

.02 647–1830

.022 Periods of Arab and Berber rule, 647–1516

Including 7th century

For 600–647, see 939.7106

.024 Period of Ottoman Empire, 1516–1830

.03 Period of French rule, 1830–1962

Class here 19th century

For 1800–1830, see 965.024; for 1900–1962, see 965.04

.04 1900–1962

Class here 20th century

For 1962–1999, see 965.05

.046 ‡Period of Revolution, 1954–1962

.05 1962–

.051 1962–1965

.052 1965–1979

.053 Administration of Chadli Bendjedid, 1979–1992

.054 1992–

Class here administration of Abdelaziz Bouteflika, 1999 to present

.5 *Northeastern provinces

For early history to 647, see 939.72

(.501) Early history to 647

Class here Numidia

(Optional number; prefer 939.72)

Add to base number 965.501 the numbers following 939.720 in 939.7201–939.7206, e.g., Roman period 965.5014

*Add as instructed under 930–990
‡Add as instructed under 940–990

.7   ***Sahara provinces**

For early history to 647, see 939.77

(.701)   Early history to 647

Class here Gaetulia

(Optional number; prefer 939.77)

966   *West Africa and offshore islands

SUMMARY

966.01–.03	**Historical periods**	
.1	**Mauritania**	
.2	**Mali, Burkina Faso, Niger**	
.3	**Senegal**	
.4	**Sierra Leone**	
.5	**Gambia, Guinea, Guinea-Bissau, Cape Verde**	
.6	**Liberia and Côte d'Ivoire**	
.7	**Ghana**	
.8	**Togo and Benin**	
.9	**Nigeria**	

.01–.03   Historical periods

Add to base number 966.0 the numbers following 960 in 960.1–960.3, e.g., early history to 640 966.01

.1   ***Mauritania**

.101   Early history to 1903

.101 6   300–1200

Class here comprehensive works on period of Ghana Empire

For period of Ghana Empire in Mali history, see 966.2301

.101 7   1200–1500

Class here period of Mali Empire

.103   French period, 1903–1960

Class here 20th century

For 1900–1903, see 966.101; for 1960–1999, see 966.105

.105   1960–2005

.105 1   1960–1978

Class here administration of Mokhtar Ould Daddah, 1961–1978

.105 2   1978–1984

Class here administration of Khouna Ould Haidallah, 1980–1984

---

*Add as instructed under 930–990

.105 3	1984–2005

        Class here administration of Maawiya Ould Sid'Ahmed Taya, 1992–2005

.106	2005–
.2	***Mali, Burkina Faso, Niger**
.201	Early history to ca. 1900
.201 7	1200–1400

        Class here period of Mali Empire

        For period of Mali Empire in Mauritanian history, see 966.1017

.201 8	1400–1500

        Class here period of Songhai Empire

.202	French period, ca. 1900–1960

        Class here 20th century

        For 1960–1999, see 966.203

.203	1960–
.23	*Mali
.230 1	Early history to 1902

        Class comprehensive works on Mali Empire in 966.2017

.230 3	Period as French Sudan, 1902–1960

        Class here 20th century, French period

        For 1900–1902, see 966.2301; for 1960–1999, see 966.2305

.230 5	1960–
.230 51	1960–1991

        Class here administration of Moussa Traoré, 1968–1991

.230 52	1991–2002

        Class here administration of Alpha Oumar Konaré, 1992–2002

.230 53	Administration of Ahmadou Touré, 2002–
.25	*Burkina Faso
.250 1	Early history to 1897

        Including kingdom of Mossi

*Add as instructed under 930–990

.250 3	French period, 1897–1960

Class here 20th century; period as Upper Volta, 1919–1932 and 1947–1984

For 1960–1999, see 966.2505

.250 5	1960–
.250 51	1960–1983
.250 52	Administration of Thomas Sankara, 1983–1987
.250 53	Administration of Blaise Compaoré, 1987–
.26	*Niger
.260 1	Early history to 1900
.260 3	French period, 1900–1960

Class here 20th century

For 1960–1999, see 966.2605

.260 5	1960–
.260 51	Administration of Hamani Diori, 1960–1974
.260 52	1974–1999

Including administration of Seyni Kountché, 1974–1987

.260 53	Administration of Mamadou Tandja, 1999–2010
.260 54	2010–
.3	***Senegal**
.301	Early history to 1895

Including kingdom of Tekrur

.303	French period, 1895–1960

Class here 20th century

For 1960–1999, see 966.305

.305	1960–
.305 1	1960–2000

Including administration of Abdou Diouf, 1981–2000; Confederation of Senegambia, 1982–1989

For Gambian part of Senegambia, see 966.51031

.305 2	Administration of Abdoulaye Wade, 2000–
.4	***Sierra Leone**
.401	Early history to 1787

*Add as instructed under 930–990

.402	Period as a British colony, 1787–1896
.403	Period as both colony and protectorate, 1896–1961

> Class here 20th century
>
> *For 1961–1999, see 966.404*

.404	1961–2007
.404 1	1961–1971
.404 2	Administration of Siaka Probyn Stevens, 1971–1985
.404 3	Administration of Joseph Saidu Momoh, 1985–1992
.404 4	‡1992–1998

> Class here chairmanship of Valentine E. M. Strasser, 1992–1996; Sierra Leone civil war, 1991–2002
>
> *For Sierra Leone civil war during 1991–1992, see 966.4043*

.404 5	Administration of Amad Tejan Kabbah, 1998–2007
.405	2007–
.5	***Gambia, Guinea, Guinea-Bissau, Cape Verde**
.51	*Gambia
.510 1	Early history to 1807
.510 2	Period as a British colony, 1807–1965

> Class here 20th century
>
> *For 1965–1999, see 966.5103*

.510 3	1965–
.510 31	Administration of Dawda Kairaba Jawara, 1965–1994

> Including period as a part of Senegambia, 1982–1989
>
> Class comprehensive works on Senegambia in 966.305

.510 32	Administration of A. J. J. Jammeh, 1994–
.52	*Guinea
.520 1	Early history to 1882
.520 3	Period as French Guinea, 1882–1958

> Class here 20th century
>
> *For 1958–1999, see 966.5205*

.520 5	1958–
.520 51	Administration of Ahmed Sékou Touré, 1958–1984

*Add as instructed under 930–990

‡ Add as instructed under 940–990

.520 52	Administration of Lansana Conte, 1984–2008
.520 53	2008–

.57   *Guinea-Bissau

.570 1	Early history to 1879
.570 2	Period as Portuguese Guinea, 1879–1974
.570 3	1974–
.570 31	1974–1980
.570 32	First administration of João Bernardo Vieira, 1980–1999
.570 33	1999–2005
.570 34	Second administration of João Bernardo Vieira, 2005–2009
.570 35	2009–

.58   *Cape Verde

.580 1	Early history to 1900
.580 2	1900–1975
.580 3	1975–
.580 31	Administration of Aristides Pereira, 1975–1991
.580 32	Administration of António Mascarenhas Monteiro, 1991–2001
.580 33	Administration of Pedro Verona Rodrigues Pires, 2001–

.6   Liberia and Côte d'Ivoire

.62   *Liberia

.620 1	Early history to 1847
.620 2	1847–1945

Class here 19th century

For 1800–1847, see 966.6201

.620 3	1945–

Class here 20th century

For 1900–1945, see 966.6202

.620 31	1945–1980
.620 32	Administration of Samuel K. Doe, 1980–1990
.620 33	1990–2003

Class here administration of Charles Ghankay Taylor, 1997–2003

---

*Add as instructed under 930–990

.620 34	2003–
	Class here administration of Ellen Johnson-Sirleaf, 2006 to present
.68	*Côte d'Ivoire (Ivory Coast)
.680 1	Early history to 1904
.680 3	French period, 1904–1960
	Class here 20th century
	For 1900–1904, see 966.6801; for 1960–1999, see 966.6805
.680 5	1960–
.680 51	Administration of Félix Houphouët-Boigny, 1960–1993
.680 52	Administration of Henri Konan Bédié, 1993–1999
.680 53	1999–
	Class here administration of Laurent Gbagbo, 2000 to present
.7	***Ghana**
	See also 966.1016 for Ghana Empire
.701	Early history to 1874
.701 6	Period of Akan states, 1295–1740
	Including Akwamu, Bono kingdoms
.701 8	Period of Asante (Ashanti) empire, 1740–1874
	Including 18th century
	For 1700–1740, see 966.7016
.703	Period as Gold Coast, 1874–1957
	Including British Togoland, 1914–1957
	Class here 20th century, British period
	For 1957–1999, see 966.705
.705	1957–
.705 1	1957–1979
	Including administration of Kwame Nkrumah, 1957–1966
.705 2	1979–2001
	Class here administration of Jerry J. Rawlings, 1981–2001
.705 3	Administration of John Agyekum Kufuor, 2001–2009
.705 4	2009–
.8	**Togo and Benin**

*Add as instructed under 930–990

.81	*Togo	
.810 1	Early history to 1894	
.810 2	Period as Togoland, 1894–1914	
.810 3	Period as French Togoland, 1914–1960	

Class here 20th century

For 1900–1914, see 966.8102; for 1960–1999, see 966.8104

.810 4	1960–
.810 41	1960–1967
.810 42	Administration of Gnassingbé Eyadéma, 1967–2005
.810 43	Administration of Faure Gnassingbé, 2005–
.83	*Benin

See also 966.9301 for kingdom of Benin

.830 1	Early history to 1904
.830 18	Period of kingdom of Dahomey, 1600–1904
.830 3	French period, 1904–1960

Class here 20th century

For 1900–1904, see 966.83018; for 1960–1999, see 966.8305

.830 5	1960–
.830 51	1960–1991

Class here first administration of Mathieu Kérékou, 1972–1991

.830 52	Administration of Nicéphore Dieudonné Soglo, 1991–1996
.830 53	Second administration of Mathieu Kérékou, 1996–2006
.830 54	Administration of Boni Yayi, 2006–
.9	***Nigeria**
.901	Early history to 1886
.903	Period as a British colony, 1886–1960

Class here 20th century

For 1960–1999, see 966.905

.905	1960–
.905 1	1960–1967
.905 2	Period of Nigerian Civil War, 1967–1970

*Add as instructed under 930–990

.905 3	1970–1999
	Including administration of Ibrahim Badamosi Babangida, 1985–1993
.905 4	Administration of Olusegun Obasanjo, 1999–2007
.905 5	Administration of Umaru Musa Yar'adua, 2007–2010
.905 6	2010–

967   *Central Africa and offshore islands

Class here Sub-Saharan Africa (Africa south of the Sahara)

For each specific part of Sub-Saharan Africa not provided for here, see the part, e.g., Nigeria 966.9

SUMMARY

967.01–.03	**Historical periods**
.1	**Cameroon, Sao Tome and Principe, Equatorial Guinea**
.2	**Gabon and Republic of the Congo**
.3	**Angola**
.4	**Central African Republic and Chad**
.5	**Democratic Republic of the Congo, Rwanda, Burundi**
.6	**Uganda and Kenya**
.7	**Djibouti and Somalia**
.8	**Tanzania**
.9	**Mozambique**

.01–.03	Historical periods
	Add to base number 967.0 the numbers following 960 in 960.1–960.3, e.g., early history to 967.01

.1	***Cameroon, Sao Tome and Principe, Equatorial Guinea**
	Class here Islands of Gulf of Guinea, Lower Guinea area
.11	*Cameroon
.110 1	Early history to 1884
.110 2	Period as Kamerun, 1884–1916
	Class here German period
.110 3	Anglo-French period, 1916–1959
	Class here 20th century
	For 1900–1916, see 967.1102; for 1960–1999, see 967.1104
.110 4	1960–
.110 41	Administration of Ahmadou Ahidjo, 1960–1982
.110 42	Administration of Paul Biya, 1982–
.15	*Sao Tome and Principe
.150 1	Early history to 1975

*Add as instructed under 930–990

.150 2	Period of Republic, 1975–
.150 21	Administration of Manuel Pinto da Costa, 1975–1991
.150 22	Administration of Miguel Trovoada, 1991–2001
.150 23	Administration of Fradique Bandiera Melo de Menezes, 2001–

.18   *Equatorial Guinea

| .180 1 | Early history to 1469 |
| .180 2 | Portuguese, British, Spanish periods, 1469–1968 |

Including 20th century

For 1968–1999, see 967.1803

.180 3	1968–
.180 31	Administration of Francisco Macías Nguema, 1968–1979
.180 32	Administration of Teodoro Obiang Nguema Mbasogo, 1979–

.2   *Gabon and Republic of the Congo

.201   Early history to 1910

.203   Period as French Equatorial Africa, 1910–1959

Class here 20th century; comprehensive works on French Equatorial Africa

For 1900–1910, see 967.201; for 1959–1999, see 967.205; for Ubangi-Shari as part of French Equatorial Africa, see 967.4103; for Chad as part of French Equatorial Africa, see 967.4302

.205   1959–

.21   *Gabon

.210 1   Early history to 1839

.210 2   French period, 1839–1960

Including period as a part of French Equatorial Africa; 19th century, 20th century

Class comprehensive works on French Equatorial Africa in 967.203

For 1800–1839, see 967.2101; for 1960–1999, see 967.2104

.210 4	1960–
.210 41	1960–1967
.210 42	Administration of Omar Bongo, 1967–2009
.210 43	2009–

.24   *Republic of the Congo

.240 1   Early history to 1885

*Add as instructed under 930–990

.240 3	Period as Middle Congo, 1885–1960

Class here 20th century, French period

Class comprehensive works on French Equatorial Africa in 967.203

For 1960–1999, see 967.2405

.240 5	1960–
.240 51	1960–1979
.240 52	First administration of Denis Sassou Nguesso, 1979–1992
.240 53	1992–1997
.240 54	Second administration of Denis Sassou Nguesso, 1997–

.3 *Angola

.301	Early history to 1648
.302	1648–1899

Including 17th century

For 1600–1648, see 967.301

.303	1900–1975
.304	1975–
.304 1	Administration of António Agostinho Neto, 1975–1979
.304 2	‡Administration of José Eduardo dos Santos, 1979–

Class here Angolan Civil War, 1975–2002

For Angolan Civil War during 1975–1979, see 967.3041

.4 *Central African Republic and Chad

.41	*Central African Republic
.410 1	Early history to 1890
.410 3	Period as Ubangi-Shari, 1890–1960

Class here 20th century, French period, period as part of French Equatorial Africa

Class comprehensive works on French Equatorial Africa in 967.203

For 1960–1999, see 967.4105

.410 5	1960–
.410 51	1960–1979
.410 52	1979–1993

Class here administration of André Kolingba, 1981–1993

*Add as instructed under 930–990
‡Add as instructed under 940–990

.410 53	Administration of Ange-Félix Patasse, 1993–2003
.410 54	Administration of François Bozizé, 2003–
.43	*Chad
.430 1	Early history to 1850

Including 19th century, kingdom of Kanem

Class Kanem-Bornu in 966.9801

For 1850–1899, see 967.4302

.430 2	Colonial period, 1850–1960

Including period as part of French Equatorial Africa; 20th century

Class comprehensive works on French Equatorial Africa in 967.203

For 1960–1999, see 967.4304

.430 4	1960–
.430 41	1960–1975
.430 42	1975–1982
.430 43	Administration of Hissein Habré, 1982–1990
.430 44	1990–
.5	***Democratic Republic of the Congo, Rwanda, Burundi**
.51	*Democratic Republic of the Congo
.510 1	Early history to 1885
.510 2	Belgian period, 1885–1960
.510 22	Period as Congo Free State, 1885–1908
.510 24	Period as Belgian Congo, 1908–1960

Class here 20th century

For 1900–1908, see 967.51022; for 1960–1999, see 967.5103

.510 3	1960–
.510 31	1960–1965
.510 33	Administration of Mobutu Sese Seko, 1965–1997

Class here period as Zaire, 1971–1997

.510 34	1997–
.57	*Rwanda and Burundi
.570 1	Early history to 1899
.570 2	German period, 1899–1917

*Add as instructed under 930–990

.570 3	Belgian period, 1917–1962
	Class here 20th century
	For 1900–1917, see 967.5702; for 1962–1999, see 967.5704
.570 4	1962–
.571	*Rwanda
.571 01	Early history to 1899
.571 02	German period, 1899–1917
.571 03	Belgian period, 1917–1962
	Class here 20th century
	For 1900–1917, see 967.57102; for 1962–1999, see 967.57104
.571 04	1962–
.571 041	1962–1973
.571 042	Administration of Juvénal Habyarimana, 1973–1994
.571 043	1994–
.571 043 1	Civil War of 1994
.572	*Burundi
.572 01	Early history to 1899
.572 02	German period, 1899–1917
.572 03	Belgian period, 1917–1962
	Class here 20th century
	For 1900–1917, see 967.57202; for 1962–1999, see 967.57204
.572 04	1962–
.572 041	1962–1993
.572 041 5	Administration of Jean-Baptiste Bagaza, 1976–1987
.572 042	1993–2005
.572 043	2005–
.6	***Uganda and Kenya**
	Class here East Africa
.601	Early history to 1894
.603	1894–1961
	Class here 20th century
	For 1961–1999, see 967.604

*Add as instructed under 930–990

.604	1961–1999
.605	2000–
.605 1	2000–2009
.605 2	2010–2019
.61	*Uganda
.610 1	Early history to 1894

Including kingdoms of Ankole, Buganda, Bunyoro, Busoga, Karagwe

.610 3	British period, 1894–1962

Class here 20th century

For 1962–1999, see 967.6104

.610 4	1962–
.610 41	First administration of A. Milton Obote, 1962–1971
.610 42	Administration of Idi Amin, 1971–1979
.610 43	Second administration of A. Milton Obote, 1980–1985
.610 44	Administration of Yoweri Museveni, 1986–
.62	*Kenya
.620 1	Early history to 1895
.620 3	British period, 1895–1963

Class here 20th century

For 1963–1999, see 967.6204

.620 4	1963–
.620 41	Administration of Jomo Kenyatta, 1963–1978
.620 42	Administration of Daniel Arap Moi, 1978–2002
.620 43	Administration of Mwai Kibaki, 2002–
.7	***Djibouti and Somalia**

Class here Somaliland

.71	*Djibouti
.710 1	Early history to 1881
.710 3	French period, 1881–1977
.710 32	Period as French Somaliland, 1881–1967

Class here 20th century

For 1967–1977, see 967.71034; for 1977–1999, see 967.7104

*Add as instructed under 930–990

.710 34	Period as French Territory of the Afars and Issas, 1967–1977
.710 4	1977–
.710 41	Administration of Hassan Gouled Aptidon, 1977–1999
.710 42	Administration of Ismail Omar Guelleh, 1999–
.73	*Somalia
.730 1	Early history to 1884
	Including kingdom of Mogadishu
.730 3	Period of British and Italian control, 1884–1960
	Class here 20th century
	For 1960–1999, see 967.7305
.730 5	1960–
.730 51	1960–1969
.730 52	Administration of Maxamed Siyaad Barre, 1969–1991
	Including 1990–1991 [*formerly* 967.73053]
	Class Somali-Ethiopian conflicts, 1978–1991, in 963.071
.730 53	1991–
	Class here Civil War, 1991 to present
	1990–1991 relocated to 967.73052
.8	***Tanzania**
.801	Early history to 1884
.802	German period, 1884–1916
.803	1916–1964
	Class here British period, 1916–1961; 20th century
	For 1900–1916, see 967.802; for 1964–1999, see 967.804
.804	Period as United Republic, 1964
.804 1	Administration of Julius K. Nyerere, 1964–1985
.804 2	Administration of Ali Hassan Mwinyi, 1985–1995
.804 3	Administration of Benjamin W. Mkapa, 1995–2005
.804 4	Administration of Jakaya Khalfan Mrisho Kikwete, 2005–
.81	*Zanzibar and Pemba regions
.810 1	Early history to 1700
.810 2	Period of Arab rule, 1700–1890

*Add as instructed under 930–990

.810 3	Period as a British protectorate, 1890–1963
	Class here 20th century
	For 1963–1999, see 967.8104
.810 4	1963–
.810 41	1963–1985
.810 42	1985–1995
.810 43	1995–2005
.810 44	2005–
.82	*Mainland regions
.820 1	Early history to 1884
.820 2	German period, 1884–1916
.820 3	Period as Tanganyika, 1916–1961
	Class here 20th century, British period
	For 1900–1916, see 967.8202; for 1961–1999, see 967.8204
.820 4	1961–
.820 41	1961–1985
.820 42	1985–1995
.820 43	1995–2005
.820 44	2005–
.9	***Mozambique**
.901	Early history to 1648
.902	1648–1900
	Including 17th century
	Class here Portuguese period, 1648–1975
	For 1600–1648, see 967.901; for 1900–1975, see 967.903
.903	1900–1975
.905	1975–
.905 1	Administration of Samora Machel, 1975–1986
.905 2	Administration of Joaquim Alberto Chissano, 1986–2005
.905 3	Administration of Armando Emílio Guebuza, 2005–

*Add as instructed under 930–990

968 Republic of South Africa and neighboring southern African countries

Class here southern Africa

SUMMARY

968.000 1–.000 9	Standard subdivisions of southern Africa
.001–.009	Standard subdivisions of Republic of South Africa
.02–.06	Historical periods of Republic of South Africa
.2	Gauteng, North-West, Limpopo, Mpumalanga, former homelands (national states) of Republic of South Africa
.4	KwaZulu-Natal
.5	Free State
.7	Northern Cape, Western Cape, Eastern Cape
.8	Namibia, Botswana, Lesotho, Swaziland
.9	Zimbabwe, Zambia, Malawi

.000 1–.000 8   Standard subdivisions of southern Africa

As modified under 930–990

.000 9   Historical periods; areas, regions, places; biography of southern Africa

.000 901–.000 905   Historical periods

Add to base number 968.00090 the numbers following —090 in notation 0901–0905 from Table 1, e.g., southern Africa during 20th century 968.000904

.000 91–.000 99   Areas, regions, places in general; biography

As modified under 930–990

.001–.009   Standard subdivisions of Republic of South Africa

As modified under 930–990

> 968.02–968.06 Historical periods of Republic of South Africa

Class comprehensive works in 968

.02   Early history to 1488

03   Period of European exploration and settlement, 1488–1814

.04   1814–1910

.041   1814–1835

Class here Mfecane (Difaqane)

.042   Great Trek, 1835–1838

.044   1838–1854

.045   1854–1899

See also 968.2046 for First Anglo-Boer War

.048	‡South African War (Second Anglo-Boer War), 1899–1902
	(Option: Class South African War [Second Anglo-Boer War] in 941.081)
.048 3	Participation of specific groups of countries, of specific countries, localities, groups
	Number built according to instructions under 940–990
	Class military participation of specific countries, localities, groups in 968.0484. Class a specific activity with the activity, e.g., efforts to preserve or restore peace 968.0481
.048 31	Great Britain
.048 32	Orange Free State and South African Republic
	Standard subdivisions are added for either or both topics in heading
[.048 34–.048 39]	Participation of specific countries and localities
	Do not use; class in 968.0483
.049	1902–1910
.05	Period of Union, 1910–1961
	Class here 20th century
	For 1900–1902, see 968.048; for 1902–1910, see 968.049; for 1961–1999, see 968.06
.052	Prime ministership of Louis Botha, 1910–1919
.053	First prime ministership of Jan Christiaan Smuts, 1919–1924
.054	Prime ministership of James Barry Munnik Hertzog, 1924–1939
.055	Second prime ministership of Jan Christiaan Smuts, 1939–1948
.056	Prime ministership of Daniel François Malan, 1948–1954
.057	Prime ministership of Johannes Gerhardus Strijdom, 1954–1958
.058	Prime ministership of Hendrik Frensch Verwoerd, 1958–1966
	Including Sharpeville Massacre, 1960
	For 1961–1966, see 968.061
.06	Period as Republic, 1961–
.061	Period of prime ministership of Hendrik Frensch Verwoerd under republic, 1961–1966
.062	Prime ministership of B. J. Vorster, 1966–1978
.062 7	1976–1977
	Class here Soweto and related riots
.063	Administration of P. W. Botha, 1978–1989

‡Add as instructed under 940–990

.064	Administration of F. W. de Klerk, 1989–1994
.065	Administration of Nelson Mandela, 1994–1999
.066	Administration of Thabo Mbeki, 1999–2008
.067	Administration of Kgalema Motlanthe, 2008–2009
.068	Administration of Jacob Zuma, 2009–

.2 ***Gauteng, North-West, Limpopo, Mpumalanga, former homelands (national states) of Republic of South Africa**

.203   Early history to 1835

.204   1835–1910

  Class here 19th century

  For 1800–1835, see 968.203

.204 2   Period of Great Trek and Boer settlement, 1835–1852

.204 5   Period as South African Republic, 1852–1877

.204 6   Period of British control, 1877–1881

  Including First Anglo-Boer War, 1880–1881

.204 7   1881–1899

.204 75   Jameson raid, 1895–1896

.204 8   Period of South African (Second Anglo-Boer) War, 1899–1902

.204 9   Period as Transvaal Colony, 1902–1910

.205   Period of Union, 1910–1961

  Class here 20th century; period as province of Transvaal, 1910–1996

  Add to base number 968.205 the numbers following 968.05 in 968.052–968.058, e.g., period of World War II 968.2055

  For 1900–1902, see 968.2048; for 1902–1910, see 968.2049; for 1961–1999, see 968.206

.206   Period of Republic, 1961

  Add to base number 968.206 the numbers following 968.06 in 968.061–968.068, e.g., period of administration of Nelson Mandela 968.2065

.29   Former homelands (national states [South Africa])

  Limited to pre-1997 periods

  For a specific homeland or part of a homeland, see the homeland or the part, e.g., Ciskei 968.755

.4 ***KwaZulu-Natal**

  Province of Republic of South Africa

*Add as instructed under 930–990

.403	Early history to 1824
.403 8	Period of early Nguni kingdoms, ca. 1500–1816
	Including kingdoms of Mthethwa, Ndwandwe, Qwabe
.403 9	Reign of Shaka, 1816–1828

For reign of Shaka during 1824–1828, see 968.4041

.404	1824–1910

Class here period of Zululand, 1816–1879

For reign of Shaka, see 968.4039

.404 1	Period of early British settlement, 1824–1835

Class here reign of Dingaan, 1828–1840

For reign of Dingaan during 1835–1840, see 968.4042

.404 2	Period of Great Trek and Boer settlement, 1835–1843

Including Battle of Blood River, 1838; republic of Natalia

.404 5	Period as a British colony, 1843–1899

Including reign of Cetewayo, 1872–1879; Zulu War, 1879; annexation of Zululand, 1897

.404 8	Period of South African (Second Anglo-Boer) War, 1899–1902
.404 9	1902–1910
.405	Period of Union, 1910–1961

Class here 20th century; period as province of Natal, 1910–1996

Add to base number 968.405 the numbers following 968.05 in 968.052–968.058, e.g., period of World War II 968.4055

For 1900–1902, see 968.4048; for 1902–1910, see 968.4049; for 1961–1999, see 968.406

.406	Period of Republic, 1961–

Add to base number 968.406 the numbers following 968.06 in 968.061–968.068, e.g., period of administration of Nelson Mandela 968.4065

.5	***Free State**

Province of Republic of South Africa

.503	Early history to 1828
.504	1828–1910

Class here 19th century

For 1800–1828, see 968.503

*Add as instructed under 930–990

| .504 2 | Periods of Great Trek and as Orange River Sovereignty, 1835–1854 |

.504 2   Periods of Great Trek and as Orange River Sovereignty, 1835–1854

.504 5   Period as Orange Free State, 1854–1899

.504 8   Period of South African (Second Anglo-Boer) War, 1899–1902

.504 9   Period as Orange River Colony, 1902–1910

.505   Period of Union, 1910–1961

> Class here 20th century; period as province of Orange Free State, 1910–1996
>
> Add to base number 968.505 the numbers following 968.05 in 968.052–968.058, e.g., period of World War II 968.5055
>
> > *For 1900–1902, see 968.5048; for 1902–1910, see 968.5049; for 1961–1999, see 968.506*

.506   Period of Republic, 1961–

> Add to base number 968.506 the numbers following 968.06 in 968.061–968.068, e.g., period of administration of Nelson Mandela 968.5065

.7   *Northern Cape, Western Cape, Eastern Cape

Provinces of Republic of South Africa

.702   Early history to 1488

.703   Period of exploration and settlement, 1488–1814

.703 1   1488–1652

> Including 17th century
>
> > *For 1652–1699, see 968.7032*

.703 2   Period of Dutch control, 1652–1795

> Class period of control by Batavian Republic in 968.7033

.703 3   1795–1806

> Including periods of British occupation, 1795–1803, control by Batavian Republic, 1803–1806

.704   1806–1910

.704 2   Period of British control, 1806–1854

> Including period of Great Trek
>
> Class period of British occupation, 1795–1803, in 968.7033

.704 5   Period of self-government, 1854–1899

.704 8   Period of South African (Second Anglo-Boer) War, 1899–1902

.704 9   1902–1910

*Add as instructed under 930–990

.705   Period of Union, 1910–1961

Class here 20th century; period as province of Cape of Good Hope, 1910–1996

Add to base number 968.705 the numbers following 968.05 in 968.052–968.058, e.g., period of World War II 968.7055

For 1900–1902, see 968.7048; for 1902–1910, see 968.7049; for 1961–1999, see 968.706

.706   Period of Republic, 1961–

Add to base number 968.706 the numbers following 968.06 in 968.061–968.068, e.g., period of administration of Nelson Mandela 968.7065

.8   *Namibia, Botswana, Lesotho, Swaziland

.801–.803   Historical periods

Add to base number 968.80 the numbers following 960 in 960.1–960.3, e.g., 20th century 968.8031

.81   *Namibia

.810 1   Early history to 1884

.810 2   German period, 1884–1915

.810 3   South African period, 1915–1990

.810 4   1990–

.810 41   Administration of Sam Nujoma, 1990–2005

.810 42   Administration of Hifikepunye Lucas Pohamba, 2005–

.83   *Botswana

.830 1   Early history to 1885

.830 2   Period as Bechuanaland, 1885–1966

Class here 20th century, British period

For 1966–1999, see 968.8303

.830 3   1966–

.830 31   Administration of Seretse Khama, 1966–1980

1980–1990 relocated to 968.83032

.830 32   Administration of Sir Ketumile Masire, 1980–1998

Including 1980–1990 [*formerly* 968.83031]

.830 33   Administration of Festus Gontebanye Mogae, 1998–2008

.830 34   Administration of Seretse Khama Ian Khama, 2008–

.85   *Lesotho

*Add as instructed under 930–990

.850 1	Early history to 1868
.850 2	Period as Basutoland, 1868–1966
	Including 20th century
	Class here British period
	For 1966–1999, see 968.8503
.850 3	1966–
.850 31	First reign of Moshoeshoe II, 1966–1990
	Class here prime ministership of Leabua Jonathan, 1966–1986
.850 32	1990–
	Including second reign of Moshoeshoe II, 1995–1996; prime ministership of Pakalitha Bethuel Mosisili, 1998 to present
	Class here reigns of Letsie III, 1990–1995 and 1996 to present
.87	*Swaziland
.870 1	Early history to 1840
.870 2	British period, 1840–1968
	Including 19th century, 20th century
	For 1800–1840, see 968.8701; for 1968–1999, see 968.8703
.870 3	1968–
	Including reigns of Sobhuza II, 1968–1982; Mswati III, 1986 to present
.9	***Zimbabwe, Zambia, Malawi**
.901	Early history to 1888
.902	Period of British control, 1888–1953
	Class here 20th century
	For 1953–1963, see 968.903; for 1964–1999, see 968.904
.903	Period as Federation of Rhodesia and Nyasaland (Central African Federation), 1953–1963
	Class here prime ministership of Roy Welensky, 1956–1963
.904	1964–
.91	*Zimbabwe
.910 1	Early history to 1889
	Including Karanga kingdoms of Changamire, the Monomotapas

*Add as instructed under 930–990

.910 2	Period as Southern Rhodesia, 1889–1953
	Class here 20th century, British period
	For 1953–1963, see 968.9103; for 1964–1980, see 968.9104; for 1980–1999, see 968.9105
.910 3	Period of federation, 1953–1963
.910 4	Period as Rhodesia, 1964–1980
	Class here prime ministership of Ian Douglas Smith, 1965–1979
.910 5	Period as Republic of Zimbabwe, 1980–
.910 51	Prime ministership of Robert Gabriel Mugabe, 1980–
.94	*Zambia
.940 1	Early history to 1890
	Including kingdoms of the Barotse, of the Bemba
.940 2	Period of British control, 1890–1953
	Including periods as North-eastern Rhodesia and North-western Rhodesia provinces, 1890–1911; as Northern Rhodesia, 1911–1953
	Class here 20th century
	For 1953–1963, see 968.9403; for 1964–1999, see 968.9404
.940 3	Period of federation, 1953–1963
.940 4	Period as Republic of Zambia, 1964–
.940 41	Administration of Kenneth D. Kaunda, 1964–1991
.940 42	Administration of Frederick Chiluba, 1991–2002
.940 43	Administration of Levy P. Mwanawasa, 2002–2008
.940 44	2008–
.97	*Malawi
.970 1	Early history to 1891
	Including kingdom of Malawi
.970 2	Period as Nyasaland, 1891–1953
	Class here 20th century, British period
	For 1953–1963, see 968.9703; for 1964–1999, see 968.9704
.970 3	Period of federation, 1953–1963
.970 4	1964–
.970 41	Administration of H. Kamuzu Banda, 1964–1994
.970 42	Administration of Bakili Muluzi, 1994–2004

*Add as instructed under 930–990

.970 43   Administration of B. W. T. Mutharika, 2004–

969   †South Indian Ocean islands

.1   ***Madagascar**

.101   Early history to 1895

                     Including kingdoms of Betsimisaraka, Boina, Menabe, Merina

.103   French period, 1895–1960

                     Class here 20th century

                     For 1960–1999, see 969.105

.105   1960–

.105 1   1960–1975

                        Class here administration of Philibert Tsiranana, 1960–1972

.105 2   First administration of Didier Ratsiraka, 1975–1993

.105 3   1993–1997

.105 4   Second administration Didier Ratsiraka, 1997–2002

.105 5   Administration of Marc Ravalomanana, 2002–2009

.105 6   2009–

.4   **†Comoro Islands**

.41   †Comoros (Federal and Islamic Republic of the Comoros)

.45   †Mayotte

.6   **†Seychelles**

.7   **†Chagos Islands**

.8   **†Réunion and Mauritius**

.81   *Réunion

.810 2   Early history to 1946

.810 4   Period as a Department of France, 1946–

                       Class here 20th century

                       For 1900–1946, see 969.8102

.82   *Mauritius

.820 1   Early history to 1810

---

*Add as instructed under 930–990

†Add as instructed under 930–990; however, do not add historical periods

.820 2	Period of British rule, 1810–1968

Including 20th century

For 1968–1999, see 969.8203

.820 3	1968–1992
.820 4	Period as republic, 1992–
.820 41	Administration of Cassam Uteem, 1992–2002
.820 42	2002–

Class here administration of Aneerood Jugnauth, 2003 to present

.9   †Isolated islands

Including Amsterdam, Cocos (Keeling), Crozet, Kerguelen, Prince Edward, Saint Paul

970   History of North America

SUMMARY

970.001–.009	**Standard subdivisions**
.01–.05	**Historical periods**
971	**Canada**
972	**Mexico, Central America, West Indies, Bermuda**
973	**United States**
974	**Northeastern United States (New England and Middle Atlantic states)**
975	**Southeastern United States (South Atlantic states)**
976	**South central United States**
977	**North central United States**
978	**Western United States**
979	**Great Basin and Pacific Slope region of United States**

.001–.003	Standard subdivisions
.004	Ethnic and national groups
.004 05–.004 09	Specific ethnic and national groups with ethnic origins from more than one continent, of European descent

Add to base number 970.0040 the numbers following —0 in notation 05–09 from Table 5, e.g., general history and civilization of people of European descent in North America 970.00409

.004 1–.004 9	Specific ethnic and national groups

Add to base number 970.004 notation 1–9 from Table 5, e.g., general history and civilization of North American native peoples in North America 970.00497
    (Option: Class North American native peoples in North America in 970.1; class specific native peoples in 970.3)

Class history and civilization of North American native peoples in a specific place before European discovery and conquest with the place, without using notation 00497 from add table under 930–990, e.g., Aztecs before 1519 972.018

†Add as instructed under 930–990; however, do not add historical periods

.005–.009   Standard subdivisions

As modified under 930–990

>   970.01–970.05   Historical periods

Class comprehensive works in 970

.01   Early history to 1599

.011   Early history to 1492

Including pre-Columbian claims

For Chinese claims, see 970.012; for Norse claims, see 970.013; for Welsh claims, see 970.014

.012   Chinese claims

.013   Norse claims

.014   Welsh claims

>   970.015–970.019   Period of European discovery and exploration

Class comprehensive works in 970.01

.015   Discoveries by Columbus

.016   Spanish and Portuguese explorations

Standard subdivisions are added for either or both topics in heading

.017   English explorations

.018   French explorations

.019   Explorations by other nations

.02   1600–1699

.03   1700–1799

.04   1800–1899

.05   1900–

.051   1900–1918

Class here period of World War I, 1914–1918

.052   1918–1945

Class here period of World War II, 1939–1945

.053   1945–1999

Class here 20th century

For 1900–1918, see 970.051; for 1918–1945, see 970.052

.053 4   1945–1949

.053 5   1950–1959

.053 6	1960–1969
.053 7	1970–1979
.053 8	1980–1989
.053 9	1990–1999
.054	2000–
.054 1	2000–2019
.054 11	2000–2009
.054 12	2010–2019

(.1)   **North American native peoples**

(Optional number; prefer 970.00497)

Class special topics in 970.3–970.5

(.3)   **Specific native peoples**

(Optional number; prefer 971–979 with use of subdivision 00497 from table under 930–990, e.g., the Hopi in Arizona 979.100497458)

Arrange alphabetically by name of people

Class government relations with specific native peoples in 970.5

(.4)   **Native peoples in specific places in North America**

(Optional number; prefer 971–979 with use of subdivision 00497 from table under 930–990, e.g., native peoples in United States 973.0497, in Arizona 979.100497)

Add to base number 970.4 the numbers following —7 in notation 71–79 from Table 2, e.g., Indians in Arizona 970.491

Class specific native peoples in specific places in 970.3; class government relations in specific places in 970.5

(.5)   **Government relations with North American native peoples**

(Optional number; prefer 323.1197 for comprehensive works; a specific subject with the subject, e.g., Black Hawk War 973.56, relation to the state in Canada 323.1197071)

History and policy

>   **971–979   Countries and localities**

Class comprehensive works in 970. Class specific native peoples in a specific place with the place in 971–979 with use of subdivision 00497 from table under 930–990, e.g., the Hopi in Arizona 979.100497458
    (Option: Class native peoples in specific places in North America in 970.4)

971   ***Canada**

---

*Add as instructed under 930–990

SUMMARY

SUMMARY

.01   Early history to 1763

.011   Early history to 1632

.011 1   Period before European discovery and exploration

.011 2   Norse explorations

.011 3   French explorations

.011 4   English explorations

.016   Period of French and English expansion, 1632–1689

                Class here 17th century

                For 1600–1632, see 971.011; for 1689–1699, see 971.018

.016 2   Period of Company of New France, 1632–1663

.016 3   1663–1689

.018   Period of struggle of France and England for supremacy, 1689–1763

Including periods of War of the League of Augsburg, 1688–1697; War of the Spanish Succession, 1701–1714; War of the Austrian Succession, 1740–1748

(Option: Class here North American aspects of War of the League of Augsburg, War of the Spanish Succession; prefer 973.25. Class here North American aspects of War of the Austrian Succession; prefer 973.26)

Class here comprehensive works on period as a French royal province, 1663–1763; 18th century

Class North American aspects of War of the League of Augsburg, War of the Spanish Succession in 973.25; class North American aspects of War of the Austrian Succession in 973.26; class comprehensive works on War of the League of Augsburg in 940.2525; class comprehensive works on War of the Spanish Succession in 940.2526; class comprehensive works on War of the Austrian Succession in 940.2532

For 1663–1689, see 971.0163; for 1763–1791, see 971.02; for 1791–1799, see 971.032

[.018 7]   Expulsion of Acadians, 1755

Relocated to 971.5017

.018 8   Period of Seven Years' War, 1756–1763

Class North American aspects of Seven Years' War in 973.26; class comprehensive works on Seven Years' War in 940.2534

(Option: Class here North American aspects of Seven Years' War; prefer 973.26)

Expulsion of Acadians, 1758, relocated to 971.5017

.02   Period of early British rule, 1763–1791

.022   1763–1774

Including Quebec Act, 1774

(Option: Class here Pontiac's conspiracy, 1763–1764; prefer 973.27)

.024   Period of American Revolution, 1774–1783

Including settlement of Loyalists from United States, 1774–1789

For settlement of Loyalists during 1783–1789, see 971.028

.028   1783–1791

Class here Constitutional Act, 1791

.03   Period of Upper and Lower Canada, 1791–1841

Class here 19th century

For 1841–1867, see 971.04; for 1867–1899, see 971.05

.032   1791–1812

.034	Period of War of 1812, 1812–1814

.034 (Option: Class here War of 1812; prefer 973.52)

.036	1814–1837

.038	Period of rebellions of 1837–1838

Including Family Compact of Upper Canada, Chateau Clique of Lower Canada

.039	1838–1841

Class here Durham mission and report, 1838–1839; Act of Union, 1840

.04	Period of Province of Canada, 1841–1867

.042	1841–1864

.048	Period of Fenian activities, 1866–1871

.049	Period of Confederation, 1864–1867

Including Charlottetown and Quebec Conferences, 1864; British North America Act, 1867

For period of Fenian activities, see 971.048

.05	Period of Dominion of Canada, 1867–

For 1911–1999, see 971.06; for 2000 to present, see 971.07

.051	First prime ministership of Sir John A. Macdonald, 1867–1873

Including Riel's first (Red River) rebellion, 1869–1870

For Fenian activities during 1867–1871, see 971.048

.052	Prime ministership of Alexander Mackenzie, 1873–1878

.054	Second prime ministership of Sir John A. Macdonald, 1878–1891

Including Riel's second (Northwest) rebellion, 1885

.055	1891–1896

Including prime ministerships of Sir John J. C. Abbott, 1891–1892; of Sir John Sparrow Thompson, 1892–1894; of Sir Mackenzie Bowell, 1894–1896, of Sir Charles Tupper, 1896

.056	Prime ministership of Sir Wilfrid Laurier, 1896–1911

.06	1911–1999

.061	1911–1921

.061 2	Prime ministership of Sir Robert Laird Borden, 1911–1920

.061 3	First prime ministership of Arthur Meighen, 1920–1921

.062	1921–1935

.062 2	First and second prime ministerships of William Lyon Mackenzie King, 1921–1930

Including second prime ministership of Arthur Meighen, 1926

.062 3	Prime ministership of Richard Bedford Bennett, 1930–1935
.063	1935–1957
.063 2	Third prime ministership of William Lyon Mackenzie King, 1935–1948
.063 3	Prime ministership of Louis Stephen Saint-Laurent, 1948–1957
.064	1957–1999
.064 2	Prime ministership of John G. Diefenbaker, 1957–1963
.064 3	Prime ministership of Lester B. Pearson, 1963–1968
.064 4	First prime ministership of Pierre Elliott Trudeau, 1968–1979
.064 5	Prime ministership of Joe (Charles Joseph) Clark, 1979–1980
.064 6	Second prime ministership of Pierre Elliott Trudeau, 1980–1984

Including prime ministership of John Turner, 1984

.064 7	Prime ministership of Brian Mulroney, 1984–1993

Including prime ministership of Kim Campbell, 1993

.064 8	1993–1999

Class here prime ministership of Jean Chrétien, 1993–2003

> *For prime ministership of Jean Chrétien during 2000–2003, see 971.071*

.07	2000–
.071	Later portion of prime ministership of Jean Chrétien, 2000–2003
.072	Prime ministership of Paul Martin, 2003–2006
.073	Prime ministership of Stephen Harper, 2006–
.1	***British Columbia**
.101	Early history to 1790
.102	Period of settlement and colony, 1790–1871

Including colony of New Caledonia

Class here 19th century

> *For 1871–1899, see 971.103*

.103	Period as a Province of Canada, 1871–

> *For 1945–1999, see 971.104; for 2000 to present, see 971.105*

.104	1945–1999

Class here 20th century

> *For 1900–1945, see 971.103*

.105	2000–

*Add as instructed under 930–990

.2	***Prairie Provinces**
.201	Early history to 1869
	Including Rupert's Land
.202	1869–1945
.203	1945–1999
	Class here 20th century
	For 1900–1945, see 971.202
.204	2000–
.3	***Ontario**
.301	Early history to 1791
.302	Period of Upper Canada and Act of Union, 1791–1867
	Class here 19th century
	For 1867–1899, see 971.303
.303	Period as a Province of Canada, 1867–
	For 1945–1999, see 971.304; for 2000 to present, see 971.305
.304	1945–1999
	Class here 20th century
	For 1900–1945, see 971.303
.305	2000–
.4	***Quebec**
.401	Early history to 1763
.401 2	Early history to 1608
	Including period of explorations by Jacques Cartier, 1534–1535
.401 4	French period, 1608–1763
	Including 18th century
	For 1763–1799, see 971.402
.402	British period, 1763–1867
	Including period of Lower Canada, 1791–1841; 19th century
	For 1867–1899, see 971.403
.403	Period as a Province of Canada, 1867–
	For 1945–1999, see 971.404; for 2000 to present, see 971.405

*Add as instructed under 930–990

.404	1945–1999

        Class here 20th century

        For 1900–1945, see 971.403

.405	2000–

.5   *Atlantic Provinces*

        Class here Maritime Provinces

        For Nova Scotia, see 971.6; for Prince Edward Island, see 971.7; for Newfoundland and Labrador, see 971.8

.501	Early history to 1763

        Including 18th century

        For 1763–1799, see 971.502

.501 7	1604–1763

        Class here expulsion of Acadians, 1755 [*formerly* 971.0187] and 1758 [*formerly* 971.0188]; comprehensive works on Acadia [*formerly* 971.601]

        For a specific part of Acadia not provided for here, see the part, e.g., Acadia in Nova Scotia 971.601

.502	Period as British colonies, 1763–1867

        Including 19th century

        For 1867–1899, see 971.503

.503	Period as provinces of Canada, 1867–

        For 1945–1999, see 971.504; for 2000 to present, see 971.505

.504	1945–1999

        Class here 20th century

        For 1900–1945, see 971.503

.505	2000–
.51	*New Brunswick
.510 1	Early history to 1784

        For expulsion of Acadians, see 971.5017

.510 2	Period as separate province, 1784–1867

        Including 19th century

        For 1867–1899, see 971.5103

.510 3	Period as a Province of Canada, 1867–

        For 1945–1999, see 971.5104; for 2000 to present, see 971.5105

---

*Add as instructed under 930–990

.510 4	1945–1999
	Class here 20th century
	For 1900–1945, see 971.5103
.510 5	2000–

.6 ***Nova Scotia**

.601	Early history to 1763
	Including 18th century
	For expulsion of Acadians, see 971.5017; for 1763–1799, see 971.602
	Comprehensive works on Acadia relocated to 971.5017
.602	Period as a British colony, 1763–1867
	Including 19th century
	For 1867–1899, see 971.603
.603	Period as a Province of Canada, 1867–
	For 1945–1999, see 971.604; for 2000 to present, see 971.605
.604	1945–1999
	Class here 20th century
	For 1900–1945, see 971.603
.605	2000–

.7 ***Prince Edward Island**

.701	Early history to 1769
	Including 18th century
	For expulsion of Acadians, see 971.5017; for 1769–1799, see 971.702
.702	Period as separate province, 1769–1873
	Including 19th century
	For 1873–1899, see 971.703
.703	Period as a Province of Canada, 1873–
	For 1945–1999, see 971.704; for 2000 to present, see 971.705
.704	1945–1999
	Class here 20th century
	For 1900–1945, see 971.703
.705	2000–

*Add as instructed under 930–990

.8   ***Newfoundland and Labrador, Saint Pierre and Miquelon**

Class here Newfoundland

\>   971.801–971.805 Historical periods for Newfoundland and Labrador

Class comprehensive works in 971.8

.801   Early history to 1855

Including 19th century

For 1855–1899, see 971.802

.802   1855 1934

.803   Period of suspension of parliamentary government, 1934–1949

.804   Period as a Province of Canada, 1949–

Class here 20th century

For 1900–1934, see 971.802; for 1934–1949, see 971.803; for 2001 to present, see 971.805

.805   2001–

.82   *Labrador

.820 1   Early history to 1763

Including 18th century

For 1763–1799, see 971.8202

.820 2   Period when claimed by Lower Canada (Quebec) and Newfoundland, 1763–1927

.820 3   Period as dependency of Newfoundland, 1927–1949

.820 4   Period as part of Province of Newfoundland and Labrador, 1949–

Class here 20th century

For 1900–1927, see 971.8202; for 1927–1949, see 971.8203; for 2001 to present, see 971.8205

.820 5   2001–

.88   †Saint Pierre and Miquelon

.9   ***Northern territories**

.901   Early history to 1870

Including 19th century

For 1870–1899, see 971.902

.902   1870–1945

---

*Add as instructed under 930–990
†Add as instructed under 930–990; however, do not add historical periods

.903	1945–1999
	Class here 20th century
	For 1900–1945, see 971.902
.904	1999–
.91	*Yukon
.910 1	Early history to 1898
.910 2	1898–1945
.910 3	1945–1999
	Class here 20th century
	For 1900–1945, see 971.9102
.910 4	1999–
.92	*Northwest Territories (1870–1999)

See also 971.93 for Northwest Territories (1999–); also 971.95 for Nunavut

.920 1–.920 4	Historical periods

Add to base number 971.920 the numbers following 971.90 in 971.901–971.904, e.g., 1945–1999 971.9203

.93	*Northwest Territories (1999–)

See also 971.92 for Northwest Territories (1870–1999)

.930 1–.930 4	Historical periods

Add to base number 971.930 the numbers following 971.90 in 971.901–971.904, e.g., 1945–1999 971.9303

.95	*Nunavut
.950 1–.950 4	Historical periods

Add to base number 971.950 the numbers following 971.90 in 971.901–971.904, e.g., 1945–1999 971.9503

972 Mexico, Central America, West Indies, Bermuda

Class here Middle America

SUMMARY

972.000 1–.000 9	**Standard subdivisions of Mexico, Central America, West Indies, Bermuda together**
.001–.009	**Standard subdivisions of Mexico**
.01–.08	**Historical periods of Mexico**
.8	**Central America**
.9	**West Indies (Antilles) and Bermuda**

*Add as instructed under 930–990

.000 1–.000 8	Standard subdivisions of Mexico, Central America, West Indies, Bermuda together
	As modified under 930–990
.000 9	Historical periods; areas, regions, places in general; biography of Mexico, Central America, West Indies, Bermuda together
.000 901–.000 905	Historical periods

Add to base number 972.00090 the numbers following —090 in notation 0901–0905 from Table 1, e.g., Mexico, Central America, West Indies, Bermuda together during 20th century 972.000904

.000 91 .000 99	Areas, regions, places in general; biography
	As modified under 930–990
.001–.009	Standard subdivisions of Mexico
	As modified under 930–990

> 972.01–972.08 Historical periods of Mexico

Class comprehensive works in 972

.01	Early history to 1519
.016	Classical period, ca. 100–ca. 900
.017	Ca. 900–1325

Class here period of Toltec empire, ca. 900–ca. 1200

.018	Aztec period, 1325–1519

Including 14th century

For 1300–1325, see 972.017

.02	Conquest and colonial period, 1519–1810
.03	Revolutionary period and period of independence, 1810–1822
.04	Periods of first empire and republic, 1822–1845

Class here 19th century

For a part of 19th century not provided for here, see the part, e.g., period of second empire 972.07

.05	Period of war with United States, 1845–1848

(Option: Class here Mexican War; prefer 973.62)

.06	Period of reaction and reform, 1848–1861

.07   Period of European intervention, 1861–1867

Class here period of second empire, 1864–1867; comprehensive works on administration of Benito Juárez, 1858–1872

For administration of Benito Juárez during 1858–1861, see 972.06; for administration of Benito Juárez during 1867–1872, see 972.0812

.08   Period of Republic, 1867–

.081   1867–1917

.081 2   1867–1876

.081 4   Porfiriato, 1876–1910

Class here administrations of Porfirio Díaz, 1876–1880, 1884–1910

.081 6   Period of Mexican Revolution, 1910–1917

.082   1917–1964

Class here 20th century

For 1900–1910, see 972.0814; for 1910–1917, see 972.0816; for 1964–1999, see 972.083

.082 1   Administrations of Venustiano Carranza and Adolfo de la Huerta, 1917–1920

.082 2   Administration of Alvaro Obregón, 1920–1924

.082 3   Administration of Plutarco Elías Calles, 1924–1928

.082 4   Administrations of Emilio Portes Gil, Pascual Ortiz Rubio, Abelardo L. Rodríguez, 1928–1934

.082 42   Administration of Emilio Portes Gil, 1928–1930

.082 43   Administration of Pascual Ortiz Rubio, 1930–1932

.082 44   Administration of Abelardo L. Rodríguez, 1932–1934

.082 5   Administration of Lázaro Cárdenas, 1934–1940

.082 6   Administration of Manuel Avila Camacho, 1940–1946

082 7   Administration of Miguel Alemán, 1946–1952

.082 8   Administration of Adolfo Ruiz Cortines, 1952–1958

.082 9   Administration of Adolfo López Mateos, 1958–1964

.083   1964–2000

.083 1   Administration of Gustavo Díaz Ordaz, 1964–1970

.083 2   Administration of Luis Echeverría, 1970–1976

.083 3   Administration of José López Portillo, 1976–1982

.083 4   Administration of Miguel de la Madrid Hurtado, 1982–1988

.083 5   Administration of Carlos Salinas de Gortari, 1988–1994

.083 6   Administration of Ernesto Zedillo Ponce de León, 1994–2000

.084	2000–
.084 1	Administration of Vicente Fox Quesada, 2000–2006
.084 2	Administration of Felipe Calderón Hinojosa, 2006–

> ### 972.8–972.9 Other parts of Middle America

Class comprehensive works in 972

.8　　***Central America**

.801	Early history to 1502
.802	Period of European discovery, exploration, conquest, 1502–1535
.803	Colonial period, 1535–1821

Including 16th century

For 1500–1502, see 978.801; for 1502–1535, see 978.802

.804	1821–1899

Including period of United Provinces of Central America, 1823–1840

.805	1900–
.805 1	1900–1944

Class here 20th century

For 1944–1979, see 972.8052; for 1979–1999, see 972.8053

.805 2	1944–1979
.805 3	1979–1999
.805 4	2000–
.81	*Guatemala
.810 1	Early history to 1502
.810 16	Mayan period, ca. 300–ca. 900

Class here comprehensive works on Mayan period in Middle America

For a specific aspect of the Mayan period not provided for here, see the aspect, e.g., Mayan period from ca. 900 to 1325 in Mexico 972.6017

.810 2	Period of European discovery, exploration, conquest, 1502–1524
.810 3	Colonial period, 1524–1821

Including 16th century

For 1500–1502, see 972.8101; for 1502–1524, see 972.8102

---

*Add as instructed under 930–990

.810 4	1821–1871
	Class here 19th century
	For 1800–1821, see 972.8103; for 1871–1899, see 972.81051
.810 42	1821–1839
	Class here period as a part of United Provinces of Central America, 1823–1839
.810 44	1839–1871
	Class here administration of Rafael Carrera, 1839–1865
.810 5	1871–
.810 51	1871–1931
.810 52	1931–1986
	Including Civil War, 1960–1996
	Class here 20th century
	For 1900–1931, see 972.81051; for 1986–1999, see 972.810531
.810 53	1986–
.810 531	1986–2000
.810 532	Administration of Alfonso Portillo, 2000–2004
.810 533	Administration of Oscar Berger Perdomo, 2004–2008
.810 534	Administration of Álvaro Colom Caballeros, 2008–
.82	*Belize
.820 1	Early history to 1502
.820 2	Period of Spanish discovery and colonization, 1502–1638
.820 3	1638–1862
	Including 17th century, 19th century
	Class here period of British involvement, 1638–1963; 18th century
	For 1600–1638, see 972.8202; for 1862–1963, see 972.8204
.820 4	Period as a British colony, 1862–1981
	Including period as self-governing colony, 1964–1981 [*formerly* 972.8205]
	Class here 20th century
	For 1981–1999, see 972.8205
.820 5	1981–
	Period as self-governing colony, 1964–1981 relocated to 972.8204

*Add as instructed under 930–990

.83	*Honduras
.830 1	Early history to 1502
.830 2	Period of Spanish discovery, exploration, conquest, 1502–1542
.830 3	Colonial period, 1542–1821

Including 16th century

For 1500–1502, see 972.8301; for 1502–1542, see 972.8302

.830 4	1821–1838

Class here period as a part of United Provinces of Central America, 1823–1838

.830 5	1838–
.830 51	1838–1924

Class here 19th century

For 1800–1821, see 972.8303; for 1821–1838, see 972.8304

.830 52	1924–1978

Class here 20th century

For 1900–1924, see 972.83051; for 1978–1999, see 972.83053

.830 53	1978–
.830 531	1978–1982
.830 532	Administration of Roberto Suazo Córdova, 1982–1986
.830 533	Administration of José Azcona H., 1986–1990
.830 534	Administration of Rafael Leonardo Callejas Romero, 1990–1994
.830 535	Administration of Carlos Roberto Reina, 1994–1998
.830 536	Administration of Carlos Flores Facussé, 1998–2002
.830 537	Administration of Ricardo Maduro, 2002–2006
.830 538	2006–
.84	*El Salvador
.840 1	Early history to 1524
.840 2	Period of Spanish discovery, exploration, conquest, 1524–1542
.840 3	Colonial period, 1542–1821

Including 16th century

For 1500–1524, see 972.8401; for 1524–1542, see 972.8402

*Add as instructed under 930–990

.840 4	1821–1859
	Class here 19th century
	For 1800–1821, see 972.8403; for 1859–1899, see 972.8451
.840 42	1821–1839
	Class here period as a part of United Provinces of Central America, 1823–1839
.840 44	1839–1859
.840 5	1859–
.840 51	1859–1931
.840 52	1931–1979
	Class here 20th century
	For 1900–1931, see 972.84051; for 1979–1994, see 972.84053; for 1994–1999, see 972.84054
.840 53	1979–1994
.840 54	1994–
.840 541	Administration of Armando Calderón Sol, 1994–1999
.840 542	Administration of Francisco Flores Pérez, 1999–2004
.840 543	Administration of Elías Antonio Saca, 2004–2009
.840 544	Administration of Carlos Mauricio Funes, 2009–
.85	*Nicaragua
.850 1	Early history to 1502
.850 2	Period of Spanish discovery, exploration, conquest, 1502–1527
.850 3	Colonial period, 1527–1821
	Including 16th century
	For 1500–1502, see 972.8501; for 1502–1527, see 972.8502
.850 4	1821–1893
	Class here 19th century
	For 1800–1821, see 972.8503; for 1893–1899, see 972.85051
.850 42	1821–1838
	Class here period as a part of United Provinces of Central America, 1823–1838
.850 44	1838–1893
.850 5	1893–

*Add as instructed under 930–990

.850 51	1893–1934
	Class here period of interventions by United States, 1909–1933
.850 52	1934–1979
	Class here 20th century
	For 1900–1934, see 972.85051; for 1979–1990, see 972.85053; for 1990–1999, see 972.85054
.850 53	1979–1990
	Including first administration of Daniel Ortega, 1985–1990
.850 54	1990–
.850 541	Administration of Violeta Barrios de Chamorro, 1990–1997
.850 542	Administration of Arnoldo Alemán, 1997–2002
.850 543	Administration of Enrique Bolaños Geyer, 2002–2007
.850 544	Second administration of Daniel Ortega, 2007–
.86	*Costa Rica
.860 1	Early history to 1502
.860 2	Period of Spanish discovery, exploration, conquest, 1502–1560
.860 3	Colonial period, 1560–1821
	Including 16th century
	For 1500–1502, see 972.8601; for 1502–1560, see 972.8602
.860 4	1821–1948
.860 42	1821–1838
	Class here period as a part of United Provinces of Central America, 1823–1838
.860 44	1838–1948
.860 5	1948–
	Class here 20th century
	For 1900–1948, see 972.86044
.860 51	1948–1986
.860 52	1986–
.860 521	First administration of Óscar Arias Sánchez, 1986–1990
.860 522	Administration of Rafael Angel Calderón Fournier, 1990–1994
.860 523	Administration of José María Figueres, 1994–1998
.860 524	Administration of Miguel Angel Rodríguez, 1998–2002

*Add as instructed under 930–990

.860 525	Administration of Abel Pacheco, 2002–2006
.860 526	Second administration of Óscar Arias Sánchez, 2006–2010
.860 527	Administration of Laura Chinchilla, 2010–
.87	*Panama
.870 1	Early history to 1514
.870 11	Early history to 1501
.870 12	Period of Spanish discovery, exploration, conquest, 1501–1514
.870 2	Colonial period, 1514–1821
	Including period as a part of Viceroyalty of New Granada, 1739–1810
.870 3	Period as a part of Colombia, 1821–1903
.870 5	1903–
.870 51	1903–1977
.870 53	1977–1999
.870 54	1999–
.870 541	Administration of Mireya Moscoso, 1999–2004
.870 542	Administration of Martín Torrijos Espino, 2004–2009
.870 543	Administration of Ricardo Alberto Martinelli Berrocal, 2009–

.9 *West Indies (Antilles) and Bermuda

Class here Caribbean Area

For a part of Caribbean Area not provided for here, see the part, e.g., Venezuela 987

.901	Early history to 1492
.902	Period of European discovery and early colonial period, 1492–1608
.903	1608–1801
.904	1801–1902
.905	1902–
.905 1	1902–1945
.905 2	1945–1999
	Class here 20th century
	For 1900–1902, see 972.904; for 1902–1945, see 972.9051
.905 3	2000–
.91	*Cuba
.910 1	Early history to 1492

*Add as instructed under 930–990

.910 2	Period of European discovery, exploration, conquest, 1492–1514
.910 3	1514–1763

Including 18th century

For 1763–1799, see 972.9104

.910 4	1763–1810
.910 5	1810–1899

For Spanish-American War, see 973.89

.910 6	1899–

Class here period of Republic, 1902 to present

For 2008 to present, see 972.9107

.910 61	Period of American military occupation, 1899–1902
.910 62	1902–1933
.910 63	1933–1958
.910 64	Period of Fidel Castro, 1959–2008
.910 7	2008–
.92	*Jamaica and Cayman Islands

Subdivisions are added for Jamaica and Cayman Islands together, for Jamaica alone

———————————

> 972.920 1–972.920 6 Historical periods of Jamaica

Class comprehensive works in 972.92

.920 1	Early history to 1494
.920 2	1494–1607
.920 3	1607–1832
.920 31	Last period of Spanish rule, 1607–1655
.920 32	1655–1692

Including Great Earthquake, 1692

Class here 17th century

For a specific part of 17th century not provided for here, see the part, e.g., 1600–1607 972.9202

.920 33	1692–1782
.920 34	1782–1832

*Add as instructed under 930–990

.920 4	1832–1904
	Class here 19th century
	For 1801–1832, see 972.92034
.920 5	1904–1962
	Class here 20th century
	For 1901–1904, see 972.9204; for 1962–1999, see 972.9206
.920 6	1962–
.921	†Cayman Islands
.93	*Dominican Republic
.930 1	Early history to 1492
.930 2	Period of European discovery and early colonial period, 1492–1608
.930 3	1608–1801
.930 4	1801–1902
.930 5	1902–
.930 52	1902–1930
.930 53	Period of Rafael Léonidas Trujillo Molina, 1930–1961
.930 54	1961–2000
.930 55	2000–
.94	*Haiti
.940 1	Early history to 1492
.940 2	Period of Spanish rule, 1492–1625
.940 3	Period as a French colony, 1625–1804
.940 4	1804–1915
.940 5	Period of American occupation, 1915–1934
.940 6	1934–1957
	Class here 20th century
	For 1900–1915, see 972.9404; for 1915–1934, see 972.9405; for 1957–1999, see 972.9407
.940 7	1957–
.940 72	Periods of François Duvalier and Jean-Claude Duvalier, 1957–1986
.940 73	1986–
.95	*Puerto Rico

*Add as instructed under 930–990
†Add as instructed under 930–990; however, do not add historical periods

.950 1	Early history to 1493
.950 2	Period of European discovery and early colonial period, 1493–1602
.950 3	1602–1804
.950 4	1804–1899
.950 5	1900–
.950 52	1900–1952

Class here 20th century

For 1952–1999, see 972.95053

.950 53	Period of Commonwealth, 1952–
.96	†Bahama Islands
.97	†Leeward Islands

For Dominica, see 972.9841

.972	†Virgin Islands
.973	†Anguilla and Saint Kitts-Nevis
.974	†Antigua and Barbuda
.975	†Montserrat
.976	†Guadeloupe
.977	†Leeward Netherlands islands
.98	†Windward and other southern islands
.981	†Barbados
.982	†Martinique
.983	*Trinidad and Tobago
.983 01	Early history to 1498
.983 02	Spanish period, 1498–1797
.983 03	British period, 1797–1962

Including 20th century

For 1962–1999, see 972.98304

.983 04	1962–
.984	†Windward Islands
.984 1	†Dominica
.984 3	†Saint Lucia

*Add as instructed under 930–990
†Add as instructed under 930–990; however, do not add historical periods

.984 4　　　　　　　†Saint Vincent and the Grenadines

For Carriacou, see 972.9845

.984 5　　　　　　　†Grenada and Carriacou

.986　　　　　　†Netherlands islands

For Leeward Netherlands islands, see 972.977

.99　　　　†Bermuda

973　　United States

For specific states, see 974–979

SUMMARY

973.01–.09	**Standard subdivisions**
.1	**Early history to 1607**
.2	**Colonial period, 1607–1775**
.3	**Periods of Revolution and Confederation, 1775–1789**
.4	**Constitutional period, 1789–1809**
.5	**1809–1845**
.6	**1845–1861**
.7	**Administration of Abraham Lincoln, 1861–1865**
.8	**Reconstruction period, 1865–1901**
.9	**1901–**

.01–.09　　Standard subdivisions

As modified under 930–990

(If optional notation 734–739 from Table 2 is chosen, use 973.01–973.09 for historical periods, and 973.001–973.009 for standard subdivisions)

.1　　Early history to 1607

Add to base number 973.1 the numbers following 970.01 in 970.011–970.019, e.g., French explorations 973.18

.2　　Colonial period, 1607–1775

> 973.21–973.22 Period of early settlements, 1607–1643

Class comprehensive works in 973.21. Class a specific European settlement with the settlement in 974–975, e.g., settlement of New Plymouth Colony 974.48202, of Jamestown 975.5425101

.21　　Period of Virginia settlements, 1607–1620

.22　　Period of other early settlements, 1620–1643

Including Pequot War, 1636–1638

.23　　1643–1664

.24　　1664–1689

Including King Philip's War, 1675–1676

Add as instructed under 930–990; however, do not add historical periods

.25	1689–1732

> Including King William's War (North American aspect of War of the League of Augsburg), 1688–1697; Queen Anne's War (North American aspects of War of the Spanish Succession), 1701–1714
>> (Option: Class North American aspects of War of the League of Augsburg, War of the Spanish Succession in 971.018)
>
> Class here 18th century
>
> Class comprehensive works on War of the League of Augsburg in 940.2525; class comprehensive works on War of the Spanish Succession in 940.2526
>
> *For a specific part of 18th century not provided for here, see the part, e.g., 1175–1789 973.3*

.26	Period of extension of English rule, 1732–1763

> Including King George's War (North American aspects of War of the Austrian Succession), 1740–1748; French and Indian War (North American aspects of Seven Year's War), 1756–1763
>> (Option: Class North American aspects of War of the Austrian Succession in 971.018; class Seven Years' War in 971.0188)
>
> Class comprehensive works on War of the Austrian Succession in 940.2532; class comprehensive works on Seven Years' War in 940.2534

.27	End of colonial period, 1763–1775

> Including Pontiac's Conspiracy, 1763–1764
>> (Option: Class Pontiac's Conspiracy in 971.022)
>
> Class events of 1763–1775 as causes of American Revolution in 973.311

.3	**Periods of Revolution and Confederation, 1775–1789**

> Standard subdivisions are added for periods of Revolution and Confederation together, for period of Revolution alone

.31	Social, political, economic history

> *For diplomatic history, see 973.32*

.311	Causes
.311 1	Stamp Act, 1765–1766
.311 2	Commercial restrictions

> Including Navigation Acts, Townshend Acts, burning of the Gaspée, 1772
>
> *For tax on tea, see 973.3115*

.311 3	Quartering of troops and Boston Massacre, 1770
.311 4	Taxation and representation
.311 5	Tax on tea and Boston Tea Party, 1773
.311 6	Boston Port Bill, 1774
.312	Continental Congress
.313	Declaration of Independence, 1776

.314	Loyalists (Tories)

Class settlement of Loyalists in Canada in 971.024

.316	Results

For Treaty of Peace, see 973.317

.317	Definitive Treaty of Peace Between Great Britain and the United States (Treaty of Paris), 1783

Class here Definitive Treaty of Peace with Spain (Treaty of Versailles), 1783

.318	Period of confederation, 1783–1789

>   973.32–973.38 Aspects of American Revolution

Class comprehensive works in 973.3

.32	Diplomatic history

Class here relations of United States with other nations

For Treaty of Paris, see 973.317

[.320 941–.320 949]	Relations with European nations

Do not use; class in 973.321–973.329

.321–.329	Relations with European nations

Add to base number 973.32 the numbers following —4 in notation 41–49 from Table 2, e.g., relations with France 973.324

.33	Operations

Class here military history

For military units, see 973.34; for naval operations, see 973.35

.331	Operations of 1775
.331 1	Battles of Lexington and Concord, 1775
.331 2	Battle of Bunker Hill, 1775
.332	Operations of 1776–January 3, 1777
.333	Operations of 1777

For Battle of Princeton, see 973.332; for winter at Valley Forge, see 973.3341

.334	Operations of 1778
.334 1	Winter at Valley Forge, 1777–1778
.335	Operations of 1779
.336	Operations of 1780
.337	Operations of 1781
.338	Operations of 1782

.339	Operations of 1783

.34	Military units

Class here organization, history, rosters, service records

Class operations of military units in 973.33. Class units engaged in a special service with the service, e.g., privateering 973.35

For naval units, see 973.35; for rolls of honor, lists of dead, see 973.36

.341	British troops

For mercenary troops, see 973.342; for American native peoples as allies, see 973.343

.342	Mercenary troops

.343	American native peoples as allies of British

.344–.345	American troops

Add to base number 973.34 the numbers following —7 in notation 74–75 from Table 2, e.g., Pennsylvania troops 973.3448

.346	Auxiliary troops on American side

Including Polish, Spanish, Swedish

For French troops, see 973.347

.347	French troops

.35	Naval history

Including privateering

Class here operations, ships, units

.36	Celebrations, commemorations, memorials

Including rolls of honor, lists of dead

Class celebrations, commemorations, memorials of a specific event with the event, e.g., Battle of Bunker Hill 973.3312

.37	Prisoners of war, medical and social services

.371	Prisoners of war

Including British prisons and prison ships, exchange of prisoners

For American prisons, see 973.372

.372	American prisons

.375	Medical services

For hospitals, see 973.376

.376	Hospitals

.38	Other topics of American Revolution

Including deserters, military life and customs, military personnel missing in action

.381 Treason

> *For treason of Benedict Arnold, see 973.382; for treason of Charles Lee, see 973.383*

.382 Treason of Benedict Arnold

.383 Treason of Charles Lee

.385 American secret service and spies

> Class here comprehensive works on secret service and spies

> *For British secret service and spies, see 973.386*

.386 British secret service and spies

.388 Propaganda

.4 Constitutional period, 1789–1809

.41 Administration of George Washington, 1789–1797

> *For second term, see 973.43*

.43 Second term of the administration of George Washington, 1793–1797

.44 Administration of John Adams, 1797–1801

.46 Administration of Thomas Jefferson, 1801–1809

> *For Tripolitan War, see 973.47; for second term, see 973.48*

.47 Tripolitan War, 1801–1805

> (Option: Class in 961.023)

.48 Second term of the administration of Thomas Jefferson, 1805–1809

.5 1809–1845

> Class here 19th century

> Class events of 1809–1845 as causes of Civil War in 973.711

> *For a specific part of 19th century not provided for here, see the part, e.g., Civil War 973.7*

.51 Administration of James Madison, 1809–1817

> *For War of 1812, see 973.52; for war with Algiers, see 973.53*

.52 ‡War of 1812, 1812–1815

> (Option: Class in 971.034)

‡Add as instructed under 940–990

.523	Military operations

> Do not use for participation of specific groups of countries, of specific countries, localities, groups; class in 973.52

> Class here land operations, military history

> > *For naval operations, see 973.525. For an aspect of military history not provided for here, see the aspect, e.g., prisoner-of-war camps 973.527*

.523 8	Operations in the South

> > *For Battle of New Orleans, see 973.5239*

.523 9	Battle of New Orleans, 1815
.524	Military units

> Number built according to instructions under 940–990

> Do not use for military operations, land operations, military history; class in 973.523. Do not use for naval operations; class in 973.525

.524 1	British troops
.524 2	American native peoples as allies of the British
.524 4–.524 7	American troops

> Add to base number 973.524 the numbers following —7 in notation 74–77 from Table 2, e.g., Pennsylvania troops 973.52448

.525	Naval operations

> Class here ships, units

> Including privateering

.525 4	Battle of Lake Erie, 1813
.525 6	Battle of Lake Champlain, 1814
.53	War with Algiers, 1815

> (Option: Class in 961.023)

.54	Administration of James Monroe, 1817–1825

> Including First Seminole War, 1818; Missouri Compromise, 1820

> > *See also 973.7113 for Missouri Compromise as a cause of Civil War*

.55	Administration of John Quincy Adams, 1825–1829
.56	Administration of Andrew Jackson, 1829–1837

> Including Black Hawk War, 1832
> (Option: Class Black Hawk War in 970.5)

.561	Nullification movement
.57	Administration of Martin Van Buren, 1837–1841

> Including Second Seminole War, 1835–1842

.58   Administrations of William Henry Harrison and John Tyler, 1841–1845

.6   1845–1861

           Class events of 1845–1861 as causes of Civil War in 973.711

.61   Administration of James Knox Polk, 1845–1849

               Including Wilmot Proviso, 1847

                   For Mexican War, see 973.62

                   See also 973.7113 for Wilmot Proviso as a cause of Civil War

.62   ‡Mexican War, 1845–1848

               (Option: Class in 972.05)

.63   Administration of Zachary Taylor, 1849–1850

.64   Administration of Millard Fillmore, 1850–1853

               Including Compromise of 1850

                   See also 973.7113 for Compromise of 1850 as a cause of Civil War

.66   Administration of Franklin Pierce, 1853–1857

.68   Administration of James Buchanan, 1857–1861

                   For Dred Scott decision, see 973.7115; for John Brown's Raid, see 973.7116

.7   Administration of Abraham Lincoln, 1861–1865

           Class here Civil War

SUMMARY

973.701–.709	**Standard subdivisions**
.71	**Social, political, economic history**
.72	**Diplomatic history**
.73	**Operations**
.74	**Military units**
.75	**Naval history**
.76	**Celebrations, commemorations, memorials**
.77	**Prisoners of war; medical and social services**
.78	**Other military topics and personal narratives**

.708   Groups of people

               Do not use for southern Union sympathizers; class in 973.717. Do not use for northern Confederate sympathizers; class in 973.718

[.708 691 4]   Displaced persons

               Relocated to 973.714

.709 2   Biography

               Do not use for personal narratives; class in 973.781–973.782

‡Add as instructed under 940–990

.71	Social, political, economic history

For diplomatic history, see 973.72

.711	Causes

For the South and secession, see 973.713

.711 2	Extension of slavery
.711 3	Wilmot Proviso, 1847, and compromises

Including Missouri Compromise, 1820; Compromise of 1850

.711 4	Abolition movement
.711 5	Fugitive slaves

Including underground railroad, Dred Scott decision

.711 6	John Brown's Raid, 1859
.712	Efforts to preserve or restore peace

For compromises, see 973.7113

.713	The South and secession

Confederate States of America in the war

.714	Results

Including displaced persons [*formerly* 973.7086914], movement of people; Emancipation Proclamation, 1863; establishment of Freedmen's Bureau, 1865

Class a result as a specific event with the event, e.g., Reconstruction 973.8

.717	Southern Union sympathizers
.718	Northern Confederate sympathizers
.72	Diplomatic history
.721	Relations of Confederacy with other nations
.722	Relations of Union with other nations
.73	Operations

For naval operations, see 973.75

.730 1	Strategy

Do not use for philosophy and theory; class in 973.73

.730 12	Union side
.730 13	Confederate side
.731	Opening phase, 1861–April, 1862
.732	May–August, 1862
.733	September, 1862 May, 1863

.733 6	Lee's invasion of Maryland, 1862
.734	June–August, 1863
.734 4	Siege and fall of Vicksburg, 1863
.734 9	Battle of Gettysburg, 1863
.735	September–December, 1863
.735 9	Chattanooga campaign, 1863
.736	January–May, 1864

For Atlanta Campaign, see 973.7371

.737	June–December, 1864
.737 1	Atlanta Campaign, 1864
.737 8	Sherman's March to the Sea and Savannah campaign, 1864
.738	1865
.74	Military units

Class here organization, history, rosters, service records

Class operations of military units in 973.73. Class units engaged in a special service with the service, e.g., privateering 973.75

For naval units, see 973.75; for rolls of honor, lists of dead, see 973.76

.741	Union troops

For state units, see 973.744–973.749

.741 5	African American troops
.742	Confederate troops

For state units, see 973.744–973.749

.744–.749	State units

Add to base number 973.74 the numbers following —7 in notation 74–79 from Table 2, e.g., Ohio troops 973.7471

.75	Naval history

Including operations, privateering, blockade running

.752	Battle of Monitor and Merrimac, 1862
.754	Battle of Kearsarge and Alabama, 1864
.757	Confederate Navy

Ships and units

.758	Union navy

Ships and units

.76	Celebrations, commemorations, memorials

Including rolls of honor, lists of dead

Class celebrations, commemorations, memorials of a specific event with the event, e.g., Battle of Antietam 973.7336

.77	Prisoners of war; medical and social services
.771	Confederate prisoner-of-war camps

Including exchange of prisoners

Class here prisoners of war

For Union prisoner-of-war camps, see 973.772

.772	Union prisoner-of-war camps
.775	Medical services

For hospitals, see 973.776

.776	Hospitals
.777	Welfare services

Including United States Sanitary Commission

.778	Religious life and chaplain services
.78	Other military topics and personal narratives

Including deserters, military personnel missing in action

.781	Personal narratives of individuals from Union side

Class here comprehensive works on personal narratives

Class personal narratives on a specific subject with the subject, e.g., on prisoner-of-war camps 973.771

For personal narratives of individuals from Confederate side, see 973.782

.782	Personal narratives of individuals from Confederate side
.783	Military life and customs of Union side

Class here comprehensive works on military life and customs

For military life and customs of Confederate side, see 973.784

.784	Military life and customs of Confederate side
.785	Union secret service and spies

Class here comprehensive works on secret service and spies

For Confederate secret service and spies, see 973.786

.786	Confederate secret service and spies
.788	Propaganda
.8	**Reconstruction period, 1865–1901**

.81	Administration of Andrew Johnson, 1865–1869
.82	Administration of Ulysses Simpson Grant, 1869–1877
.83	Administration of Rutherford Birchard Hayes, 1877–1881
.84	Administrations of James Abram Garfield and Chester Alan Arthur, 1881–1885
.85	First administration of Grover Cleveland, 1885–1889
.86	Administration of Benjamin Harrison, 1889–1893
.87	Second administration of Grover Cleveland, 1893–1897
.88	Administration of William McKinley, 1897–1901

> *For Spanish-American War, see 973.89*

.89	‡Spanish-American War, 1898

> (Option: Class in 946.074)

.893	Military operations

> Do not use for participation of specific groups of countries, of specific countries, localities, groups; class in 973.89
>
> Class here land operations, military history
>
> > *For naval operations, see 973.895. For an aspect of military history not provided for here, see the aspect, e.g., prisoner-of-war camps 973.897*

.893 3	Cuban campaign, 1898
.893 5	Puerto Rican campaign, 1898
.893 7	Philippine campaign, 1898
.894	Military units

> Number built according to instructions under 940–990
>
> Do not use for military operations, land operations, military history; class in 973.893. Do not use for naval operations; class in 973.895

.895	Naval operations

> Class here ships, units

.9	**1901–**
.91	1901–1953

> Class here 20th century
>
> > *For 1900–1901, see 973.88; for 1953–1999, see 973.92*

.911	Administration of Theodore Roosevelt, 1901–1909
.912	Administration of William Howard Taft, 1909–1913

‡Add as instructed under 940–990

.913	Administration of Woodrow Wilson, 1913–1921
.914	Administration of Warren Gamaliel Harding, 1921–1923
.915	Administration of Calvin Coolidge, 1923–1929
.916	Administration of Herbert Clark Hoover, 1929–1933
.917	Administration of Franklin Delano Roosevelt, 1933–1945
.918	Administration of Harry S Truman, 1945–1953
.92	1953–2001
.921	Administration of Dwight David Eisenhower, 1953–1961
.922	Administration of John Fitzgerald Kennedy, 1961–1963
.923	Administration of Lyndon Baines Johnson, 1963–1969

> Class here period of Vietnamese War, 1961–1975

> *For 1961–1963 period of Vietnamese War, see 973.922; for 1969–1974 period of Vietnamese War, see 973.924; for 1974–1975 period of Vietnamese War, see 973.925*

.924	Administration of Richard Milhous Nixon, 1969–1974
.925	Administration of Gerald Rudolph Ford, 1974–1977
.926	Administration of Jimmy (James Earl) Carter, 1977–1981
.927	Administration of Ronald Reagan, 1981–1989
.928	Administration of George Bush, 1989–1993
.929	Administration of Bill Clinton, 1993–2001
.93	2001–
.931	Administration of George W. Bush, 2001–2009
.932	Administration of Barack Obama, 2009–

> ## 974–979 Specific states of United States

Class comprehensive works in 973

For Hawaii, see 996.9

> ## 974–975 Northeastern and southeastern United States

Add to each subdivision identified by † as follows:

01	Early history to 1620
02	Colonial period, 1620–1776
03	1776–1865

       Class here 19th century

         For 1865–1899, see 041

04	1865–
041	1865–1918
042	1918–1945
043	1945–1999

       Class here 20th century

         For 1900–1918, see 041; for 1918–1945, see 042

044	2000–

Class comprehensive works in 974

974   *†Northeastern United States (New England and Middle Atlantic states)

.1   *†Maine

.2   *†New Hampshire

.3   *†Vermont

.4   *†Massachusetts

.5   *†Rhode Island

.6   *†Connecticut

.7   *†New York

.8   *†Pennsylvania

.9   *†New Jersey

975   *†Southeastern United States (South Atlantic states)

.1   *†Delaware

.2   *†Maryland

.3   *District of Columbia (Washington)

.301   Early history to 1799

.302   1800–1865

         Class here 19th century

         For 1865–1899, see 975.303

*Add as instructed under 930–990

†Add historical periods as instructed under 974–975

.303	1865–1933	
.304	1933–	
.304 1	1933–1999	

                                 Class here 20th century

                                   For 1900–1933, see 975.303

.304 2	2000–	
.4	***†West Virginia**	
.5	***†Virginia**	
.6	***†North Carolina**	
.7	***†South Carolina**	
.8	***†Georgia**	
.9	***Florida**	
.901	Early history to 1763	

                                 Including 18th century

                                 For 1763–1783, see 975.902; for 1783–1799, see 975.903

.902	English period, 1763–1783	
.903	Spanish period, 1783–1821	
.904	Territorial period, 1821–1845	

                                 Class here 19th century

                                 For a specific part of 19th century not provided for here, see the part, e.g., 1865–1899 975.9061

.905	Early statehood period, 1845–1865	
.906	1865–	
.906 1	1865–1918	
.906 2	1918–1945	
.906 3	1945–1999	

                                 Class here 20th century

                                 For 1900–1918, see 975.9061; for 1918–1945, see 975.9062

.906 4	2000–	

976   *South central United States

.01	Early history to 1700	

---

*Add as instructed under 930–990
†Add historical periods as instructed under 974–975

.02	1700–1799
.03	1800–1865

Class here 19th century

For 1865–1899, see 976.041

.04	1865–
.041	1865–1918
.042	1918–1945
.043	1945–1999

Class here 20th century

For 1900–1918, see 976.041; for 1918–1945, see 976.042

.044	2000–

.1   *Alabama

.101	Early history to 1701
.102	French period, 1701–1763

Class here 18th century

For 1763–1783, see 976.103; for 1783–1799, see 976.104

.103	British period, 1763–1783
.104	Spanish and territorial periods, 1783–1817
.105	Territorial and early statehood periods, 1817–1865

Class here 19th century

For 1800–1817, see 976.104; for 1865–1899, see 976.1061

.106	1865–
.106 1	1865–1918
.106 2	1918–1945
.106 3	1945–1999

Class here 20th century

For 1900–1918, see 976.1061; for 1918–1945, see 976.1062

.106 4	2000–

.2   *Mississippi

.201–.206	Historical periods

Add to base number 976.20 the numbers following 976.10 in 976.101–976.106, e.g., British period 976.203

*Add as instructed under 930–990

.3	***Louisiana**
.301	Early history to 1718
.302	French period, 1718–1763

        Class here 18th century

          For 1700–1718, see 976.301; for 1763–1799, see 976.303

.303	1763–1803

        Including French period, 1800–1803

        Class here Spanish period, 1763–1800

.304	Territorial period, 1803–1812
.305	Early statehood period, 1812–1865

        Class here 19th century

          For a specific part of 19th century not provided for here, see the part, e.g., 1865–1899 976.3061

.306	1865–
.306 1	1865–1918
.306 2	1918–1945
.306 3	1945–1999

        Class here 20th century

          For 1900–1918, see 976.3061; for 1918–1945, see 976.3062

.306 4	2000–
.4	***Texas**
.401	Early history to 1680
.402	Spanish and French periods, 1680–1821
.403	Mexican period, 1821–1836
.404	Period of the Republic, 1836–1846
.405	Early statehood period, 1846–1865

        Class here 19th century

          For a specific part of 19th century not provided for here, see the part, e.g., 1836–1846 976.404

.406	1865–
.406 1	1865–1918
.406 2	1918–1945

*Add as instructed under 930–990

.406 3	1945–1999

        Class here 20th century

          For 1900–1918, see 976.4061; for 1918–1945, see 976.4062

.406 4	2000–

.6   *Oklahoma

.601	Early history to 1682
.602	French and Spanish periods, 1682–1803
.603	Period of Indian Territory, 1803–1866

        Class here 19th century

          For 1800–1803, see 976.602; for 1866–1899, see 976.604

.604	Territorial and early statehood periods, 1866–1907
.605	1907–
.605 2	1907–1945
.605 3	1945–1999

        Class here 20th century

          For 1900–1907, see 976.604; for 1907–1945, see 976.6052

.605 4	2000–

.7   *Arkansas

.701	Early history to 1686
.702	French and Spanish periods, 1686–1803
.703	Preterritorial and territorial periods, 1803–1836
.704	Early statehood period, 1836–1865

        Class here 19th century

          For a specific part of 19th century not provided for here, see the part, e.g., 1865–1899 976.7051

.705	1865–
.705 1	1865–1918
.705 2	1918–1945
.705 3	1945–1999

        Class here 20th century

          For 1900–1918, see 976.7051; for 1918–1945, see 976.7052

.705 4	2000–

*Add as instructed under 930–990

.8 ***Tennessee**

.801 Early history to 1682

.802 French, Spanish, English periods, 1682–1769

Class here 18th century

For 1769–1796, see 976.803; for 1796–1799, see 976.804

.803 Early settlement and territorial periods, 1769–1796

Including District of Washington, State of Franklin

.804 Early statehood period, 1796–1865

Class here 19th century

For 1865–1899, see 976.8051

.805 1865–

.805 1 1865–1918

.805 2 1918–1945

.805 3 1945–1999

Class here 20th century

For 1900–1918, see 976.8051; for 1918–1945, see 976.8052

.805 4 2000–

.9 ***Kentucky**

.901 Early history to 1736

.902 1736–1792

Class here 18th century

Including periods of French, British, Virginian control; Transylvania Colony

For 1700–1736, see 976.901; for 1792–1799, see 976.903

.903 Early statehood period, 1792–1865

Class here 19th century

For 1865–1899, see 976.9041

.904 1865–

.904 1 1865–1918

.904 2 1918–1945

.904 3 1945–1999

Class here 20th century

For 1900–1918, see 976.9041; for 1918–1945, see 976.9042

*Add as instructed under 930–990

.904 4   2000–

977   *North central United States

.01   Early history to 1787

.02   1787–1865

              Class here 19th century

                  For 1865–1899, see 977.031

.03   1865–

.031   1865–1918

.032   1918–1945

.033   1945–1999

                  Class here 20th century

                      For 1900–1918, see 977.031; for 1918–1945, see 977.032

.034   2000–

.1   *Ohio

.101   Early history to 1763

                  Including 18th century

                      For 1763–1787, see 977.102; for 1787–1799, see 977.103

.102   British and early United States periods, 1763–1787

.103   Territorial and early statehood periods, 1787–1865

                  Class here 19th century

                      For 1865–1899, see 977.1041

.104   1865–

.104 1   1865–1918

.104 2   1918–1945

.104 3   1945–1999

                  Class here 20th century

                      For 1900–1918, see 977.1041; for 1918–1945, see 977.1042

.104 4   2000–

.2   *Indiana

.201–.204   Historical periods

                  Add to base number 977.20 the numbers following 977.10 in
                  977.101–977.104, e.g., territorial period 977.203

*Add as instructed under 930–990

.3   *Illinois

.301–.304   Historical periods

> Add to base number 977.30 the numbers following 977.10 in 977.101–977.104, e.g., territorial period 977.303

.4   *Michigan

.401–.404   Historical periods

> Add to base number 977.40 the numbers following 977.10 in 977.101–977.104, e.g., territorial period 977.403

.5   *Wisconsin

.501–.504   Historical periods

> Add to base number 977.50 the numbers following 977.10 in 977.101–977.104, e.g., territorial period 977.503

.6   *Minnesota

.601   Early history to 1660

> Including 17th century
>
> *For 1660–1699, see 977.602*

.602   French period, 1660–1783

.603   Preterritorial period, 1783–1849

.604   Territorial and early statehood periods, 1849–1900

> Class here 19th century
>
> *For 1800–1849, see 977.603*

.605   1900–

.605 1   1900–1918

.605 2   1918–1945

.605 3   1945–1999

> Class here 20th century
>
> *For 1900–1918, see 977.6051; for 1918–1945, see 977.6052*

.605 4   2000–

.7   *Iowa

.701   Early history to 1838

.702   Territorial and early statehood periods, 1838–1899

> Class here 19th century
>
> *For 1800–1838, see 977.701*

*Add as instructed under 930–990

.703	1900–
.703 1	1900–1918
.703 2	1918–1945
.703 3	1945–1999

Class here 20th century

For 1900–1918, see 977.7031; for 1918–1945, see 977.7032

.703 4	2000–

.8   *Missouri

.801	Early history to 1750

Including 18th century

For 1750–1799, see 977.802

.802	French and Spanish periods, 1750–1803
.803	Territorial and early statehood periods, 1803–1899
.804	1900–
.804 1	1900–1918
.804 2	1918–1945
.804 3	1945–1999

Class here 20th century

For 1900–1918, see 977.8041; for 1918–1945, see 977.8042

.804 4	2000–

978   *Western United States

.01	Early history to 1799
.02	1800–1899
.03	1900
.031	1900–1918
.032	1918–1945
.033	1945–1999

Class here 20th century

For 1900–1918, see 978.031; for 1918–1945, see 978.032

.034	2000–

.1   *Kansas

.101	Early history to 1803

*Add as instructed under 930–990

| .102 | Territorial period, 1803–1861 |
| | Class here 19th century |

    For 1800–1803, see 978.101; for 1861–1899, see 978.1031

.103	Statehood period, 1861–
.103 1	1861–1918
.103 2	1918–1945
.103 3	1945–1999
	Class here 20th century

    For 1900–1918, see 978.1031; for 1918–1945, see 978.1032

.103 4	2000–
.2	***Nebraska**
.201	Early history to 1854
	Including 19th century

    For 1854–1867, see 978.202; for 1867–1899, see 978.2031

.202	Territorial period, 1854–1867
.203	Statehood period, 1867–
.203 1	1867–1918
.203 2	1918–1945
.203 3	1945–1999
	Class here 20th century

    For 1900–1918, see 978.2031; for 1918–1945, see 978.2032

.203 4	2000–
.3	***South Dakota**
.301	Early history to 1861
	Including 19th century

    For 1861–1889, see 978.302; for 1889–1899, see 978.3031

.302	Territorial period, 1861–1889
.303	Statehood period, 1889–
.303 1	1889–1918
.303 2	1918–1945

*Add as instructed under 930–990

.303 3	1945–1999
	Class here 20th century
	For 1900–1918, see 978.3031; for 1918–1945, see 978.3032
.303 4	2000–

.4 *North Dakota

.401–.403	Historical periods
	Add to base number 978.40 the numbers following 978.30 in 978.301–978.303, e.g., territorial period 978.402

.6 *Montana

.601	Early history to 1864
	Including 19th century
	For 1864–1889, see 978.602; for 1889–1899, see 978.6031
.602	Territorial period, 1864–1889
.603	Statehood period, 1889–
.603 1	1889–1918
.603 2	1918–1945
.603 3	1945–1999
	Class here 20th century
	For 1900–1918, see 978.6031; for 1918–1945, see 978.6032
.603 4	2000–

.7 *Wyoming

.701	Early history to 1868
	Including 19th century
	For 1868–1890, see 978.702; for 1890–1899, see 978.7031
.702	Territorial period, 1868–1890
.703	Statehood period, 1890–
.703 1	1890–1918
.703 2	1918–1945
.703 3	1945–1999
	Class here 20th century
	For 1900–1918, see 978.7031; for 1918–1945, see 978.7032
.703 4	2000–

Add as instructed under 930–990

.8	***Colorado**
.801	Early history to 1803
.802	Acquisition and territorial periods, 1803–1876

         Class here 19th century

            For 1800–1803, see 978.801; for 1876–1899, see 978.8031

.803	Statehood period, 1876–
.803 1	1876–1918
.803 2	1918–1945
.803 3	1945–1999

         Class here 20th century

            For 1900–1918, see 978.8031; for 1918–1945, see 978.8032

.803 4	2000–
.9	***New Mexico**
.901	Early history to 1598
.902	Spanish period, 1598–1821
.903	Mexican period, 1821–1848
.904	Territorial period, 1848–1912

         Class here 19th century

            For 1800–1821, see 978.902; for 1821–1848, see 978.903

.905	Statehood period, 1912–
.905 2	1912–1945
.905 3	1945–1999

         Class here 20th century

            For 1900–1912, see 978.904; for 1912–1945, see 978.9052

.905 4	2000–

979   **Great Basin and Pacific Slope region of United States*

.01–.03	Historical periods

         Add to base number 979.0 the numbers following 978.0 in 978.01–978.03, e.g., 1900 to present 979.03

.1	***Arizona**

*Add as instructed under 930–990

.101–.105	Historical periods	

Add to base number 979.10 the numbers following 978.90 in 978.901–978.905, e.g., territorial period 979.104

.2   *Utah

.201   Early history to 1848

.202   Territorial period, 1848–1896

Class here 19th century

For 1800–1848, see 979.201; for 1896–1899, see 979.2031

.203   Statehood period, 1896–

.203 1   1896–1918

.203 2   1918–1945

.203 3   1945–1999

Class here 20th century

For 1900–1918, see 979.2031; for 1918–1945, see 979.2032

.203 4   2000–

.3   *Nevada

.301   Early history to 1861

Including 19th century

For 1861–1899, see 979.302

.302   Territorial and early statehood periods, 1861–1899

.303   1900–

.303 1   1900–1918

.303 2   1918–1945

.303 3   1945–1999

Class here 20th century

For 1900–1918, see 979.3031; for 1918–1945, see 979.3032

.303 4   2000–

.4   *California

.401   Early history to 1769

Including 18th century

For 1769–1799, see 979.402

.402   Spanish period, 1769–1822

Add as instructed under 930–990

.403	Mexican period, 1822–1848
.404	Territorial and early statehood periods, 1848–1899

Class here 19th century

> For 1800–1822, see 979.402; for 1822–1848, see 979.403

.405	1900–
.405 1	1900–1918
.405 2	1918–1945
.405 3	1945–1999

Class here 20th century

> For 1900–1918, see 979.4051; for 1918–1945, see 979.4052

.405 4	2000–
.5	***Oregon**
.501	Early history to 1778
.502	Spanish and British periods, 1778–1819
.503	Preterritorial and territorial periods, 1819–1859

Class here 19th century

> For 1800–1819, see 979.502; for 1859–1899, see 979.5041

.504	Statehood period, 1859–
.504 1	1859–1918
.504 2	1918–1945
.504 3	1945–1999

Class here 20th century

> For 1900–1918, see 979.5041; for 1918–1945, see 979.5042

.504 4	2000–
.6	***Idaho**
.601	Early history to 1863

Including 19th century

> For 1863–1890, see 979.602; for 1889–1899, see 979.6031

.602	Territorial period, 1863–1890
.603	Statehood period, 1890–
.603 1	1890–1918
.603 2	1918–1945

*Add as instructed under 930–990

.603 3	1945–1999
	Class here 20th century
	For 1900–1918, see 979.6031; for 1918–1945, see 979.6032
.603 4	2000–

.7 ***Washington**

.701	Early history to 1818
.702	British and preterritorial periods, 1818–1853
.703	Territorial period, 1853–1889
	Class here 19th century
	For a specific part of 19th century not provided for here, see the part, e.g., 1889–1899 979.7041
.704	Statehood period, 1889–
.704 1	1889–1918
.704 2	1918–1945
.704 3	1945–1999
	Class here 20th century
	For 1900–1918, see 979.7041; for 1918–1945, see 979.7042
.704 4	2000–

.8 ***Alaska**

.801	Early history to 1799
.802	Russian period, 1799–1867
	Class here 19th century
	For 1867–1899, see 979.803
.803	Preterritorial period, 1867–1912
.804	Territorial period, 1912–1959
	Class here 20th century
	For 1900–1912, see 979.803; for 1959–1999, see 979.8051
.805	Statehood period, 1959–
.805 1	1959–1999
.805 2	2000–

---

*Add as instructed under 930–990

980   History of South America

Class here Latin America

For Middle America, see 972

SUMMARY

980.001–.009	**Standard subdivisions**
.01–.04	**Historical periods**
981	**Brazil**
982	**Argentina**
983	**Chile**
984	**Bolivia**
985	**Peru**
986	**Colombia and Ecuador**
987	**Venezuela**
988	**Guiana**
989	**Paraguay and Uruguay**

.001–.003   Standard subdivisions

.004   Ethnic and national groups

.004 05–.004 09   Specific ethnic and national groups with ethnic origins from more than one continent, of European descent

Add to base number 980.0040 the numbers following —0 in notation 05–09 from Table 5, e.g., general history and civilization of people of European descent in South America 980.00409

.004 1–.004 9   Specific ethnic and national groups

Add to base number 980.004 notation 1–9 from Table 5, e.g., general history and civilization of South American native peoples in South America 980.00498
(Option: Class South American native peoples in South America in 980.1; class specific native peoples in 980.3)

Class prehispanic history and civilization of South American native peoples in a specific place with the place, without using notation 00498 from add table under 930–990, e.g., Incas before 1519 985.019

.005–.009   Standard subdivisions

As modified under 930–990

>   980.01–980.04   Historical periods

Class comprehensive works in 980

.01   Early history to 1806

.012   Early history to 1498

.013   Period of European discovery, exploration, colonization, 1498–1806

.02   Period of struggles for independence, 1806–1830

.03   1830–1999

.031	1830–1899

> Class here 19th century
>
> *For 1801–1806, see 980.013; for 1806–1830, see 980.02*

.032	1900–1918
.033	1918–1949

> Class here 20th century
>
> *For a specific part of 20th century not provided for here, see the part, e.g., 1950–1959 980.035*

.035	1950–1959
.036	1960–1969
.037	1970–1979
.038	1980–1989
.039	1990–1999
.04	2000–
.041	2000–2019
.041 1	2000–2009
.041 2	2010–2019

(.1)   **South American native peoples (Indians)**

> (Optional number; prefer 980.00498)
>
> Class special topics in 980.3–980.5

(.3)   **Specific native peoples**

> (Optional number; prefer 981–989 with use of subdivision 00498 from table under 930–990, e.g., Quechua in Potosí department of Bolivia 984.1400498323)
>
> Arrange alphabetically by name of people
>
> Class government relations with specific native peoples in 980.5

(.4)   **Native peoples in specific places in South America**

> (Optional number; prefer 981–989 with use of subdivision 00498 from table under 930–990, e.g., native peoples in Brazil 981.00498)
>
> Add to base number 980.4 the numbers following —8 in notation 81–89 from Table 2, e.g., native peoples in Brazil 980.41
>
> Class specific native peoples in specific places in 980.3; class government relations in specific places in 980.5

(.5)   **Government relations with native South Americans**

> (Optional number; prefer 323.1198 for comprehensive works; a specific subject with the subject, e.g., conquest of Incas by Pizarro 985.02, relation to state in Chile 323.1198083)

> ## 981–989 Countries and localities

Class comprehensive works in 980. Class a specific native people in a specific place with the place in 981–989 with use of subdivision 00498 from table under 930–990, e.g., Quechua in Potosí department of Bolivia 984.1400498323
 (Option: Class South American native peoples in specific places in South America in 980.4)

981   *Brazil

.01   Early history to 1500

.03   Colonial period, 1500–1822

.031   Period of European explorations, 1500–1533

.032   Period of hereditary captaincies, 1533–1762

           Including 16th century, 18th century

           Class here 17th century

              For 1500–1533, see 981.031; for 1762–1799, see 981.033

.033   1762–1822

.04   Period of Empire, 1822–1889

           Class here 19th century

              For 1800–1822, see 981.033; for 1889–1899, see 981.05; for Paraguayan War, see 989.205

.05   Period of First Republic, 1889–1930

.06   Period of Second Republic, 1930–

           Class here 20th century

              For 1901–1930, see 981.05

.061   Period of Getúlio Vargas, 1930–1954

           Including administrations of José Finol Linhares and Eurico Gaspar Dutra, 1945–1951

.062   1954–1964

.063   Period of military presidents, 1964–1985

.064   1985–2002

           Including administrations of José Sarney, Fernando Affonso Collor de Mello, Itamar Franco, Fernando Henrique Cardoso

.065   Administration of Luiz Inácio Lula da Silva, 2003–2011

.066   2011–

982   *Argentina

*Add as instructed under 930–990

.01   Early history to 1516

.02   Period of European discovery, conquest, colonization, 1516–1810

.022   Period of European discovery and conquest, 1516–1580

Class here 16th century

For 1500–1516, see 982.01; for 1580–1599, see 982.023

.023   Colonial period, 1580–1810

For period of viceroyalty of La Plata, 1776–1810, see 982.024

.024   Period of viceroyalty of La Plata, 1776–1810

.03   Period of struggle for independence, 1810–1829

.04   1829–1861

Class here 19th century

For 1801–1810, see 982.024; for 1810–1829, see 982.03; for 1861–1900, see 982.05

.05   1861–1910

For Paraguayan War, see 989.205

.06   1910–1999

.061   1910–1946

.062   First administration of Juan Domingo Perón, 1946–1955

.063   1955–1973

.064   1973–1989

Including second administration of Juan Domingo Perón, 1973–1974; administration of Isabel Perón, 1974–1976

.065   Administration of Carlos Saúl Menem, 1989–1999

.07   1999–

.071   1999–2003

Class here administrations of Fernando de la Rúa, 1999–2001, Eduardo Alberto Duhalde, 2002–2003

.072   Administration of Néstor Kirchner, 2003–2007

.073   Administration of Cristina Fernández de Kirchner, 2007–

983   *Chile

.01   Early history to 1535

*Add as instructed under 930–990

.02	Period of European discovery and conquest, 1535–1560

         Class here 16th century

         For 1500–1535, see 983.01; for 1560–1599, see 983.03

.03	Colonial period, 1560–1810
.04	Period of early republics, 1810–1861

         Class here 19th century

         For period of autocratic republic, 1830–1861, see 983.05. For a specific part of 19th century not provided for here, see the part, e.g., 1879–1883 983.0616

.05	Period of autocratic republic, 1830–1861
.06	Period of later republics, 1861–
.061	Period of liberal republic, 1861–1891
.061 6	‡War of the Pacific, 1879–1883

         (Option: Class Bolivian aspects of War of the Pacific in 984.045; Peruvian aspects of War of the Pacific in 985.061)

.062	Revolution of 1891
.063	Period of parliamentary republic, 1891–1925
.064	1925–1973

         Class here 20th century

         For 1901–1925, see 983.063; for 1973–1990, see 983.065; for 1990–1999, see 983.066

.064 1	1925–1932
.064 2	1932–1946
.064 3	1946–1958
.064 4	Administration of Jorge Alessandri, 1958–1964
.064 5	Administration of Eduardo Frei Montalva, 1964–1970
.064 6	Administration of Salvador Allende Gossens, 1970–1973
.065	Period of military rule, 1973–1990
.066	1990–
.066 1	Administration of Patricio Aylwin Azócar, 1990–1994
.066 2	Administration of Eduardo Frei Ruiz-Tagle, 1994–2000
.066 3	Administration of Ricardo Lagos Escobar, 2000–2006
.066 4	Administration of Michelle Bachelet, 2006–

‡Add as instructed under 940–990

984   *Bolivia

.01	Early history to 1532
.02	Period of European discovery and conquest, 1532–1559

> Class here 16th century
>
> *For 1500–1532, see 984.01; for 1559–1599, see 984.03*

.03	Colonial period, 1559–1809
.04	1809–1899
.041	Period of struggle for independence, 1809–1825
.042	Period of formation of the Republic, 1825–1831
.044	Administration of Andrés Santa Cruz, 1831–1839

> Including Peru-Bolivian Confederation, 1836–1839

.045	1839–1883

> (Option: Class here War of the Pacific; prefer 983.0616)

.046	Period of conservative republic, 1883–1899
.05	1899–
.051	1899–1952

> Class here 20th century
>
> *For 1952–1999, see 984.052*
>
> (Option: Class here Chaco War; prefer 989.20716)

.052	1952–1982

> Including revolution of 1952

.053	1982–1997
.054	1997–
.054 1	1997–2006

> Including second administration of Hugo Banzer Suárez, 1997–2001

.054 2	Administration of Evo Morales Ayma, 2006–

985   *Peru

.01	Early history to 1519
.019	Period of Inca (Inka) empire, ca. 1438–1519

> *For a part of Inca empire not provided for here, see the part, e.g.,
> Inca empire in Bolivia 984.01*

*Add as instructed under 930–990

.02	Period of European discovery and conquest, 1519–1555

Class here 16th century

For 1500–1519, see 985.019; for 1555–1599, see 985.031

(Option: Class conquest in 980.5)

.03	Colonial period, 1555–1808
.031	1555–1599
.032	1600–1699
.033	1700–1808
.04	Period of struggle for independence, 1808–1824
.05	1824–1867

Class here 19th century

Including Peru-Bolivian Confederation, 1836–1839

For a specific part of 19th century not provided for here, see the part, e.g., 1867–1883 985.061

.06	1867–
.061	1867–1883

(Option: Class here War of the Pacific, 1879–1883; prefer 983.0616)

.062	Period of reconstruction, 1883–1895
.063	1895–1980
.063 1	1895–1930
.063 2	1930–1968
.063 3	Period of the Revolutionary Government, 1968–1980
.064	1980–
.064 3	Administration of Alberto Fujimori, 1990–2000
.064 4	2000–2006

Class here administration of Alejandro Toledo Manrique, 2001–2006

.064 5	Administration of Alan García, 2006–

986   *Colombia and Ecuador

.1   *Colombia

.101	Early history to 1550

Including 16th century

For 1550–1599, see 986.102

*Add as instructed under 930–990

.102	Colonial period, 1550–1810

Including periods as Viceroyalty of New Granada, 1718–1724 and 1740–1810

Class here comprehensive works on Viceroyalty of New Granada

For Panama as part of Viceroyalty of New Granada, see 972.8702; for Ecuador as part of Viceroyalty of New Granada, see 986.602; for Venezuela as part of Viceroyalty of New Granada, see 987.03

.103	Period of struggle for independence, 1810–1819
.104	Period of Gran Colombia, 1819–1832

Class here comprehensive works on Gran Colombia

For Panama as a part of Gran Colombia, see 972.8703; for Ecuador as part of Gran Colombia, see 986.604; for Venezuela as part of Gran Colombia, see 987.05

.105	1832–1863

Class here 19th century

For a specific part of 19th century not provided for here, see the part, e.g., 1810–1819 986.103

.105 2	Period of Republic of New Granada, 1832–1858

Class here comprehensive works on Republic of New Granada

For Panama as part of Republic of New Granada, see 972.8703

.105 3	Period of Granadine Confederation, 1858–1863

Class here comprehensive works on Granadine Confederation

For Panama as part of Granadine Confederation, see 972.8703

.106	1863–
.106 1	Period of United States of Colombia, 1863–1886

Class here comprehensive works on United States of Colombia

For Panama as part of United States of Colombia, see 972.8703

.106 2	Period of Republic of Colombia, 1886–

For Panama as part of Republic of Colombia, see 972.8703; for Colombian history from 1930 to present, see 986.1063

.106 3	1930–

Class here 20th century

For 1901–1930, see 986.1062

.106 31	Period of liberal domination, 1930–1946
.106 32	1946–1958
.106 33	Period of National Front, 1958–1974
.106 34	1974–1991

.106 35	1991–

.6   ***Ecuador**

.601   Early history to 1562

     Including 16th century

      For 1562–1599, see 986.602

.602   Colonial period, 1562–1810

     Including period as part of Viceroyalty of New Granada, 1740–1810

.603   Period of struggle for independence, 1810–1822

.604   Period as part of Gran Colombia, 1822–1830

     Class here Quito Presidency

.605   1830–1859

     Including period of formation of Republic

     Class here 19th century

      For a specific part of 19th century not provided for here, see the part, e.g., 1810–1822 986.603

.606   1860–1895

.607   1896–

.607 1   1896–1925

     Class here 20th century

      For a specific part of 20th century not provided for here, see the part, e.g., 1960–1999 986.6074

.607 2   1925–1948

.607 3   1948–1960

.607 4   1960–2000

.607 5   2000–

987   *Venezuela

.01   Early history to 1498

.02   Period of discovery and conquest, 1498–1528

.03   Colonial period, 1528–1810

     Including period of Welsers, 1528–1556; period as part of Viceroyalty of New Granada, 1740–1810; 16th century

      For 1500–1528, see 987.02

.04   Period of struggle for independence, 1810–1821

*Add as instructed under 930–990

.05	Period as part of Gran Colombia, 1821–1830
.06	Period of Republic, 1830–
.061	1830–1848
.062	1848–1899

Including Revolution of April 1870

Class here 19th century

For a specific part of 19th century not provided for here, see the part, e.g., 1810–1821 987.04

.062 8	1870–1899

Class here administration of Antonio Guzmán Blanco, 1870–1888

.063	1899–1989
.063 1	1899–1945
.063 12	Period of Cipriano Castro, 1899–1908
.063 13	Period of Juan Vicente Gómez, 1908–1935
.063 14	Administration of Eleazar López Contreras, 1935–1941
.063 15	Administration of Isaías Medina Angarita, 1941–1945
.063 2	1945–1958

Including Revolution of October 1945

.063 3	1958–1989

Including Revolution of 1958

.064	1989–
.064 2	Administration of Hugo Chávez Frias, 1999–

988   *Guiana

.01	Early history to 1815
.02	1815–1945
.03	1945–

Class here 20th century

For 1901–1945, see 988.02

.1   *Guyana

.101	Early history to 1815
.102	1815–1945

*Add as instructed under 930–990

.103	1945–
	Class here 20th century
	For 1901–1945, see 988.102
.103 1	1945–1966
.103 2	1966–1992
.103 3	1992–
.103 31	Administration of Cheddi Jagan, 1992–1997
.103 32	Administration of Janet Jagan, 1997–1999
.103 33	Administration of Bharrat Jagdeo, 1999–
.2	**†French Guiana (Guyane)**
.3	***Suriname**
.301	Early history to 1815
.302	1815–1945
.303	1945–
	Class here 20th century
	For 1901–1945, see 988.302
.303 1	1945–1975
.303 2	1975–
.303 21	1975–1991
.303 22	First administration of Runaldo Ronald Venetiaan, 1991–1996
.303 23	Administration of Jules A. Wijdenbosch, 1996–2000
.303 24	Second administration of Runaldo Ronald Venetiaan, 2000–

989   †Paraguay and Uruguay

.2	***Paraguay**
.201	Early history to 1524
.202	Period of European discovery, exploration, conquest, 1524–1537
.203	Colonial period, 1537–1811
	Including 16th century
	For 1500–1524, see 989.201; for 1524–1537, see 989.202
.204	Period of struggle for independence, 1811–1814

*Add as instructed under 930–990
†Add as instructed under 930–990; however, do not add historical periods

.205	Period of dictatorship, 1814–1870

Including Paraguayan War (War of the Triple Alliance), 1865–1870

Class here 19th century

For a specific part of 19th century not provided for here, see the part, e.g., 1811–1814 989.204

.206	1870–1902
.207	1902–
.207 1	1902–1940
.207 16	‡Chaco War, 1933–1935

(Option: Class in 984.051)

.207 2	1940–1954

1954–1958 relocated to 989.2073

.207 3	Administration of Alfredo Stroessner, 1954–1989

Including 1954–1958 [*formerly* 989.2072]

.207 4	1989–
.207 41	Administration of Andrés Rodríguez, 1989–1993
.207 42	Administration of Juan Carlos Wasmosy, 1993–1998
.207 43	Administration of Raúl Cubas Grau, 1998–1999
.207 44	Administration of Luis Angel González Macchi, 1999–2003
.207 45	Administration of Nicanor Duarte Frutos, 2003–2008
.207 46	Administration of Fernando Lugo Méndez, 2008–
.5	***Uruguay**
.501	Early history to 1516
.502	Period of European discovery and conquest, 1516–1724
.503	Colonial period, 1724–1811
.504	Period of struggle for independence, 1811–1830
.505	Period of Republic, 1830–

Class here 19th century

For Paraguayan War, see 989.205; for 1886 to present, see 989.506. For a specific part of 19th century not provided for here, see the part, e.g., 1811–1830 989.504

.506	1886–
.506 1	1886–1917

*Add as instructed under 930–990
‡Add as instructed under 940–990

.506 2	1917–1933
.506 3	1933–1951
.506 4	1951–1966
.506 5	1966–1973
.506 6	1973–1985
.506 7	1985–
.506 71	First administration of Julio María Sanguinetti, 1985–1990
.506 72	Administration of Luis Albert Lacalle Herrera, 1990–1995
.506 73	Second administration of Julio María Sanguinetti, 1995–2000
.506 74	Administration of Jorge Batlle Ibáñez, 2000–2005
.506 75	Administration of Tabaré Vázquez, 2005–2010
.506 76	Administration of José Alberto Mujica Cordano, 2010–

990 History of Australasia, Pacific Ocean islands, Atlantic Ocean islands, Arctic islands, Antarctica, extraterrestrial worlds

.01–.09   Standard subdivisions of Australasia, Pacific Ocean islands, Atlantic Ocean islands, Arctic islands, Antarctica, extraterrestrial worlds together; of Australasia alone; of Pacific Ocean islands alone

> As modified under 930–990

[991] [Unassigned]

> Most recently used in Edition 17

[992] [Unassigned]

> Most recently used in Edition 17

993 *New Zealand

.01   Early history to 1840

> Including history of Maori before European settlement, of European settlers

.02   Colonial period, 1840–1908

> Class here 19th century

> *For 1800–1840, see 993.01*

.021   Period as a Crown colony, 1840–1853

> Including New Zealand Wars of 1843–1847

*Add as instructed under 930–990

.022	Period of provincial governments, 1853–1876
	Class here comprehensive works on New Zealand Wars
	For New Zealand Wars of 1843–1847, see 993.021
.023	Period of centralized government, 1876–1908
.03	1908–1999
	Class here Dominion period, 1908–1947
.031	1908–1918
.032	1918–1945
.035	1945–1969
.037	1970–1984
.038	1984–1999
.04	2000–
.041	2000–2019
.041 1	2000–2009
.041 2	2010–2019

994 *Australia

.01	Early history to 1788
.02	Period of settlement and growth, 1788–1851
	Class here 19th century
	For 1851–1899, see 994.03
.03	Period of development of self government, 1851–1901
.031	Period of gold discovery and consolidation, 1851–1891
.032	1891–1901
.04	Period of Commonwealth, 1901–
	Class here 20th century
	For 1945–1966, see 994.05; for 1966–1999, see 994.06; for 2000 to present, see 994.07
.041	1901–1922
.042	1922–1945
	Including first prime ministership of Robert Menzies, 1939–1941
.05	1945–1966
	Class here second prime ministership of Robert Menzies, 1949–1966

*Add as instructed under 930–990

.06	1966–1999
.061	1966–1972
.062	Prime ministership of Gough Whitlam, 1972–1975
.063	Prime ministership of Malcolm Fraser, 1975–1983
.064	Prime ministership of Bob Hawke, 1983–1991
.065	Prime ministership of Paul Keating, 1991–1996
.066	1996–1999

> Class here prime ministership of John Howard, 1996–2007

> *For prime ministership of John Howard during 2000–2007, see 994.071*

.07	2000–
.071	Later part of prime ministership of John Howard, 2000–2007
.072	2007–

995 †New Guinea and neighboring countries of Melanesia

Class here Oceania

Subdivisions are added for New Guinea and neighboring countries of Melanesia together, for New Guinea alone

Class Polynesia in 996

> **995.1–995.7 New Guinea**

Class comprehensive works in 995

.1 *Western New Guinea (Irian Barat)

| .101–.104 | Historical periods |

> Add to base number 995.10 the numbers following 959.80 in 959.801–959.804, e.g., period of administration of Soekarno 995.1035

.3 *Papua New Guinea

Class here New Guinea region

> *For Papuan region, see 995.4; for Highlands region, see 995.6; for Momase region, see 995.7; for Bismarck Archipelago, see 995.8; for North Solomons Province, see 995.92*

| .301 | Early history to 1884 |

---

*Add as instructed under 930–990
†Add as instructed under 930–990; however, do not add historical periods

.302	1884–1942

> Class here 20th century
>
> *For 1942–1945, see 995.303; for 1945–1975, see 995.304; for 1975–1999, see 995.305*

.302 1	1884–1921

> Class here German New Guinea

.302 2	1921–1942

> Class here period as Territory of New Guinea, 1921–1949
>
> *For 1942–1945, see 995.303; for 1945–1949, see 995.304*

.303	Period of World War II, 1942–1945
.304	1945–1975

> Class here Territory of Papua and New Guinea, 1949–1975

.305	Period of independence, 1975–

.4   *Papuan region

.401	Early history to 1884
.402	1884–1942

> Class here 20th century
>
> *For 1942–1945, see 995.403; for 1945–1975, see 995.404; for 1975–1999, see 995.405*

.402 1	Period as British New Guinea, 1884–1906
.402 2	1906–1942

> Class here period as Territory of Papua, 1906–1949
>
> *For 1942–1945, see 995.403; for 1945–1949, see 995.404*

.403	Period of World War II, 1942–1945
.404	1945–1975

> Class here Papuan region as a part of Territory of Papua and New Guinea, 1949–1975

.405	Period of independence, 1975–

.6   *Highlands region

.601–.605	Historical periods

> Add to base number 995.60 the numbers following 995.30 in 995.301–995.305, e.g., period of World War II 995.603

.7   *Momase (Northern coastal) region

*Add as instructed under 930–990

.701–.705   Historical periods

> Add to base number 995.70 the numbers following 995.30 in 995.301–995.305, e.g., period of World War II 995.703

.8   *Bismarck Archipelago

.801–.805   Historical periods

> Add to base number 995.80 the numbers following 995.30 in 995.301–995.305, e.g., period of World War II 995.803

.9   †Other parts of Melanesia

.92   *North Solomons Province

.920 1–.920 5   Historical periods

> Add to base number 995.920 the numbers following 995.30 in 995.301–995.305, e.g., period of World War II 995.9203

.93   †Solomon Islands

.95   †Vanuatu

.97   †New Caledonia

996   Polynesia and other Pacific Ocean islands

.001–.009   Standard subdivisions of Polynesia and other Pacific Ocean islands together, of Polynesia alone

> As modified under 930–990

.1   †Southwest central Pacific, and isolated islands of southeast Pacific

.11   †Fiji

.12   †Tonga (Friendly Islands)

.13   †American Samoa

.14   †Samoa

.15   †Tokelau (Union Islands)

.16   †Wallis and Futuna Islands

.18   †Isolated islands of southeast Pacific

.2   †South central Pacific Ocean islands

.3   †Southeast central Pacific Ocean islands

> *For isolated islands of southeast Pacific, see 996.18*

.4   †Line Islands (Equatorial Islands)

.5   †West central Pacific Ocean islands (Micronesia)

---

*Add as instructed under 930–990

†Add as instructed under 930–990; however, do not add historical periods

.6   †**Federated States of Micronesia and Republic of Palau**

.7   †**Mariana Islands**

.8   †**Islands of eastern Micronesia**

.81   †Kiribati

.82   †Tuvalu

.83   †Marshall Islands

.85   †Nauru (Pleasant Island)

.9   **Hawaii and neighboring north central Pacific Ocean islands**

.900 01–.900 08   Standard subdivisions of north central Pacific islands

> As modified under 930–990

.900 09   Historical periods; areas, regions, places in general; biography of north central Pacific islands

.900 090 1–.900 090 5   Historical periods

> Add to base number 996.900090 the numbers following —090 in notation 0901–0905 from Table 1, e.g., north central Pacific islands during 20th century 996.9000904

.900 091–.900 099   Areas, regions, places in general; biography

> As modified under 930–990

.900 1–.900 9   Standard subdivisions of Hawaii

> As modified under 930–990

>   996.902–996.904 Historical periods of Hawaii

> Class comprehensive works in 996.9

.902   Early history to 1898

.902 7   Period of kingdom, 1810–1893

.902 8   Period of republic, 1893–1898

.903   Territorial period, 1898–1959

> Class here 20th century

> *For 1959–1999, see 996.9041*

.904   Statehood period, 1959–

.904 1   1959–1999

.904 2   2000–

.99   †Outlying islands

†Add as instructed under 930–990; however, do not add historical periods

997 †Atlantic Ocean islands

> *For each specific island or group of islands not provided for here, see the island or group of islands, e.g., Azores 946.99*

.1 †**Falkland Islands, South Georgia and South Sandwich Islands, Bouvet Island**

.11 *Falkland Islands (Islas Malvinas)

.110 1 Early history to 1832

Including French, British, Spanish, Argentine presence

.110 2 British period, 1832–

Including 19th century

> *For 1800–1832, see 997.1101*

.110 24 ‡Falkland Islands War, 1982

.3 †**Saint Helena and dependencies**

998 †Arctic islands and Antarctica

.2 †**Greenland**

999 Extraterrestrial worlds

Class here extraterrestrial civilization, extraterrestrial intelligence, SETI (search for extraterrestrial intelligence)

Do not add from table under 930–990

---

*Add as instructed under 930–990
†Add as instructed under 930–990; however, do not add historical periods
‡Add as instructed under 940–990

The 23rd edition of the Dewey Decimal Classification was produced using the fourth generation of the Editorial Support System (ESS), developed by OCLC Online Computer Library Center, Inc. ESS includes a print module developed by Pansoft GmbH, Karlsruhe, Germany, under an agreement with OCLC. Composition was done in Times Roman and Arial under the supervision of Michael Panzer. The book was printed and bound by Edwards Brothers, Inc., Ann Arbor, Michigan.